COLLINS POCKET REFERENCE

PUZZLE SOLVER

COLLINS POCKET REFERENCE

PUZZLE SOLVER

HarperCollins*Publishers*

HarperCollins Publishers
PO Box, Glasgow G4 ONB

First Published 1994
© HarperCollins Publishers 1994
ISBN 0 00 470672-2

Editorial Staff

Managing Editor
Marian Makins

Editor
Ian Brookes

Editorial Assistance
Anne Young

Typeset by Barbers Ltd
Wrotham, England

Produced by Maury-Eurolivres S.A.
45300 Manchecourt – France

How to Use This Book

Collins Pocket Reference Puzzle Solver helps you to find the answer you need in a crossword or other word game quickly and easily. It contains over 54,000 possible answer words and phrases which are arranged according to the number of letters they contain.

If, for instance, you are looking for a word of six letters, you turn to the section of the book in which, at the left-hand side of the page, you will find the heading *6 letters*. There you will find all the words of six letters grouped together in alphabetical order.

Each answer word or phrase is followed by a label, printed in red, which shows the topic or subject area to which it belongs. So if, for example, you know, or suspect, that the six-letter word you are looking for has something to do with *clothes*, you can look through the six-letter words quickly to find the ones in this category. Possible answers are: *afghan, angora, anorak,* and so on.

If an answer word can fall into more than one subject area, then it is given its full range of subject areas, with each separately identified. For instance, the word *anthem* is given twice, once labelled *music* and once labelled *relig (religion)*. This ensures that you can find the answer whatever the context of the clue you are tackling. Some labels are abbreviated to save space, and a full list of the labels is given on pages vii-viii.

When you are looking for a word, it may be helpful to remember that some of the subject areas overlap. So, if the word you are looking for is the name of a plant, it is worth looking at words labelled *cereal, fruit, flowers,* and *veg*, as well as those with the *plants* label. Similarly names of animals can be labelled *birds, fish,* and *insects,* as well as *animals*.

Also bear in mind that the words in this book are usually singular forms. If the word you are looking for is plural, it may be useful to look at words with one letter fewer than that word. For instance, if you want to find a ten-letter word meaning "rituals", you could look at nine-letter words labelled *relig* and add an "s" to come up with the word you need: perhaps *catechisms, sacraments, or sacrifices.*

Names of geographical features are given in full, so a lake with five letters might be found with the nine-letter words *(Lake Garda, Lake Huron,* etc.), while a mountain with six letters is likely to appear with the eleven-letter words *(Mount Erebus, Mount Hermon,* etc.).

In order to make it easier to scan through the words and relate them to a word puzzle grid, a special typeface has been used that keeps the letters of each word vertically in line with those of the words above and below it. The following symbols are used when the answer consists of more than one word:

      | = a word space, as in hammer|and|tongs

      ı = a hyphen, as in dairyıfarm

      ı = an apostrophe, as in ladyıs|finger

Key to Subject Area Labels

abbrev	Abbreviations
agric	Agriculture
animals	Animals
archit	Architecture
art	Visual Arts
artists	Artists
astron	Astronomy
Bible	Biblical Names
biol	Biological Sciences
birds	Birds
cereal	Cereals
chem	Chemical Sciences
cities	Cities
clothes	Clothes
colour	Colours
comput	Computing
drink	Drink
educ	Education
family	Relations
film/TV	Cinema and Television
fish	Fish
flowers	Flowers
food	Food
foreign	Foreign Words and Phrases
fruit	Fruit
geog	Geography
govt	Government
herald	Heraldry
house	Furniture and Household Items
insects	Insects, Reptiles, etc.
islands	Islands
jewels	Jewelry
jobs	Occupations
lakes	Lakes
law	Law
leaders	Political Leaders
lit	Literature
machine	Machinery

Key to Subject Area Labels

marine	The Marine World
maths	Mathematics
measure	Measurement
medic	Medicine
mineral	Minerals
money	Money
mounts	Mountains
muses	Muses
music	Music
myth	Mythology
names	First Names
people	Character Types
physics	Physical Sciences
plants	Plants
relig	Religion
rivers	Rivers
seas	Oceans and Seas
Shakesp	Shakespearean Characters
sins	Deadly Sins
sport	Sports, Games and Pastimes
theatre	Theatre
time	Time
titles	Titles of Works of Literature and Music
tools	Tools
trade	Trade
travel	Travel, Transport and Communications
trees	Trees
USpres	Presidents of the USA
veg	Vegetables
virtues	Virtues
war	Warfare
weather	The Weather
wonders	Wonders of the World
writers	Writers
zodiac	Signs of the Zodiac

2 LETTERS

AA *abbrev*	CA *trade*	DP *abbrev*	go *educ*	kr *abbrev*
AA *travel*	CB *abbrev*	Dr *abbrev*	go *travel*	Kt *abbrev*
AB *abbrev*	cc *abbrev*	Dr *educ*	GP *jobs*	KT *abbrev*
AB *jobs*	CC *abbrev*	Dr *medic*	GP *medic*	LA *abbrev*
AB *war*	CD *abbrev*	DS *music*	gr *abbrev*	la *music*
ac *abbrev*	CD *govt*	DV *abbrev*	GR *abbrev*	lb *measure*
AC *abbrev*	cf *abbrev*	EC *abbrev*	gs *abbrev*	lc *abbrev*
ad *abbrev*	CF *abbrev*	ed *abbrev*	GS *abbrev*	Ld *abbrev*
AD *time*	ch *abbrev*	Ed *abbrev*	GT *travel*	lh *abbrev*
AG *abbrev*	Ch *abbrev*	Ed *lit*	gu *abbrev*	LM *abbrev*
AI *abbrev*	CH *abbrev*	eg *abbrev*	gu *music*	LP *music*
ai *animals*	CI *abbrev*	em *lit*	HC *abbrev*	Lt *abbrev*
am *time*	cl *abbrev*	en *lit*	HE *abbrev*	LT *abbrev*
as *money*	cm *abbrev*	EP *music*	hf *abbrev*	LV *abbrev*
AU *physics*	c|o *abbrev*	ER *abbrev*	HM *abbrev*	MA *educ*
av *abbrev*	Co *abbrev*	Ex *abbrev*	ho *abbrev*	ma *family*
AV *abbrev*	CO *abbrev*	Ez *abbrev*	HP *trade*	MA *jobs*
BA *abbrev*	co *trade*	FA *abbrev*	HQ *abbrev*	mb *abbrev*
BA *educ*	cp *abbrev*	fa *music*	hr *abbrev*	MB *abbrev*
BA *jobs*	CP *abbrev*	FD *abbrev*	HT *abbrev*	MC *abbrev*
BB *abbrev*	cr *abbrev*	ff *music*	ib *abbrev*	MC *jobs*
BC *time*	CR *abbrev*	fl *abbrev*	i|c *abbrev*	MD *jobs*
BD *abbrev*	CS *abbrev*	FM *abbrev*	id *abbrev*	MD *medic*
bf *abbrev*	ct *abbrev*	FO *abbrev*	id *fish*	me *music*
bk *abbrev*	cu *abbrev*	fp *abbrev*	ie *abbrev*	mf *abbrev*
BL *abbrev*	Cu *abbrev*	FP *abbrev*	in *abbrev*	mg *abbrev*
BM *abbrev*	cv *abbrev*	fp *music*	IQ *educ*	MG *abbrev*
bn *abbrev*	DA *abbrev*	fr *abbrev*	Ir *abbrev*	MI *abbrev*
Bp *abbrev*	DC *abbrev*	Fr *abbrev*	Is *abbrev*	mk *abbrev*
BP *abbrev*	DC *music*	ft *abbrev*	It *abbrev*	ml *abbrev*
br *abbrev*	DD *jobs*	FT *abbrev*	JP *law*	mm *abbrev*
Br *abbrev*	DF *abbrev*	GB *abbrev*	Jr *abbrev*	MM *abbrev*
BR *abbrev*	DG *abbrev*	GC *abbrev*	KB *abbrev*	MN *abbrev*
Bt *abbrev*	DJ *abbrev*	GI *war*	KC *law*	MO *jobs*
ca *abbrev*	DM *abbrev*	Gh *abbrev*	KG *abbrev*	MO *medic*
CA *abbrev*	do *abbrev*	gm *abbrev*	km *abbrev*	mo *time*
CA *jobs*	do *music*	GM *abbrev*	KO *sport*	MP *govt*

MP	*jobs*	OR	*abbrev*	PR	*abbrev*	RT	*abbrev*	TT	*sport*
MP	*war*	or	*herald*	Ps	*abbrev*	RU	*abbrev*	Tu	*abbrev*
MR	*abbrev*	OS	*abbrev*	PS	*abbrev*	RV	*abbrev*	TV	*film/TV*
Mr	*jobs*	os	*medic*	ps	*lit*	ry	*abbrev*	UK	*abbrev*
Ms	*abbrev*	OT	*abbrev*	pt	*abbrev*	sc	*abbrev*	UN	*govt*
MS	*abbrev*	OU	*abbrev*	PT	*sport*	sc	*abbrev*	UP	*abbrev*
MS	*lit*	ox	*animals*	PU	*abbrev*	sd	*abbrev*	Ur	*Bible*
Mt	*abbrev*	oz	*measure*	pw	*abbrev*	SE	*abbrev*	US	*abbrev*
mv	*abbrev*	pa	*abbrev*	QC	*law*	SF	*abbrev*	ut	*music*
MW	*abbrev*	PA	*abbrev*	q1	*abbrev*	sf	*music*	UU	*abbrev*
NB	*abbrev*	pa	*family*	QM	*abbrev*	SI	*abbrev*	ux	*abbrev*
nd	*abbrev*	PA	*jobs*	qr	*abbrev*	Si	*rivers*	vb	*abbrev*
NE	*abbrev*	pc	*abbrev*	qt	*abbrev*	SJ	*abbrev*	VC	*abbrev*
NI	*abbrev*	PC	*abbrev*	qv	*abbrev*	SM	*abbrev*	VD	*abbrev*
nl	*abbrev*	PC	*govt*	RA	*abbrev*	SO	*abbrev*	VE	*abbrev*
no	*abbrev*	pd	*abbrev*	RA	*archit*	sp	*abbrev*	VJ	*abbrev*
nr	*abbrev*	PE	*abbrev*	RA	*war*	SP	*abbrev*	vo	*abbrev*
NS	*abbrev*	PG	*abbrev*	RB	*abbrev*	sq	*abbrev*	VP	*abbrev*
NT	*abbrev*	pH	*abbrev*	RC	*abbrev*	Sr	*abbrev*	vs	*abbrev*
NW	*abbrev*	pi	*maths*	rd	*abbrev*	SS	*abbrev*	vt	*abbrev*
NY	*abbrev*	pl	*abbrev*	Rd	*abbrev*	st	*abbrev*	VW	*abbrev*
NZ	*abbrev*	pm	*abbrev*	RD	*abbrev*	St	*abbrev*	wc	*abbrev*
ob	*abbrev*	PM	*abbrev*	rd	*trade*	SU	*abbrev*	wc	*archit*
OB	*abbrev*	pm	*govt*	RE	*abbrev*	SW	*abbrev*	WD	*abbrev*
Ob	*rivers*	PM	*jobs*	re	*music*	TA	*abbrev*	WI	*abbrev*
OC	*abbrev*	pm	*time*	RE	*war*	TB	*medic*	wk	*abbrev*
OE	*abbrev*	po	*abbrev*	RF	*abbrev*	TD	*abbrev*	WO	*abbrev*
OK	*abbrev*	PO	*abbrev*	rh	*abbrev*	te	*music*	wp	*abbrev*
OM	*rivers*	Po	*rivers*	RI	*abbrev*	Th	*abbrev*	WS	*abbrev*
op	*abbrev*	pp	*abbrev*	RN	*war*	tp	*abbrev*	wt	*abbrev*
OP	*abbrev*	pp	*music*	ro	*abbrev*	tr	*abbrev*	yd	*abbrev*
op	*lit*	pr	*abbrev*	RS	*abbrev*	TT	*abbrev*	yr	*abbrev*
op	*music*	Pr	*abbrev*						

3 LETTERS

AAA	*abbrev*	Abe	*names*	ace	*travel*	act	*lit*
ABC	*educ*	Abp	*abbrev*	act	*film/TV*	act	*music*
ABC	*lit*	acc	*abbrev*	act	*govt*	act	*theatre*
ABC	*travel*	ace	*sport*	act	*law*	Ada	*names*

ADC	*abbrev*	APR	*abbrev*	Bax	*music*	bob	*trade*
add	*maths*	APT	*abbrev*	bay	*animals*	BOC	*abbrev*
adj	*abbrev*	arc	*maths*	bay	*archit*	bog	*geog*
adv	*abbrev*	are	*measure*	bay	*marine*	bop	*music*
AEC	*abbrev*	ark	*relig*	bay	*travel*	bor	*abbrev*
aet	*abbrev*	ark	*travel*	bay	*trees*	Bor	*myth*
AEU	*abbrev*	arm	*medic*	BBC	*film/TV*	BOT	*abbrev*
AFC	*abbrev*	arm	*war*	BCC	*abbrev*	BOT	*trade*
AFM	*abbrev*	ARP	*abbrev*	Bea	*names*	bow	*music*
aft	*travel*	Arp	*artists*	BEd	*abbrev*	bow	*sport*
aga	*govt*	arr	*abbrev*	bed	*flowers*	bow	*theatre*
age	*time*	ART	*art*	bed	*geog*	bow	*war*
agm	*abbrev*	ASA	*abbrev*	bed	*house*	box	*house*
ago	*time*	ASH	*abbrev*	bed	*medic*	box	*sport*
agr	*abbrev*	ash	*trees*	bee	*insects*	box	*theatre*
AID	*abbrev*	asp	*insects*	BEF	*abbrev*	box	*trees*
ail	*medic*	ass	*animals*	beg	*govt*	bra	*clothes*
aim	*sport*	ass	*people*	Bel	*myth*	Bro	*abbrev*
air	*geog*	ATC	*abbrev*	Bel	*names*	BRS	*abbrev*
air	*music*	Ate	*myth*	BEM	*abbrev*	BSA	*abbrev*
air	*travel*	ATS	*abbrev*	ben	*geog*	BSc	*jobs*
ait	*geog*	ATV	*abbrev*	Ben	*names*	BSM	*abbrev*
aka	*abbrev*	AUC	*abbrev*	ben	*trees*	BST	*abbrev*
alb	*clothes*	Aug	*abbrev*	bet	*sport*	BTA	*abbrev*
alb	*relig*	auk	*birds*	bey	*govt*	Btu	*abbrev*
Ald	*abbrev*	AVM	*abbrev*	bhp	*abbrev*	BTU	*measure*
ale	*drink*	awl	*tools*	BHS	*abbrev*	bud	*flowers*
Alf	*names*	awn	*cereal*	bib	*clothes*	bug	*govt*
alp	*geog*	axe	*tools*	bib	*fish*	bug	*insects*
Als	*islands*	axe	*war*	bib	*house*	Bug	*rivers*
alt	*abbrev*	Aya	*myth*	bid	*sport*	bun	*clothes*
ami	*foreign*	aye	*time*	bid	*trade*	bun	*food*
amp	*measure*	Bab	*names*	BIM	*abbrev*	bur	*plants*
amp	*physics*	bag	*clothes*	bin	*drink*	bus	*travel*
amt	*abbrev*	bag	*trade*	bin	*food*	buy	*trade*
Amy	*names*	bar	*archit*	bit	*money*	BVM	*abbrev*
ana	*lit*	bar	*herald*	bit	*theatre*	BWV	*abbrev*
Ann	*names*	bar	*house*	bit	*tools*	bye	*sport*
ans	*abbrev*	bar	*law*	BMA	*abbrev*	CAB	*abbrev*
ant	*insects*	bar	*lit*	BMJ	*abbrev*	cab	*measure*
Anu	*myth*	bar	*machine*	BMW	*abbrev*	cab	*travel*
aob	*abbrev*	bar	*music*	boa	*clothes*	cad	*people*
aor	*abbrev*	bar	*trade*	bob	*clothes*	cal	*abbrev*
ape	*animals*	bat	*animals*	bob	*money*	Cal	*abbrev*
Apr	*abbrev*	bat	*sport*	Bob	*names*	cam	*machine*

cam	*travel*	col	*geog*	cwt	*measure*	Dir	*abbrev*
can	*food*	con	*abbrev*	dab	*fish*	Dis	*myth*
CAP	*abbrev*	con	*educ*	dad	*family*	div	*abbrev*
cap	*clothes*	con	*govt*	dam	*animals*	DIY	*sport*
cap	*lit*	con	*trade*	dam	*geog*	DNA	*abbrev*
cap	*sport*	coo	*birds*	Dan	*Bible*	DNB	*abbrev*
cap	*trade*	cop	*law*	Dan	*abbrev*	dob	*abbrev*
cap	*war*	Cor	*abbrev*	Dan	*names*	doc	*jobs*
car	*machine*	Cos	*islands*	dan	*sport*	doc	*medic*
car	*travel*	cos	*maths*	dau	*abbrev*	DOE	*abbrev*
CAT	*abbrev*	Cos	*myth*	daw	*birds*	doe	*animals*
cat	*animals*	cos	*veg*	day	*time*	dog	*animals*
cat	*music*	cot	*archit*	DBE	*abbrev*	doh	*music*
cat	*sport*	cot	*house*	dbl	*abbrev*	dom	*abbrev*
cat	*travel*	cot	*maths*	DCL	*abbrev*	don	*govt*
caw	*birds*	cow	*animals*	DCM	*abbrev*	don	*jobs*
cay	*geog*	cow	*tools*	DDR	*abbrev*	Don	*names*
CBE	*abbrev*	cox	*sport*	DDT	*abbrev*	Don	*rivers*
CBI	*abbrev*	cox	*travel*	DEA	*abbrev*	dor	*insects*
CCF	*abbrev*	Cpl	*abbrev*	dea	*myth*	dot	*govt*
Cdr	*abbrev*	CPR	*abbrev*	deb	*jobs*	dot	*lit*
CET	*abbrev*	CRE	*abbrev*	dec	*abbrev*	dot	*music*
cfi	*abbrev*	cry	*animals*	Dec	*abbrev*	Dot	*names*
CGS	*abbrev*	cry	*birds*	Dee	*rivers*	dot	*trade*
ChB	*abbrev*	CSE	*abbrev*	def	*abbrev*	doz	*abbrev*
Chr	*abbrev*	CST	*abbrev*	deg	*abbrev*	DPP	*abbrev*
Cia	*abbrev*	CSV	*abbrev*	del	*abbrev*	DSC	*abbrev*
CIA	*abbrev*	CTC	*abbrev*	den	*animals*	DSO	*abbrev*
CID	*govt*	cub	*animals*	den	*archit*	dsp	*abbrev*
CID	*jobs*	cue	*film/TV*	den	*educ*	DSS	*abbrev*
Cie	*abbrev*	cue	*music*	den	*house*	DTI	*abbrev*
cif	*abbrev*	cue	*sport*	dep	*abbrev*	DTs	*medic*
CMG	*abbrev*	cue	*theatre*	Dep	*abbrev*	dud	*war*
CMS	*abbrev*	CUP	*abbrev*	DEP	*abbrev*	due	*time*
CND	*abbrev*	cup	*house*	DES	*abbrev*	due	*trade*
cob	*animals*	cup	*medic*	dew	*geog*	dun	*colour*
cob	*fruit*	cup	*sport*	DFC	*abbrev*	dun	*trade*
cod	*abbrev*	cur	*animals*	DFM	*abbrev*	duo	*music*
cod	*fish*	cut	*art*	Dia	*myth*	dux	*educ*
COD	*trade*	cut	*medic*	die	*sport*	dux	*jobs*
cog	*machine*	cut	*war*	die	*tools*	dye	*art*
cog	*travel*	CVO	*abbrev*	dig	*tools*	dye	*chem*
COI	*abbrev*	cwm	*geog*	Dip	*abbrev*	ear	*agric*
col	*abbrev*	cwo	*abbrev*	dip	*geog*	ear	*cereal*
Col	*abbrev*	CWS	*abbrev*	dip	*govt*	ear	*medic*

ebb	*marine*	ETA	*abbrev*	fig	*trees*	gas	*travel*
EBU	*abbrev*	etc	*abbrev*	fin	*fish*	gat	*war*
ECG	*medic*	ETD	*abbrev*	fin	*travel*	Gay	*music*
ECO	*abbrev*	ETU	*abbrev*	fir	*fruit*	Gay	*names*
EDC	*abbrev*	Eva	*lit*	fir	*trees*	GBA	*abbrev*
EEC	*abbrev*	Eva	*names*	FIS	*abbrev*	gbh	*abbrev*
EEC	*trade*	Eve	*Bible*	fit	*medic*	GBS	*abbrev*
EEG	*medic*	Eve	*names*	Flo	*names*	GCB	*abbrev*
eel	*fish*	eve	*time*	flu	*medic*	GCE	*abbrev*
e'en	*time*	ewe	*animals*	fly	*birds*	GDP	*abbrev*
e'er	*time*	Exc	*abbrev*	fly	*insects*	GDR	*abbrev*
EFL	*abbrev*	Exe	*rivers*	fly	*travel*	GEC	*abbrev*
eft	*insects*	eye	*geog*	fob	*abbrev*	gel	*chem*
egg	*food*	eye	*medic*	fob	*clothes*	gem	*jewels*
EIS	*abbrev*	fag	*educ*	foc	*abbrev*	gem	*lit*
eld	*time*	fah	*music*	foe	*war*	gem	*mineral*
elf	*myth*	fam	*abbrev*	fog	*geog*	gen	*abbrev*
Eli	*Bible*	fan	*film/TV*	fog	*plants*	Gen	*abbrev*
elk	*animals*	fan	*house*	fop	*clothes*	Geo	*abbrev*
ell	*measure*	fan	*jobs*	fop	*people*	ger	*abbrev*
elm	*trees*	fan	*machine*	for	*abbrev*	Ger	*names*
Ely	*Shakesp*	fan	*sport*	fox	*animals*	GHQ	*abbrev*
EMI	*abbrev*	fan	*theatre*	Fox	*leaders*	Gib	*abbrev*
Ems	*rivers*	fan	*travel*	FPA	*abbrev*	gig	*travel*
emu	*birds*	FAO	*abbrev*	Fri	*abbrev*	gin	*drink*
Ena	*names*	fas	*abbrev*	FRS	*abbrev*	gin	*machine*
ENE	*abbrev*	fat	*medic*	fry	*food*	gin	*sport*
eng	*abbrev*	fay	*myth*	Fry	*writers*	GLC	*abbrev*
Eng	*abbrev*	Fay	*names*	fun	*sport*	GMC	*abbrev*
ENT	*medic*	FBA	*abbrev*	fur	*abbrev*	GMT	*geog*
Eos	*myth*	FBI	*govt*	fur	*animals*	GMT	*time*
Eos	*time*	FCA	*abbrev*	fur	*clothes*	GNP	*abbrev*
Eph	*abbrev*	FCO	*abbrev*	fut	*abbrev*	gnu	*animals*
era	*time*	fcp	*abbrev*	fwd	*abbrev*	GOC	*abbrev*
ere	*time*	FDR	*abbrev*	Gad	*Bible*	god	*myth*
erg	*measure*	Feb	*abbrev*	gad	*travel*	Gog	*myth*
erg	*physics*	fec	*abbrev*	gag	*theatre*	GOM	*abbrev*
ESE	*abbrev*	Fed	*govt*	Gal	*abbrev*	Gov	*abbrev*
Esk	*rivers*	fee	*trade*	gam	*animals*	goy	*relig*
ESN	*abbrev*	fem	*abbrev*	gap	*geog*	GPI	*abbrev*
esp	*abbrev*	fen	*geog*	gar	*fish*	GTC	*abbrev*
ESP	*abbrev*	feu	*law*	gas	*chem*	gue	*music*
Esq	*abbrev*	fez	*clothes*	gas	*geog*	gum	*art*
est	*abbrev*	fig	*abbrev*	gas	*house*	gum	*medic*
ESU	*abbrev*	fig	*fruit*	gas	*medic*	gum	*trees*

gun	*machine*	HMS	*travel*	ind	*abbrev*	Joe	*names*
gun	*war*	HMV	*abbrev*	inf	*abbrev*	jog	*travel*
GUS	*abbrev*	HNC	*abbrev*	ink	*educ*	jot	*educ*
Gus	*names*	HND	*abbrev*	ink	*lit*	Joy	*names*
gut	*medic*	hob	*animals*	inn	*archit*	Jud	*abbrev*
guy	*jobs*	hob	*house*	Ino	*myth*	jug	*drink*
Guy	*names*	Hob	*myth*	int	*abbrev*	jug	*law*
guy	*travel*	hod	*tools*	IOM	*abbrev*	Jul	*abbrev*
gym	*sport*	hoe	*tools*	ion	*chem*	jus	*law*
Hab	*abbrev*	hog	*animals*	IOU	*trade*	jut	*geog*
HAC	*abbrev*	Hon	*abbrev*	IOW	*abbrev*	Kay	*names*
Hag	*abbrev*	hop	*fruit*	IPC	*abbrev*	KBE	*abbrev*
hag	*fish*	hop	*sport*	IRA	*abbrev*	KCB	*abbrev*
hag	*people*	hop	*travel*	Ira	*myth*	kea	*birds*
Ham	*Bible*	hor	*abbrev*	Isa	*names*	key	*house*
ham	*food*	Hos	*abbrev*	ITN	*abbrev*	key	*machine*
ham	*people*	hoy	*travel*	ITV	*film/TV*	key	*music*
ham	*theatre*	HRH	*abbrev*	ivy	*plants*	key	*travel*
Han	*rivers*	HSE	*abbrev*	jab	*sport*	KGB	*abbrev*
har	*geog*	HTV	*abbrev*	jam	*food*	kid	*animals*
hat	*clothes*	hub	*machine*	Jan	*abbrev*	kid	*clothes*
haw	*fruit*	hub	*travel*	Jan	*names*	kid	*jobs*
hay	*agric*	hue	*art*	jar	*house*	Kim	*names*
hay	*music*	hum	*music*	Jas	*abbrev*	Kim	*titles*
hay	*plants*	Hun	*war*	jaw	*medic*	kin	*family*
Hay	*writers*	hut	*archit*	jay	*birds*	kip	*archit*
HCF	*abbrev*	Ian	*names*	JCR	*abbrev*	kit	*animals*
Heb	*abbrev*	IBA	*abbrev*	jct	*abbrev*	kit	*music*
Hel	*myth*	IBM	*abbrev*	Jer	*abbrev*	Kit	*names*
hem	*clothes*	ice	*food*	jet	*geog*	kit	*sport*
hen	*birds*	ice	*weather*	jet	*machine*	KKK	*abbrev*
her	*abbrev*	ICI	*abbrev*	jet	*travel*	KLM	*abbrev*
hex	*people*	ICS	*abbrev*	jeu	*sport*	kmh	*abbrev*
hey	*music*	icy	*weather*	jib	*machine*	kob	*animals*
HGV	*abbrev*	Ida	*myth*	jib	*travel*	ktl	*abbrev*
hip	*fruit*	ide	*fish*	jig	*music*	Kyd	*writers*
hip	*medic*	ill	*abbrev*	jig	*sport*	Lab	*abbrev*
hit	*music*	ill	*medic*	jig	*tools*	lab	*biol*
hit	*sport*	ILO	*abbrev*	Jim	*names*	lab	*chem*
hit	*theatre*	ILP	*abbrev*	Jno	*abbrev*	lab	*medic*
HLI	*abbrev*	IMF	*abbrev*	Jnr	*abbrev*	lab	*physics*
HMC	*abbrev*	imp	*abbrev*	Job	*Bible*	lac	*art*
HMG	*abbrev*	imp	*myth*	job	*jobs*	lad	*jobs*
HMI	*abbrev*	Ina	*names*	Job	*titles*	lag	*law*
HMS	*govt*	inc	*abbrev*	job	*trade*	lag	*travel*

lah	music	Lok	myth	Mgr	abbrev	nav	abbrev
lap	sport	loo	sport	Mic	abbrev	NBC	abbrev
lap	travel	loq	abbrev	mil	abbrev	nbg	abbrev
lat	abbrev	Lot	Bible	mil	money	NCB	abbrev
Lat	abbrev	lot	trade	min	abbrev	NCO	war
law	law	low	animals	Min	abbrev	NEB	abbrev
lay	lit	Low	artists	mis	abbrev	NEC	abbrev
lay	music	low	weather	MIT	abbrev	Ned	names
lbw	sport	LPO	abbrev	MLR	abbrev	nef	archit
LCC	abbrev	LSA	abbrev	Mme	abbrev	neg	abbrev
LCJ	abbrev	LSD	abbrev	moa	birds	Neh	abbrev
lcm	abbrev	LSD	medic	mod	abbrev	net	clothes
LDS	medic	LSE	abbrev	MOD	abbrev	Net	names
LDV	abbrev	LSO	abbrev	MOH	abbrev	net	sport
LEA	abbrev	LTA	abbrev	Mon	abbrev	net	trade
lea	agric	Ltd	trade	moo	animals	NFS	abbrev
lea	cereal	Lug	myth	mop	house	NFT	abbrev
lee	travel	lur	music	mot	lit	NFU	abbrev
Lee	war	LWT	abbrev	Mot	myth	NGA	abbrev
Lee	writers	Lyn	names	MOT	travel	NHI	abbrev
leg	food	Lys	rivers	mow	agric	NHS	abbrev
leg	medic	Mab	myth	mow	plants	nil	maths
leg	sport	mac	clothes	mph	measure	nip	drink
leg	travel	mag	abbrev	mph	travel	nip	geog
lei	flowers	mag	money	MPS	abbrev	nis	myth
Len	names	Maj	abbrev	MRA	abbrev	nit	insects
Leo	myth	Mal	abbrev	MRC	abbrev	nix	myth
Leo	names	man	jobs	Mrs	abbrev	NNE	abbrev
Leo	zodiac	map	geog	Mrs	jobs	NNW	abbrev
Ler	myth	map	travel	MSC	abbrev	nob	govt
let	sport	Mar	abbrev	msl	abbrev	Nod	Bible
Lev	abbrev	mat	house	mss	abbrev	nom	abbrev
lex	law	max	abbrev	MTB	abbrev	NOP	abbrev
lie	sport	Max	names	mud	geog	Nov	abbrev
lip	medic	May	names	mug	house	Nox	myth
lip	music	May	time	mug	theatre	NPL	abbrev
lit	abbrev	MBE	abbrev	mum	family	NSW	abbrev
Liz	names	MCC	abbrev	mus	abbrev	NUJ	abbrev
LLB	abbrev	Mc|s	abbrev	MVO	abbrev	Num	abbrev
lob	sport	Meg	names	nag	animals	NUM	abbrev
log	abbrev	MEP	abbrev	Nan	names	nun	jobs
log	house	met	abbrev	nap	clothes	NUR	abbrev
log	lit	mew	animals	nat	abbrev	NUS	abbrev
log	travel	mfd	abbrev	Nat	abbrev	NUT	abbrev
log	trees	MFH	abbrev	Nat	names	nut	food

nut	*fruit*	OSB	*abbrev*	PGA	*abbrev*	Pru	*names*
nut	*machine*	OTC	*abbrev*	PhD	*abbrev*	psc	*abbrev*
nut	*music*	OUP	*abbrev*	phr	*abbrev*	PTA	*abbrev*
Nut	*myth*	ova	*biol*	pie	*birds*	Pte	*abbrev*
Nye	*names*	owe	*trade*	pie	*food*	PTO	*abbrev*
Nym	*Shakesp*	owl	*birds*	pie	*lit*	pub	*archit*
NYO	*abbrev*	Oxf	*abbrev*	pie	*money*	pug	*animals*
Nyx	*myth*	Oya	*myth*	pie	*relig*	pun	*lit*
oaf	*people*	pad	*animals*	pig	*animals*	pup	*animals*
oak	*trees*	pad	*house*	pin	*clothes*	pus	*medic*
OAP	*abbrev*	pad	*lit*	pin	*sport*	put	*trade*
oar	*travel*	pal	*people*	pip	*fruit*	PVC	*abbrev*
OAS	*abbrev*	Pam	*names*	Pip	*names*	pye	*relig*
oat	*cereal*	pan	*house*	pit	*geog*	pyx	*relig*
OBE	*abbrev*	Pan	*myth*	Pit	*sport*	QED	*abbrev*
obi	*myth*	pap	*abbrev*	pit	*theatre*	QEF	*abbrev*
obj	*abbrev*	pap	*geog*	pit	*trade*	QEH	*abbrev*
oct	*abbrev*	par	*abbrev*	PLA	*abbrev*	QMG	*abbrev*
Oct	*abbrev*	par	*sport*	PLC	*abbrev*	QPR	*abbrev*
ode	*lit*	par	*trade*	PLO	*abbrev*	qty	*abbrev*
ode	*music*	pat	*abbrev*	PLP	*abbrev*	Rab	*names*
OED	*abbrev*	Pat	*names*	PLR	*abbrev*	RAC	*abbrev*
oft	*time*	paw	*animals*	ply	*travel*	rad	*measure*
ohm	*measure*	pay	*jobs*	PMG	*abbrev*	Rae	*names*
oil	*art*	pay	*trade*	PMO	*abbrev*	RAF	*war*
oil	*food*	PBI	*abbrev*	poa	*plants*	rag	*clothes*
oil	*geog*	PCC	*abbrev*	pod	*animals*	rag	*lit*
oil	*medic*	pea	*veg*	pod	*veg*	rag	*music*
oil	*travel*	ped	*music*	Poe	*writers*	rag	*theatre*
Oka	*rivers*	peg	*house*	poi	*food*	RAM	*abbrev*
old	*time*	Peg	*names*	pom	*animals*	ram	*animals*
ONC	*abbrev*	peg	*sport*	pop	*abbrev*	ram	*machine*
OND	*abbrev*	PEN	*abbrev*	pop	*drink*	ram	*travel*
ono	*abbrev*	pen	*art*	pop	*music*	ram	*war*
oof	*trade*	pen	*birds*	pos	*abbrev*	Ran	*myth*
opp	*abbrev*	pcn	*educ*	pot	*art*	rat	*animals*
Ops	*abbrev*	pen	*lit*	pot	*house*	Rat	*lit*
Ops	*myth*	Pen	*names*	pot	*sport*	rat	*people*
opt	*abbrev*	PEP	*abbrev*	POW	*war*	rat	*war*
orb	*geog*	pep	*medic*	pox	*medic*	ray	*fish*
orb	*herald*	pes	*music*	ppc	*abbrev*	ray	*music*
ord	*abbrev*	pet	*animals*	PPE	*abbrev*	Ray	*names*
ore	*mineral*	pet	*birds*	PPS	*abbrev*	ray	*physics*
Ore	*myth*	pew	*house*	PRO	*abbrev*	RBA	*abbrev*
ort	*food*	pew	*relig*	pro	*trade*	RCM	*abbrev*

RCO	abbrev	roe	food	SCE	abbrev	sod	plants
RCT	abbrev	Rom	abbrev	SCM	abbrev	soh	music
RDC	abbrev	row	war	SCR	abbrev	sol	chem
rec	abbrev	Roy	names	SDP	abbrev	sol	money
red	colour	RPI	abbrev	sea	geog	sol	music
red	govt	rpm	abbrev	sea	marine	Sol	myth
Red	rivers	RPM	abbrev	sea	travel	son	family
ref	abbrev	RPO	abbrev	Seb	myth	sop	abbrev
Reg	names	RRE	abbrev	Sec	abbrev	SOS	govt
rem	measure	RSA	abbrev	sec	maths	SOS	travel
rep	jobs	RSM	abbrev	sec	time	sot	people
rep	theatre	RTE	abbrev	see	relig	sot	veg
rev	travel	RTZ	abbrev	Sen	abbrev	sou	money
rex	govt	rub	medic	SEN	abbrev	sow	animals
Rex	names	RUC	abbrev	sen	money	sow	cereal
RFA	abbrev	rue	plants	seq	abbrev	sow	flowers
RFC	abbrev	rue	veg	ser	abbrev	sox	clothes
RFU	abbrev	rug	house	set	animals	soy	cereal
RGS	abbrev	rum	drink	set	film/TV	spa	medic
RHA	abbrev	run	animals	set	lit	spy	jobs
RHS	abbrev	run	music	Set	myth	spy	war
ria	geog	run	sport	set	sport	sqn	abbrev
rib	archit	run	theatre	set	theatre	Sri	myth
rib	medic	run	travel	SET	trade	SRN	abbrev
RIC	abbrev	rut	travel	SFA	abbrev	SSE	abbrev
rig	clothes	rye	agric	sfz	abbrev	SSW	abbrev
rig	machine	rye	cereal	She	titles	std	abbrev
rig	trade	RYS	abbrev	shy	sport	STD	abbrev
rig	travel	sac	biol	Sid	names	STD	travel
rip	geog	sac	medic	sin	maths	str	abbrev
rip	people	sae	abbrev	sin	relig	STV	abbrev
RIP	relig	sag	trade	sir	jobs	sty	animals
Rly	abbrev	Sal	names	Sis	names	sty	medic
RMA	abbrev	sal	trees	sit	art	sub	abbrev
RMO	abbrev	Sam	abbrev	ska	music	sub	travel
RMP	abbrev	SAM	abbrev	ski	sport	sub	war
RMS	abbrev	Sam	names	ski	travel	sue	law
rob	law	sap	trees	sky	astron	Sue	names
ROC	abbrev	sap	war	SMO	abbrev	Suk	music
roc	birds	SAS	abbrev	SMP	abbrev	sum	maths
rod	govt	Sat	abbrev	SNP	abbrev	sum	trade
rod	herald	saw	lit	sob	abbrev	Sun	abbrev
rod	measure	saw	tools	Soc	abbrev	sun	astron
rod	war	sax	music	soc	law	sup	food
roe	fish	Say	Shakesp	sod	geog	tab	clothes

tab	*theatre*	tod	*animals*	urn	*drink*	Wal	*names*
tag	*clothes*	toe	*medic*	USA	*abbrev*	wan	*medic*
tag	*sport*	tom	*animals*	Usk	*rivers*	war	*war*
tag	*trade*	Tom	*names*	USN	*abbrev*	wax	*geog*
Tam	*names*	ton	*measure*	USS	*abbrev*	wax	*music*
tan	*colour*	ton	*sport*	usu	*abbrev*	way	*travel*
tan	*maths*	ton	*travel*	usw	*abbrev*	WEA	*abbrev*
tap	*house*	top	*sport*	uva	*fruit*	web	*insects*
tap	*machine*	top	*travel*	Vac	*myth*	Wed	*abbrev*
tar	*jobs*	tot	*drink*	VAD	*abbrev*	wef	*abbrev*
tar	*travel*	tow	*travel*	val	*abbrev*	wen	*medic*
tax	*govt*	toy	*sport*	Val	*names*	wet	*geog*
tax	*trade*	try	*law*	Van	*myth*	wet	*govt*
Tay	*rivers*	try	*sport*	van	*travel*	WHO	*abbrev*
TCD	*abbrev*	TSB	*abbrev*	van	*war*	wig	*clothes*
tea	*drink*	tub	*travel*	var	*abbrev*	wig	*law*
tea	*medic*	TUC	*abbrev*	vat	*drink*	win	*sport*
tea	*plants*	Tue	*abbrev*	vat	*machine*	wit	*people*
Ted	*names*	tug	*travel*	VAT	*trade*	WNW	*abbrev*
teg	*animals*	tui	*birds*	VDU	*abbrev*	wok	*food*
tel	*abbrev*	Tum	*myth*	veg	*abbrev*	wow	*physics*
Tem	*myth*	tup	*animals*	vel	*abbrev*	wpb	*abbrev*
ten	*abbrev*	TVA	*abbrev*	Ven	*abbrev*	wpm	*abbrev*
Thu	*abbrev*	tyg	*drink*	vet	*jobs*	WSW	*abbrev*
tic	*medic*	Tyr	*myth*	vet	*medic*	WVS	*abbrev*
tie	*archit*	Tyr	*war*	vet	*war*	Wye	*rivers*
tie	*clothes*	UAE	*abbrev*	VHF	*abbrev*	yak	*animals*
tie	*music*	UAR	*abbrev*	via	*travel*	yam	*fruit*
tie	*sport*	UDC	*abbrev*	Vic	*names*	yaw	*travel*
Tim	*abbrev*	UDI	*govt*	vid	*abbrev*	yen	*money*
Tim	*names*	UDR	*abbrev*	VIP	*abbrev*	yet	*time*
tin	*house*	UFO	*travel*	Vis	*islands*	yew	*trees*
tin	*mineral*	UHF	*abbrev*	Viv	*names*	YOP	*abbrev*
tin	*trade*	UHT	*abbrev*	viz	*abbrev*	Zan	*myth*
tip	*trade*	uke	*music*	voc	*abbrev*	Zio	*myth*
Tit	*abbrev*	Ull	*myth*	vol	*abbrev*	zip	*clothes*
tit	*birds*	ult	*time*	vow	*relig*	Ziu	*myth*
Tiu	*myth*	Una	*names*	VSO	*abbrev*	Zoe	*names*
Tiw	*myth*	UNO	*govt*	wad	*geog*	zoo	*animals*
TNT	*war*	urn	*art*	wad	*trade*	zoo	*birds*

Abba	*Bible*	aide	*jobs*	anat	*abbrev*	army	*war*
abbr	*abbrev*	AIDS	*medic*	Anax	*myth*	Arne	*music*
abed	*medic*	Aire	*rivers*	Andy	*names*	Arno	*rivers*
Abel	*Bible*	Ajax	*Shakesp*	ankh	*herald*	arty	*art*
Abel	*names*	Ajax	*myth*	anna	*money*	arum	*flowers*
Abie	*names*	akee	*trees*	Anna	*myth*	asap	*abbrev*
ABTA	*abbrev*	Alan	*names*	Anna	*names*	Askr	*myth*
ACAS	*abbrev*	alap	*music*	Anne	*Shakesp*	Asst	*abbrev*
ACGB	*abbrev*	alar	*biol*	Anne	*names*	Aten	*myth*
ache	*medic*	alba	*clothes*	anon	*lit*	at|no	*abbrev*
acid	*chem*	Aldo	*names*	anon	*time*	atom	*chem*
acne	*medic*	Alea	*myth*	Anta	*myth*	atom	*measure*
acre	*measure*	ally	*govt*	ante	*sport*	atom	*physics*
Adad	*myth*	Ally	*names*	ante	*time*	Aton	*myth*
Adam	*Bible*	ally	*war*	A￿one	*travel*	at|wt	*abbrev*
Adam	*Shakesp*	Alma	*names*	apex	*geog*	AUEW	*abbrev*
Adam	*artists*	alms	*relig*	apex	*maths*	Auge	*myth*
Adam	*music*	alod	*govt*	Apis	*myth*	aula	*archit*
Adam	*names*	aloe	*fruit*	apse	*archit*	aunt	*family*
adit	*archit*	Alps	*mounts*	apse	*relig*	auto	*travel*
adit	*geog*	alto	*music*	Arab	*animals*	Avis	*names*
adze	*tools*	alum	*chem*	Aran	*islands*	Avon	*rivers*
Aeon	*myth*	ambo	*educ*	arch	*abbrev*	A￿war	*war*
aeon	*time*	ambo	*house*	arch	*archit*	away	*sport*
AERE	*abbrev*	ambo	*relig*	arch	*geog*	AWOL	*war*
Afer	*myth*	AMDG	*abbrev*	arco	*music*	AWRE	*abbrev*
Afro	*clothes*	Amen	*myth*	area	*archit*	axes	*maths*
Agag	*Bible*	amen	*relig*	area	*geog*	axil	*biol*
ages	*time*	Amis	*writers*	area	*measure*	axis	*govt*
agio	*trade*	ammo	*war*	Ares	*myth*	axis	*maths*
Agni	*myth*	Amon	*Bible*	Ares	*war*	axle	*travel*
ague	*medic*	Amor	*myth*	Argo	*astron*	ayre	*music*
Ahab	*Bible*	Amos	*Bible*	Argo	*myth*	Baal	*Bible*
Ahaz	*Bible*	Amos	*names*	aria	*music*	Baal	*myth*
ahoy	*travel*	Amun	*myth*	arid	*geog*	babe	*jobs*
Aida	*lit*	amyl	*chem*	arms	*herald*	Babs	*names*
Aida	*titles*	anas	*lit*	arms	*war*	baby	*jobs*

Bach	*music*	bell	*relig*
back	*medic*	Bell	*writers*
back	*trade*	belt	*clothes*
back	*travel*	belt	*geog*
bags	*clothes*	bema	*archit*
bail	*law*	bema	*relig*
bail	*sport*	bend	*herald*
bail	*travel*	bend	*sport*
bait	*sport*	bend	*travel*
Baku	*cities*	bent	*plants*
Bala	*lakes*	berg	*geog*
bald	*medic*	Berg	*music*
bale	*agric*	berm	*archit*
Bali	*islands*	Bert	*names*
balk	*archit*	Bess	*names*
ball	*sport*	Beth	*names*
ball	*war*	bevy	*birds*
balm	*medic*	BFPO	*abbrev*
balm	*plants*	bias	*clothes*
band	*clothes*	bias	*sport*
band	*medic*	Bibl	*abbrev*
band	*music*	bier	*relig*
band	*war*	biga	*travel*
bang	*clothes*	bike	*insects*
bank	*geog*	bike	*sport*
bank	*machine*	bike	*travel*
bank	*sport*	bile	*medic*
bank	*trade*	bill	*birds*
bank	*travel*	bill	*geog*
BAOR	*abbrev*	bill	*govt*
barb	*fish*	bill	*law*
barb	*war*	Bill	*names*
bard	*herald*	bill	*theatre*
bard	*jobs*	bill	*war*
bard	*lit*	bind	*music*
bard	*music*	bind	*sport*
bard	*war*	biog	*abbrev*
Bari	*cities*	biol	*abbrev*
bark	*travel*	bird	*birds*
bark	*trees*	bird	*war*
barn	*agric*	bite	*food*
barn	*archit*	bitt	*travel*
Bart	*abbrev*	bixa	*plants*
Bart	*names*	blay	*fish*
base	*archit*	bldg	*abbrev*
base	*music*	bley	*insects*
base	*sport*	blip	*travel*
bass	*fish*	bloc	*govt*
bass	*music*	blot	*educ*
bass	*trees*	blow	*music*
Bast	*myth*	Blow	*music*
bast	*trees*	blow	*sport*
bath	*house*	blow	*weather*
baud	*comput*	blue	*colour*
Baum	*writers*	blue	*sport*
Bawd	*Shakesp*	Blum	*leaders*
BCal	*abbrev*	BMus	*abbrev*
BCom	*abbrev*	BNOC	*abbrev*
bead	*archit*	BOAC	*abbrev*
bead	*clothes*	boar	*animals*
beak	*animals*	boat	*travel*
beak	*jobs*	Boaz	*Bible*
beak	*law*	body	*medic*
beak	*travel*	body	*trade*
beam	*archit*	boil	*food*
beam	*house*	boil	*medic*
beam	*physics*	bola	*war*
beam	*travel*	bold	*lit*
bean	*money*	bole	*trees*
bean	*veg*	bolt	*food*
bear	*animals*	bolt	*geog*
bear	*jobs*	bolt	*machine*
bear	*trade*	bolt	*war*
beat	*govt*	Bolt	*writers*
beat	*lit*	bomb	*geog*
beat	*music*	bomb	*machine*
beat	*sport*	bomb	*war*
beau	*jobs*	Bona	*Shakesp*
beck	*geog*	bond	*govt*
Beds	*abbrev*	bond	*trade*
beef	*food*	bone	*medic*
beer	*drink*	bone	*war*
beet	*veg*	Bonn	*cities*
Belg	*abbrev*	book	*educ*
bell	*archit*	book	*lit*
bell	*house*	boom	*machine*
bell	*music*	boom	*trade*
		boom	*travel*
		boot	*clothes*
		boot	*travel*
		Bora	*astron*
		Bora	*myth*
		bore	*geog*

bore	*machine*	bull	*jobs*	calm	*geog*	cell	*archit*
bore	*people*	bull	*lit*	calx	*chem*	cell	*biol*
bosk	*trees*	bull	*relig*	calx	*sport*	cell	*law*
boss	*archit*	bull	*trade*	camp	*govt*	cell	*machine*
boss	*art*	buna	*chem*	camp	*war*	cell	*medic*
boss	*herald*	bunk	*house*	Cana	*Bible*	cell	*physics*
boss	*jobs*	bunk	*travel*	cane	*plants*	cell	*relig*
boss	*machine*	buoy	*travel*	cant	*lit*	cent	*abbrev*
bout	*sport*	BUPA	*abbrev*	cant	*relig*	cent	*money*
bout	*war*	burn	*geog*	cant	*trade*	cert	*abbrev*
bowl	*house*	burn	*medic*	cape	*clothes*	cess	*trade*
bowl	*sport*	burp	*medic*	cape	*geog*	Ceto	*myth*
bowl	*theatre*	burr	*plants*	caps	*abbrev*	Ceyx	*myth*
brae	*geog*	bury	*trade*	Capt	*abbrev*	Chad	*names*
brag	*sport*	Bush	*USpres*	Cara	*names*	chap	*abbrev*
bran	*food*	bush	*geog*	Card	*abbrev*	chap	*jobs*
Bran	*myth*	bush	*machine*	CARD	*abbrev*	char	*fish*
brat	*people*	bush	*trees*	card	*lit*	char	*jobs*
bray	*animals*	busk	*theatre*	card	*sport*	char	*trade*
Bren	*war*	buss	*travel*	Carl	*names*	Chas	*abbrev*
brew	*drink*	bust	*art*	carp	*fish*	chat	*birds*
Brig	*abbrev*	Buto	*myth*	cart	*agric*	chef	*jobs*
brig	*govt*	butt	*machine*	cart	*travel*	Chem	*abbrev*
brig	*travel*	butt	*war*	Cary	*writers*	chin	*medic*
brim	*clothes*	Byng	*war*	case	*house*	chip	*comput*
brio	*music*	Byrd	*music*	case	*law*	chip	*money*
Brit	*abbrev*	byre	*agric*	case	*lit*	chip	*sport*
Brno	*cities*	byre	*animals*	case	*machine*	chip	*trade*
Bron	*myth*	byre	*archit*	case	*medic*	choc	*abbrev*
Bros	*abbrev*	byte	*comput*	case	*travel*	chop	*food*
BThU	*measure*	Cade	*Shakesp*	cash	*money*	chop	*sport*
bubo	*medic*	cadi	*law*	cash	*trade*	chow	*animals*
buck	*animals*	cafe	*drink*	cask	*drink*	chow	*food*
buck	*money*	cafe	*food*	cast	*art*	chub	*fish*
buck	*sport*	cage	*animals*	cast	*film/TV*	chum	*fish*
buck	*trade*	Cage	*music*	cast	*medic*	chum	*people*
Buck	*writers*	Cain	*Bible*	cast	*theatre*	CIGS	*abbrev*
buff	*colour*	cake	*food*	cath	*abbrev*	CinC	*abbrev*
buff	*machine*	calf	*agric*	Cath	*abbrev*	circ	*abbrev*
bulb	*flowers*	calf	*animals*	Cato	*Shakesp*	Ciss	*names*
bulb	*house*	calf	*geog*	cave	*geog*	city	*geog*
bulk	*trade*	calf	*medic*	cavy	*animals*	Civa	*myth*
bull	*agric*	calk	*art*	CCPR	*abbrev*	clam	*fish*
bull	*animals*	call	*animals*	Cebu	*islands*	clan	*govt*
bull	*govt*	call	*trade*	CEGB	*abbrev*	clap	*theatre*

claw	*animals*	cold	*medic*	coup	*herald*	cyte	*biol*
claw	*birds*	cold	*weather*	coup	*sport*	czar	*govt*
claw	*fish*	cole	*veg*	cove	*archit*	DAAG	*abbrev*
clay	*agric*	Coll	*islands*	cove	*marine*	dace	*fish*
clay	*art*	colt	*animals*	cove	*people*	dado	*archit*
clay	*geog*	Colt	*war*	cowl	*clothes*	dais	*archit*
clay	*mineral*	coma	*medic*	cowl	*machine*	dais	*theatre*
clef	*music*	comb	*clothes*	cowl	*relig*	dale	*geog*
cleg	*insects*	comb	*insects*	CPRE	*abbrev*	Dali	*artists*
Clem	*names*	comp	*abbrev*	crab	*fish*	dame	*govt*
Cleo	*names*	cone	*biol*	crab	*fruit*	damp	*geog*
Clio	*lit*	cone	*maths*	crag	*geog*	Dane	*writers*
Clio	*muses*	cone	*trees*	cram	*educ*	dart	*clothes*
Clio	*myth*	conj	*abbrev*	cran	*measure*	dart	*sport*
clog	*clothes*	cony	*animals*	crew	*film/TV*	dart	*war*
clot	*medic*	cook	*jobs*	crew	*jobs*	dash	*lit*
club	*sport*	coon	*animals*	crew	*sport*	dash	*music*
club	*war*	coop	*birds*	crew	*travel*	dash	*sport*
coal	*house*	coop	*trade*	crib	*educ*	dash	*travel*
coal	*mineral*	coot	*birds*	crib	*house*	data	*maths*
coat	*clothes*	cope	*clothes*	CRMP	*abbrev*	date	*fruit*
coat	*herald*	cope	*relig*	croc	*insects*	date	*time*
coca	*trees*	copy	*art*	crop	*agric*	daub	*art*
cock	*machine*	copy	*educ*	crop	*cereal*	Dave	*names*
cock	*war*	copy	*lit*	crop	*trade*	Davy	*Shakesp*
coco	*trees*	Cora	*myth*	crow	*birds*	dawn	*geog*
coda	*music*	cord	*clothes*	CSYS	*abbrev*	Dawn	*names*
code	*law*	core	*fruit*	Cuba	*islands*	dawn	*time*
code	*lit*	core	*physics*	cube	*maths*	daze	*medic*
code	*travel*	Cork	*cities*	cuff	*clothes*	Dday	*war*
coed	*educ*	Cork	*herald*	culm	*plants*	deaf	*medic*
CofE	*abbrev*	cork	*travel*	curb	*trade*	deal	*sport*
CofI	*abbrev*	cork	*trees*	curb	*travel*	deal	*trade*
CofS	*abbrev*	corm	*flowers*	curd	*food*	dean	*educ*
coho	*fish*	corn	*agric*	cure	*jobs*	dean	*jobs*
coif	*clothes*	corn	*cereal*	cure	*medic*	dean	*relig*
coif	*herald*	corn	*medic*	cure	*relig*	dear	*trade*
coif	*war*	corn	*trade*	curl	*clothes*	debt	*trade*
coil	*machine*	Corp	*abbrev*	cusp	*archit*	deck	*sport*
coil	*physics*	cosh	*abbrev*	cusp	*maths*	deck	*travel*
coin	*archit*	cosh	*maths*	cusp	*medic*	decl	*abbrev*
coin	*lit*	cosh	*war*	Cuyp	*artists*	deed	*govt*
coin	*money*	cost	*trade*	cyma	*archit*	deep	*geog*
coin	*trade*	cote	*archit*	cyme	*flowers*	deer	*animals*
coke	*drink*	coth	*abbrev*	cyst	*medic*	deil	*myth*

dele	*lit*	dine	*food*	doxy	*jobs*	dune	*geog*
deli	*food*	Dion	*Shakesp*	drag	*clothes*	dung	*agric*
dell	*geog*	Dirk	*names*	drag	*sport*	dupe	*people*
Dell	*writers*	dirk	*war*	drag	*travel*	dusk	*time*
demo	*govt*	dirt	*geog*	dram	*drink*	dust	*geog*
demy	*educ*	disc	*music*	dram	*measure*	dust	*trade*
demy	*jobs*	dish	*food*	draw	*art*	duty	*govt*
demy	*lit*	dish	*house*	draw	*sport*	duty	*trade*
dent	*law*	disk	*music*	draw	*travel*	duty	*war*
dept	*abbrev*	dist	*abbrev*	dray	*animals*	dyad	*chem*
derv	*abbrev*	dita	*trees*	dray	*travel*	dyer	*jobs*
desk	*educ*	diva	*jobs*	Drew	*names*	dyke	*geog*
desk	*house*	diva	*music*	drey	*animals*	dyne	*measure*
desk	*trade*	diva	*theatre*	drip	*archit*	earl	*govt*
deus	*myth*	dive	*sport*	drip	*medic*	Earl	*names*
Deut	*abbrev*	dive	*travel*	drip	*people*	earn	*trade*
Deva	*myth*	DMus	*abbrev*	drop	*theatre*	east	*geog*
Devi	*myth*	dock	*law*	drug	*medic*	eats	*food*
Dewa	*myth*	dock	*plants*	drug	*trade*	eave	*archit*
dhak	*trees*	dock	*theatre*	drum	*archit*	Ebor	*abbrev*
dhow	*travel*	dock	*travel*	drum	*machine*	Ebro	*rivers*
dial	*abbrev*	dodo	*birds*	drum	*music*	Eccl	*abbrev*
dial	*machine*	doge	*foreign*	duck	*birds*	Echo	*myth*
dial	*time*	doge	*law*	duck	*clothes*	echo	*physics*
dial	*travel*	doit	*money*	duck	*food*	Edam	*food*
diam	*abbrev*	dole	*trade*	duck	*sport*	Edda	*myth*
Dian	*myth*	doll	*people*	duck	*travel*	eddy	*marine*
dibs	*trade*	doll	*sport*	duck	*war*	Eden	*Bible*
dice	*sport*	dolt	*people*	duct	*geog*	Eden	*leaders*
Dick	*Shakesp*	dome	*archit*	duct	*machine*	Eden	*myth*
dick	*jobs*	dome	*relig*	duct	*medic*	Eden	*rivers*
Dick	*names*	door	*archit*	dude	*people*	Edin	*abbrev*
dict	*abbrev*	door	*house*	duel	*sport*	edit	*lit*
Dido	*lit*	dope	*art*	duel	*war*	Edna	*names*
Dido	*myth*	dope	*medic*	dues	*trade*	Edom	*Bible*
diet	*food*	Dora	*names*	duet	*music*	EFTA	*trade*
diet	*govt*	dory	*fish*	duff	*food*	Eigg	*islands*
diet	*medic*	dory	*travel*	duke	*govt*	ElAl	*abbrev*
diff	*abbrev*	dose	*medic*	Duke	*names*	elan	*clothes*
digs	*archit*	dots	*theatre*	DUKW	*abbrev*	Elan	*rivers*
Dike	*myth*	dove	*birds*	Dull	*Shakesp*	Elba	*islands*
dike	*war*	dove	*govt*	dumb	*medic*	Elbe	*rivers*
dill	*plants*	dove	*war*	dump	*music*	ELDO	*abbrev*
dill	*veg*	down	*birds*	dump	*trade*	elec	*abbrev*
dime	*money*	down	*geog*	dump	*war*	Elia	*writers*

Ella	*names*	eyre	*law*	file	*govt*	flue	*machine*
Elma	*names*	Eyre	*writers*	file	*sport*	flue	*music*
Elsa	*lit*	eyry	*birds*	file	*tools*	flux	*art*
Elsa	*names*	Ezek	*abbrev*	file	*trade*	flux	*geog*
emir	*govt*	Ezra	*Bible*	file	*war*	flux	*medic*
Emma	*names*	face	*archit*	film	*art*	flux	*physics*
Emma	*titles*	face	*medic*	film	*film/TV*	foal	*animals*
Enid	*names*	fact	*educ*	fine	*law*	foam	*marine*
ENSA	*abbrev*	fade	*medic*	fine	*music*	foam	*physics*
envy	*sins*	fail	*educ*	fine	*trade*	Foch	*war*
Enyo	*myth*	fair	*trade*	fire	*art*	foci	*physics*
EOKA	*abbrev*	fall	*geog*	fire	*trade*	foil	*sport*
epee	*sport*	fall	*medic*	fire	*war*	foil	*theatre*
epee	*war*	fall	*sport*	firm	*jobs*	foil	*war*
epic	*lit*	fall	*time*	firm	*trade*	fold	*clothes*
epic	*theatre*	Fang	*Shakesp*	firn	*geog*	fold	*geog*
EPNS	*abbrev*	fang	*animals*	fisc	*trade*	Fons	*myth*
epos	*lit*	fare	*food*	fish	*fish*	font	*lit*
Erda	*myth*	fare	*sport*	fish	*sport*	font	*relig*
Eric	*myth*	fare	*travel*	fish	*war*	food	*food*
Eric	*names*	farm	*agric*	fist	*sport*	Fool	*Shakesp*
Eris	*myth*	farm	*archit*	flag	*archit*	fool	*food*
erne	*birds*	fast	*relig*	flag	*flowers*	fool	*people*
Eros	*Shakesp*	fast	*time*	flag	*herald*	fool	*theatre*
Eros	*myth*	fast	*travel*	flak	*war*	foot	*herald*
Erua	*myth*	Fate	*myth*	flam	*colour*	foot	*lit*
Esau	*Bible*	Faun	*myth*	flan	*food*	foot	*measure*
Esth	*abbrev*	fawn	*animals*	flat	*archit*	foot	*medic*
et|al	*abbrev*	fawn	*colour*	flat	*art*	Ford	*Shakesp*
etch	*art*	feed	*food*	flat	*music*	Ford	*USpres*
etna	*chem*	feed	*jobs*	flat	*theatre*	ford	*travel*
Etty	*artists*	fees	*trade*	flax	*plants*	Ford	*writers*
Evan	*names*	fell	*geog*	flea	*insects*	fore	*sport*
even	*time*	felt	*clothes*	flee	*travel*	fore	*time*
ever	*time*	feod	*law*	flex	*machine*	fore	*travel*
Ewan	*names*	fern	*plants*	flex	*physics*	fork	*geog*
ewer	*house*	feud	*law*	flip	*drink*	fork	*house*
exam	*educ*	feud	*war*	flit	*travel*	fork	*tools*
exec	*abbrev*	FIAT	*abbrev*	floe	*geog*	fork	*travel*
exit	*archit*	fiat	*law*	flop	*theatre*	form	*animals*
Exon	*abbrev*	FIDO	*abbrev*	flow	*geog*	form	*art*
exon	*war*	Fido	*animals*	flow	*travel*	form	*educ*
eyas	*birds*	fief	*govt*	fl|oz	*abbrev*	form	*music*
Eyck	*artists*	FIFA	*abbrev*	flue	*archit*	form	*sport*
eyot	*geog*	fife	*music*	flue	*house*	fort	*archit*

fort	*war*	garb	*clothes*	girl	*jobs*	grip	*medic*
foss	*archit*	gash	*medic*	giro	*trade*	grip	*sport*
foss	*geog*	gate	*archit*	Giza	*cities*	grit	*geog*
foul	*sport*	gate	*sport*	Glam	*abbrev*	grog	*drink*
fowl	*birds*	Gath	*Bible*	glee	*music*	grub	*food*
fowl	*food*	GATT	*abbrev*	glen	*geog*	grub	*insects*
fray	*war*	gaur	*animals*	Glos	*abbrev*	Guam	*islands*
FRCP	*abbrev*	Gaza	*Bible*	glue	*art*	guan	*birds*
FRCS	*abbrev*	GCMG	*abbrev*	glut	*trade*	guin	*abbrev*
Fred	*names*	GCVO	*abbrev*	Glyn	*writers*	gulf	*marine*
free	*trade*	Gdns	*abbrev*	Gman	*jobs*	gull	*birds*
fret	*archit*	gean	*fruit*	gnat	*insects*	gull	*people*
fret	*herald*	gear	*clothes*	goal	*sport*	guns	*war*
fret	*music*	gear	*machine*	goat	*animals*	guru	*educ*
Frey	*myth*	gear	*sport*	goby	*fish*	guru	*people*
Fria	*myth*	gear	*travel*	gods	*theatre*	guru	*relig*
Frig	*myth*	gene	*biol*	Gogh	*artists*	gust	*weather*
frog	*animals*	gene	*foreign*	gold	*colour*	guts	*medic*
frog	*clothes*	Gene	*names*	gold	*jewels*	Gwen	*names*
fuel	*house*	gent	*abbrev*	gold	*mineral*	Gwyn	*names*
fund	*trade*	geog	*abbrev*	gold	*trade*	gyro	*travel*
Fury	*myth*	geol	*abbrev*	golf	*sport*	gyve	*law*
fuse	*machine*	geom	*abbrev*	Goll	*myth*	haar	*weather*
fuse	*physics*	Gerd	*myth*	gong	*house*	hack	*animals*
Gaea	*myth*	Gere	*myth*	gong	*music*	hack	*jobs*
gaff	*sport*	germ	*biol*	good	*trade*	hack	*lit*
gaff	*travel*	germ	*medic*	gore	*clothes*	hack	*travel*
Gaia	*myth*	gest	*lit*	Gota	*rivers*	hade	*geog*
Gail	*names*	geum	*flowers*	gout	*medic*	haha	*archit*
gain	*trade*	Gide	*writers*	gown	*clothes*	Haig	*war*
gait	*travel*	gift	*trade*	gown	*educ*	haik	*clothes*
gala	*sport*	Gifu	*cities*	Goya	*artists*	hail	*geog*
gale	*plants*	gila	*insects*	Gozo	*islands*	hair	*medic*
gale	*weather*	Gila	*rivers*	grab	*machine*	hake	*fish*
gall	*medic*	gild	*art*	grad	*educ*	half	*maths*
gall	*plants*	gild	*trade*	gram	*measure*	hall	*archit*
gamb	*herald*	Gill	*artists*	Gray	*writers*	hall	*house*
game	*birds*	gill	*fish*	Graz	*cities*	hall	*theatre*
game	*food*	gill	*geog*	Grey	*Shakesp*	Hall	*writers*
game	*medic*	gill	*measure*	grey	*colour*	halo	*geog*
game	*sport*	Gill	*names*	Grey	*leaders*	halo	*relig*
game	*trade*	gilt	*art*	grid	*machine*	Hals	*artists*
gamp	*clothes*	gilt	*clothes*	grid	*sport*	halt	*medic*
gang	*geog*	gilt	*trade*	grid	*theatre*	hand	*jobs*
gaol	*law*	Gina	*names*	grig	*insects*	hand	*measure*

hand	*medic*	hemp	*medic*	holm	*geog*	hump	*animals*
hand	*sport*	hemp	*plants*	holy	*relig*	Hunt	*artists*
hang	*law*	Hera	*myth*	home	*archit*	hunt	*sport*
hank	*sport*	herb	*plants*	home	*geog*	Hunt	*writers*
Hapi	*myth*	herb	*veg*	home	*medic*	hurt	*medic*
hare	*animals*	herd	*agric*	home	*sport*	husk	*agric*
harm	*medic*	herd	*animals*	Home	*writers*	husk	*cereal*
harp	*music*	hern	*animals*	Homs	*cities*	huso	*fish*
harp	*relig*	Hero	*Shakesp*	honk	*birds*	Hwar	*war*
hart	*animals*	hero	*film/TV*	Hons	*abbrev*	hyke	*clothes*
hash	*food*	hero	*jobs*	hood	*clothes*	hymn	*music*
hasp	*machine*	hero	*lit*	hood	*travel*	hymn	*relig*
hate	*war*	Hero	*myth*	Hood	*writers*	hype	*clothes*
haul	*trade*	hero	*theatre*	hoof	*animals*	hype	*people*
haul	*travel*	hero	*war*	hook	*geog*	hype	*sport*
hawk	*birds*	Hess	*leaders*	hook	*sport*	hype	*trade*
hawk	*govt*	hick	*people*	hoop	*clothes*	hypo	*medic*
hawk	*trade*	HIDB	*abbrev*	hoop	*sport*	Iago	*Shakesp*
hawk	*war*	hide	*animals*	hoot	*birds*	Iago	*lit*
haze	*geog*	hi-fi	*house*	Hope	*names*	Iain	*names*
head	*archit*	hi-fi	*machine*	hope	*virtues*	iamb	*lit*
head	*art*	hi-fi	*music*	Hope	*writers*	IATA	*abbrev*
head	*educ*	high	*geog*	Hora	*myth*	ibex	*animals*
head	*geog*	hike	*sport*	horn	*animals*	ibid	*abbrev*
head	*jobs*	hike	*travel*	horn	*machine*	ibis	*birds*
head	*medic*	hill	*geog*	horn	*music*	ICBM	*war*
head	*travel*	hilt	*war*	horn	*travel*	icon	*myth*
heal	*medic*	hind	*animals*	hose	*clothes*	icon	*relig*
heap	*trade*	hips	*medic*	hose	*house*	idea	*lit*
heat	*physics*	hire	*trade*	hose	*tools*	Iden	*Shakesp*
heat	*sport*	hist	*abbrev*	host	*jobs*	Ides	*time*
heat	*weather*	hive	*trade*	host	*war*	idle	*trade*
Hebe	*astron*	Hler	*myth*	Hoth	*myth*	idle	*travel*
Hebe	*myth*	HMSO	*abbrev*	hove	*travel*	idol	*myth*
heel	*clothes*	hoar	*weather*	howl	*animals*	idol	*relig*
heel	*medic*	hobo	*jobs*	Hugh	*names*	idol	*theatre*
heel	*people*	hock	*animals*	Hugo	*names*	Idun	*myth*
heel	*travel*	hock	*drink*	Hugo	*writers*	ILEA	*abbrev*
heir	*family*	Hodr	*myth*	hulk	*travel*	ilex	*trees*
heir	*law*	hold	*sport*	Hull	*cities*	Ilia	*lit*
hell	*myth*	hold	*trade*	hull	*fruit*	ilia	*medic*
Hell	*relig*	hold	*travel*	hull	*travel*	Ilus	*myth*
helm	*herald*	hold	*war*	huma	*myth*	imam	*govt*
helm	*travel*	hole	*animals*	Hume	*Shakesp*	impi	*war*
helm	*war*	hole	*sport*	Hume	*writers*	Inar	*myth*

Inca	*govt*	jade	*mineral*	Jove	*myth*	kelp	*plants*
inch	*measure*	Jael	*Bible*	juba	*music*	kelt	*fish*
incl	*abbrev*	jail	*law*	Juba	*rivers*	Kent	*Shakesp*
in|re	*foreign*	Jake	*names*	Jude	*Bible*	kepi	*clothes*
INRI	*abbrev*	jamb	*archit*	Judg	*abbrev*	kerb	*travel*
Inst	*abbrev*	jamb	*herald*	judo	*sport*	keta	*fish*
inst	*time*	jamb	*house*	Judy	*names*	KGCB	*abbrev*
Iole	*myth*	jamb	*war*	juju	*myth*	khor	*geog*
Iona	*islands*	Jamy	*Shakesp*	July	*time*	kibe	*medic*
Iona	*names*	Jane	*names*	jump	*sport*	Kiel	*cities*
iota	*measure*	jape	*sport*	junc	*abbrev*	Kiev	*cities*
IOUS	*abbrev*	Java	*islands*	June	*names*	kill	*sport*
IOUS	*trade*	jazz	*music*	June	*time*	kill	*war*
Ipoh	*cities*	jean	*clothes*	junk	*medic*	kiln	*art*
Iras	*Shakesp*	Jean	*names*	junk	*travel*	kiln	*machine*
Irel	*abbrev*	jeep	*travel*	Juno	*Shakesp*	kilo	*measure*
irid	*flowers*	jeep	*war*	Juno	*astron*	kilt	*clothes*
Iris	*Shakesp*	Jeff	*names*	Juno	*myth*	kine	*agric*
iris	*flowers*	Jehu	*Bible*	jupe	*clothes*	kine	*animals*
iris	*medic*	jess	*agric*	Jura	*islands*	king	*govt*
Iris	*myth*	Jess	*names*	Jura	*mounts*	king	*sport*
Iris	*names*	jest	*sport*	jury	*law*	kink	*medic*
iron	*house*	jiff	*time*	just	*law*	kirk	*relig*
iron	*machine*	jill	*animals*	jute	*plants*	kite	*birds*
iron	*medic*	Jill	*names*	kadi	*law*	kite	*sport*
iron	*mineral*	jinn	*myth*	kail	*sport*	kite	*travel*
iron	*sport*	jinx	*myth*	kaka	*birds*	kith	*family*
Isis	*myth*	jive	*music*	kale	*veg*	kiwi	*birds*
isle	*geog*	jive	*sport*	Kali	*myth*	Klee	*artists*
I|spy	*sport*	Joan	*names*	Kama	*myth*	knee	*medic*
ital	*abbrev*	Jock	*names*	Kama	*rivers*	knob	*machine*
itch	*medic*	Jock	*war*	kame	*geog*	knot	*clothes*
item	*trade*	Joel	*Bible*	kami	*myth*	knot	*measure*
Ivan	*names*	John	*Bible*	Kano	*cities*	knot	*travel*
Ives	*music*	John	*Shakesp*	Kant	*writers*	Knox	*writers*
Ivor	*names*	John	*artists*	Kapi	*myth*	Kobe	*cities*
jack	*govt*	John	*names*	Karl	*names*	KoKo	*lit*
jack	*herald*	joke	*lit*	Kate	*names*	kola	*drink*
jack	*music*	joke	*sport*	KCMG	*abbrev*	kora	*birds*
Jack	*names*	joke	*theatre*	KCVO	*abbrev*	kris	*war*
jack	*sport*	Josh	*abbrev*	keel	*travel*	kudu	*animals*
jack	*tools*	Josh	*names*	keen	*music*	Kura	*rivers*
jack	*travel*	joss	*myth*	keen	*relig*	kyat	*money*
jack	*war*	joss	*relig*	keep	*archit*	kyle	*marine*
jade	*jewels*	jota	*music*	keep	*war*	lace	*clothes*

lady	govt	left	govt	ling	animals	Lond	abbrev
lair	animals	Lely	artists	ling	plants	long	abbrev
lake	art	Lena	names	link	machine	long	trade
lake	colour	Lena	rivers	link	measure	loom	machine
lake	geog	lend	trade	linn	geog	loom	sport
Lalo	music	lens	art	lint	medic	loon	birds
lama	relig	lens	machine	lint	plants	loop	sport
lamb	agric	lens	medic	lion	animals	loop	travel
lamb	animals	lens	physics	lion	herald	Loos	writers
lamb	food	Lent	time	lips	medic	lord	geog
Lamb	writers	Leon	names	lira	money	lord	law
lame	clothes	Leto	myth	lira	music	lore	educ
lame	medic	Levi	Bible	Lisa	names	lory	birds
lamp	house	levy	govt	lisp	medic	loss	trade
land	geog	levy	trade	list	archit	lost	travel
land	travel	levy	war	list	clothes	lout	people
lane	sport	liar	people	list	trade	love	sport
lane	travel	lias	geog	list	travel	love	virtues
lang	abbrev	lice	insects	Livy	writers	LRAM	abbrev
Lang	writers	lido	sport	load	war	LRCP	abbrev
lard	food	lied	music	loaf	food	LRCS	abbrev
lark	birds	lien	law	loam	agric	Luce	Shakesp
lark	sport	lieu	geog	loam	geog	luce	fish
lass	jobs	lift	archit	loan	trade	Lucy	Shakesp
last	machine	lift	house	lobe	medic	Lucy	names
late	time	lift	machine	loch	geog	ludo	sport
lava	mineral	lift	sport	lock	clothes	luff	machine
lawn	clothes	lift	travel	lock	house	luff	travel
lawn	plants	lilt	music	lock	machine	luge	sport
lead	jobs	lily	flowers	lock	sport	Luke	Bible
lead	machine	Lily	names	lock	travel	Luke	names
lead	mineral	Lima	cities	lock	war	Lulu	lit
lead	music	limb	geog	lode	mineral	Lulu	titles
lead	theatre	limb	medic	Lodz	cities	Luna	myth
leaf	lit	lime	agric	LofC	abbrev	lune	maths
leaf	plants	lime	fruit	loft	archit	lung	medic
Leah	Bible	lime	geog	loft	house	lure	herald
Leah	names	limn	art	loft	theatre	lure	music
leap	sport	limp	medic	Loge	lit	lure	sport
Lear	Shakesp	line	art	loge	theatre	lush	agric
Lear	writers	line	lit	loin	food	lust	sins
Lech	rivers	line	maths	Lois	names	lute	music
Leda	myth	line	theatre	Loke	myth	Lyly	writers
leek	veg	line	trade	Loki	myth	Lynn	names
lees	drink	line	travel	Lola	names	lynx	animals

Lynx	*astron*	masc	*abbrev*	mile	*measure*	mole	*animals*
Lyon	*herald*	mash	*food*	mile	*sport*	mole	*archit*
lyra	*astron*	mask	*art*	milk	*agric*	mole	*measure*
lyra	*music*	mask	*clothes*	milk	*drink*	mole	*medic*
Lyra	*myth*	mask	*medic*	Milk	*rivers*	mole	*tools*
lyre	*music*	mask	*theatre*	milk	*trade*	mole	*travel*
Maas	*rivers*	mass	*measure*	mill	*archit*	mole	*war*
mace	*govt*	mass	*music*	mill	*machine*	moly	*plants*
mace	*veg*	mass	*physics*	mill	*money*	mona	*animals*
mach	*abbrev*	mass	*relig*	mill	*trade*	monk	*jobs*
Mach	*travel*	mast	*machine*	Mill	*writers*	monk	*relig*
Magi	*Bible*	mast	*travel*	Mime	*lit*	mood	*lit*
magi	*jobs*	math	*abbrev*	mime	*theatre*	mood	*music*
magi	*myth*	Math	*myth*	Mimi	*lit*	moon	*astron*
Maia	*myth*	Matt	*abbrev*	mina	*birds*	moon	*time*
maid	*jobs*	Matt	*names*	mine	*machine*	moor	*geog*
mail	*travel*	maud	*clothes*	mine	*war*	moor	*travel*
mail	*war*	Maud	*names*	mini	*clothes*	mora	*lit*
maim	*medic*	Maud	*titles*	mini	*travel*	More	*leaders*
main	*marine*	maxi	*clothes*	mink	*animals*	More	*writers*
Main	*rivers*	mead	*drink*	mink	*clothes*	MORI	*abbrev*
make	*trade*	meal	*food*	mint	*money*	morn	*abbrev*
mall	*sport*	meat	*food*	mint	*plants*	morn	*time*
malt	*food*	mech	*abbrev*	mint	*trade*	Mors	*myth*
malt	*medic*	meed	*trade*	mint	*veg*	moss	*geog*
mana	*myth*	meet	*sport*	minx	*people*	moss	*plants*
mane	*animals*	Meir	*leaders*	mire	*geog*	Moth	*Shakesp*
Mann	*writers*	meld	*sport*	MIRV	*war*	moth	*insects*
Mara	*myth*	memo	*govt*	miss	*jobs*	MRCP	*abbrev*
mare	*agric*	Ment	*myth*	mist	*geog*	Muck	*islands*
mare	*animals*	menu	*food*	mite	*insects*	muff	*clothes*
marg	*abbrev*	meow	*animals*	mite	*money*	Muir	*names*
Mark	*Bible*	mere	*geog*	mitt	*clothes*	Muir	*writers*
mark	*art*	mere	*war*	Mlle	*abbrev*	mule	*animals*
mark	*educ*	merk	*money*	Moab	*Bible*	mule	*clothes*
mark	*money*	mesa	*geog*	moat	*archit*	mule	*machine*
Mark	*names*	mews	*animals*	moat	*war*	mull	*geog*
marl	*mineral*	mews	*archit*	mode	*clothes*	Mull	*islands*
Mars	*astron*	mica	*mineral*	mode	*educ*	muon	*chem*
Mars	*war*	Mick	*names*	mode	*lit*	muse	*lit*
mart	*trade*	midi	*geog*	mode	*music*	Muse	*myth*
Marx	*leaders*	mike	*film/TV*	Mods	*abbrev*	musk	*animals*
Marx	*writers*	mike	*machine*	mods	*educ*	must	*drink*
Mary	*Bible*	Mike	*names*	moke	*animals*	mute	*birds*
Mary	*names*	mild	*geog*	moke	*travel*	mute	*govt*

mute	*medic*	ness	*geog*	nude	*art*	open	*music*
mute	*music*	nest	*birds*	numb	*medic*	Opie	*artists*
mute	*theatre*	neut	*abbrev*	Oahu	*islands*	opus	*lit*
mutt	*animals*	neve	*geog*	Oaks	*sport*	opus	*music*
myna	*animals*	newt	*insects*	oars	*sport*	oral	*educ*
Myra	*names*	next	*time*	oars	*travel*	oral	*medic*
myth	*lit*	NFER	*abbrev*	oath	*law*	Oran	*cities*
Nabu	*myth*	Nice	*cities*	oath	*relig*	Orff	*music*
NADA	*abbrev*	nick	*govt*	oats	*agric*	orig	*abbrev*
Naga	*myth*	nick	*law*	oats	*cereal*	orle	*herald*
Nagy	*leaders*	Nick	*names*	Obad	*abbrev*	ORTF	*abbrev*
nail	*machine*	nide	*birds*	obdt	*abbrev*	oryx	*animals*
nail	*medic*	Nike	*myth*	oboe	*music*	Oslo	*cities*
nail	*trade*	Nile	*rivers*	obol	*money*	otic	*medic*
Nana	*myth*	Nina	*names*	OCTU	*abbrev*	otto	*chem*
naos	*archit*	Nita	*names*	odds	*sport*	otto	*plants*
naos	*relig*	Noah	*Bible*	Oder	*rivers*	OUDS	*abbrev*
nape	*medic*	nock	*sport*	Odin	*myth*	Ouse	*rivers*
nape	*medic*	node	*geog*	Odin	*war*	ouzo	*drink*
Nash	*artists*	node	*maths*	OEEC	*abbrev*	Oval	*sport*
Nash	*writers*	node	*music*	ogee	*archit*	oven	*art*
NATO	*abbrev*	noel	*music*	ogre	*myth*	oven	*house*
naut	*abbrev*	Noel	*names*	ogre	*people*	over	*sport*
nave	*archit*	Noel	*time*	Ohio	*rivers*	over	*time*
nave	*relig*	noma	*medic*	OHMS	*govt*	Ovid	*writers*
navy	*colour*	Nona	*myth*	oils	*art*	ovum	*biol*
navy	*travel*	Nono	*music*	Oise	*rivers*	Owen	*names*
navy	*war*	nonU	*abbrev*	okra	*fruit*	Owen	*writers*
naze	*geog*	nook	*archit*	okra	*veg*	oxen	*animals*
Nazi	*abbrev*	nook	*house*	Olaf	*names*	Oxon	*abbrev*
NCCL	*abbrev*	noon	*time*	Olga	*names*	Oxus	*rivers*
Neal	*names*	norm	*chem*	olio	*food*	oyer	*law*
neap	*marine*	norm	*measure*	olla	*food*	oyes	*govt*
neat	*agric*	Norn	*myth*	Omri	*Bible*	oyez	*govt*
neat	*animals*	nose	*medic*	Omsk	*cities*	paca	*animals*
Nebo	*myth*	nose	*travel*	once	*time*	pace	*measure*
neck	*geog*	nosh	*food*	onyx	*jewels*	pace	*sport*
neck	*medic*	note	*educ*	onyx	*mineral*	pace	*travel*
neck	*music*	note	*lit*	Oona	*names*	pack	*animals*
NEDC	*abbrev*	note	*music*	oont	*animals*	pack	*sport*
neep	*agric*	note	*trade*	ooze	*geog*	pact	*govt*
Neil	*names*	Nott	*myth*	opah	*fish*	Page	*Shakesp*
Nell	*names*	noun	*lit*	opal	*jewels*	page	*jobs*
neon	*chem*	nous	*educ*	opal	*mineral*	page	*lit*
Neph	*myth*	nova	*astron*	OPEC	*abbrev*	paid	*trade*

pail	*house*	peas	*veg*	pile	*archit*	pole	*physics*
pain	*medic*	peat	*agric*	pile	*herald*	Polk	*USpres*
pale	*archit*	peat	*geog*	pile	*machine*	poll	*animals*
pale	*herald*	peat	*plants*	pile	*physics*	poll	*govt*
pale	*medic*	peba	*animals*	pill	*medic*	polo	*sport*
pall	*relig*	peck	*measure*	pina	*fruit*	pome	*fruit*
palm	*medic*	peel	*food*	pine	*trees*	pomp	*govt*
palm	*trees*	peel	*fruit*	pink	*colour*	pond	*geog*
paly	*herald*	Peel	*leaders*	pink	*flowers*	pons	*medic*
pane	*archit*	peel	*war*	pink	*govt*	pony	*animals*
pang	*medic*	peer	*govt*	pint	*measure*	pony	*money*
Para	*rivers*	peer	*jobs*	pinx	*abbrev*	Pooh	*lit*
pard	*animals*	pelt	*animals*	pion	*physics*	pool	*geog*
park	*archit*	peon	*jobs*	pipe	*house*	pool	*sport*
park	*geog*	peon	*war*	pipe	*machine*	pool	*trade*
park	*travel*	peor	*myth*	pith	*fruit*	poop	*travel*
parr	*fish*	pepo	*fruit*	Pitt	*leaders*	pope	*jobs*
part	*film/TV*	perf	*abbrev*	plan	*archit*	Pope	*relig*
part	*lit*	perh	*abbrev*	plan	*lit*	Pope	*writers*
part	*music*	peri	*myth*	plat	*geog*	pore	*medic*
part	*theatre*	perk	*trade*	play	*film/TV*	pork	*food*
pass	*abbrev*	pern	*birds*	play	*lit*	port	*drink*
pass	*educ*	pers	*abbrev*	play	*sport*	port	*music*
pass	*geog*	peso	*money*	play	*theatre*	port	*sport*
pass	*sport*	pest	*agric*	plea	*law*	port	*travel*
pass	*travel*	pest	*animals*	plot	*film/TV*	pose	*art*
past	*lit*	pest	*insects*	plot	*lit*	post	*archit*
past	*time*	pest	*medic*	plot	*maths*	post	*time*
pate	*food*	Pete	*names*	plot	*theatre*	post	*trade*
path	*archit*	Peto	*Shakesp*	plug	*house*	post	*travel*
path	*travel*	Phil	*abbrev*	plug	*machine*	post	*war*
Paul	*Bible*	Phil	*names*	plug	*medic*	posy	*flowers*
Paul	*names*	phon	*abbrev*	plum	*fruit*	pout	*fish*
Pavo	*astron*	phon	*measure*	plum	*money*	prad	*animals*
pavo	*birds*	phon	*physics*	plup	*abbrev*	pram	*travel*
pawn	*sport*	phot	*measure*	plur	*abbrev*	pray	*relig*
pawn	*trade*	phys	*abbrev*	plus	*maths*	Preb	*abbrev*
PAYE	*trade*	pica	*lit*	pock	*medic*	prep	*abbrev*
PDSA	*abbrev*	pick	*music*	poem	*lit*	prep	*educ*
peag	*trade*	pick	*tools*	poet	*jobs*	Pres	*abbrev*
peak	*clothes*	pier	*archit*	poet	*lit*	prey	*animals*
peak	*geog*	pier	*travel*	poke	*clothes*	prig	*people*
peal	*music*	pika	*animals*	poke	*flowers*	Prin	*abbrev*
pean	*herald*	pike	*fish*	pole	*geog*	prob	*abbrev*
pear	*fruit*	pike	*war*	pole	*measure*	Prof	*abbrev*

prof	*educ*	rack	*war*	read	*lit*	ring	*clothes*
Prom	*music*	RADA	*abbrev*	real	*money*	ring	*geog*
prop	*abbrev*	RADC	*abbrev*	reap	*cereal*	ring	*herald*
prop	*theatre*	RAEC	*abbrev*	reap	*trade*	ring	*sport*
prop	*travel*	raft	*sport*	recd	*abbrev*	ring	*theatre*
Prot	*abbrev*	raft	*travel*	reed	*archit*	ring	*travel*
Prov	*abbrev*	raga	*music*	reed	*music*	rink	*sport*
prow	*travel*	raga	*relig*	reed	*plants*	riot	*war*
prox	*time*	rags	*clothes*	reef	*marine*	ripe	*fruit*
Prut	*rivers*	rags	*trade*	reef	*travel*	rise	*archit*
PSBR	*abbrev*	Rahu	*myth*	reel	*machine*	risk	*trade*
Ptah	*myth*	raid	*trade*	reel	*music*	Rita	*names*
puce	*colour*	rail	*archit*	reel	*sport*	rite	*relig*
Puck	*Shakesp*	rail	*birds*	reel	*sport*	RNAS	*abbrev*
Puck	*myth*	rail	*travel*	regt	*abbrev*	RNIB	*abbrev*
puck	*sport*	rain	*weather*	rein	*animals*	RNLI	*abbrev*
puff	*food*	raja	*govt*	reis	*money*	RNVR	*abbrev*
puff	*lit*	rake	*agric*	REME	*abbrev*	road	*archit*
Puff	*lit*	rake	*people*	Rene	*names*	road	*travel*
pull	*lit*	rake	*tools*	rent	*govt*	roam	*travel*
pull	*travel*	Rama	*myth*	rent	*trade*	roan	*animals*
puma	*animals*	RAMC	*abbrev*	rest	*medic*	roar	*animals*
pump	*clothes*	ramp	*archit*	rest	*music*	robe	*clothes*
pump	*machine*	rand	*money*	Rhea	*astron*	robe	*relig*
pump	*tools*	rani	*govt*	rhea	*birds*	rock	*food*
punt	*travel*	rank	*govt*	Rhea	*myth*	rock	*mineral*
pupa	*insects*	rank	*music*	rhea	*plants*	rock	*music*
purl	*geog*	rank	*war*	rhet	*abbrev*	rock	*war*
push	*travel*	rant	*theatre*	Rhum	*islands*	role	*film/TV*
puss	*animals*	RAOC	*abbrev*	Rhys	*names*	role	*theatre*
putt	*sport*	RAPC	*abbrev*	rial	*money*	Rolf	*names*
pyre	*relig*	rape	*agric*	rias	*geog*	roll	*art*
quad	*archit*	rape	*law*	RIBA	*abbrev*	roll	*educ*
quad	*educ*	rape	*plants*	ribs	*medic*	roll	*food*
quad	*lit*	rare	*food*	rice	*cereal*	roll	*music*
quay	*travel*	rash	*medic*	Rick	*names*	roll	*trade*
quid	*money*	rate	*trade*	ride	*travel*	roll	*travel*
quiz	*educ*	rath	*war*	rift	*geog*	Rome	*cities*
quiz	*sport*	RAVC	*abbrev*	Riga	*cities*	rood	*measure*
race	*geog*	rave	*theatre*	rill	*geog*	rood	*relig*
race	*sport*	rays	*physics*	rima	*archit*	roof	*archit*
rack	*geog*	raze	*archit*	rime	*weather*	roof	*archit*
rack	*govt*	RCMP	*abbrev*	rind	*archit*	roof	*medic*
rack	*house*	read	*comput*	rind	*fruit*	rook	*birds*
rack	*machine*	read	*educ*	Rind	*myth*	rook	*sport*

room *archit*	rush *theatre*	sash *archit*	seer *relig*
root *agric*	rush *war*	sash *clothes*	sell *trade*
root *lit*	rusk *food*	sash *house*	Sept *abbrev*
root *maths*	rust *chem*	SATB *abbrev*	serf *govt*
root *medic*	rust *colour*	Sati *myth*	serf *jobs*
root *music*	rust *plants*	Saul *Bible*	Serg *abbrev*
root *trees*	Ruth *Bible*	Saul *names*	Seth *Bible*
root *veg*	Ruth *names*	save *trade*	Seth *myth*
roro *abbrev*	ryal *money*	saxe *colour*	sett *animals*
Rory *names*	Ryan *names*	scab *medic*	sext *relig*
rosa *flowers*	Saar *rivers*	scab *people*	shad *fish*
Rosa *names*	sack *clothes*	scab *trade*	shah *govt*
rose *colour*	sack *drink*	scad *fish*	shaw *agric*
rose *herald*	sack *govt*	scan *lit*	Shaw *writers*
Rose *names*	sack *trade*	scar *geog*	shed *archit*
Ross *Shakesp*	safe *house*	scar *medic*	Shem *Bible*
Ross *herald*	safe *trade*	scat *music*	shin *medic*
Ross *names*	saga *clothes*	Scot *abbrev*	ship *travel*
rota *govt*	saga *lit*	scow *travel*	shoe *clothes*
rote *music*	Saga *myth*	scud *geog*	shoe *machine*
roup *trade*	sage *colour*	scup *fish*	shop *archit*
rout *animals*	sage *educ*	SDLP *abbrev*	shop *trade*
rout *war*	sage *jobs*	seal *animals*	shot *art*
rove *travel*	sage *plants*	seal *art*	shot *film/TV*
RSPB *abbrev*	sage *veg*	seal *clothes*	shot *medic*
RSVP *abbrev*	saic *travel*	seal *govt*	shot *sport*
ruby *jewels*	sail *sport*	seal *herald*	shot *theatre*
ruby *lit*	sail *travel*	seal *machine*	shot *war*
ruby *mineral*	sake *drink*	seam *clothes*	show *art*
Ruby *names*	saki *animals*	seam *geog*	show *film/TV*
ruck *sport*	Saki *writers*	Sean *names*	show *theatre*
rudd *fish*	sale *trade*	seat *archit*	Shri *myth*
ruff *birds*	SALT *abbrev*	seat *educ*	sial *geog*
ruff *clothes*	salt *food*	seat *geog*	sick *medic*
ruff *sport*	salt *jobs*	seat *govt*	side *sport*
ruin *trade*	salt *mineral*	seat *house*	side *theatre*
rule *govt*	salt *trade*	seat *sport*	sign *herald*
rule *machine*	salt *travel*	sect *abbrev*	silk *clothes*
rule *measure*	sand *geog*	sect *relig*	silk *jobs*
rule *physics*	Sand *writers*	seed *agric*	silk *law*
rule *sport*	Sara *names*	seed *flowers*	sill *archit*
rump *food*	sard *jewels*	seed *fruit*	sill *geog*
rune *lit*	sari *clothes*	seed *sport*	silo *agric*
runt *animals*	sark *clothes*	seer *jobs*	silo *archit*
rush *plants*	Sark *islands*	seer *myth*	silt *geog*

sima	geog	slur	machine	span	travel	stop	music
sine	maths	slur	music	spar	mineral	stot	animals
sing	abbrev	Smee	lit	spar	travel	stud	animals
sing	music	smew	birds	SPCK	abbrev	stud	clothes
sinh	maths	smog	weather	Spes	myth	stye	medic
sink	house	snap	art	Spey	rivers	Styx	myth
sink	trade	snap	sport	spin	sport	subj	abbrev
sink	travel	SNCF	abbrev	spin	travel	suet	food
sire	family	snob	people	spit	geog	Suir	rivers
site	archit	snow	weather	spit	house	suit	clothes
site	geog	Snow	writers	spit	war	suit	law
sium	veg	Snug	Shakesp	spot	geog	suit	sport
Siva	myth	soap	house	spot	medic	sumo	sport
size	measure	sock	clothes	spot	sport	sump	machine
skat	sport	sock	theatre	spot	theatre	sums	maths
skep	agric	soda	chem	SPQR	abbrev	Supt	abbrev
skid	sport	soda	house	spud	veg	surd	maths
skid	travel	sofa	house	spur	flowers	surf	marine
skin	medic	soil	agric	spur	geog	swab	medic
skip	clothes	soil	geog	spur	herald	swag	law
skip	machine	soke	govt	spur	war	swan	birds
skip	sport	sold	trade	stab	medic	Swan	rivers
skip	travel	sole	clothes	stab	war	swap	trade
skis	sport	sole	fish	stab	war	swat	educ
skis	travel	sole	medic	stag	animals	sway	govt
skit	theatre	solo	music	stag	trade	swim	sport
skua	birds	solo	sport	Stan	names	swot	educ
Skye	islands	solo	theatre	star	astron	syst	abbrev
slab	archit	Solr	abbrev	star	film/TV	tabu	myth
slag	geog	Soma	myth	star	jobs	tack	sport
slam	sport	soma	plants	star	lit	tack	travel
slaw	veg	song	lit	star	plants	Taff	rivers
sled	travel	song	music	star	theatre	Taft	USpres
slim	medic	soon	time	stay	travel	tail	animals
Slim	war	soph	educ	stem	flowers	tail	birds
slip	clothes	sorb	trees	stem	lit	tail	fish
slip	lit	sord	birds	stem	travel	tail	govt
slip	sport	sore	medic	step	archit	tail	theatre
sloe	fruit	soul	relig	step	measure	tail	travel
slow	time	soup	art	step	travel	talc	biol
slug	insects	soup	drink	stet	lit	talc	clothes
slug	lit	sown	herald	stew	food	talc	mineral
slug	trade	soya	cereal	stir	law	tale	lit
slug	war	span	archit	stoa	archit	talk	educ
slum	archit	span	time	STOL	abbrev	tana	govt

Tana *rivers*	Thos *abbrev*	tome *lit*	tuna *fish*
tanh *abbrev*	thou *money*	tone *art*	tuna *food*
tank *biol*	thug *law*	tone *music*	tune *music*
tank *house*	thug *people*	tone *physics*	turf *plants*
tank *machine*	Thur *abbrev*	Tony *names*	turf *sport*
tank *travel*	tice *sport*	tool *art*	turn *art*
tank *war*	tick *clothes*	tool *tools*	turn *medic*
tape *measure*	tick *insects*	toot *music*	turn *music*
Tara *myth*	tick *time*	tope *archit*	turn *theatre*
Tare *myth*	tick *trade*	tope *fish*	tusk *animals*
tare *plants*	tide *marine*	tope *relig*	tutu *clothes*
tare *trade*	tide *time*	torc *clothes*	tutu *theatre*
tarn *geog*	tide *travel*	tort *law*	twig *trees*
taro *plants*	tidy *house*	Tory *govt*	twin *family*
tart *food*	tige *archit*	toss *sport*	twit *people*
task *jobs*	tike *animals*	tour *travel*	tyke *animals*
task *trade*	Tiki *myth*	tout *trade*	Tyne *rivers*
TASS *abbrev*	tile *archit*	town *geog*	type *lit*
taxi *travel*	tile *art*	tram *travel*	tyre *travel*
TCCB *abbrev*	tile *clothes*	trap *geog*	tyro *educ*
teak *trees*	tile *house*	trap *sport*	tyro *jobs*
teal *animals*	till *agric*	trap *travel*	tyro *myth*
team *animals*	till *geog*	tray *house*	UCCA *abbrev*
team *sport*	till *machine*	tree *trees*	UEFA *abbrev*
tech *abbrev*	till *time*	trek *travel*	Ullr *myth*
tech *educ*	till *trade*	trig *maths*	ulna *medic*
Tees *rivers*	tilt *geog*	trim *travel*	umbo *herald*
temp *abbrev*	time *music*	Trin *abbrev*	umbo *medic*
tent *archit*	time *time*	trio *music*	unau *animals*
tent *medic*	tint *art*	trip *travel*	undy *herald*
term *educ*	titi *animals*	trot *sport*	unit *film/TV*
term *lit*	Tito *leaders*	trot *travel*	unit *maths*
term *time*	toad *animals*	Troy *myth*	unit *physics*
tern *birds*	Toby *drink*	tsar *govt*	unit *theatre*
Tess *names*	Toby *names*	tuba *music*	unit *war*
test *educ*	TocH *abbrev*	tube *machine*	Univ *abbrev*
text *lit*	toff *people*	tube *travel*	Unst *islands*
text *relig*	toft *archit*	tuck *clothes*	unto *time*
text *theatre*	toft *govt*	tuck *food*	upas *trees*
TGWU *abbrev*	toga *clothes*	tuck *music*	Upis *myth*
thaw *weather*	toga *herald*	tuck *war*	Ural *rivers*
Thea *myth*	togs *clothes*	Tues *abbrev*	ursa *animals*
then *time*	Tojo *leaders*	tufa *mineral*	Urth *myth*
Theo *names*	toll *travel*	tuff *mineral*	urus *animals*
Thor *myth*	tomb *relig*	tuft *plants*	urva *animals*

USAF	*abbrev*	vole	*animals*	watt	*measure*	wing	*insects*
USSR	*abbrev*	volt	*measure*	watt	*physics*	wing	*sport*
Vaal	*rivers*	volt	*physics*	wave	*marine*	wing	*theatre*
Vach	*myth*	vote	*govt*	wave	*physics*	wing	*war*
vair	*herald*	vows	*relig*	WAVE	*war*	wino	*drink*
vale	*geog*	VSOP	*abbrev*	wavy	*herald*	wire	*machine*
Vale	*myth*	VTOL	*abbrev*	WCdr	*abbrev*	wire	*sport*
Vali	*myth*	vulg	*abbrev*	weal	*medic*	wire	*travel*
vamp	*clothes*	WAAC	*abbrev*	wear	*clothes*	wisp	*birds*
vamp	*music*	WAAF	*war*	Wear	*rivers*	wits	*medic*
vane	*archit*	WACS	*war*	Webb	*writers*	woad	*plants*
vane	*geog*	wadi	*geog*	weed	*agric*	wold	*geog*
vane	*machine*	wage	*jobs*	weed	*plants*	wolf	*animals*
vang	*travel*	wage	*trade*	week	*time*	Wolf	*music*
Vans	*myth*	wage	*war*	weft	*clothes*	womb	*medic*
vase	*art*	wain	*travel*	weir	*archit*	wood	*music*
vase	*house*	wait	*music*	weir	*geog*	wood	*sport*
Vaux	*Shakesp*	wake	*relig*	weka	*birds*	wood	*trees*
Vayu	*myth*	wake	*travel*	well	*archit*	woof	*clothes*
veal	*food*	wale	*medic*	well	*geog*	wool	*clothes*
veer	*travel*	walk	*sport*	welt	*clothes*	word	*lit*
vega	*agric*	walk	*travel*	welt	*medic*	work	*art*
Vega	*astron*	wall	*archit*	west	*geog*	work	*jobs*
veil	*clothes*	wall	*medic*	West	*writers*	work	*lit*
veil	*relig*	wall	*war*	WFTU	*abbrev*	work	*music*
vein	*medic*	Walt	*names*	when	*time*	work	*trade*
vein	*mineral*	wane	*geog*	whet	*food*	worm	*insects*
veld	*geog*	wane	*physics*	whey	*food*	wort	*flowers*
vena	*medic*	ward	*geog*	Whig	*govt*	WRAC	*abbrev*
vend	*trade*	ward	*govt*	whin	*trees*	WRAF	*abbrev*
vent	*clothes*	ward	*jobs*	whip	*govt*	wrap	*clothes*
vent	*travel*	ward	*medic*	whip	*jobs*	Wren	*artists*
Vera	*names*	ward	*war*	whip	*sport*	wren	*birds*
verb	*lit*	ware	*trade*	wide	*sport*	Wren	*writers*
vert	*herald*	warm	*geog*	will	*law*	writ	*law*
vest	*clothes*	warm	*weather*	Will	*names*	WRNS	*abbrev*
veto	*law*	warp	*clothes*	wilt	*medic*	WRVS	*abbrev*
vice	*machine*	warp	*travel*	wimp	*people*	Xmas	*time*
view	*art*	Wart	*Shakesp*	wind	*music*	Xray	*medic*
Vili	*myth*	wart	*medic*	wind	*weather*	Xray	*physics*
viol	*music*	wash	*art*	wine	*colour*	yale	*machine*
visa	*govt*	wash	*geog*	wine	*drink*	Yalu	*rivers*
visa	*trade*	wash	*travel*	wing	*archit*	Yama	*myth*
vivo	*foreign*	wasp	*insects*	wing	*birds*	yard	*archit*
void	*geog*	Wate	*myth*	wing	*food*	yard	*measure*

yard	*travel*	yoke	*animals*	Yule	*time*	zeta	*archit*
yarn	*clothes*	yoke	*clothes*	Yves	*names*	Zeus	*myth*
yarn	*lit*	yoke	*machine*	zany	*theatre*	zinc	*mineral*
yawl	*travel*	yolk	*food*	zarf	*house*	Zion	*myth*
yawn	*medic*	yomp	*war*	zeal	*relig*	zoic	*geog*
yaws	*medic*	yore	*time*	zebu	*animals*	Zola	*writers*
year	*time*	York	*Shakesp*	zein	*chem*	zone	*geog*
yelp	*animals*	York	*herald*	Zemi	*myth*	zone	*war*
yeti	*myth*	yowl	*animals*	zero	*maths*	zoom	*travel*
YMCA	*abbrev*	yoyo	*sport*	zest	*food*	Zulu	*war*
Ymir	*myth*						

5 LETTERS

AAgun	*war*	actor	*jobs*	adyta	*archit*	agent	*trade*
AAQMG	*abbrev*	actor	*theatre*	Aegir	*myth*	Aggie	*names*
Aaron	*Bible*	acute	*lit*	aegis	*govt*	aggro	*law*
Aaron	*Shakesp*	acute	*maths*	aegis	*herald*	Agnes	*names*
Aaron	*names*	acute	*medic*	aegis	*myth*	agony	*medic*
abaca	*plants*	adage	*lit*	aegis	*war*	agora	*archit*
abaft	*travel*	Adams	*USpres*	Aegle	*myth*	agora	*govt*
abbey	*archit*	Adana	*cities*	aerie	*birds*	Aidan	*names*
abbey	*relig*	addax	*animals*	Aeson	*myth*	aidos	*foreign*
Abbie	*names*	adder	*insects*	Aesop	*writers*	Ailie	*names*
abbot	*jobs*	addio	*foreign*	affix	*lit*	Ailsa	*names*
abbot	*relig*	Adele	*names*	afoot	*travel*	aisle	*archit*
abele	*trees*	ademi	*food*	afoul	*travel*	aisle	*relig*
abies	*trees*	adhoc	*foreign*	afrit	*myth*	Aisne	*rivers*
Abihu	*Bible*	Adige	*rivers*	again	*time*	album	*lit*
Abner	*Bible*	adios	*foreign*	agama	*insects*	album	*music*
abode	*archit*	adlib	*music*	agami	*birds*	alder	*trees*
Abomb	*war*	adlib	*theatre*	agape	*relig*	Alfie	*names*
abovo	*foreign*	adman	*jobs*	agate	*jewels*	algae	*biol*
Abram	*Bible*	admin	*abbrev*	agate	*mineral*	algae	*plants*
abrus	*plants*	adobe	*archit*	agave	*flowers*	algid	*medic*
abysm	*geog*	adobe	*geog*	agene	*chem*	Algie	*names*
abyss	*geog*	adrem	*foreign*	agent	*chem*	ALGOL	*abbrev*
Accra	*cities*	adsum	*foreign*	agent	*govt*	Algol	*astron*
acorn	*trees*	adult	*jobs*	agent	*jobs*	Algol	*comput*
actor	*film/TV*	adval	*abbrev*	agent	*theatre*	Algol	*myth*

algum	*trees*	angle	*maths*	Arges	*myth*	at|bay	*war*
alias	*govt*	angle	*measure*	argil	*geog*	Athor	*myth*
alibi	*law*	angle	*sport*	argon	*chem*	atlas	*educ*
Alice	*Shakesp*	Angus	*Shakesp*	Argos	*myth*	atlas	*geog*
Alice	*lit*	Angus	*names*	argot	*lit*	atlas	*lit*
Alice	*names*	anion	*physics*	Argun	*rivers*	Atlas	*myth*
Aline	*clothes*	anise	*fruit*	argus	*birds*	Atman	*myth*
Aline	*names*	anise	*plants*	Argus	*myth*	atoll	*marine*
alive	*medic*	Anita	*names*	Ariel	*Shakesp*	atomy	*medic*
alkyl	*chem*	Anjou	*Shakesp*	Ariel	*astron*	atone	*music*
Allah	*relig*	ankle	*medic*	Ariel	*myth*	at|par	*trade*
alley	*archit*	annal	*lit*	Aries	*myth*	attic	*archit*
alley	*sport*	Annas	*Bible*	Aries	*zodiac*	attic	*house*
alley	*travel*	annat	*law*	Arion	*myth*	at|war	*war*
alloy	*mineral*	Annie	*names*	arith	*abbrev*	Auber	*music*
almug	*relig*	annum	*time*	armed	*war*	Auden	*writers*
almug	*trees*	anode	*machine*	armet	*war*	audit	*trade*
aloft	*travel*	anode	*physics*	Arran	*islands*	auger	*tools*
Alpha	*relig*	anvil	*machine*	arras	*house*	aural	*medic*
Altai	*mounts*	anvil	*medic*	array	*clothes*	Auric	*music*
altar	*relig*	Anzac	*abbrev*	array	*war*	avian	*birds*
Alvin	*names*	ANZUS	*abbrev*	arris	*archit*	avion	*travel*
Alwyn	*music*	aodai	*clothes*	arrow	*sport*	Avril	*names*
amass	*trade*	aorta	*medic*	arrow	*war*	awash	*travel*
amban	*govt*	apage	*foreign*	arsis	*lit*	aweto	*insects*
amber	*geog*	apery	*animals*	arson	*law*	axiom	*lit*
amber	*jewels*	aphid	*insects*	Artio	*myth*	azure	*colour*
ambit	*geog*	aphis	*insects*	Asdic	*machine*	azure	*geog*
amble	*travel*	apple	*fruit*	Asher	*Bible*	azure	*herald*
ambry	*house*	appro	*abbrev*	ashet	*house*	Babel	*Bible*
ambry	*relig*	April	*names*	Aside	*music*	Bacon	*artists*
amice	*clothes*	April	*time*	aside	*theatre*	bacon	*food*
amice	*relig*	apron	*clothes*	ASLEF	*abbrev*	Bacon	*writers*
amide	*chem*	apron	*house*	aspen	*trees*	badge	*clothes*
amine	*chem*	apron	*relig*	asper	*money*	badge	*herald*
Amman	*cities*	apsis	*astron*	aspic	*food*	baffy	*sport*
Ammon	*myth*	apsis	*relig*	aspic	*plants*	Bagot	*Shakesp*
ancon	*archit*	araba	*travel*	assai	*music*	baize	*clothes*
ancon	*medic*	arbor	*trees*	assay	*chem*	baker	*jobs*
Andes	*mounts*	Arcas	*myth*	assay	*trade*	Baldr	*myth*
angel	*money*	areca	*fruit*	asset	*trade*	baler	*agric*
angel	*relig*	arena	*archit*	Assoc	*abbrev*	baler	*machine*
angel	*theatre*	arena	*sport*	aster	*flowers*	Balfe	*music*
angel	*trade*	arena	*theatre*	ASTMS	*abbrev*	Baloo	*lit*
anger	*sins*	arena	*war*	as|yet	*time*	BALPA	*abbrev*

balsa *travel*	beach *travel*	Bevan *leaders*	blind *house*
balsa *trees*	beads *jewels*	bevel *machine*	blind *medic*
Banda *leaders*	beads *relig*	bevel *maths*	blind *sport*
B and B *abbrev*	beans *trade*	Bevin *leaders*	Bliss *music*
b and s *abbrev*	beard *clothes*	Bevis *Shakesp*	BLitt *abbrev*
bands *clothes*	bears *trade*	Bhaga *myth*	blitz *war*
bangs *clothes*	beast *animals*	bible *lit*	Bloch *music*
banjo *music*	bebop *music*	Bible *relig*	block *art*
banns *relig*	Becca *names*	Biddy *names*	block *machine*
Barak *Bible*	bedew *geog*	bidet *house*	block *trade*
barge *travel*	beech *trees*	bidup *trade*	blond *clothes*
baron *govt*	begum *govt*	bifid *biol*	blood *medic*
baron *trade*	Behan *writers*	bight *marine*	bloom *flowers*
Barra *islands*	beige *colour*	Bigot *Shakesp*	blowy *weather*
barre *theatre*	Belch *Shakesp*	bigot *relig*	blues *clothes*
Barry *names*	belch *medic*	bijou *jewels*	blues *music*
Bart's *abbrev*	Belem *cities*	bilge *travel*	bluff *geog*
BASIC *abbrev*	belga *money*	billy *animals*	bluff *sport*
basic *chem*	Bella *names*	bingo *sport*	Blunt *Shakesp*
Basic *comput*	belle *jobs*	biped *animals*	blunt *trade*
Basil *names*	bells *music*	birch *law*	blurb *lit*
basil *plants*	belly *music*	birch *trees*	board *educ*
basil *veg*	below *travel*	birth *medic*	board *govt*
basin *house*	Belus *myth*	bison *animals*	board *house*
basin *marine*	bench *house*	bitch *animals*	board *sport*
Basle *cities*	bench *law*	Bizet *music*	board *trade*
Basra *cities*	Bones *leaders*	black *colour*	board *travel*
basse *fish*	Benny *names*	blade *plants*	bobby *law*
basso *music*	beret *clothes*	blade *sport*	Boche *war*
batch *trade*	Beria *leaders*	blade *war*	bogey *myth*
Batea *myth*	Berio *music*	blain *fish*	bogey *sport*
Bates *Shakesp*	Berks *abbrev*	blain *medic*	boggy *geog*
Bates *writers*	Berne *cities*	Blake *artists*	bogus *trade*
bathe *medic*	Berry *artists*	Blake *war*	Boito *music*
bathe *sport*	berry *fruit*	Blake *writers*	bolas *war*
baths *medic*	Berry *names*	blank *war*	bolus *medic*
baths *sport*	berth *archit*	blast *war*	bomoh *medic*
batik *art*	berth *travel*	blast *weather*	bonds *govt*
batik *clothes*	beryl *jewels*	bleak *fish*	bones *music*
baton *music*	beryl *mineral*	bleak *geog*	bones *trade*
baton *sport*	Beryl *names*	bleat *animals*	bongo *animals*
baton *war*	beset *war*	bleed *medic*	bonus *trade*
bayou *geog*	besom *house*	bless *relig*	booby *birds*
beach *geog*	Betsy *names*	blimp *govt*	books *lit*
beach *marine*	Betty *names*	blimp *travel*	boost *trade*

booth	*archit*	brake	*trees*
booth	*trade*	Brand	*titles*
boots	*clothes*	brand	*trade*
boots	*jobs*	brant	*birds*
booty	*govt*	brash	*geog*
booze	*drink*	brash	*medic*
borax	*chem*	brass	*music*
borax	*medic*	brass	*trade*
borax	*mineral*	brave	*war*
borer	*animals*	brawl	*music*
Boris	*names*	bread	*food*
boron	*chem*	break	*medic*
Bosch	*artists*	break	*sport*
bosun	*jobs*	break	*theatre*
bosun	*travel*	bream	*fish*
botch	*medic*	breve	*lit*
Botha	*leaders*	breve	*music*
bothy	*agric*	Brian	*music*
bothy	*archit*	Brian	*names*
bough	*trees*	briar	*trees*
boule	*govt*	bribe	*law*
Boult	*Shakesp*	brick	*archit*
bound	*sport*	brief	*law*
bourn	*geog*	brief	*lit*
bowel	*medic*	brief	*time*
bower	*archit*	brier	*trees*
bower	*sport*	brill	*fish*
bowls	*sport*	briny	*marine*
boxer	*animals*	brize	*insects*
boxer	*jobs*	broad	*geog*
boxer	*sport*	broad	*measure*
Boyce	*music*	broch	*archit*
Boyet	*Shakesp*	broch	*geog*
Boyne	*rivers*	broch	*war*
brace	*birds*	brock	*animals*
brace	*lit*	brogh	*archit*
brace	*medic*	brogh	*geog*
brace	*tools*	broil	*house*
bract	*plants*	broke	*trade*
Bragi	*myth*	brood	*animals*
braid	*clothes*	brook	*geog*
brail	*travel*	broom	*trees*
brain	*medic*	broth	*drink*
brake	*machine*	brown	*colour*
brake	*travel*	Bruce	*names*

Bruch	*music*	by₁law	*law*
Bruin	*animals*	Byron	*writers*
Bruno	*names*	byway	*travel*
brush	*animals*	cabal	*govt*
brush	*art*	Cabal	*myth*
brush	*geog*	cabby	*travel*
brush	*house*	caber	*sport*
brush	*machine*	cabin	*archit*
brush	*trees*	cabin	*travel*
brute	*animals*	cable	*film/TV*
Brute	*myth*	cable	*machine*
B₁side	*music*	cable	*travel*
Bucks	*abbrev*	cacao	*fruit*
bucks	*trade*	cacao	*trees*
buffo	*theatre*	Cacus	*myth*
Buffs	*war*	caddy	*house*
buggy	*travel*	caddy	*jobs*
bugle	*music*	caddy	*sport*
build	*medic*	cadet	*herald*
bulla	*govt*	cadet	*jobs*
bulla	*medic*	cadge	*sport*
bulls	*trade*	cadge	*trade*
bully	*food*	cadre	*war*
bully	*sport*	ca₁ira	*foreign*
bunce	*trade*	cairn	*relig*
bunny	*animals*	Cairo	*cities*
burgh	*geog*	Caius	*Shakesp*
burgh	*govt*	Caleb	*Bible*
burin	*art*	Caleb	*names*
burin	*tools*	calve	*agric*
Burke	*writers*	calyx	*flowers*
Burns	*writers*	camas	*plants*
burro	*animals*	Cambs	*abbrev*
bursa	*biol*	camel	*animals*
Bursa	*cities*	cameo	*art*
bursa	*medic*	cameo	*jewels*
burst	*war*	campo	*geog*
busby	*clothes*	CAMRA	*abbrev*
Bushy	*Shakesp*	Camus	*writers*
butte	*geog*	canal	*geog*
Butts	*Shakesp*	canal	*medic*
buyer	*jobs*	canal	*travel*
buyer	*trade*	candy	*food*
buy₁up	*trade*	Canis	*myth*
by₁bid	*trade*	canna	*plants*

canoe	*sport*	Celia	*Shakesp*	chess	*sport*	Circe	*myth*
canoe	*travel*	Celia	*names*	chest	*house*	circs	*abbrev*
canon	*geog*	cella	*archit*	chest	*medic*	civet	*animals*
canon	*jobs*	cella	*relig*	chest	*medic*	civic	*govt*
canon	*law*	cello	*music*	Chiba	*cities*	claim	*law*
canon	*lit*	CENTO	*abbrev*	chick	*birds*	clamp	*machine*
canon	*music*	Ceres	*Shakesp*	chief	*govt*	Clara	*names*
canon	*relig*	Ceres	*myth*	chief	*herald*	Clare	*names*
canto	*lit*	Cerus	*myth*	chief	*jobs*	Clare	*writers*
canto	*music*	Cetus	*astron*	chill	*weather*	Clark	*artists*
Capek	*writers*	Cetus	*myth*	chime	*music*	clary	*plants*
caper	*plants*	chafe	*medic*	china	*art*	clash	*war*
caper	*sport*	chain	*clothes*	chine	*geog*	clasp	*jewels*
caper	*veg*	chain	*geog*	chink	*trade*	class	*biol*
caple	*animals*	chain	*machine*	Chios	*islands*	class	*educ*
capon	*birds*	chain	*measure*	chips	*food*	class	*govt*
capon	*food*	chair	*educ*	chips	*jobs*	clava	*medic*
Capri	*islands*	chair	*govt*	chips	*sport*	clear	*trade*
Capta	*myth*	chair	*house*	chips	*trade*	cleat	*travel*
capul	*animals*	chalk	*art*	chirp	*birds*	Cleon	*Shakesp*
carat	*jewels*	chalk	*educ*	chirp	*insects*	clerk	*jobs*
carat	*measure*	chalk	*geog*	chive	*veg*	clerk	*trade*
cards	*sport*	chant	*music*	Chloe	*names*	cliff	*geog*
caret	*lit*	chant	*relig*	choir	*music*	Cliff	*names*
cargo	*trade*	Chaos	*myth*	choir	*relig*	climb	*sport*
cargo	*travel*	chaps	*clothes*	choke	*machine*	climb	*travel*
Caria	*myth*	chard	*veg*	choke	*travel*	clime	*geog*
Carla	*names*	charm	*birds*	choky	*law*	clime	*weather*
carob	*trees*	charm	*jewels*	chord	*maths*	clink	*law*
carol	*music*	charm	*myth*	chord	*music*	Clive	*names*
Carol	*names*	chart	*geog*	chore	*house*	Clive	*war*
carol	*relig*	chase	*art*	chore	*jobs*	cloak	*clothes*
carom	*sport*	chase	*geog*	chore	*trade*	clock	*house*
Carpo	*myth*	chase	*machine*	Chris	*names*	clock	*machine*
carve	*art*	chase	*sport*	Chron	*abbrev*	clock	*time*
Casca	*Shakesp*	chasm	*geog*	chuck	*food*	clogs	*clothes*
caste	*govt*	cheap	*trade*	churn	*agric*	clone	*biol*
catch	*animals*	check	*clothes*	chute	*sport*	close	*archit*
catch	*medic*	check	*sport*	chute	*travel*	close	*geog*
catch	*sport*	check	*trade*	chute	*war*	close	*music*
Cathy	*names*	cheek	*archit*	cibol	*veg*	cloth	*house*
cause	*govt*	cheek	*medic*	cider	*drink*	cloth	*theatre*
cavie	*birds*	cheep	*birds*	cigar	*house*	cloud	*weather*
Cecil	*names*	cheer	*food*	Cilea	*music*	clove	*plants*
cedar	*trees*	chela	*relig*	Cinna	*Shakesp*	clove	*veg*

clown	*theatre*	coomb	*geog*	crank	*machine*	crown	*clothes*
clubs	*sport*	co,opt	*govt*	crank	*travel*	crown	*govt*
cluck	*birds*	copse	*trees*	crape	*clothes*	crown	*herald*
clump	*flowers*	coral	*jewels*	craps	*sport*	crown	*money*
Clyde	*rivers*	coral	*mineral*	crash	*clothes*	cruet	*house*
coach	*educ*	Coral	*names*	crash	*trade*	crumb	*food*
coach	*jobs*	Corfu	*islands*	crash	*travel*	cruse	*house*
coach	*sport*	Corin	*Shakesp*	crate	*machine*	crust	*food*
coach	*travel*	Corin	*names*	crate	*travel*	crust	*geog*
coast	*geog*	corno	*music*	crawl	*animals*	crypt	*archit*
coast	*travel*	Corot	*artists*	crawl	*sport*	crypt	*relig*
coati	*animals*	corps	*govt*	cream	*colour*	cubeb	*trees*
cobia	*fish*	corps	*theatre*	cream	*drink*	cubeb	*veg*
coble	*travel*	corps	*war*	credo	*relig*	cubed	*maths*
COBOL	*abbrev*	cosec	*maths*	creed	*relig*	cubic	*maths*
Cobol	*comput*	costs	*trade*	creek	*geog*	cubit	*measure*
cobra	*insects*	cotta	*clothes*	Creon	*myth*	cuddy	*animals*
cocoa	*drink*	cotta	*relig*	crepe	*clothes*	culex	*insects*
cocoa	*fruit*	couch	*house*	cresc	*abbrev*	cumin	*plants*
codex	*lit*	couch	*plants*	cress	*veg*	Cupid	*Shakesp*
Coeus	*myth*	cough	*medic*	crest	*birds*	Cupid	*myth*
cohoe	*fish*	count	*govt*	crest	*herald*	Curan	*Shakesp*
cohog	*fish*	count	*maths*	Crete	*islands*	curds	*food*
COHSE	*abbrev*	count	*sport*	Creus	*myth*	curia	*govt*
coign	*archit*	coupe	*sport*	crick	*medic*	curie	*measure*
colic	*medic*	coupe	*travel*	crier	*jobs*	curie	*physics*
Colin	*names*	Court	*Shakesp*	crime	*law*	Curio	*Shakesp*
colon	*lit*	court	*archit*	Crius	*myth*	curio	*art*
colon	*medic*	court	*law*	croak	*insects*	curry	*food*
colon	*money*	court	*sport*	crock	*art*	curse	*relig*
Comdr	*abbrev*	coven	*myth*	crock	*house*	curve	*maths*
comet	*astron*	cover	*house*	croft	*archit*	cusec	*abbrev*
comic	*lit*	cover	*lit*	Crome	*artists*	cycad	*plants*
comic	*theatre*	cover	*war*	crone	*jobs*	cycle	*geog*
comma	*lit*	covey	*birds*	crony	*jobs*	cycle	*measure*
comma	*music*	coypu	*animals*	crook	*herald*	cycle	*physics*
Comus	*myth*	crack	*geog*	crook	*jobs*	cycle	*sport*
Comus	*titles*	craft	*art*	crook	*law*	cycle	*time*
conch	*medic*	craft	*trade*	crook	*music*	cycle	*trade*
coney	*animals*	craft	*travel*	croon	*music*	cycle	*travel*
conge	*sport*	craig	*geog*	crops	*agric*	cymar	*clothes*
Congo	*rivers*	crake	*birds*	cross	*herald*	Cyril	*names*
conic	*maths*	cramp	*medic*	cross	*relig*	Cyrus	*Bible*
contd	*abbrev*	crane	*birds*	croup	*medic*	Cyrus	*names*
conto	*money*	crane	*machine*	crown	*archit*	cyton	*biol*

Dacca	*cities*	decoy	*jobs*	Dilys	*names*	Donne	*writers*
Dagda	*myth*	decoy	*sport*	Dinah	*Bible*	donor	*jobs*
dagga	*medic*	deeds	*govt*	Dinah	*names*	donor	*medic*
dagga	*plants*	deeps	*geog*	dinar	*money*	Doric	*archit*
Dagon	*Bible*	Defoe	*writers*	d'Indy	*music*	Doris	*names*
Dagon	*myth*	Degas	*artists*	diner	*house*	dormy	*sport*
daily	*lit*	deify	*myth*	dingo	*animals*	dorse	*fish*
daily	*time*	deity	*myth*	diode	*machine*	Dorus	*myth*
dairy	*agric*	dekad	*time*	Dione	*astron*	dough	*food*
daisy	*flowers*	delay	*time*	Dione	*myth*	dough	*trade*
Daisy	*names*	delft	*art*	diota	*house*	Douro	*rivers*
daman	*animals*	Delhi	*cities*	Dip|Ed	*abbrev*	dowel	*archit*
Damia	*myth*	Delia	*names*	Diral	*myth*	dowel	*machine*
Danae	*myth*	Delos	*islands*	Dirce	*myth*	dower	*law*
dance	*herald*	delta	*geog*	dirge	*music*	downs	*geog*
dance	*music*	delve	*tools*	disco	*music*	dowry	*law*
dance	*sport*	demon	*jobs*	ditch	*agric*	dowry	*trade*
D|and|C	*abbrev*	demon	*relig*	ditch	*archit*	doyen	*govt*
dandy	*clothes*	denim	*clothes*	ditch	*geog*	doyen	*jobs*
dandy	*medic*	Denis	*names*	ditch	*travel*	Doyle	*writers*
dandy	*travel*	Denny	*Shakesp*	ditch	*war*	dozen	*measure*
Danny	*names*	depot	*trade*	ditto	*lit*	DPhil	*abbrev*
Dante	*writers*	depth	*measure*	ditty	*music*	Draco	*astron*
Darby	*names*	Derby	*Shakesp*	divan	*govt*	Draco	*myth*
D'Arcy	*names*	derby	*clothes*	divan	*house*	draft	*govt*
daric	*money*	Derby	*leaders*	divan	*lit*	draft	*lit*
darts	*sport*	Derby	*sport*	diver	*birds*	draft	*trade*
datum	*maths*	Derek	*names*	diver	*jobs*	draft	*war*
Davao	*cities*	desto	*music*	diver	*sport*	drain	*archit*
David	*Bible*	deuce	*sport*	Dives	*trade*	drain	*drink*
David	*artists*	devil	*jobs*	divot	*sport*	drain	*machine*
David	*lit*	devil	*lit*	dizzy	*medic*	drain	*medic*
David	*names*	Devil	*myth*	DLitt	*abbrev*	drake	*birds*
Davie	*names*	Devil	*relig*	dodge	*travel*	Drake	*war*
davit	*machine*	dhole	*animals*	Dodie	*names*	drama	*film/TV*
davit	*travel*	dhoti	*clothes*	dogie	*animals*	drama	*lit*
Dayan	*war*	Diana	*Shakesp*	dogma	*relig*	drama	*theatre*
death	*medic*	Diana	*myth*	doily	*house*	drape	*clothes*
debit	*trade*	Diana	*names*	dolce	*music*	Drava	*rivers*
debut	*sport*	Diane	*names*	dolly	*machine*	drawn	*art*
debut	*theatre*	diary	*lit*	Dolly	*names*	dregs	*chem*
decay	*medic*	diary	*time*	dolly	*travel*	dregs	*drink*
decor	*archit*	dicer	*food*	domus	*archit*	dress	*clothes*
decor	*house*	digit	*maths*	Donar	*myth*	drier	*machine*
decor	*theatre*	digit	*medic*	Donna	*names*	drift	*geog*

drift	*travel*	dwale	*herald*	elder	*trees*	Erato	*myth*
drill	*agric*	dwarf	*geog*	elect	*govt*	erica	*plants*
drill	*animals*	dwarf	*myth*	elegy	*lit*	Erlik	*myth*
drill	*clothes*	Dyaus	*myth*	elegy	*music*	ERNIE	*abbrev*
drill	*medic*	dying	*medic*	Elgar	*music*	Ernie	*machine*
drill	*theatre*	Dylan	*myth*	Elias	*Bible*	Ernie	*names*
drill	*tools*	Dylan	*names*	Elias	*names*	Ernie	*trade*
drink	*drink*	Dymas	*myth*	Elihu	*Bible*	erode	*geog*
drink	*geog*	eagle	*birds*	Eliot	*names*	Errol	*names*
drive	*archit*	eagle	*money*	Eliot	*writers*	esker	*geog*
drive	*sport*	eagle	*sport*	Elise	*names*	essay	*educ*
drive	*travel*	eagre	*geog*	elite	*govt*	essay	*lit*
drive	*war*	Eamon	*names*	Eliza	*names*	Essen	*cities*
drome	*travel*	early	*time*	Ellen	*names*	Essex	*Shakesp*
drone	*insects*	earth	*animals*	Ellis	*names*	ester	*chem*
drone	*music*	earth	*geog*	Ellis	*writers*	Etara	*myth*
drops	*medic*	earth	*machine*	Elmer	*names*	Ethel	*names*
dross	*geog*	easel	*art*	Elsie	*names*	ether	*chem*
drove	*animals*	eaves	*archit*	elves	*myth*	ether	*geog*
druid	*relig*	E｢boat	*travel*	embus	*travel*	ether	*medic*
drums	*music*	ebony	*trees*	emery	*geog*	ethyl	*chem*
drupe	*fruit*	eclat	*theatre*	Emily	*names*	et|seq	*abbrev*
druse	*geog*	ecole	*educ*	emmet	*insects*	etude	*music*
dryad	*myth*	Eddie	*names*	enact	*film/TV*	Eurus	*myth*
dryer	*art*	edema	*medic*	enact	*theatre*	Eurus	*weather*
dry|up	*theatre*	Edgar	*Shakesp*	Endor	*Bible*	Evans	*Shakesp*
ducat	*money*	Edgar	*names*	enemy	*war*	Evans	*writers*
duchy	*govt*	edges	*machine*	Enlil	*myth*	evens	*sport*
ducks	*clothes*	edict	*govt*	Enoch	*Bible*	event	*sport*
Dukas	*music*	edify	*educ*	Enoch	*names*	exact	*trade*
dulia	*relig*	Edith	*names*	entry	*archit*	exile	*relig*
dulse	*plants*	Edwin	*names*	entry	*trade*	ex|lib	*abbrev*
Dumas	*writers*	Effie	*names*	envoi	*lit*	extol	*relig*
dummy	*jobs*	Egeus	*Shakesp*	envoy	*jobs*	extra	*film/TV*
dummy	*lit*	Egill	*myth*	envoy	*lit*	extra	*jobs*
dummy	*sport*	egret	*birds*	epact	*time*	extra	*lit*
dunce	*educ*	Ehlis	*myth*	ephod	*clothes*	extra	*theatre*
dunes	*geog*	eider	*birds*	ephod	*relig*	eyass	*sport*
Durer	*artists*	Eiger	*mounts*	ephor	*law*	eyrie	*birds*
Durga	*myth*	eland	*animals*	epoch	*time*	fable	*lit*
durra	*cereal*	Elbow	*Shakesp*	epode	*lit*	fable	*myth*
dutch	*jobs*	elbow	*medic*	Epona	*myth*	facia	*archit*
duvet	*house*	elder	*govt*	equal	*maths*	facia	*travel*
Dvina	*rivers*	elder	*jobs*	Erato	*muses*	Fagin	*lit*
dwale	*flowers*	elder	*relig*	Erato	*music*	Fagus	*myth*

faint *medic*	fetch *myth*	flare *machine*	focus *physics*
fairy *myth*	Fetes *titles*	flare *travel*	focus *theatre*
Faith *names*	fever *medic*	flash *clothes*	foggy *weather*
faith *relig*	fibre *biol*	flash *time*	foist *travel*
faith *virtues*	fibre *medic*	flask *chem*	folio *lit*
fakir *jobs*	fiche *machine*	flask *house*	folio *measure*
falls *geog*	fichu *clothes*	flats *archit*	folly *archit*
fanal *archit*	field *animals*	flats *geog*	foots *theatre*
fanal *travel*	field *cereal*	fleet *travel*	foray *war*
fancy *music*	field *herald*	fleet *war*	force *physics*
Fanny *names*	field *maths*	flesh *medic*	forel *lit*
fanon *clothes*	Field *music*	Fleur *names*	forge *machine*
fanon *relig*	field *physics*	flick *film/TV*	forge *trade*
farad *measure*	field *sport*	flier *travel*	forte *music*
farce *lit*	field *war*	flies *theatre*	Forth *rivers*
farce *music*	fiend *myth*	fling *sport*	forth *travel*
farce *theatre*	fifer *jobs*	flint *geog*	forum *archit*
fasti *time*	fifer *music*	flint *mineral*	forum *educ*
fault *geog*	fifth *music*	float *trade*	forum *govt*
fault *sport*	fight *sport*	float *travel*	fossa *animals*
fauna *animals*	fight *war*	flock *animals*	fossa *medic*
fauna *biol*	filch *govt*	flood *geog*	fosse *archit*
fauna *geog*	files *trade*	Flood *relig*	fosse *war*
Fauna *myth*	filly *animals*	floor *archit*	fount *lit*
Faust *myth*	final *educ*	floor *theatre*	foyer *archit*
Faust *titles*	final *lit*	flora *biol*	foyer *theatre*
feast *food*	final *music*	flora *flowers*	Foyle *rivers*
feint *sport*	final *sport*	flora *geog*	frame *art*
feint *war*	finch *birds*	Flora *myth*	frame *govt*
Felix *names*	Finzi *music*	Flora *names*	frame *house*
felon *jobs*	Fiona *names*	flota *travel*	frame *machine*
felon *law*	fiord *geog*	flour *cereal*	frame *medic*
femur *medic*	fired *art*	fluid *chem*	frame *sport*
fence *archit*	firth *geog*	fluke *fish*	franc *money*
fence *govt*	fitch *animals*	fluke *insects*	Frank *names*
fence *jobs*	fitch *plants*	fluke *travel*	fraud *law*
fence *machine*	fiver *money*	flunk *educ*	Frayn *writers*
fence *war*	fives *sport*	fluor *geog*	Freda *names*
feoff *law*	fjord *geog*	fluor *mineral*	fresh *educ*
feral *animals*	flail *war*	flush *archit*	Freud *writers*
feral *relig*	flame *colour*	flush *medic*	Freya *myth*
fermi *measure*	flame *physics*	Flute *Shakesp*	friar *jobs*
ferry *travel*	flank *food*	flute *archit*	friar *relig*
fesse *herald*	flank *war*	flute *music*	Frigg *myth*
Feste *Shakesp*	flare *clothes*	focus *geog*	frill *clothes*

Frith *artists*	gauze *medic*	girth *animals*	gouty *medic*
frith *geog*	gavel *law*	glade *trees*	Gower *Shakesp*
frith *trees*	Gavin *names*	gland *machine*	goyim *relig*
frock *clothes*	gayal *animals*	gland *medic*	grace *music*
frock *relig*	gecko *insects*	glare *geog*	Grace *myth*
frond *plants*	geese *birds*	glass *archit*	Grace *names*
front *govt*	gelid *geog*	glass *art*	grace *relig*
front *theatre*	gemma *biol*	glass *house*	grade *educ*
front *war*	gemma *plants*	glaze *art*	graft *flowers*
front *weather*	genes *biol*	glean *cereal*	graft *fruit*
frost *weather*	genet *animals*	glebe *archit*	graft *govt*
Froth *Shakesp*	genie *myth*	glebe *relig*	graft *medic*
froth *geog*	Genoa *cities*	glede *birds*	grail *geog*
fruit *agric*	genre *art*	glide *travel*	grail *relig*
fruit *fruit*	genre *lit*	globe *geog*	grain *agric*
fucus *plants*	genus *animals*	gloom *plants*	grain *cereal*
fudge *food*	genus *biol*	glory *relig*	grain *measure*
fugue *medic*	genus *birds*	gloss *art*	grand *money*
fugue *music*	genus *fish*	gloss *educ*	Grant *USpres*
funds *trade*	genus *insects*	gloss *lit*	grape *fruit*
fungi *plants*	geode *geog*	glove *clothes*	grape *war*
furze *trees*	Geoff *names*	Gluck *music*	graph *maths*
fusee *war*	geoid *geog*	glyph *archit*	grass *agric*
fusil *herald*	gerah *measure*	glyph *art*	grass *jobs*
fusil *war*	Gerda *names*	gnome *lit*	grass *plants*
gable *archit*	geste *lit*	gnome *myth*	grass *sport*
Galen *jobs*	get¦up *clothes*	gnome *trade*	grate *archit*
Galen *medic*	Ghats *mounts*	Goffe *Shakesp*	grate *house*
galop *music*	Ghost *Shakesp*	Gogol *writers*	grave *art*
gamba *music*	ghost *jobs*	going *sport*	grave *lit*
gamut *music*	ghost *lit*	going *travel*	grave *music*
G¦and¦S *abbrev*	ghost *myth*	gonad *medic*	grave *relig*
gaper *fish*	ghoul *myth*	goods *trade*	gravy *food*
gaper *fish*	ghyll *geog*	goody *food*	graze *agric*
garbo *jobs*	giant *myth*	goose *birds*	graze *medic*
garda *law*	Gibil *myth*	goose *food*	grebe *birds*
Garry *names*	gigot *food*	gored *medic*	Green *Shakesp*
Garth *names*	gigue *music*	gorge *food*	green *colour*
gaudy *educ*	Gilda *lit*	gorge *geog*	Green *rivers*
gauge *machine*	Giles *artists*	Gorki *writers*	green *sport*
gauge *measure*	Giles *names*	Gorky *cities*	grego *clothes*
gault *mineral*	gilts *trade*	gorse *trees*	Greta *names*
Gauri *myth*	Ginny *names*	Gouda *food*	grice *animals*
gauss *physics*	gipsy *jobs*	gouge *tools*	Grieg *music*
gauze *clothes*	giron *herald*	gourd *fruit*	grill *food*

Grimm	*writers*	Hadad	*myth*	Hekla	*mounts*	Hoder	*myth*
grind	*educ*	Hades	*myth*	Helen	*Shakesp*	hoist	*archit*
gripe	*medic*	Hades	*relig*	Helen	*myth*	hoist	*machine*
groat	*money*	hadji	*educ*	Helen	*names*	hoist	*travel*
groin	*archit*	Haifa	*cities*	Helga	*names*	Holda	*myth*
gross	*measure*	Haiti	*islands*	helio	*colour*	holly	*trees*
gross	*trade*	hakim	*law*	helix	*archit*	Holst	*music*
group	*biol*	halfa	*plants*	helix	*maths*	homer	*birds*
grove	*geog*	Halle	*cities*	helix	*medic*	homer	*measure*
grove	*trees*	halma	*sport*	Helle	*myth*	Homer	*writers*
growl	*animals*	Haman	*Bible*	henna	*colour*	honey	*food*
gruel	*food*	h‚and‚c	*abbrev*	henna	*trees*	Honor	*names*
grunt	*animals*	Hanoi	*cities*	Henry	*Shakesp*	Horae	*myth*
guana	*insects*	Hants	*abbrev*	henry	*measure*	horse	*agric*
guano	*agric*	hardy	*flowers*	Henry	*names*	horse	*animals*
guard	*govt*	Hardy	*writers*	henry	*physics*	horse	*travel*
guard	*jobs*	harpy	*birds*	Henry	*writers*	Horus	*myth*
guard	*sport*	Harpy	*myth*	Henty	*writers*	Hosea	*Bible*
guard	*travel*	Harry	*names*	Henze	*music*	hotel	*archit*
guard	*war*	harry	*war*	herbs	*medic*	hound	*animals*
guava	*fruit*	haste	*travel*	Herod	*Bible*	houri	*myth*
guest	*jobs*	hatch	*archit*	heron	*birds*	house	*archit*
guide	*educ*	hatch	*art*	Herse	*myth*	house	*educ*
guide	*jobs*	hatch	*birds*	Herts	*abbrev*	house	*theatre*
guide	*machine*	hatch	*travel*	hertz	*measure*	house	*trade*
guide	*sport*	Hatra	*myth*	hertz	*physics*	hovel	*archit*
guide	*travel*	haulm	*agric*	Hetty	*names*	humid	*weather*
guild	*govt*	haunt	*myth*	hewer	*jobs*	humus	*agric*
guild	*trade*	Havel	*rivers*	hexad	*chem*	humus	*geog*
guilt	*law*	hawse	*travel*	H‚hour	*war*	Hunts	*abbrev*
guimp	*clothes*	Haydn	*music*	hiker	*travel*	hurry	*travel*
guise	*clothes*	Hayes	*USpres*	Hilda	*names*	hurst	*trees*
gules	*herald*	hazel	*fruit*	hilum	*medic*	husky	*animals*
gully	*geog*	Hazel	*names*	hinge	*archit*	hutch	*animals*
gully	*sport*	H‚bomb	*war*	hinge	*house*	hutch	*archit*
gumbo	*drink*	heads	*lit*	hinny	*animals*	hutia	*animals*
gumbo	*fruit*	heart	*medic*	hippo	*animals*	Hyads	*myth*
gumma	*medic*	heath	*geog*	Hiram	*Bible*	Hydra	*astron*
gunny	*clothes*	Heath	*leaders*	Hiram	*names*	hydra	*fish*
guppy	*fish*	heath	*plants*	hives	*medic*	Hydra	*myth*
gusty	*weather*	heave	*sport*	hoard	*trade*	hyena	*animals*
Gyges	*myth*	heavy	*theatre*	hoary	*weather*	Hylas	*myth*
gyron	*herald*	hedge	*agric*	hobby	*birds*	Hymen	*Shakesp*
gyrus	*medic*	hedge	*trees*	hobby	*sport*	Hymen	*myth*
habit	*clothes*	Heine	*writers*	hobby	*travel*	hyoid	*medic*

hypha	*biol*	Innes	*writers*	jelly	*food*	Judas	*people*
hyrax	*animals*	input	*comput*	jemmy	*tools*	judge	*jobs*
Iasus	*myth*	intro	*abbrev*	jenny	*animals*	judge	*law*
Ibert	*music*	Ionic	*archit*	jenny	*birds*	judge	*relig*
Ibiza	*islands*	Ionic	*lit*	jenny	*machine*	juice	*house*
Ibsen	*writers*	Irene	*myth*	Jenny	*names*	julep	*drink*
ichor	*myth*	Irene	*names*	jerid	*war*	Julia	*Shakesp*
icing	*food*	Irmin	*myth*	jerks	*medic*	Julie	*names*
ictus	*lit*	irony	*lit*	Jerry	*names*	Jumbo	*animals*
ictus	*medic*	Isaac	*Bible*	Jerry	*war*	jumbo	*travel*
ictus	*music*	Isaac	*names*	Jesse	*Bible*	Jumna	*rivers*
idiom	*lit*	Ishim	*rivers*	Jesse	*names*	junco	*birds*
Idmon	*myth*	Islam	*relig*	jetty	*archit*	junta	*govt*
idyll	*lit*	Islay	*islands*	jetty	*sport*	junto	*govt*
idyll	*music*	islet	*geog*	jetty	*travel*	jupon	*clothes*
igloo	*archit*	issue	*jobs*	jewel	*jewels*	jurat	*law*
ileum	*medic*	issue	*lit*	Jewry	*relig*	juror	*jobs*
Iliad	*myth*	issue	*trade*	jiffy	*time*	juror	*law*
ilium	*medic*	Istar	*myth*	jihad	*war*	Jurua	*rivers*
image	*art*	Ister	*myth*	Jimmy	*names*	jutty	*archit*
imago	*insects*	ivory	*colour*	jimmy	*tools*	kaama	*animals*
imbue	*educ*	ivory	*jewels*	jingo	*war*	Kabul	*cities*
incus	*medic*	izard	*animals*	jinni	*myth*	Kafka	*writers*
indef	*abbrev*	Izmir	*cities*	jodel	*music*	kails	*sport*
index	*lit*	jabot	*clothes*	joint	*archit*	Karen	*names*
index	*maths*	Jacky	*names*	joint	*food*	Karna	*myth*
index	*trade*	Jacob	*Bible*	joint	*geog*	karoo	*geog*
indiv	*abbrev*	Jacob	*names*	joint	*medic*	Kasai	*rivers*
Indra	*myth*	James	*Bible*	joist	*archit*	kayak	*sport*
Indus	*astron*	James	*names*	joker	*people*	kayak	*travel*
Indus	*rivers*	James	*rivers*	joker	*sport*	Kazan	*cities*
inert	*chem*	James	*writers*	jolly	*travel*	Keats	*writers*
ingle	*archit*	Jamie	*names*	Jonah	*Bible*	kebab	*food*
ingot	*mineral*	Janet	*names*	Jones	*writers*	kedge	*travel*
ingot	*trade*	Janey	*names*	Joppa	*Bible*	Keith	*names*
Inigo	*names*	Janus	*myth*	jorum	*drink*	Kelly	*artists*
inion	*medic*	Japan	*art*	Josie	*names*	kelpy	*myth*
inlaw	*law*	jarul	*trees*	joule	*measure*	kendo	*sport*
inlay	*archit*	Jason	*myth*	joust	*sport*	ketch	*travel*
inlay	*art*	Jason	*names*	jowls	*medic*	Kevin	*names*
inlay	*medic*	jaunt	*travel*	Joyce	*names*	Keyes	*war*
inlet	*geog*	Jayne	*names*	Joyce	*writers*	khaki	*colour*
inlet	*machine*	jazzy	*music*	Jubal	*Bible*	khoja	*educ*
inloc	*abbrev*	jeans	*clothes*	Judah	*Bible*	kiang	*animals*
inner	*sport*	Jeans	*writers*	Judas	*Bible*	kiosk	*archit*

Kipps	*titles*	lance	*machine*
kitty	*animals*	lance	*medic*
Kitty	*names*	Lance	*names*
kitty	*sport*	lance	*war*
knave	*people*	Lancs	*abbrev*
knave	*sport*	LaPaz	*cities*
knell	*relig*	lapel	*clothes*
knife	*house*	lapin	*animals*
knife	*tools*	lapis	*jewels*
knife	*war*	lapse	*geog*
knoll	*geog*	larch	*trees*
koala	*animals*	Lares	*myth*
kokra	*trees*	large	*music*
kokum	*trees*	largo	*music*
Komos	*myth*	larus	*birds*
kopje	*geog*	larva	*insects*
Koran	*relig*	larva	*myth*
Kotys	*myth*	LASER	*abbrev*
kraal	*geog*	laser	*machine*
krait	*insects*	laser	*physics*
kraut	*veg*	latch	*house*
krona	*money*	later	*time*
krone	*money*	latex	*chem*
kudos	*educ*	lathe	*machine*
kukri	*war*	lauds	*relig*
kulan	*animals*	Laura	*names*
Kyoga	*lakes*	Laval	*leaders*
Kyoto	*cities*	laver	*relig*
kyrie	*music*	lay|by	*travel*
Laban	*Bible*	layer	*geog*
label	*herald*	lazar	*medic*
ladle	*house*	leach	*chem*
ladle	*machine*	learn	*educ*
Lafeu	*Shakesp*	lease	*law*
Lagan	*rivers*	lease	*trade*
lager	*drink*	leash	*animals*
lager	*war*	leave	*war*
Lagos	*cities*	ledge	*archit*
laird	*govt*	leech	*insects*
laird	*jobs*	leech	*medic*
Laius	*myth*	leech	*travel*
LaMer	*titles*	Leeds	*cities*
lamia	*myth*	legal	*law*
Lamos	*myth*	Lehar	*music*
lance	*fish*	Leics	*abbrev*

Leila	*names*	limey	*jobs*
lemma	*maths*	Lincs	*abbrev*
lemna	*plants*	Linda	*names*
lemon	*colour*	Lindy	*names*
lemon	*fruit*	linen	*clothes*
lemur	*animals*	linen	*house*
Lenin	*leaders*	liner	*travel*
Lenny	*names*	lines	*art*
lento	*music*	lines	*educ*
Leona	*names*	lines	*theatre*
leper	*medic*	lingo	*lit*
leper	*relig*	linin	*biol*
Lepus	*astron*	links	*sport*
Lepus	*myth*	Lippi	*artists*
Lethe	*myth*	lisle	*clothes*
levee	*geog*	lists	*sport*
level	*archit*	Liszt	*music*
level	*geog*	litho	*machine*
level	*measure*	litre	*measure*
lever	*tools*	liver	*food*
Levis	*clothes*	liver	*medic*
Lewis	*Shakesp*	livre	*measure*
Lewis	*islands*	llama	*animals*
Lewis	*names*	llano	*geog*
Lewis	*writers*	Lloyd	*names*
Leyte	*islands*	loach	*educ*
liana	*plants*	lobby	*archit*
Liard	*rivers*	lobby	*govt*
Libby	*names*	lobby	*house*
libel	*law*	local	*geog*
Liber	*myth*	local	*jobs*
libra	*measure*	local	*medic*
Libra	*myth*	Locke	*music*
Libra	*zodiac*	Locke	*writers*
licit	*law*	locum	*jobs*
liege	*govt*	locum	*medic*
lie|to	*travel*	locus	*geog*
Lieut	*abbrev*	locus	*maths*
liger	*animals*	lodge	*archit*
light	*physics*	Lodge	*writers*
light	*travel*	loess	*geog*
lilac	*colour*	Logos	*relig*
lilac	*trees*	Loire	*rivers*
limax	*insects*	loose	*sport*
limbo	*myth*	loran	*travel*

Lorca	*writers*	lyric	*lit*	manse	*archit*	Medea	*myth*
loris	*animals*	lyric	*music*	manse	*relig*	Medea	*titles*
Lorna	*names*	lysin	*biol*	manta	*clothes*	Medes	*relig*
lorry	*travel*	lysis	*medic*	manto	*clothes*	Media	*relig*
loser	*jobs*	Mabel	*lit*	manul	*animals*	medic	*jobs*
loser	*sport*	Mabel	*names*	Maori	*jobs*	medic	*medic*
lotto	*sport*	macaw	*birds*	maple	*trees*	Medoc	*drink*
lotus	*archit*	macho	*people*	March	*Shakesp*	melee	*war*
lotus	*flowers*	madam	*jobs*	March	*herald*	melic	*music*
lough	*geog*	madge	*birds*	march	*music*	melon	*fruit*
louis	*money*	Madge	*names*	march	*sport*	Melun	*Shakesp*
Louis	*names*	Maeve	*names*	March	*time*	Menas	*Shakesp*
louse	*insects*	Mafia	*law*	march	*travel*	Mensa	*astron*
Lovel	*Shakesp*	Magda	*names*	Marco	*lit*	merit	*educ*
lover	*jobs*	magma	*geog*	marge	*geog*	merle	*birds*
Lowry	*artists*	magma	*mineral*	Marge	*names*	Merle	*names*
Lt.Col	*abbrev*	Magog	*myth*	Margo	*names*	meson	*physics*
Lt.Gen	*abbrev*	magus	*myth*	Maria	*Shakesp*	metal	*mineral*
Lucan	*writers*	magus	*relig*	Maria	*names*	meter	*machine*
luces	*herald*	mains	*archit*	Marie	*names*	meter	*measure*
Lucia	*names*	maize	*agric*	Mario	*names*	meths	*abbrev*
Lucio	*Shakesp*	maize	*cereal*	marly	*geog*	Metis	*myth*
lucre	*trade*	major	*educ*	Marne	*rivers*	metre	*lit*
Luger	*war*	major	*govt*	marsh	*geog*	metre	*measure*
Lully	*music*	major	*jobs*	Marty	*names*	metre	*music*
lumen	*measure*	major	*music*	Marut	*myth*	Meuse	*rivers*
lunar	*astron*	maker	*jobs*	mason	*jobs*	mezzo	*music*
lunch	*food*	Maker	*relig*	Mason	*writers*	Miami	*cities*
lunge	*sport*	maker	*trade*	match	*sport*	miaow	*animals*
lungi	*clothes*	Malmo	*cities*	mater	*family*	miasm	*medic*
lungs	*medic*	Malta	*islands*	maths	*abbrev*	Micah	*Bible*
Lupus	*astron*	malva	*flowers*	matin	*time*	micro	*comput*
Lupus	*myth*	mamba	*insects*	Maude	*names*	Midas	*myth*
lurex	*clothes*	mambo	*sport*	mauve	*colour*	Midas	*trade*
luter	*jobs*	Mamie	*names*	mavis	*birds*	Middx	*abbrev*
luter	*music*	mamma	*medic*	Mavis	*names*	midge	*insects*
Luzon	*islands*	Manet	*artists*	maxim	*lit*	mid on	*sport*
lycee	*educ*	mango	*fruit*	mayor	*govt*	Milan	*cities*
Lycus	*myth*	manis	*animals*	mayor	*jobs*	miler	*sport*
Lydia	*myth*	manna	*food*	Mazda	*myth*	Miles	*names*
Lydia	*names*	manna	*relig*	Mazda	*relig*	Milly	*names*
lymph	*biol*	Manny	*names*	means	*trade*	Milne	*writers*
lymph	*medic*	Manon	*titles*	Mecca	*cities*	mimer	*theatre*
Lynne	*names*	manor	*archit*	Mecca	*relig*	mimic	*myth*
Lyons	*cities*	manor	*govt*	medal	*sport*	mimic	*theatre*

mince	*food*	Moray	*names*	mummy	*family*	Nelly	*names*
miner	*jobs*	mores	*law*	mumps	*medic*	Nerio	*myth*
minim	*measure*	Morna	*myth*	mural	*art*	nerve	*medic*
minim	*music*	Morna	*names*	mural	*house*	Netty	*names*
minor	*educ*	moron	*people*	murex	*fish*	neume	*music*
minor	*govt*	morra	*sport*	murre	*birds*	never	*time*
minor	*jobs*	morse	*animals*	murry	*fish*	Nevis	*islands*
minor	*music*	morse	*travel*	musak	*music*	nevus	*medic*
Minos	*myth*	Morta	*myth*	Musca	*astron*	newel	*archit*
minus	*maths*	Moses	*Bible*	musci	*plants*	Niall	*names*
miser	*people*	Moses	*names*	Muses	*lit*	niche	*archit*
miser	*trade*	Mosul	*cities*	music	*music*	Nicky	*names*
misty	*weather*	motel	*archit*	Myles	*names*	Nicol	*names*
mitre	*archit*	motet	*music*	Myrna	*names*	nidus	*birds*
mitre	*herald*	motet	*relig*	myrrh	*relig*	niece	*family*
mitre	*relig*	motif	*art*	myrrh	*trees*	Nigel	*names*
Mitzi	*names*	motif	*clothes*	NAAFI	*abbrev*	Niger	*rivers*
mixer	*house*	motif	*music*	nabob	*govt*	night	*time*
mixer	*machine*	motor	*machine*	nadir	*astron*	ninon	*clothes*
mocha	*drink*	motor	*travel*	Nahum	*Bible*	Ninos	*myth*
modal	*music*	motto	*herald*	naiad	*myth*	ninth	*music*
model	*art*	motto	*lit*	naker	*music*	Niobe	*myth*
model	*clothes*	mould	*art*	Nancy	*names*	nisse	*myth*
model	*jobs*	mould	*flowers*	nandu	*birds*	nitre	*chem*
Mogul	*govt*	mould	*geog*	Nanna	*myth*	nixie	*myth*
mohur	*money*	mould	*machine*	nanny	*animals*	Nixon	*USpres*
Moira	*myth*	moult	*birds*	nanny	*jobs*	Njord	*myth*
Moira	*names*	mound	*relig*	Nanny	*names*	nobid	*sport*
moire	*clothes*	mound	*war*	Naomi	*Bible*	noble	*govt*
molar	*medic*	mount	*animals*	Naomi	*names*	noble	*money*
Molly	*names*	mount	*geog*	nappy	*clothes*	nodes	*geog*
Momos	*myth*	mount	*travel*	nasal	*medic*	nomad	*people*
Momus	*myth*	mouse	*animals*	naval	*travel*	nomad	*travel*
monad	*chem*	mouse	*people*	navel	*medic*	nonce	*time*
Monet	*artists*	mouth	*geog*	navvy	*jobs*	nones	*relig*
money	*trade*	mouth	*medic*	nawab	*govt*	nonet	*music*
monte	*sport*	movie	*film/TV*	Naxos	*islands*	noose	*govt*
month	*time*	mower	*agric*	nebel	*music*	Norma	*astron*
Moore	*war*	mower	*tools*	Neddy	*animals*	Norma	*lit*
Moore	*writers*	mufti	*clothes*	Neddy	*govt*	Norma	*names*
moose	*animals*	mufti	*law*	Negeb	*relig*	Norma	*titles*
Mopsa	*Shakesp*	muggy	*weather*	Negro	*rivers*	north	*geog*
Morag	*names*	mulch	*agric*	negus	*govt*	North	*leaders*
moral	*lit*	mulct	*law*	Nehru	*leaders*	notch	*sport*
moray	*birds*	mules	*clothes*	neigh	*animals*	notes	*music*

Notts *abbrev*	opera *music*	ovary *medic*	panic *plants*
Notus *geog*	opera *theatre*	ovate *biol*	panic *trade*
Notus *myth*	opium *medic*	ovine *agric*	pansy *flowers*
novel *lit*	optic *physics*	ovoid *biol*	pants *clothes*
Noyes *writers*	orang *animals*	ovolo *archit*	paolo *money*
NSPCC *abbrev*	orbit *astron*	ovule *biol*	papaw *fruit*
nurse *jobs*	orbit *physics*	owing *trade*	paper *educ*
nurse *medic*	orbit *travel*	owlet *birds*	paper *lit*
nylon *chem*	Orcus *myth*	owner *jobs*	paper *trade*
nylon *clothes*	Orczy *writers*	ox,bow *geog*	Parca *myth*
nymph *insects*	order *archit*	oxeye *birds*	Paris *Shakesp*
nymph *myth*	order *biol*	OXFAM *abbrev*	Paris *cities*
oasis *geog*	order *herald*	oxide *chem*	Paris *myth*
obang *money*	order *trade*	oxlip *flowers*	parka *clothes*
obeah *myth*	oread *myth*	ozone *chem*	Parry *music*
obiit *foreign*	organ *lit*	ozone *geog*	parry *sport*
Obote *leaders*	organ *medic*	paddy *cereal*	parry *war*
ocean *marine*	organ *music*	Paddy *names*	parse *lit*
ochre *colour*	orgue *war*	padre *jobs*	party *govt*
ochre *mineral*	oriel *archit*	padre *relig*	party *jobs*
ochre *trade*	Orion *astron*	Padua *cities*	pasha *govt*
ocrea *flowers*	Orion *myth*	paean *lit*	passe *time*
octad *maths*	Orlon *clothes*	paean *music*	pasta *food*
octet *maths*	ormer *fish*	Paean *myth*	paste *jewels*
octet *music*	ornis *birds*	paean *relig*	pasty *food*
odeon *film/TV*	Orpen *artists*	pagan *myth*	patch *clothes*
odeon *music*	orpin *plants*	pagan *relig*	patch *veg*
odeum *theatre*	orris *fruit*	Paine *writers*	paten *relig*
odist *jobs*	Orson *names*	paint *art*	pater *family*
odist *lit*	Osage *rivers*	paint *clothes*	Pater *writers*
offal *food*	Osaka *cities*	paint *house*	patio *archit*
offer *trade*	oscar *film/TV*	pairs *sport*	Patna *cities*
often *time*	Oscar *lit*	palay *trees*	patte *clothes*
ogive *archit*	Oscar *names*	paled *herald*	patty *food*
okapi *animals*	osier *plants*	pales *herald*	Patty *names*
olive *fruit*	Osmin *lit*	Pales *myth*	Paula *names*
Omaha *cities*	Osric *Shakesp*	palsy *medic*	pause *music*
ombre *sport*	otary *animals*	Panay *islands*	pause *time*
Omega *relig*	otter *animals*	panda *animals*	pavan *music*
on,cue *theatre*	Ouida *writers*	P,and,O *abbrev*	pavis *war*
onion *veg*	Ouija *sport*	panel *archit*	Peace *rivers*
onset *war*	ounce *animals*	panel *govt*	peach *colour*
on,tow *travel*	ouphe *myth*	panel *house*	peach *fruit*
op,art *art*	ousel *birds*	panel *machine*	pearl *jewels*
op,cit *abbrev*	ouzel *birds*	panel *medic*	pearl *lit*

Pearl	*names*	picus	*birds*	place	*geog*	point	*art*
Pearl	*rivers*	pidog	*animals*	plaid	*clothes*	point	*clothes*
pease	*veg*	piece	*art*	plain	*geog*	point	*geog*
pecan	*food*	piece	*lit*	plain	*herald*	point	*lit*
pecan	*fruit*	piece	*money*	plait	*clothes*	point	*maths*
Pecos	*rivers*	piece	*music*	plane	*maths*	point	*music*
pedal	*machine*	piece	*theatre*	plane	*tools*	point	*sport*
pedal	*music*	piece	*trade*	plane	*travel*	point	*time*
pedal	*travel*	piety	*relig*	plane	*trees*	poise	*chem*
peggy	*birds*	piggy	*animals*	plant	*agric*	poker	*birds*
Peggy	*names*	pilaf	*food*	plant	*machine*	poker	*house*
pekan	*birds*	pilaw	*food*	plant	*plants*	poker	*sport*
pence	*money*	pilot	*jobs*	plant	*trade*	polar	*geog*
penny	*money*	pilot	*sport*	plash	*geog*	polar	*physics*
Penny	*names*	pilot	*travel*	plate	*art*	polio	*medic*
peony	*flowers*	Pinch	*Shakesp*	plate	*herald*	polka	*music*
Pepys	*writers*	pinch	*law*	plate	*house*	polka	*sport*
Perce	*names*	pinna	*fish*	plate	*machine*	polls	*govt*
perch	*fish*	pinna	*medic*	plate	*medic*	Polly	*birds*
perch	*measure*	pinon	*fruit*	Plate	*rivers*	Polly	*names*
Percy	*Shakesp*	pinta	*measure*	plate	*war*	polyp	*fish*
Percy	*names*	pinto	*animals*	Plato	*writers*	polyp	*medic*
Peron	*leaders*	pinup	*art*	playa	*geog*	pongo	*animals*
Perry	*names*	pinup	*jobs*	plaza	*archit*	pooch	*animals*
perse	*colour*	pious	*relig*	plaza	*geog*	pools	*sport*
perse	*foreign*	pipal	*trees*	plead	*law*	Poona	*cities*
Perth	*cities*	Piper	*artists*	pleat	*clothes*	poppy	*flowers*
petal	*flowers*	piper	*jobs*	plebs	*govt*	porch	*archit*
Peter	*Bible*	piper	*music*	pleno	*music*	porch	*house*
Peter	*Shakesp*	pipit	*birds*	Pliny	*writers*	porgy	*fish*
Peter	*names*	pique	*clothes*	pluck	*music*	Porte	*govt*
petri	*biol*	pique	*sport*	plumb	*measure*	poser	*educ*
petty	*law*	pitch	*archit*	plume	*clothes*	posse	*govt*
pewit	*birds*	pitch	*music*	plume	*lit*	posse	*jobs*
phase	*astron*	pitch	*sport*	plush	*clothes*	posse	*war*
phase	*physics*	pitch	*trade*	PLUTO	*abbrev*	potto	*animals*
Phebe	*Shakesp*	pitch	*travel*	Pluto	*astron*	pouch	*animals*
pheon	*herald*	piton	*sport*	Pluto	*myth*	poult	*birds*
Philo	*Shakesp*	pitta	*birds*	poach	*food*	pound	*animals*
phlox	*flowers*	Pitys	*myth*	poach	*govt*	pound	*measure*
phone	*lit*	pivot	*machine*	Poeas	*myth*	pound	*money*
photo	*art*	pivot	*sport*	poesy	*lit*	pound	*trade*
piano	*house*	pixie	*clothes*	pogge	*fish*	Pound	*writers*
piano	*music*	pixie	*myth*	poilu	*war*	power	*govt*
Piave	*rivers*	pizza	*food*	Poins	*Shakesp*	power	*maths*

power	*physics*	psalm	*music*	quill	*educ*	ranch	*archit*
power	*war*	psalm	*relig*	quill	*jobs*	RandA	*abbrev*
praam	*travel*	pseud	*abbrev*	quill	*lit*	RandD	*abbrev*
prang	*travel*	psora	*medic*	quill	*machine*	range	*archit*
prank	*sport*	Pugin	*artists*	quilt	*house*	range	*geog*
prawn	*fish*	pulse	*cereal*	quint	*music*	range	*music*
press	*house*	pulse	*medic*	Quito	*cities*	range	*sport*
press	*lit*	pulse	*music*	quoin	*archit*	range	*travel*
press	*machine*	pumps	*clothes*	quoin	*machine*	range	*war*
Priam	*Shakesp*	punch	*drink*	quota	*trade*	ranks	*war*
Priam	*myth*	Punch	*theatre*	quote	*lit*	raphe	*medic*
price	*trade*	punch	*tools*	quote	*trade*	rapid	*geog*
pride	*animals*	punto	*sport*	Rabat	*cities*	rasse	*animals*
pride	*sins*	pupil	*art*	rabbi	*jobs*	ratel	*animals*
prime	*art*	pupil	*jobs*	rabbi	*relig*	ratio	*maths*
prime	*educ*	pupil	*medic*	rabid	*medic*	Ravel	*music*
prime	*lit*	puppy	*animals*	racer	*jobs*	raven	*birds*
prime	*maths*	puppy	*people*	racer	*sport*	rayon	*clothes*
prime	*time*	puree	*food*	racer	*travel*	razed	*herald*
print	*art*	purge	*medic*	rache	*animals*	razor	*machine*
print	*clothes*	Purim	*time*	radar	*machine*	reach	*geog*
print	*lit*	purse	*clothes*	radar	*physics*	reach	*travel*
prior	*jobs*	purse	*trade*	radar	*travel*	Reade	*writers*
prior	*relig*	Purus	*rivers*	radii	*maths*	ready	*time*
prior	*time*	pussy	*animals*	radio	*film/TV*	realm	*geog*
prism	*art*	puton	*theatre*	radio	*house*	realm	*govt*
prism	*maths*	pylon	*archit*	radio	*machine*	rebec	*music*
prize	*educ*	pylon	*machine*	radio	*travel*	rebel	*govt*
prize	*trade*	pylon	*travel*	radix	*maths*	rebel	*war*
projam	*sport*	Qboat	*travel*	radix	*plants*	rebus	*herald*
probe	*medic*	quack	*birds*	radon	*chem*	rebus	*lit*
proem	*lit*	quack	*jobs*	rails	*trade*	rebuy	*trade*
proms	*music*	quack	*medic*	rains	*weather*	recce	*war*
prong	*machine*	quaff	*drink*	rainy	*weather*	recto	*lit*
proof	*govt*	quail	*birds*	rajah	*govt*	redan	*war*
proof	*lit*	quail	*food*	rally	*govt*	reeds	*music*
props	*theatre*	quark	*physics*	rally	*sport*	reeve	*birds*
prose	*lit*	quart	*measure*	rally	*trade*	reeve	*law*
prosy	*lit*	quart	*sport*	rally	*travel*	regal	*govt*
Provo	*law*	quash	*law*	rally	*war*	regal	*music*
Provo	*war*	queen	*govt*	Ralph	*names*	Regan	*Shakesp*
proxy	*govt*	queen	*sport*	ramie	*plants*	Reger	*music*
proxy	*jobs*	queer	*trade*	ramus	*medic*	Reich	*geog*
prude	*people*	queue	*clothes*	ramus	*trees*	reign	*govt*
prune	*fruit*	queue	*theatre*	ranch	*agric*	reins	*animals*

relay *machine*	robes *clothes*	RSPCA *abbrev*	salts *medic*
relay *physics*	Robin *Shakesp*	RtlHon *abbrev*	salve *medic*
relay *sport*	robin *birds*	RtlRev *abbrev*	salve *trade*
relay *travel*	Robin *names*	rubia *plants*	salvo *war*
relic *relig*	roble *trees*	Rufus *names*	Samar *islands*
remit *trade*	robot *machine*	Rugby *Shakesp*	samba *sport*
Remus *myth*	Robur *myth*	rugby *sport*	Samoa *islands*
renal *medic*	rocks *trade*	Rugen *islands*	Samos *islands*
repay *trade*	rodeo *theatre*	ruler *govt*	Samso *islands*
repel *war*	Rodge *names*	ruler *maths*	Sands *Shakesp*
reply *lit*	Rodin *artists*	ruler *measure*	Sandy *names*
reset *law*	Roger *names*	rules *sport*	Saone *rivers*
resin *chem*	rogue *people*	rumal *clothes*	sapan *trees*
resin *music*	roker *fish*	rumba *music*	Sarah *Bible*
revet *archit*	romal *clothes*	rumba *sport*	Sarah *names*
revue *theatre*	Roman *lit*	rumen *agric*	saros *astron*
revlup *travel*	Romeo *Shakesp*	rummy *sport*	Sarum *abbrev*
rheum *medic*	rondo *music*	runes *lit*	sasin *animals*
Rhine *rivers*	rooms *archit*	runic *lit*	Satan *myth*
rhino *animals*	roost *birds*	runic *music*	Satan *relig*
rhino *trade*	roots *trees*	rupee *money*	Satie *music*
Rhoda *names*	roots *veg*	rural *geog*	satin *clothes*
rhomb *maths*	ropes *travel*	sable *animals*	satyr *animals*
Rhona *names*	rosin *chem*	sable *clothes*	satyr *myth*
Rhone *rivers*	rosin *music*	sable *herald*	sauce *food*
rhyme *lit*	ROSLA *abbrev*	sabot *clothes*	sault *geog*
rider *jobs*	RoSPA *abbrev*	sabre *sport*	saury *fish*
rider *law*	rotch *birds*	Sadie *names*	saute *food*
rider *maths*	rotor *machine*	sagum *clothes*	saver *jobs*
rider *travel*	rotor *travel*	saiga *animals*	savoy *veg*
ridge *archit*	rouge *colour*	saint *people*	sawer *jobs*
ridge *geog*	rouge *sport*	saint *relig*	scald *lit*
rifle *machine*	rough *art*	Sakai *cities*	scale *archit*
rifle *war*	rough *sport*	saker *birds*	scale *fish*
Rigel *astron*	round *food*	salad *veg*	scale *geog*
right *geog*	round *music*	salle *archit*	scale *measure*
right *law*	round *sport*	Sally *names*	scale *music*
Rilke *writers*	route *travel*	sally *travel*	scalp *medic*
riser *archit*	rover *jobs*	sally *war*	scalp *trade*
rishi *jobs*	rover *sport*	salmi *food*	scamp *people*
rival *jobs*	rowan *trees*	salon *archit*	scape *art*
river *geog*	rowel *herald*	salon *house*	scarf *clothes*
rivet *machine*	rowel *war*	Salop *abbrev*	scarf *relig*
roach *fish*	royal *govt*	salse *geog*	scarp *geog*
roast *food*	royal *travel*	salts *chem*	scarp *war*

scaur *geog*	seedy *medic*	shark *trade*	shrew *animals*
sceat *money*	segno *music*	sharp *music*	shrew *people*
scena *music*	segue *music*	sharp *time*	shrub *trees*
scena *theatre*	Seine *rivers*	shawl *clothes*	shunt *machine*
scene *art*	semis *money*	shawm *music*	shunt *travel*
scene *film/TV*	senna *medic*	Sheba *Bible*	Shute *writers*
scene *lit*	senna *plants*	sheep *agric*	Siang *rivers*
scene *theatre*	Senta *lit*	sheep *animals*	Sibyl *myth*
scene *war*	Seoul *cities*	sheer *clothes*	sidle *travel*
scent *sport*	sepal *flowers*	sheer *geog*	siege *war*
sci-fi *lit*	sepia *colour*	sheer *travel*	sieve *house*
scion *family*	sepoy *war*	sheet *house*	sieve *machine*
scion *herald*	serac *geog*	sheet *lit*	sight *medic*
scold *people*	serge *clothes*	sheet *travel*	sight *sport*
scone *food*	serif *lit*	sheik *govt*	Silas *Bible*
Scoop *titles*	serin *birds*	shelf *geog*	simar *clothes*
scoop *tools*	serum *medic*	shelf *house*	Simon *Bible*
scoop *trade*	serve *sport*	shell *fish*	Simon *names*
score *measure*	serve *war*	shell *fruit*	Sinai *Bible*
score *music*	setup *lit*	shell *medic*	since *time*
score *sport*	setup *trade*	shell *travel*	sinew *medic*
score *theatre*	sewer *archit*	shell *war*	Sinon *myth*
score *trade*	sewer *jobs*	Sheol *myth*	sinus *medic*
Scott *artists*	shack *archit*	shift *clothes*	siren *music*
Scott *writers*	shade *art*	shift *trade*	siren *myth*
scout *jobs*	shade *geog*	shift *travel*	siren *people*
scout *war*	shade *myth*	shire *animals*	Siris *myth*
scrag *food*	SHAEF *abbrev*	shire *geog*	sisal *plants*
scree *geog*	shaft *archit*	shirt *clothes*	sixth *music*
screw *law*	shaft *geog*	Shiva *myth*	sizar *educ*
screw *machine*	shaft *machine*	shoal *fish*	skald *lit*
screw *sport*	shaft *sport*	shoal *marine*	skart *birds*
screw *travel*	shaft *travel*	shoat *agric*	skate *fish*
scrim *clothes*	shaft *war*	shoat *animals*	skean *war*
scrip *lit*	shake *music*	shock *medic*	skein *birds*
scrip *trade*	shake *time*	shoes *clothes*	skein *clothes*
scrub *plants*	shako *clothes*	shoot *flowers*	skier *sport*
scrum *sport*	shako *war*	shoot *fruit*	skiff *sport*
SCUBA *abbrev*	shale *mineral*	shoot *sport*	skiff *travel*
scull *sport*	shank *food*	shoot *war*	skill *trade*
sculp *art*	shank *machine*	shore *archit*	skink *insects*
SEATO *abbrev*	SHAPE *abbrev*	shore *marine*	skirt *clothes*
sedan *travel*	shape *art*	short *time*	skirt *travel*
sedge *insects*	share *trade*	short *trade*	skull *medic*
sedge *plants*	shark *fish*	Shree *myth*	skull *travel*

skunk	*animals*	smock	*clothes*	sound	*medic*	Spohr	*music*
slack	*mineral*	smoke	*geog*	sound	*music*	spook	*myth*
SLADE	*abbrev*	smolt	*fish*	sound	*physics*	spool	*art*
slang	*lit*	Smuts	*leaders*	Sousa	*music*	spool	*machine*
slant	*lit*	snack	*food*	south	*geog*	spoon	*house*
slash	*trade*	snail	*insects*	sowar	*war*	spoon	*sport*
slate	*archit*	snake	*insects*	sower	*jobs*	spore	*biol*
slate	*educ*	Snake	*rivers*	Spaak	*leaders*	sport	*people*
slate	*govt*	snake	*war*	space	*lit*	sport	*sport*
slate	*lit*	Snare	*Shakesp*	space	*music*	spots	*trade*
slate	*mineral*	snare	*music*	space	*time*	spout	*theatre*
slave	*jobs*	snarl	*animals*	spade	*tools*	sprat	*fish*
sleep	*medic*	sneak	*people*	spahi	*war*	spray	*flowers*
sleet	*mineral*	Sneer	*lit*	spark	*people*	spray	*machine*
sleet	*weather*	snide	*trade*	spark	*physics*	spray	*war*
slide	*art*	snipe	*birds*	Spark	*writers*	Spree	*rivers*
slide	*biol*	snood	*clothes*	spars	*travel*	sprig	*flowers*
slide	*music*	snook	*fish*	spasm	*medic*	sprig	*plants*
slide	*sport*	snort	*animals*	spate	*geog*	sprit	*travel*
sling	*medic*	Snout	*Shakesp*	spats	*clothes*	spume	*marine*
sling	*war*	snout	*animals*	spawn	*fish*	spurs	*war*
slink	*animals*	Snowy	*rivers*	spear	*cereal*	squab	*birds*
slips	*sport*	Soane	*artists*	spear	*sport*	squad	*war*
slips	*travel*	socie	*archit*	spear	*war*	squid	*fish*
sloop	*travel*	Sodom	*Bible*	specs	*clothes*	SSAFA	*abbrev*
slope	*geog*	solar	*time*	Speed	*Shakesp*	stack	*geog*
slops	*food*	Sofia	*cities*	speed	*travel*	staff	*educ*
sloth	*animals*	SOGAT	*abbrev*	spell	*educ*	staff	*govt*
sloth	*sins*	solan	*birds*	spell	*lit*	staff	*herald*
slump	*trade*	solar	*astron*	spell	*myth*	staff	*jobs*
slums	*archit*	soldo	*money*	spell	*time*	staff	*music*
slush	*geog*	solfa	*music*	spend	*trade*	staff	*relig*
smack	*travel*	solid	*maths*	speos	*archit*	staff	*war*
smart	*medic*	Solon	*law*	Spica	*astron*	stage	*archit*
Smart	*writers*	Solon	*relig*	spice	*food*	stage	*theatre*
smash	*sport*	solum	*geog*	spiel	*trade*	stage	*travel*
smash	*trade*	solve	*physics*	spike	*cereal*	stagy	*theatre*
smash	*travel*	Somme	*rivers*	spike	*war*	stain	*art*
smear	*art*	Sonia	*names*	spill	*travel*	stair	*archit*
smelt	*fish*	sonny	*family*	spine	*medic*	stake	*herald*
Smike	*lit*	sopor	*medic*	spire	*archit*	stake	*sport*
Smith	*artists*	sordo	*music*	spire	*relig*	stake	*trade*
smith	*jobs*	sough	*archit*	spitz	*animals*	stalk	*flowers*
smith	*trade*	sough	*geog*	splay	*archit*	stalk	*fruit*
Smith	*writers*	sound	*marine*	Spode	*art*	stalk	*sport*

stall	*animals*	stint	*trade*	strut	*travel*	swede	*veg*
stall	*archit*	stipe	*fruit*	study	*archit*	sweep	*sport*
stall	*medic*	stoat	*animals*	study	*art*	sweep	*travel*
stall	*relig*	stock	*agric*	study	*educ*	sweet	*food*
stall	*theatre*	stock	*clothes*	study	*house*	swell	*marine*
stall	*trade*	stock	*drink*	study	*lit*	swell	*music*
stall	*travel*	stock	*flowers*	study	*music*	Swift	*writers*
stamp	*art*	stock	*trade*	stuff	*clothes*	swill	*food*
stamp	*lit*	stoep	*archit*	stunt	*theatre*	swine	*animals*
stamp	*travel*	stoic	*people*	stunt	*travel*	swing	*music*
stand	*theatre*	stole	*clothes*	stupa	*archit*	swing	*sport*
stand	*trade*	stole	*relig*	stupa	*relig*	swirl	*geog*
starr	*plants*	stoma	*plants*	stupe	*medic*	swoon	*medic*
stars	*astron*	stone	*archit*	style	*art*	sword	*sport*
start	*travel*	stone	*art*	style	*clothes*	sword	*war*
state	*geog*	stone	*fruit*	style	*flowers*	Sybil	*names*
stave	*music*	stone	*measure*	style	*lit*	sylph	*myth*
stays	*clothes*	stone	*mineral*	style	*time*	Synge	*writers*
steak	*food*	stone	*war*	subst	*abbrev*	synod	*relig*
steam	*physics*	stool	*house*	sucre	*money*	syrup	*drink*
steam	*travel*	STOPP	*abbrev*	suede	*clothes*	tabby	*animals*
steed	*animals*	store	*trade*	sugar	*food*	tabby	*clothes*
steel	*mineral*	stork	*birds*	suite	*archit*	taber	*relig*
steel	*war*	storm	*war*	suite	*house*	tabes	*medic*
steer	*animals*	storm	*weather*	suite	*music*	tabid	*medic*
Steer	*artists*	story	*lit*	sumac	*trees*	tabla	*music*
steer	*sport*	stoup	*relig*	Sumba	*islands*	table	*food*
Stein	*writers*	stout	*drink*	Sumer	*relig*	table	*geog*
stele	*archit*	stove	*house*	summa	*lit*	table	*house*
stere	*measure*	stove	*machine*	sunny	*weather*	table	*maths*
stern	*travel*	Stowe	*writers*	sunup	*time*	table	*music*
Stern	*writers*	Strad	*music*	Surat	*cities*	taboo	*myth*
Steve	*names*	straw	*agric*	surge	*geog*	tabor	*music*
stick	*machine*	straw	*cereal*	Surya	*myth*	tacet	*music*
stick	*war*	straw	*house*	Susan	*names*	Tagus	*rivers*
stile	*archit*	stray	*animals*	Susie	*names*	tails	*clothes*
still	*art*	stray	*travel*	swale	*geog*	taint	*medic*
still	*biol*	stria	*archit*	Swale	*rivers*	takin	*animals*
still	*machine*	stria	*geog*	SWALK	*abbrev*	tally	*sport*
still	*theatre*	strip	*sport*	swamp	*geog*	tally	*trade*
still	*time*	strip	*travel*	SWAPO	*abbrev*	talma	*clothes*
stilt	*birds*	strop	*trade*	sward	*plants*	talon	*animals*
sting	*fish*	strum	*music*	swarm	*insects*	talon	*archit*
sting	*insects*	strut	*archit*	swear	*law*	talus	*geog*
sting	*medic*	strut	*machine*	sweat	*medic*	talus	*medic*

tambo	*music*	theme	*lit*
tammy	*clothes*	theme	*music*
Tampa	*cities*	theol	*abbrev*
tango	*music*	theos	*myth*
tango	*sport*	therm	*measure*
Tania	*names*	Thess	*abbrev*
tansy	*plants*	thief	*jobs*
Tanya	*names*	thief	*law*
Taper	*lit*	thigh	*medic*
tapir	*animals*	third	*measure*
tapis	*house*	third	*music*
targe	*war*	thole	*machine*
tarot	*sport*	thole	*travel*
tasse	*war*	thorn	*flowers*
Tasso	*writers*	thorn	*trees*
tatou	*animals*	Thoth	*myth*
Tatum	*names*	throb	*medic*
taupe	*colour*	throb	*music*
tawny	*colour*	throe	*medic*
taxes	*trade*	throw	*art*
taxis	*biol*	thrum	*clothes*
Tbone	*food*	thrum	*music*
teach	*educ*	Thrym	*myth*
teeth	*medic*	Thule	*myth*
Telex	*travel*	thumb	*medic*
telly	*film/TV*	thyme	*plants*
tempo	*music*	thyme	*veg*
tempo	*time*	tiara	*clothes*
tench	*fish*	tiara	*herald*
tenne	*herald*	tiara	*relig*
tenor	*jobs*	Tiber	*rivers*
tenor	*music*	tibia	*medic*
tense	*lit*	tiger	*animals*
tenth	*maths*	tigon	*animals*
tepee	*archit*	tilde	*lit*
terms	*trade*	tiler	*jobs*
Terra	*myth*	tilia	*trees*
terry	*clothes*	Tilly	*names*
Terry	*names*	tilth	*agric*
Tessa	*lit*	timer	*house*
Texel	*islands*	timer	*machine*
thane	*govt*	Timon	*Shakesp*
theft	*law*	Timor	*islands*
Theia	*myth*	tinct	*art*
thema	*lit*	tinge	*art*

tired	*medic*	torso	*medic*
Tiree	*islands*	torte	*food*
Titan	*astron*	torus	*archit*
Titan	*myth*	Tosca	*lit*
tithe	*maths*	Tosca	*titles*
tithe	*trade*	totem	*myth*
title	*lit*	touch	*music*
title	*sport*	touch	*sport*
Titus	*Bible*	towel	*house*
Titus	*Shakesp*	tower	*archit*
toady	*people*	tower	*machine*
toast	*food*	toxin	*chem*
today	*time*	trace	*art*
toddy	*drink*	trace	*medic*
toise	*measure*	track	*sport*
token	*trade*	track	*travel*
Tokyo	*cities*	tract	*geog*
toman	*money*	tract	*lit*
tommy	*jobs*	tract	*medic*
tommy	*war*	tract	*relig*
tommy	*war*	Tracy	*names*
Tomsk	*cities*	trade	*jobs*
Tonga	*islands*	trade	*trade*
tongs	*house*	trail	*travel*
tongs	*tools*	train	*clothes*
tonic	*medic*	train	*machine*
tonic	*music*	train	*travel*
tonne	*measure*	train	*war*
tonup	*measure*	tramp	*jobs*
tonup	*sport*	tramp	*travel*
tonup	*travel*	trans	*abbrev*
tooth	*machine*	trave	*archit*
tooth	*medic*	tread	*archit*
topaz	*jewels*	tread	*travel*
topaz	*mineral*	treas	*abbrev*
topee	*clothes*	treat	*drink*
toper	*people*	treal	*food*
topic	*lit*	treat	*medic*
toque	*clothes*	treat	*trade*
Torah	*relig*	trend	*trade*
torch	*house*	Trent	*rivers*
torch	*machine*	tress	*clothes*
Torne	*rivers*	trews	*clothes*
torse	*herald*	triad	*maths*
torsk	*birds*	triad	*music*

trial	law	tupek	archit	Uriel	myth	verse	music
tribe	govt	tupik	archit	urine	medic	verso	lit
trice	time	Turin	cities	usage	lit	verso	money
trick	sport	turps	art	usher	educ	vespa	insects
trier	people	tutor	educ	usher	jobs	Vesta	myth
trike	travel	tutor	jobs	usher	law	vetch	plants
trill	birds	tutti	music	usher	theatre	vibes	music
trill	music	TV set	machine	usine	archit	vicar	jobs
tripe	food	Twain	writers	usurp	govt	vicar	relig
Troad	myth	tweed	clothes	usury	trade	Vicky	names
troll	music	Tweed	rivers	utter	trade	Vidar	myth
troll	myth	tweet	birds	U tube	chem	video	film/TV
Tromp	war	twill	clothes	U turn	travel	villa	archit
troop	animals	twins	family	uvula	medic	villi	medic
troop	war	twist	lit	UWIST	abbrev	Vince	names
trope	lit	twist	sport	vagus	medic	viner	jobs
trope	music	Tyche	myth	vakil	law	vinyl	chem
trout	fish	Tyler	USpres	valet	jobs	Viola	Shakesp
truce	govt	U boat	travel	valse	music	viola	flowers
truce	war	U boat	war	valse	sport	viola	music
truck	machine	udder	animals	value	maths	Viola	names
truck	trade	uhlan	jobs	value	trade	viper	insects
truck	travel	uhlan	war	valve	machine	vireo	birds
trump	sport	ulcer	medic	valve	medic	Virgo	myth
trunk	animals	ulema	law	valve	music	Virgo	zodiac
trunk	archit	ulnar	medic	valve	travel	virtu	art
trunk	house	umbel	plants	V and A	abbrev	virus	biol
trunk	medic	umber	colour	Vanir	myth	virus	medic
trunk	travel	umber	fish	Varah	myth	visit	travel
trunk	trees	umbra	astron	Varro	Shakesp	visne	law
trust	govt	umiak	travel	vault	archit	visor	herald
trust	law	UMIST	abbrev	vault	geog	visor	war
trust	trade	uncia	measure	vault	relig	Vithi	myth
Tubal	Shakesp	uncle	family	veery	birds	Vitim	rivers
tuber	agric	uncus	medic	vegan	food	vixen	animals
tuber	veg	unfit	medic	veldt	agric	vixen	people
tulip	flowers	UNRRA	abbrev	veldt	geog	V neck	clothes
tulle	clothes	until	time	venal	trade	vocab	abbrev
tummy	medic	up bow	music	venue	sport	vodka	drink
tuned	music	upper	clothes	Venus	astron	voice	lit
tuner	jobs	Urals	mounts	Venus	lit	voice	music
tunic	clothes	urban	geog	Venus	myth	voile	clothes
tunic	relig	uredo	chem	Verdi	music	Volga	rivers
Tunis	cities	Uriah	Bible	Verne	writers	volta	music
tunny	fish	urial	animals	verse	lit	Volta	rivers

volte	*music*	weald	*geog*	Wilts	*abbrev*	xerox	*machine*
vomer	*medic*	weave	*clothes*	wince	*medic*	Xingu	*rivers*
vomit	*medic*	Weber	*music*	winch	*machine*	Xrays	*maths*
voter	*govt*	wedge	*sport*	winds	*music*	Xtian	*abbrev*
vowel	*lit*	wedge	*tools*	windy	*weather*	xylem	*chem*
WAACS	*war*	Weill	*music*	wings	*theatre*	yacht	*travel*
WAAFS	*war*	weird	*myth*	witch	*jobs*	Yasna	*myth*
Wabun	*myth*	Wells	*writers*	Wodan	*myth*	years	*time*
wacke	*mineral*	welsh	*trade*	Woden	*myth*	yeast	*chem*
waddy	*war*	wench	*jobs*	Woden	*war*	yeast	*plants*
wader	*birds*	Wendy	*names*	Wolfe	*war*	Yeats	*writers*
wafer	*food*	Weser	*rivers*	woman	*jobs*	yield	*agric*
wager	*sport*	whale	*animals*	woods	*music*	yield	*trade*
wages	*jobs*	wharf	*travel*	Woolf	*writers*	yodel	*music*
wages	*trade*	wheal	*medic*	Worcs	*abbrev*	yokel	*jobs*
wagon	*agric*	wheat	*agric*	words	*lit*	Yorks	*abbrev*
waist	*clothes*	wheat	*cereal*	works	*lit*	young	*time*
waist	*medic*	wheel	*art*	works	*trade*	Young	*writers*
waits	*music*	wheel	*machine*	world	*geog*	youth	*jobs*
waler	*animals*	wheel	*travel*	worth	*trade*	youth	*time*
wally	*people*	whelk	*fish*	Wotan	*lit*	yucca	*plants*
waltz	*music*	whelk	*medic*	Wotan	*myth*	Yukon	*rivers*
waltz	*sport*	whelp	*animals*	wound	*medic*	yulan	*flowers*
wamus	*clothes*	Whigs	*govt*	wound	*war*	Zadok	*Bible*
Wanda	*names*	while	*time*	woven	*clothes*	zamia	*trees*
wares	*trade*	whisk	*house*	wrack	*plants*	Zbend	*travel*
waste	*geog*	whist	*sport*	WRACS	*war*	zebra	*animals*
watch	*clothes*	white	*colour*	wrath	*sins*	zibet	*animals*
watch	*time*	Widor	*music*	wreck	*medic*	Zimri	*Bible*
water	*drink*	widow	*family*	Wrens	*war*	zombi	*myth*
Watts	*artists*	wigan	*clothes*	wrist	*medic*	zooid	*biol*
Waugh	*writers*	Wilde	*writers*	Wyatt	*artists*	zoril	*animals*
wayin	*travel*	wilds	*geog*	xebec	*travel*	zorro	*animals*
Wayne	*names*	wilds	*geog*	xenon	*chem*	Zweig	*writers*

6 LETTERS

Aachen	*cities*	abacus	*trade*	abattu	*foreign*
abacus	*machine*	Abadan	*cities*	abbess	*jobs*
abacus	*maths*	abatis	*war*	abbess	*relig*

Abdiel	*rivers*	
Abessa	*lit*	
ab|init	*abbrev*	
abjure	*law*	
Ablast	*physics*	
aboard	*travel*	
abrege	*lit*	
abroad	*travel*	
abroma	*trees*	
abseil	*sport*	
absurd	*theatre*	
acacia	*plants*	
acajou	*trees*	
acarus	*insects*	
accent	*lit*	
accent	*music*	
accept	*trade*	
access	*travel*	
accord	*music*	
accrue	*trade*	
acetic	*chem*	
achene	*fruit*	
aching	*medic*	
achkan	*clothes*	
acinus	*fruit*	
ack|ack	*war*	
acting	*theatre*	
action	*chem*	
action	*law*	
action	*lit*	
action	*theatre*	
action	*war*	
act|out	*theatre*	
actual	*time*	
adagio	*music*	
addict	*medic*	
adding	*comput*	
adding	*maths*	
addled	*food*	
admass	*jobs*	
admass	*trade*	
Adonai	*myth*	
Adonis	*myth*	
Adrian	*Shakesp*	
Adrian	*names*	
adrift	*travel*	
advent	*time*	
adverb	*lit*	
adytum	*archit*	
Aeacus	*myth*	
Aeetes	*myth*	
Aegean	*seas*	
Aegeon	*Shakesp*	
Aegeus	*myth*	
Aegina	*islands*	
Aegina	*myth*	
Aeneas	*Shakesp*	
Aeneas	*lit*	
Aeneas	*myth*	
Aeneid	*myth*	
Aeolus	*myth*	
Aeolus	*weather*	
aerial	*house*	
aerial	*machine*	
aerial	*physics*	
aerobe	*biol*	
Aethra	*myth*	
afford	*trade*	
afghan	*clothes*	
afloat	*travel*	
afreet	*myth*	
agamic	*biol*	
agaric	*plants*	
Agatha	*names*	
agency	*trade*	
agenda	*govt*	
agenda	*trade*	
Agenor	*myth*	
Aglaia	*myth*	
agnate	*family*	
agouta	*animals*	
agouti	*animals*	
agrege	*foreign*	
Aileen	*names*	
ailing	*medic*	
air|ace	*jobs*	
air|arm	*war*	
airbus	*travel*	
airgas	*chem*	
airgun	*war*	
airing	*travel*	
air|log	*travel*	
airman	*jobs*	
airman	*travel*	
air|ram	*travel*	
airway	*travel*	
akimbo	*sport*	
Albany	*Shakesp*	
Albany	*herald*	
albedo	*astron*	
albedo	*physics*	
albert	*colour*	
Albert	*names*	
albino	*animals*	
albino	*jobs*	
albino	*medic*	
albino	*plants*	
Alcaic	*lit*	
Alcina	*titles*	
alcove	*archit*	
alcove	*house*	
Aldine	*lit*	
Aldous	*names*	
Alecto	*myth*	
Aleppo	*cities*	
alevin	*fish*	
alexia	*medic*	
Alexis	*names*	
Alfred	*names*	
Alfred	*war*	
Alfven	*music*	
Alicia	*names*	
alidad	*maths*	
alight	*travel*	
Alison	*names*	
alkali	*chem*	
allons	*foreign*	
almain	*music*	
almand	*music*	
almond	*food*	
almond	*fruit*	
alnage	*clothes*	
Alonso	*Shakesp*	
alpaca	*animals*	
alpaca	*clothes*	

alpeen *war*	angora *animals*	appeal *trade*
alpine *geog*	angora *clothes*	appear *theatre*
Alseid *myth*	anguis *insects*	approx *abbrev*
althea *flowers*	animal *agric*	Aquila *astron*
Althea *names*	animus *war*	aquila *birds*
alumna *educ*	Ankara *cities*	Aquila *myth*
alumna *jobs*	anklet *clothes*	Arabel *names*
always *time*	annals *lit*	arabis *plants*
Amager *islands*	annato *colour*	arable *agric*
Amalek *Bible*	anneal *chem*	aralia *plants*
Amanda *names*	annexe *archit*	aranea *insects*
Amazon *myth*	annual *flowers*	Ararat *Bible*
Amazon *people*	annual *lit*	Ararat *mounts*
Amazon *rivers*	annual *time*	arbour *archit*
Amazon *war*	anoint *medic*	arbute *trees*
ambush *war*	anoint *relig*	arcade *archit*
Amelia *names*	anorak *clothes*	archer *jobs*
Amelia *titles*	anorak *sport*	archer *sport*
AmenₐRa *myth*	Anstey *writers*	archer *war*
Amenti *myth*	answer *music*	Archer *writers*
Amiens *Shakesp*	ant|cow *insects*	Archie *names*
amoeba *biol*	anthem *music*	Archie *war*
Amores *myth*	anthem *relig*	archon *law*
amount *trade*	anther *flowers*	arctic *geog*
ampere *measure*	antiar *trees*	Arctic *seas*
ampere *physics*	antler *animals*	areola *medic*
amulet *myth*	Antlia *astron*	argala *birds*
amulet *relig*	Antony *Shakesp*	argali *animals*
amylum *chem*	Antony *names*	argent *herald*
amytal *medic*	antrum *medic*	argosy *travel*
ananas *fruit*	Anubis *myth*	argosy *war*
anchor *sport*	Anytus *myth*	arioso *music*
anchor *travel*	Anzacs *war*	aristo *govt*
Andrea *names*	aorist *lit*	Arline *names*
Andrew *Bible*	aoudad *animals*	armada *travel*
Andrew *names*	apache *people*	armada *war*
Andros *islands*	apercu *lit*	Armado *Shakesp*
anemia *medic*	apiary *insects*	armful *measure*
anemic *medic*	apnoea *medic*	armlet *clothes*
Angara *rivers*	apogee *astron*	armlet *relig*
Angela *names*	apogee *maths*	armour *herald*
Angelo *Shakesp*	Apollo *lit*	armour *war*
angina *medic*	Apollo *music*	armpit *medic*
angler *fish*	Apollo *myth*	arnica *medic*
angler *sport*	appeal *law*	Arnold *music*

Arnold	*names*	atomic	*physics*	avenir	*foreign*
Arnold	*writers*	atonal	*music*	avenue	*archit*
arolla	*trees*	at|once	*time*	avenue	*travel*
arpent	*measure*	Atreus	*myth*	aviary	*birds*
arrear	*trade*	atrium	*archit*	avocet	*birds*
arrest	*law*	attack	*medic*	aweigh	*travel*
arrive	*travel*	attack	*sport*	awning	*archit*
artery	*medic*	attack	*war*	awning	*house*
artery	*travel*	Attica	*myth*	axilla	*medic*
Arthur	*Shakesp*	Attila	*war*	aye|aye	*animals*
Arthur	*USpres*	attire	*clothes*	Ayesha	*lit*
Arthur	*myth*	Attlee	*leaders*	Aylwin	*names*
Arthur	*names*	attrib	*abbrev*	azalea	*flowers*
artist	*art*	aubade	*music*	azo|dye	*art*
artist	*jobs*	Aubrey	*names*	Azores	*islands*
ascent	*sport*	auburn	*colour*	Azrael	*myth*
ascent	*travel*	Audrey	*Shakesp*	Babbar	*myth*
Asgard	*myth*	Audrey	*names*	baboon	*animals*
ash|bin	*house*	au|fait	*foreign*	backer	*jobs*
ash|can	*house*	au|fond	*foreign*	backer	*theatre*
Asimov	*writers*	August	*time*	backer	*trade*
askari	*war*	auklet	*birds*	back|up	*travel*
Asmara	*cities*	auntie	*family*	badger	*animals*
aspect	*archit*	au|pair	*jobs*	baffle	*machine*
assail	*war*	aureus	*money*	baffle	*physics*
Assama	*myth*	Auriga	*astron*	bagnio	*archit*
assets	*trade*	Auriga	*myth*	bailer	*sport*
astern	*travel*	aurist	*jobs*	Bailey	*writers*
asthma	*medic*	aurist	*medic*	bailie	*law*
astral	*astron*	Aurora	*myth*	Bairam	*time*
astral	*myth*	Aurora	*names*	Balaam	*Bible*
Astrid	*names*	Aurora	*time*	Balboa	*war*
asylum	*govt*	aurora	*weather*	Balder	*myth*
asylum	*law*	Austen	*writers*	Baldur	*myth*
ataxia	*medic*	Auster	*myth*	baleen	*animals*
Atbara	*rivers*	Austin	*cities*	ballad	*lit*
at|cost	*trade*	Austin	*names*	ballad	*music*
at|ease	*sport*	author	*jobs*	ballet	*music*
a|tempo	*music*	author	*lit*	ballet	*theatre*
Athena	*myth*	autumn	*geog*	ballot	*govt*
Athene	*myth*	autumn	*time*	balsam	*medic*
Athene	*names*	avails	*trade*	balsam	*plants*
Athens	*cities*	Avalon	*myth*	Baltic	*seas*
atocia	*medic*	avanti	*foreign*	Balzac	*writers*
atomic	*chem*	avatar	*myth*	bamboo	*plants*

banana	*fruit*	barrow	*relig*	bedpan	*medic*
bandit	*govt*	barrow	*travel*	bedsit	*archit*
bandit	*jobs*	barter	*trade*	beefly	*insects*
bandog	*animals*	Bartok	*music*	beetle	*insects*
banger	*food*	barton	*animals*	beggar	*jobs*
banger	*travel*	barton	*archit*	Beirut	*cities*
Bangka	*islands*	baryta	*chem*	belair	*foreign*
bangle	*jewels*	basalt	*mineral*	beldam	*jobs*
banker	*jobs*	basket	*house*	belfry	*archit*
banker	*sport*	basket	*travel*	Belial	*Bible*
banker	*trade*	basque	*clothes*	Belial	*myth*
banner	*herald*	Basset	*Shakesp*	Belloc	*writers*
Banquo	*Shakesp*	basset	*animals*	bellow	*animals*
bantam	*birds*	bateau	*travel*	bellum	*war*
banyan	*trees*	bathos	*lit*	beluga	*animals*
baobab	*trees*	batman	*jobs*	beluga	*fish*
barbel	*fish*	batman	*war*	BenHur	*titles*
barbel	*war*	batten	*archit*	benign	*medic*
barber	*jobs*	batter	*food*	Benson	*writers*
Barber	*music*	batter	*jobs*	Berber	*jobs*
barbet	*birds*	battle	*war*	Berlin	*cities*
bargee	*jobs*	bauble	*clothes*	berlin	*travel*
bargee	*travel*	Baucis	*myth*	bertha	*clothes*
Barham	*writers*	bawbee	*money*	Bertha	*names*
barite	*chem*	bayard	*animals*	bester	*fish*
barium	*chem*	bazaar	*trade*	Bethel	*Bible*
barker	*jobs*	beacon	*machine*	Beulah	*myth*
barker	*theatre*	beacon	*travel*	Bewick	*artists*
barker	*trade*	beadle	*jobs*	bezant	*herald*
Barkis	*lit*	beadle	*relig*	bharal	*animals*
barley	*agric*	beagle	*animals*	Bianca	*Shakesp*
barley	*cereal*	beaker	*chem*	bibber	*drink*
barman	*jobs*	beaker	*house*	bibber	*people*
Barney	*names*	bearer	*jobs*	biceps	*medic*
Baroda	*cities*	bearer	*trade*	bidder	*sport*
barony	*govt*	beater	*jobs*	bident	*animals*
barque	*travel*	Beatty	*war*	bigamy	*law*
barrel	*machine*	beauty	*people*	biglend	*machine*
barrel	*measure*	beaver	*animals*	biglend	*travel*
barrel	*war*	beaver	*clothes*	biggin	*clothes*
barren	*animals*	beaver	*herald*	biggin	*house*
Barrie	*writers*	beaver	*war*	biggun	*war*
barrow	*archit*	Becket	*titles*	BigTop	*theatre*
barrow	*geog*	bedaub	*art*	bikini	*clothes*
barrow	*machine*	bedbug	*insects*	Bikini	*islands*

Bilbao	cities
billet	archit
billet	herald
billet	war
Billie	names
binary	comput
binary	maths
binate	maths
binder	agric
binder	lit
binder	machine
binder	medic
Binyon	writers
biogen	biol
bionic	biol
biopsy	medic
biotin	biol
birdie	sport
bireme	travel
bisect	maths
bishop	jobs
bishop	relig
bishop	sport
bisque	art
bisque	drink
bisque	sport
bistro	archit
bite|in	art
Blaise	names
Blanch	Shakesp
blanch	medic
blazer	clothes
blazon	art
blazon	herald
bleach	house
blenny	birds
blintz	food
blocks	sport
blonde	colour
Blount	Shakesp
blouse	clothes
blower	machine
blow|up	art
bluing	house
boards	theatre

boatel	travel
boater	clothes
Bobbie	names
bobbin	machine
bobcat	animals
bob|saw	tools
Bochum	cities
bodice	clothes
bodkin	clothes
bodkin	tools
boffin	chem
boffin	jobs
boffin	physics
bog|oak	trees
Bogota	cities
boiler	house
boiler	machine
bolero	clothes
bolero	music
Boleyn	Shakesp
bolide	astron
bolide	physics
Bombay	cities
bomber	travel
bomber	war
bonbon	food
bonito	birds
bon|mot	lit
bonnet	clothes
bonnet	travel
bon|ton	foreign
boodle	trade
bookie	jobs
bookie	sport
bootee	clothes
Bootes	astron
Bootes	myth
borage	plants
borage	veg
borate	chem
border	flowers
border	geog
border	herald
border	theatre
boreal	weather

Boreas	myth
Boreas	weather
Borneo	islands
borrow	sport
borrow	trade
Borrow	writers
borsch	drink
borzoi	animals
Boston	cities
boston	sport
botany	biol
botfly	insects
bo|tree	trees
bottle	drink
Bottom	Shakesp
bottom	geog
boucle	clothes
bought	trade
bounce	trade
bounty	trade
bourse	trade
bovate	measure
bovine	animals
bowels	medic
bowfin	fish
bowing	music
bowled	sport
bowler	clothes
bowler	sport
bowman	jobs
bowman	sport
bowser	travel
bow|tie	clothes
bow|wow	animals
boxing	sport
braced	herald
bracer	medic
bracer	sport
braces	clothes
braces	travel
Brahma	myth
Brahma	relig
Brahms	music
brains	educ
brainy	educ

branch	*geog*	Brooke	*writers*	bureau	*trade*
branch	*trade*	brough	*archit*	burgee	*herald*
Brandt	*leaders*	brough	*geog*	burial	*relig*
brandy	*drink*	Browne	*writers*	burlap	*clothes*
bransh	*trees*	browse	*educ*	burner	*house*
Braque	*artists*	browse	*lit*	burnet	*insects*
brayer	*machine*	bruise	*medic*	burnet	*plants*
breach	*law*	brumal	*time*	Burney	*writers*
breast	*food*	brumal	*weather*	burrow	*animals*
breast	*medic*	brunch	*food*	burrow	*geog*
breath	*medic*	Brutus	*Shakesp*	bursar	*educ*
Brecht	*writers*	Bryant	*writers*	bursar	*jobs*
breech	*machine*	Bryony	*names*	bursar	*trade*
breech	*war*	bryony	*plants*	burton	*machine*
breeze	*insects*	Buchan	*writers*	bus|bar	*machine*
breeze	*weather*	bucket	*house*	bushel	*measure*
breezy	*weather*	bucket	*travel*	busker	*jobs*
Bremen	*cities*	buckle	*clothes*	buskin	*clothes*
Brenda	*names*	Buddha	*myth*	buskin	*theatre*
brevet	*govt*	Buddha	*relig*	busman	*travel*
brewer	*myth*	budget	*trade*	Busoni	*music*
Briard	*animals*	buffer	*machine*	bustle	*clothes*
bricks	*sport*	buffet	*food*	butler	*jobs*
bridge	*archit*	bugler	*jobs*	Butler	*writers*
bridge	*music*	bugler	*music*	butter	*agric*
Bridge	*music*	bugler	*war*	butter	*food*
bridge	*sport*	bulbul	*birds*	button	*clothes*
bridge	*travel*	bulger	*sport*	button	*trade*
Bridie	*writers*	bulimy	*medic*	buying	*trade*
bridle	*animals*	Bullen	*Shakesp*	buy|out	*trade*
briefs	*clothes*	bullet	*war*	bye|law	*law*
Bright	*leaders*	Bumble	*lit*	by|lane	*travel*
broach	*machine*	bumper	*sport*	by|pass	*travel*
broads	*geog*	bumper	*travel*	bypath	*travel*
brogan	*clothes*	bunion	*medic*	byroad	*travel*
brogue	*clothes*	bunker	*house*	by|room	*archit*
broker	*jobs*	bunker	*sport*	byssus	*clothes*
broker	*trade*	bunker	*war*	byword	*lit*
brolly	*clothes*	bunsen	*chem*	cabbie	*jobs*
bronco	*animals*	Bunyan	*writers*	Cabiri	*myth*
Bronte	*writers*	burbot	*fish*	cachou	*food*
bronze	*art*	burden	*lit*	cackle	*animals*
bronze	*colour*	burden	*music*	cacoon	*plants*
bronze	*mineral*	bureau	*govt*	cactus	*plants*
brooch	*jewels*	bureau	*house*	caddie	*jobs*

caddie	*sport*	
cadent	*music*	
cadger	*people*	
Cadmus	*myth*	
Cadwal	*Shakesp*	
caecum	*medic*	
Caelum	*astron*	
Caesar	*Shakesp*	
Caesar	*govt*	
Caesar	*leaders*	
Caesar	*war*	
Caesar	*writers*	
caftan	*clothes*	
caique	*travel*	
calash	*clothes*	
calash	*travel*	
calcar	*chem*	
calico	*clothes*	
caligo	*medic*	
caliph	*govt*	
caller	*jobs*	
call|up	*travel*	
callus	*medic*	
calory	*measure*	
calque	*art*	
Calvin	*names*	
calxes	*chem*	
camail	*herald*	
camail	*war*	
camass	*plants*	
camber	*archit*	
camber	*travel*	
cambio	*trade*	
camera	*archit*	
camera	*art*	
camera	*film/TV*	
camera	*machine*	
camise	*clothes*	
camper	*jobs*	
campus	*educ*	
Canaan	*Bible*	
canape	*food*	
canard	*travel*	
canary	*birds*	
can,can	*music*	
can,can	*sport*	
Cancer	*fish*	
cancer	*medic*	
Cancer	*myth*	
Cancer	*zodiac*	
candle	*house*	
canine	*animals*	
canker	*medic*	
cannon	*sport*	
cannon	*war*	
canopy	*archit*	
canopy	*geog*	
Cantab	*abbrev*	
canter	*people*	
canter	*sport*	
canter	*travel*	
canton	*geog*	
canton	*herald*	
cantor	*jobs*	
cantor	*music*	
cantor	*relig*	
cantus	*music*	
canvas	*art*	
canvas	*clothes*	
canvas	*travel*	
canyon	*geog*	
Caphis	*Shakesp*	
caplin	*fish*	
capote	*clothes*	
captor	*jobs*	
carafe	*drink*	
carapa	*trees*	
carbon	*chem*	
carboy	*chem*	
careen	*travel*	
career	*jobs*	
career	*trade*	
career	*travel*	
carfax	*travel*	
caribe	*fish*	
caries	*medic*	
carina	*travel*	
Carmel	*Bible*	
Carmen	*lit*	
Carmen	*names*	
Carmen	*titles*	
Carole	*names*	
carpel	*flowers*	
carper	*people*	
carpet	*house*	
carpus	*medic*	
Carrie	*names*	
carrot	*veg*	
car|run	*sport*	
Carson	*leaders*	
cartel	*trade*	
Carter	*USpres*	
carter	*jobs*	
carved	*art*	
carver	*art*	
carver	*house*	
carver	*jobs*	
casein	*chem*	
cashew	*food*	
cashew	*fruit*	
cash|in	*trade*	
casino	*sport*	
casket	*relig*	
Caspar	*names*	
casque	*clothes*	
casque	*herald*	
casque	*war*	
cassia	*trees*	
Cassio	*Shakesp*	
Cassio	*lit*	
cassis	*drink*	
Casson	*artists*	
caster	*house*	
caster	*machine*	
castle	*archit*	
castle	*sport*	
castle	*war*	
castor	*animals*	
Castor	*astron*	
castor	*clothes*	
castor	*house*	
castor	*machine*	
Castor	*myth*	
Castro	*leaders*	
casual	*jobs*	

casual *war*	chafer *insects*	chisel *tools*
catchy *music*	chaise *travel*	chiton *clothes*
catgut *music*	chalet *archit*	choker *clothes*
cation *physics*	Chandi *myth*	choler *medic*
catkin *trees*	change *trade*	chopin *clothes*
cat|nap *animals*	chanty *music*	chopin *measure*
catnip *plants*	chapel *archit*	choral *music*
catsup *food*	chapel *relig*	chorea *medic*
cattle *agric*	charge *herald*	chorus *lit*
cattle *animals*	charge *law*	chorus *music*
caucus *govt*	charge *physics*	chorus *theatre*
caudex *trees*	charge *trade*	chough *birds*
caulis *plants*	charge *war*	chrism *relig*
Caurus *astron*	Charis *myth*	chroma *art*
caveat *law*	Charon *myth*	chrome *mineral*
cavern *geog*	chased *art*	chukka *sport*
caviar *food*	chaser *art*	church *archit*
cavity *medic*	chaser *theatre*	church *relig*
cayman *animals*	chaser *tools*	cicada *insects*
Cedric *names*	chasse *sport*	cicala *insects*
Ceefax *film/TV*	cheeky *herald*	Cicero *Shakesp*
celery *veg*	cheese *food*	Cicero *writers*
cellar *archit*	Chekov *writers*	cilice *clothes*
cellar *drink*	Chenab *rivers*	Cimber *Shakesp*
cement *archit*	cheque *trade*	cinema *film/TV*
censer *relig*	cherry *fruit*	circle *geog*
censor *govt*	Cherry *names*	circle *maths*
censor *jobs*	cherry *sport*	circle *theatre*
censor *law*	cherub *myth*	circus *animals*
census *govt*	cherub *relig*	circus *archit*
centre *archit*	Cheryl *names*	circus *sport*
centre *sport*	cheven *fish*	circus *theatre*
cerate *chem*	chevin *fish*	cirque *geog*
cereal *agric*	chiasm *medic*	cirrus *weather*
cereal *cereal*	chigoe *insects*	cistus *flowers*
cerise *colour*	chilli *veg*	cither *music*
cerium *chem*	chilly *weather*	citole *music*
cerium *mineral*	chimer *clothes*	citric *chem*
cervix *medic*	chimer *relig*	citron *fruit*
cestus *clothes*	chimes *music*	citrus *fruit*
cestus *sport*	chinch *insects*	Claire *names*
cet|par *abbrev*	chintz *clothes*	claque *theatre*
cha|cha *sport*	Chiron *Shakesp*	claret *drink*
chacma *animals*	Chiron *myth*	Claude *artists*
chafed *medic*	chisel *art*	Claude *names*

clause	*govt*	
clause	*law*	
clause	*lit*	
clavus	*medic*	
clayey	*geog*	
cleche	*herald*	
clergy	*relig*	
cleric	*jobs*	
cleric	*relig*	
cliche	*lit*	
client	*jobs*	
client	*trade*	
climax	*lit*	
clinic	*medic*	
clique	*govt*	
Clitus	*Shakesp*	
cloche	*clothes*	
clonus	*medic*	
closet	*archit*	
closet	*house*	
Cloten	*Shakesp*	
Clotho	*myth*	
cloudy	*weather*	
Clough	*writers*	
clover	*agric*	
clover	*plants*	
clunch	*geog*	
clutch	*birds*	
clutch	*machine*	
clutch	*travel*	
coaita	*animals*	
coaler	*travel*	
coatee	*clothes*	
Coates	*music*	
cobalt	*chem*	
cobalt	*colour*	
cobalt	*mineral*	
cobble	*travel*	
cobnut	*fruit*	
Cobweb	*Shakesp*	
coccus	*biol*	
coccyx	*medic*	
cocker	*animals*	
cockle	*fish*	
cockle	*food*	
cockle	*plants*	
cockle	*travel*	
cocoon	*insects*	
codein	*medic*	
codger	*people*	
codist	*jobs*	
coelom	*medic*	
coeval	*time*	
coffee	*drink*	
coffee	*plants*	
coffer	*archit*	
coffer	*house*	
coffer	*trade*	
coffin	*relig*	
cognac	*drink*	
coheir	*govt*	
coheir	*jobs*	
cohort	*biol*	
cohort	*war*	
collar	*clothes*	
collar	*herald*	
collar	*machine*	
collet	*clothes*	
collie	*animals*	
collop	*food*	
colmar	*house*	
colony	*biol*	
colony	*geog*	
colony	*govt*	
colour	*art*	
colour	*lit*	
colter	*agric*	
colugo	*animals*	
column	*archit*	
column	*lit*	
column	*war*	
colure	*geog*	
combat	*war*	
comber	*fish*	
comedo	*medic*	
comedy	*film/TV*	
comedy	*lit*	
comedy	*theatre*	
comfit	*food*	
coming	*time*	
common	*geog*	
comper	*sport*	
concha	*archit*	
concha	*medic*	
condor	*birds*	
conger	*fish*	
conker	*sport*	
conman	*govt*	
conman	*people*	
conner	*travel*	
Connor	*names*	
Conrad	*names*	
Conrad	*writers*	
conrod	*machine*	
conrod	*travel*	
consol	*trade*	
consul	*govt*	
consul	*jobs*	
convex	*archit*	
convoy	*travel*	
convoy	*war*	
cooker	*house*	
cooker	*machine*	
cookie	*food*	
cooler	*law*	
cooler	*machine*	
coolie	*jobs*	
cooper	*jobs*	
Cooper	*writers*	
copeck	*money*	
copier	*jobs*	
coping	*archit*	
copper	*colour*	
copper	*govt*	
copper	*jobs*	
copper	*mineral*	
copper	*money*	
copper	*trade*	
copter	*travel*	
copula	*lit*	
corban	*relig*	
corbel	*archit*	
Corbet	*artists*	
corbie	*birds*	
cordon	*govt*	

cordon	war	county	geog	crisis	trade
corium	medic	county	govt	critic	film/TV
corium	war	couped	herald	critic	jobs
corkir	plants	couper	jobs	critic	lit
cornea	medic	coupon	trade	critic	theatre
cornel	trees	course	archit	crocus	flowers
corner	archit	course	educ	Cronin	writers
corner	sport	course	food	Cronus	myth
corner	trade	course	geog	crosse	sport
cornet	food	course	sport	crotal	plants
cornet	music	course	travel	croton	plants
corona	archit	cousin	family	Crotus	myth
corona	astron	covert	birds	croute	food
corona	flowers	coward	people	cruise	sport
corona	music	Coward	writers	cruise	travel
Corona	myth	cowboy	jobs	cruive	animals
corpse	medic	cowman	agric	crusta	medic
corral	animals	cowpea	veg	crutch	medic
corral	geog	cowpox	medic	cubism	art
corrie	geog	cowrie	trade	cubist	art
corset	clothes	coyote	animals	cuboid	maths
Cortes	govt	coypou	animals	cuboid	medic
Cortes	war	Crabbe	writers	cuckoo	birds
cortex	medic	Cracow	cities	cudgel	war
Corvus	astron	cradle	house	cueing	music
Corvus	myth	cradle	sport	cuisse	herald
corymb	flowers	crambo	lit	cuisse	war
coryza	medic	crambo	sport	culver	birds
cosech	abbrev	cranny	archit	cummin	plants
cosine	maths	crater	geog	cuneus	medic
cosinh	maths	Crater	myth	cupful	measure
cosmic	astron	cravat	clothes	cupola	archit
cosmos	astron	crayon	art	cuptie	sport
cosmos	flowers	crease	sport	curacy	relig
costal	medic	creche	educ	curate	jobs
costar	jobs	credit	trade	curate	relig
coster	jobs	creese	war	curfew	govt
costly	trade	crenel	archit	curfew	time
Cotman	artists	Creole	jobs	curfew	war
cotton	clothes	Creusa	myth	curium	chem
cotton	plants	crewel	clothes	curler	clothes
cottus	fish	crible	art	curler	sport
coucal	birds	Cripps	leaders	curlew	birds
cougar	animals	crisis	medic	curtal	animals
coulee	geog	crisis	time	curtal	war

Curtis *Shakesp*	Daniel *names*	defend *war*
Curzon *leaders*	Danube *rivers*	defile *geog*
cuscus *animals*	Daphne *myth*	defray *trade*
cushat *birds*	Daphne *names*	degage *foreign*
custom *trade*	daphne *trees*	degree *educ*
cutler *jobs*	dapper *clothes*	degree *maths*
cutlet *food*	Daquin *music*	degree *measure*
cutout *machine*	Darius *Bible*	degree *physics*
cutout *travel*	darnel *plants*	degree *weather*
cutter *agric*	Darsey *names*	deicer *travel*
cutter *jobs*	darter *birds*	dejavu *foreign*
cutter *travel*	darter *fish*	dejure *foreign*
cuttle *fish*	dartre *medic*	Dekker *writers*
Cybele *myth*	dassie *animals*	delate *law*
cyclic *maths*	dative *lit*	delete *lit*
cygnet *birds*	dauber *art*	delict *law*
Cygnus *astron*	Daudet *writers*	Delius *music*
Cygnus *myth*	Davies *writers*	deluge *geog*
cymbal *music*	Davina *names*	Deluge *relig*
Cyprus *islands*	daybed *house*	demand *trade*
cytode *biol*	dayfly *insects*	demise *medic*
Czerny *music*	Dayton *cities*	denary *maths*
dacapo *music*	deacon *jobs*	dengue *medic*
Dacron *clothes*	deacon *relig*	denial *law*
dactyl *lit*	deadly *medic*	denier *clothes*
daemon *myth*	dealer *jobs*	denier *measure*
dagger *lit*	dealer *sport*	denier *money*
dagger *war*	dealer *trade*	Denise *names*
dahlia *flowers*	dealin *trade*	Dennis *Shakesp*
daimio *govt*	debate *educ*	dental *medic*
dainty *food*	debate *govt*	dentil *archit*
Daland *lit*	Debbie *names*	Denver *cities*
Dallas *cities*	debtee *trade*	deodar *trees*
damage *medic*	debtor *jobs*	depart *travel*
damask *clothes*	debtor *trade*	depict *art*
Damian *names*	decade *time*	depict *lit*
damper *archit*	decane *chem*	depict *theatre*
damper *house*	decani *music*	depths *geog*
damper *music*	decare *measure*	depute *govt*
damsel *jobs*	decked *travel*	deputy *govt*
damson *fruit*	decree *law*	deputy *jobs*
Danaus *myth*	Decuma *myth*	dermis *medic*
dancer *jobs*	dedans *sport*	Dermot *names*
dancer *theatre*	defeat *war*	derTag *foreign*
Daniel *Bible*	defect *medic*	desert *geog*

design	*art*	dirndl	*clothes*	dorsum	*medic*
desman	*animals*	dishes	*house*	dosage	*medic*
despot	*govt*	dittos	*clothes*	dosser	*archit*
detail	*war*	divert	*travel*	dossil	*medic*
detour	*travel*	divide	*maths*	dotage	*time*
device	*herald*	divine	*jobs*	dotard	*people*
device	*machine*	divine	*relig*	double	*jobs*
devout	*relig*	diving	*sport*	double	*music*
dewbow	*geog*	diving	*travel*	Dougal	*names*
dewlap	*animals*	dobbin	*animals*	dowser	*jobs*
dexter	*herald*	docent	*educ*	drachm	*measure*
dharma	*law*	docker	*jobs*	drachm	*money*
diadem	*herald*	doctor	*educ*	dragee	*food*
diadem	*jewels*	doctor	*jobs*	dragon	*animals*
diadem	*relig*	doctor	*medic*	dragon	*herald*
Dianne	*names*	dodger	*people*	dragon	*myth*
diaper	*clothes*	dogate	*law*	draper	*jobs*
dibble	*tools*	dogger	*travel*	drawer	*art*
dicker	*trade*	doghip	*fruit*	drawer	*house*
dickey	*clothes*	dogleg	*sport*	drawer	*jobs*
dictum	*law*	dolium	*house*	drawer	*trade*
dictum	*lit*	dollar	*money*	dredge	*machine*
diesel	*machine*	dolman	*clothes*	driver	*jobs*
diesis	*lit*	dolmen	*geog*	driver	*sport*
diesis	*music*	dolmen	*relig*	driver	*travel*
digest	*govt*	domain	*geog*	Dromio	*Shakesp*
digest	*lit*	domain	*govt*	drones	*music*
digger	*agric*	Donald	*names*	drongo	*birds*
digger	*tools*	Donets	*rivers*	dropsy	*medic*
dikdik	*animals*	donjon	*archit*	drudge	*jobs*
dilute	*chem*	donjon	*war*	dryair	*weather*
dimity	*clothes*	donkey	*animals*	Dryden	*writers*
dinghy	*travel*	doodle	*art*	dryfly	*sport*
dingle	*geog*	doodle	*lit*	dryice	*chem*
dining	*food*	Dorado	*astron*	dryrot	*archit*
dinner	*food*	dorado	*fish*	dryrun	*travel*
diplon	*chem*	Dorcas	*Bible*	dryrun	*war*
dipody	*lit*	Dorcas	*Shakesp*	Dublin	*cities*
dipole	*physics*	Doreen	*names*	Dublin	*herald*
dipper	*astron*	doremi	*music*	Duccio	*artists*
dipper	*birds*	dorfly	*insects*	Dudley	*names*
dipsas	*insects*	dormer	*archit*	duello	*war*
direct	*music*	dormie	*sport*	duenna	*educ*
direct	*theatre*	dorsal	*archit*	duenna	*jobs*
dirhem	*measure*	Dorset	*Shakesp*	duffel	*clothes*

duffer *people*	editor *jobs*	Emilia *names*
Dugald *names*	editor *lit*	Emmaus *Bible*
dugong *animals*	Edmund *Shakesp*	empire *geog*
dugout *travel*	Edmund *names*	empire *govt*
dugout *war*	Edward *Shakesp*	Empson *writers*
dulcet *music*	Edward *names*	emptio *trade*
Dulcie *names*	Edwina *names*	emptor *law*
Dulles *leaders*	Eeyore *lit*	emquad *lit*
dumdum *war*	effect *theatre*	enamel *art*
Duncan *Shakesp*	effigy *art*	encore *music*
Duncan *names*	efflux *geog*	encore *theatre*
Dundee *cities*	Egbert *names*	ending *lit*
Dunelm *abbrev*	Egeria *myth*	endive *veg*
dunlin *birds*	eggbox *food*	energy *physics*
dunner *trade*	eggcup *house*	enfete *foreign*
Duparc *music*	eggnog *drink*	engild *art*
duplex *archit*	egoist *people*	engine *machine*
Durban *cities*	egress *travel*	engine *travel*
durbar *archit*	eighth *music*	engram *medic*
durbar *govt*	Eileen *names*	enlist *war*
durgan *myth*	Eilidh *names*	enrich *trade*
durian *fruit*	Eirene *myth*	EnSaga *titles*
during *time*	Elaine *names*	ensign *herald*
duster *house*	elanet *birds*	ensign *jobs*
Dustin *names*	elapse *time*	ensign *war*
Dvorak *music*	eleven *sport*	entail *law*
Dwight *names*	elevon *travel*	entire *animals*
dyeing *art*	Elijah *Bible*	entree *food*
dynamo *machine*	Elinor *Shakesp*	enzyme *biol*
dynamo *physics*	Elinor *names*	Eocene *geog*
dynast *govt*	Elisha *Bible*	eolith *tools*
eaglet *birds*	Elisha *names*	eothen *geog*
EandOE *abbrev*	elixir *medic*	eparch *govt*
earing *travel*	ellops *fish*	Epirus *myth*
earwig *insects*	ellops *insects*	eponym *lit*
Easter *names*	ElPaso *cities*	epopee *lit*
Easter *relig*	Elvira *names*	equine *animals*
Easter *time*	embalm *relig*	equipe *sport*
eatout *art*	embark *travel*	equity *law*
eatout *food*	emblem *herald*	Equity *theatre*
ecbole *music*	embryo *animals*	equity *trade*
eclair *food*	embryo *biol*	eraser *educ*
eczema *medic*	embryo *medic*	erbium *chem*
eddies *marine*	emetic *medic*	erbium *mineral*
edible *food*	Emilia *Shakesp*	Erebus *myth*

ere|now	*time*	Evelyn	*writers*	farina	*cereal*
eringo	*plants*	examen	*educ*	farmer	*agric*
Erinys	*myth*	exarch	*govt*	Farnol	*writers*
ermine	*animals*	excise	*trade*	farrow	*animals*
ermine	*clothes*	exedra	*archit*	fasces	*govt*
ermine	*herald*	Exeter	*Shakesp*	fascia	*archit*
Ernest	*names*	Exmoor	*mounts*	fascia	*clothes*
Erotes	*myth*	Exocet	*war*	fascia	*medic*
errand	*trade*	Exodus	*Bible*	father	*family*
errata	*lit*	exodus	*theatre*	Father	*relig*
escape	*travel*	exodus	*travel*	fathom	*measure*
escarp	*war*	exotic	*flowers*	Faunus	*myth*
eschar	*medic*	expend	*trade*	favour	*lit*
escort	*jobs*	expert	*jobs*	fawner	*people*
escort	*war*	export	*trade*	fedora	*clothes*
escudo	*money*	expose	*lit*	Feeble	*Shakesp*
Eskimo	*jobs*	extant	*time*	feeder	*clothes*
Esmond	*names*	eyelid	*medic*	feeder	*geog*
estate	*archit*	Fabian	*Shakesp*	feeder	*jobs*
estate	*law*	Fabian	*govt*	feeder	*theatre*
estate	*trade*	fabler	*jobs*	feline	*animals*
Esther	*Bible*	fabler	*lit*	fellow	*educ*
Esther	*names*	fabric	*archit*	fellow	*jobs*
etcher	*art*	fabric	*clothes*	fellow	*people*
etcher	*jobs*	facade	*archit*	felony	*law*
etcher	*machine*	facial	*clothes*	fencer	*sport*
ethane	*chem*	facies	*geog*	fender	*house*
ethnic	*geog*	facing	*archit*	fender	*travel*
Etolia	*myth*	facing	*clothes*	fennec	*animals*
etymon	*lit*	factor	*jobs*	fennel	*veg*
Euboea	*islands*	factor	*maths*	Fenton	*Shakesp*
euchre	*sport*	fading	*music*	Fergus	*names*
Euclid	*maths*	faggot	*govt*	ferial	*time*
Eugene	*names*	faggot	*machine*	ferine	*animals*
eulogy	*lit*	faggot	*people*	ferret	*animals*
Eunice	*Bible*	faille	*clothes*	fescue	*plants*
Eunice	*names*	falcon	*birds*	fester	*medic*
eunuch	*relig*	fallal	*clothes*	Festus	*Bible*
euphon	*music*	fallow	*agric*	fetish	*myth*
eureka	*maths*	famine	*geog*	fetter	*law*
Europa	*geog*	famine	*relig*	fewter	*war*
Europa	*myth*	fannel	*clothes*	fiacre	*travel*
Euryte	*myth*	fannel	*relig*	fiasco	*house*
Evadne	*names*	fantod	*people*	fibber	*people*
Evelyn	*names*	farcer	*theatre*	fibrin	*biol*

fibula	*jewels*	flight	*sport*	foxbat	*animals*
fibula	*medic*	flight	*travel*	foxfur	*clothes*
FidDef	*abbrev*	flight	*war*	France	*writers*
fiddle	*music*	flimsy	*lit*	Franck	*music*
fidonc	*foreign*	flinty	*mineral*	Franco	*leaders*
Figaro	*lit*	flitch	*food*	Franco	*war*
figure	*art*	floats	*theatre*	frappe	*food*
figure	*lit*	floret	*flowers*	Fraser	*rivers*
figure	*maths*	floret	*veg*	frater	*family*
figure	*medic*	florid	*flowers*	Frazer	*writers*
figure	*music*	florin	*money*	freeze	*trade*
figure	*trade*	Flotow	*music*	freeze	*weather*
filler	*theatre*	flower	*flowers*	fresco	*archit*
fillet	*archit*	fluent	*maths*	fresco	*art*
fillet	*clothes*	flunky	*jobs*	fretty	*herald*
fillet	*herald*	flurry	*geog*	Freyia	*myth*
fillip	*medic*	fluted	*archit*	Freyja	*myth*
filter	*art*	flying	*sport*	Friday	*time*
filter	*chem*	flying	*travel*	fridge	*food*
filter	*machine*	flyman	*jobs*	fridge	*house*
finale	*music*	flyman	*theatre*	friend	*jobs*
finale	*theatre*	Flysch	*mineral*	frieze	*archit*
finals	*educ*	focsle	*travel*	frieze	*house*
finery	*clothes*	fodder	*agric*	Frigga	*myth*
fingan	*house*	fodder	*food*	frills	*clothes*
finger	*measure*	foeman	*war*	fringe	*clothes*
finger	*medic*	foetus	*biol*	Frunze	*cities*
finial	*archit*	foetus	*medic*	fucoid	*plants*
finite	*maths*	fogash	*fish*	fugato	*music*
firing	*art*	fogbow	*weather*	Fuhrer	*govt*
firing	*music*	folder	*lit*	Fukoka	*cities*
fiscal	*law*	foldup	*trade*	fuller	*jobs*
fiscal	*trade*	foment	*biol*	fulmar	*birds*
fisher	*sport*	fondue	*food*	fundus	*medic*
fitche	*herald*	forage	*agric*	fungus	*medic*
fitchy	*herald*	forage	*food*	fungus	*plants*
fitter	*jobs*	forage	*war*	funnel	*chem*
flacon	*house*	forces	*war*	funnel	*travel*
flagon	*house*	forest	*trees*	furrow	*agric*
flamen	*relig*	forger	*jobs*	Fushun	*cities*
flanch	*herald*	forger	*law*	fusion	*chem*
flange	*machine*	fornix	*medic*	future	*lit*
flatus	*weather*	fossil	*animals*	future	*time*
fleche	*archit*	founds	*archit*	future	*trade*
flight	*birds*	fourth	*music*	fylfot	*herald*

gabbro	*mineral*	
gabion	*war*	
gadfly	*insects*	
gadget	*tools*	
gaffer	*jobs*	
gaggle	*birds*	
gagman	*jobs*	
gagman	*theatre*	
gaiter	*clothes*	
galaxy	*astron*	
galena	*chem*	
galena	*mineral*	
galiot	*travel*	
galley	*house*	
galley	*lit*	
galley	*machine*	
galley	*travel*	
gallon	*measure*	
gallop	*sport*	
gallop	*travel*	
galoot	*war*	
galosh	*clothes*	
gamash	*clothes*	
gambet	*birds*	
Gambia	*rivers*	
gambit	*sport*	
gamete	*biol*	
gaming	*sport*	
gammon	*food*	
gander	*birds*	
Ganesa	*myth*	
ganger	*jobs*	
Ganges	*rivers*	
gangue	*mineral*	
gannet	*birds*	
gantry	*machine*	
gaoler	*jobs*	
gaoler	*law*	
garage	*archit*	
garage	*house*	
garage	*trade*	
garage	*travel*	
garcon	*jobs*	
garden	*archit*	
garden	*flowers*	

garden	*veg*	
Gareth	*names*	
gargle	*medic*	
garlic	*veg*	
garnet	*jewels*	
garnet	*machine*	
garnet	*mineral*	
garret	*archit*	
garret	*house*	
garron	*animals*	
garrot	*birds*	
garter	*clothes*	
garter	*herald*	
garuda	*birds*	
Garuda	*myth*	
garvie	*fish*	
gasbag	*people*	
gas|jar	*biol*	
gas|jar	*chem*	
gas|jet	*house*	
gas|jet	*travel*	
gasket	*machine*	
gasket	*travel*	
gas|tap	*house*	
Gaston	*names*	
gatcau	*food*	
gaucho	*jobs*	
gavial	*insects*	
Gawain	*myth*	
gay|dog	*people*	
gazebo	*archit*	
gazump	*trade*	
G|clamp	*machine*	
Gdansk	*cities*	
geegee	*animals*	
Gehazi	*Bible*	
Geiger	*physics*	
gemels	*herald*	
Gemini	*myth*	
Gemini	*zodiac*	
gender	*lit*	
genera	*animals*	
Geneva	*cities*	
genius	*educ*	
genius	*myth*	

genius	*people*	
gennet	*animals*	
gentry	*govt*	
geodes	*geog*	
George	*names*	
Gerald	*names*	
Gerard	*names*	
gerbil	*animals*	
German	*jobs*	
Gertie	*names*	
gerund	*lit*	
Geryon	*myth*	
gewgaw	*jewels*	
geyser	*geog*	
geyser	*house*	
Ghandi	*leaders*	
ghetto	*archit*	
Ghosts	*titles*	
gibbon	*animals*	
Gibbon	*writers*	
Gibeon	*Bible*	
giblet	*food*	
Gideon	*Bible*	
Gideon	*names*	
gigolo	*jobs*	
Gilboa	*Bible*	
Gilead	*Bible*	
Gilgal	*Bible*	
gillie	*jobs*	
gimlet	*tools*	
gimmer	*agric*	
ginger	*veg*	
gingko	*trees*	
Giotto	*artists*	
girder	*archit*	
girdle	*clothes*	
giusto	*music*	
glacis	*war*	
Gladys	*names*	
glaive	*war*	
glazed	*art*	
glazer	*jobs*	
glider	*sport*	
glider	*travel*	
Gliere	*music*	

Glinka *music*	grader *educ*	groove *geog*
Gloria *names*	grader *machine*	groper *fish*
glover *jobs*	grades *educ*	grotto *geog*
gluten *chem*	gradin *archit*	grouch *people*
gnawer *animals*	gradus *educ*	ground *archit*
gneiss *mineral*	gradus *lit*	ground *educ*
gnomic *lit*	Graeae *myth*	ground *geog*
gnomon *astron*	Graham *names*	ground *machine*
gnomon *time*	Graham *writers*	ground *sport*
goatee *clothes*	grains *agric*	grouse *birds*
gobang *sport*	gramme *measure*	grouse *food*
gobble *animals*	grange *agric*	grower *jobs*
gobble *sport*	grange *archit*	growth *flowers*
goblet *drink*	granny *archit*	growth *medic*
goblin *myth*	grater *house*	growth *trade*
gobony *herald*	grater *tools*	growth *veg*
gocart *travel*	gratis *trade*	Grumio *Shakesp*
godown *archit*	gravel *archit*	guenon *animals*
godown *trade*	gravel *geog*	guidon *herald*
godson *family*	graven *art*	guilty *law*
godwit *birds*	graver *art*	guinea *money*
Goethe *writers*	graver *jobs*	guinea *trade*
goitre *medic*	Graves *writers*	guiser *theatre*
gokart *sport*	grazia *music*	guitar *music*
golfer *jobs*	grease *trade*	gulden *money*
golfer *sport*	greatC *music*	gullet *medic*
googly *sport*	greats *educ*	gulley *geog*
gooney *birds*	greave *clothes*	gundog *animals*
gopher *animals*	greave *war*	gunman *jobs*
gopura *archit*	Greene *writers*	gunman *law*
Gordon *names*	greens *veg*	gunnel *travel*
Gordon *war*	Gregor *names*	gunner *jobs*
Gordon *writers*	Gremio *Shakesp*	gunner *war*
gorget *herald*	Gretel *lit*	gunshy *war*
gorget *war*	Gretel *names*	Gurkha *war*
Gorgon *myth*	Gretry *music*	gurnet *fish*
Goshen *Bible*	griffe *archit*	Gurney *Shakesp*
goslow *trade*	grille *archit*	gusset *clothes*
gospel *relig*	grilse *fish*	gusset *war*
gossip *people*	gripes *medic*	gutter *archit*
Gothic *archit*	grippe *medic*	gutter *machine*
Gothic *lit*	grison *animals*	gutter *sport*
Gounod *music*	grivet *animals*	Gwenda *names*
graces *music*	groats *cereal*	gypsum *mineral*
Graces *myth*	grocer *jobs*	haboob *weather*

hackee	*animals*	Hassan	*lit*	hedera	*plants*
hacker	*comput*	Hassan	*titles*	hegoat	*animals*
hackle	*animals*	hassle	*people*	heifer	*agric*
Haemon	*myth*	hat|box	*clothes*	heifer	*animals*
hagbut	*war*	Hathor	*myth*	height	*measure*
Haggai	*Bible*	hatpin	*clothes*	Hekate	*myth*
haggle	*trade*	hatter	*jobs*	Helena	*Shakesp*
Hainan	*islands*	Hattie	*names*	Helena	*titles*
hairdo	*clothes*	haul|to	*travel*	Helios	*myth*
halide	*chem*	Havana	*cities*	helium	*chem*
hallow	*relig*	Hawaii	*islands*	helmet	*clothes*
hallux	*medic*	hawhaw	*archit*	helmet	*herald*
Halsey	*war*	hawker	*jobs*	helmet	*sport*
Hamish	*names*	hawker	*trade*	helmet	*war*
Hamlet	*Shakesp*	Hawkes	*writers*	helper	*jobs*
hamlet	*geog*	hawser	*travel*	Hemans	*writers*
hammer	*medic*	hazard	*sport*	henbit	*flowers*
hammer	*music*	Hblast	*physics*	Henley	*writers*
hammer	*sport*	header	*archit*	henrun	*birds*
hammer	*tools*	header	*sport*	hepcat	*music*
hammer	*trade*	healer	*jobs*	hepcat	*people*
hammer	*war*	healer	*medic*	heptad	*maths*
hamper	*house*	health	*medic*	herald	*birds*
Handel	*music*	hearse	*relig*	herald	*herald*
hand|in	*sport*	hearse	*travel*	herald	*jobs*
handle	*house*	hearth	*archit*	heresy	*relig*
handle	*machine*	hearth	*house*	heriot	*law*
hangar	*archit*	hearts	*sport*	Hermes	*myth*
hangar	*travel*	hearty	*medic*	Hermia	*Shakesp*
hanger	*war*	heater	*house*	hermit	*jobs*
hanjar	*war*	heater	*machine*	hermit	*relig*
hankie	*clothes*	heaume	*herald*	hernia	*medic*
Hannah	*Bible*	heaume	*war*	heroic	*lit*
Hannah	*names*	heaven	*astron*	heroin	*medic*
Hansel	*lit*	heaven	*myth*	Herold	*music*
hansom	*travel*	Heaven	*relig*	Hesiod	*writers*
harass	*war*	Hebrew	*relig*	Hester	*names*
Harbin	*cities*	Hebron	*Bible*	hetman	*jobs*
hard|up	*trade*	Hebrus	*myth*	heyday	*time*
harman	*law*	Hecate	*Shakesp*	hiatus	*geog*
Harold	*names*	Hecate	*myth*	hiatus	*lit*
harper	*music*	Hector	*Shakesp*	hiemal	*geog*
harrow	*agric*	Hector	*myth*	hiemal	*time*
harrow	*tools*	Hector	*names*	high|up	*jobs*
Harvey	*names*	Hecuba	*myth*	hiking	*sport*

Hilary	*names*
hippie	*jobs*
hippie	*people*
Hitler	*leaders*
Hobbes	*writers*
Hobbit	*myth*
hockey	*sport*
Hoenir	*myth*
hogget	*animals*
hograt	*animals*
holder	*govt*
holdup	*law*
hollow	*geog*
Holmes	*writers*
Holtby	*writers*
homage	*govt*
homage	*relig*
homily	*educ*
homily	*lit*
homily	*relig*
hominy	*cereal*
honker	*birds*
honour	*law*
honour	*sport*
HonSec	*abbrev*
Honshu	*islands*
hoodoo	*myth*
hooker	*sport*
hooker	*travel*
hookey	*sport*
hooper	*birds*
hoopla	*sport*
hoopoe	*birds*
Hoover	*USpres*
hooves	*animals*
hopfly	*insects*
hopper	*agric*
hopper	*machine*
Horace	*names*
Horace	*writers*
Horner	*Shakesp*
horner	*music*
hornet	*insects*
hosier	*jobs*
hostel	*archit*

hotair	*weather*
hotday	*weather*
hotdog	*food*
hotpot	*food*
hotrod	*travel*
hotwar	*war*
houdah	*animals*
hourly	*time*
hoveto	*travel*
Howard	*names*
Howard	*writers*
howdah	*animals*
howlet	*birds*
hubcap	*travel*
Hubert	*names*
Hudson	*rivers*
Hughes	*writers*
Humber	*rivers*
humble	*animals*
humbug	*food*
humbug	*people*
hummel	*animals*
Hummel	*music*
humour	*medic*
hunter	*animals*
hunter	*jobs*
Hunter	*names*
hurdle	*sport*
hurley	*sport*
hurtle	*travel*
hussar	*jobs*
hussar	*war*
hustle	*travel*
Huxley	*writers*
Hyades	*astron*
Hyades	*myth*
hyaena	*animals*
hybrid	*animals*
hybrid	*biol*
hybrid	*flowers*
hybrid	*lit*
Hydrus	*astron*
Hyllus	*myth*
hymnal	*music*
hymner	*jobs*

hymner	*music*
hyphen	*lit*
hyssop	*plants*
iambic	*lit*
iambus	*lit*
Iasion	*myth*
Iasius	*myth*
Ibadan	*cities*
Iberia	*titles*
ibidem	*foreign*
Icarus	*myth*
Iceage	*geog*
Iceage	*time*
iceaxe	*sport*
icebox	*house*
icecap	*geog*
iceman	*jobs*
icicle	*geog*
idling	*travel*
ignite	*physics*
Iguacu	*rivers*
iguana	*insects*
Ijssel	*rivers*
imbibe	*drink*
immune	*medic*
Imogen	*Shakesp*
Imogen	*names*
impact	*travel*
impact	*war*
impala	*animals*
impale	*war*
import	*trade*
impose	*lit*
impose	*trade*
impost	*archit*
impost	*trade*
inarms	*war*
inbulk	*trade*
incash	*trade*
incise	*art*
income	*trade*
incorp	*abbrev*
Indara	*myth*
indebt	*trade*
indecl	*abbrev*

indict *law*	Irving *names*	jargon *mineral*
indigo *colour*	Isabel *Shakesp*	jarool *trees*
indigo *plants*	Isabel *names*	jarrah *trees*
indium *chem*	Isaiah *Bible*	jasper *jewels*
indium *mineral*	Isaiah *names*	jasper *mineral*
Indore *cities*	Ischia *islands*	Jasper *names*
induna *govt*	Iseult *myth*	Jeeves *lit*
infamy *law*	Ishtar *myth*	jemima *clothes*
infant *educ*	island *geog*	Jemima *names*
infant *family*	island *travel*	jennet *animals*
infirm *medic*	Ismene *myth*	Jenufa *lit*
influx *geog*	isobar *physics*	Jenufa *titles*
infula *clothes*	isobar *weather*	jerboa *animals*
infuse *educ*	Isobel *names*	jereed *war*
Ingram *names*	isohel *weather*	Jeremy *names*
Ingres *artists*	Isolde *lit*	jerkin *clothes*
Ingrid *names*	Isolde *myth*	Jerome *names*
injury *medic*	Isolde *names*	Jerome *writers*
inkpot *educ*	isomer *chem*	jersey *clothes*
inland *geog*	Israel *Bible*	Jersey *islands*
inmate *jobs*	Israel *names*	Jervis *war*
in|pain *medic*	Israel *relig*	jesses *sport*
inroad *war*	italic *lit*	Jessie *names*
insect *insects*	Ithaca *islands*	jester *jobs*
insole *clothes*	Ithunn *myth*	jester *theatre*
instar *animals*	jabiru *birds*	Jesuit *relig*
instep *medic*	jacana *birds*	jet|age *time*
insula *archit*	jackal *animals*	Jethro *Bible*
insula *medic*	jacket *clothes*	jet|lag *travel*
intake *travel*	jacket *lit*	jetsam *travel*
intern *jobs*	Jackie *names*	jet|set *jobs*
intern *medic*	jaeger *animals*	jet|set *people*
in|time *time*	jaguar *animals*	jet|set *travel*
in|tray *trade*	jailer *jobs*	Jewish *relig*
in|trim *travel*	jailer *law*	Jhelum *rivers*
in|tune *music*	Jaipur *cities*	jib|guy *travel*
inulin *chem*	Jairus *Bible*	jigger *insects*
in|vivo *foreign*	jalopy *travel*	jigger *travel*
iodide *chem*	jam|jar *food*	jigsaw *sport*
iodine *chem*	jampot *food*	jigsaw *tools*
iodine *medic*	Janice *names*	jingal *war*
Iolcus *myth*	Japura *rivers*	jingle *lit*
iolite *mineral*	Jaques *Shakesp*	jingle *music*
Ireton *war*	jargon *jewels*	jinnee *myth*
Irtysh *rivers*	jargon *lit*	Joanna *names*

Joanne	*names*	junior	*jobs*	kimono	*clothes*
jobber	*jobs*	junior	*law*	kindle	*animals*
jobber	*trade*	junker	*govt*	kipper	*fish*
job|lot	*trade*	junker	*jobs*	kipper	*food*
jockey	*jobs*	junket	*food*	kirsch	*drink*
jockey	*sport*	junket	*travel*	Kirsty	*names*
joiner	*jobs*	junkie	*people*	kirtle	*clothes*
Jonson	*writers*	jurant	*law*	Kishon	*Bible*
Joplin	*music*	jurist	*law*	kiss|me	*plants*
Jordan	*Bible*	Justin	*names*	kit|bag	*travel*
Jordan	*relig*	Kabuki	*theatre*	kit|fox	*animals*
Jordan	*rivers*	kaftan	*clothes*	kitten	*animals*
Joseph	*Bible*	kagool	*clothes*	kittul	*trees*
Joseph	*names*	Kaiser	*govt*	klaxon	*machine*
Joshua	*Bible*	kakapo	*birds*	klaxon	*travel*
Joshua	*names*	kalmia	*trees*	knawel	*plants*
Josiah	*Bible*	Kanpur	*cities*	Knight	*artists*
Josiah	*names*	kaolin	*mineral*	knight	*govt*
josser	*relig*	karate	*sport*	knight	*sport*
jostle	*sport*	kaross	*house*	kobold	*myth*
jostle	*travel*	karroo	*geog*	Kodaly	*music*
jotter	*educ*	kation	*physics*	Kolyma	*rivers*
jubbah	*relig*	Kaunda	*leaders*	koodoo	*animals*
Judaea	*Bible*	keener	*jobs*	kopeck	*money*
Judith	*names*	keener	*music*	kraken	*myth*
jujube	*food*	keener	*relig*	Kronos	*myth*
jujube	*trees*	keeper	*govt*	Kumasi	*cities*
Julian	*names*	keeper	*jobs*	kumiss	*drink*
Julian	*time*	kelpie	*myth*	kummel	*drink*
Juliet	*Shakesp*	Kenelm	*names*	Kundry	*lit*
Juliet	*names*	kennel	*animals*	Kunlun	*mounts*
Julius	*names*	kennel	*archit*	Kyushu	*islands*
jumart	*animals*	kernel	*food*	laager	*war*
jumart	*myth*	kernel	*fruit*	labial	*medic*
jumble	*house*	ketone	*chem*	labile	*chem*
jumper	*clothes*	kettle	*house*	labour	*medic*
jumper	*jobs*	kettle	*music*	labour	*trade*
jumper	*machine*	keyway	*machine*	labrys	*war*
jumper	*sport*	Khulna	*cities*	laches	*law*
jungle	*animals*	kidnap	*law*	lackey	*jobs*
jungle	*geog*	kidney	*food*	lacuna	*biol*
jungle	*plants*	kidney	*medic*	ladder	*house*
jungle	*trees*	kilerg	*measure*	lagena	*house*
junior	*educ*	killer	*animals*	lagoon	*geog*
junior	*family*	killer	*jobs*	Lahore	*cities*

laid│up	*medic*	lawyer	*law*	lessee	*jobs*
lalang	*plants*	layers	*geog*	lessee	*law*
lambda	*medic*	layman	*people*	lesson	*educ*
lament	*music*	leader	*govt*	lessor	*law*
lamina	*biol*	leader	*jobs*	Lester	*names*
Lammas	*law*	leader	*lit*	lethal	*law*
Lammas	*time*	leader	*machine*	letter	*lit*
lanate	*biol*	leader	*music*	letter	*travel*
lancer	*jobs*	leader	*people*	levant	*geog*
lancer	*war*	leader	*sport*	Levite	*jobs*
lancet	*archit*	leader	*trade*	liable	*trade*
lancet	*medic*	league	*measure*	Libera	*myth*
landau	*travel*	lean│to	*archit*	lichen	*medic*
Landor	*writers*	leaser	*law*	lichen	*plants*
langur	*animals*	leaven	*food*	lictor	*law*
lanner	*birds*	Le│Beau	*Shakesp*	Lieder	*music*
lap│dog	*animals*	lector	*educ*	Liffey	*rivers*
lappet	*clothes*	lector	*jobs*	Ligeti	*music*
lappet	*medic*	lector	*relig*	lights	*theatre*
lapsed	*time*	ledger	*trade*	lignum	*trees*
Laputa	*myth*	Ledoux	*artists*	Lilian	*names*
larder	*house*	leeway	*travel*	Lilith	*myth*
lariat	*sport*	legacy	*law*	limber	*theatre*
Larkin	*writers*	legate	*govt*	limner	*art*
Larrie	*names*	legate	*jobs*	limner	*jobs*
larynx	*medic*	legato	*music*	limpet	*fish*
lascar	*jobs*	leg│bye	*sport*	linden	*trees*
lascar	*travel*	legend	*lit*	linear	*measure*
Lassus	*music*	legion	*war*	lining	*clothes*
Laszlo	*artists*	legist	*law*	linnet	*birds*
lateen	*travel*	legume	*veg*	lintel	*archit*
lately	*time*	Leitha	*rivers*	lintel	*house*
latest	*time*	Lemnos	*islands*	Lionel	*names*
latish	*time*	lemuel	*relig*	lionet	*animals*
latria	*relig*	lender	*jobs*	lipase	*biol*
Launce	*Shakesp*	lender	*trade*	lipoma	*medic*
launce	*fish*	length	*measure*	liquid	*drink*
launch	*travel*	Lennox	*Shakesp*	liquor	*drink*
laurel	*trees*	Lenski	*lit*	Lisbon	*cities*
Laurie	*names*	lentil	*cereal*	listel	*archit*
lavage	*medic*	lepton	*money*	litany	*relig*
Lavery	*artists*	Lesbos	*islands*	litchi	*fruit*
lawful	*law*	lesion	*medic*	Lit│Hum	*abbrev*
lawman	*law*	Lesley	*names*	litmus	*chem*
lawyer	*jobs*	Leslie	*names*	litter	*animals*

litter	*travel*	lowrie	*animals*	maggot	*insects*
livery	*clothes*	Luanda	*cities*	magian	*relig*
livery	*herald*	Lubeck	*cities*	magilp	*art*
living	*jobs*	Lucina	*myth*	magnet	*machine*
living	*trade*	Lucius	*Shakesp*	magnet	*physics*
lizard	*insects*	Lucius	*names*	magnum	*drink*
loafer	*people*	Lugaid	*myth*	magnum	*measure*
lobule	*medic*	lugger	*travel*	Magnus	*names*
locale	*geog*	lumber	*medic*	magpie	*birds*
loc|cit	*abbrev*	lunate	*geog*	maguey	*flowers*
lochan	*geog*	lunula	*medic*	magyar	*clothes*
locker	*house*	lupine	*animals*	Mahler	*music*
locket	*clothes*	lupine	*flowers*	mahout	*jobs*
lock|up	*travel*	Lusaka	*cities*	mahout	*travel*
Locris	*myth*	lustre	*colour*	maiden	*jobs*
locust	*fruit*	lustre	*time*	maigre	*fish*
locust	*insects*	lutein	*chem*	mailed	*war*
lodged	*herald*	Luther	*names*	Mailer	*writers*
lodger	*jobs*	lutist	*jobs*	maimed	*medic*
log|bin	*house*	lutist	*music*	Maisie	*names*
loggia	*archit*	luxury	*house*	maison	*archit*
log|log	*maths*	luxury	*trade*	Majlis	*govt*
Lolita	*names*	lyceum	*archit*	make|up	*clothes*
Lolita	*titles*	lyceum	*educ*	make|up	*film/TV*
Londin	*abbrev*	lyceum	*theatre*	make|up	*lit*
London	*cities*	lychee	*fruit*	make|up	*theatre*
London	*writers*	lyrist	*jobs*	malady	*medic*
Lonrho	*abbrev*	lyrist	*lit*	Malaga	*cities*
looper	*insects*	lyrist	*music*	Malang	*cities*
loquat	*trees*	lysine	*chem*	mallee	*plants*
lorcha	*travel*	Lytton	*writers*	mallet	*art*
lorica	*herald*	Mabuse	*artists*	mallet	*sport*
lorica	*war*	mackle	*lit*	mallet	*tools*
lotion	*medic*	macron	*lit*	mallow	*flowers*
Lottie	*names*	macule	*lit*	Malory	*writers*
Louisa	*names*	madder	*art*	maltha	*mineral*
Louise	*names*	madder	*colour*	mammal	*animals*
lounge	*archit*	madder	*plants*	mammee	*fruit*
lounge	*house*	mad|dog	*animals*	Mammon	*myth*
louvre	*archit*	madman	*people*	mammon	*trade*
louvre	*house*	Madras	*cities*	manana	*time*
lovage	*fruit*	madras	*clothes*	manati	*animals*
Lovell	*Shakesp*	Madrid	*cities*	Man|Dir	*abbrev*
lowboy	*house*	maenad	*myth*	manege	*animals*
lowing	*animals*	Maggie	*names*	manege	*sport*

manger	*agric*
manger	*animals*
manger	*relig*
mangle	*house*
Manila	*cities*
manioc	*plants*
manito	*myth*
mantel	*archit*
mantid	*insects*
mantis	*insects*
mantle	*clothes*
mantle	*herald*
mantle	*relig*
mantra	*relig*
mantua	*clothes*
manual	*educ*
manual	*lit*
manual	*music*
manual	*relig*
Manuel	*names*
manuka	*trees*
manure	*agric*
map	out	*geog*
maquis	*plants*
maquis	*war*
marble	*archit*
marble	*art*
marble	*mineral*
marble	*sport*
marcel	*clothes*
Marcia	*names*
Marcus	*names*
Marduk	*myth*
margay	*animals*
Margie	*names*
margin	*geog*
margin	*lit*
Marian	*names*
Marina	*Shakesp*
marina	*sport*
marina	*travel*
marine	*jobs*
marine	*marine*
marine	*war*
Marion	*names*

Marius	*names*
marker	*jobs*
marker	*travel*
marlin	*fish*
Marmar	*myth*
marmot	*animals*
maroon	*colour*
marram	*plants*
marrow	*medic*
marrow	*veg*
marrum	*plants*
marshy	*geog*
marten	*animals*
Martha	*Bible*
Martha	*names*
Martha	*titles*
martin	*birds*
Martin	*names*
martyr	*people*
martyr	*relig*
mascle	*herald*
mascot	*myth*
mascot	*sport*
mashie	*sport*
masque	*theatre*
massif	*geog*
master	*art*
master	*educ*
master	*govt*
master	*jobs*
matins	*relig*
matrix	*machine*
matrix	*maths*
matron	*educ*
matron	*jobs*
matron	*medic*
matter	*chem*
matter	*lit*
maundy	*relig*
Mauser	*war*
Maxine	*names*
maxixe	*music*
maxixe	*sport*
maybug	*insects*
May|day	*time*

mayday	*travel*
mayfly	*insects*
mayhem	*govt*
meadow	*agric*
meagre	*fish*
mealie	*cereal*
measly	*medic*
meatus	*medic*
medick	*plants*
medico	*jobs*
medico	*medic*
medium	*art*
medium	*jobs*
medius	*medic*
medlar	*fruit*
medley	*music*
medusa	*fish*
Medusa	*myth*
Medway	*rivers*
Megara	*myth*
megilp	*art*
megohm	*measure*
megohm	*physics*
megrim	*fish*
megrim	*medic*
Mekong	*rivers*
melody	*music*
melton	*clothes*
Melvin	*names*
Melvyn	*names*
member	*jobs*
member	*medic*
Memnon	*myth*
memoir	*lit*
menage	*house*
menhir	*geog*
menial	*jobs*
meninx	*medic*
mentor	*educ*
mentor	*jobs*
Mentor	*myth*
mentum	*medic*
mercer	*jobs*
merger	*trade*
merils	*sport*

merino	*agric*	
merino	*animals*	
merlin	*animals*	
Merlin	*lit*	
Merlin	*myth*	
Merlin	*names*	
merlon	*war*	
merman	*fish*	
merman	*myth*	
Merope	*myth*	
Mersey	*rivers*	
Mervyn	*names*	
Messrs	*abbrev*	
meteor	*astron*	
method	*theatre*	
methyl	*chem*	
metope	*archit*	
metric	*lit*	
metric	*physics*	
miasma	*medic*	
Michel	*names*	
Mickey	*names*	
micron	*measure*	
micron	*physics*	
midday	*time*	
mid off	*sport*	
midrib	*medic*	
Midway	*islands*	
Mignon	*titles*	
mikado	*govt*	
mikado	*jobs*	
milady	*govt*	
milieu	*archit*	
miller	*jobs*	
Miller	*writers*	
millet	*agric*	
Millet	*artists*	
millet	*cereal*	
milord	*govt*	
milter	*fish*	
Milton	*writers*	
mimosa	*flowers*	
mincer	*house*	
mincer	*machine*	
minion	*jobs*	
minion	*lit*	
minium	*clothes*	
Minnie	*names*	
minnie	*war*	
minnow	*fish*	
minuet	*music*	
minuet	*sport*	
minute	*maths*	
minute	*measure*	
minute	*time*	
minute	*trade*	
mirage	*geog*	
Miriam	*Bible*	
Miriam	*names*	
mirror	*house*	
mirror	*physics*	
mirror	*travel*	
misere	*sport*	
missal	*relig*	
mister	*jobs*	
Mithra	*myth*	
mitten	*clothes*	
Mizpah	*Bible*	
mizzen	*travel*	
mob cap	*clothes*	
mobile	*art*	
mobile	*house*	
mobile	*travel*	
Mobutu	*leaders*	
mock up	*art*	
mod con	*abbrev*	
modena	*colour*	
modern	*time*	
module	*archit*	
module	*travel*	
moduli	*maths*	
Moerae	*myth*	
Moeran	*music*	
mohair	*clothes*	
moiety	*govt*	
moiler	*jobs*	
Moirai	*myth*	
Moldau	*rivers*	
Molech	*myth*	
mollah	*law*	
Moloch	*myth*	
molten	*mineral*	
Moltke	*war*	
moment	*time*	
Monday	*time*	
moneys	*trade*	
monger	*jobs*	
monger	*trade*	
mongol	*medic*	
Monica	*names*	
monies	*trade*	
monkey	*animals*	
monkey	*machine*	
monkey	*money*	
monody	*lit*	
monody	*music*	
Monroe	*USpres*	
mopoke	*birds*	
moppet	*jobs*	
morass	*geog*	
morbid	*medic*	
moreen	*clothes*	
Morgan	*Shakesp*	
Morgan	*names*	
Morgan	*writers*	
morgue	*lit*	
morion	*herald*	
morion	*mineral*	
morion	*war*	
Morley	*music*	
Mormon	*relig*	
Morrie	*names*	
Morris	*artists*	
Morris	*names*	
morris	*sport*	
Morris	*writers*	
morrow	*time*	
morsel	*food*	
mortal	*jobs*	
mortar	*archit*	
mortar	*machine*	
mortar	*war*	
Morton	*Shakesp*	
Morven	*names*	
mosaic	*archit*	

mosaic	*art*	Muriel	*names*	Nagpur	*cities*
Moscow	*cities*	murine	*fish*	nandoo	*birds*
Moslem	*relig*	murphy	*veg*	nankin	*clothes*
mosque	*archit*	murray	*fish*	nannie	*jobs*
mosque	*relig*	Murray	*names*	Nantes	*cities*
mother	*family*	Murray	*rivers*	napkin	*house*
motion	*govt*	murrey	*colour*	Naples	*cities*
motion	*music*	murrey	*fish*	nasion	*medic*
motion	*travel*	Mus|Bac	*abbrev*	Nasser	*leaders*
motive	*law*	muscat	*drink*	Nathan	*Bible*
motive	*music*	muscat	*fruit*	Nathan	*names*
motley	*theatre*	muscle	*medic*	nation	*geog*
motmot	*birds*	Mus|Doc	*abbrev*	native	*geog*
motuka	*insects*	museum	*archit*	native	*jobs*
Mouldy	*Shakesp*	museum	*art*	natron	*chem*
mouser	*animals*	musico	*jobs*	Nat|Sci	*abbrev*
mousse	*animals*	musico	*music*	nausea	*medic*
mousse	*food*	musket	*war*	Nazism	*govt*
movies	*film/TV*	musk|ox	*animals*	nebula	*geog*
Mowgli	*lit*	muslin	*clothes*	Neckar	*rivers*
Mozart	*music*	mussel	*fish*	nectar	*drink*
Mr|Mole	*lit*	Musset	*writers*	nectar	*flowers*
Mr|Toad	*lit*	muster	*animals*	nectar	*myth*
mucous	*medic*	muster	*war*	needle	*clothes*
mud|eel	*fish*	mutiny	*govt*	needle	*machine*
mud|hut	*archit*	mutism	*medic*	needle	*medic*
mud|pie	*sport*	Mutius	*Shakesp*	needle	*music*
muffin	*food*	mutton	*food*	Neisse	*rivers*
mugger	*insects*	mutule	*archit*	nekton	*biol*
mulish	*animals*	muzzle	*animals*	nekton	*fish*
mullah	*educ*	muzzle	*machine*	Neleus	*myth*
mullah	*relig*	muzzle	*war*	nelson	*sport*
muller	*tools*	myopic	*medic*	Nelson	*war*
mullet	*fish*	myriad	*measure*	nem|con	*abbrev*
mullet	*herald*	myrica	*plants*	nephew	*family*
Multan	*cities*	Myrrha	*myth*	Nereid	*astron*
mummer	*jobs*	Myrtle	*names*	nereid	*insects*
mummer	*theatre*	myrtle	*trees*	Nereid	*myth*
Munich	*cities*	Mysore	*cities*	Nereus	*myth*
munshi	*educ*	mystic	*jobs*	Nergal	*myth*
munshi	*jobs*	mystic	*relig*	Nessie	*names*
muntin	*archit*	Naaman	*Bible*	Nessus	*myth*
murder	*law*	Naboth	*Bible*	Nestor	*Shakesp*
murder	*sport*	Nadine	*names*	Nestor	*myth*
murena	*fish*	naevus	*medic*	Nettie	*names*

nettle	*plants*	notice	*lit*	octroi	*law*
net|ton	*measure*	notice	*trade*	octroi	*trade*
neumes	*music*	nougat	*food*	oculus	*archit*
neuron	*medic*	nought	*maths*	oculus	*medic*
neuter	*lit*	novena	*relig*	odd|job	*jobs*
Newark	*cities*	novice	*educ*	odd|job	*trade*
new|day	*time*	novice	*jobs*	odd|lot	*trade*
Newman	*writers*	novice	*relig*	Odessa	*cities*
niacin	*chem*	nowell	*music*	Odette	*names*
NIBMAR	*govt*	nozzle	*machine*	Oeneus	*myth*
nickel	*mineral*	Nuages	*titles*	offcut	*lit*
nickel	*money*	nuclei	*physics*	off|day	*time*
Nicola	*names*	nudist	*jobs*	office	*archit*
Nicole	*names*	nugget	*trade*	office	*govt*
nilgai	*animals*	number	*lit*	office	*jobs*
nilgau	*animals*	number	*maths*	office	*relig*
nimbus	*relig*	number	*theatre*	office	*trade*
nimbus	*weather*	numina	*myth*	off|key	*music*
Nimrod	*Bible*	nuncio	*govt*	offset	*lit*
Nimrod	*myth*	nuncio	*jobs*	of|late	*time*
nip|off	*travel*	nuncle	*family*	ogress	*myth*
nipple	*machine*	nutmeg	*food*	ogress	*people*
nipple	*medic*	nutmeg	*fruit*	oilcan	*war*
nipter	*relig*	nutter	*people*	Oileus	*myth*
Nivose	*time*	nylons	*clothes*	oil|gun	*tools*
no|ball	*sport*	obelus	*lit*	oilman	*jobs*
nobile	*music*	Oberon	*Shakesp*	oil|rig	*machine*
nobody	*people*	Oberon	*astron*	old|age	*time*
Noelle	*names*	Oberon	*myth*	old|boy	*educ*
noggin	*drink*	Oberon	*titles*	old|boy	*people*
nonage	*govt*	obi|man	*myth*	old|lag	*law*
nonary	*maths*	object	*lit*	Old|Ned	*myth*
non|com	*abbrev*	oblong	*maths*	old|saw	*lit*
Noncon	*abbrev*	oboist	*jobs*	Oliver	*Shakesp*
non|seq	*abbrev*	oboist	*music*	Oliver	*names*
noodle	*food*	occult	*myth*	Olivia	*Shakesp*
Norman	*jobs*	ocelot	*animals*	omelet	*food*
Norman	*names*	o'clock	*time*	onager	*animals*
Norris	*names*	octane	*chem*	on|call	*trade*
Norroy	*herald*	octane	*travel*	oncost	*trade*
Norvic	*abbrev*	Octans	*astron*	on|deck	*travel*
nose|up	*travel*	octant	*maths*	Ondine	*myth*
nostoc	*plants*	octave	*lit*	one|act	*theatre*
notary	*jobs*	octave	*music*	one|day	*time*
notice	*govt*	octavo	*lit*	O'Neill	*writers*

oneway	*travel*	
onfoot	*travel*	
online	*comput*	
onoath	*law*	
ontick	*trade*	
ontime	*time*	
ontour	*theatre*	
onward	*travel*	
Oonagh	*names*	
opaque	*art*	
opaque	*physics*	
opener	*sport*	
opiate	*medic*	
Oporto	*cities*	
optics	*physics*	
optime	*educ*	
optime	*jobs*	
option	*trade*	
oracle	*jobs*	
oracle	*myth*	
orange	*colour*	
orange	*fruit*	
Orange	*rivers*	
orator	*govt*	
orator	*jobs*	
orchid	*flowers*	
orchis	*flowers*	
ordain	*relig*	
ordeal	*govt*	
Oriana	*names*	
Orient	*geog*	
origan	*plants*	
oriole	*birds*	
orison	*relig*	
Ormuzd	*myth*	
oroide	*mineral*	
orphan	*family*	
orpine	*plants*	
Orsino	*Shakesp*	
Orwell	*writers*	
Osbert	*names*	
oscine	*birds*	
Osiris	*myth*	
osmium	*chem*	
osmium	*mineral*	

osprey	*birds*
Ossian	*myth*
osteal	*medic*
ostler	*jobs*
ostrea	*fish*
Oswald	*Shakesp*
Oswald	*names*
Otello	*lit*
Otello	*titles*
ottava	*music*
Ottawa	*cities*
Ottawa	*rivers*
outbid	*trade*
outcry	*trade*
outfit	*clothes*
outfit	*war*
outing	*travel*
outlaw	*jobs*
outlaw	*law*
outlay	*trade*
outlet	*geog*
outlet	*machine*
outlet	*trade*
output	*trade*
outset	*travel*
ovisac	*biol*
oxalis	*plants*
oxbird	*birds*
oxcart	*travel*
Oxford	*Shakesp*
Oxford	*cities*
oxgang	*measure*
oxgate	*measure*
oxland	*measure*
oxtail	*drink*
oxtail	*food*
oxygen	*chem*
oyster	*fish*
packer	*jobs*
packet	*trade*
packet	*travel*
paddle	*sport*
paddle	*travel*
paella	*food*
pagoda	*archit*

pagoda	*relig*
palace	*archit*
palace	*relig*
palais	*archit*
palama	*birds*
palate	*medic*
paling	*archit*
pallah	*animals*
Pallas	*myth*
pallor	*medic*
palolo	*insects*
Pamela	*names*
Pamina	*lit*
Pamirs	*mounts*
pampas	*geog*
pampas	*plants*
panada	*food*
panama	*clothes*
Pandar	*Shakesp*
pandit	*educ*
Panini	*artists*
panisc	*myth*
panisk	*myth*
pantry	*house*
panzer	*war*
papacy	*govt*
papacy	*relig*
papaya	*fruit*
papaya	*trees*
pappus	*plants*
papule	*medic*
parade	*war*
parage	*govt*
Parana	*rivers*
Parcae	*myth*
pardon	*law*
parent	*family*
parget	*archit*
parget	*art*
pariah	*animals*
pariah	*people*
parish	*geog*
parish	*relig*
parity	*trade*
Parker	*writers*

parkin	*food*	peanut	*fruit*	period	*music*
parole	*law*	peapod	*veg*	period	*sport*
parole	*war*	pearls	*jewels*	period	*time*
parrot	*birds*	pebble	*geog*	Pernod	*drink*
parsec	*measure*	pectin	*chem*	person	*lit*
parson	*jobs*	Pedant	*Shakesp*	person	*theatre*
parson	*relig*	pedant	*educ*	peruke	*clothes*
partan	*fish*	pedant	*people*	peruse	*educ*
parure	*clothes*	peddle	*trade*	peseta	*money*
parvis	*archit*	pedlar	*jobs*	Petain	*war*
Pascal	*writers*	pedlar	*trade*	petard	*war*
passer	*birds*	peeler	*law*	petrel	*birds*
pastel	*art*	pecwee	*birds*	petrol	*chem*
pastel	*colour*	peewit	*birds*	petrol	*travel*
pastor	*animals*	Peking	*cities*	Petrus	*names*
pastor	*jobs*	Peleus	*myth*	Petula	*names*
pastor	*relig*	Pelham	*leaders*	pewter	*mineral*
pastry	*food*	Pelias	*myth*	pharos	*archit*
patent	*clothes*	pellet	*herald*	pharos	*machine*
patent	*herald*	pellet	*war*	pharos	*travel*
pathos	*lit*	pelmet	*house*	phenol	*chem*
patina	*house*	Pelops	*myth*	Philip	*Shakesp*
Patmos	*Bible*	pelota	*sport*	Philip	*names*
patois	*lit*	pelvis	*medic*	phlegm	*medic*
patrol	*govt*	Penang	*cities*	phobia	*medic*
patrol	*war*	pencil	*art*	Phocis	*myth*
patron	*govt*	pencil	*educ*	phoebe	*birds*
patron	*jobs*	pencil	*lit*	Phoebe	*myth*
patron	*theatre*	penman	*jobs*	Phoebe	*names*
patron	*trade*	penman	*lit*	pholas	*fish*
patter	*theatre*	penned	*lit*	photon	*measure*
Patton	*war*	pennon	*herald*	phrase	*lit*
pauper	*trade*	penpal	*jobs*	phrase	*music*
pavane	*music*	penpal	*lit*	phylum	*animals*
pavise	*war*	pentad	*maths*	phylum	*biol*
pavone	*birds*	peplos	*clothes*	phylum	*plants*
pawpaw	*fruit*	peplum	*clothes*	physic	*medic*
payday	*trade*	pepper	*food*	piazza	*archit*
payfor	*trade*	pepper	*veg*	picket	*archit*
paying	*trade*	pepper	*war*	picket	*jobs*
payoff	*trade*	pepsin	*chem*	picket	*trade*
payola	*trade*	peptic	*medic*	picket	*war*
payout	*trade*	period	*educ*	pickle	*food*
peahen	*birds*	period	*geog*	pickup	*machine*
peanut	*food*	period	*lit*	pickup	*travel*

picnic *food*	piston *travel*	poison *chem*
Pictor *astron*	pitman *jobs*	poison *medic*
pieman *jobs*	pitman *theatre*	polder *geog*
Pierce *USpres*	placer *geog*	police *law*
pierce *war*	Placia *myth*	policy *govt*
pigeon *birds*	plague *medic*	policy *trade*
piglet *agric*	plague *relig*	polish *house*
piglet *animals*	plaice *fish*	polity *govt*
Piglet *lit*	plains *geog*	pollan *fish*
pigrat *animals*	planet *astron*	pollen *flowers*
pigsty *agric*	plaque *art*	pollen *fruit*
pigsty *animals*	plaque *house*	Pollux *astron*
pilaff *food*	plasma *biol*	Pollux *myth*
Pilate *Bible*	plasma *geog*	pomade *clothes*
pileup *travel*	plasma *jewels*	pomato *fruit*
pillar *archit*	plasma *medic*	pomelo *fruit*
pillow *house*	platan *trees*	pommel *sport*
pimple *medic*	platen *machine*	Pommie *jobs*
Pindar *writers*	plater *jobs*	Pompey *Shakesp*
Pindus *mounts*	player *jobs*	Pompey *war*
Pinero *writers*	player *music*	pompom *clothes*
pinery *trees*	player *sport*	pompom *war*
pinion *machine*	player *theatre*	poncho *clothes*
Pinkie *lit*	pledge *govt*	pongee *clothes*
Pinter *writers*	pledge *trade*	Pontus *myth*
pintle *machine*	plenum *geog*	poodle *animals*
pipeup *music*	pleura *medic*	poorly *medic*
pippin *fruit*	plexus *medic*	poplart *art*
piquet *sport*	pliers *tools*	popgun *sport*
piracy *law*	plinth *archit*	poplar *trees*
pirana *fish*	plough *agric*	poplin *clothes*
pirate *jobs*	plough *tools*	porker *agric*
pirate *law*	plover *birds*	porker *animals*
pirate *trade*	plunge *sport*	portal *archit*
Pisano *artists*	plunge *trade*	porter *drink*
pisces *fish*	Plutus *trade*	porter *jobs*
Pisces *myth*	pocket *clothes*	porter *travel*
Pisces *zodiac*	pocket *sport*	Portia *Shakesp*
pistil *flowers*	pocket *trade*	posada *archit*
Pistol *Shakesp*	podium *archit*	posset *drink*
pistol *machine*	podium *theatre*	possum *animals*
pistol *war*	poetry *lit*	poster *art*
piston *machine*	Pogner *lit*	postil *lit*
piston *music*	pogrom *govt*	postil *relig*
Piston *music*	pogrom *war*	potage *drink*

potash	*chem*	
potato	*agric*	
potato	*veg*	
potent	*herald*	
Pothos	*myth*	
potion	*medic*	
potted	*lit*	
potter	*art*	
potter	*jobs*	
pouffe	*house*	
pouter	*birds*	
powder	*clothes*	
powder	*war*	
pow,pow	*war*	
pow,wow	*govt*	
Poznan	*cities*	
Prague	*cities*	
prater	*jobs*	
praxis	*lit*	
prayer	*relig*	
preach	*educ*	
preach	*relig*	
precis	*lit*	
prefab	*archit*	
prefix	*lit*	
presto	*music*	
presto	*time*	
prewar	*time*	
priest	*jobs*	
priest	*relig*	
primer	*art*	
primer	*educ*	
primer	*lit*	
primus	*relig*	
prince	*govt*	
priory	*relig*	
prison	*law*	
privet	*trees*	
profit	*trade*	
prolix	*lit*	
prompt	*theatre*	
prompt	*time*	
pronto	*time*	
propel	*travel*	
pro,tem	*time*	
proton	*measure*	
proton	*physics*	
Proust	*writers*	
prunus	*trees*	
Psyche	*myth*	
ptisan	*medic*	
public	*trade*	
puddle	*geog*	
Puebla	*cities*	
puffer	*fish*	
puffin	*birds*	
pug,dog	*animals*	
puisne	*govt*	
pullet	*birds*	
pulley	*house*	
pulley	*machine*	
pulpit	*relig*	
pumice	*mineral*	
puncta	*medic*	
pundit	*educ*	
pundit	*lit*	
pundit	*people*	
punica	*fruit*	
punter	*jobs*	
puppet	*govt*	
puppet	*people*	
puppet	*sport*	
puppet	*theatre*	
purist	*lit*	
purist	*people*	
purlin	*archit*	
purple	*colour*	
purser	*jobs*	
pursue	*travel*	
purvey	*trade*	
putter	*sport*	
puzzle	*sport*	
pye,dog	*animals*	
pyemia	*medic*	
pyrite	*mineral*	
Pythia	*myth*	
python	*insects*	
Python	*myth*	
QARANC	*abbrev*	
quagga	*animals*	
quaggy	*geog*	
quahog	*fish*	
Quaker	*relig*	
quango	*abbrev*	
quarry	*mineral*	
quarry	*sport*	
quarte	*sport*	
quarto	*lit*	
quartz	*mineral*	
quasar	*astron*	
quasar	*physics*	
quaver	*music*	
queach	*trees*	
queasy	*medic*	
Quebec	*cities*	
Quemoy	*islands*	
quiche	*food*	
Quince	*Shakesp*	
quince	*fruit*	
quinsy	*medic*	
quinze	*sport*	
quiver	*war*	
quoits	*sport*	
quorum	*govt*	
quotes	*lit*	
rabbit	*animals*	
Rabbit	*lit*	
rabbit	*people*	
rabbit	*sport*	
rabies	*medic*	
raceme	*flowers*	
Rachel	*Bible*	
Rachel	*names*	
rachis	*medic*	
Racine	*writers*	
racing	*sport*	
racket	*music*	
racket	*sport*	
racket	*trade*	
racoon	*animals*	
radial	*medic*	
radial	*travel*	
radian	*maths*	
radian	*measure*	
radish	*veg*	

radium	*chem*	ratlin	*travel*	reefer	*clothes*
radium	*mineral*	rattan	*trees*	reefer	*travel*
radius	*maths*	rattle	*music*	reflex	*medic*
radome	*physics*	rave_up	*sport*	reflux	*chem*
rafale	*war*	ravine	*geog*	reform	*govt*
raffia	*plants*	ray_gun	*war*	refuge	*archit*
raffle	*sport*	razzia	*war*	refund	*trade*
raffle	*trade*	reader	*educ*	regent	*govt*
rafter	*archit*	reader	*jobs*	reggae	*music*
raglan	*clothes*	reader	*lit*	regime	*govt*
Raglan	*war*	Reagan	*USpres*	Regina	*names*
ragman	*jobs*	realty	*trade*	region	*geog*
ragout	*food*	reaper	*agric*	regius	*educ*
raguly	*herald*	reaper	*jobs*	regius	*jobs*
raisin	*fruit*	rebate	*trade*	reglet	*archit*
Rajput	*war*	rebato	*clothes*	reglet	*machine*
rallus	*birds*	rebeck	*music*	regula	*archit*
ramble	*sport*	rebuff	*war*	reject	*trade*
ramble	*travel*	recant	*lit*	relate	*lit*
Rameau	*music*	recent	*time*	relief	*archit*
ramjet	*machine*	recess	*archit*	relief	*art*
ramjet	*travel*	recess	*govt*	relief	*medic*
ramrod	*tools*	recipe	*food*	relief	*theatre*
ramrod	*war*	recite	*educ*	relish	*food*
ramson	*plants*	record	*govt*	remand	*law*
randem	*travel*	record	*lit*	remark	*lit*
ranger	*animals*	record	*music*	remedy	*medic*
ranger	*jobs*	record	*sport*	remedy	*trade*
ransom	*govt*	recoup	*trade*	remise	*sport*
ranula	*medic*	rector	*educ*	remora	*fish*
rapids	*geog*	rector	*jobs*	remove	*educ*
rapids	*sport*	rector	*relig*	remove	*house*
rapier	*sport*	red_ant	*insects*	render	*trade*
rapier	*war*	red_bud	*trees*	rennet	*fruit*
rapine	*govt*	redcap	*birds*	Renoir	*artists*
rappel	*war*	redeem	*trade*	rental	*trade*
rarely	*time*	redeye	*fish*	repast	*food*
rascal	*people*	redfin	*fish*	repeat	*music*
rasher	*food*	red_fir	*trees*	repeat	*theatre*
rating	*govt*	red_fox	*animals*	replay	*sport*
rating	*jobs*	Red_Sea	*seas*	report	*educ*
rating	*trade*	red_sky	*weather*	report	*law*
rating	*travel*	redtop	*plants*	report	*lit*
ration	*food*	reduit	*war*	report	*war*
ration	*trade*	reebok	*animals*	resale	*trade*

reseda	*colour*	rigger	*jobs*	Rommel	*war*
resell	*trade*	rigger	*travel*	Romney	*artists*
resign	*trade*	rigout	*clothes*	Ronald	*names*
result	*sport*	rillet	*geog*	rondel	*lit*
resume	*lit*	ringer	*jobs*	rookie	*jobs*
retail	*trade*	ring|up	*theatre*	rookie	*war*
re|take	*theatre*	ring|up	*travel*	roquet	*sport*
retina	*medic*	rioter	*jobs*	rosary	*relig*
retire	*trade*	rioter	*war*	rosery	*flowers*
retort	*chem*	rip|off	*law*	Rosina	*lit*
return	*trade*	ripple	*geog*	rotter	*people*
return	*travel*	rip|saw	*tools*	rouble	*money*
Reuben	*Bible*	ritual	*relig*	rounce	*machine*
Reuben	*names*	Rivers	*Shakesp*	rounds	*music*
Reuter	*lit*	roamer	*people*	Rowena	*names*
revers	*clothes*	robalo	*fish*	rowing	*sport*
review	*lit*	robber	*jobs*	Roxana	*names*
review	*theatre*	robber	*law*	rozzer	*law*
revise	*lit*	Robert	*names*	rubato	*music*
revolt	*war*	Robina	*names*	rubber	*educ*
reward	*govt*	Rob|Roy	*titles*	rubber	*sport*
reward	*trade*	robust	*medic*	rubble	*archit*
rhesus	*animals*	rochet	*clothes*	rubble	*geog*
rhesus	*medic*	rochet	*relig*	Rubbra	*music*
Rhodes	*islands*	rocker	*house*	Rubens	*artists*
Rhodus	*myth*	rocket	*fruit*	rubric	*law*
rhumba	*sport*	rocket	*machine*	rubric	*relig*
rhymer	*jobs*	rocket	*travel*	rudder	*machine*
rhymer	*lit*	rocket	*war*	rudder	*travel*
rhymic	*lit*	rococo	*archit*	ruelle	*house*
rhythm	*music*	rococo	*art*	ruffle	*clothes*
rhyton	*house*	rodent	*animals*	rugger	*sport*
rialto	*trade*	Rodney	*names*	ruined	*trade*
Ribble	*rivers*	Rodney	*war*	ruling	*law*
ribbon	*clothes*	Rokeby	*titles*	rummer	*drink*
ribose	*chem*	Roland	*names*	Rumour	*Shakesp*
riches	*trade*	roller	*agric*	runlet	*geog*
rictus	*medic*	roller	*birds*	runnel	*geog*
riddle	*machine*	roller	*clothes*	runner	*flowers*
riddle	*sport*	roller	*marine*	runner	*jobs*
riddle	*tools*	roller	*medic*	runner	*machine*
riding	*geog*	roller	*tools*	runner	*sport*
riding	*sport*	roll|in	*sport*	runner	*travel*
Rienzi	*titles*	Romans	*Bible*	runner	*veg*
rigged	*travel*	Romany	*people*	run|off	*lit*

runway	*travel*	saloon	*archit*
Rupert	*names*	saloon	*travel*
Rupert	*war*	saluki	*animals*
rushes	*film/TV*	salute	*war*
Ruskin	*artists*	salver	*house*
Ruskin	*writers*	salvia	*flowers*
russet	*colour*	sambar	*animals*
russet	*fruit*	Sambre	*rivers*
rustic	*geog*	samiel	*weather*
rustic	*people*	samite	*clothes*
rustre	*herald*	sampan	*travel*
rutile	*mineral*	Samson	*Bible*
SABENA	*abbrev*	Samuel	*Bible*
Sabina	*names*	Samuel	*names*
Sabine	*rivers*	sandal	*clothes*
sachem	*govt*	Sandra	*names*
sacque	*clothes*	sangar	*war*
sacred	*relig*	Santos	*cities*
sacrum	*medic*	sapium	*plants*
saddle	*animals*	sapota	*trees*
saddle	*food*	sappan	*trees*
saddle	*geog*	sapper	*jobs*
saddle	*machine*	sapper	*war*
sadist	*people*	Sappho	*writers*
safari	*sport*	sarong	*clothes*
sailor	*jobs*	sarsen	*geog*
sailor	*travel*	sartor	*jobs*
Saipan	*islands*	Sartre	*writers*
salade	*herald*	sateen	*clothes*
salade	*war*	satire	*lit*
Salado	*rivers*	satire	*theatre*
salami	*food*	satrap	*govt*
salary	*trade*	satrap	*relig*
salina	*geog*	Saturn	*astron*
saline	*chem*	Saturn	*myth*
saliva	*medic*	saucer	*house*
sallet	*herald*	savage	*jobs*
sallet	*war*	savant	*educ*
sallow	*trees*	savant	*jobs*
salmon	*fish*	savate	*sport*
salmon	*food*	save up	*trade*
Salome	*Bible*	saving	*trade*
Salome	*lit*	savory	*fruit*
Salome	*names*	savory	*veg*
Salome	*titles*	sawfly	*insects*

sawyer	*jobs*
Sayers	*writers*
saying	*lit*
Scales	*Shakesp*
scales	*house*
scales	*machine*
scarab	*clothes*
scarab	*insects*
Scarus	*Shakesp*
scenic	*theatre*
scheme	*lit*
schism	*relig*
schist	*geog*
school	*animals*
school	*archit*
school	*art*
school	*educ*
Schutz	*music*
scilla	*flowers*
Sciron	*myth*
sconce	*archit*
sconce	*govt*
sconce	*house*
sconce	*war*
scorer	*jobs*
scorer	*music*
scorer	*sport*
scoria	*mineral*
Scotch	*drink*
scoter	*birds*
scotia	*archit*
scouse	*jobs*
scrape	*medic*
scrawl	*lit*
screed	*lit*
screen	*archit*
screen	*art*
screen	*film/TV*
screen	*house*
scribe	*jobs*
scribe	*lit*
Scribe	*relig*
script	*film/TV*
script	*lit*
script	*theatre*

scrive	*lit*	secant	*maths*	serdab	*house*
scroll	*archit*	second	*jobs*	serein	*weather*
scroll	*educ*	second	*measure*	Serena	*names*
scroll	*lit*	second	*music*	serial	*film/TV*
Scroop	*Shakesp*	second	*sport*	serial	*lit*
scudos	*money*	second	*time*	series	*film/TV*
sculls	*sport*	sector	*geog*	series	*lit*
sculls	*travel*	sector	*maths*	series	*maths*
sculpt	*art*	sector	*measure*	seriph	*lit*
scurvy	*medic*	sedile	*relig*	sermon	*educ*
scutum	*herald*	seeder	*machine*	sermon	*lit*
scutum	*war*	seeing	*medic*	sermon	*relig*
Scylla	*myth*	seesaw	*sport*	serous	*medic*
scythe	*tools*	Sekume	*myth*	serran	*fish*
sea air	*marine*	seldom	*time*	serval	*animals*
sea ape	*animals*	Selene	*astron*	server	*jobs*
sea bat	*fish*	Selene	*myth*	sesame	*plants*
sea bed	*marine*	Selina	*names*	sestet	*lit*
sea cat	*fish*	seller	*jobs*	sestet	*music*
sea cob	*birds*	sell up	*trade*	set gun	*war*
sea cow	*animals*	Selwyn	*names*	set out	*travel*
sea dog	*animals*	Semele	*myth*	settee	*house*
sea dog	*jobs*	Semele	*titles*	setter	*animals*
sea ear	*fish*	Semite	*relig*	settle	*house*
sea eel	*fish*	semmit	*clothes*	settle	*trade*
sea fog	*marine*	sempre	*music*	Seurat	*artists*
sea fox	*fish*	senary	*maths*	Severn	*rivers*
sea god	*myth*	senate	*govt*	sexist	*people*
sea hog	*fish*	sender	*travel*	sextet	*lit*
sealer	*jobs*	Seneca	*writers*	sextet	*music*
seaman	*jobs*	senior	*educ*	sexton	*jobs*
seaman	*travel*	senior	*family*	sexton	*relig*
seamat	*plants*	senior	*jobs*	Seyton	*Shakesp*
sea mew	*birds*	senses	*medic*	Shadow	*Shakesp*
seance	*sport*	sensor	*physics*	shadow	*art*
sea owl	*birds*	sentry	*jobs*	shadow	*geog*
sea pen	*fish*	sentry	*war*	shadow	*jobs*
sea pig	*fish*	sepsis	*medic*	shaman	*relig*
search	*law*	septet	*music*	shandy	*drink*
Searle	*music*	septic	*medic*	shanty	*archit*
season	*geog*	sequel	*lit*	shanty	*music*
season	*theatre*	sequin	*jewels*	shares	*trade*
season	*time*	sequin	*money*	Sharon	*names*
seaway	*marine*	serape	*clothes*	shaver	*tools*
seaway	*travel*	seraph	*myth*	shears	*tools*

sheath	*clothes*	
sheave	*agric*	
Sheena	*names*	
sheets	*travel*	
sheila	*jobs*	
Sheila	*names*	
shekel	*measure*	
shekel	*money*	
shelty	*animals*	
sherry	*drink*	
shield	*herald*	
shield	*war*	
shimmy	*sport*	
shiner	*fish*	
shinny	*sport*	
shinty	*sport*	
Shiraz	*cities*	
shoddy	*clothes*	
shofar	*music*	
shogun	*govt*	
shoran	*travel*	
shorts	*clothes*	
shorts	*sport*	
shorts	*trade*	
shovel	*house*	
shovel	*tools*	
shower	*house*	
shower	*jobs*	
shrike	*birds*	
shrimp	*fish*	
shrine	*relig*	
shrink	*jobs*	
shroud	*clothes*	
shroud	*relig*	
shroud	*travel*	
Sicily	*islands*	
sicken	*medic*	
sickle	*tools*	
sickly	*medic*	
siding	*travel*	
Sidney	*names*	
Sidney	*writers*	
sienna	*colour*	
sierra	*geog*	
signal	*travel*	

signet	*herald*
silage	*agric*
silene	*flowers*
silica	*chem*
silica	*mineral*
Silius	*Shakesp*
silver	*colour*
silver	*jewels*
silver	*mineral*
silver	*trade*
Silvia	*Shakesp*
Silvia	*names*
Simeon	*Bible*
simian	*animals*
simile	*lit*
Simios	*myth*
simony	*law*
simony	*trade*
simoom	*weather*
Simple	*Shakesp*
simple	*medic*
simple	*plants*
simurg	*birds*
Sinbad	*myth*
singer	*jobs*
singer	*music*
singer	*theatre*
sinner	*people*
sinner	*relig*
sinter	*chem*
sinter	*geog*
siphon	*machine*
siphon	*physics*
sircar	*govt*
sirdar	*govt*
Sirius	*astron*
Sirius	*myth*
Sisera	*Bible*
siskin	*birds*
Sisley	*artists*
sister	*family*
sister	*jobs*
sister	*medic*
sister	*relig*
sit com	*film/TV*

Siward	*Shakesp*
skater	*jobs*
skater	*sport*
skates	*travel*
skerry	*geog*
sketch	*art*
sketch	*lit*
sketch	*theatre*
skewer	*house*
ski cap	*clothes*
skiing	*sport*
skivvy	*jobs*
skygod	*myth*
skyman	*jobs*
Skyros	*islands*
skyway	*travel*
slacks	*clothes*
slalom	*sport*
slater	*jobs*
slavey	*jobs*
slayer	*jobs*
sledge	*sport*
sledge	*travel*
sleeve	*clothes*
sleeve	*herald*
sleeve	*machine*
sleigh	*travel*
sleuth	*animals*
sleuth	*jobs*
slip on	*clothes*
slogan	*war*
slough	*geog*
slough	*insects*
slough	*medic*
sluice	*archit*
sluice	*machine*
slurry	*geog*
smalls	*educ*
smilax	*flowers*
smithy	*machine*
smithy	*trade*
smoker	*jobs*
smoker	*travel*
snatch	*music*
sneeze	*medic*

sniper	jobs	sphere	geog	spurry	plants
sniper	war	sphere	maths	spying	war
sobole	plants	sphinx	animals	squall	weather
socage	govt	sphinx	insects	squama	fish
soccer	sport	Sphynx	myth	square	archit
socket	machine	spider	insects	square	machine
sodium	chem	spigot	tools	square	maths
soffit	archit	spikes	sport	square	measure
solano	geog	spinal	medic	square	people
solder	physics	spinel	jewels	squash	drink
solidi	money	spinel	mineral	squash	fruit
Somnus	myth	spinet	music	squash	sport
sonata	music	spiral	archit	squill	plants
sonnet	lit	spiral	sport	squint	medic
sooner	time	spiral	trade	squire	govt
Sophia	names	spiral	travel	squire	jobs
Sophie	lit	spirit	chem	Squire	writers
Sophie	names	spirit	drink	stable	agric
sorrel	animals	spirit	myth	stable	animals
sorrel	plants	splash	geog	stable	archit
sortie	travel	spleen	medic	stable	chem
sortie	war	splice	travel	stable	trade
souari	trees	splint	medic	Staffa	islands
source	geog	sponge	fish	Staffs	abbrev
soutar	jobs	sponge	food	stager	theatre
souter	jobs	sponge	house	staker	trade
soviet	govt	sponge	trade	stakes	sport
sowbug	insects	sports	sport	Stalin	leaders
sowing	agric	spotty	medic	Stalky	lit
sowter	jobs	spouse	family	stalls	relig
spades	sport	sprain	medic	stalls	theatre
spadix	flowers	spread	food	stamen	flowers
sparks	jobs	spread	herald	stance	sport
sparks	travel	spread	lit	stanza	lit
Sparta	myth	spread	trade	stanza	music
sparth	war	spring	archit	stanza	theatre
spathe	flowers	spring	geog	stapes	medic
spatum	medic	spring	machine	staple	biol
specie	money	spring	time	starch	chem
specie	trade	spring	travel	starch	house
speech	govt	sprint	sport	starry	astron
speech	law	sprite	myth	stasis	medic
speech	theatre	sprout	veg	stater	money
spence	archit	spruce	trees	stator	machine
Spence	artists	spurge	plants	Stator	myth

statue	*art*	
status	*govt*	
status	*jobs*	
Steele	*writers*	
Stella	*names*	
steppe	*geog*	
Sterne	*writers*	
Steven	*names*	
Stheno	*myth*	
sticks	*sport*	
stigma	*flowers*	
stigma	*medic*	
stilts	*sport*	
stitch	*medic*	
stiver	*money*	
St|John	*rivers*	
stocks	*law*	
stocks	*trade*	
stocks	*travel*	
stoker	*jobs*	
stoker	*travel*	
stolon	*plants*	
stooge	*people*	
stooge	*theatre*	
storax	*plants*	
storey	*archit*	
stormy	*weather*	
St|Paul	*cities*	
strafe	*war*	
strain	*lit*	
strain	*music*	
strait	*marine*	
strake	*travel*	
strand	*marine*	
strata	*geog*	
strath	*geog*	
Strato	*Shakesp*	
stream	*geog*	
street	*archit*	
street	*travel*	
stress	*lit*	
stress	*physics*	
strial	*geog*	
stride	*travel*	
strike	*sport*	
strike	*trade*	
strike	*war*	
Strine	*lit*	
string	*animals*	
string	*house*	
string	*music*	
strium	*medic*	
stroke	*machine*	
stroke	*medic*	
stroke	*sport*	
stroll	*sport*	
stroll	*travel*	
struma	*medic*	
Struma	*rivers*	
Strymo	*myth*	
Stuart	*names*	
Stubbs	*artists*	
stucco	*archit*	
studio	*archit*	
studio	*art*	
studio	*film/TV*	
stuffy	*weather*	
stumps	*sport*	
stupor	*medic*	
stylet	*medic*	
stylus	*lit*	
stylus	*tools*	
stymie	*sport*	
subito	*music*	
suburb	*archit*	
suburb	*geog*	
subway	*travel*	
sucker	*fish*	
sucker	*flowers*	
sudden	*time*	
suffer	*medic*	
suffix	*lit*	
suitor	*family*	
suitor	*jobs*	
suitor	*law*	
sultan	*govt*	
sultan	*law*	
sultry	*weather*	
sumach	*trees*	
summer	*animals*	
summer	*archit*	
summer	*geog*	
summer	*time*	
summit	*geog*	
summit	*govt*	
sundae	*food*	
Sunday	*relig*	
Sunday	*time*	
sundew	*plants*	
sundog	*geog*	
sundry	*trade*	
sungod	*myth*	
sunhat	*clothes*	
sunset	*time*	
supper	*food*	
supply	*trade*	
Surrey	*Shakesp*	
surrey	*travel*	
surtax	*trade*	
Sutlej	*rivers*	
sutler	*jobs*	
suttee	*relig*	
suture	*medic*	
swampy	*geog*	
sweeps	*sport*	
sweets	*food*	
swerve	*travel*	
swings	*trade*	
switch	*clothes*	
switch	*house*	
switch	*machine*	
swivel	*sport*	
swivel	*war*	
Sydney	*cities*	
Sydney	*names*	
sylvan	*trees*	
Sylvia	*names*	
Sylvia	*titles*	
symbol	*art*	
symbol	*chem*	
symbol	*herald*	
syndic	*educ*	
syndic	*govt*	
syntax	*lit*	
syphon	*physics*	

syrinx	*music*	tanker	*travel*	temple	*medic*
syrinx	*myth*	tanner	*jobs*	temple	*relig*
system	*biol*	Tannoy	*machine*	tenail	*war*
syzygy	*astron*	Tannoy	*travel*	tenant	*jobs*
tabard	*clothes*	tappet	*machine*	tenant	*law*
tabard	*herald*	target	*sport*	tender	*medic*
tables	*maths*	target	*war*	tender	*trade*
tablet	*archit*	tariff	*trade*	tender	*travel*
tablet	*lit*	tarots	*sport*	tendon	*medic*
tablet	*medic*	tarpan	*animals*	tenner	*money*
tablet	*relig*	tarpon	*fish*	tennis	*sport*
tabret	*music*	tarsus	*medic*	tenor|C	*music*
Tabriz	*cities*	tartan	*clothes*	tenrec	*animals*
tackle	*machine*	tartan	*travel*	tenths	*trade*
tackle	*sport*	Tartar	*jobs*	tenure	*law*
tackle	*travel*	tassle	*clothes*	tenuto	*music*
Tadema	*artists*	taster	*jobs*	tercet	*lit*
taenia	*archit*	tatter	*jobs*	tercet	*music*
Tagore	*writers*	tattoo	*music*	teredo	*insects*
Tahiti	*islands*	taught	*educ*	terzet	*music*
tailor	*jobs*	Taurus	*Shakesp*	tester	*money*
Taipei	*cities*	taurus	*animals*	teston	*money*
Taiwan	*islands*	Taurus	*myth*	Tethys	*astron*
Talbot	*Shakesp*	Taurus	*zodiac*	Tethys	*myth*
talcum	*clothes*	tautog	*fish*	tetrad	*maths*
talent	*art*	tavern	*archit*	tetter	*medic*
talent	*jobs*	taxman	*trade*	tettix	*clothes*
talent	*relig*	Taylor	*USpres*	Teucer	*myth*
talent	*theatre*	tea,bag	*drink*	Teuton	*jobs*
Talinn	*cities*	teacup	*drink*	Thaisa	*Shakesp*
talion	*war*	teapot	*house*	thaler	*money*
talkie	*film/TV*	teapoy	*house*	Thalia	*muses*
Tallis	*music*	teasel	*plants*	Thalia	*myth*
Talmud	*relig*	teaser	*educ*	Thalia	*theatre*
tamale	*food*	teaser	*theatre*	Thallo	*myth*
tamara	*food*	teaset	*house*	Thames	*rivers*
Tamino	*lit*	tea,urn	*house*	Thasos	*islands*
Tammuz	*myth*	tedder	*tools*	thatch	*archit*
Tamora	*Shakesp*	teetee	*animals*	Thebus	*myth*
tampon	*medic*	teledu	*animals*	Thelma	*names*
tampon	*music*	teller	*jobs*	Themis	*myth*
Tamsin	*names*	teller	*trade*	theory	*biol*
tam,tam	*music*	Tellus	*myth*	theory	*chem*
tandem	*travel*	temper	*music*	theory	*educ*
tangle	*plants*	temple	*archit*	theory	*lit*

theory	*physics*	tiller	*jobs*	tomato	*veg*
thesis	*lit*	tiller	*travel*	tomcat	*animals*
Thetis	*myth*	timbal	*music*	tomtom	*music*
Thisbe	*lit*	timber	*archit*	tomtom	*war*
tholos	*archit*	timber	*travel*	Tonans	*myth*
tholus	*archit*	timber	*trees*	tongue	*clothes*
Thomas	*Bible*	timbre	*music*	tongue	*food*
Thomas	*Shakesp*	timely	*time*	tongue	*lit*
Thomas	*names*	timing	*theatre*	tongue	*medic*
Thomas	*writers*	tincan	*travel*	tooter	*music*
thorax	*medic*	tingle	*medic*	tophat	*clothes*
thoron	*chem*	tinhat	*clothes*	Tophet	*myth*
thrall	*myth*	tinker	*jobs*	topper	*clothes*
thread	*clothes*	tinner	*jobs*	topten	*music*
threes	*sport*	tipcat	*sport*	torero	*sport*
thrift	*plants*	tippet	*clothes*	Tories	*govt*
thrips	*insects*	tippet	*relig*	torque	*clothes*
throat	*medic*	tipple	*drink*	torque	*machine*
throes	*medic*	tiptoe	*sport*	torque	*physics*
throne	*govt*	tipula	*insects*	torque	*travel*
thrush	*birds*	tisane	*medic*	torsel	*archit*
thrush	*medic*	tissue	*biol*	totter	*travel*
thrust	*physics*	tissue	*clothes*	toucan	*birds*
thrust	*sport*	tissue	*medic*	touche	*sport*
thrust	*war*	Titans	*myth*	toupee	*clothes*
Thunor	*myth*	titbit	*food*	towage	*trade*
Thurio	*Shakesp*	Tithon	*myth*	towbar	*travel*
thwart	*sport*	Titian	*artists*	towhee	*birds*
thymus	*medic*	titian	*colour*	toxoid	*chem*
ticker	*machine*	Tityus	*myth*	toybox	*house*
ticker	*medic*	tivoli	*sport*	toydog	*animals*
ticker	*trade*	toarms	*war*	toygun	*sport*
ticker	*travel*	Tobago	*islands*	tracer	*animals*
ticket	*govt*	tocsin	*govt*	trader	*jobs*
ticket	*theatre*	tocsin	*war*	trader	*trade*
ticket	*trade*	todate	*time*	trades	*weather*
ticket	*travel*	toddle	*travel*	tragic	*theatre*
tickle	*sport*	toecap	*clothes*	tragus	*medic*
tiepin	*clothes*	toffee	*food*	Tranio	*Shakesp*
tierce	*relig*	toggle	*travel*	transf	*abbrev*
tiewig	*law*	toiler	*jobs*	travel	*travel*
tiffin	*food*	toilet	*archit*	treaty	*govt*
tights	*clothes*	Toledo	*cities*	treaty	*trade*
tights	*theatre*	Toledo	*war*	treble	*music*
Tigris	*rivers*	tomato	*fruit*	tremor	*geog*

tremor	*medic*	trunks	*clothes*	Tybalt	*Shakesp*
trench	*archit*	tsetse	*insects*	Tyburn	*govt*
trench	*geog*	Tshirt	*clothes*	tycoon	*jobs*
trench	*war*	TTrace	*sport*	tycoon	*trade*
trepan	*machine*	Tucana	*astron*	Tydeus	*myth*
trepan	*medic*	tucker	*clothes*	tymbal	*music*
Trevor	*names*	tucker	*food*	tympan	*machine*
Tricia	*names*	tucket	*music*	tympan	*music*
tricot	*clothes*	tuckin	*food*	Typhon	*myth*
trifle	*food*	tulwar	*war*	typist	*jobs*
trigon	*maths*	tumour	*medic*	tyrant	*govt*
trilby	*clothes*	tundra	*geog*	tyrant	*jobs*
Trilby	*titles*	tuneup	*music*	Ulrica	*lit*
triode	*machine*	tuning	*music*	ulster	*clothes*
tripod	*art*	tunnel	*archit*	Ulster	*herald*
tripod	*chem*	tunnel	*geog*	umbles	*food*
tripod	*machine*	tunnel	*insects*	umlaut	*lit*
tripos	*educ*	tunnel	*travel*	umpire	*govt*
Triton	*astron*	turban	*clothes*	umpire	*jobs*
triton	*fish*	turbot	*fish*	umpire	*sport*
Triton	*myth*	turbot	*food*	uncial	*lit*
trivet	*house*	turdus	*birds*	undine	*myth*
trivet	*machine*	tureen	*house*	UNESCO	*abbrev*
Trixie	*names*	turkey	*birds*	ungula	*maths*
trocar	*medic*	turkey	*food*	unholy	*relig*
troche	*medic*	Turner	*artists*	UNICEF	*abbrev*
trogon	*birds*	turner	*jobs*	unisex	*clothes*
troika	*travel*	turnip	*agric*	unison	*music*
tromba	*music*	turnip	*geog*	unload	*trade*
troops	*war*	turnip	*veg*	unmoor	*travel*
trophy	*sport*	Turnus	*lit*	unpaid	*trade*
tropic	*geog*	turret	*archit*	unripe	*fruit*
troppo	*music*	turret	*machine*	unwell	*medic*
trough	*agric*	turret	*travel*	upbeat	*music*
trough	*geog*	turret	*war*	update	*time*
troupe	*theatre*	turtle	*insects*	upland	*geog*
trowel	*tools*	tusker	*animals*	upleft	*theatre*
truant	*educ*	tussah	*clothes*	uppers	*clothes*
truant	*govt*	tusser	*clothes*	uraeus	*herald*
truant	*jobs*	tuxedo	*clothes*	Urania	*muses*
truant	*sport*	TVshow	*film/TV*	Urania	*myth*
trudge	*travel*	twaite	*fish*	Uranus	*astron*
Trudie	*names*	tweeds	*clothes*	Uranus	*myth*
truism	*lit*	twinge	*medic*	urchin	*fish*
Truman	*USpres*	twitch	*plants*	urchin	*jobs*

ureter *medic*	Vernon *Shakesp*	voided *herald*
ursine *animals*	Verona *cities*	volant *travel*
Ursula *Shakesp*	versin *maths*	volary *birds*
Ursula *names*	versus *sport*	volery *machine*
Ushant *islands*	vertex *maths*	volley *sport*
usurer *jobs*	vervet *animals*	volley *war*
usurer *trade*	vesica *medic*	volume *lit*
Utopia *myth*	Vesper *myth*	volume *maths*
Utopia *titles*	vesper *time*	volume *measure*
vacuum *physics*	vessel *house*	volute *archit*
vakass *relig*	vessel *medic*	vomica *medic*
valise *travel*	vessel *travel*	voodoo *myth*
valley *geog*	vestry *relig*	vortex *geog*
vallum *archit*	viande *food*	vortex *physics*
vallum *war*	viands *food*	Vosges *mounts*
valour *war*	victor *jobs*	voting *govt*
valuer *jobs*	Victor *myth*	voyage *travel*
valuta *trade*	Victor *names*	voyeur *medic*
vandal *people*	victor *war*	voyeur *people*
Vandal *war*	vicuna *animals*	Vulcan *astron*
vanman *jobs*	vielle *music*	Vulcan *myth*
VanRyn *artists*	Vienna *cities*	Wabash *rivers*
vapour *chem*	viewer *art*	waders *clothes*
Varese *music*	vigils *relig*	waffle *food*
Varuna *myth*	Viking *jobs*	waggon *travel*
vassal *govt*	Villon *writers*	Wagner *music*
vector *maths*	villus *medic*	waiter *jobs*
vector *medic*	Vilyui *rivers*	Walden *titles*
vellum *educ*	vinery *fruit*	walkon *jobs*
vellum *lit*	violet *colour*	walkon *theatre*
velure *clothes*	violet *flowers*	Waller *writers*
velvet *clothes*	Violet *names*	wallet *clothes*
vendor *jobs*	violin *music*	wallet *trade*
vendor *trade*	virago *people*	Wallis *names*
vendue *trade*	Virgil *writers*	walnut *food*
veneer *house*	viscus *medic*	walnut *trees*
Venice *cities*	Vishnu *myth*	walrus *animals*
verbal *lit*	vision *myth*	Walter *names*
verger *jobs*	vision *relig*	Walton *music*
verger *relig*	vitals *medic*	Walton *writers*
Verges *Shakesp*	vivace *music*	wampum *trade*
Verity *names*	Vivian *names*	wampus *clothes*
vermin *animals*	Vivien *names*	wander *travel*
vernal *geog*	vizier *govt*	wapiti *animals*
vernal *time*	voices *music*	warble *agric*

warble	*birds*	wherry	*travel*	wraith	*myth*
war|cry	*war*	whilst	*time*	wrasse	*fish*
warden	*govt*	whinny	*animals*	wreath	*flowers*
warden	*jobs*	whisky	*drink*	wreath	*herald*
warder	*jobs*	whisky	*travel*	wrench	*medic*
warder	*law*	whites	*clothes*	wrench	*tools*
war|dog	*war*	wicket	*archit*	wretch	*people*
war|god	*myth*	wicket	*sport*	wright	*jobs*
war|god	*war*	wigeon	*birds*	wright	*trade*
Warhol	*artists*	wigwam	*archit*	writer	*jobs*
warm|up	*theatre*	Wilbur	*names*	writer	*lit*
Warner	*names*	Wilbye	*music*	writer	*theatre*
warren	*animals*	Wilcox	*writers*	writhe	*medic*
Warren	*names*	wild|ox	*animals*	wyvern	*animals*
Warsaw	*cities*	willet	*birds*	wyvern	*herald*
washer	*house*	Willie	*names*	wyvern	*myth*
washer	*machine*	Willis	*names*	xylose	*chem*
Watson	*people*	willow	*sport*	xyster	*medic*
wattle	*trees*	willow	*trees*	Yahweh	*myth*
Wavell	*war*	Wilson	*USpres*	yarrow	*flowers*
waxing	*music*	Wilson	*leaders*	yearly	*time*
way|out	*travel*	Wilson	*writers*	ye|gods	*myth*
weaken	*medic*	wimple	*clothes*	Yehudi	*names*
weakly	*medic*	window	*archit*	yellow	*colour*
wealth	*trade*	window	*geog*	yeoman	*govt*
weapon	*war*	window	*house*	yeoman	*jobs*
weasel	*animals*	winger	*sport*	yeoman	*war*
weaver	*birds*	winner	*jobs*	yester	*time*
weaver	*jobs*	winner	*sport*	ynambu	*birds*
Webern	*music*	Winnie	*names*	yoicks	*sport*
weekly	*lit*	winter	*geog*	yorker	*sport*
weekly	*time*	winter	*time*	Yum|Yum	*lit*
weever	*fish*	Winton	*abbrev*	Yvette	*names*
weevil	*agric*	wiring	*house*	Yvonne	*names*
weevil	*insects*	wizard	*jobs*	Zagreb	*cities*
weight	*physics*	wizard	*myth*	zambra	*music*
welder	*jobs*	Wolsey	*Shakesp*	zealot	*people*
welkin	*geog*	Wolsey	*leaders*	zealot	*relig*
Wesker	*writers*	wombat	*animals*	zenith	*geog*
Wesley	*names*	womera	*war*	zephyr	*geog*
wester	*geog*	woofer	*machine*	Zephyr	*myth*
wether	*animals*	woolly	*clothes*	Zethus	*myth*
whaler	*jobs*	worker	*jobs*	zeugma	*lit*
whaler	*travel*	worker	*trade*	zinnia	*flowers*
Wharfe	*rivers*	worthy	*people*	zircon	*jewels*

zircon *mineral*	zombie *people*	zufolo *music*
zither *music*	zoning *archit*	Zurich *cities*
zodiac *astron*	zoster *clothes*	zygoma *medic*
zombie *myth*	Zouave *war*	zymase *biol*

7 LETTERS

Abaddon *Bible*	accuser *law*	acyclic *biol*
Abaddon *myth*	ace|high *sport*	acyclic *chem*
a|bad|egg *people*	acerose *plants*	adamant *jewels*
abalone *fish*	acetate *chem*	adamant *mineral*
abattis *war*	acetone *chem*	adaptor *house*
abaxial *maths*	acetose *chem*	adaptor *physics*
abdomen *medic*	Achalia *myth*	ad|astra *foreign*
abetter *jobs*	acharne *foreign*	addenda *lit*
abiding *time*	Achates *myth*	Addison *writers*
Abidjan *cities*	Acheron *myth*	address *archit*
Abigail *Bible*	acid|dye *art*	address *sport*
abigail *jobs*	acid|dye *chem*	address *travel*
Abigail *names*	acidity *chem*	ad|finem *foreign*
Abilene *Bible*	acidity *medic*	adjourn *govt*
Abraham *Bible*	ack|cmma *time*	adjourn *law*
Abraham *Shakesp*	acolyte *jobs*	adjunct *lit*
Abraham *names*	acolyte *relig*	ad|litem *foreign*
abraxas *jewels*	aconite *flowers*	admiral *govt*
abridge *lit*	aconite *medic*	admiral *jobs*
Absalom *Bible*	Acrilan *clothes*	Adonais *titles*
Absalom *lit*	acrobat *jobs*	adrenal *medic*
abscess *medic*	acrobat *sport*	Adriana *names*
abscond *law*	acrobat *theatre*	Adullam *Bible*
abscond *trade*	acronym *lit*	advance *war*
absinth *drink*	Actaeon *myth*	adviser *govt*
abstain *govt*	act|drop *theatre*	adviser *jobs*
academy *archit*	actinon *physics*	ad|vivum *foreign*
academy *educ*	actress *film/TV*	Aemilia *Shakesp*
acaleph *fish*	actress *jobs*	aeolian *weather*
accidie *sins*	actress *theatre*	aerator *physics*
account *lit*	actuary *jobs*	aerobic *biol*
account *trade*	actuary *trade*	aerobus *travel*
accused *law*	acushla *art*	aerosol *chem*

affaire *foreign*	a|lamode *foreign*	almirah *house*
affiche *foreign*	Alarbus *Shakesp*	almoner *jobs*
Afriana *Shakesp*	Albeniz *music*	almoner *relig*
agacant *foreign*	albumen *biol*	alodium *law*
AgaKhan *govt*	albumen *food*	already *time*
ageless *time*	albumin *biol*	also|ran *people*
ages|ago *time*	Alcaeus *myth*	also|ran *sport*
agitato *music*	alcaide *foreign*	altesse *foreign*
Agrippa *Shakesp*	alcalde *law*	althaea *flowers*
aground *travel*	alchemy *chem*	althorn *music*
Ahriman *myth*	Alcmene *myth*	alumnus *educ*
ailanto *trees*	alcohol *chem*	alumnus *jobs*
aileron *travel*	alcohol *drink*	alyssum *flowers*
ailment *medic*	alcohol *medic*	Amadeus *titles*
air|base *travel*	al|conto *foreign*	amalgam *chem*
airboat *travel*	Alcoran *relig*	amanita *plants*
air|crew *travel*	Alcyone *myth*	amateur *educ*
airdrop *travel*	alecost *plants*	amateur *jobs*
air|duct *archit*	alembic *chem*	amateur *sport*
air|flow *travel*	Alencon *Shakesp*	ambages *travel*
airfoil *travel*	alewife *fish*	ambatch *trees*
air|jump *travel*	alfalfa *plants*	Amboina *islands*
air|lane *travel*	Alfreda *names*	Ambrose *names*
air|legs *travel*	algebra *maths*	ammeter *physics*
airlift *travel*	Algiers *cities*	ammonia *chem*
airline *travel*	Ali|Baba *myth*	Amneris *lit*
airlock *machine*	alidade *maths*	amnesty *govt*
airlock *physics*	aliment *food*	amnesty *law*
air|mass *weather*	alimony *law*	amnesty *war*
air|miss *travel*	aliquot *maths*	Amphion *myth*
airpark *travel*	Alister *names*	amphora *house*
airport *travel*	alkanet *plants*	ampoule *chem*
air|pump *machine*	Allegri *music*	ampulla *medic*
air|pump *physics*	allegro *music*	amylase *biol*
air|raid *war*	Allenby *war*	anaemia *medic*
airship *travel*	Allende *leaders*	anaemic *medic*
airsick *medic*	allergy *medic*	anagram *lit*
airsick *travel*	allheal *medic*	analogy *maths*
air|taxi *travel*	allheal *plants*	analyst *jobs*
Alabama *rivers*	allonge *trade*	analyst *medic*
Aladdin *lit*	all|over *time*	Ananias *Bible*
Aladdin *myth*	all|star *theatre*	anarchy *govt*
Aladdin *titles*	alluvia *geog*	anatomy *biol*
a|lamode *clothes*	almanac *geog*	anatomy *medic*
alamode *clothes*	almanac *time*	anchovy *fish*

anchovy *food*	Antiope *myth*	Ariadne *myth*
ancient *people*	Antipas *Bible*	Ariadne *names*
ancient *time*	antique *house*	arietta *music*
Andaman *islands*	antique *lit*	armband *clothes*
andante *music*	ant|lion *insects*	arm|hold *sport*
anemone *flowers*	Antonia *names*	armhole *clothes*
aneroid *physics*	Antonio *Shakesp*	armiger *govt*
angelic *relig*	antonym *lit*	armiger *herald*
angelus *relig*	Antwerp *cities*	armilla *plants*
angling *sport*	anytime *time*	arm|lock *sport*
anguine *insects*	apatite *mineral*	armoire *house*
angular *maths*	aphasia *medic*	armoury *archit*
angular *physics*	aphonia *medic*	armoury *herald*
aniline *art*	aphotic *physics*	armoury *war*
aniline *chem*	apostil *lit*	army|ant *insects*
animato *music*	apostle *jobs*	Arragon *Shakesp*
aniseed *drink*	apostle *relig*	arraign *law*
aniseed *plants*	apparel *clothes*	arrange *music*
Annabel *names*	appulse *astron*	arrears *trade*
annelid *insects*	apraxia *medic*	arrival *travel*
Annette *names*	apricot *colour*	arsenal *archit*
annuity *govt*	apricot *fruit*	arsenal *machine*
annuity *trade*	a|priori *foreign*	arsenal *war*
anodyne *medic*	apsides *astron*	arsenic *chem*
anomaly *biol*	aquaria *biol*	art|deco *art*
Anouilh *writers*	aquatic *fish*	Artemis *myth*
antacid *chem*	Aquilon *myth*	art|form *art*
antacid *medic*	Aquinas *writers*	article *lit*
Antaeus *myth*	Arallis *myth*	article *trade*
Antares *astron*	Aral|Sea *lakes*	artisan *jobs*
ant|bear *animals*	Aral|Sea *seas*	artiste *jobs*
antbird *birds*	arbiter *jobs*	artiste *theatre*
antenna *insects*	arbiter *law*	art|song *music*
antenna *machine*	arbutus *trees*	art|work *art*
antenna *physics*	Arcadia *myth*	ascents *relig*
Antenor *Shakesp*	arcanum *medic*	ascetic *people*
Antenor *myth*	archaic *time*	ashtray *house*
Anteros *myth*	archery *sport*	asinine *animals*
antheap *insects*	archery *war*	asphalt *archit*
ant|hill *insects*	archlet *archit*	asphalt *mineral*
Anthony *names*	archway *archit*	aspirin *medic*
anthrax *agric*	arc|lamp *machine*	assault *law*
antigen *medic*	areaway *archit*	assault *sport*
Antigua *islands*	Argolis *myth*	assault *war*
Antioch *Bible*	Ariadne *lit*	assayer *jobs*

assegai	*war*	
assizes	*law*	
assuage	*medic*	
Astarte	*myth*	
astylar	*archit*	
Ataturk	*leaders*	
atavism	*biol*	
atebrin	*medic*	
atelier	*art*	
atelier	*trade*	
Athamas	*myth*	
atheist	*relig*	
athlete	*jobs*	
athlete	*sport*	
Atlanta	*cities*	
at|night	*time*	
atom|gun	*war*	
atomics	*physics*	
atomism	*physics*	
atom|war	*war*	
atrazin	*chem*	
atrophy	*medic*	
Atropos	*myth*	
attacca	*music*	
attache	*jobs*	
attired	*herald*	
attuned	*music*	
auction	*trade*	
auditor	*jobs*	
auditor	*trade*	
Aumerle	*Shakesp*	
au|mieux	*foreign*	
Aurelia	*names*	
aureola	*weather*	
aureole	*physics*	
auricle	*medic*	
auricle	*plants*	
aurochs	*animals*	
Auslese	*foreign*	
autarky	*govt*	
autobus	*travel*	
autocar	*travel*	
automat	*trade*	
autonym	*lit*	
autopsy	*law*	
autopsy	*medic*	
autovac	*travel*	
Avallon	*myth*	
avenger	*people*	
average	*trade*	
Avernus	*myth*	
aviator	*jobs*	
aviator	*travel*	
aviette	*travel*	
avocado	*fruit*	
Axierus	*myth*	
axolotl	*insects*	
Azapane	*myth*	
Azariah	*Bible*	
azimuth	*astron*	
azimuth	*geog*	
azimuth	*physics*	
Azucena	*lit*	
azurite	*mineral*	
Babbitt	*titles*	
babbler	*people*	
baboosh	*clothes*	
babussu	*trees*	
baby|jib	*travel*	
Babylon	*Bible*	
Babylon	*relig*	
Bacardi	*drink*	
Bacchus	*myth*	
bacilli	*medic*	
backing	*trade*	
backing	*weather*	
back|row	*sport*	
bad|calx	*sport*	
bad|debt	*trade*	
bad|luck	*myth*	
bad|peri	*myth*	
baggage	*travel*	
Baghdad	*cities*	
bagpipe	*music*	
Bahamas	*islands*	
Bahrein	*islands*	
bailiff	*jobs*	
bailiff	*law*	
bail|out	*travel*	
balance	*chem*	
balance	*machine*	
balance	*sport*	
balance	*trade*	
balcony	*archit*	
balcony	*theatre*	
baldric	*clothes*	
baldric	*war*	
Baldwin	*leaders*	
Baldwin	*names*	
Balfour	*leaders*	
ballade	*lit*	
ballade	*music*	
ballast	*machine*	
ballast	*sport*	
ballast	*trade*	
ballast	*travel*	
ballboy	*jobs*	
balloon	*sport*	
balloon	*travel*	
bandage	*medic*	
band|aid	*govt*	
bandana	*clothes*	
bandbox	*clothes*	
bandeau	*clothes*	
bandman	*jobs*	
bandman	*music*	
bandore	*music*	
bandsaw	*tools*	
Bangkok	*cities*	
banking	*trade*	
banking	*travel*	
bannock	*food*	
banquet	*food*	
banshee	*myth*	
banting	*food*	
baptism	*relig*	
Baptist	*relig*	
Barbara	*names*	
bar|beat	*music*	
bar|bell	*sport*	
bargain	*trade*	
barge|in	*travel*	
barking	*animals*	
bar|line	*music*	
barmaid	*jobs*	

barmkin	*archit*	
Barnaby	*names*	
Barnaul	*cities*	
barn|owl	*birds*	
baronet	*govt*	
baronet	*jobs*	
baroque	*archit*	
baroque	*art*	
barrack	*archit*	
barrack	*war*	
barrage	*war*	
barrens	*geog*	
barrier	*war*	
bar|shot	*war*	
baryton	*music*	
bas|bleu	*foreign*	
basenji	*animals*	
basinet	*herald*	
basinet	*war*	
Bassano	*artists*	
bassist	*jobs*	
bassist	*music*	
bassoon	*music*	
bastion	*war*	
Bath|bun	*food*	
bathing	*sport*	
bath|oil	*clothes*	
bath|tub	*house*	
batiste	*clothes*	
batsman	*sport*	
battery	*machine*	
battery	*music*	
battery	*physics*	
battery	*travel*	
battery	*war*	
bat|tick	*insects*	
battuta	*music*	
bauxite	*mineral*	
bay|leaf	*veg*	
bay|line	*travel*	
bayonet	*war*	
bazooka	*music*	
bazooka	*war*	
beading	*archit*	
beading	*clothes*	

bean|fly	*insects*	
bear|cat	*animals*	
bearing	*archit*	
bearing	*herald*	
bearing	*machine*	
bearing	*maths*	
beatnik	*people*	
beat|off	*war*	
beavery	*animals*	
bebeeru	*trees*	
Beckett	*writers*	
bedding	*geog*	
bedding	*house*	
bedfast	*medic*	
Bedford	*Shakesp*	
bedroom	*archit*	
bedroom	*house*	
bedsore	*medic*	
bedtime	*time*	
beef|tea	*drink*	
bee|hive	*insects*	
beeline	*insects*	
beeline	*travel*	
beemoth	*insects*	
beer|mug	*drink*	
begonia	*flowers*	
beguine	*sport*	
belated	*time*	
belcher	*clothes*	
beldame	*jobs*	
Belfast	*cities*	
Belinda	*lit*	
Belinda	*names*	
bellboy	*jobs*	
bellhop	*jobs*	
Bellini	*artists*	
Bellini	*music*	
bell|jar	*chem*	
Bellona	*myth*	
Bellona	*war*	
bellows	*machine*	
bellows	*music*	
Beltane	*law*	
bencher	*law*	

benefit	*theatre*	
Benelux	*abbrev*	
Ben|Gunn	*lit*	
Bennett	*music*	
Bennett	*writers*	
benthos	*biol*	
benthos	*fish*	
benthos	*marine*	
benthos	*plants*	
benzene	*chem*	
Beowulf	*titles*	
bequest	*law*	
Berbice	*rivers*	
berceau	*foreign*	
bergylt	*fish*	
Berlioz	*music*	
Bermuda	*islands*	
Bernard	*names*	
Bernice	*names*	
Bernini	*artists*	
Berowne	*Shakesp*	
berries	*trade*	
Bertram	*Shakesp*	
Bertram	*names*	
bestial	*animals*	
best|man	*family*	
beta|ray	*physics*	
betimes	*time*	
bewitch	*myth*	
bezants	*herald*	
bezique	*sport*	
bibelot	*house*	
bicycle	*sport*	
bicycle	*travel*	
bidding	*sport*	
bidding	*trade*	
Bifrost	*myth*	
big|game	*animals*	
big|game	*sport*	
big|guns	*war*	
bighorn	*animals*	
Bighorn	*rivers*	
big|name	*jobs*	
big|shot	*jobs*	
big|shot	*war*	

bilious *medic*	Blucher *war*	book|fed *lit*
bindery *machine*	bluecap *fish*	booking *theatre*
binding *law*	blue|eye *birds*	booking *travel*
binding *lit*	blue|fox *animals*	bookish *educ*
binocle *physics*	bluegum *trees*	bookish *lit*
biology *biol*	blue|jay *birds*	booklet *lit*
biotite *mineral*	blue|sky *weather*	bookman *educ*
biparty *govt*	blue|tit *birds*	bookman *jobs*
biplane *travel*	Blunden *writers*	booster *biol*
bipolar *physics*	bluster *weather*	booster *machine*
bird|dog *animals*	boarder *educ*	booster *medic*
birdman *travel*	boarder *jobs*	booster *travel*
biretta *clothes*	boat|fly *insects*	booster *war*
biretta *relig*	boating *sport*	bordure *herald*
biscuit *art*	boating *travel*	bornite *mineral*
biscuit *food*	boatman *jobs*	Borodin *music*
bismuth *chem*	boatman *travel*	borough *govt*
bismuth *medic*	bobstay *travel*	borscht *drink*
bistort *plants*	Boeotia *myth*	borstal *law*
bit|part *jobs*	Boer|War *war*	boscage *trees*
bit|part *theatre*	bogbean *plants*	Boswell *lit*
bittern *birds*	boggart *myth*	Boswell *writers*
bitters *drink*	bog|moss *plants*	bottoms *geog*
bitumen *chem*	boiling *chem*	Boucher *artists*
bivalve *fish*	boiling *food*	boudoir *archit*
bivouac *sport*	Bolivar *leaders*	boudoir *house*
bladder *medic*	bollard *travel*	boulder *geog*
bladder *sport*	Bologna *cities*	bouncer *jobs*
Blanche *names*	bolster *house*	bounder *people*
blanket *house*	bombard *music*	bouquet *drink*
blanket *machine*	bombard *war*	bouquet *flowers*
blaster *sport*	bombast *clothes*	bouquet *house*
blawort *flowers*	bomb|bay *travel*	Bourbon *Shakesp*
blender *jobs*	bombing *war*	bourbon *drink*
blender *machine*	Bona|Dea *myth*	bourdon *music*
blesbok *animals*	bonanza *trade*	bourree *music*
blessed *relig*	bondage *relig*	bow|fast *travel*
blewits *veg*	bondage *trade*	bow|legs *medic*
blister *medic*	bondman *relig*	bowline *travel*
blister *travel*	bone|bed *geog*	bowling *sport*
blossom *flowers*	bonfire *sport*	boxhaul *travel*
blossom *fruit*	bonjour *foreign*	box|kite *sport*
blowfly *insects*	bonkers *people*	box|kite *travel*
blowgun *war*	bonsoir *foreign*	boxroom *archit*
blubber *biol*	bookery *lit*	boxroom *house*

boxseat	*travel*	
boxwood	*trees*	
boycott	*trade*	
boyhood	*time*	
bracing	*archit*	
bracing	*sport*	
bracken	*plants*	
bracket	*archit*	
bracket	*maths*	
bradawl	*tools*	
Bradley	*war*	
Braille	*educ*	
bramble	*fruit*	
Brandon	*Shakesp*	
brantub	*sport*	
brasses	*music*	
brassie	*sport*	
bravado	*war*	
bravura	*music*	
breaker	*geog*	
breaker	*marine*	
breccia	*mineral*	
breeder	*biol*	
breeder	*jobs*	
Brendan	*names*	
Brengun	*war*	
Brescia	*cities*	
brevier	*lit*	
bribery	*law*	
bricole	*war*	
Bridges	*writers*	
Bridget	*names*	
brigade	*war*	
brigand	*jobs*	
brinjal	*fruit*	
brisket	*food*	
Bristol	*cities*	
Britten	*music*	
brittle	*food*	
britzka	*travel*	
brocade	*clothes*	
Brocken	*mounts*	
brocket	*animals*	
broiler	*food*	
bromide	*chem*	

bromide	*medic*
bromine	*chem*
Brontes	*myth*
Bronwen	*names*
brooder	*birds*
brother	*family*
brother	*relig*
brownie	*myth*
brushup	*educ*
bubbles	*sport*
bubonic	*medic*
buccina	*music*
buckeye	*fruit*
buckler	*herald*
buckler	*war*
buckram	*clothes*
bucolic	*lit*
bucolic	*people*
buffalo	*animals*
Buffalo	*cities*
buffoon	*people*
buffoon	*theatre*
bugaboo	*myth*
bugbear	*myth*
bugloss	*plants*
builder	*jobs*
bulimia	*medic*
bullace	*trees*
bullbat	*animals*
bulldog	*animals*
bulldog	*war*
bullets	*trade*
bullion	*trade*
bullock	*agric*
bullock	*animals*
bulrush	*plants*
bulwark	*archit*
bulwark	*travel*
bulwark	*war*
bummalo	*fish*
bumpkin	*people*
bunkbed	*house*
bunting	*birds*
bunting	*clothes*
bunting	*herald*

burdash	*clothes*
burdock	*plants*
burette	*chem*
burgeon	*flowers*
burglar	*jobs*
burglar	*law*
burnous	*clothes*
bursary	*educ*
bursary	*trade*
burying	*relig*
bushcat	*animals*
bushman	*jobs*
bushtit	*birds*
buskins	*relig*
busline	*travel*
busstop	*travel*
bustard	*birds*
butcher	*jobs*
buttery	*house*
buttons	*jobs*
buyback	*trade*
buzzard	*birds*
buzzing	*travel*
buzzoff	*travel*
buzzsaw	*tools*
byandby	*time*
bycoket	*clothes*
cabaret	*archit*
cabaret	*theatre*
cabbage	*agric*
cabbage	*trade*
cabbage	*veg*
cabbala	*relig*
Cabeiri	*myth*
cabinet	*govt*
caboose	*travel*
cacique	*govt*
caconym	*lit*
cadaver	*medic*
cadence	*music*
cadency	*music*
cadenza	*music*
cadmium	*chem*
cadmium	*mineral*
cadrans	*tools*

caesium *chem*	Cameron *names*	captain *jobs*
caesura *lit*	Camilla *names*	captain *sport*
cagoule *clothes*	Camilla *titles*	captain *travel*
caisson *machine*	Camillo *Shakesp*	captive *govt*
caisson *war*	camp|bed *sport*	captive *jobs*
caitiff *war*	camphor *medic*	capture *geog*
cajuput *trees*	camping *sport*	capture *sport*
cake|mix *food*	campion *flowers*	capuche *clothes*
cake|tin *house*	Campion *writers*	capuche *relig*
calamus *lit*	Candida *names*	Capulet *Shakesp*
calamus *plants*	Candida *titles*	carabus *insects*
calando *music*	Candide *titles*	caracal *animals*
Calchas *Shakesp*	candies *food*	Caracas *cities*
calcite *mineral*	cannery *machine*	caracol *archit*
calcium *medic*	Canning *leaders*	caramba *foreign*
calcium *mineral*	cannula *medic*	caramel *food*
caldera *geog*	Canopus *astron*	caravan *travel*
calends *time*	cantata *music*	caravel *travel*
Caliban *Shakesp*	canteen *archit*	caraway *plants*
calibre *war*	canteen *house*	caraway *veg*
caliver *war*	cantina *archit*	carbide *chem*
call|box *travel*	cantrip *myth*	carbine *war*
callboy *jobs*	Cantuar *relig*	carcase *animals*
callboy *theatre*	canvass *govt*	carcass *animals*
calling *jobs*	canzona *music*	carcass *medic*
calling *trade*	canzone *music*	carcass *war*
calomel *chem*	cap|a|pie *war*	cardiac *medic*
calomel *medic*	capelin *fish*	Cardiff *cities*
calorie *biol*	Capella *myth*	cardoon *veg*
calorie *food*	capital *archit*	cariama *birds*
calotte *clothes*	capital *govt*	caribou *animals*
calotte *relig*	capital *lit*	carioca *music*
caltrop *plants*	capital *trade*	carioca *sport*
caltrop *war*	Capitol *govt*	cariole *travel*
Calvary *Bible*	caprice *music*	carious *medic*
calving *agric*	capsize *travel*	carlinc *plants*
Calydon *myth*	capstan *machine*	Carlton *names*
calypso *music*	capstan *travel*	Carlyle *writers*
Calypso *myth*	capsule *chem*	carmine *colour*
camaieu *art*	capsule *fruit*	Carolyn *names*
cambist *jobs*	capsule *lit*	carouse *drink*
cambist *trade*	capsule *medic*	carpark *travel*
cambium *plants*	capsule *physics*	carport *house*
cambric *clothes*	capsule *travel*	carport *travel*
Camelot *myth*	captain *govt*	carrack *travel*

Carrick *herald*	cat's eye *travel*	chamade *war*
carrier *jobs*	catspaw *marine*	chamber *archit*
carrier *medic*	cat suit *clothes*	Chamber *govt*
carrier *travel*	cattalo *animals*	chamber *house*
carrier *war*	catwalk *theatre*	chamber *machine*
Carroll *writers*	catwalk *travel*	chamber *physics*
carsick *medic*	caulker *jobs*	chamber *war*
cartoon *art*	cautery *medic*	chambre *archit*
cartoon *film/TV*	caution *law*	chamise *trees*
carving *archit*	Cavalli *music*	chamiso *trees*
carving *art*	cavalry *war*	chamois *animals*
cascade *geog*	caveman *jobs*	chamois *clothes*
cascara *medic*	cavetto *archit*	chamois *house*
case law *law*	caviare *food*	chancel *archit*
cash box *trade*	cayenne *food*	chancel *relig*
cashier *jobs*	Cecilia *names*	chancre *medic*
cashier *law*	Cecrops *myth*	channel *marine*
cashier *trade*	cedilla *lit*	channel *travel*
cashier *war*	ceiling *archit*	chanson *music*
cassava *plants*	ceiling *house*	chanter *music*
cassino *sport*	ceiling *trade*	chantry *music*
Cassius *Shakesp*	Celebes *islands*	chantry *relig*
cassock *clothes*	celesta *music*	chapeau *clothes*
cassock *relig*	Celeste *names*	chaplet *clothes*
casting *theatre*	Cellini *artists*	chaplet *flowers*
casuals *clothes*	cellist *jobs*	chaplet *herald*
catalpa *trees*	cellist *music*	chaplet *relig*
catarrh *medic*	cell sap *biol*	chapman *relig*
catawba *fruit*	cembalo *music*	chapman *trade*
catbird *birds*	centaur *animals*	chapter *archit*
catboat *travel*	centaur *myth*	chapter *lit*
cat call *theatre*	century *sport*	chapter *relig*
catcher *sport*	century *time*	charade *sport*
catchup *food*	Cepheus *astron*	charade *theatre*
Catesby *Shakesp*	Cepheus *myth*	Chardin *artists*
catfish *fish*	ceramic *art*	charged *herald*
cat flea *insects*	Cercyon *myth*	charger *animals*
cat head *travel*	Cerimon *Shakesp*	charger *machine*
cathode *machine*	cervine *animals*	charger *war*
cathode *physics*	cestoid *insects*	chariot *travel*
catling *animals*	cetacea *animals*	Charity *names*
catmint *plants*	Cezanne *artists*	charity *relig*
cat's ear *plants*	Chagall *artists*	charity *trade*
cat's eye *clothes*	chalice *house*	charity *virtues*
cat's eye *mineral*	chalone *medic*	Charles *Shakesp*

Charles	names	Chicago	sport	Christy	names
Charlie	names	chicane	sport	chronic	medic
charmer	myth	chicken	birds	chuckie	mineral
charmer	people	chicken	food	chukker	sport
charnel	archit	chicken	war	chutist	travel
charnel	relig	chicory	veg	chutney	food
charpoy	house	chiffon	clothes	cichlid	fish
charqui	food	chigger	insects	ciliary	medic
charter	govt	chignon	clothes	Cimabue	artists
charter	law	chikara	animals	cipolin	archit
charter	sport	chikara	music	circuit	law
charter	travel	chiliad	measure	circuit	machine
chasing	art	chiliad	time	circuit	physics
chassis	machine	chimera	animals	circuit	sport
chassis	travel	chimera	myth	circuit	theatre
chateau	archit	chimere	clothes	circuit	travel
Chatham	Shakesp	chimere	relig	Cisseus	myth
chattel	law	chiming	music	cistern	archit
chatter	machine	chimney	archit	cistern	house
Chaucer	writers	chimney	geog	citadel	archit
chauvin	people	chimney	house	citadel	war
cheater	people	chimney	sport	cithara	music
chechia	clothes	chindit	jobs	cithern	music
checker	herald	chinker	trade	citizen	jobs
cheetah	animals	chinook	weather	citrate	chem
Chekhov	writers	chipper	sport	citrine	colour
chemise	clothes	chirrup	birds	citrine	mineral
chemism	chem	chlamys	clothes	cittern	music
chemist	chem	Chloris	myth	civvies	clothes
chemist	jobs	cholera	medic	clachan	geog
chemist	medic	choltry	archit	clapper	music
Chemosh	myth	chopine	clothes	clapper	theatre
Chengtu	cities	chopper	house	Clarice	names
Cherith	Bible	chopper	tools	clarion	music
chervil	veg	chopper	travel	clarkia	flowers
Chester	herald	chorale	music	classic	art
Cheviot	animals	chorale	relig	classic	lit
cheviot	clothes	chorine	music	classic	music
chevron	clothes	chorine	theatre	classic	sport
chevron	herald	chorion	medic	Claudia	names
chewink	birds	chorist	jobs	Claudio	Shakesp
chezmoi	archit	chorist	music	clavier	music
chianti	drink	choroid	medic	cleaner	jobs
chiasma	medic	chowder	food	cleaver	house
Chicago	cities	Chrissy	names	cleaver	tools

Clement	*names*	
clement	*weather*	
Clemmie	*names*	
Cleopas	*Bible*	
climate	*weather*	
climber	*flowers*	
climber	*jobs*	
clinker	*trade*	
Clinton	*USpres*	
clipper	*travel*	
clippie	*jobs*	
clivers	*plants*	
clobber	*clothes*	
cloison	*archit*	
closeby	*art*	
closeup	*theatre*	
closure	*govt*	
clotbur	*plants*	
clothes	*clothes*	
cluster	*geog*	
Clymene	*myth*	
coacher	*educ*	
coalman	*jobs*	
coaltar	*chem*	
coaltit	*birds*	
coastal	*marine*	
coaster	*house*	
coaster	*travel*	
coating	*art*	
Cobbett	*writers*	
cobbler	*drink*	
cobbler	*jobs*	
cobwall	*archit*	
cocaine	*medic*	
cochlea	*medic*	
cockade	*clothes*	
cockade	*herald*	
cockney	*jobs*	
cockpit	*travel*	
coconut	*fruit*	
coconut	*house*	
Cocteau	*writers*	
Cocytus	*myth*	
codetta	*music*	
codfish	*fish*	

codices	*lit*
codicil	*law*
codling	*fish*
cognate	*family*
coinage	*lit*
coinage	*trade*
coining	*trade*
cojuror	*law*
colanut	*fruit*
coldair	*weather*
coldsaw	*tools*
coldwar	*war*
Colette	*writers*
colibri	*birds*
colicky	*medic*
colitis	*medic*
collage	*art*
collard	*veg*
collect	*relig*
colleen	*jobs*
college	*educ*
college	*herald*
collide	*travel*
collier	*jobs*
collier	*travel*
Colline	*lit*
Collins	*writers*
colloid	*chem*
colobus	*animals*
Cologne	*cities*
Colombo	*cities*
colonel	*govt*
colonel	*jobs*
colours	*art*
colours	*herald*
Columba	*astron*
combine	*agric*
combine	*machine*
COMECON	*abbrev*
comedia	*theatre*
command	*govt*
command	*war*
comment	*lit*
commere	*jobs*
commere	*theatre*

commode	*house*
commons	*food*
Commons	*govt*
commune	*geog*
commute	*travel*
compact	*clothes*
compact	*govt*
company	*jobs*
company	*theatre*
company	*trade*
company	*war*
compass	*geog*
compass	*machine*
compass	*maths*
compass	*measure*
compass	*music*
compass	*sport*
compass	*travel*
compend	*lit*
compere	*film/TV*
compere	*jobs*
compere	*theatre*
complex	*maths*
complin	*relig*
compose	*lit*
compose	*music*
compost	*agric*
compote	*food*
comrade	*jobs*
conbrio	*music*
concave	*archit*
concern	*trade*
concert	*music*
conchie	*war*
concord	*music*
conduct	*music*
conduit	*archit*
conduit	*geog*
condyle	*medic*
conflux	*geog*
congame	*govt*
congeal	*biol*
conifer	*trees*
conmoto	*music*
conquer	*war*

Conrade	*Shakesp*	Corinth	*Bible*	coupler	*music*
console	*archit*	cork‚oak	*trees*	couplet	*lit*
Consols	*abbrev*	corncob	*cereal*	coupure	*war*
consols	*trade*	cornett	*music*	courage	*war*
consort	*family*	cornice	*archit*	Courbet	*artists*
consort	*govt*	cornist	*music*	courier	*jobs*
consort	*music*	corn‚pit	*trade*	courier	*travel*
contact	*trade*	corolla	*flowers*	courser	*animals*
contact	*travel*	coroner	*jobs*	courser	*war*
context	*lit*	coroner	*law*	couture	*clothes*
contour	*archit*	coroner	*medic*	cowbane	*plants*
contour	*geog*	coronet	*govt*	cowbird	*birds*
control	*machine*	coronet	*herald*	cowherd	*agric*
control	*physics*	coronet	*jewels*	cowherd	*jobs*
convent	*relig*	corrode	*chem*	cowpoke	*jobs*
convert	*jobs*	corsage	*clothes*	cowshed	*agric*
convert	*relig*	corsage	*flowers*	cowshed	*animals*
convert	*trade*	corsair	*govt*	cowslip	*flowers*
convict	*jobs*	corsair	*jobs*	cow‚tree	*trees*
convict	*law*	Corsica	*islands*	cow‚weed	*plants*
cookery	*food*	corslet	*herald*	coxcomb	*clothes*
cooking	*food*	corslet	*war*	coxcomb	*people*
coon‚cat	*animals*	cortege	*relig*	coxcomb	*theatre*
co‚pilot	*jobs*	Corunna	*cities*	cracker	*food*
co‚pilot	*travel*	Cossack	*jobs*	crack‚up	*travel*
Copland	*music*	cossack	*war*	crammer	*educ*
coppers	*trade*	Costard	*Shakesp*	crampon	*sport*
coppice	*trees*	costume	*clothes*	cranium	*medic*
copy‚cat	*people*	costume	*theatre*	Cranmer	*Shakesp*
copyist	*art*	coterie	*lit*	crannog	*geog*
copyist	*jobs*	cothurn	*theatre*	creases	*sport*
copyman	*jobs*	cotinga	*birds*	creator	*jobs*
copyman	*lit*	cottage	*archit*	creator	*lit*
coquito	*trees*	cottons	*trade*	Creator	*relig*
coracle	*travel*	couloir	*geog*	creeper	*birds*
corcass	*geog*	couloir	*sport*	creeper	*plants*
cordate	*biol*	coulomb	*measure*	Cremona	*music*
cordial	*drink*	council	*govt*	Creston	*music*
cordial	*medic*	counsel	*govt*	crevice	*geog*
cordite	*war*	counsel	*jobs*	crewcut	*clothes*
Cordoba	*cities*	counsel	*law*	crewman	*travel*
cordoba	*money*	counter	*maths*	cricket	*insects*
Corelli	*music*	counter	*sport*	cricket	*sport*
Corelli	*writers*	counter	*trade*	cricoid	*medic*
Corinna	*names*	country	*geog*	crimson	*colour*

crinoid	*plants*	
cripple	*medic*	
croaker	*animals*	
crochet	*clothes*	
crocket	*archit*	
crock|up	*travel*	
Croesus	*trade*	
crofter	*jobs*	
crooner	*jobs*	
crooner	*music*	
cropper	*jobs*	
croquet	*sport*	
crosier	*relig*	
crottle	*plants*	
crowbar	*tools*	
crozier	*herald*	
crozier	*relig*	
cruiser	*travel*	
crumpet	*food*	
crusade	*relig*	
crusade	*war*	
crusado	*money*	
cry|baby	*people*	
crystal	*chem*	
crystal	*geog*	
crystal	*house*	
crystal	*physics*	
cubical	*maths*	
cubicle	*archit*	
cuckold	*people*	
cuculla	*clothes*	
cudgels	*war*	
cue|ball	*sport*	
cuirass	*herald*	
cuirass	*war*	
cuisine	*food*	
culotte	*clothes*	
culprit	*people*	
culture	*biol*	
culture	*educ*	
culvert	*archit*	
culvert	*geog*	
cumquat	*fruit*	
cumshaw	*trade*	
cumulus	*weather*	

cupcake	*food*
cupping	*medic*
cuprite	*chem*
curacao	*drink*
Curacao	*islands*
curator	*jobs*
curb|bit	*sport*
curcuma	*plants*
cure|all	*medic*
Curetes	*myth*
curling	*sport*
currant	*fruit*
current	*marine*
current	*physics*
current	*time*
current	*weather*
curtain	*house*
curtain	*theatre*
curtain	*war*
curtall	*music*
curtana	*war*
cushion	*archit*
cushion	*house*
cushion	*sport*
custard	*drink*
custode	*jobs*
custody	*law*
customs	*trade*
Customs	*trade*
cuticle	*medic*
cutlass	*sport*
cutlass	*war*
cutlery	*house*
cut|rate	*trade*
cutting	*flowers*
cutworm	*insects*
cyanide	*chem*
cycling	*sport*
cyclist	*jobs*
cyclist	*sport*
cyclist	*travel*
cycloid	*maths*
cyclone	*weather*
cyclops	*fish*
cyclops	*myth*

cymbals	*music*
Cynthia	*myth*
Cynthia	*names*
cypress	*trees*
Cythera	*islands*
Cyzicus	*myth*
czarina	*govt*
dabbler	*educ*
dabbler	*people*
d'accord	*foreign*
Dadaism	*art*
dagwood	*trees*
dallier	*people*
damages	*law*
damages	*trade*
dancing	*sport*
dancing	*theatre*
Dandini	*lit*
danseur	*jobs*
danseur	*theatre*
darling	*people*
Darling	*rivers*
dash|off	*art*
dash|off	*lit*
dastard	*war*
dasyure	*animals*
Daumier	*artists*
Da|Vinci	*artists*
dawning	*time*
daybook	*lit*
daybook	*trade*
day|lily	*flowers*
daylong	*time*
day|peep	*time*
daysman	*jobs*
daysman	*relig*
day|star	*astron*
daytime	*time*
day|trip	*sport*
day|trip	*travel*
deadpan	*theatre*
Dead|Sea	*lakes*
Dead|Sea	*relig*
Dead|Sea	*seas*
dealing	*trade*

deanery	*relig*	
Deasura	*myth*	
deathly	*medic*	
debacle	*geog*	
debater	*jobs*	
Deborah	*Bible*	
Deborah	*names*	
de|Burgh	*Shakesp*	
Debussy	*music*	
decagon	*maths*	
decease	*medic*	
deciare	*measure*	
decibel	*measure*	
decibel	*physics*	
decider	*sport*	
decimal	*maths*	
declare	*sport*	
declare	*trade*	
decline	*lit*	
decline	*medic*	
decoder	*machine*	
deed|box	*govt*	
deed|box	*house*	
deep|fry	*food*	
deepsea	*marine*	
deerdog	*animals*	
deer,fly	*insects*	
deer,hog	*animals*	
deerlet	*animals*	
de|Falla	*music*	
default	*trade*	
defence	*law*	
defence	*sport*	
defence	*war*	
deficit	*trade*	
deflate	*trade*	
degrees	*educ*	
De|Hooch	*artists*	
Deipyle	*myth*	
Deirdre	*names*	
delator	*law*	
delenda	*lit*	
Delibes	*music*	
Delilah	*Bible*	
deltoid	*biol*	

deltoid	*medic*	
demesne	*geog*	
demesne	*law*	
Demeter	*myth*	
demigod	*myth*	
demotic	*lit*	
denarii	*money*	
denizen	*animals*	
denizen	*jobs*	
density	*physics*	
dentine	*biol*	
dentist	*jobs*	
dentist	*medic*	
deodand	*law*	
deodate	*relig*	
deposit	*chem*	
deposit	*law*	
deposit	*trade*	
derange	*medic*	
derrick	*archit*	
derrick	*machine*	
dervish	*myth*	
Derwent	*rivers*	
descant	*lit*	
descant	*music*	
descent	*sport*	
descent	*travel*	
Desmond	*names*	
Despina	*lit*	
dessert	*fruit*	
detrain	*travel*	
Detroit	*cities*	
deutzia	*plants*	
develop	*art*	
deviser	*trade*	
devotee	*people*	
devotee	*relig*	
dew|claw	*animals*	
dextrin	*chem*	
diabase	*mineral*	
diabolo	*sport*	
diagram	*maths*	
diagram	*physics*	
dialect	*lit*	
dialyse	*chem*	

diamond	*jewels*	
diamond	*lit*	
diamond	*mineral*	
diamond	*sport*	
diarchy	*govt*	
Diarmid	*names*	
dibasic	*chem*	
dicebox	*sport*	
Dickens	*writers*	
dictate	*govt*	
Didymus	*Bible*	
diehard	*people*	
digging	*agric*	
digital	*maths*	
dika|nut	*fruit*	
diluent	*chem*	
dilutee	*people*	
dimeter	*lit*	
dine|out	*food*	
dinette	*archit*	
dinette	*house*	
diocese	*relig*	
Dionyza	*Shakesp*	
diorama	*art*	
diorite	*mineral*	
dioxide	*chem*	
diploid	*biol*	
diploma	*educ*	
Dip|Tech	*abbrev*	
diptych	*relig*	
disband	*war*	
discard	*sport*	
discord	*music*	
disease	*medic*	
dish|mop	*house*	
dissect	*biol*	
distaff	*war*	
distich	*lit*	
dittany	*plants*	
diurnal	*geog*	
diurnal	*time*	
divided	*maths*	
diviner	*jobs*	
diviner	*relig*	
divisor	*maths*	

divorce	*law*	
Dnieper	*rivers*	
Dnotice	*govt*	
dockage	*trade*	
dodgems	*travel*	
Dodgson	*writers*	
Doenitz	*war*	
doeskin	*clothes*	
dogbane	*plants*	
dogcart	*travel*	
dogdays	*geog*	
dogdays	*time*	
dogfish	*fish*	
dogrose	*flowers*	
dogstar	*astron*	
dogstar	*myth*	
dogwood	*trees*	
Dolores	*names*	
dolphin	*animals*	
dolphin	*herald*	
Dominic	*names*	
dominie	*educ*	
dominie	*jobs*	
Donetsk	*cities*	
DonJose	*lit*	
DonJuan	*titles*	
doorman	*jobs*	
doorway	*archit*	
doorway	*house*	
dopping	*birds*	
Doppler	*physics*	
dorhawk	*birds*	
dormant	*herald*	
Dorothy	*names*	
dossier	*law*	
doubleC	*music*	
doubles	*music*	
doubles	*sport*	
doublet	*clothes*	
doubter	*people*	
doubter	*relig*	
Douglas	*Shakesp*	
Douglas	*names*	
Douglas	*writers*	
dovecot	*birds*	
dowager	*family*	
dowager	*govt*	
Dowding	*war*	
Dowland	*music*	
downbow	*music*	
drachma	*money*	
Dracula	*titles*	
dragnet	*law*	
dragoon	*jobs*	
dragoon	*war*	
draught	*art*	
draught	*drink*	
draught	*medic*	
draught	*travel*	
draught	*war*	
drawers	*clothes*	
drawing	*art*	
drawing	*sport*	
drawout	*trade*	
drayman	*jobs*	
drayman	*travel*	
Drayton	*writers*	
dreamer	*people*	
dredger	*machine*	
dredger	*travel*	
Dresden	*cities*	
dresser	*house*	
dresser	*jobs*	
dressup	*clothes*	
dressup	*theatre*	
dribble	*sport*	
drifter	*people*	
drifter	*travel*	
driller	*jobs*	
drivein	*theatre*	
drivein	*travel*	
driving	*sport*	
drizzle	*weather*	
droguet	*clothes*	
dropout	*people*	
droshky	*travel*	
drought	*agric*	
drought	*weather*	
drugget	*clothes*	
drummer	*jobs*	
drummer	*music*	
drycell	*machine*	
drycell	*physics*	
drydock	*travel*	
dryfire	*war*	
dryland	*travel*	
DryMass	*relig*	
drypint	*measure*	
drywine	*drink*	
duarchy	*govt*	
Dubawnt	*rivers*	
duchess	*govt*	
dudgeon	*war*	
duebill	*trade*	
dueller	*war*	
dukedom	*govt*	
dullard	*people*	
Dumaine	*Shakesp*	
dumping	*trade*	
Dunciad	*educ*	
dungeon	*archit*	
dungeon	*law*	
dungeon	*war*	
dunnock	*birds*	
Dunsany	*writers*	
duramen	*trees*	
durmast	*trees*	
Durrell	*writers*	
dustbin	*house*	
dustman	*jobs*	
dustpan	*house*	
dyarchy	*govt*	
dynasty	*govt*	
earache	*medic*	
eardrum	*medic*	
earldom	*govt*	
earlier	*time*	
earlobe	*medic*	
earring	*jewels*	
earshot	*medic*	
earworm	*insects*	
ebauche	*art*	
ebbtide	*marine*	
echelon	*war*	
echidna	*insects*	

Echidna	*myth*	embargo	*trade*	Epigoni	*myth*
echinus	*animals*	embassy	*govt*	epigram	*lit*
echinus	*archit*	embassy	*jobs*	episode	*lit*
eclipse	*astron*	emerald	*colour*	episode	*music*
eclogue	*lit*	emerald	*jewels*	epistle	*lit*
ecology	*biol*	emerald	*mineral*	epitaph	*lit*
economy	*trade*	Emerson	*writers*	epitaph	*relig*
ecorche	*art*	emperor	*govt*	epithem	*medic*
edibles	*food*	emperor	*insects*	epithet	*lit*
edifice	*archit*	emplane	*travel*	epitome	*lit*
edition	*lit*	empress	*govt*	epizoon	*animals*
eelpout	*fish*	emption	*trade*	epochal	*time*
effects	*trade*	emuwren	*birds*	eponymy	*lit*
eggbird	*birds*	enation	*biol*	Epstein	*artists*
eggcell	*biol*	enchase	*art*	equerry	*jobs*
eggflip	*drink*	enclave	*govt*	equinox	*astron*
egghead	*educ*	encoder	*machine*	equinox	*time*
egghead	*people*	endgame	*sport*	Erasmus	*names*
eggplum	*fruit*	endless	*time*	Erasmus	*writers*
eggyolk	*food*	endorse	*trade*	eremite	*people*
egotist	*people*	endplay	*sport*	Erewhon	*titles*
ejector	*machine*	enfeoff	*law*	Erginus	*myth*
ejector	*travel*	engaged	*travel*	Erinyes	*myth*
elapsed	*time*	English	*lit*	erlking	*myth*
elastic	*clothes*	engrail	*herald*	erodium	*flowers*
elastic	*physics*	engrave	*art*	erosion	*agric*
Eleanor	*Shakesp*	engross	*trade*	erosion	*medic*
Eleanor	*names*	enlarge	*art*	erratum	*lit*
Eleazar	*Bible*	enomoty	*war*	erudite	*educ*
Eleazar	*relig*	enprise	*sport*	Escalus	*Shakesp*
elector	*govt*	enroute	*travel*	Escanes	*Shakesp*
Electra	*myth*	enstamp	*lit*	escapee	*jobs*
Electra	*titles*	entasis	*archit*	escaper	*jobs*
elegiac	*lit*	entrain	*travel*	escheat	*law*
element	*chem*	entrant	*educ*	esparto	*plants*
element	*weather*	entrant	*jobs*	esquirc	*govt*
Eleusis	*myth*	entrant	*sport*	esquire	*jobs*
ElGreco	*artists*	entropy	*physics*	essence	*chem*
Elkanah	*Bible*	entrust	*trade*	essence	*food*
ellipse	*maths*	epergne	*house*	Essenes	*relig*
elogist	*jobs*	Ephesus	*Bible*	Estella	*names*
Elspeth	*names*	Ephraim	*Bible*	estival	*time*
Elysian	*myth*	epicure	*food*	estoile	*herald*
Emanuel	*names*	epicure	*people*	estover	*law*
embargo	*govt*	epidote	*mineral*	estrade	*archit*

estreat *law*	eyewash *medic*	Fascism *govt*
etching *art*	Ezekiel *Bible*	Fascist *govt*
ethmoid *medic*	Ezekiel *names*	fashion *clothes*
Eubulus *myth*	fabliau *lit*	fast|day *time*
Eugenia *names*	faction *govt*	fast|dye *art*
Eunomia *myth*	factory *archit*	fasting *relig*
Eupheme *myth*	factory *machine*	fathead *people*
euphony *music*	factory *trade*	fatigue *medic*
Euphues *titles*	factual *lit*	fatigue *physics*
Euratom *abbrev*	faculae *astron*	Faustus *myth*
EURATOM *physics*	faculty *educ*	Fauvism *art*
euripus *marine*	faddist *people*	feather *birds*
Euryale *myth*	fad|word *lit*	feather *clothes*
Eurytus *myth*	fagotto *music*	feature *film/TV*
eustyle *archit*	faience *art*	feature *lit*
Euterpe *muses*	faience *house*	febrile *medic*
Euterpe *music*	failing *medic*	federal *govt*
Euterpe *myth*	failure *educ*	feel|ill *medic*
eutropy *chem*	failure *trade*	feeling *medic*
evening *time*	fair|cop *law*	fee|tail *law*
evil|eye *myth*	Fairfax *war*	felonry *law*
Evil|one *myth*	fairing *travel*	felspar *mineral*
ewe|lamb *animals*	fairway *sport*	felt|hat *clothes*
exactly *time*	fairway *travel*	felucca *travel*
ex|aequo *foreign*	fall|due *trade*	femoral *medic*
examine *educ*	fall|guy *people*	fencing *archit*
excerpt *lit*	fall|out *physics*	fencing *sport*
exciter *machine*	fall|out *war*	fend|off *war*
exergue *money*	falsies *clothes*	Fenella *names*
exhaust *chem*	fanatic *people*	feoffee *law*
exhaust *machine*	fanatic *relig*	fermata *music*
exhaust *travel*	fanbelt *machine*	ferment *chem*
expense *trade*	fan|club *sport*	fern|owl *birds*
expired *time*	fan|club *theatre*	ferrule *clothes*
explain *educ*	fanfare *music*	ferrule *machine*
exploit *trade*	Faninal *lit*	fertile *agric*
explore *travel*	fantail *birds*	fertile *biol*
exports *trade*	fantasy *lit*	festoon *archit*
expound *educ*	fantasy *medic*	fetch|up *travel*
express *travel*	farceur *jobs*	fetlock *animals*
extinct *animals*	farceur *theatre*	feu|duty *law*
extinct *time*	farcist *jobs*	fibroid *medic*
extract *lit*	farcist *theatre*	fiction *lit*
eyeball *medic*	farming *agric*	fiddle|G *music*
eyebrow *medic*	farrier *jobs*	fiddler *jobs*

fiddler	*music*	flanche	*herald*
Fidelio	*titles*	flaneur	*people*
fidgets	*medic*	flannel	*clothes*
fielder	*sport*	flapper	*birds*
fifteen	*sport*	flapper	*jobs*
fighter	*jobs*	flare⎮up	*machine*
fighter	*war*	flattop	*travel*
fig⎮leaf	*clothes*	Flavius	*Shakesp*
fig⎮leaf	*trees*	Fleance	*Shakesp*
fig⎮roll	*food*	Flecker	*writers*
figures	*maths*	flesher	*jobs*
figwort	*flowers*	flexure	*maths*
filbert	*fruit*	flicker	*birds*
filemot	*colour*	flicker	*film/TV*
filibeg	*clothes*	flipper	*fish*
filling	*medic*	flivver	*travel*
film⎮set	*film/TV*	Floreal	*time*
fimbria	*medic*	florist	*jobs*
finance	*trade*	Florrie	*names*
finback	*animals*	Flossie	*names*
fine⎮leg	*sport*	flounce	*clothes*
finesse	*sport*	flowers	*lit*
finnock	*fish*	fluency	*lit*
fir⎮cone	*trees*	flushed	*medic*
firearm	*war*	flutina	*music*
firefly	*insects*	fluting	*archit*
fire⎮god	*myth*	fluting	*music*
fireman	*jobs*	flutist	*music*
Firenze	*cities*	flutter	*trade*
fishing	*sport*	fluxion	*maths*
fissile	*physics*	flyblow	*insects*
fission	*physics*	flyboat	*travel*
fistula	*biol*	fly⎮half	*sport*
fistula	*medic*	flyleaf	*lit*
fitchet	*animals*	flyover	*travel*
fitchew	*animals*	fly⎮past	*travel*
fitment	*archit*	foghorn	*machine*
fitting	*clothes*	foliage	*trees*
fitting	*house*	foliose	*trees*
fixture	*archit*	fondant	*food*
fixture	*house*	Foochow	*cities*
fixture	*sport*	foot⎮bow	*sport*
flaccid	*biol*	footboy	*jobs*
flag⎮day	*time*	foot⎮lot	*trade*
flagman	*jobs*	footman	*jobs*

footpad	*jobs*
footpad	*law*
foramen	*medic*
forceps	*biol*
forceps	*medic*
forceps	*tools*
forearm	*medic*
foreleg	*animals*
foreman	*jobs*
foreman	*law*
foreman	*trade*
forepaw	*animals*
foretop	*travel*
forever	*time*
forfeit	*law*
forgery	*law*
forgery	*trade*
for⎮good	*time*
forlana	*music*
for⎮life	*time*
Formosa	*islands*
formula	*chem*
formula	*maths*
formula	*sport*
formula	*travel*
for⎮sale	*trade*
Forster	*writers*
fortify	*war*
fortlet	*war*
FORTRAN	*abbrev*
Fortran	*comput*
Fortuna	*myth*
fortune	*trade*
forward	*sport*
Fossway	*archit*
foulard	*clothes*
foumart	*animals*
founder	*jobs*
founder	*travel*
foundry	*machine*
foundry	*trade*
four⎮oar	*travel*
foxhole	*war*
fox⎮hunt	*sport*
foxtail	*plants*

foxtrot	*music*	
foxtrot	*sport*	
frailty	*medic*	
frame up	*law*	
Frances	*names*	
Francis	*Shakesp*	
Francis	*names*	
freckle	*clothes*	
freckle	*medic*	
freebie	*trade*	
free end	*archit*	
free hit	*sport*	
freeway	*travel*	
freight	*trade*	
freshen	*weather*	
fresher	*educ*	
freshet	*geog*	
fretsaw	*tools*	
frigate	*travel*	
Frisbee	*sport*	
frisket	*machine*	
fritter	*food*	
friture	*foreign*	
frocked	*clothes*	
frogbit	*plants*	
frog fly	*insects*	
frogged	*clothes*	
frogman	*jobs*	
frogman	*sport*	
frogman	*travel*	
frontal	*medic*	
frontal	*relig*	
fuchsia	*flowers*	
fulcrum	*machine*	
fulcrum	*maths*	
full lot	*trade*	
full sun	*geog*	
funeral	*relig*	
funfair	*sport*	
furbish	*house*	
fur coat	*clothes*	
furioso	*music*	
furlana	*music*	
furlong	*measure*	
furnace	*art*	

furnace	*house*	
furnace	*machine*	
furnish	*house*	
furrier	*jobs*	
fur seal	*animals*	
fusarol	*archit*	
fuse box	*house*	
fuse box	*machine*	
fustian	*clothes*	
futtock	*travel*	
futures	*trade*	
fuzzbox	*music*	
gabbler	*people*	
gabelle	*trade*	
Gabriel	*Bible*	
Gabriel	*myth*	
Gabriel	*names*	
gadwall	*birds*	
gaiters	*clothes*	
gaiters	*relig*	
Galahad	*myth*	
Galatea	*myth*	
Galilee	*Bible*	
galilee	*archit*	
gallant	*people*	
gallant	*war*	
galleon	*travel*	
gallery	*archit*	
gallery	*art*	
gallery	*sport*	
gallery	*theatre*	
gallery	*war*	
galleys	*travel*	
gallfly	*insects*	
Gallico	*writers*	
gallium	*chem*	
gallium	*mineral*	
Gallius	*Shakesp*	
gallows	*law*	
gambler	*jobs*	
gamboge	*colour*	
gambrel	*animals*	
game leg	*medic*	
game pie	*food*	
gametes	*biol*	

gangway	*travel*	
gardant	*herald*	
garfish	*fish*	
garland	*archit*	
garland	*flowers*	
garland	*herald*	
garland	*lit*	
garment	*clothes*	
Garonne	*rivers*	
garotte	*law*	
gar pike	*fish*	
gas bomb	*war*	
Gaskell	*writers*	
gas mask	*war*	
gas ring	*house*	
gastric	*medic*	
gateman	*jobs*	
gateman	*theatre*	
gateway	*archit*	
Gauguin	*artists*	
gavotte	*music*	
gavotte	*sport*	
gazelle	*animals*	
gazette	*lit*	
gearbox	*machine*	
gearbox	*travel*	
Gehenna	*myth*	
gelatin	*food*	
gelding	*animals*	
gemsbok	*animals*	
general	*govt*	
general	*jobs*	
Genesis	*Bible*	
genesis	*biol*	
genipap	*trees*	
genista	*plants*	
gentian	*flowers*	
Gentile	*Bible*	
gentile	*relig*	
geodesy	*geog*	
geodesy	*measure*	
geogony	*chem*	
geogony	*geog*	
geology	*chem*	
geology	*geog*	

Geordie	names	
georgic	lit	
Geraint	names	
germ|war	war	
Gestalt	foreign	
Gestapo	govt	
getaway	travel	
get|lost	travel	
gherkin	veg	
ghillie	jobs	
giantry	myth	
Gibbons	artists	
Gibbons	music	
gibbous	astron	
giblets	food	
gift|box	trade	
gigabit	comput	
gilbert	measure	
Gilbert	names	
gilbert	physics	
Gilbert	writers	
gilding	art	
Gillian	names	
Gillray	artists	
gimbals	physics	
gin|fizz	drink	
gingham	clothes	
ginseng	plants	
giocoso	music	
giraffe	animals	
girasol	clothes	
girasol	mineral	
gisarme	war	
Giselle	names	
Giselle	titles	
gizzard	animals	
glacial	geog	
glacier	geog	
Glasgow	cities	
glasses	clothes	
glasses	medic	
Glaucus	myth	
glazier	jobs	
gleaner	jobs	
gliadin	biol	

gliding	sport	
gliding	travel	
Glitnir	myth	
glorify	relig	
glowfly	insects	
glucose	chem	
glucose	food	
glutton	animals	
glutton	food	
glutton	people	
glyphic	art	
glyptic	art	
gnocchi	food	
gnu|goat	animals	
go|ahead	travel	
goat|god	myth	
gobbler	birds	
go|below	travel	
go|broke	trade	
go|by|air	travel	
goddess	myth	
godetia	flowers	
go|devil	travel	
Godfrey	names	
godhead	relig	
godling	myth	
godroon	archit	
Goering	leaders	
goggles	sport	
goldbug	insects	
goldeye	birds	
Golding	writers	
golf|bag	sport	
golfing	sport	
golf|tie	sport	
Goliath	Bible	
gondola	travel	
Goneril	Shakesp	
Gonzalo	Shakesp	
good|buy	trade	
good|fun	sport	
good|man	relig	
good|sum	trade	
gorcock	birds	
gor|crow	birds	

gorilla	animals	
goshawk	birds	
gosling	birds	
gothite	mineral	
Gotland	islands	
go|to|war	war	
gouache	art	
goulash	food	
go|under	trade	
gourmet	food	
gourmet	people	
grackle	birds	
gradine	archit	
gradino	relig	
gradual	music	
grafted	herald	
grammar	educ	
grammar	lit	
grampus	animals	
granary	archit	
grandee	govt	
granish	food	
granite	archit	
granite	mineral	
granule	measure	
grapery	fruit	
graphic	art	
graphic	lit	
grapnel	travel	
grapnel	war	
grassum	law	
grating	archit	
graving	art	
gravity	physics	
gravure	art	
great|go	educ	
greaves	herald	
gregale	weather	
Gregory	Shakesp	
Gregory	names	
gremlin	myth	
Grenada	islands	
grenade	war	
grey|fox	animals	
grey|hen	birds	

greylag	birds	gunlock	war	halfwit	people
greyowl	birds	gunmoll	jobs	halibut	fish
greysky	weather	gunnage	war	halling	music
griddle	house	gunnery	war	hallway	archit
griffin	animals	gunning	war	halogen	chem
griffin	myth	gunpark	war	halyard	travel
griffon	animals	gunplay	war	Hamburg	cities
griffon	herald	gunport	war	hamitup	theatre
griffon	myth	gunroom	war	hammock	house
grimace	theatre	gunshot	war	hammock	travel
grinder	educ	gurnard	fish	Hampden	leaders
gripper	tools	guyrope	sport	hamster	animals
grocery	food	guyrope	travel	handbag	clothes
grogram	clothes	Gwalior	cities	handbag	travel
grommet	machine	Gwyneth	names	handjar	war
Gropius	artists	gymnast	jobs	handler	jobs
grounds	archit	gymnast	sport	handoff	sport
grounds	sport	gymslip	clothes	handout	lit
grouper	fish	gyrocar	travel	handsaw	tools
groupie	people	gyronny	herald	hangdog	people
growler	travel	habitat	animals	hanging	law
grownup	jobs	habitat	biol	hangman	jobs
Gruyere	food	habitat	geog	hangman	law
gryphon	animals	hachure	geog	Hanover	cities
grysbok	animals	hackbut	war	hanuman	animals
Gstring	clothes	hacking	sport	Hanuman	myth
Gstring	music	hackney	animals	hapenny	money
guanaco	animals	hackney	travel	haploid	biol
guarana	plants	hacksaw	tools	harbour	geog
guayule	plants	haddock	fish	harbour	law
gudgeon	fish	hafnium	chem	harbour	marine
guerdon	trade	hafnium	mineral	harbour	travel
guereza	animals	haggard	birds	Harding	USpres
guichet	travel	haggard	medic	hardman	people
guilder	money	Haggard	writers	hardtop	travel
guipure	clothes	haggler	people	haricot	veg
gumboil	medic	haircut	clothes	harmony	music
gumboot	clothes	hairnet	clothes	harmost	govt
gumdrop	food	hairpin	clothes	harness	animals
gumtree	trees	hairpin	sport	harness	travel
gunboat	travel	halberd	war	harness	war
gunboat	war	halcyon	birds	Harnett	writers
gundeck	travel	halfape	animals	Harpies	myth
gundeck	war	halfday	trade	harpist	jobs
gunfire	war	halfgod	myth	harpist	music

harpoon	sport	hearsay	law	Herrick	writers
harrier	animals	heathen	relig	herring	fish
harrier	sport	Heather	names	Hertzog	leaders
Harriet	names	heather	plants	Hesione	myth
Hartley	writers	heating	house	hessian	clothes
harvest	agric	heating	physics	Hessian	war
harvest	cereal	heavens	astron	hexagon	maths
harvest	fruit	heave to	travel	hexapod	animals
harvest	time	Hebrews	Bible	heyduck	war
harvest	trade	Hebrews	relig	hickory	house
has been	people	heckler	jobs	hickory	trees
hashish	medic	hectare	measure	hidalgo	govt
hatband	clothes	heiress	family	high art	art
hatchet	tools	heiress	jobs	high day	time
hatchet	war	heiress	law	high hat	clothes
hauberk	herald	Helenus	Shakesp	high sea	marine
hauberk	war	Helenus	myth	high tea	house
haulage	trade	helibus	travel	highway	travel
haulier	jobs	Helicon	lit	hillock	geog
hautboy	music	Helicon	mounts	hilltop	geog
haut ton	foreign	helipad	travel	Himeros	myth
hawk bit	plants	hellcat	people	Himmler	leaders
hawking	sport	hellier	people	hindleg	animals
hawk owl	birds	hellion	myth	hindpaw	animals
haycart	agric	Helmand	rivers	hip bath	house
hayfork	tools	helping	food	hipbone	medic
hayrake	tools	hemline	clothes	hip boot	clothes
hayrick	agric	hemlock	plants	hip roof	archit
hayseed	plants	henbane	plants	hipster	jobs
haywain	travel	hen coop	birds	hircine	animals
Hazlitt	writers	hennery	birds	his nibs	govt
head boy	jobs	heralds	herald	histoid	biol
head for	travel	herbage	plants	history	lit
heading	lit	Herbert	Shakesp	history	medic
headman	jobs	Herbert	names	history	time
head off	travel	Herbert	writers	histrio	jobs
headset	travel	heretic	people	histrio	theatre
head tax	trade	heretic	relig	hit song	music
headway	travel	heritor	law	hit tune	music
heal all	medic	heroine	film/TV	hive bee	insects
healing	medic	heroine	jobs	hoatzin	birds
healthy	medic	heroine	lit	Hobbema	artists
hearing	educ	heroine	myth	Hockney	artists
hearing	law	heroine	theatre	Hogarth	artists
hearing	medic	heroism	war	hog deer	animals

hogfish	*fish*	hospice	*medic*	iceberg	*geog*
hogwash	*animals*	hostage	*war*	ice|bird	*birds*
hogweed	*plants*	hostess	*jobs*	iceboat	*travel*
Holbein	*artists*	hot|bath	*medic*	ice|cave	*geog*
holdall	*house*	hot|cake	*food*	ice|cold	*weather*
holdall	*travel*	hothead	*people*	ice|cube	*food*
holding	*trade*	hot|jazz	*music*	iced|tea	*drink*
hold|off	*war*	hot|line	*travel*	icefall	*geog*
holiday	*time*	hot|seat	*govt*	ice|f'loe	*geog*
Holland	*Shakesp*	Hotspur	*Shakesp*	Iceland	*islands*
holmium	*chem*	hotspur	*people*	ice|pack	*geog*
holmium	*mineral*	housing	*archit*	ice|pick	*sport*
holmoak	*trees*	Housman	*writers*	ice|raft	*geog*
holster	*sport*	Houston	*cities*	ice|rink	*sport*
holster	*war*	Howells	*music*	ice|worm	*insects*
holy|day	*relig*	huitain	*lit*	Ichabod	*Bible*
holy|day	*time*	humerus	*medic*	Ichabod	*relig*
holy|see	*relig*	humming	*music*	ich|dien	*foreign*
holy|war	*relig*	hummock	*geog*	icterus	*medic*
holy|war	*war*	hundred	*measure*	icy|wind	*weather*
homburg	*clothes*	hunting	*sport*	idyllic	*lit*
homelyn	*fish*	hurdler	*sport*	igneous	*mineral*
Homeric	*lit*	hurling	*sport*	ikebana	*sport*
homonym	*lit*	hurry|up	*travel*	Ile|de|Re	*islands*
honesty	*plants*	husband	*family*	illicit	*law*
honours	*educ*	hustler	*people*	illness	*medic*
honours	*sport*	Hwang|Ho	*rivers*	ill|wind	*weather*
hoodlum	*people*	hyalite	*mineral*	Illyria	*myth*
Hooghly	*rivers*	hydrant	*archit*	imagery	*lit*
hoot|owl	*birds*	hydrant	*machine*	imagism	*art*
hop|flea	*insects*	hydrate	*chem*	imagist	*jobs*
Hopkins	*writers*	hydride	*chem*	impaled	*herald*
hop|tree	*trees*	Hygieia	*myth*	impeach	*law*
Horatii	*myth*	hygiene	*medic*	impetus	*travel*
Horatio	*Shakesp*	hymnary	*relig*	impiety	*relig*
Horatio	*names*	hymnist	*jobs*	impious	*relig*
horizon	*geog*	hymnist	*music*	imports	*trade*
hormone	*medic*	hymnody	*music*	impress	*lit*
hornbug	*insects*	hyped|up	*people*	imprint	*lit*
hornfly	*insects*	hyperon	*chem*	impulse	*physics*
hornist	*music*	Iacchus	*myth*	impulse	*travel*
hornowl	*birds*	Iachimo	*Shakesp*	incense	*relig*
Hosanna	*relig*	Iapetus	*myth*	incised	*art*
hosiery	*clothes*	Icarius	*myth*	incisor	*medic*
hospice	*archit*	ice|bear	*animals*	incline	*geog*

incubus	*myth*	Ireland	*music*	jam|tart	*food*
indices	*maths*	iridium	*chem*	Janacek	*music*
inertia	*maths*	iridium	*mineral*	janitor	*jobs*
inertia	*physics*	Irkutsk	*cities*	jankers	*war*
infancy	*time*	Iron|Age	*time*	January	*time*
infanta	*govt*	iron|men	*trade*	Japheth	*Bible*
inferno	*myth*	iron|ore	*mineral*	jargoon	*jewels*
infidel	*people*	iron|pan	*mineral*	jargoon	*mineral*
infidel	*relig*	iron|red	*colour*	jasmine	*flowers*
infield	*sport*	ischium	*medic*	Java|Sea	*seas*
inflate	*trade*	Isfahan	*cities*	javelin	*sport*
in|funds	*trade*	Ishmael	*Bible*	javelin	*war*
ingenue	*theatre*	isobase	*geog*	jawbone	*medic*
ingesta	*food*	isochor	*maths*	jawfish	*fish*
ingress	*travel*	isohyet	*weather*	jaw|rope	*travel*
initial	*lit*	isotone	*physics*	Jeffrey	*names*
inkhorn	*educ*	isotope	*chem*	Jehovah	*relig*
inkwell	*educ*	isotope	*physics*	jejunum	*medic*
innards	*medic*	isotopy	*chem*	jemedar	*jobs*
innings	*sport*	isotron	*chem*	jeofail	*law*
in|print	*lit*	isotype	*maths*	Jericho	*Bible*
inquest	*law*	isthmus	*geog*	Jessica	*Shakesp*
inquiry	*law*	italics	*lit*	Jessica	*names*
insides	*medic*	Iuturna	*myth*	jet|pipe	*travel*
insight	*lit*	Ivanhoe	*titles*	jewfish	*fish*
instant	*time*	ivories	*music*	Jezebel	*Bible*
instill	*educ*	Iwo|Jima	*islands*	Jezebel	*people*
insular	*geog*	jacamar	*birds*	Jezreel	*Bible*
insulin	*medic*	jacchus	*animals*	jib|boom	*travel*
integer	*maths*	jacinth	*jewels*	jibstay	*travel*
interim	*time*	jacinth	*mineral*	jingler	*trade*
intrada	*music*	jackass	*animals*	jobbers	*trade*
intrans	*abbrev*	jackdaw	*birds*	jobbing	*trade*
introit	*music*	jackman	*war*	jobless	*trade*
introit	*relig*	jackpot	*sport*	Jocasta	*myth*
intrust	*trade*	Jackson	*USpres*	Jocelyn	*names*
in|utero	*foreign*	Jack|Tar	*jobs*	Joe|Soap	*people*
in|vacuo	*foreign*	Jack|Tar	*travel*	jogging	*sport*
invader	*war*	jaconet	*clothes*	John|Doe	*law*
invalid	*jobs*	j'adoube	*sport*	Johnson	*USpres*
invalid	*medic*	jaegers	*clothes*	Johnson	*writers*
in|vitro	*foreign*	Jakarta	*cities*	jollies	*war*
invoice	*trade*	Jamaica	*islands*	jonquil	*flowers*
Ionesco	*writers*	jambeau	*war*	journal	*lit*
Ireland	*islands*	jam|roll	*food*	journal	*time*

journal *trade*	Kenneth *names*	Krishna *rivers*
journey *travel*	keratin *chem*	krypton *chem*
joy|ride *sport*	kerogen *mineral*	kumquat *fruit*
joy|ride *travel*	kestrel *birds*	Kwangju *cities*
jubilee *relig*	ketchup *food*	kyanite *mineral*
jubilee *time*	keyhole *archit*	labarum *herald*
Judaism *relig*	keyhole *house*	labiate *plants*
juggler *jobs*	key|note *music*	Lacerta *astron*
jugular *medic*	khamsin *weather*	lacerta *insects*
ju|jitsu *sport*	Kharkov *cities*	Lachlan *names*
juke|box *music*	khedive *govt*	Lachlan *rivers*
Juliana *names*	kick|off *sport*	laconic *lit*
jump|jet *war*	killdee *birds*	lacquer *art*
June|bug *insects*	killick *travel*	lacquer *chem*
June|fly *insects*	killing *trade*	lacquer *house*
juniper *trees*	killock *travel*	lactase *biol*
junkman *jobs*	kiloton *measure*	lactate *chem*
Jupiter *astron*	kiloton *physics*	lactose *chem*
Jupiter *myth*	kilt|pin *clothes*	ladrone *law*
jury|box *law*	kindred *family*	ladybug *insects*
juryman *law*	kingcup *flowers*	lady|cow *insects*
jussive *lit*	kingdom *geog*	Lady|day *time*
justice *jobs*	king|pin *people*	ladyfly *insects*
justice *law*	kinsman *family*	Laertes *Shakesp*
justice *virtues*	Kipling *writers*	Laertes *myth*
justify *lit*	Kirstie *names*	lagging *archit*
Justine *names*	kitchen *archit*	lagging *house*
just|now *time*	kitchen *house*	laid|low *medic*
Juvenal *writers*	klinker *archit*	lakelet *geog*
Kai|Lung *lit*	knacker *jobs*	Lake|Tuz *lakes*
Kala|Nag *lit*	kneecap *medic*	Lake|Van *lakes*
kalends *time*	kneepan *medic*	Lakshmi *myth*
Kalinin *cities*	Knesset *govt*	lambast *war*
Karachi *cities*	knifing *war*	lambert *measure*
karakul *animals*	knitter *jobs*	Lambert *music*
Kara|Sea *seas*	knock|up *sport*	Lambeth *relig*
Katrina *names*	know|all *people*	lambing *agric*
katydid *insects*	know|how *jobs*	lambkin *animals*
keelson *travel*	knuckle *food*	lamboys *war*
keening *music*	kola|nut *fruit*	lamella *biol*
keening *relig*	Kosygin *leaders*	lampfly *insects*
keep|fit *sport*	Kowloon *cities*	lampoon *lit*
keep|off *travel*	Kremlin *govt*	lamprey *fish*
keitloa *animals*	kremlin *war*	lancers *sport*
Kennedy *USpres*	Krishna *myth*	land|ice *geog*

landing	*archit*
landing	*house*
landing	*sport*
landing	*travel*
Landler	*foreign*
Landler	*music*
land,rat	*animals*
land|tax	*govt*
land|tax	*trade*
lanolin	*chem*
lanolin	*medic*
lantern	*archit*
lantern	*house*
lanyard	*travel*
Laocoon	*myth*
Laodice	*myth*
La|Plata	*cities*
Laputan	*myth*
lapwing	*birds*
larceny	*law*
lardoon	*food*
larmier	*archit*
last|act	*theatre*
last|lap	*sport*
lateral	*biol*
latitat	*law*
lattice	*archit*
lattice	*house*
lattice	*maths*
laus|Deo	*foreign*
Lavache	*Shakesp*
Lavinia	*Shakesp*
Lavinia	*names*
law|list	*law*
law|lord	*law*
lawsuit	*law*
layette	*clothes*
lazaret	*medic*
Lazarus	*Bible*
L|driver	*travel*
Leacock	*writers*
leaders	*lit*
leading	*trade*
leafage	*flowers*
leafage	*trees*

leaflet	*flowers*
leaflet	*lit*
leaflet	*trees*
Leander	*myth*
learned	*educ*
learner	*educ*
learner	*jobs*
learner	*travel*
leather	*clothes*
Lebanon	*relig*
lectern	*educ*
lectern	*relig*
lection	*relig*
lecture	*educ*
lee|helm	*travel*
lee|tack	*travel*
leeward	*travel*
leewide	*travel*
leftist	*govt*
legatee	*law*
legator	*law*
leg|hold	*sport*
leghorn	*clothes*
leg|show	*theatre*
leg|side	*sport*
Lehmann	*writers*
Leipzig	*cities*
lemming	*animals*
lending	*trade*
lentigo	*medic*
lentisk	*trees*
Leonard	*names*
Leonato	*Shakesp*
Leonine	*Shakesp*
leonine	*animals*
Leonine	*lit*
Leonora	*lit*
Leonora	*names*
Leontes	*Shakesp*
leopard	*animals*
leopard	*herald*
Leopold	*names*
leotard	*clothes*
leotard	*theatre*
Lepidus	*Shakesp*

leprosy	*medic*
leprous	*medic*
Lessing	*writers*
let|ball	*sport*
Letitia	*names*
letters	*educ*
letters	*lit*
lettuce	*trade*
lettuce	*veg*
leucine	*chem*
leveret	*animals*
lexicon	*educ*
lexicon	*lit*
libelee	*govt*
Liberal	*govt*
liberal	*people*
library	*archit*
library	*house*
library	*lit*
lich,owl	*birds*
lie,abed	*people*
lift,off	*travel*
lighter	*machine*
lighter	*travel*
lignite	*mineral*
Lillian	*names*
lily|pad	*flowers*
limeade	*drink*
limited	*trade*
limiter	*machine*
limniad	*myth*
Limpopo	*rivers*
Lincoln	*USpres*
linctus	*medic*
Lindsey	*names*
lineman	*jobs*
line|out	*sport*
Linette	*names*
linkboy	*jobs*
linkman	*jobs*
linocut	*art*
linsang	*animals*
linseed	*plants*
lioness	*animals*
lipoids	*chem*

liqueur *drink*	lowbrow *people*	Madeira *islands*
Lismore *islands*	lowland *geog*	Madeira *rivers*
literal *lit*	LowMass *relig*	Madison *USpres*
lithium *chem*	lowrise *archit*	madoqua *animals*
lithium *mineral*	lowtide *marine*	madrona *trees*
lithoid *mineral*	lozenge *food*	maestro *educ*
Litolff *music*	lozenge *herald*	maestro *jobs*
litotes *lit*	lozenge *medic*	maestro *music*
liturgy *relig*	Lplates *travel*	MaeWest *clothes*
loafers *clothes*	lucerne *agric*	MaeWest *travel*
lobelia *flowers*	lucerne *plants*	mafioso *law*
lobster *fish*	Lucetta *Shakesp*	magenta *colour*
lobworm *insects*	Luciana *Shakesp*	magnate *jobs*
lockjaw *medic*	Lucifer *myth*	magneto *machine*
lockman *jobs*	Lucille *names*	magneto *travel*
locknut *machine*	Lucinda *names*	mahseer *fish*
lockout *trade*	Lucknow *cities*	mailman *jobs*
lodging *archit*	Luddite *people*	mailvan *travel*
logbook *lit*	luggage *travel*	maintop *travel*
logbook *travel*	lugsail *travel*	majesty *govt*
logwood *trees*	lugworm *insects*	Majorca *islands*
Lombard *trade*	lullaby *music*	majorin *educ*
longago *time*	lumbago *medic*	makefor *travel*
longbob *clothes*	lumpsum *trade*	makeoff *travel*
longbow *sport*	lunatic *people*	makewar *war*
longbow *war*	lunette *archit*	Malachi *Bible*
longhop *sport*	lunette *war*	malaise *medic*
longleg *sport*	lurcher *animals*	malaria *medic*
longrun *theatre*	lustrum *time*	Malcolm *Shakesp*
longrun *time*	Luthuli *leaders*	Malcolm *names*
longrun *trade*	Lycidas *titles*	malines *clothes*
LongTom *war*	lycopod *plants*	mallard *birds*
longton *measure*	lyddite *war*	malleus *medic*
lookout *jobs*	Lymoges *Shakesp*	malmsey *drink*
lookout *war*	lymphad *travel*	malmsey *fruit*
looting *law*	Lynceus *myth*	Malraux *writers*
lording *govt*	lyrical *lit*	mammoth *animals*
LordJim *titles*	macaque *animals*	manacle *law*
Lorelei *myth*	Macbeth *Shakesp*	manager *jobs*
Lorenzo *Shakesp*	Macbeth *titles*	manager *theatre*
lorimer *jobs*	MacCunn *music*	manager *trade*
lottery *sport*	Macduff *Shakesp*	Managua *cities*
lottery *trade*	machair *geog*	manakin *birds*
lounger *people*	machete *war*	manatee *animals*
lowbrow *educ*	Madeira *drink*	mandate *govt*

Mandela	*leaders*	marshal	*jobs*	Maureen	*names*
mandola	*music*	marshal	*law*	Mauriac	*writers*
mandora	*music*	Marsyas	*myth*	Maurice	*names*
Manfred	*titles*	Martext	*Shakesp*	Maurois	*writers*
manhood	*time*	martial	*war*	MaVlast	*titles*
manhour	*time*	Martial	*writers*	mawworm	*insects*
maniple	*clothes*	Martian	*travel*	maxilla	*medic*
maniple	*relig*	Martina	*names*	maximum	*measure*
maniple	*war*	Martine	*names*	maxwell	*measure*
mankind	*family*	martini	*drink*	Maxwell	*names*
manmade	*trade*	Martinu	*music*	maylily	*flowers*
manowar	*travel*	Martius	*Shakesp*	maypole	*sport*
Manrico	*lit*	martlet	*birds*	mayweed	*plants*
mansard	*archit*	martlet	*herald*	Mazeppa	*titles*
mansion	*archit*	Marvell	*writers*	mazurka	*music*
mansman	*people*	Marxism	*govt*	mazurka	*sport*
manteau	*clothes*	Marxist	*govt*	meander	*geog*
manteel	*clothes*	Marxist	*people*	meander	*travel*
mantlet	*war*	Masaryk	*leaders*	meaning	*lit*
Manxcat	*animals*	mascara	*clothes*	measles	*medic*
marabou	*birds*	Masetto	*lit*	measure	*govt*
marbles	*sport*	masonry	*archit*	measure	*lit*
Marcade	*Shakesp*	massage	*medic*	measure	*machine*
marcato	*music*	masseur	*jobs*	measure	*music*
Marchen	*lit*	masseur	*medic*	meatman	*jobs*
Marcius	*Shakesp*	mastaba	*relig*	meatpie	*food*
Mardian	*Shakesp*	mastiff	*animals*	meccano	*sport*
Margery	*names*	mastoid	*medic*	Mechlin	*clothes*
margosa	*trees*	matador	*jobs*	meddler	*people*
Mariana	*Shakesp*	matador	*sport*	mediant	*music*
Marilyn	*names*	matches	*house*	mediate	*govt*
marimba	*music*	matelot	*jobs*	medical	*medic*
mariner	*jobs*	matelot	*travel*	Medtner	*music*
mariner	*travel*	Mathias	*music*	medulla	*medic*
marines	*war*	Matilda	*names*	meerkat	*animals*
Maritsa	*rivers*	matinal	*time*	Megaera	*myth*
markhor	*animals*	matinee	*theatre*	megaron	*archit*
marline	*travel*	Matisse	*artists*	megaton	*physics*
Marlowe	*writers*	matrass	*chem*	megaton	*war*
Marmion	*titles*	matross	*war*	Melanie	*names*
marmose	*animals*	Matthew	*Bible*	melanin	*chem*
marquee	*archit*	Matthew	*names*	melding	*sport*
marquee	*theatre*	mattock	*tools*	melilot	*plants*
marquis	*govt*	matzoth	*food*	melisma	*music*
Marryat	*writers*	Maugham	*writers*	Melissa	*names*

melodia	*music*	Miletus	*myth*	mistral	*weather*
melodic	*music*	milfoil	*plants*	mitosis	*biol*
Memlinc	*artists*	Milhaud	*music*	mixture	*chem*
memoirs	*lit*	militia	*govt*	mixture	*medic*
memoria	*relig*	militia	*war*	mixture	*music*
Memphis	*cities*	milkcan	*agric*	mob|rule	*govt*
Mendips	*mounts*	milk|cow	*animals*	mobsman	*govt*
Menotti	*music*	milking	*agric*	mobsman	*jobs*
menthol	*medic*	milk|leg	*medic*	mobster	*govt*
Menzies	*leaders*	milkman	*jobs*	mobster	*jobs*
mercury	*chem*	milk|run	*travel*	modesty	*clothes*
mercury	*mineral*	Millais	*artists*	Modesty	*names*
Mercury	*myth*	mill|run	*geog*	modicum	*measure*
Merimee	*writers*	milreis	*money*	modiste	*clothes*
merling	*fish*	mimicry	*theatre*	modiste	*jobs*
mermaid	*fish*	mimulus	*flowers*	modulus	*maths*
mermaid	*myth*	minaret	*archit*	moellon	*archit*
Meshach	*Bible*	minaret	*relig*	mofette	*geog*
message	*lit*	Mindoro	*islands*	moidore	*money*
Messala	*Shakesp*	mineral	*mineral*	mole|rat	*animals*
Messiah	*Bible*	Minerva	*myth*	Moliere	*writers*
Messiah	*relig*	minibus	*travel*	mollusc	*fish*
Messiah	*titles*	minicab	*travel*	mollusk	*fish*
Messias	*relig*	minicar	*travel*	Molokai	*islands*
Messina	*cities*	minimum	*measure*	Molotov	*leaders*
metamer	*chem*	minisub	*travel*	Mombasa	*cities*
metazoa	*animals*	minor|in	*educ*	monarch	*govt*
methane	*chem*	minster	*relig*	moneyed	*trade*
metonym	*lit*	mintage	*trade*	mongrel	*animals*
micelle	*chem*	minuend	*maths*	monitor	*biol*
Michael	*Bible*	minutes	*govt*	monitor	*educ*
Michael	*Shakesp*	Miocene	*geog*	monitor	*insects*
Michael	*myth*	Mirabel	*names*	monitor	*jobs*
Michael	*names*	miracle	*relig*	monitor	*machine*
microbe	*biol*	miracle	*theatre*	monitor	*physics*
microbe	*medic*	mirador	*archit*	monitor	*travel*
middle|C	*music*	Miranda	*Shakesp*	monocle	*clothes*
Midgard	*myth*	Miranda	*names*	monsoon	*weather*
midiron	*sport*	missile	*physics*	monster	*animals*
mid|week	*time*	missile	*war*	montage	*art*
midwife	*jobs*	mission	*relig*	Montagu	*names*
midwife	*medic*	mission	*trade*	Montano	*Shakesp*
migrant	*birds*	mission	*travel*	monthly	*lit*
migrant	*travel*	mission	*war*	monthly	*time*
Mildred	*names*	missive	*lit*	Montjoy	*Shakesp*

moorhen	*birds*	Musetta	*lit*	necktie	*clothes*
mooring	*travel*	musette	*music*	nemesia	*flowers*
morceau	*lit*	musical	*film/TV*	Nemesis	*myth*
mordent	*music*	musical	*music*	Neogene	*geog*
Mordred	*myth*	musical	*theatre*	neology	*lit*
morello	*fruit*	musimon	*animals*	Nephele	*myth*
morendo	*music*	muskhog	*animals*	Neptune	*astron*
mormaor	*govt*	muskrat	*animals*	Neptune	*myth*
morning	*time*	mustang	*animals*	Nerissa	*Shakesp*
Morocco	*Shakesp*	mustard	*food*	Nerthus	*myth*
morrion	*war*	mustard	*plants*	nervous	*medic*
Moselle	*drink*	mutular	*archit*	nestegg	*trade*
Moselle	*rivers*	Mycenae	*myth*	netball	*sport*
mouflon	*animals*	Myfanwy	*names*	netcord	*sport*
moulded	*art*	myology	*biol*	netgain	*trade*
moulder	*art*	myringa	*medic*	network	*biol*
moulder	*jobs*	mystery	*lit*	network	*film/TV*
mourner	*jobs*	mystery	*theatre*	network	*machine*
mourner	*relig*	mytilus	*fish*	neutral	*govt*
Mowbray	*Shakesp*	Nabokov	*writers*	neutral	*war*
mozetta	*clothes*	Nabucco	*titles*	neutron	*measure*
MrDarcy	*lit*	nacelle	*travel*	neutron	*physics*
MrRight	*people*	nailbed	*medic*	Neville	*names*
mudfish	*fish*	Nairobi	*cities*	newblue	*colour*
mudhook	*travel*	nandine	*animals*	Newbolt	*writers*
mudlark	*birds*	nankeen	*clothes*	newborn	*time*
mudlark	*jobs*	Nanking	*cities*	NewDeal	*govt*
mudpack	*clothes*	NanLing	*mounts*	NewLook	*clothes*
mudsill	*archit*	NanShan	*mounts*	newmoon	*astron*
mudwort	*plants*	Nariman	*myth*	newmown	*agric*
muezzin	*relig*	narrate	*lit*	newsboy	*jobs*
muffler	*clothes*	narrows	*marine*	newsman	*jobs*
muffler	*machine*	narthex	*archit*	newsman	*lit*
mullein	*flowers*	narthex	*relig*	newtown	*archit*
mullion	*archit*	narwhal	*animals*	NewWave	*theatre*
mummery	*theatre*	nascent	*biol*	newwine	*drink*
mummify	*relig*	Natalie	*names*	newword	*lit*
mundane	*geog*	Natasha	*names*	NewYear	*time*
munting	*archit*	nathist	*abbrev*	niblick	*sport*
muonium	*chem*	NATSOPA	*abbrev*	Nicanor	*Shakesp*
muraena	*fish*	natural	*music*	Nichols	*writers*
Murdoch	*names*	NatWest	*abbrev*	Nicolas	*names*
Murdoch	*writers*	navarch	*jobs*	Nielsen	*music*
muridae	*animals*	nebulae	*weather*	Niflhel	*myth*
Murillo	*artists*	necking	*archit*	nigella	*flowers*

niggard	*people*	
nightie	*clothes*	
nightly	*time*	
ninepin	*sport*	
Nineveh	*Bible*	
niobium	*chem*	
niobium	*mineral*	
Nirvana	*myth*	
Nisroch	*myth*	
nitrate	*chem*	
nitride	*chem*	
nitrite	*chem*	
Nkrumah	*leaders*	
No|drama	*theatre*	
no|entry	*travel*	
nombril	*herald*	
nominal	*lit*	
nonacid	*chem*	
non|obst	*abbrev*	
nonsuit	*law*	
nonuple	*maths*	
nookman	*lit*	
noonday	*time*	
Norfolk	*Shakesp*	
nosebag	*animals*	
nosegay	*flowers*	
nostril	*medic*	
nostrum	*medic*	
notepad	*lit*	
nothing	*maths*	
notions	*trade*	
no|trump	*sport*	
novella	*lit*	
nuclear	*physics*	
nucleon	*physics*	
nucleus	*physics*	
nuclide	*chem*	
null|set	*maths*	
numeral	*maths*	
numeric	*maths*	
nummary	*money*	
nummary	*trade*	
nunnery	*relig*	
nursery	*archit*	
nursery	*educ*	

nursery	*house*	
nurture	*food*	
nut|case	*people*	
Nyerere	*leaders*	
nymphet	*myth*	
Oakland	*cities*	
oak|leaf	*herald*	
oakling	*trees*	
oarfish	*fish*	
oarsman	*jobs*	
oarsman	*sport*	
oarsman	*travel*	
oatcake	*food*	
oatmeal	*cereal*	
Obadiah	*Bible*	
Obadiah	*names*	
obelisk	*archit*	
obelisk	*lit*	
obelisk	*relig*	
obesity	*medic*	
oblique	*maths*	
obovate	*biol*	
obovoid	*biol*	
obverse	*money*	
ocarina	*music*	
occiput	*medic*	
Oceania	*islands*	
oceanic	*marine*	
Oceanid	*myth*	
Oceanus	*myth*	
octagon	*maths*	
octapla	*lit*	
Octavia	*Shakesp*	
octette	*music*	
October	*time*	
octopod	*fish*	
octopus	*fish*	
octuple	*maths*	
oculist	*jobs*	
oculist	*medic*	
oddball	*people*	
oddment	*trade*	
odyssey	*travel*	
Oedipus	*myth*	
offbeat	*music*	

offence	*law*	
offence	*war*	
officer	*govt*	
officer	*jobs*	
offices	*archit*	
off|line	*comput*	
off|peak	*physics*	
offside	*sport*	
offside	*travel*	
off|tone	*art*	
ohmeter	*physics*	
oilbird	*birds*	
oil|lamp	*house*	
oil|silk	*clothes*	
oilskin	*clothes*	
Okinawa	*islands*	
old|blue	*colour*	
old|fogy	*people*	
old|girl	*educ*	
old|gold	*colour*	
old|joke	*lit*	
old|maid	*people*	
old|maid	*sport*	
Old|Nick	*myth*	
old|salt	*jobs*	
old|salt	*travel*	
olitory	*veg*	
olivine	*jewels*	
olivine	*mineral*	
Olympus	*myth*	
omentum	*medic*	
omnibus	*jobs*	
omnibus	*lit*	
omnibus	*travel*	
Omphale	*myth*	
on|board	*travel*	
one|step	*music*	
one|step	*sport*	
one|time	*time*	
ongoing	*travel*	
on|guard	*sport*	
on|guard	*war*	
on|offer	*trade*	
on|paper	*lit*	
on|stage	*theatre*	

on terms	*trade*	ossicle	*medic*	padlock	*machine*
on the go	*travel*	ossuary	*archit*	paenula	*clothes*
on trial	*law*	ossuary	*relig*	pageant	*govt*
on trust	*trade*	ostrich	*birds*	pageant	*herald*
opening	*trade*	Othello	*Shakesp*	pageant	*theatre*
opening	*travel*	Othello	*titles*	page boy	*clothes*
open war	*war*	otology	*medic*	page boy	*jobs*
operate	*medic*	Ottilie	*names*	painter	*animals*
Ophelia	*Shakesp*	ottoman	*house*	painter	*art*
Ophelia	*names*	Ouranos	*myth*	painter	*jobs*
ophidia	*insects*	outcast	*people*	painter	*travel*
opossum	*animals*	outline	*art*	paisley	*clothes*
oppidan	*educ*	outline	*lit*	pajamas	*clothes*
opulent	*trade*	outlook	*archit*	paladin	*war*
opuntia	*plants*	outpost	*war*	Palawan	*islands*
opuscle	*lit*	outride	*travel*	palazzo	*archit*
oratory	*relig*	outsize	*clothes*	Palermo	*cities*
oratrix	*jobs*	out tray	*trade*	paletot	*clothes*
orbital	*medic*	outwork	*archit*	palette	*art*
orbital	*travel*	outwork	*war*	palette	*machine*
orchard	*fruit*	ovaries	*medic*	palfrey	*animals*
orderly	*jobs*	overact	*theatre*	pallium	*clothes*
orderly	*medic*	overall	*clothes*	pallium	*relig*
ordinal	*maths*	overall	*house*	pallone	*sport*
oregano	*veg*	overarm	*sport*	palmcat	*animals*
Orestes	*myth*	overdue	*time*	palm nut	*fruit*
Oresund	*seas*	overlay	*machine*	palmyra	*trees*
organdy	*clothes*	over par	*sport*	panacea	*medic*
organic	*medic*	overrun	*lit*	panache	*clothes*
organum	*music*	oxalate	*chem*	pancake	*food*
organza	*clothes*	Oxfords	*clothes*	pandect	*educ*
Orinoco	*rivers*	oxidant	*chem*	pandect	*lit*
Orkneys	*islands*	oxidase	*biol*	Pandion	*myth*
Orlando	*Shakesp*	oxidase	*chem*	pandora	*music*
Orleans	*Shakesp*	oxonium	*chem*	Pandora	*myth*
Orpheus	*music*	oxyacid	*chem*	pandore	*music*
Orpheus	*myth*	oxytone	*lit*	pandura	*music*
orphrey	*clothes*	pabulum	*food*	panicle	*flowers*
Orthrus	*myth*	package	*trade*	pannier	*archit*
ortolan	*birds*	pack rat	*animals*	pannier	*clothes*
Osborne	*writers*	padding	*clothes*	panoply	*herald*
osmosis	*chem*	paddock	*agric*	panoply	*war*
osmunda	*plants*	paddock	*animals*	Panpipe	*music*
osseous	*medic*	paddock	*sport*	panther	*animals*
osseter	*fish*	padella	*house*	Panthus	*myth*

panties	*clothes*	passade	*sport*	peasant	*people*
pantile	*archit*	passado	*sport*	pea|soup	*weather*
papaver	*flowers*	passage	*archit*	peccary	*animals*
papilio	*insects*	passage	*lit*	peccavi	*foreign*
papilla	*medic*	passage	*medic*	Pechora	*rivers*
paprika	*food*	passage	*music*	peddlar	*trade*
papyrus	*educ*	passage	*travel*	pedicel	*biol*
papyrus	*lit*	passant	*herald*	pedicel	*flowers*
papyrus	*plants*	pas|seul	*music*	pedrero	*war*
papyrus	*relig*	pass|key	*house*	peerage	*govt*
parable	*lit*	passman	*educ*	peeress	*govt*
parable	*relig*	passman	*jobs*	Pegasus	*animals*
paracme	*biol*	pass|out	*medic*	Pegasus	*astron*
parados	*war*	pastern	*animals*	Pegasus	*myth*
paradox	*lit*	pastime	*sport*	pegtops	*clothes*
paragon	*lit*	pasture	*agric*	pelagic	*marine*
paragon	*people*	patella	*medic*	pelican	*birds*
parapet	*archit*	pathway	*travel*	pelisse	*clothes*
parapet	*war*	patient	*jobs*	Pelleas	*lit*
parasol	*clothes*	patient	*medic*	pellock	*fish*
paresis	*medic*	Patmore	*writers*	pelorus	*measure*
parfait	*food*	Patrick	*names*	penalty	*law*
parking	*travel*	patriot	*govt*	penalty	*sport*
parlour	*archit*	patriot	*people*	Penates	*myth*
parlour	*house*	patriot	*war*	pendant	*archit*
parlour	*trade*	patroon	*jobs*	pendant	*clothes*
Parnell	*leaders*	pattern	*art*	pendant	*herald*
parolee	*law*	pattern	*clothes*	pending	*time*
parotid	*medic*	pattern	*machine*	pending	*trade*
parquet	*archit*	Paulina	*Shakesp*	penguin	*birds*
parquet	*house*	Pauline	*names*	pen|name	*lit*
parsing	*lit*	Paul|Pry	*people*	pennant	*herald*
parsley	*veg*	payable	*trade*	pension	*archit*
parsnip	*veg*	pay|cash	*trade*	pension	*govt*
partial	*music*	payload	*travel*	pension	*trade*
parting	*herald*	payment	*trade*	pentode	*machine*
parting	*travel*	pay|rise	*trade*	pentose	*chem*
Partlet	*birds*	payroll	*trade*	peptide	*chem*
partlet	*clothes*	payslip	*trade*	percale	*clothes*
partner	*family*	Peachum	*lit*	per|cent	*maths*
partner	*jobs*	peacock	*birds*	Perdita	*Shakesp*
partner	*sport*	Peacock	*writers*	Perdita	*names*
parvenu	*people*	peafowl	*birds*	perfect	*lit*
parvenu	*trade*	pearler	*jobs*	perform	*film/TV*
Pasmore	*artists*	peasant	*jobs*	perform	*theatre*

perfume	*clothes*	physics	*physics*	pinball	*sport*
pergola	*archit*	piacere	*music*	pincers	*tools*
periapt	*relig*	pianist	*jobs*	pinched	*law*
peridot	*clothes*	pianist	*music*	pin|curl	*clothes*
peridot	*mineral*	pianola	*music*	pinetum	*trees*
perigee	*astron*	piastre	*money*	pinfall	*sport*
periwig	*clothes*	pibroch	*music*	pinguin	*birds*
perjury	*law*	picador	*jobs*	pinguin	*plants*
Perseus	*astron*	picador	*sport*	pin|high	*sport*
Perseus	*myth*	Picasso	*artists*	pinkeye	*medic*
Pervati	*myth*	piccolo	*music*	pinnace	*travel*
pesante	*music*	pickaxe	*tools*	pinnock	*birds*
pessary	*medic*	picquet	*sport*	pinocle	*sport*
pctasus	*clothes*	picture	*art*	pintado	*birds*
pet|bank	*trade*	picture	*house*	pintail	*birds*
petiole	*flowers*	piddock	*fish*	pinworm	*insects*
petrary	*war*	piebald	*animals*	pioneer	*jobs*
Petrina	*names*	pie|dish	*house*	pip|emma	*time*
petunia	*flowers*	pierced	*herald*	piragua	*travel*
pfennig	*money*	pierrot	*jobs*	piranha	*fish*
Phaedra	*myth*	Pierrot	*theatre*	pirogue	*travel*
phaeton	*travel*	pietism	*relig*	Pisanio	*Shakesp*
phalanx	*medic*	piffero	*music*	piscina	*relig*
phalanx	*war*	pig|boat	*travel*	piscine	*fish*
phantom	*myth*	pig|deer	*animals*	pismire	*insects*
Pharaoh	*Bible*	piggery	*agric*	pitcher	*house*
Pharaoh	*govt*	pig|iron	*mineral*	pitcher	*sport*
pharynx	*medic*	pigment	*art*	pith|hat	*clothes*
phasmid	*insects*	pigment	*biol*	pit|pony	*animals*
Phidias	*artists*	pigment	*medic*	pit|stop	*sport*
philtre	*drink*	pigskin	*clothes*	placebo	*medic*
philtre	*myth*	pigtail	*clothes*	plafond	*archit*
Phineus	*myth*	pikelet	*food*	planner	*jobs*
Phoebus	*myth*	pikeman	*war*	planter	*jobs*
Phoenix	*astron*	pilgrim	*jobs*	planter	*machine*
phoenix	*birds*	pilgrim	*relig*	plaster	*archit*
Phoenix	*cities*	pillage	*govt*	plaster	*art*
Phoenix	*myth*	pillbox	*clothes*	plaster	*medic*
phone|in	*film/TV*	pillbox	*medic*	plastid	*biol*
phoneme	*lit*	pillbox	*war*	platane	*trees*
Phorcys	*myth*	pill|bug	*insects*	platoon	*war*
Phrynia	*Shakesp*	pillion	*travel*	platter	*house*
Phryxus	*myth*	pillory	*law*	play|act	*theatre*
Phyllis	*lit*	pimento	*food*	playboy	*people*
Phyllis	*names*	pimento	*fruit*	playing	*theatre*

playlet	*lit*	pontiff	*jobs*	poultry	*food*
playlet	*theatre*	pontiff	*relig*	poundal	*measure*
playoff	*sport*	pontoon	*sport*	Poussin	*artists*
playpen	*house*	pontoon	*travel*	praetor	*govt*
pleader	*law*	PoohBah	*lit*	prairie	*agric*
pledget	*medic*	poorman	*jobs*	prairie	*geog*
Pleione	*myth*	poorman	*trade*	praline	*food*
plumage	*birds*	popcorn	*food*	prayers	*relig*
plumber	*jobs*	popidol	*jobs*	prebend	*relig*
plumcot	*fruit*	popidol	*theatre*	precede	*travel*
plunder	*govt*	popover	*food*	precept	*educ*
plunger	*trade*	popsong	*music*	precept	*govt*
Pluvius	*myth*	popstar	*film/TV*	preempt	*trade*
poacher	*govt*	popstar	*jobs*	preface	*lit*
poacher	*jobs*	popstar	*theatre*	prefect	*educ*
pochard	*birds*	porcine	*animals*	prefect	*govt*
podagra	*medic*	porkpie	*clothes*	prefect	*jobs*
podesta	*govt*	porkpie	*food*	prelate	*jobs*
poetess	*jobs*	portage	*trade*	prelate	*relig*
poetess	*lit*	portico	*archit*	prelims	*lit*
poetics	*lit*	portray	*art*	prelude	*music*
poetise	*lit*	portray	*film/TV*	Premier	*govt*
pointer	*animals*	portray	*lit*	premier	*jobs*
pointer	*educ*	portray	*theatre*	premium	*trade*
poisson	*food*	positon	*physics*	prepaid	*trade*
polacca	*travel*	postage	*travel*	prepupa	*insects*
polacre	*travel*	postboy	*jobs*	present	*film/TV*
Polaris	*astron*	postern	*archit*	present	*lit*
poleaxe	*war*	postman	*jobs*	present	*theatre*
polecat	*animals*	postman	*travel*	present	*time*
PolEcon	*abbrev*	postwar	*time*	presser	*jobs*
politic	*govt*	potable	*drink*	pressup	*sport*
pollack	*birds*	potherb	*veg*	pretzel	*food*
pollard	*trees*	pothole	*geog*	preview	*art*
pollman	*jobs*	potlids	*music*	preview	*theatre*
polltax	*trade*	Potomac	*rivers*	pricing	*trade*
poloist	*jobs*	potshot	*sport*	pricket	*animals*
poloist	*sport*	pottage	*food*	primary	*art*
polygon	*maths*	pottery	*art*	primary	*biol*
polypod	*animals*	pottery	*house*	primary	*educ*
pomfret	*fish*	pottery	*machine*	primary	*govt*
pompano	*fish*	poulard	*birds*	primate	*animals*
pomposo	*music*	Poulenc	*music*	primate	*biol*
ponceau	*archit*	poultry	*agric*	primate	*jobs*
poniard	*war*	poultry	*birds*	primate	*relig*

primula *flowers*	protein *food*	puttock *birds*
printed *lit*	protest *govt*	pyaemia *medic*
printer *jobs*	Proteus *Shakesp*	pyjamas *clothes*
printer *lit*	Proteus *myth*	Pylades *myth*
privado *jobs*	proverb *lit*	pylorus *medic*
private *jobs*	proverb *theatre*	pyralis *insects*
private *war*	provide *trade*	pyramid *archit*
probate *law*	proviso *govt*	pyramid *maths*
problem *educ*	Provost *Shakesp*	pyramid *medic*
problem *maths*	provost *jobs*	pyramid *relig*
proceed *travel*	provost *law*	pyramid *sport*
process *govt*	prowess *sport*	pyramid *trade*
Procris *myth*	prowler *jobs*	pyretic *medic*
proctor *educ*	prox|acc *abbrev*	pyrexia *medic*
proctor *geog*	proximo *time*	pyrites *mineral*
proctor *jobs*	pruning *flowers*	Pyrrhus *myth*
proctor *law*	pruning *trees*	pyx|veil *relig*
Procyon *astron*	Psalter *music*	quadrat *lit*
Procyon *myth*	Psalter *relig*	qualify *educ*
prodigy *people*	pterion *medic*	quantum *physics*
produce *film/TV*	publish *lit*	quarrel *war*
produce *theatre*	Publius *Shakesp*	quarter *geog*
produce *trade*	Puccini *music*	quarter *herald*
produce *veg*	pudding *food*	quarter *measure*
product *maths*	puddler *jobs*	quarter *sport*
profane *relig*	Pullman *travel*	quarter *time*
profile *art*	pull|out *travel*	quartet *music*
profile *geog*	pumpkin *veg*	quassia *medic*
profile *lit*	punctum *medic*	Queenie *names*
profits *trade*	punster *jobs*	Quentin *names*
progeny *family*	Purcell *music*	questor *law*
program *comput*	puritan *people*	quetzal *birds*
project *physics*	Puritan *relig*	quietus *geog*
promote *trade*	purlieu *archit*	Quilter *music*
pronoun *lit*	purloin *law*	quinary *maths*
proofer *jobs*	pursuer *jobs*	quinine *medic*
proofer *lit*	pursuit *trade*	quintal *measure*
prophet *jobs*	purview *govt*	quintet *music*
prophet *relig*	push|car *travel*	Quintus *Shakesp*
pro|rata *trade*	Pushkin *writers*	qui|vive *foreign*
prosaic *lit*	push|rod *machine*	quondam *time*
prosody *lit*	pustule *medic*	rabboni *relig*
prosper *trade*	putamen *fruit*	raccoon *animals*
protege *jobs*	putamen *medic*	rackets *sport*
protein *biol*	puttees *clothes*	Radames *lit*

radiant	geog	rathole	animals	red|tape	govt
radiant	maths	rations	food	red|wine	drink
radical	govt	ratline	travel	redwing	birds
radical	people	rat|race	jobs	redwood	trees
radical	physics	rattler	animals	re|enact	theatre
radicle	biol	ravelin	war	re|entry	travel
Raeburn	artists	ravioli	food	referee	govt
Raffles	lit	Raymond	names	referee	jobs
ragazza	foreign	reactor	machine	referee	sport
rag|doll	sport	reactor	physics	refrain	lit
ragtime	music	read|for	educ	refrain	music
ragweed	flowers	reading	educ	refugee	govt
ragwort	flowers	reagent	chem	refugee	jobs
railing	archit	realgar	mineral	refusal	trade
railman	jobs	realism	art	regalia	herald
railway	travel	reality	govt	regatta	sport
raiment	clothes	realize	trade	regency	govt
raiment	relig	realtor	jobs	regimen	govt
rainbow	weather	realtor	trade	regimen	medic
raingod	myth	reaping	agric	Reg|Prof	abbrev
raining	weather	rearing	agric	regrate	trade
Raleigh	war	Rebecca	names	regular	jobs
Ramadan	relig	Rebecca	titles	regular	war
Ramadan	time	Rebekah	Bible	Regulus	astron
rambler	flowers	rebound	sport	reissue	lit
ramekin	house	rebound	travel	reissue	trade
Rameses	relig	receipt	trade	relapse	medic
rampage	war	recital	music	releasc	lit
rampant	herald	recluse	people	release	trade
rampart	archit	recount	govt	relievo	art
rampart	war	recount	lit	religio	relig
rampick	trees	recruit	war	removal	medic
rampike	trees	rectory	relig	remover	jobs
rampion	flowers	red|army	war	rentier	jobs
rancher	agric	redbird	birds	reprint	lit
rancher	jobs	red|cent	money	reprise	music
Rangoon	cities	redcoat	war	rep|show	theatre
Raphael	artists	red|deer	animals	reptile	insects
Raphael	myth	redfish	fish	repulse	war
Raphael	names	redoubt	war	requiem	music
ratafia	food	red|pine	trees	requiem	relig
ratchet	machine	redpoll	animals	requite	trade
rat|flea	insects	red|root	plants	reredos	archit
Rathaus	archit	red|rose	flowers	reredos	relig
Rathlin	islands	redskin	jobs	rescuer	jobs

reserve	*jobs*	ringlet	*clothes*	roomman	*trade*
reserve	*sport*	ringoff	*travel*	rooster	*birds*
reserve	*trade*	RiotAct	*law*	rootage	*plants*
respond	*music*	ripcord	*sport*	ropetow	*travel*
retable	*relig*	ripcord	*travel*	ropeway	*travel*
retinue	*jobs*	ripeage	*time*	rorqual	*animals*
retiral	*trade*	ripieno	*music*	rosalia	*music*
retrace	*travel*	riposte	*sport*	Rosalie	*names*
retreat	*travel*	riposte	*war*	Rosario	*cities*
retreat	*war*	riptide	*marine*	Roscius	*theatre*
returns	*govt*	risotto	*food*	rosebay	*flowers*
returns	*trade*	rissole	*food*	rosebud	*flowers*
Reunion	*islands*	rivulet	*geog*	rosebug	*insects*
revenue	*trade*	roadhog	*travel*	rosehip	*fruit*
reverse	*money*	roadmap	*geog*	rosella	*birds*
reverse	*travel*	roadmap	*travel*	roselle	*flowers*
reverso	*lit*	roadtax	*travel*	rosette	*archit*
reviser	*lit*	Roanoke	*rivers*	rosette	*clothes*
reviver	*medic*	roaster	*house*	rosette	*sport*
rewrite	*lit*	robbery	*law*	Rossini	*music*
Reynard	*animals*	Roberta	*names*	RossSea	*seas*
Reynaud	*leaders*	rockcod	*fish*	rostrum	*archit*
rhenium	*chem*	rockers	*sport*	rostrum	*theatre*
rhenium	*mineral*	rockery	*flowers*	rotator	*tools*
rhizome	*plants*	Rockies	*mounts*	rotifer	*animals*
rhodium	*chem*	Rodolfo	*lit*	rotunda	*archit*
rhombic	*maths*	Rodrigo	*music*	roulade	*music*
rhombus	*maths*	roebuck	*animals*	rouleau	*trade*
rhubarb	*fruit*	roedeer	*animals*	roundel	*herald*
rhyming	*lit*	rollers	*trade*	roundel	*lit*
ribcage	*medic*	rolling	*travel*	Roussel	*music*
ribible	*music*	romance	*lit*	routine	*jobs*
Richard	*Shakesp*	romance	*music*	rowboat	*travel*
Richard	*names*	rompers	*clothes*	rowlock	*sport*
richman	*jobs*	Romulus	*myth*	rowlock	*travel*
richman	*trade*	rondeau	*lit*	royalet	*govt*
rickets	*medic*	rondeau	*music*	royalty	*govt*
rideout	*travel*	rondino	*music*	royalty	*trade*
riffler	*tools*	rontgen	*measure*	rubbers	*clothes*
rigging	*trade*	rontgen	*physics*	rubella	*medic*
rigging	*travel*	roofage	*archit*	rubeola	*medic*
Rigsdag	*govt*	roofing	*archit*	rubicon	*sport*
RigVeda	*myth*	rooftop	*archit*	rubyred	*colour*
Riksdag	*govt*	rookery	*birds*	ruddock	*birds*
Rimbaud	*writers*	roomlet	*archit*	ruddock	*fruit*

Rudolph	*names*	
Rudyard	*names*	
ruellia	*fruit*	
ruffian	*people*	
rug|gown	*clothes*	
rum|baba	*food*	
runaway	*people*	
run|away	*travel*	
run|down	*medic*	
run|into	*travel*	
runners	*travel*	
running	*sport*	
rupture	*medic*	
Russell	*leaders*	
Russell	*names*	
Russell	*writers*	
rustler	*agric*	
rustler	*jobs*	
Rutland	*Shakesp*	
Sabaoth	*war*	
sabaton	*war*	
Sabbath	*relig*	
Sabbath	*time*	
Sabrina	*names*	
saccule	*medic*	
sackbut	*music*	
sacking	*clothes*	
sacking	*govt*	
sacking	*trade*	
saddler	*jobs*	
sad|sack	*people*	
saffron	*colour*	
saffron	*flowers*	
sagaman	*jobs*	
sagaman	*lit*	
sagathy	*clothes*	
sage|hen	*birds*	
Sagitta	*astron*	
Sagitta	*myth*	
saguaro	*plants*	
sailing	*sport*	
sailing	*travel*	
saimiri	*animals*	
salable	*trade*	
Saladin	*war*	
Salamis	*islands*	
Salanio	*Shakesp*	
Salazar	*leaders*	
salband	*geog*	
salicet	*music*	
salient	*herald*	
salient	*war*	
Salieri	*lit*	
Salieri	*music*	
salsify	*fruit*	
salsify	*veg*	
saltant	*biol*	
saltant	*herald*	
saltier	*herald*	
Saltire	*herald*	
salt|pan	*geog*	
salt|tax	*trade*	
salvage	*trade*	
Salween	*rivers*	
sambuca	*music*	
samisen	*music*	
Sammael	*myth*	
samovar	*house*	
Samoyed	*animals*	
sampire	*plants*	
Sampson	*Shakesp*	
samurai	*govt*	
samurai	*jobs*	
samurai	*war*	
sanctum	*archit*	
sanctum	*house*	
sanctum	*relig*	
Sanctus	*music*	
sandals	*clothes*	
sandals	*relig*	
sandbag	*war*	
sandbar	*marine*	
sand|eel	*fish*	
sand|fly	*insects*	
sandman	*jobs*	
sandman	*myth*	
sand|pie	*sport*	
sand|pit	*sport*	
San|Jose	*cities*	
San|Juan	*cities*	
Santa|Fe	*cities*	
sapajou	*animals*	
sapling	*trees*	
Sapphic	*lit*	
Sapporo	*cities*	
sapwood	*trees*	
sarafan	*clothes*	
Saratov	*cities*	
sarcasm	*lit*	
sarcoma	*medic*	
sardine	*fish*	
sardine	*food*	
Sargent	*artists*	
Saroyan	*writers*	
Sassoon	*writers*	
satchel	*educ*	
satchel	*travel*	
saunter	*travel*	
saurian	*insects*	
sausage	*food*	
sautoir	*jewels*	
savanna	*agric*	
savanna	*geog*	
saveloy	*food*	
savings	*trade*	
saviour	*people*	
Saviour	*relig*	
Savitri	*myth*	
savoury	*food*	
sawbuck	*money*	
sawfish	*fish*	
sawmill	*machine*	
saxhorn	*music*	
saxtuba	*music*	
scabies	*medic*	
scaldic	*lit*	
scalene	*maths*	
scallop	*fish*	
scalpel	*medic*	
scalpel	*tools*	
scalper	*jobs*	
scamper	*travel*	
scanner	*biol*	
scanner	*machine*	
scapula	*medic*	

scarlet	colour	sea cock	fish	secular	time
Scarpia	lit	sea cook	jobs	sedilia	relig
sceatta	money	seadace	fish	seedbox	plants
scenery	theatre	seadove	birds	seedpod	flowers
scenist	art	seaduck	birds	seedpod	fruit
scenist	jobs	seafood	food	seedpod	veg
scenist	theatre	seagull	birds	segment	maths
sceptic	people	seahare	fish	seizure	medic
sceptic	relig	seahawk	birds	self bow	war
sceptre	govt	seakale	fruit	selling	trade
sceptre	herald	seakale	veg	sell out	trade
Scheldt	rivers	seaking	jobs	seltzer	food
scherzo	music	sealane	travel	seltzer	medic
Schloss	archit	sealark	birds	selvage	clothes
scholar	educ	sealegs	travel	seminar	educ
scholar	jobs	sealion	animals	seminar	jobs
scholia	lit	sealoch	marine	Semitic	relig
schools	educ	sealord	jobs	senator	govt
Schuman	music	seamaid	myth	senator	jobs
science	biol	seamist	marine	send off	travel
science	chem	seapike	fish	Senegal	rivers
science	physics	seapink	flowers	sensory	medic
scomber	fish	seareed	plants	septuor	music
scooter	sport	seasick	medic	sequoia	trees
scooter	travel	seasick	travel	Serapis	myth
scoring	music	seaslug	fish	seriema	birds
Scorpio	myth	seastar	fish	Serpens	astron
Scorpio	zodiac	seatang	plants	Serpens	myth
scourge	relig	Seattle	cities	serpent	insects
scraper	jobs	seawall	archit	serpent	music
scraper	tools	seaward	travel	serpent	myth
scratch	art	seaweed	plants	serpent	relig
scratch	medic	seawife	fish	servant	jobs
scratch	sport	seawolf	fish	service	house
Scrooge	people	seawolf	jobs	service	jobs
scruple	measure	seaworm	fish	service	music
sculpin	fish	sebacic	chem	service	relig
scupper	travel	seconal	medic	service	sport
scuttle	travel	seconds	trade	service	trade
seabass	fish	section	biol	service	trees
seabear	fish	section	geog	service	war
Seabees	war	section	lit	serving	house
seabird	birds	section	medic	session	relig
seablue	colour	section	war	sestina	lit
seacalf	fish	secular	relig	set sail	travel

settled	*geog*	shipway	*travel*	Simenon	*writers*
settler	*govt*	Shirley	*names*	Simpcox	*Shakesp*
settler	*jobs*	Shirley	*titles*	simurgh	*birds*
setwall	*flowers*	shocker	*lit*	sine die	*time*
seventh	*music*	shoebox	*drink*	singing	*music*
seven up	*sport*	shoot at	*war*	singles	*sport*
Seville	*cities*	shooter	*war*	singlet	*clothes*
sextans	*money*	shopman	*jobs*	singlet	*sport*
sextant	*maths*	shopman	*trade*	sinkage	*archit*
sextant	*measure*	shopper	*jobs*	sinking	*medic*
sextile	*astron*	shopper	*trade*	Siobhan	*names*
shackle	*law*	shore up	*archit*	Sirenes	*titles*
shackle	*machine*	shoring	*archit*	sirenia	*animals*
shad fly	*insects*	shortly	*time*	sirgang	*birds*
shading	*art*	shotgun	*war*	sirloin	*food*
Shaitan	*myth*	shot put	*sport*	sirocco	*weather*
shallop	*travel*	showery	*weather*	sistrum	*relig*
shallot	*veg*	showman	*jobs*	Sitwell	*writers*
Shallow	*Shakesp*	showman	*people*	sixfoil	*herald*
Shamash	*myth*	showman	*theatre*	sixfold	*measure*
Shammah	*relig*	show off	*people*	sizzler	*weather*
shampoo	*clothes*	show off	*theatre*	skating	*sport*
Shankar	*music*	shuffle	*sport*	skew put	*archit*
Shannon	*rivers*	shutter	*archit*	Skiddaw	*mounts*
sharper	*jobs*	shutter	*art*	skid lid	*sport*
shearer	*jobs*	shutter	*machine*	skid pan	*travel*
shebeen	*archit*	shuttle	*sport*	skid row	*archit*
she goat	*animals*	shuttle	*tools*	skiffle	*music*
shekels	*trade*	shuttle	*travel*	skilled	*trade*
Shelagh	*names*	Shylock	*Shakesp*	skillet	*house*
shellac	*biol*	shyster	*govt*	skimmer	*birds*
Shelley	*names*	shyster	*people*	skimmer	*clothes*
Shelley	*writers*	siamang	*animals*	skin man	*medic*
shelter	*archit*	sibling	*family*	skinner	*jobs*
shelves	*house*	sickbay	*medic*	skipper	*jobs*
sherbet	*drink*	sickbed	*medic*	skipper	*travel*
sheriff	*jobs*	Sickert	*artists*	skirret	*veg*
sheriff	*law*	sidecar	*travel*	sky blue	*colour*
Sherman	*war*	Sigmund	*myth*	skylark	*birds*
Shikoku	*islands*	Si Kiang	*rivers*	skyline	*geog*
shingle	*archit*	Silence	*Shakesp*	skysail	*travel*
shingle	*clothes*	Silenus	*myth*	slacker	*people*
shingle	*geog*	silicon	*chem*	slander	*law*
shingle	*marine*	silk hat	*clothes*	slating	*archit*
shippon	*animals*	Silvius	*Shakesp*	sleeper	*machine*

sleeper	*travel*	sorosis	*fruit*	spiraea	*flowers*
Slender	*Shakesp*	souffle	*food*	spireme	*chem*
slicker	*clothes*	sounder	*animals*	spirits	*chem*
slipway	*travel*	sounder	*animals*	spirits	*drink*
sloe|gin	*drink*	soupcon	*food*	spitoon	*medic*
smacker	*money*	soursop	*fruit*	spondee	*lit*
smash|up	*travel*	soutane	*clothes*	sponger	*people*
smelter	*machine*	soutane	*relig*	sponger	*trade*
smelter	*trade*	souther	*geog*	sponsor	*film/TV*
Smetana	*music*	Southey	*writers*	sponsor	*jobs*
snaffle	*sport*	soybean	*veg*	sporran	*clothes*
snooker	*sport*	spangle	*jewels*	spotter	*jobs*
snorkel	*sport*	spaniel	*animals*	spouter	*animals*
snow|bed	*geog*	spanker	*travel*	sprayer	*tools*
snow|cap	*geog*	spanner	*tools*	springs	*medic*
Snowdon	*mounts*	sparrer	*sport*	spritza	*drink*
soapbox	*govt*	sparrow	*birds*	sprouts	*veg*
soapbox	*theatre*	spartan	*jobs*	spurrey	*plants*
soccage	*law*	Spartan	*war*	Sputnik	*physics*
society	*sport*	sparthe	*war*	Sputnik	*travel*
sockeye	*fish*	spastic	*medic*	spy|hole	*house*
Socotra	*islands*	spatula	*art*	spy|ring	*govt*
soft|hat	*clothes*	spatula	*chem*	squails	*sport*
soft|toy	*sport*	spatula	*house*	squally	*weather*
soldier	*jobs*	spatula	*tools*	squared	*maths*
soldier	*war*	spawner	*fish*	squeeze	*trade*
solidus	*money*	Speaker	*govt*	stadium	*sport*
Solinus	*Shakesp*	speaker	*jobs*	stadium	*theatre*
soloist	*jobs*	speaker	*machine*	stagery	*theatre*
soloist	*music*	special	*lit*	staging	*theatre*
Solomon	*Bible*	spectre	*myth*	Stainer	*music*
Solomon	*names*	Spencer	*artists*	stamina	*sport*
solvent	*chem*	spencer	*clothes*	Stamitz	*music*
solvent	*trade*	Spencer	*names*	stammel	*clothes*
some|day	*time*	Spencer	*writers*	stammer	*medic*
sondeli	*animals*	Spender	*writers*	stamnos	*house*
song|hit	*music*	Spenser	*writers*	stand|by	*jobs*
Soochow	*cities*	spieler	*theatre*	stand|by	*theatre*
soother	*medic*	spignel	*plants*	stand|in	*theatre*
soprano	*jobs*	spinach	*veg*	staniel	*birds*
soprano	*music*	spindle	*machine*	Stanley	*Shakesp*
sorcery	*myth*	spinner	*jobs*	Stanley	*names*
sordino	*music*	spinner	*war*	stapler	*tools*
sorghum	*plants*	spinney	*trees*	stardom	*theatre*
sorites	*lit*	Spinoza	*writers*	starlet	*jobs*

starlet	*theatre*	St Kilda	*islands*	succory	*fruit*
starman	*jobs*	St Kitts	*islands*	succory	*veg*
starter	*jobs*	St Leger	*sport*	sucrose	*chem*
starter	*machine*	St Louis	*cities*	Sudeten	*mounts*
starter	*sport*	St Lucia	*islands*	Suffolk	*Shakesp*
starter	*travel*	stomach	*medic*	Sukkoth	*time*
startup	*travel*	stopped	*music*	sulphur	*chem*
statant	*herald*	stopway	*travel*	sulphur	*medic*
statice	*plants*	storage	*trade*	sulphur	*mineral*
station	*archit*	storied	*archit*	sultana	*fruit*
station	*geog*	storied	*lit*	sultana	*govt*
station	*govt*	straits	*marine*	Sulu Sea	*seas*
station	*jobs*	stratum	*geog*	Sumatra	*islands*
station	*travel*	Strauss	*music*	Sumbawa	*islands*
statist	*govt*	stretch	*geog*	summary	*lit*
statute	*law*	stretch	*law*	summons	*law*
steamer	*house*	stretch	*time*	sumpter	*animals*
steamer	*travel*	stretto	*music*	sunbath	*medic*
steeple	*archit*	striges	*birds*	sunbath	*sport*
steeple	*relig*	strigil	*insects*	sunbeam	*geog*
stellar	*astron*	striker	*sport*	sunbear	*animals*
stencil	*art*	striker	*trade*	sunbird	*birds*
stengun	*war*	strings	*music*	sundari	*trees*
Stephen	*Bible*	strophe	*lit*	sundial	*archit*
Stephen	*names*	strudel	*food*	sundial	*house*
stepson	*family*	stubble	*agric*	sundial	*time*
sterile	*medic*	student	*educ*	sundown	*geog*
sternum	*medic*	student	*jobs*	sundown	*time*
stetson	*clothes*	studier	*educ*	sunfish	*fish*
Stettin	*cities*	studies	*educ*	Sun King	*govt*
steward	*govt*	stumped	*sport*	sunlamp	*medic*
steward	*jobs*	sturnus	*birds*	sunrise	*time*
steward	*travel*	stutter	*medic*	sunspot	*astron*
Stewart	*names*	subacid	*chem*	sunsuit	*clothes*
stewpot	*house*	subaqua	*sport*	support	*govt*
stickup	*law*	subbase	*archit*	support	*theatre*
stimuli	*biol*	subject	*lit*	supremo	*govt*
stipend	*jobs*	subject	*music*	supremo	*jobs*
stipend	*relig*	sublime	*medic*	supremo	*war*
stipend	*trade*	subrosa	*flowers*	surbase	*archit*
stipple	*art*	subsidy	*trade*	surcoat	*clothes*
stipule	*plants*	subsoil	*agric*	surcoat	*herald*
stirrer	*machine*	subsoil	*geog*	surface	*geog*
stirrup	*medic*	suburbs	*geog*	surface	*travel*
stirrup	*sport*	subzero	*weather*	surgeon	*jobs*

surgeon	*medic*	
surplus	*trade*	
Surtees	*writers*	
surtout	*clothes*	
Surtsey	*islands*	
Susanna	*lit*	
Susanna	*names*	
suspect	*law*	
suspect	*people*	
Suzanne	*names*	
swaddle	*clothes*	
swagman	*jobs*	
swallow	*birds*	
swear|in	*govt*	
swear|in	*law*	
sweater	*clothes*	
sweeper	*house*	
sweeper	*machine*	
sweeper	*travel*	
sweltry	*weather*	
swifter	*travel*	
swindle	*law*	
swindle	*trade*	
swinger	*people*	
sworn|in	*govt*	
sworn|in	*law*	
sylphid	*myth*	
symptom	*medic*	
synapse	*biol*	
syncope	*medic*	
syncope	*music*	
synergy	*biol*	
synesis	*lit*	
synonym	*lit*	
syntone	*medic*	
syntony	*medic*	
syringa	*trees*	
syringe	*biol*	
syringe	*medic*	
syrphus	*insects*	
tabaret	*clothes*	
tabasco	*food*	
tableau	*art*	
tableau	*theatre*	
tabloid	*lit*	

taborer	*music*
taboret	*music*
tabular	*maths*
tachism	*art*
Tacitus	*writers*
tacking	*sport*
tackler	*travel*
tactics	*sport*
tactics	*war*
tactile	*medic*
tadpole	*animals*
Tadpole	*lit*
taenial	*medic*
taffeta	*clothes*
taffety	*clothes*
tagetes	*flowers*
tail|end	*travel*
tail|fin	*travel*
take|ill	*medic*
take|off	*sport*
take|off	*travel*
takings	*trade*
talipes	*medic*
tallage	*govt*
tallboy	*house*
tally|ho	*sport*
tamarin	*animals*
tambura	*music*
tampion	*medic*
tanager	*animals*
tangelo	*fruit*
tangent	*maths*
tangent	*music*
tanghin	*plants*
tangram	*sport*
tankard	*house*
tannery	*machine*
tantivy	*sport*
tant|pis	*foreign*
tapetum	*medic*
tapioca	*cereal*
taproot	*trees*
tapster	*jobs*
Taranto	*cities*
tarbush	*clothes*

tarnish	*chem*
tarsier	*animals*
tartane	*travel*
Tartini	*music*
tarweed	*plants*
Tatiana	*lit*
tatters	*clothes*
tatting	*clothes*
tattler	*birds*
taxable	*trade*
tax|free	*trade*
taxicab	*travel*
taxiing	*travel*
taxiway	*travel*
Taygete	*myth*
Tbilisi	*cities*
teacake	*food*
teacher	*educ*
teacher	*jobs*
teach|in	*educ*
tea|cosy	*house*
tea|gown	*clothes*
tea|leaf	*drink*
tear|bag	*medic*
tear|gas	*war*
tearoom	*house*
tea|rose	*flowers*
tea|tray	*house*
tea|tree	*trees*
teenage	*time*
Teheran	*cities*
Telamon	*archit*
Telamon	*myth*
Tel|Aviv	*cities*
televox	*machine*
telling	*lit*
telpher	*travel*
Telstar	*travel*
tempera	*art*
tempest	*weather*
Templar	*govt*
tenable	*war*
tenancy	*law*
tendril	*plants*
Tenedos	*islands*

tenfold	*measure*	
Tenniel	*artists*	
tenpins	*sport*	
tensile	*physics*	
tension	*physics*	
ten|spot	*money*	
tent|peg	*sport*	
tequila	*drink*	
terbium	*chem*	
terbium	*mineral*	
terebra	*machine*	
Terence	*names*	
Terence	*writers*	
termini	*travel*	
termite	*insects*	
ternary	*maths*	
ternion	*maths*	
terpene	*chem*	
terrace	*archit*	
terrain	*geog*	
terrier	*animals*	
terrier	*trade*	
tertian	*time*	
tessera	*art*	
testate	*law*	
test|hop	*travel*	
testify	*law*	
testoon	*money*	
testudo	*war*	
tetanus	*medic*	
textile	*clothes*	
textual	*lit*	
texture	*clothes*	
Thaumus	*myth*	
the|arts	*art*	
the|arts	*educ*	
theatre	*archit*	
theatre	*educ*	
theatre	*medic*	
theatre	*theatre*	
theatre	*war*	
the|blue	*weather*	
the|city	*trade*	
the|fray	*war*	
the|gods	*myth*	

the|gods	*theatre*	
the|line	*geog*	
themata	*lit*	
theNine	*lit*	
theNine	*music*	
The|Oaks	*sport*	
theorbo	*music*	
theorem	*maths*	
The|Oval	*sport*	
Theresa	*names*	
theriac	*medic*	
The|Ring	*titles*	
thermae	*medic*	
thermal	*chem*	
thermal	*geog*	
thermos	*house*	
Theseus	*Shakesp*	
Theseus	*myth*	
Thespis	*theatre*	
The|Wash	*seas*	
thicket	*trees*	
thimble	*house*	
thinker	*educ*	
thinker	*people*	
thinner	*art*	
this|day	*time*	
thistle	*plants*	
Thomson	*music*	
Thomson	*writers*	
Thoreau	*writers*	
thorium	*chem*	
thorium	*mineral*	
three|R's	*educ*	
throw|in	*sport*	
thulium	*chem*	
thulium	*mineral*	
thunder	*weather*	
Thurber	*writers*	
Thyreus	*Shakesp*	
thyroid	*medic*	
thyrsus	*flowers*	
ticking	*clothes*	
ticking	*house*	
tiddler	*fish*	
tideway	*geog*	

tidy|sum	*trade*	
tie|beam	*archit*	
tie|game	*sport*	
Tiepolo	*artists*	
tiercel	*birds*	
tiffany	*clothes*	
tigress	*animals*	
tilbury	*travel*	
tile|hat	*clothes*	
tile|red	*colour*	
tillage	*agric*	
tilling	*agric*	
tilting	*sport*	
timbrel	*music*	
time|lag	*time*	
time|was	*time*	
Timothy	*Bible*	
Timothy	*names*	
timothy	*plants*	
timpani	*music*	
tinamou	*birds*	
tinfoil	*chem*	
tin|mine	*mineral*	
tinting	*art*	
tintype	*art*	
Tippett	*music*	
tippler	*people*	
tipster	*jobs*	
tirasse	*music*	
Tirpitz	*war*	
Titania	*Shakesp*	
Titania	*astron*	
Titania	*myth*	
titlark	*birds*	
titling	*birds*	
titling	*fish*	
titrate	*chem*	
toaster	*house*	
toaster	*machine*	
tobacco	*plants*	
Toby|jug	*house*	
toccata	*music*	
toe|hold	*sport*	
toenail	*medic*	
toheroa	*fish*	

to|horse	travel	tourney	sport	trawler	travel
toisech	govt	towards	travel	treacle	food
Tolkien	writers	towboat	travel	treadle	machine
Tolstoy	writers	towpath	travel	treason	law
toluene	chem	towrope	travel	treat|of	lit
tombola	sport	toxemia	medic	treble|C	music
tonight	time	tracery	archit	tree|fox	animals
tonneau	measure	tracery	art	trefoil	archit
tonneau	travel	trachea	medic	trefoil	herald
tonsils	medic	tracing	art	trefoil	plants
tonsure	clothes	tracker	machine	trellis	archit
tonsure	relig	tracker	music	trellis	house
too|late	time	tractor	agric	tremolo	music
toolbox	tools	tractor	machine	trepang	fish
tooling	art	tractor	travel	Tressel	Shakesp
tool|kit	house	trade|in	trade	tribune	archit
too|soon	time	trading	trade	tribune	law
top|boot	clothes	traffic	trade	triceps	medic
topcoat	clothes	traffic	travel	trickle	geog
top|deck	travel	tragedy	film/TV	tricorn	clothes
top|hose	clothes	tragedy	lit	Trieste	cities
topical	geog	tragedy	theatre	trigger	machine
topknot	clothes	trailer	film/TV	trigger	war
topmast	travel	trailer	travel	trilogy	lit
top|note	music	trainee	educ	Trinity	relig
topsail	travel	trainee	jobs	trinket	clothes
topside	travel	trainer	jobs	triolet	lit
topsoil	geog	trainer	sport	trional	medic
torchon	clothes	traipse	travel	triplet	lit
tormina	medic	traitor	law	triplet	music
tornado	weather	traitor	people	tripody	lit
Toronto	cities	traitor	war	Tripoli	cities
torpedo	fish	tramcar	travel	tripoli	mineral
torpedo	war	tramway	travel	tripper	jobs
Torpids	sport	tranche	trade	tripper	travel
torrent	geog	transit	astron	trireme	travel
torsion	physics	transit	travel	triseme	lit
torsion	travel	transom	archit	Tristan	lit
torture	govt	transom	house	Tristan	myth
Toryism	govt	trapeze	maths	tritium	chem
tosspot	people	trapper	jobs	tritone	music
totient	maths	travail	medic	trochee	lit
touch|up	art	travels	travel	Troilus	Shakesp
tourist	jobs	Travers	Shakesp	Troilus	myth
tourist	travel	trawler	jobs	trolley	house

trolley	*machine*	twinjet	*travel*	uptonow	*time*
trolley	*travel*	twinkle	*time*	uranide	*chem*
trooper	*jobs*	twinset	*clothes*	uranium	*chem*
trooper	*war*	twinter	*animals*	uranium	*mineral*
tropics	*geog*	twister	*people*	urethra	*medic*
Trotsky	*leaders*	twitter	*birds*	urodele	*animals*
trotter	*animals*	twobits	*money*	Urswick	*Shakesp*
trouper	*jobs*	twofold	*measure*	Uruguay	*rivers*
trouper	*theatre*	twosome	*sport*	Ustinov	*writers*
Trudeau	*leaders*	twostep	*music*	usually	*time*
trueman	*people*	twostep	*sport*	utensil	*house*
truffle	*food*	twotwos	*time*	utensil	*machine*
truffle	*plants*	Tynwald	*law*	utility	*trade*
trumpet	*music*	typeset	*lit*	Utrecht	*cities*
trundle	*travel*	typhoid	*medic*	utricle	*medic*
trustee	*law*	typhoon	*weather*	Utrillo	*artists*
trustee	*trade*	Tyrrell	*Shakesp*	vacancy	*trade*
trypsin	*biol*	Uccello	*artists*	vaccine	*animals*
trysail	*travel*	ukelele	*music*	vaccine	*biol*
Tsangpo	*rivers*	ukulele	*music*	vaccine	*medic*
tsarina	*govt*	Ulysses	*Shakesp*	vagrant	*travel*
tuatara	*insects*	Ulysses	*myth*	valance	*house*
Tuesday	*time*	Ulysses	*titles*	valence	*chem*
tugboat	*travel*	umpteen	*measure*	valency	*chem*
tuition	*educ*	unction	*medic*	Valeria	*Shakesp*
tumbler	*birds*	unction	*relig*	Valerie	*names*
tumbler	*house*	undress	*clothes*	vampire	*animals*
tumbler	*jobs*	unguent	*medic*	vampire	*myth*
tumbler	*sport*	unguled	*herald*	VanDyck	*artists*
tumbler	*theatre*	unicorn	*animals*	Vanessa	*names*
tumbrel	*travel*	unicorn	*herald*	VanEyck	*artists*
tumbril	*travel*	unicorn	*myth*	VanGogh	*artists*
tumbril	*war*	uniform	*clothes*	vanilla	*food*
tumulus	*archit*	uniform	*govt*	vanilla	*plants*
tumulus	*relig*	uniform	*herald*	vantage	*sport*
tuneful	*music*	uniform	*war*	vapours	*medic*
tunicle	*clothes*	unitary	*maths*	variola	*medic*
tunicle	*relig*	unready	*time*	varlect	*abbrev*
turbine	*machine*	unsound	*medic*	varnish	*art*
turfman	*jobs*	uplands	*geog*	varnish	*house*
turning	*travel*	upright	*archit*	Varrius	*Shakesp*
turnkey	*law*	upright	*music*	varsity	*educ*
turnups	*clothes*	upright	*theatre*	vascula	*biol*
tussock	*plants*	upstage	*theatre*	Vatican	*govt*
tweeter	*machine*	upstart	*people*	Vatican	*relig*

Vaughan	*Shakesp*	villein	*govt*	Wallace	*writers*
Vaughan	*names*	Vincent	*names*	Walpole	*leaders*
vaulter	*sport*	vinegar	*chem*	Walpole	*writers*
veering	*weather*	vinegar	*food*	Walther	*lit*
vehicle	*theatre*	vintage	*drink*	wanigan	*travel*
vehicle	*travel*	vintage	*fruit*	warbler	*birds*
veiling	*clothes*	vintner	*jobs*	warbler	*music*
velours	*clothes*	violist	*music*	war|bond	*trade*
vending	*trade*	violone	*music*	war|club	*sport*
venison	*food*	virelay	*lit*	war|club	*war*
Ventose	*time*	virgate	*measure*	ward|off	*war*
venture	*trade*	virgule	*lit*	war|drum	*war*
veranda	*archit*	visa|vis	*travel*	warfare	*war*
verbena	*flowers*	viscera	*medic*	war|game	*sport*
verbose	*lit*	visitor	*jobs*	war|game	*war*
verb|sap	*abbrev*	visitor	*travel*	warhead	*war*
verdant	*flowers*	Vistula	*rivers*	warlike	*war*
verdant	*plants*	vitamin	*biol*	Warlock	*music*
verdict	*law*	vitamin	*food*	warlock	*myth*
verdure	*flowers*	vitamin	*medic*	warlord	*war*
verdure	*plants*	vitrail	*archit*	warm|air	*weather*
Vermeer	*artists*	vitriol	*chem*	warpath	*war*
vermeil	*herald*	Vivaldi	*music*	warrant	*law*
vernier	*measure*	vocable	*lit*	warrant	*trade*
vernier	*physics*	voiture	*travel*	warring	*war*
veronal	*medic*	volante	*travel*	warrior	*jobs*
verruca	*medic*	volcano	*geog*	warrior	*war*
versify	*lit*	Volpone	*titles*	warship	*travel*
vertigo	*medic*	voltage	*physics*	warship	*war*
vervain	*plants*	voucher	*trade*	war|song	*music*
vespers	*music*	voyager	*travel*	war|song	*war*
vespers	*relig*	Vulgate	*relig*	warthog	*animals*
vespoid	*insects*	vulpine	*animals*	Warwick	*Shakesp*
veteran	*jobs*	vulture	*birds*	washday	*house*
veteran	*war*	vulture	*people*	washout	*weather*
viaduct	*archit*	wage|war	*war*	washtub	*house*
viaduct	*travel*	wagoner	*agric*	wassail	*drink*
vibrato	*music*	wagtail	*birds*	wassail	*music*
viceroy	*govt*	Waikato	*rivers*	wastrel	*people*
viceroy	*jobs*	Waitaki	*rivers*	water|ox	*animals*
victory	*war*	walking	*sport*	Watteau	*artists*
vihuela	*music*	walkout	*trade*	wavelet	*marine*
village	*geog*	wallaby	*animals*	waxmoth	*insects*
villain	*govt*	Wallace	*names*	wax|tree	*trees*
villain	*people*	Wallace	*war*	waxwing	*birds*

waybill	*travel*	
wayfare	*travel*	
wayworn	*travel*	
wealthy	*trade*	
weapons	*war*	
weather	*weather*	
webbing	*clothes*	
web,foot	*birds*	
webster	*jobs*	
Webster	*writers*	
web,toed	*animals*	
webworm	*insects*	
weed,out	*flowers*	
weed,out	*veg*	
weekday	*time*	
weekend	*time*	
Weelkes	*music*	
welcher	*people*	
welcome	*travel*	
welding	*machine*	
welfare	*trade*	
wellies	*clothes*	
well,off	*trade*	
welsher	*people*	
welsher	*trade*	
Werther	*titles*	
West,end	*geog*	
western	*lit*	
wet,cell	*machine*	
whatnot	*house*	
whereon	*time*	
whipcat	*people*	
whipper	*jobs*	
whippet	*animals*	
whisker	*animals*	
whiskey	*drink*	
whistle	*music*	
whiting	*fish*	
whitlow	*medic*	
Whitman	*writers*	
whitsun	*time*	
widgeon	*birds*	
widower	*family*	
Wieland	*myth*	
wild,ass	*animals*	

wild,cat	*animals*
wildcat	*trade*
wild,oat	*cereal*
Wilfred	*names*
William	*Shakesp*
William	*names*
wind,bag	*people*
wind,god	*myth*
wind,gun	*war*
winding	*machine*
Windsor	*herald*
Windsor	*names*
wine,gum	*food*
Wingate	*war*
winging	*travel*
wing,nut	*machine*
wingtip	*travel*
Winston	*names*
wise,guy	*people*
wiseman	*jobs*
wistiti	*animals*
withers	*animals*
witless	*medic*
witness	*jobs*
witness	*law*
wolf,cub	*jobs*
wolf,dog	*animals*
Wolfram	*lit*
wolfram	*mineral*
wood,ant	*insects*
woodcut	*art*
woodman	*jobs*
wood,owl	*birds*
wood,rat	*animals*
woodsaw	*tools*
woolman	*jobs*
woomera	*war*
wordage	*lit*
workday	*trade*
workman	*jobs*
workout	*sport*
workshy	*people*
worktop	*house*
worldly	*geog*
worship	*relig*

worsted	*clothes*
wounded	*war*
Wozzeck	*lit*
Wozzeck	*titles*
wrecker	*people*
wrecker	*travel*
wren,tit	*birds*
wrestle	*sport*
wringer	*house*
wringer	*machine*
write,up	*lit*
writing	*educ*
writing	*lit*
written	*educ*
written	*lit*
wryneck	*birds*
wych,elm	*trees*
Wyndham	*names*
Yangtze	*rivers*
yard,ant	*insects*
yardarm	*travel*
yashmak	*clothes*
yatagan	*war*
Yenisei	*rivers*
yoghurt	*food*
Yolande	*names*
yolk,sac	*biol*
yomping	*war*
yttrium	*chem*
yttrium	*mineral*
Yule,log	*trees*
Zadkiel	*myth*
Zambezi	*rivers*
Zealand	*islands*
Zebedee	*Bible*
zedoary	*plants*
Zeeland	*islands*
zeolite	*mineral*
Zerlina	*lit*
ziganka	*music*
ziganka	*sport*
zillion	*measure*
zincite	*mineral*
zizania	*plants*
Zoffany	*artists*

zoology	*biol*	zootomy	*biol*	zymurgy	*chem*
zooming	*travel*	zymotic	*medic*		

8 LETTERS

aardvark	*animals*	acanthus	*plants*	Adam Zero	*titles*
aardwolf	*animals*	accentor	*birds*	addition	*maths*
aasvogel	*birds*	accident	*medic*	additive	*chem*
abamurus	*archit*	accolade	*govt*	Adelaide	*cities*
Abanazar	*lit*	accolade	*herald*	Adenauer	*leaders*
abat jour	*archit*	accredit	*trade*	adenoids	*medic*
abattoir	*animals*	accuracy	*maths*	adherent	*jobs*
abat voix	*archit*	accusant	*law*	adhesion	*biol*
abbatoir	*archit*	aceldama	*war*	adhesion	*medic*
abdicate	*govt*	Achelous	*myth*	adhesive	*biol*
abductor	*jobs*	Achernar	*astron*	adjutant	*birds*
abductor	*law*	Achernar	*myth*	adjutant	*jobs*
Abednego	*Bible*	Achilles	*Shakesp*	Adonijah	*Bible*
Aberdeen	*cities*	Achilles	*myth*	Adrastus	*myth*
Aberdeen	*leaders*	acid bath	*chem*	Adriatic	*seas*
Abhorson	*Shakesp*	acid drop	*food*	Adrienne	*names*
Abinadab	*Bible*	acid kiln	*art*	ad summum	*foreign*
ablative	*lit*	acidosis	*medic*	adultery	*law*
abnormal	*medic*	acid salt	*chem*	advocate	*jobs*
abortion	*medic*	acid test	*chem*	advocate	*law*
above par	*trade*	Acrisius	*myth*	aegrotat	*educ*
abrasion	*medic*	acrolith	*archit*	Aegyptus	*myth*
abrogate	*govt*	acromion	*medic*	Aemilius	*Shakesp*
abruptly	*time*	acrostic	*lit*	aerobics	*sport*
absentee	*people*	actinism	*chem*	aerodyne	*travel*
absinthe	*drink*	actinium	*chem*	aerofoil	*travel*
absorber	*machine*	actinoid	*chem*	aerogram	*travel*
abstract	*art*	activate	*chem*	aerolite	*astron*
abstract	*lit*	activate	*war*	aerology	*physics*
Absyrtus	*myth*	activism	*govt*	aeronaut	*jobs*
Abu Dhabi	*islands*	activity	*chem*	aeronaut	*travel*
abutilon	*plants*	actuator	*machine*	aerostat	*physics*
abutment	*archit*	Adam Bede	*lit*	aerostat	*travel*
academic	*educ*	Adam Bede	*titles*	aesculus	*fruit*
acanthus	*archit*	Adam s ale	*drink*	aesthete	*art*

aesthete	*people*	air,to,air	*war*	a|long|day	*time*
aetheist	*relig*	airwoman	*travel*	alopecia	*medic*
affluent	*geog*	Akeldama	*Bible*	Aloysius	*names*
affluent	*trade*	Akeldama	*relig*	alphabet	*lit*
after|tax	*trade*	Akimiski	*islands*	alpha|ray	*physics*
agacerie	*foreign*	a|la|carte	*food*	alta|moda	*foreign*
Aganippe	*myth*	alarmist	*people*	alter|ego	*people*
agar|agar	*chem*	Alasdair	*names*	altitude	*geog*
agar|agar	*medic*	Alastair	*names*	altitude	*travel*
agiotage	*trade*	albacore	*birds*	alto|clef	*music*
agitator	*people*	Alberich	*lit*	alto|horn	*music*
agitprop	*educ*	albinism	*medic*	alto|viol	*music*
agnostic	*people*	Albinoni	*music*	altruist	*people*
agnostic	*relig*	alburnum	*trees*	amadavat	*birds*
Agnus|Dei	*music*	alcahest	*chem*	amandine	*chem*
agraphia	*medic*	alcatras	*birds*	amaranth	*flowers*
Agricola	*war*	Alcatraz	*islands*	ambivert	*jobs*
agronomy	*agric*	Alcestis	*titles*	ambrosia	*food*
agronomy	*trade*	aldehyde	*chem*	ambrosia	*myth*
Aidoneus	*myth*	alderman	*jobs*	Ameinias	*myth*
aigrette	*birds*	Alderney	*islands*	amethyst	*jewels*
aigrette	*clothes*	algorism	*maths*	amethyst	*mineral*
aigrette	*jewels*	alienate	*govt*	Amfortas	*lit*
ailantus	*trees*	alienist	*jobs*	amitosis	*biol*
air|borne	*travel*	aliquant	*maths*	ammo|dump	*war*
air|brake	*machine*	alkahest	*chem*	ammonium	*chem*
air|brake	*travel*	alkaline	*chem*	Amonasro	*lit*
air|coach	*travel*	all|at|sea	*travel*	Amorites	*Bible*
aircraft	*travel*	all|clear	*war*	amortize	*law*
air|drain	*archit*	allegory	*lit*	amortize	*trade*
air|drill	*tools*	allergic	*medic*	amputate	*medic*
Airedale	*animals*	alleyway	*travel*	Amritsar	*cities*
airfield	*travel*	all|fours	*sport*	Amu|Darya	*rivers*
air|force	*war*	alliance	*govt*	amygdule	*mineral*
airframe	*travel*	alliance	*war*	Anabasis	*titles*
airliner	*travel*	allopath	*jobs*	anabasis	*war*
air|motor	*machine*	allopath	*medic*	anabatic	*geog*
air|rifle	*war*	allspice	*food*	anaconda	*insects*
air|route	*travel*	allspice	*trees*	anaglyph	*art*
airscape	*art*	allusion	*lit*	analecta	*lit*
air|scout	*travel*	alluvial	*geog*	analects	*lit*
airscrew	*travel*	alluvion	*geog*	analogue	*chem*
airspace	*travel*	alluvium	*geog*	analogue	*lit*
air|speed	*travel*	Almagest	*astron*	analogue	*maths*
airstrip	*travel*	Almighty	*relig*	analyser	*chem*

analysis *chem*	antihero *lit*	Apuleius *writers*
analysis *lit*	antihero *people*	aqualung *sport*
analysis *medic*	Antilles *islands*	aquarium *biol*
analytic *chem*	Antilope *animals*	Aquarius *myth*
anapaest *lit*	antimask *theatre*	Aquarius *zodiac*
anaphora *lit*	antimine *war*	aquatics *sport*
anathema *relig*	antimony *chem*	aquatint *art*
anatomic *medic*	antimony *mineral*	aqueduct *archit*
ancestor *family*	antinode *physics*	aquiline *birds*
ancestor *herald*	antiphon *music*	Arabella *names*
Anchises *lit*	antipope *people*	Arabella *titles*
Anchises *myth*	antipope *relig*	arachnid *insects*
anchoret *jobs*	antpipit *birds*	arapunga *birds*
Andersen *writers*	aperient *medic*	arbalest *war*
Andropov *leaders*	aperitif *drink*	arboreal *trees*
anecdote *lit*	aperture *archit*	arcature *archit*
angelica *food*	aphelion *astron*	archaism *lit*
angelica *plants*	aphorism *lit*	archduke *govt*
Angelico *artists*	apiacere *music*	archives *archit*
Angeline *names*	apodosis *lit*	archives *lit*
Anglesey *islands*	Apollyon *lit*	archlute *music*
Anglican *relig*	Apollyon *myth*	Arcturus *astron*
angstrom *measure*	apologia *lit*	Arcturus *myth*
angstrom *physics*	apologue *lit*	areacode *travel*
anguilla *fish*	apophyge *archit*	Argestes *myth*
Anguilla *islands*	apoplexy *medic*	argonaut *animals*
animalia *animals*	apostate *people*	Argonaut *myth*
anisette *drink*	aposteme *medic*	argonite *mineral*
annalist *lit*	Apostles *relig*	argument *govt*
annotate *lit*	apothegm *lit*	argument *maths*
anoderay *physics*	Appelles *Bible*	Arimaspi *myth*
anserine *birds*	appendix *lit*	Arkansas *rivers*
anserous *birds*	appendix *medic*	armagnac *drink*
anteater *animals*	appetite *food*	armament *machine*
antedate *time*	appetite *medic*	armament *war*
antelope *animals*	applause *theatre*	armature *machine*
antennae *insects*	applepie *food*	armature *physics*
antepast *food*	applepip *fruit*	armature *war*
anteroom *archit*	applique *clothes*	armchair *house*
anteroom *food*	appraise *trade*	armguard *sport*
anthesis *flowers*	approach *sport*	armorial *herald*
antibody *medic*	approach *travel*	armorist *jobs*
antidote *medic*	apresski *sport*	armoured *war*
Antigone *myth*	apterous *birds*	armourer *jobs*
Antigone *titles*	apterous *insects*	armsrace *war*

army⎮worm	insects	asteroid	astron	autology	biol
arpeggio	music	Asterope	myth	automate	trade
arquebus	war	asthenia	medic	autonomy	govt
arranger	jobs	Astraeus	myth	autotype	art
arranger	music	astragal	archit	autotype	lit
arrogate	govt	Astyanax	myth	autotypy	art
arsenate	chem	Astyoche	myth	autumnal	geog
arsenide	chem	Atalanta	myth	autunite	mineral
art⎮autre	art	at⎮anchor	travel	Auvergne	Shakesp
art⎮class	art	at⎮a⎮price	trade	aux⎮armes	foreign
artcraft	art	atheling	govt	AveMaria	music
artefact	archit	Atlantes	archit	AveMaria	relig
artefact	art	Atlantic	seas	aventail	war
arterial	travel	Atlantis	myth	averment	govt
arteries	medic	atmology	physics	aviation	travel
articled	law	atom⎮bomb	war	aviatrix	travel
articles	law	atomizer	house	avicular	insects
artifact	art	atomizer	physics	avifauna	birds
artiness	art	atropine	medic	Avogadro	physics
artistic	art	attacker	jobs	away⎮game	sport
artistry	art	attacker	war	axemaker	jobs
art⎮of⎮war	war	Atticism	lit	Baalpeor	myth
art⎮paper	art	attorney	jobs	babouche	clothes
arum⎮lily	flowers	attorney	law	baby⎮blue	colour
asbestos	chem	Auckland	cities	baccarat	sport
asbestos	mineral	audience	film/TV	bacchant	myth
Ascot⎮tie	clothes	audience	theatre	bachelor	family
ash⎮blond	colour	audit⎮ale	drink	bacillus	medic
Ashkelon	Bible	auditing	trade	backache	medic
ash⎮plant	trees	audition	theatre	backbone	medic
Asian⎮flu	medic	Aufidius	Shakesp	backdoor	archit
Asmodeus	myth	au⎮gratin	foreign	backdoor	house
asphodel	plants	Augsburg	cities	backdrop	theatre
asphyxia	medic	Augustus	leaders	backfire	travel
aspirant	govt	Augustus	names	backhand	sport
assassin	govt	aularian	archit	backheel	sport
assassin	jobs	aularian	educ	backlash	law
assay⎮ton	measure	Aurelian	war	backlash	machine
Assembly	govt	au⎮revoir	foreign	back⎮seat	travel
assessor	govt	auricula	flowers	backspin	sport
assessor	jobs	autacoid	medic	backstay	travel
as⎮soon⎮as	time	autarchy	govt	backwash	travel
assuager	medic	autobahn	travel	bacteria	medic
astatine	chem	autocarp	fruit	bactrian	animals
asterisk	lit	autogyro	travel	bad⎮fairy	myth

badlyoff	*trade*	Baptista	*Shakesp*
badmoney	*trade*	Barabbas	*Bible*
bagmaker	*jobs*	barathea	*clothes*
bagpiper	*music*	Barbados	*islands*
bagpipes	*music*	barbecue	*food*
baguette	*archit*	barbecue	*house*
bailball	*sport*	barberry	*trees*
bakedegg	*food*	barbette	*war*
Bakelite	*chem*	barbican	*archit*
baldness	*medic*	barbican	*war*
baldpate	*birds*	barbital	*medic*
balkline	*sport*	Barbizon	*art*
ballader	*lit*	Bardolph	*Shakesp*
ballcock	*house*	bargeman	*jobs*
balletic	*theatre*	bargeman	*travel*
ballgame	*sport*	baritone	*jobs*
ballista	*machine*	baritone	*music*
ballista	*war*	Barnabas	*Bible*
balloter	*govt*	Barnabas	*names*
ballroom	*house*	barnacle	*birds*
ballyhoo	*trade*	barnacle	*travel*
Balmoral	*clothes*	baronage	*govt*
baluster	*archit*	baroness	*govt*
banality	*lit*	barouche	*travel*
bandelet	*archit*	barracks	*war*
banderol	*archit*	barstool	*house*
banderol	*war*	bartisan	*archit*
bandfish	*fish*	bartisan	*war*
bandsman	*music*	barytone	*music*
banister	*archit*	basanite	*mineral*
banister	*house*	baseball	*sport*
banjoist	*jobs*	baseclef	*music*
banjoist	*music*	basecoin	*money*
bankbook	*trade*	basecoin	*trade*
bankloan	*trade*	baselard	*war*
banknote	*trade*	baseline	*archit*
bankroll	*trade*	baseline	*sport*
bankrupt	*govt*	basement	*archit*
bankrupt	*jobs*	basement	*house*
bankrupt	*trade*	basenote	*music*
banksman	*jobs*	baseviol	*music*
banlieue	*foreign*	basicdye	*art*
banneret	*herald*	basicity	*chem*
bannerol	*archit*	basicpay	*trade*
banterer	*people*	basidium	*biol*
		basilica	*archit*
		basilica	*relig*
		basilisk	*insects*
		basquine	*clothes*
		Bassanio	*Shakesp*
		bassdrum	*music*
		basshorn	*music*
		bassinet	*house*
		bassoboe	*music*
		basswood	*trees*
		bastardy	*law*
		Bastille	*govt*
		bathcube	*clothes*
		bathcube	*house*
		bathrobe	*clothes*
		bathroom	*archit*
		bathsoap	*house*
		battalia	*war*
		battling	*war*
		beadroll	*relig*
		beadsman	*jobs*
		beadsman	*relig*
		beagling	*sport*
		beamends	*travel*
		beamtree	*trees*
		beararms	*war*
		bearings	*geog*
		bearings	*herald*
		bearings	*machine*
		bearings	*travel*
		bearpool	*trade*
		bearraid	*trade*
		bear'sear	*flowers*
		bearskin	*clothes*
		beatdown	*trade*
		Beatrice	*Shakesp*
		Beatrice	*names*
		beattime	*music*
		Beaufort	*Shakesp*
		Beaufort	*weather*
		Beaumont	*writers*
		becalmed	*marine*
		becalmed	*travel*
		bedcover	*house*
		bedesman	*jobs*

bedesman	*relig*	
bedlinen	*house*	
bedmaker	*jobs*	
bedsocks	*clothes*	
bedstead	*house*	
bedstraw	*plants*	
beechnut	*fruit*	
beeeater	*birds*	
beefwood	*trees*	
Beerbohm	*writers*	
beetroot	*fruit*	
beetroot	*veg*	
beginner	*educ*	
beginner	*jobs*	
beginner	*people*	
Behemoth	*Bible*	
Belarius	*Shakesp*	
belcanto	*foreign*	
Belgrade	*cities*	
believer	*relig*	
Belitung	*islands*	
bellbird	*birds*	
bellpull	*house*	
belltent	*archit*	
Belmonte	*lit*	
belowpar	*trade*	
Benedick	*Shakesp*	
Benedict	*music*	
Benedict	*names*	
benefice	*jobs*	
Benjamin	*Bible*	
Benjamin	*music*	
Benjamin	*names*	
BenNevis	*mounts*	
Benvolio	*Shakesp*	
benzoate	*chem*	
berceuse	*music*	
bergamot	*fruit*	
berghaan	*birds*	
beriberi	*medic*	
Berkeley	*Shakesp*	
Berkeley	*music*	
Berkeley	*writers*	
Bernardo	*Shakesp*	
Bertrand	*names*	

besieger	*war*
bestroom	*archit*
betarays	*physics*
betatron	*physics*
betelnut	*food*
betelnut	*fruit*
Bethesda	*Bible*
Betjeman	*writers*
betrayer	*people*
betrayer	*war*
bevatron	*physics*
Beveland	*islands*
beverage	*drink*
Beverley	*names*
biannual	*time*
biathlon	*sport*
bicamera	*govt*
bicuspid	*medic*
biennial	*flowers*
biennial	*time*
bifocals	*medic*
bigamist	*jobs*
bignoise	*people*
bignonia	*plants*
bigscene	*theatre*
bilander	*travel*
bilberry	*fruit*
bileduct	*medic*
billhook	*tools*
billycan	*house*
bindweed	*plants*
binnacle	*travel*
binomial	*maths*
bioblast	*biol*
biochemy	*chem*
biometer	*biol*
biophore	*biol*
bioscope	*film/TV*
birdbath	*birds*
birdbath	*house*
birdcage	*birds*
birdcall	*birds*
bird'segg	*birds*
bird'seye	*flowers*
birretta	*clothes*

birthday	*time*
Bismarck	*leaders*
bistable	*comput*
bistoury	*medic*
bivalent	*chem*
biweekly	*lit*
biweekly	*time*
blackant	*insects*
blackart	*myth*
blackbox	*travel*
blackcap	*birds*
blackcap	*law*
blackcat	*animals*
blackeye	*medic*
blackfly	*insects*
blackfox	*animals*
blackice	*weather*
blackleg	*jobs*
blackleg	*trade*
blackout	*medic*
blackrat	*animals*
BlackRod	*govt*
BlackSea	*seas*
blacktie	*clothes*
blastema	*biol*
blauwbok	*animals*
blazoner	*herald*
blazonry	*herald*
bleeding	*medic*
blessing	*relig*
blessyou	*relig*
blighter	*people*
blindeye	*medic*
blinding	*archit*
blindman	*jobs*
blinkers	*animals*
blizzard	*weather*
blockade	*war*
blockage	*medic*
blocking	*sport*
bloodred	*colour*
bloomers	*clothes*
bloomery	*machine*
blowhole	*animals*
blowover	*weather*

blowpipe	machine	bondmaid	relig	boutique	trade
blowpipe	war	bondsman	jobs	boutrime	lit
bludgeon	war	bonecave	geog	bowmaker	jobs
blueback	fish	bonefish	fish	bowsprit	travel
bluebell	flowers	bongrace	clothes	boxmaker	jobs
bluebill	birds	boniface	jobs	boyscout	jobs
bluebird	birds	bonspiel	sport	bracelet	jewels
bluebuck	animals	bookcase	house	brachial	medic
bluechip	trade	bookcase	lit	brackets	lit
bluefish	fish	bookclub	lit	brackets	maths
bluehare	animals	bookends	house	brackets	sport
bluemoon	time	bookends	lit	Bradford	cities
bluenose	people	booklice	insects	Bradshaw	travel
blueweed	plants	booklore	educ	braggart	people
bluewing	birds	bookmark	lit	braiding	clothes
boardlot	trade	bookrack	lit	brakeman	jobs
boardman	jobs	bookread	lit	brancard	animals
boardman	trade	bookrest	lit	brancard	travel
boatbill	birds	bookroom	lit	Brancusi	artists
boatdeck	travel	bookshop	lit	Brangane	lit
boathook	travel	bookworm	educ	Brangwyn	artists
boatline	travel	bookworm	insects	Brasilia	cities
boatneck	clothes	bookworm	lit	brassard	herald
boatrace	sport	boomtown	geog	brasshat	clothes
boatsong	music	boomtown	trade	brasshat	govt
boattail	birds	boondock	geog	brassica	veg
bobbinet	clothes	bootlace	clothes	brattice	archit
bobolink	birds	Borachio	Shakesp	brattice	war
bobwhite	birds	Bordeaux	cities	breakage	trade
bodyblow	sport	Bordeaux	drink	breakout	medic
bodycell	biol	borecole	veg	breeches	clothes
bodysuit	clothes	borehole	geog	breeding	agric
bodywork	travel	BornFree	titles	brethren	relig
boggrass	plants	Bornholm	islands	breviary	relig
Bohemian	jobs	borrower	jobs	Brezhnev	leaders
Bohemian	people	borrower	trade	Briareus	myth
boldface	lit	Bosporus	seas	brickbat	war
boldhand	lit	bosshead	machine	Brisbane	cities
bollworm	insects	botanist	jobs	brisling	fish
boltrope	travel	bouffant	clothes	broachto	travel
bombrack	war	bouffons	music	broadaxe	war
bombsite	war	Boughton	music	Broadway	theatre
bonafide	foreign	bouillon	drink	brocatel	clothes
BonarLaw	leaders	boundary	geog	broccoli	veg
bondager	trade	boundary	sport	brochure	lit

brochure	*trade*	burglary	*law*	calendar	*time*
bromelia	*fruit*	Burgoyne	*war*	Caligula	*leaders*
brookite	*mineral*	Burgundy	*Shakesp*	calipers	*measure*
brooklet	*geog*	Burgundy	*colour*	calipers	*tools*
brougham	*travel*	Burgundy	*drink*	callgirl	*jobs*
Browning	*war*	burinist	*art*	Calliope	*lit*
Browning	*writers*	burletta	*theatre*	Calliope	*muses*
brownowl	*birds*	bushbaby	*animals*	Calliope	*music*
brownrat	*animals*	bushbuck	*animals*	Calliope	*myth*
Bruckner	*music*	bushwren	*birds*	Callisto	*myth*
Brueghel	*artists*	business	*jobs*	calotype	*art*
Brumaire	*time*	business	*theatre*	calyptra	*clothes*
brunette	*colour*	business	*trade*	Cambrian	*geog*
brunette	*jobs*	bustline	*clothes*	camellia	*flowers*
Brussels	*cities*	busybody	*people*	camisole	*clothes*
Buchanan	*USpres*	buttress	*archit*	camomile	*flowers*
buckbean	*plants*	buttress	*war*	camomile	*veg*
buckshot	*war*	buyingin	*trade*	campaign	*govt*
buckskin	*clothes*	buzzbomb	*war*	campaign	*trade*
Budapest	*cities*	buzzword	*lit*	campaign	*war*
Buddhist	*relig*	caatinga	*trees*	Campbell	*writers*
buddleia	*flowers*	Cabeirus	*myth*	Campeius	*Shakesp*
building	*archit*	cabinboy	*jobs*	campfire	*sport*
Bulawayo	*cities*	cabinboy	*travel*	Campinas	*cities*
Bulganin	*leaders*	cablecar	*travel*	campsite	*sport*
bulkhead	*archit*	cableway	*travel*	camshaft	*machine*
bulkhead	*travel*	cachalot	*animals*	camshaft	*travel*
Bullcalf	*Shakesp*	cachelot	*animals*	canaigre	*plants*
bullcalf	*animals*	cachepot	*house*	Canaries	*islands*
bulletin	*lit*	cacology	*lit*	Canberra	*cities*
bulletin	*medic*	caduceus	*herald*	canephor	*archit*
bullfrog	*animals*	caduceus	*myth*	Canicula	*astron*
bullhead	*fish*	Caesarea	*Bible*	Canidius	*Shakesp*
bullpool	*trade*	caffeine	*medic*	canister	*house*
bullraid	*trade*	Cagliari	*cities*	cannabis	*medic*
bullring	*sport*	Caiaphas	*Bible*	cannibal	*animals*
bull'seye	*archit*	cakewalk	*sport*	cannonry	*war*
bull'seye	*food*	calabash	*fruit*	canoeing	*sport*
bull'seye	*sport*	calamary	*fish*	canoness	*jobs*
bullyoff	*sport*	calamite	*trees*	canonics	*relig*
bulwarks	*travel*	calciole	*geog*	canonize	*relig*
bummaree	*jobs*	calculus	*maths*	canonlaw	*law*
bungalow	*archit*	Calcutta	*cities*	canthook	*tools*
burberry	*clothes*	calendar	*law*	canticle	*music*
Burghley	*leaders*	calendar	*lit*	canticle	*relig*

canticum	*music*	
cantoned	*archit*	
cantoned	*herald*	
cantoris	*music*	
canzonet	*music*	
Capareus	*myth*	
capeline	*clothes*	
Capetown	*cities*	
capparis	*fruit*	
caprifig	*fruit*	
capsicum	*veg*	
capstone	*archit*	
capuchin	*animals*	
capuchin	*clothes*	
capuchin	*relig*	
Capucius	*Shakesp*	
capybara	*animals*	
caracara	*birds*	
caracole	*archit*	
caracole	*travel*	
carapace	*animals*	
carapace	*fish*	
carbonyl	*chem*	
carcajou	*animals*	
carcanet	*jewels*	
cardamom	*plants*	
card|game	*sport*	
cardigan	*clothes*	
Cardigan	*war*	
cardinal	*birds*	
cardinal	*jobs*	
cardinal	*maths*	
cardinal	*relig*	
carditis	*medic*	
cargoose	*birds*	
cariacou	*animals*	
carillon	*music*	
Carlisle	*Shakesp*	
Carlotta	*names*	
carnauba	*trees*	
Carnaval	*titles*	
carnival	*sport*	
carnival	*theatre*	
Carnival	*titles*	
Carolina	*names*	

Caroline	*names*
carotene	*biol*
carousel	*sport*
carouser	*people*
car|rally	*sport*
carriage	*trade*
carriage	*travel*
carucate	*measure*
caryatid	*archit*
casemate	*war*
casement	*archit*
casement	*house*
caseworm	*insects*
cashbook	*trade*
cash|down	*trade*
cashmere	*clothes*
cash|sale	*trade*
cassette	*physics*
Castalia	*myth*
castaway	*jobs*
cast|away	*travel*
cast|iron	*mineral*
castling	*sport*
castrate	*animals*
casualty	*medic*
catacomb	*archit*
catacomb	*geog*
catalyse	*chem*
catalyst	*chem*
catapult	*sport*
catapult	*travel*
catapult	*war*
cataract	*geog*
cataract	*medic*
catchfly	*flowers*
catching	*medic*
catheter	*medic*
cathexis	*medic*
Cathleen	*names*
catholic	*relig*
Catriona	*names*
Catriona	*titles*
cat's|eyes	*travel*
cat's|foot	*plants*
cat's|tail	*plants*

cat|stick	*sport*
Catullus	*writers*
Caucasus	*mounts*
caudillo	*govt*
cauldron	*house*
caulicle	*plants*
causerie	*lit*
causeway	*geog*
causeway	*travel*
cavalier	*war*
cavatina	*music*
cave|bear	*animals*
cavicorn	*animals*
Celanese	*clothes*
celeriac	*veg*
cell|wall	*biol*
cemetery	*relig*
cenobite	*people*
cenotaph	*relig*
centaury	*plants*
centiare	*measure*
centrode	*maths*
centroid	*maths*
centuple	*maths*
cephalic	*medic*
Cephalus	*myth*
Cepheids	*astron*
ceramics	*art*
ceramist	*jobs*
cerastes	*insects*
ceratops	*animals*
Cerberus	*animals*
Cerberus	*myth*
cerebral	*medic*
ceremony	*govt*
ceremony	*relig*
cerulean	*marine*
cervical	*medic*
cetacean	*animals*
Cevennes	*mounts*
Chabrier	*music*
chaconne	*music*
chaffron	*war*
chainsaw	*tools*
chair|bed	*house*

chair‚leg	*house*	chess|set	*sport*	chromism	*art*
chairman	*govt*	chestnut	*animals*	chromite	*mineral*
chairman	*jobs*	chestnut	*colour*	chromium	*chem*
chambers	*govt*	chestnut	*fruit*	chromium	*mineral*
chambers	*jobs*	chestnut	*lit*	Chrysaor	*myth*
chamfron	*herald*	chestnut	*trees*	chthonic	*myth*
chamfron	*war*	cheverel	*clothes*	churinga	*jewels*
champion	*govt*	cheveron	*herald*	cicatrix	*medic*
champion	*jobs*	Cheviots	*mounts*	cicerone	*jobs*
champion	*sport*	Cheyenne	*rivers*	cicisbeo	*jobs*
champion	*war*	chez|nous	*archit*	ciclaton	*clothes*
chancery	*law*	chiasmus	*lit*	cigar|box	*house*
chandler	*jobs*	chick|pea	*veg*	Cimarosa	*music*
chantage	*law*	children	*family*	Cimmerii	*myth*
chanting	*music*	chimaera	*animals*	cinchona	*trees*
chapatti	*food*	chimaera	*myth*	cincture	*archit*
chapbook	*lit*	chinampa	*flowers*	cincture	*clothes*
chaperon	*clothes*	China|tea	*drink*	cincture	*relig*
chaperon	*jobs*	Chindwin	*rivers*	Cinerama	*film/TV*
chapiter	*archit*	chin|hold	*sport*	cingulum	*clothes*
chaplain	*jobs*	chipmuck	*animals*	cinnabar	*mineral*
chaplain	*relig*	chipmunk	*animals*	cinnamon	*food*
chaptrel	*archit*	chip|shot	*sport*	cinnamon	*trees*
charades	*sport*	Chirripo	*mounts*	cinqfoil	*herald*
charcoal	*art*	chivalry	*war*	Circinus	*astron*
charcoal	*chem*	chlorate	*chem*	circular	*lit*
Charites	*myth*	chloride	*chem*	circular	*trade*
charlock	*plants*	chlorine	*chem*	ciselure	*art*
Charlton	*names*	chlorite	*chem*	citation	*govt*
Charmian	*Shakesp*	chlorite	*mineral*	citrange	*fruit*
Charmian	*names*	choirboy	*jobs*	city|desk	*lit*
chartism	*govt*	choirboy	*music*	city|room	*lit*
chasseur	*war*	choirboy	*relig*	civet|cat	*animals*
chasuble	*clothes*	choirman	*music*	civilian	*govt*
chasuble	*relig*	choleric	*medic*	civilian	*jobs*
chat|show	*film/TV*	choliamb	*lit*	civil|law	*law*
Chausson	*music*	chop|suey	*food*	civil|war	*war*
checkers	*sport*	choragus	*music*	Claggart	*lit*
chemical	*chem*	Chorazin	*Bible*	claimant	*jobs*
chemurgy	*chem*	choregus	*music*	claimant	*law*
chenille	*clothes*	chowchow	*animals*	clambake	*food*
chequers	*sport*	chow|mein	*food*	clansman	*jobs*
cherubim	*myth*	chrismal	*relig*	clappers	*music*
cherubim	*relig*	Christie	*writers*	clapping	*theatre*
chessman	*sport*	chromate	*chem*	claqueur	*theatre*

Clarence *Shakesp*	clubfoot *medic*	collagen *chem*
Clarence *names*	clubmoss *plants*	collapse *medic*
clarence *travel*	clubrush *plants*	collegno *music*
Claribel *names*	Clymenus *myth*	Collette *names*
clarinet *music*	coachbox *travel*	colliery *machine*
Clarissa *names*	coachdog *animals*	Colonsay *islands*
classics *lit*	coaching *educ*	colophon *lit*
classman *educ*	coachman *travel*	Colorado *rivers*
classman *jobs*	coachway *travel*	colorama *art*
Claudius *Shakesp*	coalfish *fish*	colossus *archit*
Claudius *names*	coalmine *geog*	colossus *myth*
clavicle *medic*	coasting *sport*	Columbia *rivers*
clawback *govt*	coasting *travel*	Columbus *cities*
claymore *war*	coauthor *jobs*	comatose *medic*
clayware *art*	coauthor *lit*	comedian *film/TV*
clearday *weather*	cobalite *chem*	comedian *jobs*
clearing *trees*	cocculus *plants*	comedian *theatre*
clearsky *weather*	cockatoo *birds*	Cominius *Shakesp*
clearway *travel*	Cockayne *myth*	commando *jobs*
cleavage *geog*	cockboat *travel*	commando *war*
cleavers *plants*	cockerel *birds*	commands *trade*
clematis *flowers*	cockeyed *medic*	commerce *trade*
Clemence *names*	cocktail *drink*	commoner *educ*
Clementi *music*	cocoanut *fruit*	commoner *jobs*
clerihew *lit*	cocopalm *fruit*	commuter *travel*
clerkess *jobs*	cocotree *trees*	compiler *jobs*
cleveite *chem*	cocowood *trees*	compiler *lit*
clientry *trade*	coenzyme *biol*	compline *relig*
Clifford *Shakesp*	cogwheel *machine*	composer *jobs*
Clifford *names*	cohesion *biol*	composer *lit*
climatic *weather*	cohesion *chem*	composer *music*
climbing *sport*	coiffure *clothes*	compound *chem*
clinical *medic*	colander *house*	compress *medic*
clippers *agric*	coldcash *trade*	computer *comput*
clippers *tools*	coldfeet *war*	computer *machine*
clithral *archit*	coldmeat *food*	conamore *music*
cloister *archit*	coldsnap *weather*	concerto *music*
cloister *relig*	coldsore *medic*	conchate *biol*
Clorinda *lit*	coldwave *clothes*	conclave *govt*
closeout *trade*	coldwave *weather*	conclave *relig*
clothcap *clothes*	coldweld *machine*	Concorde *travel*
clothier *jobs*	coldwind *weather*	concrete *archit*
clothing *clothes*	coleslaw *veg*	conferva *plants*
cloudcap *weather*	colewort *veg*	confined *medic*
clowning *theatre*	coliseum *theatre*	confines *geog*

conflict	war	corridor	archit	Cranford	titles
confuoco	foreign	corridor	geog	crapgame	sport
congoeel	fish	corridor	house	crawfish	fish
congress	govt	corridor	travel	crayfish	fish
Congreve	writers	corselet	clothes	creamjug	house
conjurer	jobs	corselet	herald	creation	art
conjurer	theatre	corselet	war	Creation	relig
conserve	food	corundum	mineral	creative	lit
consomme	drink	corvette	travel	creature	animals
constant	maths	coryphee	jobs	credence	relig
constant	physics	coryphee	theatre	credenda	relig
construe	lit	Corythus	myth	creditor	jobs
consumer	trade	cosecant	maths	creditor	trade
contango	trade	Cosgrave	leaders	creditto	trade
contempt	law	cosmetic	clothes	creepers	clothes
contents	lit	costmary	plants	crescent	herald
continuo	music	costumer	theatre	crescent	travel
contract	law	Cotopaxi	mounts	Cressida	Shakesp
contract	medic	cottabus	sport	Cressida	names
contract	sport	cottager	jobs	Cretheus	myth
contract	trade	couchant	herald	cretonne	clothes
controls	machine	coulisse	theatre	crevasse	geog
convener	jobs	counters	sport	crewneck	clothes
converge	travel	countess	govt	cribbage	sport
converts	trade	counting	trade	criminal	law
conveyor	machine	Couperin	music	criminal	people
Coolidge	USpres	coupling	machine	critical	medic
Coppelia	titles	courante	music	critique	lit
copperas	chem	coursing	sport	crockery	house
copybook	educ	courtier	jobs	Crockett	war
copybook	lit	covenant	relig	cromlech	relig
copydesk	lit	Coventry	cities	cromorna	music
copyhold	law	coverlet	house	cromorne	music
coqauvin	food	cowberry	fruit	Cromwell	Shakesp
CoralSea	seas	cowgrass	plants	Cromwell	leaders
Cordelia	Shakesp	cowhouse	animals	Cromwell	war
Cordelia	names	cowplant	plants	crooning	music
corduroy	clothes	cowwheat	plants	cropping	agric
corktree	trees	coxswain	jobs	crossbar	sport
cornflag	flowers	coxswain	sport	crossbat	sport
Cornwall	Shakesp	coxswain	travel	crossbit	tools
coronach	music	crabbing	travel	crossbow	war
coronary	medic	crackpot	people	crossbun	food
corporal	jobs	cramming	educ	crossing	travel
corporal	relig	cranefly	insects	crosslet	herald

Crossman	leaders	cuspidor	house	Dardanus	myth
crossply	travel	customer	trade	dark|blue	colour
cross|tie	archit	cut|glass	house	dark|blue	sport
crotchet	music	cut|grass	plants	darkling	geog
croupier	jobs	Cuthbert	names	darkling	time
croutons	food	cut|price	trade	darkness	geog
crown|law	law	cutpurse	jobs	darkroom	archit
crucible	chem	cuttings	lit	darkroom	art
crucible	machine	cyanogen	chem	Dartmoor	mounts
crucifer	veg	cyanosis	medic	data|bank	comput
crucifix	jewels	Cyclades	islands	database	comput
crucifix	relig	cyclamen	flowers	date|line	geog
cruising	sport	cyclonic	weather	date|line	time
cruising	travel	Cyclopes	myth	date|palm	trees
Crusader	relig	cyclosis	biol	date|plum	fruit
crush|hat	clothes	cylinder	machine	date|roll	food
crutches	medic	cylinder	maths	date|tree	trees
cruzeiro	money	cylinder	music	daughter	family
cry|havoc	war	cylinder	travel	Davy|lamp	machine
cryolite	mineral	cylinder	war	daybreak	time
cube|root	maths	cymatium	archit	day|dress	clothes
cubiform	maths	cynanche	medic	Day|Lewis	writers
cucumber	veg	Cynosura	myth	daylight	time
cucurbit	chem	Cynosure	astron	day|shift	trade
cul|de|sac	archit	cytology	biol	dead|ball	sport
cul|de|sac	travel	dabchick	birds	dead|duck	birds
culottes	clothes	dactylic	lit	dead|hand	govt
cultural	educ	Daedalus	myth	dead|head	jobs
cultured	educ	daffodil	flowers	dead|heat	sport
culverin	war	dahabeah	travel	deadline	time
cum|laude	foreign	daiquiri	drink	deadlock	sport
cupboard	archit	dairy|cow	animals	dead|shot	sport
cupboard	house	dairyman	jobs	dead|wall	archit
cup|final	sport	dalmatic	clothes	deadwood	trees
cupmaker	jobs	dalmatic	relig	deal|fish	fish
curassow	birds	dal|segno	music	dealings	trade
curative	medic	Damascus	Bible	deathbed	medic
curb|roof	archit	Damascus	cities	death|cap	plants
curculio	insects	Danaides	myth	death|cup	plants
Curiatii	myth	dancetty	herald	debility	medic
Curitiba	cities	dandruff	medic	decagram	measure
curlicue	art	danegeld	govt	decanter	house
currency	trade	Danielle	names	deceiver	people
curricle	travel	danseuse	jobs	December	time
cursitor	law	danseuse	theatre	decigram	measure

decimate	*maths*	deponent	*law*	dibstone	*mineral*
deck|hand	*jobs*	Derby|day	*time*	dicentra	*plants*
deck|hand	*travel*	Derby|dog	*animals*	dictator	*govt*
decrepit	*medic*	Dercetas	*Shakesp*	dictator	*jobs*
deedpoll	*law*	derelict	*people*	didactic	*educ*
deer|park	*animals*	derelict	*travel*	didapper	*birds*
defector	*people*	describe	*lit*	didrachm	*money*
defender	*law*	deserter	*jobs*	dies|irae	*foreign*
defender	*war*	deserter	*war*	diet|cook	*jobs*
defrayal	*trade*	designer	*art*	digestif	*medic*
de|Gaulle	*leaders*	designer	*jobs*	diggings	*archit*
Deiphyle	*myth*	despatch	*lit*	diggings	*mineral*
dejeuner	*food*	Despoina	*myth*	dihedral	*maths*
De|laMare	*writers*	destrier	*war*	dillseed	*veg*
Delaware	*rivers*	detached	*archit*	dilution	*chem*
delegate	*govt*	detainee	*jobs*	diluvium	*geog*
delegate	*jobs*	detainee	*law*	dinosaur	*animals*
delicacy	*food*	detector	*machine*	diocesan	*jobs*
delicate	*medic*	detector	*physics*	Diomedes	*Shakesp*
delictum	*law*	detritus	*geog*	Diomedes	*myth*
delirium	*medic*	Deus|vult	*foreign*	Dionysus	*myth*
delivery	*medic*	deuteron	*physics*	Dionysus	*theatre*
delivery	*sport*	de|Valera	*leaders*	Dioscuri	*myth*
delta|ray	*physics*	devaloka	*myth*	diplegia	*medic*
delubrum	*relig*	devil|god	*myth*	diplogen	*chem*
dcmagogy	*govt*	dewberry	*fruit*	diplomat	*govt*
demarche	*foreign*	dew|point	*physics*	diplomat	*jobs*
Demavend	*mounts*	dew|point	*weather*	dipstick	*machine*
demersal	*biol*	dextrose	*chem*	dipstick	*travel*
demijohn	*drink*	diabetes	*medic*	directly	*time*
demi|lion	*herald*	diadochi	*govt*	director	*film/TV*
demilune	*war*	diagnose	*medic*	director	*jobs*
demister	*machine*	diagonal	*maths*	director	*theatre*
demitint	*art*	dialogue	*theatre*	director	*trade*
demiurge	*myth*	dialysis	*chem*	dirty|dog	*people*
demi|wolf	*animals*	dialytic	*chem*	disabled	*medic*
Democrat	*govt*	diamante	*jewels*	disburse	*trade*
demonism	*myth*	diameter	*maths*	disciple	*educ*
demurrer	*law*	diamonds	*sport*	disciple	*jobs*
denarius	*money*	dianthus	*flowers*	disciple	*relig*
dendrite	*chem*	diapason	*music*	discount	*trade*
dendrite	*mineral*	diapente	*music*	diseased	*medic*
dendroid	*trees*	diastase	*biol*	disgorge	*medic*
dentures	*medic*	diatomic	*biol*	disguise	*clothes*
depicter	*art*	diatonic	*music*	disguise	*theatre*

dismount	travel	dogwatch	time	downpipe	archit
disorder	medic	dog|wheat	plants	downpour	weather
dispatch	lit	Dohnanyi	music	downtown	geog
dispense	medic	doh,rayme	music	doxology	music
disposal	trade	doldrums	marine	doxology	relig
Disraeli	leaders	doldrums	weather	dragoman	jobs
Disraeli	writers	dolerite	mineral	dragoman	travel
distance	measure	dolomite	mineral	dragonet	fish
distrain	law	doloroso	music	dragster	sport
distrait	foreign	domestic	jobs	dragster	travel
distress	law	domicile	archit	drag|wire	travel
district	geog	domicile	law	drainage	agric
ditty|bag	travel	dominant	music	drainage	geog
diuretic	medic	Dominica	islands	dramatic	lit
divalent	chem	Dominica	names	dramatic	theatre
dividend	trade	dominion	geog	Drambuie	drink
dividers	maths	dominion	govt	draughts	sport
dividers	measure	dominoes	sport	draw|lots	sport
dividers	tools	Don|Pedro	Shakesp	dream|god	myth
divinity	relig	don't,know	govt	dressage	sport
division	educ	doomsday	time	dressing	food
division	govt	doorbell	house	dressing	medic
division	maths	doorhead	archit	dress,tie	clothes
division	war	door|jamb	archit	dried|egg	food
divorcee	family	doorknob	house	driftway	travel
Dniester	rivers	doorpost	archit	drilling	clothes
dobchick	birds	doorpost	house	dripping	food
Doberman	animals	doorsill	archit	driptray	house
docimasy	chem	doorstep	house	drive|off	travel
dock|leaf	plants	doorstop	house	driveway	archit
doctrine	govt	Dordogne	rivers	driveway	travel
doctrine	relig	dormouse	animals	Dr|Jekyll	lit
document	lit	Dorothea	names	drop|curl	clothes
Dogberry	Shakesp	Dortmund	cities	drop|dead	medic
dogberry	fruit	dosology	medic	drop|goal	sport
dog|daisy	flowers	dotterel	birds	drop|kick	sport
doggerel	ltt	doubling	sport	drop|shot	sport
dog|grass	plants	doubloon	money	dropwort	plants
doggy|bag	food	doughboy	war	druggist	jobs
dog|house	animals	doughnut	food	druggist	medic
do|gooder	people	dovecote	birds	druidess	relig
dog|pound	animals	dove|grey	colour	drumbeat	music
dogsbody	jobs	downbeat	music	drum|call	war
dog's|life	animals	downhaul	travel	drumfire	war
dog|tired	medic	down|left	theatre	drumhead	medic

drumhead	music	dynamite	war	eight|oar	travel
drumhead	war	eagle|owl	birds	El|Dorado	myth
drumskin	music	eagle|ray	fish	election	govt
drunkard	people	ear|muffs	clothes	elective	educ
Drusilla	names	earnings	trade	electron	measure
Dr|Watson	lit	earphone	machine	electron	physics
dry|goods	trade	earshell	fish	elegiast	jobs
dry|nurse	educ	earth|god	myth	elegiast	lit
dry|paint	art	earth|hog	animals	elements	weather
dry|plate	art	earthnut	fruit	elephant	animals
dry|quart	measure	easterly	geog	elevator	agric
Dubonnet	drink	Eastmain	rivers	elevator	machine
duckbill	animals	east|wind	weather	elevator	travel
duck|hawk	birds	eau|de|nil	colour	elf|child	myth
duckling	birds	ebenezer	archit	elflocks	clothes
duckling	food	Ebenezer	Bible	elkhound	animals
duck|mole	birds	Ebenezer	names	ellipsis	lit
duck|pond	birds	eclectic	art	embalmer	jobs
duckweed	plants	ecliptic	astron	embattle	war
ductless	medic	ecraseur	medic	embezzle	govt
duellist	war	ectogeny	biol	embezzle	trade
duettino	music	edentate	animals	emblazon	art
duettist	jobs	edgebone	medic	embolism	medic
duettist	music	edge|tool	tools	embolism	relig
Duisburg	cities	Edmonton	cities	embracer	law
dulciana	music	educable	educ	emeritus	educ
dulcimer	music	educated	educ	emeritus	jobs
dumb|bell	sport	educator	educ	emigrant	jobs
dumb|show	theatre	educator	jobs	emigrant	travel
dumpling	food	eel|grass	plants	emigrate	travel
dunce|cap	clothes	effluent	biol	emissary	jobs
duodenum	medic	effluent	geog	Emmanuel	relig
duologue	theatre	egg|apple	veg	Emmental	food
duration	time	egg|fruit	veg	emphasis	music
dustbowl	geog	eggplant	plants	employee	jobs
dust|cart	travel	eggplant	veg	employee	trade
dust|coat	clothes	eggshell	art	employer	trade
Dutch|cap	clothes	eggshell	food	emporium	trade
Dutch|hoe	tools	eggslice	house	empty|set	maths
dwelling	archit	eggspoon	house	empyrean	astron
dyestuff	art	egg|timer	house	emulsion	art
dyestuff	chem	egg|timer	time	emulsion	chem
dyestuff	colour	eggwhisk	house	emulsion	house
dynamics	maths	egg|white	food	emulsion	medic
dynamite	machine	Eg|lamour	Shakesp	enallage	lit

enceinte	*medic*	
enchased	*art*	
endocarp	*fruit*	
endpaper	*lit*	
endrhyme	*lit*	
enduring	*time*	
Endymion	*titles*	
enfilade	*war*	
engineer	*jobs*	
engramma	*medic*	
engraved	*art*	
engraver	*art*	
engraver	*jobs*	
enlarger	*art*	
enlistee	*war*	
ensemble	*clothes*	
ensemble	*music*	
ensilage	*agric*	
entellus	*animals*	
enthalpy	*physics*	
entozoon	*biol*	
entr'acte	*music*	
entr'acte	*theatre*	
entr'acte	*time*	
entrails	*animals*	
entrails	*medic*	
entrance	*archit*	
entrance	*theatre*	
entrance	*travel*	
entrench	*war*	
entrepot	*trade*	
entresol	*archit*	
envelope	*travel*	
envelope	*war*	
Eolithic	*geog*	
epanodos	*lit*	
ephemera	*insects*	
epiblast	*biol*	
epicalyx	*flowers*	
Epicaste	*myth*	
epicpoet	*jobs*	
epicpoet	*lit*	
epidemic	*medic*	
epifocal	*geog*	
epigraph	*lit*	
epilepsy	*medic*	
epilogue	*lit*	
epilogue	*theatre*	
Epiphany	*relig*	
Epiphany	*time*	
epiploon	*medic*	
Epistles	*relig*	
epistyle	*archit*	
epitasis	*lit*	
epitasis	*theatre*	
epopoeia	*lit*	
epsomite	*mineral*	
equation	*chem*	
equation	*physics*	
equipage	*travel*	
erection	*archit*	
Eridanus	*myth*	
Erinnyes	*myth*	
Eriphyle	*myth*	
Erodanus	*astron*	
errantry	*war*	
eruption	*geog*	
eruption	*medic*	
Erytheia	*myth*	
erythema	*medic*	
escalade	*war*	
escalope	*food*	
escargot	*food*	
escarole	*veg*	
espalier	*archit*	
essayist	*jobs*	
essayist	*lit*	
estancia	*archit*	
estimate	*trade*	
etcetera	*foreign*	
Eteocles	*myth*	
eternity	*time*	
ethylene	*chem*	
etiology	*medic*	
Etoncrop	*clothes*	
Etonsuit	*clothes*	
eugenics	*biol*	
eulogist	*jobs*	
eulogium	*lit*	
Euphemia	*names*	
euphuism	*lit*	
Eurayale	*myth*	
europium	*chem*	
europium	*mineral*	
Europort	*travel*	
Eurydice	*myth*	
eutectic	*physics*	
euxenite	*mineral*	
evacuate	*travel*	
evaluate	*trade*	
evection	*astron*	
evenkeel	*sport*	
evenkeel	*travel*	
evenodds	*sport*	
evensong	*relig*	
eventide	*time*	
evermore	*time*	
everyday	*time*	
everyman	*people*	
Everyman	*titles*	
eviction	*law*	
evidence	*law*	
evildoer	*people*	
evilhour	*time*	
examinee	*jobs*	
examiner	*educ*	
excerpta	*lit*	
exchange	*trade*	
exchange	*travel*	
excision	*medic*	
excitant	*physics*	
excursus	*lit*	
excursus	*travel*	
executor	*jobs*	
executor	*law*	
exegesis	*lit*	
exegesis	*relig*	
exequial	*relig*	
exequies	*relig*	
exercise	*educ*	
exercise	*sport*	
exercise	*war*	
exgratia	*foreign*	

exhalant	*chem*	falconer	*jobs*	feast|day	*time*
exit|dose	*medic*	falconer	*sport*	feathers	*birds*
exit|line	*theatre*	falconet	*war*	February	*time*
exorcise	*myth*	falconry	*sport*	feedback	*biol*
exorcism	*myth*	falderal	*music*	feldspar	*mineral*
exorcism	*relig*	fall|back	*travel*	Felicity	*names*
expended	*trade*	false|god	*myth*	feminine	*lit*
expenses	*trade*	falsetto	*music*	feminist	*people*
explorer	*jobs*	Falstaff	*Shakesp*	fencible	*war*
exponent	*jobs*	Falstaff	*lit*	fenestra	*astron*
exponent	*maths*	Falstaff	*titles*	fernshaw	*plants*
exporter	*trade*	fan|crest	*herald*	Ferrando	*lit*
exposure	*art*	fandango	*music*	ferryman	*jobs*
exposure	*geog*	fandango	*sport*	ferryman	*travel*
exposure	*medic*	fanfaron	*jobs*	Fervidor	*time*
exterior	*archit*	fanlight	*archit*	festival	*film/TV*
exterior	*art*	fanlight	*house*	festival	*theatre*
extracts	*lit*	fanmaker	*jobs*	feverfew	*flowers*
extrados	*archit*	fantasia	*music*	field|day	*sport*
eye|drops	*medic*	fantasie	*music*	field|gun	*war*
eye|patch	*medic*	farceuse	*theatre*	Fielding	*writers*
eye|rhyme	*lit*	farcical	*theatre*	fighting	*war*
eyesalve	*medic*	farewell	*travel*	figurant	*jobs*
eyeshade	*clothes*	farm|hand	*jobs*	figurant	*theatre*
eyesight	*medic*	farmyard	*agric*	figurate	*maths*
eye|tooth	*medic*	farmyard	*archit*	figurine	*art*
fabulist	*jobs*	Farquhar	*names*	filament	*house*
fabulist	*lit*	farthing	*money*	filament	*machine*
fabulous	*lit*	fascicle	*lit*	filament	*physics*
fabulous	*myth*	fast|ball	*sport*	file|fire	*war*
faburden	*music*	fastener	*clothes*	filefish	*fish*
face|card	*sport*	fast|hold	*war*	filigree	*jewels*
face|lift	*clothes*	fast|line	*travel*	fillibeg	*clothes*
face|lift	*medic*	fastness	*archit*	Fillmore	*USpres*
face|pack	*clothes*	fastness	*war*	film|club	*film/TV*
face|ruin	*trade*	fast|pile	*physics*	film|crew	*film/TV*
factotum	*jobs*	fast|time	*time*	filmgoer	*theatre*
fail|safe	*machine*	fatigues	*clothes*	film|idol	*jobs*
fair|copy	*art*	faubourg	*archit*	film|star	*film/TV*
fair|copy	*lit*	Faulkner	*writers*	film|star	*jobs*
fair|isle	*clothes*	fauteuil	*theatre*	film|unit	*theatre*
Fair|Isle	*islands*	fauvette	*birds*	filtrate	*chem*
fair|play	*sport*	favonian	*weather*	finalist	*jobs*
faithful	*relig*	Favonius	*myth*	finalist	*sport*
falchion	*war*	Favonius	*weather*	finances	*trade*

findings	law	flannels	clothes	Fluellen	Shakesp
fine|arts	art	flapjack	food	flue|pipe	music
FineGael	govt	flapping	sport	flue|work	music
fine|lady	people	flashgun	tools	fluoride	chem
fineness	mineral	Flashman	lit	fluorine	chem
finisher	jobs	flat|arch	archit	fluorite	mineral
fin|whale	animals	flatboat	travel	fluxions	maths
fireball	war	flat|feet	medic	fly|paper	house
fireball	weather	flatfish	fish	fly|press	machine
firebird	fish	flatfoot	govt	flywheel	machine
fireboat	travel	flatfoot	jobs	flywheel	travel
firebolt	weather	flat|iron	house	fob|watch	clothes
fire|bomb	war	flat|iron	tools	fogbound	travel
firebrat	insects	flat|race	sport	fohn|wind	weather
fire|clay	art	flat|rate	trade	foilsman	sport
firelock	war	flat|roof	archit	fold|axis	geog
fire|opal	jewels	flat|spin	travel	folderol	music
fire|opal	mineral	flat|tyre	travel	folk|hero	people
fire|plug	archit	flatworm	insects	folklore	myth
fire|sale	trade	flautist	jobs	folk|rock	music
fireside	archit	flautist	music	folk|song	music
fireside	house	flaxseed	plants	folk|tale	lit
fire|stop	archit	fleeting	time	follicle	biol
fire|upon	war	flesh|fly	insects	follicle	fruit
fireweed	plants	flesh|pot	food	follicle	medic
firewood	house	Fletcher	writers	follower	people
firework	sport	Flinders	rivers	fontange	clothes
fireworm	insects	flippers	sport	foodmill	house
first|act	theatre	flip|side	music	fool's|cap	clothes
first|aid	medic	floating	sport	foolscap	educ
fish|hawk	birds	floating	travel	foolscap	lit
fishpond	fish	flocculi	astron	footfall	travel
fish|tail	clothes	flooring	archit	foothold	sport
fish|tank	fish	floorman	jobs	footnote	lit
fishwife	jobs	floorman	trade	footpath	travel
fistiana	sport	Florence	Shakesp	foot|race	sport
fistular	biol	Florence	cities	footslog	travel
fivefold	measure	Florence	names	footstep	travel
fivepins	sport	Florizel	Shakesp	footwear	clothes
fixative	art	flotilla	travel	footwork	sport
fixtures	house	flotilla	war	for|a|song	trade
flagging	travel	flounder	fish	forecast	weather
flagship	travel	flour|bin	house	foredawn	time
flamingo	birds	flourish	music	forefoot	travel
flan|case	food	floweret	flowers	forehand	sport

forehead	*medic*	fracture	*medic*	fugitive	*jobs*
fore|jack	*travel*	fragment	*lit*	fugleman	*war*
foreland	*geog*	Francine	*names*	full|back	*sport*
fore|lift	*travel*	francium	*chem*	full|draw	*sport*
foremast	*travel*	freak|out	*medic*	fullface	*lit*
forenoon	*time*	Frederic	*lit*	full|load	*travel*
forensic	*law*	free|gift	*trade*	full|moon	*astron*
foresail	*travel*	freehand	*art*	full|stop	*lit*
foreship	*travel*	freehold	*govt*	full|tide	*marine*
forestay	*travel*	free|kick	*sport*	full|toss	*sport*
forester	*jobs*	free|port	*trade*	fumarole	*geog*
Forester	*writers*	free|vote	*govt*	fumigant	*medic*
forestry	*agric*	freezing	*physics*	function	*maths*
forestry	*trees*	freezing	*weather*	function	*trade*
foretack	*travel*	frenulum	*medic*	funerary	*relig*
forewing	*birds*	frequent	*time*	funereal	*relig*
foreyard	*travel*	frescoes	*art*	funk|hole	*archit*
forfeits	*sport*	fresh|air	*weather*	funny|man	*people*
forgeman	*jobs*	freshman	*educ*	funny|man	*theatre*
fork|lift	*machine*	freshman	*jobs*	furbelow	*clothes*
forkroad	*travel*	fretwork	*art*	furlough	*war*
formerly	*time*	fretwork	*sport*	fur|stole	*clothes*
formulae	*chem*	friction	*physics*	furuncle	*medic*
formulae	*maths*	fried|egg	*food*	fusarole	*archit*
formulae	*physics*	Frimaire	*time*	fuselage	*travel*
fortress	*archit*	frippery	*clothes*	fuse|wire	*house*
fortress	*war*	frog|fish	*fish*	fuse|wire	*machine*
fossette	*archit*	frogling	*animals*	fusilier	*jobs*
foul|goal	*sport*	frontier	*geog*	fusilier	*war*
foul|line	*sport*	front|man	*jobs*	futurism	*art*
Foulness	*islands*	front|man	*people*	gable|end	*archit*
foul|play	*law*	front|row	*sport*	Gabrieli	*music*
foul|play	*sport*	front|row	*theatre*	gadabout	*people*
fountain	*archit*	frosting	*food*	gad|about	*travel*
fountain	*geog*	froth|fly	*insects*	Gadarene	*Bible*
fountain	*herald*	froufrou	*clothes*	gadgetry	*machine*
fourfold	*measure*	fructose	*fruit*	Gadshill	*Shakesp*
foursome	*sport*	fruit|bat	*animals*	gain|time	*time*
foxglove	*flowers*	fruit|cup	*drink*	galactic	*astron*
foxhound	*animals*	fruit|fly	*insects*	galleass	*travel*
foxhound	*sport*	fruit|gum	*food*	gall|gnat	*insects*
fox|shark	*fish*	fruit|pie	*film/TV*	galliard	*music*
fraction	*maths*	fuel|cell	*physics*	gallipot	*house*
fraction	*measure*	fuel|ship	*travel*	gallipot	*medic*
fracture	*geog*	fugitive	*govt*	Galloway	*animals*

gall|wasp	insects	gatepost	archit	Glasberg	myth
galoshes	clothes	Gaullist	govt	glaucoma	medic
Gamaliel	Bible	gauntlet	clothes	gleaning	agric
Gamaliel	educ	gauntlet	herald	glee|club	music
gamashes	clothes	gauntlet	sport	gloaming	time
gambados	clothes	gauntlet	war	globulin	chem
gambeson	clothes	gazetted	trade	Gloriana	titles
gambeson	war	gazumper	trade	glory|pea	plants
gambling	sport	Gehennah	Bible	glossary	educ
gamecock	birds	gelatine	chem	glossary	lit
game|fish	fish	gelatine	food	glow|worm	insects
game|laws	law	gemshorn	music	gloxinia	flowers
game|room	archit	gemstone	jewels	glutelin	chem
gamester	people	gemstone	mineral	glutenin	chem
gamester	sport	gendarme	govt	gluttony	sins
gamma|ray	physics	gendarme	jobs	glycerin	medic
ganglion	medic	genetics	biol	glycogen	chem
gangrene	medic	genitive	lit	glyptics	art
gangsman	jobs	genocide	govt	go|aboard	travel
gangster	jobs	Gentiles	relig	goal|kick	sport
gangster	law	Geoffrey	names	goalpost	sport
ganymede	astron	geometer	maths	go|ashore	travel
Ganymede	myth	geometry	maths	go|astray	travel
gaolbird	jobs	Georgina	names	goatfish	fish
gaolbird	people	geotaxis	biol	goatherd	jobs
garboard	travel	geranium	flowers	goat|moth	insects
gardener	jobs	Germinal	time	goat's|rue	flowers
gardenia	flowers	Gershwin	music	goatweed	plants
garefowl	birds	Gertrude	Shakesp	go|before	travel
Garfield	USpres	Gertrude	names	go|by|rail	travel
garganey	birds	get|ahead	travel	Godavari	rivers
gargoyle	archit	Gianetta	lit	God's|acre	relig
Gargrave	Shakesp	giantess	myth	Godspeed	travel
garrison	war	gift|shop	trade	Goebbels	leaders
garroter	jobs	gilt|edge	trade	gold|coin	money
garrotte	law	gin|and|it	drink	gold|dust	mineral
garrotte	machine	gin|rummy	sport	goldfish	fish
gas|laser	physics	gin|sling	drink	gold|lame	clothes
gaslight	machine	Giordano	music	gold|mine	mineral
gas|meter	house	girasole	jewels	gold|mine	trade
gas|meter	measure	girasole	mineral	gold|rush	mineral
gasoline	chem	Giuseppe	lit	gold|rush	trade
gasoline	travel	giveaway	trade	gold|wasp	insects
gas|plant	plants	gladioli	flowers	golf|ball	sport
gasworks	trade	glad|rags	clothes	golf|club	sport

Golgotha	*Bible*
golliwog	*sport*
Gomorrah	*Bible*
gonfalon	*herald*
Good Book	*lit*
Good Book	*relig*
good calx	*sport*
good luck	*myth*
good shot	*sport*
good will	*trade*
Gorlovka	*cities*
gossamer	*clothes*
gourmand	*people*
governor	*govt*
governor	*jobs*
governor	*machine*
governor	*relig*
gownsman	*educ*
gownsman	*jobs*
gradient	*maths*
gradient	*travel*
graduand	*educ*
graduate	*educ*
graduate	*jobs*
graffiti	*art*
graffiti	*lit*
graffito	*art*
graffito	*lit*
Grainger	*music*
gramarye	*myth*
gram atom	*measure*
Granados	*music*
grandmal	*medic*
Grandpre	*Shakesp*
grandson	*family*
granules	*geog*
graphics	*art*
graphite	*mineral*
Grasmere	*lakes*
Gratiano	*Shakesp*
gratuity	*trade*
gravemen	*law*
grayling	*fish*
Gray's Inn	*law*
great auk	*birds*

great man	*people*
Great War	*war*
Greek fir	*trees*
Greek urn	*art*
green bag	*law*
greenery	*flowers*
greenery	*plants*
greenery	*veg*
greenfly	*insects*
green pea	*veg*
green tea	*drink*
grey hair	*clothes*
grey mare	*animals*
grey wolf	*animals*
gridelin	*clothes*
gridiron	*sport*
gridiron	*theatre*
Griffith	*Shakesp*
grilling	*food*
grilling	*govt*
grimacer	*theatre*
grimoire	*myth*
gritrock	*mineral*
grosbeak	*birds*
groschen	*money*
gross ton	*measure*
grounded	*travel*
grouping	*art*
groupnik	*people*
grow rich	*trade*
guacharo	*birds*
guaiacum	*trees*
guardian	*govt*
guardian	*jobs*
guarding	*sport*
guerilla	*jobs*
guerilla	*war*
guernsey	*clothes*
Guernsey	*islands*
guidance	*educ*
gulfweed	*plants*
gunflint	*war*
Gunga Din	*lit*
gunmaker	*jobs*
gunmetal	*war*

gunpoint	*war*
gunsmith	*jobs*
gunsmith	*war*
gunstick	*war*
gunstock	*war*
gymkhana	*sport*
gym pants	*clothes*
gym shoes	*clothes*
gym shoes	*sport*
gym tunic	*clothes*
gynarchy	*govt*
gyrostat	*machine*
Habakkuk	*Bible*
habanera	*music*
habanera	*sport*
hacienda	*archit*
hagberry	*fruit*
Hail Mary	*relig*
Haiphong	*cities*
hair ball	*medic*
hair band	*clothes*
hairline	*clothes*
hair seal	*animals*
hair tail	*animals*
hair worm	*insects*
halfback	*sport*
half ball	*sport*
half blue	*sport*
half boot	*clothes*
half deck	*travel*
half hose	*clothes*
half hour	*time*
half life	*physics*
half mast	*herald*
half mile	*sport*
half moon	*astron*
half past	*time*
half rest	*music*
half shot	*sport*
half term	*educ*
half time	*sport*
half tint	*art*
half tone	*art*
hallmark	*trade*
hallowed	*relig*

ham|actor	jobs	hatching	art	heavy|gun	war
ham|actor	theatre	hatchway	travel	heavy|sea	marine
Hamilton	cities	hat|guard	clothes	heavy|sky	weather
Hamilton	rivers	hatmaker	jobs	Hebraist	jobs
handball	sport	hatstand	house	Hebrides	islands
handbell	house	hat|trick	sport	hecatomb	relig
handbell	music	hawfinch	birds	heckling	govt
handbook	lit	hawk|moth	insects	hectorer	people
handcart	travel	hawkshaw	jobs	hedgehog	animals
handicap	medic	hawkweed	flowers	hedgehog	war
handicap	sport	hawse|bag	travel	hedgepig	animals
hand|knit	clothes	hawthorn	trees	hedgerow	plants
handmaid	jobs	hay|fever	medic	hedonist	people
handrail	archit	Hay|Fever	titles	heel|bone	medic
handrail	house	hay|field	agric	heel|over	travel
handtool	tools	haymaker	agric	hegemony	govt
handyman	jobs	haymaker	jobs	heirloom	govt
hang|back	travel	haymaker	sport	helicoid	maths
hangbird	birds	haystack	agric	heliport	travel
Hangchow	cities	hazelnut	food	hell|fire	myth
hanger|on	govt	hazelnut	fruit	Hellotis	myth
hanger|on	people	haziness	weather	helminth	insects
hang|fire	war	headache	medic	helmsman	jobs
hangings	house	headband	clothes	helmsman	sport
hangover	drink	head|cook	jobs	helmsman	travel
Hannibal	war	head|fast	travel	helpmeet	family
Hanukkah	time	headgear	clothes	Helsinki	cities
harangue	educ	head|girl	jobs	hematite	mineral
Harcourt	Shakesp	head|into	travel	hemostat	machine
hard|cash	trade	headland	geog	hemostat	medic
hard|drug	medic	headline	lit	hemp|palm	trees
hard|sell	trade	headline	theatre	hemp|tree	trees
hard|tack	food	headlock	sport	henchman	govt
hardware	comput	headpost	archit	henchman	jobs
hardware	machine	headrace	geog	henequen	flowers
hardware	trade	headship	jobs	henhouse	birds
hardwood	trees	headsill	archit	hepatica	plants
harebell	flowers	headwear	clothes	heptagon	maths
Harmonia	myth	head|wind	weather	Hepworth	artists
harmonic	music	heat|haze	weather	Heracles	myth
harmonic	physics	heat|lamp	medic	heraldic	herald
Harpinna	myth	heat|sink	physics	heraldry	herald
harp|lute	music	heat|spot	medic	Hercules	astron
Harrison	USpres	heatwave	weather	Hercules	myth
Hastings	Shakesp	heavenly	astron	Hercules	names

herdsman	jobs	hip|joint	medic	Hong|Kong	islands
here|lies	relig	hipsters	clothes	Honolulu	cities
hereunto	time	hired|gun	jobs	hookworm	insects
herisson	herald	hired|man	jobs	hooligan	people
herisson	war	hireling	jobs	Horatius	myth
heritage	govt	hireling	war	hornbeak	fish
Hermione	Shakesp	historic	lit	hornbeam	trees
Hermione	names	hitherto	time	hornbill	birds
hernshaw	birds	hoarding	trade	hornbook	lit
Herodias	Bible	hoggerel	animals	hornpipe	music
Hesperis	myth	Hogmanay	time	hornpipe	sport
hexagram	maths	hogshead	measure	horntail	insects
hexapody	lit	Hokkaido	islands	hornwork	war
Hezekiah	Bible	holed|out	sport	hornworm	insects
Hiawatha	lit	hole|high	sport	horology	time
Hiawatha	myth	holiness	relig	horsebox	animals
hibernal	geog	Hollands	house	horsebox	travel
hibernal	time	holly|oak	trees	horse|fly	insects
hibiscus	plants	hologram	physics	horseman	jobs
hic|jacet	relig	holotony	medic	horseman	sport
hick|town	geog	holy|city	relig	horseman	travel
hieratic	lit	holy|coat	relig	hose|pipe	machine
highball	drink	holy|days	time	hospital	archit
highbrow	educ	Holy|Land	relig	hospital	medic
highbrow	people	Holy|Loch	lakes	hot|drink	drink
high|dive	sport	holyrood	relig	hotelier	jobs
high|heel	clothes	Holy|Week	relig	hot|flush	medic
high|jump	sport	Holy|Week	time	hothouse	archit
highland	geog	Holy|Writ	relig	hothouse	flowers
High|Mass	relig	home|game	sport	hothouse	fruit
highness	govt	home|help	jobs	hot|money	trade
high|rise	archit	homeland	geog	hot|pants	clothes
highroad	travel	home|rule	govt	hotplate	house
high|seas	marine	homesick	medic	hotplate	machine
high|seas	travel	homespun	clothes	hot|toddy	drink
high|tide	marine	homespun	house	hound|dog	animals
high|time	time	homeward	travel	house|ant	insects
high|wind	weather	homework	educ	houseboy	jobs
hijacker	jobs	homework	trade	housebug	insects
hill|fort	war	homicide	law	house|dog	animals
hillside	geog	homogamy	biol	house|fly	insects
Himantes	myth	Honegger	music	houseman	medic
himation	clothes	honey|bee	insects	housetop	archit
hind|wing	birds	honeydew	chem	howitzer	war
hip|flask	house	honeydew	plants	how's|that	sport

huckster	*trade*	idolater	*people*	inductor	*physics*
Hudibras	*titles*	idolater	*relig*	industry	*trade*
Huguenot	*relig*	idolatry	*relig*	infantry	*war*
hulagirl	*jobs*	Idomeneo	*lit*	infected	*medic*
hulahoop	*sport*	Idomeneo	*titles*	infinity	*maths*
hulahula	*sport*	idyllist	*jobs*	infinity	*time*
humanism	*educ*	idyllist	*lit*	inflamed	*medic*
humidity	*weather*	ignition	*machine*	inflight	*travel*
humorist	*lit*	ignition	*physics*	informed	*educ*
humorist	*people*	ignition	*travel*	informer	*jobs*
humpback	*animals*	Illinois	*rivers*	informer	*law*
Humphrey	*names*	illtimed	*time*	informer	*war*
humstrum	*music*	ilmenite	*mineral*	infradig	*abbrev*
hungjury	*law*	imbecile	*people*	infrared	*physics*
huntsman	*jobs*	Immanuel	*Bible*	infusion	*drink*
huntsman	*sport*	Immanuel	*relig*	infuture	*time*
hurdling	*sport*	immerser	*house*	inhalant	*medic*
Huronian	*geog*	immunity	*medic*	initiate	*jobs*
hustings	*govt*	impeller	*machine*	injector	*physics*
hyacinth	*flowers*	impeller	*physics*	inkmaker	*jobs*
hydrogen	*chem*	imperial	*govt*	inkstand	*educ*
hydromel	*drink*	impetigo	*medic*	inkstand	*lit*
hydrozoa	*animals*	importer	*jobs*	inkstone	*mineral*
hymeneal	*music*	importer	*trade*	inmotion	*travel*
Hymettus	*mounts*	impostor	*people*	innerear	*medic*
hymnbook	*relig*	impotent	*medic*	innerjib	*travel*
hymntune	*music*	inaccord	*music*	innerman	*relig*
hyperion	*astron*	inaflash	*time*	innocent	*law*
Hyperion	*myth*	inarrear	*trade*	innocent	*people*
Hyperion	*titles*	inatrice	*time*	innotime	*time*
hypogene	*geog*	incamera	*govt*	inositol	*biol*
hypogeum	*geog*	inceptor	*educ*	inpocket	*trade*
iceblink	*geog*	inceptor	*jobs*	inrelief	*art*
icebound	*travel*	inchmeal	*measure*	inscribe	*art*
icecream	*food*	inchorus	*music*	inscribe	*lit*
icefield	*geog*	inchtape	*clothes*	inscroll	*lit*
iceplant	*plants*	inchtape	*measure*	inseason	*time*
icesheet	*geog*	inchworm	*insects*	insignia	*herald*
icestorm	*weather*	incision	*medic*	insomnia	*medic*
icewater	*drink*	incivism	*govt*	instruct	*educ*
iceyacht	*sport*	increase	*trade*	intaglio	*art*
iceyacht	*travel*	indebted	*trade*	integral	*maths*
identity	*jobs*	indented	*geog*	intercom	*machine*
ideogram	*lit*	indented	*herald*	intercom	*travel*
idocrase	*mineral*	indigent	*geog*	interest	*trade*

interior	*archit*	islander	*jobs*	Jephthah	*Bible*
interior	*art*	isobront	*weather*	Jeremiah	*Bible*
interior	*geog*	isochasm	*astron*	Jeroboam	*Bible*
internal	*medic*	isocheim	*weather*	jerrican	*travel*
Interpol	*law*	isocryme	*weather*	jet|pilot	*jobs*
interval	*music*	isodomon	*archit*	jet|pilot	*travel*
interval	*theatre*	isogonic	*maths*	jet|plane	*travel*
interval	*time*	isolator	*machine*	jet|power	*travel*
in|the|red	*trade*	isomeric	*chem*	jettison	*travel*
In|the|Wet	*titles*	isostasy	*geog*	jewel|box	*house*
intimism	*art*	isoteric	*chem*	jeweller	*jobs*
intrados	*archit*	isothere	*weather*	jeweller	*trade*
intruder	*people*	isotherm	*weather*	jews|harp	*music*
in|unison	*music*	isotopic	*chem*	Jim|Dixon	*lit*
invading	*war*	isotropy	*biol*	jingoism	*govt*
invasion	*war*	Issachar	*Bible*	jingoism	*war*
invasive	*war*	issuance	*trade*	jiu|jitsu	*sport*
invected	*herald*	issue|par	*trade*	jodhpurs	*clothes*
inventor	*jobs*	Istanbul	*cities*	John|Bull	*govt*
investor	*jobs*	itch|mite	*insects*	John|Bull	*people*
investor	*trade*	jabberer	*people*	John|Dory	*fish*
involute	*biol*	jackboot	*clothes*	John|Ridd	*lit*
Iolanthe	*lit*	Jack|Cade	*Shakesp*	jointure	*govt*
Iolanthe	*titles*	jackstay	*travel*	Jokanaan	*lit*
ion|drive	*physics*	jack|tree	*trees*	Jonathan	*Bible*
ionizing	*physics*	Jacquard	*clothes*	Jonathan	*names*
Iphicles	*myth*	jailbird	*jobs*	jongleur	*jobs*
iriscope	*physics*	jailbird	*law*	jongleur	*lit*
Irish|elk	*animals*	jailbird	*people*	jongleur	*music*
Irishism	*lit*	jalousie	*house*	Jourdain	*Shakesp*
Irish|jig	*sport*	Jane|Eyre	*lit*	journeys	*travel*
iron|bark	*trees*	Jane|Eyre	*titles*	joy|rider	*travel*
ironclad	*travel*	janizary	*war*	joystick	*sport*
ironclad	*war*	Jan|Mayen	*islands*	joystick	*travel*
iron|clay	*mineral*	japonica	*flowers*	Jubilate	*music*
iron|grey	*colour*	jaundice	*medic*	judgment	*law*
iron|lung	*machine*	jawsmith	*people*	judicial	*law*
iron|lung	*medic*	jazerant	*war*	julienne	*drink*
iron|shot	*sport*	jazz|band	*music*	jumbo|jet	*travel*
ironwood	*trees*	jazzed|up	*music*	jump|area	*war*
irrigate	*geog*	Jeanette	*names*	junction	*travel*
irritant	*medic*	Jellicoe	*war*	juncture	*time*
Isabella	*Shakesp*	jelly|bag	*house*	Jungfrau	*mounts*
Iscariot	*Bible*	Jennifer	*names*	junkshop	*trade*
Iseabail	*names*	jenny|ass	*animals*	Jurassic	*geog*

jurymast	travel	Kinshasa	cities	Lake Como	lakes
jury sail	travel	kiss curl	clothes	Lake Erie	lakes
juvenile	jobs	kitemark	trade	Lake Eyre	lakes
juvenile	theatre	kitty cat	animals	Lake Kivu	lakes
Juventas	myth	kiwi kiwi	birds	lakeland	geog
Kalevala	myth	Klingsor	lit	Lake Tana	lakes
kamikaze	travel	klystron	physics	L'Allegro	titles
kangaroo	animals	knapsack	travel	lamasery	relig
Kathleen	names	knapweed	plants	lame duck	birds
Katmandu	cities	knapwood	plants	lame duck	people
Katowice	cities	knickers	clothes	lame duck	trade
Kattegat	seas	knife boy	jobs	lancegay	war
kedgeree	food	knitwear	clothes	lancelet	animals
keel over	travel	knitwork	trade	Lancelot	myth
keep shop	trade	knock out	sport	Lancelot	names
keep time	time	knotweed	plants	land ahoy	travel
keeshond	animals	knuckles	war	land army	war
Kenyatta	leaders	Koestler	writers	land crab	fish
kerchief	clothes	kohlrabi	veg	landfall	travel
kerosene	chem	kolinsky	animals	landform	geog
Ketelbey	music	Korea Bay	seas	land girl	agric
keyboard	music	korfball	sport	land girl	jobs
key bugle	music	Korngold	music	landlady	jobs
keystone	archit	Krakatoa	mounts	landlord	jobs
Khartoum	cities	Kriesler	music	landmass	geog
kickback	travel	Kruschev	leaders	land mile	measure
kickshaw	house	Kumamoto	cities	land mine	war
killadar	war	Kurwenal	lit	landrail	birds
killdeer	birds	Kweiyang	cities	Landseer	artists
kill time	time	kyrielle	lit	landslip	geog
kilogram	measure	La Boheme	titles	landsman	jobs
kilovolt	measure	labourer	jobs	langrage	war
kilowatt	measure	labourer	trade	lang syne	time
kindling	house	labrador	animals	language	lit
kingbird	birds	laburnum	trees	languish	medic
king crab	fish	lacewing	insects	lanneret	birds
king crow	birds	Lachesis	myth	Laomedon	myth
kingfish	fish	Laconica	myth	lapidary	art
King Lear	titles	laconics	lit	lapidary	jobs
kingpost	archit	lacrosse	sport	Laputian	myth
kingship	govt	ladybird	insects	larboard	travel
Kingsley	writers	lady fern	plants	largesse	trade
Kingston	cities	ladyship	govt	large sum	trade
kingwood	trees	laid back	people	larkspur	flowers
kinka jou	animals	Lake Chad	lakes	laser gun	machine

laser|gun	*physics*	learning	*educ*	libation	*drink*
last|post	*music*	lecithin	*chem*	libation	*myth*
last|post	*war*	lecturer	*educ*	libeccio	*weather*
last|time	*time*	lecturer	*jobs*	libelant	*law*
last|week	*time*	leeboard	*travel*	libretto	*lit*
lateener	*travel*	lee|sheet	*travel*	libretto	*music*
lateness	*time*	left|back	*sport*	libretto	*theatre*
Latinist	*educ*	left|bank	*geog*	licensee	*jobs*
latitude	*geog*	left|half	*sport*	lich|gate	*archit*
latterly	*time*	left|hand	*music*	lich|gate	*relig*
laudanum	*medic*	left|hook	*sport*	licorice	*food*
launcher	*travel*	left|wing	*govt*	licorice	*plants*
launcher	*war*	left|wing	*sport*	life|belt	*travel*
laureate	*lit*	legal|aid	*law*	lifeboat	*travel*
Laurence	*Shakesp*	legalism	*law*	life|buoy	*travel*
Laurence	*names*	legality	*law*	lifeline	*sport*
lava|flow	*geog*	legation	*govt*	lifeline	*travel*
lavatory	*archit*	legation	*trade*	lifelong	*time*
lavement	*medic*	leg|break	*sport*	life|peer	*jobs*
lavender	*colour*	leggiero	*music*	life|raft	*travel*
lavender	*trees*	leggings	*clothes*	life|span	*time*
Lavengro	*titles*	leg|guard	*sport*	lifetime	*time*
laverock	*birds*	Leiriope	*myth*	life|work	*jobs*
law|agent	*jobs*	lemonade	*drink*	life|work	*trade*
law|agent	*law*	lemon|dab	*fish*	lift|pump	*machine*
law|court	*law*	lenitive	*medic*	lift|wire	*travel*
lawgiver	*jobs*	lenticel	*biol*	ligament	*medic*
lawgiver	*law*	lenticle	*geog*	Ligarius	*Shakesp*
lawmaker	*jobs*	Leonardo	*Shakesp*	ligature	*lit*
lawmaker	*law*	Leonardo	*artists*	ligature	*medic*
lawn|game	*sport*	Leonatus	*Shakesp*	ligature	*music*
Lawrence	*names*	Leonidas	*war*	likeness	*art*
Lawrence	*war*	Leon|mine	*war*	Lilliput	*myth*
Lawrence	*writers*	leotards	*clothes*	lily|pond	*flowers*
laxative	*medic*	leporine	*animals*	Lima|bean	*veg*
layabout	*people*	LesNoces	*titles*	limekiln	*art*
lay|clerk	*music*	lethargy	*medic*	limerick	*lit*
lay|judge	*law*	lettered	*educ*	limoniad	*myth*
lay|vicar	*music*	leukemia	*medic*	limonite	*mineral*
lay|vicar	*relig*	levanter	*geog*	lincture	*medic*
laywoman	*jobs*	levanter	*trade*	linesman	*jobs*
lazurite	*mineral*	level|off	*travel*	linesman	*sport*
leaching	*chem*	levulose	*chem*	lingerie	*clothes*
leapfrog	*sport*	Lewis|gun	*war*	linguist	*jobs*
leap|year	*time*	Lewisian	*geog*	liniment	*medic*

link|verb	*lit*	lodestar	*geog*	love|game	*sport*
linkworm	*insects*	lodgings	*archit*	Lovelace	*writers*
linoleum	*house*	lodgment	*archit*	love|nest	*archit*
linotype	*lit*	Lodovico	*Shakesp*	love|poem	*lit*
linotype	*machine*	log|cabin	*archit*	love|seat	*house*
lion|fish	*fish*	log|canoe	*travel*	love|song	*music*
lion's|den	*animals*	logician	*jobs*	low|cloud	*weather*
liparite	*mineral*	logogram	*lit*	lowlands	*geog*
lip|brush	*clothes*	logotype	*lit*	low|lifer	*people*
lipogram	*lit*	logotype	*machine*	low|pitch	*music*
lip|rouge	*clothes*	loin|chop	*food*	low|price	*trade*
lip|salve	*clothes*	loiterer	*jobs*	low|water	*marine*
lip|salve	*medic*	lollipop	*food*	low|water	*trade*
lipstick	*clothes*	lone|wolf	*people*	loyalist	*govt*
liripipe	*educ*	longbeat	*travel*	Lucentio	*Shakesp*
liripoop	*educ*	longeron	*travel*	Lucilius	*Shakesp*
listener	*jobs*	long|game	*sport*	lucky|bag	*sport*
literacy	*educ*	longhand	*lit*	lucky|dip	*sport*
literacy	*lit*	long|haul	*travel*	Lucky|Jim	*titles*
literate	*educ*	long|horn	*animals*	Lucretia	*lit*
literate	*lit*	long|jump	*sport*	Lucullus	*Shakesp*
litharge	*chem*	long|odds	*sport*	lumberer	*jobs*
litigant	*law*	long|rush	*sport*	luminary	*astron*
litigate	*law*	long|shot	*sport*	luminary	*jobs*
little|go	*educ*	long|side	*trade*	lump|fish	*fish*
littoral	*geog*	long|stop	*sport*	lunation	*time*
littoral	*marine*	long|time	*time*	luncheon	*food*
live|high	*trade*	looker|on	*jobs*	lungfish	*fish*
livelong	*time*	loophole	*law*	lutanist	*music*
live|show	*theatre*	loophole	*war*	lutecium	*mineral*
live|well	*trade*	loosebox	*agric*	lutetium	*chem*
live|wire	*people*	loosebox	*animals*	Lutheran	*relig*
Llewelyn	*names*	loose|box	*travel*	Lycurgus	*myth*
lobbying	*govt*	Lord|Lyon	*herald*	lynching	*law*
lobbyist	*govt*	lordosis	*medic*	lynch|law	*law*
lobotomy	*medic*	Lord's|day	*relig*	Lyonesse	*myth*
location	*geog*	Lord's|day	*time*	lyricist	*jobs*
location	*theatre*	lordship	*govt*	Lysander	*Shakesp*
Loch|Earn	*lakes*	Lorraine	*names*	macaroni	*food*
Loch|Fyne	*lakes*	lose|time	*time*	macaroon	*food*
Loch|Long	*lakes*	lost|ball	*sport*	Macaulay	*writers*
Loch|Ness	*lakes*	lotus|bud	*archit*	Macavity	*lit*
lock|gate	*machine*	louis|d'or	*money*	MacHeath	*lit*
lock|weir	*machine*	lovebird	*birds*	machismo	*people*
locoweed	*fruit*	love|drug	*medic*	mackerel	*fish*

mackinaw	*clothes*	Malagasy	*islands*
MacNeice	*writers*	malaprop	*lit*
madapple	*fruit*	malarial	*medic*
madapple	*veg*	maldemer	*medic*
Madeline	*names*	Malenkov	*leaders*
madrigal	*lit*	Mallarme	*writers*
madrigal	*music*	Malvolio	*Shakesp*
Maecenas	*Shakesp*	Manasseh	*Bible*
maestoso	*music*	Mandalay	*cities*
magazine	*archit*	mandamus	*law*
magazine	*lit*	mandarin	*fruit*
magazine	*war*	mandarin	*govt*
Magdalen	*names*	mandarin	*jobs*
maggiore	*music*	mandible	*medic*
magiceye	*physics*	mandorla	*art*
magician	*jobs*	mandrake	*plants*
magician	*myth*	mandrill	*animals*
magician	*theatre*	maneater	*animals*
magnesia	*chem*	maneater	*fish*
magneton	*measure*	mangabey	*animals*
magnolia	*trees*	mangrove	*trees*
Mahadeva	*myth*	manhater	*people*
maharani	*govt*	manicure	*clothes*
mahjongg	*sport*	manifest	*trade*
mahogany	*trees*	manifold	*machine*
mailboat	*travel*	manifold	*travel*
mailclad	*war*	mannaash	*trees*
maincrop	*veg*	Mannheim	*cities*
maindeck	*travel*	manofwar	*fish*
maindish	*food*	manofwar	*travel*
mainland	*geog*	manofwar	*war*
mainlift	*travel*	manpower	*trade*
mainline	*travel*	Mantegna	*artists*
mainmast	*travel*	mantelet	*clothes*
mainroad	*travel*	mantelet	*war*
mainsail	*marine*	mantilla	*clothes*
mainstay	*travel*	mantissa	*maths*
mainyard	*travel*	mapmaker	*jobs*
majolica	*art*	marabout	*relig*
majority	*govt*	marasmus	*medic*
majorkey	*music*	Marathon	*myth*
makeabid	*trade*	marathon	*sport*
makegood	*trade*	marauder	*govt*
maketime	*time*	marauder	*jobs*
malafide	*foreign*	Marcello	*lit*

Margaret	*Shakesp*
Margaret	*names*
margrave	*govt*
Marianne	*names*
marigold	*flowers*
Marigold	*names*
marinade	*food*
marinate	*food*
maritime	*marine*
maritime	*travel*
marjoram	*plants*
marjoram	*veg*
Marjorie	*names*
markdown	*trade*
marksman	*jobs*
marksman	*sport*
marksman	*war*
marktime	*time*
marmoset	*animals*
Marnaran	*myth*
marriage	*sport*
marshgas	*chem*
martello	*archit*
martello	*war*
martinet	*govt*
martinet	*people*
Marullus	*Shakesp*
marzipan	*food*
Mascagni	*music*
massacre	*war*
Massbook	*relig*
Massenet	*music*
masseter	*medic*
masseuse	*jobs*
masseuse	*medic*
masthead	*travel*
mastodon	*animals*
matamata	*insects*
matchbox	*house*
material	*clothes*
material	*trade*
matrices	*maths*
Matthias	*Bible*
Matthias	*names*
mattress	*house*

maturant	*medic*	membrane	*medic*	militant	*war*
maturity	*trade*	memorial	*relig*	military	*war*
maverick	*animals*	memorize	*educ*	milkmaid	*jobs*
Maxim gun	*war*	mem sahib	*govt*	milk tree	*trees*
May apple	*fruit*	Menelaus	*Shakesp*	milkweed	*plants*
maybloom	*flowers*	Menelaus	*myth*	milkwood	*trees*
mayoress	*govt*	Menevian	*geog*	milkwort	*plants*
mazourka	*music*	menhaden	*fish*	Milky Way	*astron*
McCarthy	*leaders*	meniscus	*biol*	millgirl	*jobs*
McKinley	*USpres*	menology	*relig*	millhand	*jobs*
mea culpa	*foreign*	menology	*time*	milliard	*measure*
meal worm	*insects*	Menteith	*Shakesp*	milliner	*jobs*
mealy bug	*insects*	Mephisto	*myth*	millpond	*marine*
mean tide	*marine*	mercator	*jobs*	millpool	*geog*
mean time	*time*	merchant	*jobs*	millrace	*geog*
meantime	*time*	merchant	*trade*	mill rind	*herald*
mean tone	*music*	mercuric	*chem*	mince pie	*food*
measured	*lit*	Mercutio	*Shakesp*	Mindanao	*islands*
measured	*music*	Meredith	*names*	mine ship	*travel*
meat ball	*food*	Meredith	*writers*	minister	*govt*
meat loaf	*food*	meridian	*time*	minister	*jobs*
meat roll	*food*	meringue	*food*	minister	*relig*
meatsafe	*house*	meristem	*plants*	ministry	*govt*
meat stew	*food*	Merodach	*myth*	ministry	*jobs*
mechanic	*jobs*	Merriman	*writers*	ministry	*relig*
mediator	*jobs*	mesotron	*physics*	minority	*govt*
mediator	*relig*	Mesozoic	*geog*	minor key	*music*
medicago	*plants*	mesquite	*trees*	Minotaur	*animals*
medicate	*medic*	Messenia	*myth*	Minotaur	*myth*
medicine	*medic*	mess hall	*archit*	minstrel	*jobs*
medieval	*time*	mess hall	*house*	minstrel	*lit*
megalith	*relig*	Messiaen	*music*	minstrel	*music*
megapode	*birds*	Messidor	*time*	mint drop	*trade*
megavolt	*measure*	messuage	*archit*	Mirabeau	*writers*
megawatt	*measure*	messuage	*law*	miscible	*chem*
melamine	*chem*	metallic	*mineral*	misnomer	*lit*
Melampus	*myth*	metaphor	*lit*	misprint	*lit*
Meleager	*myth*	meteoric	*time*	Missouri	*rivers*
melinite	*war*	metonymy	*lit*	mistress	*educ*
melodeon	*music*	metrical	*lit*	mistress	*jobs*
melodica	*music*	Michelle	*names*	mistrial	*law*
melodics	*music*	microbar	*measure*	misusage	*lit*
melodist	*jobs*	midbrain	*medic*	mittimus	*law*
melodist	*music*	midnight	*time*	mobilize	*war*
Melville	*writers*	migraine	*medic*	Moby Dick	*titles*

moccasin	*clothes*	
moccasin	*insects*	
mock|moon	*astron*	
modelled	*art*	
modeller	*art*	
modeller	*jobs*	
moderate	*weather*	
moderato	*music*	
modifier	*lit*	
molasses	*food*	
molecule	*chem*	
molecule	*measure*	
molecule	*physics*	
moleskin	*clothes*	
molossus	*lit*	
Moluccas	*islands*	
momently	*time*	
momentum	*physics*	
momentum	*travel*	
monachal	*relig*	
monarchy	*govt*	
monastic	*relig*	
monazite	*mineral*	
monetary	*trade*	
moneybag	*trade*	
moneybox	*trade*	
mongoose	*animals*	
monition	*govt*	
monkfish	*fish*	
monk|seal	*animals*	
monogram	*house*	
monolith	*archit*	
monolith	*geog*	
monolith	*relig*	
monomial	*maths*	
monopoly	*sport*	
monopoly	*trade*	
monorail	*travel*	
monotone	*music*	
monotype	*lit*	
monotype	*machine*	
monoxide	*chem*	
mon|repos	*archit*	
Montague	*Shakesp*	
Montague	*names*	
Montcalm	*war*	
Montegna	*artists*	
monticle	*geog*	
Montreal	*cities*	
Montrose	*war*	
monument	*archit*	
monument	*art*	
monument	*relig*	
moon|base	*travel*	
moonbeam	*astron*	
moonsail	*travel*	
moon|ship	*travel*	
moonshot	*travel*	
moonwalk	*travel*	
moonwort	*plants*	
moor|cock	*birds*	
moor|fowl	*birds*	
moorings	*travel*	
moorland	*geog*	
moralist	*jobs*	
morality	*theatre*	
moralize	*educ*	
morganes	*myth*	
morpheme	*lit*	
Morpheus	*myth*	
morphine	*medic*	
Morrison	*names*	
mortgage	*law*	
mortgage	*trade*	
Mortimer	*Shakesp*	
Mortimer	*names*	
Mortimer	*writers*	
mortmain	*law*	
mortuary	*law*	
mosquito	*insects*	
moss|rose	*flowers*	
moth|ball	*house*	
mot|juste	*lit*	
motorbus	*travel*	
motorcar	*travel*	
motoring	*travel*	
motorist	*jobs*	
motorist	*sport*	
motorist	*travel*	
motorway	*travel*	
moulding	*house*	
mountain	*geog*	
Mount|Ida	*mounts*	
Mounties	*law*	
mourning	*clothes*	
mourning	*relig*	
moussaka	*food*	
movement	*art*	
movement	*govt*	
movement	*music*	
mozzetta	*relig*	
Mr|Badger	*lit*	
Mr|Dangle	*lit*	
Mrs|Grose	*lit*	
Mr|Wardle	*lit*	
mud|puppy	*insects*	
mudstone	*mineral*	
mulberry	*colour*	
mulberry	*fruit*	
mule|deer	*animals*	
muleteer	*jobs*	
muleteer	*travel*	
multi|gym	*sport*	
multi|jet	*travel*	
multiple	*maths*	
multiply	*maths*	
muniment	*war*	
munition	*war*	
Munnings	*artists*	
muralist	*jobs*	
murderer	*jobs*	
Murmansk	*cities*	
muscadin	*clothes*	
muscatel	*drink*	
muscatel	*fruit*	
muscular	*medic*	
mushroom	*food*	
mushroom	*plants*	
mushroom	*war*	
musicale	*music*	
music|box	*music*	
musician	*jobs*	
musician	*music*	
musk|duck	*birds*	
musketry	*war*	

musk pear	*fruit*	neat herd	*animals*	night owl	*birds*
musk plum	*fruit*	neckband	*clothes*	night sky	*astron*
musk rose	*flowers*	necklace	*jewels*	nihilism	*govt*
musquash	*animals*	neckline	*clothes*	nihilist	*people*
mustache	*clothes*	necrosis	*medic*	ninefold	*measure*
mutation	*biol*	negative	*art*	ninepins	*sport*
mute swan	*birds*	negative	*maths*	nitrogen	*chem*
mycology	*biol*	negative	*physics*	Noah's Ark	*relig*
mycology	*medic*	negatron	*physics*	nobelium	*chem*
mylonite	*mineral*	negligee	*clothes*	nobility	*govt*
myosotis	*flowers*	Nehemiah	*Bible*	nobleman	*govt*
myriapod	*insects*	Nelly Bly	*lit*	no charge	*trade*
Myrtilus	*myth*	nembutal	*medic*	nocturne	*music*
mythical	*lit*	neon tube	*machine*	nomology	*law*
Nagasaki	*cities*	neophyte	*educ*	nonenary	*maths*
nail file	*clothes*	neophyte	*jobs*	non metal	*chem*
nainsook	*clothes*	neophyte	*relig*	nonvoter	*govt*
naked eye	*medic*	neoplasm	*medic*	noontide	*time*
Nanki Poo	*lit*	nephrite	*mineral*	noontime	*time*
Naphtali	*Bible*	Nephthys	*myth*	Norseman	*jobs*
Napoleon	*leaders*	nepotist	*people*	North Sea	*seas*
napoleon	*money*	nerve gas	*war*	Northumb	*abbrev*
Napoleon	*people*	netmaker	*jobs*	nose band	*animals*
napoleon	*sport*	net price	*trade*	nose cone	*travel*
Napoleon	*war*	net worth	*trade*	nosedive	*sport*
narcosis	*medic*	neuritis	*medic*	nosedive	*travel*
narcotic	*medic*	neutrino	*physics*	nose down	*travel*
narratio	*govt*	new broom	*house*	nose into	*travel*
narrator	*jobs*	newcomer	*jobs*	nose ring	*clothes*
narrator	*lit*	new pence	*money*	nosogeny	*medic*
natal day	*time*	new penny	*money*	nosology	*medic*
natation	*sport*	news hawk	*jobs*	notation	*lit*
naturist	*jobs*	newsreel	*film/TV*	notation	*music*
nauplius	*fish*	New Style	*time*	notation	*trade*
Nauplius	*myth*	New World	*geog*	notebook	*educ*
nautilus	*animals*	next week	*time*	notebook	*lit*
navarchy	*travel*	Nicholas	*names*	notecase	*trade*
navicert	*govt*	nicotine	*chem*	not often	*time*
navy blue	*colour*	Niflheim	*myth*	no trumps	*sport*
Nazareth	*Bible*	night ape	*animals*	novelist	*jobs*
neap tide	*marine*	nightcap	*clothes*	novelist	*lit*
Nearctic	*geog*	nightcap	*drink*	November	*time*
Near East	*geog*	night fly	*insects*	novocain	*medic*
nearside	*travel*	nightjar	*birds*	nowadays	*time*
near silk	*clothes*	nightman	*jobs*	nucleate	*physics*

nucleole	*biol*	off|stage	*theatre*	operatic	*music*
nuisance	*people*	off|white	*colour*	operatic	*theatre*
numbness	*medic*	ofttimes	*time*	operator	*jobs*
numerary	*maths*	ogee|arch	*archit*	operator	*medic*
numskull	*people*	ohmmeter	*physics*	operator	*trade*
nurse|ant	*insects*	oilcloth	*clothes*	operator	*travel*
nutation	*astron*	oil|gauge	*travel*	operetta	*music*
nuthatch	*birds*	oilskins	*clothes*	operetta	*theatre*
nutshell	*fruit*	ointment	*medic*	ophidian	*insects*
oak|apple	*fruit*	old|crock	*travel*	opponent	*jobs*
oak|eggar	*insects*	OldHarry	*myth*	opponent	*sport*
obituary	*lit*	OldHorny	*myth*	optician	*jobs*
obituary	*relig*	old|story	*lit*	optimist	*people*
objector	*jobs*	old|times	*time*	opulence	*trade*
objector	*people*	OldWorld	*geog*	opuscule	*lit*
oblation	*relig*	oleander	*trees*	orangery	*fruit*
observer	*jobs*	oleaster	*fruit*	oratorio	*music*
obsidian	*mineral*	oleo|gear	*travel*	oratress	*jobs*
obsolete	*time*	oligarch	*govt*	ordinand	*jobs*
occasion	*time*	oliphant	*animals*	ordinary	*herald*
Occident	*geog*	olive|oil	*food*	ordinary	*trade*
occluded	*weather*	olive|oil	*medic*	ordinary	*travel*
occupant	*jobs*	Olympiad	*sport*	ordnance	*geog*
ocean|bed	*marine*	Olympian	*myth*	ordnance	*war*
octapody	*lit*	omelette	*food*	organism	*biol*
Octavian	*lit*	omnivore	*animals*	organist	*jobs*
Octavius	*names*	oncoming	*travel*	organist	*music*
octonary	*maths*	on|credit	*trade*	origanum	*plants*
oddments	*trade*	on|demand	*trade*	original	*art*
odometer	*measure*	one|horse	*travel*	original	*lit*
Odysseus	*myth*	one|sided	*maths*	orillion	*war*
Odysseus	*names*	onlooker	*jobs*	ornament	*archit*
Oenomaus	*myth*	on|strike	*trade*	ornament	*house*
off|break	*sport*	on|the|dot	*time*	ornament	*music*
off|drive	*sport*	on|the|map	*geog*	orthodox	*relig*
offender	*law*	on|the|run	*law*	ostinato	*music*
offender	*people*	on|the|run	*travel*	otoscope	*medic*
offering	*relig*	op|artist	*jobs*	ouistiti	*animals*
official	*govt*	open|book	*lit*	our|times	*time*
official	*jobs*	open|file	*sport*	outboard	*machine*
off|price	*trade*	open|fire	*war*	outboard	*travel*
offprint	*lit*	open|note	*music*	outer|jib	*travel*
offshoot	*flowers*	open|plan	*archit*	outfield	*sport*
offshoot	*plants*	open|road	*travel*	outguard	*war*
offshore	*marine*	opera|hat	*clothes*	outhouse	*archit*

outhouse	*house*	paganism	*myth*	paragoge	*lit*
outlawry	*law*	paint|box	*art*	paragram	*lit*
outsider	*people*	paintbox	*art*	Paraguay	*rivers*
outsider	*sport*	painting	*art*	parakeet	*birds*
oval|ball	*sport*	painting	*house*	parallax	*astron*
ovenbird	*birds*	palatine	*govt*	parallel	*maths*
ovenware	*house*	paleface	*people*	parallel	*music*
overalls	*clothes*	palinode	*lit*	paramour	*people*
overcast	*weather*	palisade	*archit*	parasite	*insects*
overcoat	*clothes*	palisade	*war*	parasite	*medic*
Overdone	*Shakesp*	pall|mall	*sport*	parasite	*people*
overdose	*medic*	palmette	*archit*	par|avion	*foreign*
overfold	*geog*	palmetto	*trees*	parclose	*archit*
overhang	*geog*	palm|tree	*trees*	pardoner	*jobs*
overhaul	*trade*	palomino	*animals*	pargeter	*art*
overhaul	*travel*	palstaff	*war*	parietal	*medic*
overhead	*trade*	palstave	*war*	parlando	*music*
overkill	*war*	pamphlet	*lit*	parlante	*music*
overland	*travel*	pancreas	*medic*	Parnaiba	*rivers*
overload	*physics*	panda|car	*law*	parodist	*jobs*
overlord	*govt*	Pandarus	*Shakesp*	Parolles	*Shakesp*
overlord	*jobs*	pandemia	*medic*	Parousia	*relig*
overpass	*travel*	Pandulph	*Shakesp*	paroxysm	*medic*
overrule	*govt*	pangolin	*animals*	Parsifal	*lit*
overseas	*travel*	pannakin	*house*	Parsifal	*titles*
overseer	*jobs*	panorama	*art*	parterre	*archit*
overseer	*trade*	Panpipes	*music*	parterre	*theatre*
overtake	*travel*	Panpipes	*myth*	particle	*lit*
overtime	*trade*	pansophy	*educ*	particle	*measure*
overtone	*music*	Pantheon	*archit*	particle	*physics*
overture	*music*	Pantheon	*myth*	partisan	*govt*
overture	*theatre*	Panthino	*Shakesp*	partisan	*people*
overturn	*travel*	Panufnik	*music*	partisan	*war*
Oxbridge	*educ*	Papagena	*lit*	part|song	*music*
oxidizer	*chem*	Papageno	*lit*	party|man	*govt*
ox|pecker	*birds*	papillae	*medic*	party|man	*jobs*
oxymoron	*lit*	parabema	*archit*	par|value	*trade*
pabouche	*clothes*	parabola	*maths*	Pasiphae	*myth*
pacifism	*govt*	parabole	*lit*	passbook	*trade*
pacifist	*people*	paradigm	*lit*	passer|by	*jobs*
pacifist	*war*	paradigm	*physics*	passer|by	*travel*
pack|mule	*animals*	Paradise	*myth*	pass|line	*sport*
paddling	*sport*	Paradise	*relig*	pass|mark	*educ*
paduasoy	*clothes*	paradise	*theatre*	Passover	*relig*
Paganini	*music*	paraffin	*house*	Passover	*time*

passover	travel	pedology	chem	Perpetua	names
passport	govt	peduncle	flowers	perruque	clothes
passport	travel	peduncle	medic	Pershing	war
pass roll	sport	peep show	theatre	Persides	myth
pass time	time	Peer Gynt	titles	perspire	medic
password	lit	peignoir	clothes	Perugino	artists
password	war	Pekinese	animals	Pervaneh	lit
pastiche	art	pelerine	clothes	Peshawar	cities
pastille	art	pellagra	medic	petalody	flowers
pastille	food	Pembroke	Shakesp	Peter Pan	lit
pastoral	art	pembroke	house	Peter Pan	myth
pastoral	lit	pemmican	food	petition	law
pastoral	music	penal law	law	petit mal	medic
pastoral	theatre	pencraft	lit	Petrarch	writers
pastrami	food	pendulum	house	petronel	war
patentee	govt	pendulum	machine	Phaethon	myth
patentee	jobs	Penelope	myth	phalange	medic
Patience	lit	Penelope	names	phantasy	music
Patience	names	penitent	people	Pharisee	relig
patience	sport	penitent	relig	pharmacy	medic
Patience	titles	penknife	tools	pheasant	birds
Patricia	names	penmaker	jobs	pheasant	food
patty pan	house	Pennines	mounts	phenolic	chem
pauldron	war	penny dog	animals	philabeg	clothes
pavement	travel	penology	law	Philario	Shakesp
pavilion	archit	Pentagon	govt	Philemon	Shakesp
pavonian	birds	pentagon	maths	Philemon	myth
pawn shop	trade	Pentheus	myth	Philippa	names
pay talks	trade	pentosan	chem	philomel	birds
peachery	fruit	penumbra	astron	Philotis	myth
pea green	colour	Perceval	leaders	Philotus	Shakesp
peak arch	archit	Percival	myth	philtrum	medic
peak load	physics	Percival	names	phosgene	chem
pear tree	trees	perfumer	jobs	photomap	art
peasecod	veg	Pergamus	myth	photomap	geog
peat moss	plants	perianth	flowers	phrasing	music
pectoral	medic	Periboea	myth	phthisis	medic
peculate	law	pericarp	fruit	phyllome	plants
pedagogy	educ	Pericles	Shakesp	physalia	fish
pedantic	educ	Pericles	leaders	physical	medic
pedantry	educ	Pericles	titles	physical	physics
pedestal	archit	periplus	travel	physique	medic
pedicure	clothes	perjurer	jobs	pia mater	medic
pedigree	agric	perjurer	people	pianette	music
pediment	archit	peroxide	chem	pianiste	music

piassava	trees	pipe|tune	music	Pleiades	myth
picaroon	jobs	pisiform	medic	plein|air	art
picaroon	law	Pissarro	artists	pleonasm	lit
picayune	money	pit|stall	theatre	pleurisy	medic
pickerel	fish	pittance	trade	plimsoll	clothes
pick|me|up	medic	Pittheus	myth	Plimsoll	travel
picturer	art	pit|viper	insects	Pliocene	geog
pictures	film/TV	placenta	medic	plumbago	mineral
Pierides	lit	plagiary	jobs	plumbago	plants
Pierides	music	planchet	money	plum|cake	food
Pierides	myth	plangent	music	plunging	sport
pigs|feet	food	plankton	biol	Plutarch	writers
pigswill	agric	plankton	fish	Pluviose	time
pigswill	food	plantage	plants	Plymouth	cities
pike|dive	sport	plantain	plants	pochette	clothes
pikehead	war	plantain	veg	podagric	medic
pilaster	archit	plant|pot	plants	Podarces	myth
pilchard	fish	plantule	plants	podargus	birds
pilferer	jobs	plastics	chem	podiatry	medic
pillager	jobs	platanna	animals	poethood	lit
pillwort	plants	plateaux	geog	poetizer	lit
pilotage	travel	platform	archit	poet|king	lit
pimiento	fruit	platform	govt	poetling	jobs
pinacoid	physics	platform	theatre	poetling	lit
pinafore	clothes	platform	travel	poetship	lit
pinaster	trees	platinum	chem	Pointers	astron
Pindaric	lit	platinum	jewels	pointing	archit
Pindarus	Shakesp	platinum	mineral	poisoner	jobs
pine|cone	trees	platypus	animals	pokeweed	plants
pine|tree	trees	playbook	lit	polar|cap	geog
ping|pong	sport	playbook	theatre	polar|fox	animals
pink|lady	drink	playgoer	theatre	polarity	physics
pinkroot	plants	playland	theatre	polemics	educ
pin|money	trade	playmate	sport	pole|star	astron
pinnacle	archit	playroom	archit	polisher	house
pinnacle	geog	playroom	house	polisher	jobs
pinniped	animals	playroom	sport	polisher	tools
pinochle	sport	play|suit	clothes	politico	govt
pinscher	animals	playtime	educ	politics	govt
pin|table	sport	playwork	theatre	polka|dot	clothes
pinwheel	machine	pleading	law	polliwog	animals
pipefish	fish	plebeian	people	polo|ball	sport
pipeline	machine	plectron	music	polo|neck	clothes
pipeline	trade	plectrum	music	polonium	chem
pipe|rack	house	Pleiades	astron	polonium	mineral

Polonius	*Shakesp*	
polo|pony	*animals*	
polo|pony	*sport*	
poltroon	*people*	
poltroon	*war*	
polyacid	*chem*	
Polydore	*Shakesp*	
polygamy	*govt*	
polyglot	*educ*	
polyglot	*lit*	
Polyxena	*myth*	
pomander	*clothes*	
pond|lily	*flowers*	
pondweed	*plants*	
pontifex	*jobs*	
pontifex	*relig*	
ponyskin	*clothes*	
pony|tail	*clothes*	
pony|trek	*sport*	
pool|room	*sport*	
poop|deck	*travel*	
poor|soul	*people*	
poorwill	*birds*	
pope's|eye	*food*	
pop|group	*music*	
popinjay	*birds*	
popinjay	*people*	
pop|music	*music*	
poppy|red	*colour*	
pore|over	*educ*	
pork|chop	*food*	
porkling	*animals*	
porphyry	*mineral*	
porpoise	*animals*	
porridge	*food*	
porridge	*law*	
porthole	*travel*	
Portland	*cities*	
portrait	*art*	
portrait	*house*	
Port|Said	*cities*	
portside	*travel*	
port|tack	*sport*	
port|tack	*travel*	
Portunus	*myth*	

port|wine	*drink*	
Poseidon	*myth*	
position	*geog*	
position	*jobs*	
position	*trade*	
positive	*art*	
positive	*physics*	
positron	*physics*	
posology	*medic*	
post|boat	*travel*	
postcard	*lit*	
postcard	*travel*	
postcode	*travel*	
postdate	*time*	
postgrad	*educ*	
post|horn	*music*	
postiche	*clothes*	
postlude	*music*	
post|paid	*trade*	
postpone	*time*	
potation	*drink*	
Potemkin	*war*	
potherbs	*veg*	
Potiphar	*Bible*	
potmaker	*jobs*	
pot|plant	*house*	
pot|roast	*food*	
potsherd	*art*	
poultice	*medic*	
poundage	*trade*	
powdered	*herald*	
power|cut	*physics*	
power|saw	*tools*	
practice	*jobs*	
practice	*medic*	
practice	*theatre*	
practice	*trade*	
Prairial	*time*	
praise|be	*relig*	
prattler	*people*	
preacher	*educ*	
preacher	*jobs*	
preacher	*relig*	
preamble	*govt*	
precinct	*geog*	

precinct	*law*	
predator	*animals*	
predella	*relig*	
pregnant	*medic*	
premiere	*film/TV*	
premiere	*theatre*	
premises	*trade*	
premolar	*medic*	
prenatal	*medic*	
preserve	*food*	
pressman	*jobs*	
pressman	*lit*	
pressure	*physics*	
pressure	*weather*	
Pretoria	*cities*	
previous	*time*	
price|cut	*trade*	
price|war	*trade*	
prie|dieu	*relig*	
primrose	*colour*	
primrose	*flowers*	
Primrose	*names*	
princess	*govt*	
printers	*lit*	
printery	*lit*	
printing	*art*	
printing	*lit*	
print|out	*compul*	
prioress	*jobs*	
prismoid	*maths*	
prisoner	*jobs*	
prisoner	*law*	
prizeman	*jobs*	
procaine	*medic*	
proceeds	*trade*	
producer	*film/TV*	
producer	*jobs*	
producer	*theatre*	
producer	*trade*	
pro|forma	*foreign*	
progress	*travel*	
prologue	*lit*	
prologue	*theatre*	
promisor	*law*	
promoter	*jobs*	

prompter	jobs	purblind	medic	quisling	people
prompter	theatre	purchase	trade	quisling	war
promptly	time	pure|silk	clothes	quit|rent	trade
property	archit	purlieus	geog	quiz|game	sport
property	theatre	purslane	plants	quiz|show	film/TV
property	trade	purveyor	jobs	quotient	maths
prophase	biol	pus|basin	medic	quo|vadis	war
prosaism	lit	pushball	sport	rabbitry	animals
prospect	archit	pushcart	travel	Rabelais	writers
prospect	geog	puss|moth	insects	racegoer	sport
prospect	trade	pussy|cat	animals	rack|rent	trade
Prospero	Shakesp	put|price	trade	radar|man	jobs
prostate	medic	put|to|bed	lit	radiator	house
protasis	lit	put|to|sea	travel	radiator	machine
protasis	theatre	Putumayo	rivers	radiator	physics
protocol	govt	put|up|job	govt	radiator	travel
protozoa	animals	Pyongang	cities	radio|ham	sport
province	geog	pyorrhea	medic	radio|set	machine
province	relig	pyramids	sport	raga|rock	music
Prudence	names	Pyrenees	mounts	ragtimer	music
prudence	virtues	pyroxene	mineral	rag|trade	clothes
Prunella	names	pyx|cloth	relig	rag|trade	jobs
prunello	fruit	quackery	people	rag|trade	trade
psalmody	music	quadrans	money	ragwoman	jobs
psaltery	music	quadrant	maths	railroad	travel
psaltery	relig	quadrant	measure	rain|belt	weather
psychist	jobs	quadrate	maths	raincoat	clothes
publican	jobs	quadriga	travel	rain|drop	weather
publican	relig	quaestor	law	rainfall	weather
puffball	plants	quagmire	geog	rain|tree	trees
puff|bird	birds	quandong	trees	rainy|day	trade
pugilism	sport	quantity	chem	rainy|day	weather
pugilist	jobs	quantity	maths	rakehell	people
pugilist	sport	quarrier	jobs	rambling	sport
puissant	govt	quarters	archit	Rambures	Shakesp
pullover	clothes	quatrain	lit	rambutan	trees
pulmonic	medic	queen|ant	insects	rara|avis	birds
pulsejet	machine	queen|bee	insects	rare|bird	birds
pulsejet	travel	quenelle	food	rare|book	lit
pumicite	mineral	question	educ	Rasselas	titles
pump|room	medic	question	govt	Ratcliff	Shakesp
puncheon	war	quilting	clothes	rational	maths
punctual	time	quintain	sport	ratsbane	plants
puncture	travel	Quirinus	myth	Rattigan	writers
punditry	educ	quisling	govt	raw|umber	colour

reaching	*sport*	
reactant	*chem*	
reaction	*chem*	
reaction	*medic*	
reaction	*physics*	
reactive	*chem*	
reactive	*physics*	
read|copy	*lit*	
read|up|on	*educ*	
ready|pen	*lit*	
rebuttal	*law*	
receipts	*trade*	
receiver	*jobs*	
receiver	*law*	
receiver	*machine*	
receiver	*physics*	
receiver	*travel*	
recently	*time*	
receptor	*medic*	
reckoner	*trade*	
recorder	*jobs*	
recorder	*law*	
recorder	*machine*	
recorder	*music*	
recorder	*physics*	
recorder	*trade*	
recovery	*sport*	
recovery	*trade*	
recreant	*war*	
red|algae	*plants*	
red|belly	*fish*	
redbrick	*educ*	
red|cedar	*trees*	
red|cloak	*sport*	
Red|Cross	*medic*	
red|dwarf	*astron*	
red|giant	*astron*	
red|light	*travel*	
red|maple	*trees*	
red|ochre	*colour*	
redouble	*sport*	
red|poppy	*flowers*	
red|sable	*clothes*	
redshank	*birds*	
red|shift	*physics*	

redstart	*birds*	
reedbird	*birds*	
reed|mace	*plants*	
reed|pipe	*music*	
reed|stop	*music*	
reef|band	*travel*	
reef|knot	*travel*	
refinery	*machine*	
refinery	*trade*	
reformer	*govt*	
reformer	*jobs*	
regicide	*govt*	
regiment	*war*	
Reginald	*names*	
register	*machine*	
register	*music*	
register	*trade*	
regnancy	*govt*	
regrater	*trade*	
rehearse	*theatre*	
Reignier	*Shakesp*	
reigning	*govt*	
reindeer	*animals*	
relation	*family*	
relation	*lit*	
relative	*family*	
religion	*relig*	
remedial	*medic*	
renegade	*people*	
renegade	*war*	
rent|free	*trade*	
rent|roll	*trade*	
repeater	*machine*	
repetend	*maths*	
reporter	*jobs*	
reporter	*lit*	
repousse	*art*	
reprieve	*law*	
republic	*govt*	
repulsor	*war*	
requital	*trade*	
rescript	*lit*	
research	*chem*	
research	*educ*	
research	*jobs*	

research	*physics*
reserves	*trade*
reserves	*war*
resident	*jobs*
resident	*medic*
resinoid	*chem*
resistor	*machine*
resistor	*physics*
Respighi	*music*
response	*music*
rest|cure	*medic*
retailer	*jobs*
retailer	*trade*
retainer	*jobs*
retainer	*trade*
reticule	*clothes*
reveille	*music*
reveille	*war*
reveller	*jobs*
revenant	*jobs*
revenant	*myth*
reviewer	*jobs*
reviewer	*lit*
revision	*educ*
revision	*lit*
revolver	*war*
row|writer	*jobs*
Reynaldo	*Shakesp*
rhapsode	*lit*
rhapsody	*lit*
rhapsody	*music*
rheology	*chem*
rheostat	*machine*
rheostat	*physics*
rhetoric	*lit*
rhizopod	*animals*
rhomboid	*maths*
rhyolite	*mineral*
ribgrass	*plants*
rice|beer	*drink*
rice|bird	*birds*
rice|soup	*drink*
richesse	*trade*
richling	*trade*
Richmond	*Shakesp*

Richmond	*cities*	
Richmond	*herald*	
rickshaw	*travel*	
ricochet	*sport*	
ricochet	*war*	
Riesling	*drink*	
rifleman	*jobs*	
rifleman	*war*	
rigadoon	*music*	
right|now	*time*	
ringdove	*birds*	
ring|down	*theatre*	
ringdyke	*geog*	
ring|road	*travel*	
ringtail	*birds*	
ringtime	*time*	
ringworm	*medic*	
rink|polo	*sport*	
riparian	*geog*	
ripe|corn	*cereal*	
risalder	*war*	
ritenuto	*music*	
river|bed	*geog*	
river|hog	*animals*	
riverine	*geog*	
rivetter	*jobs*	
roadgang	*jobs*	
road|sign	*travel*	
roadster	*travel*	
roborant	*medic*	
rocaille	*archit*	
rockaway	*travel*	
rock|bird	*birds*	
rock|cake	*food*	
rock|cook	*fish*	
rock|dove	*birds*	
rock|fish	*fish*	
rock|lark	*birds*	
rockling	*fish*	
rock|rose	*flowers*	
rock|salt	*food*	
rock|salt	*mineral*	
rockweed	*plants*	
Roderick	*names*	
Roderigo	*Shakesp*	
roentgen	*measure*	
roentgen	*physics*	
roll|cast	*educ*	
roly|poly	*food*	
romancer	*lit*	
romancer	*people*	
Romanism	*relig*	
Roman|law	*law*	
romantic	*lit*	
romantic	*people*	
rood|loft	*relig*	
roof|rack	*travel*	
root|beer	*drink*	
root|crop	*agric*	
root|crop	*veg*	
root|knot	*plants*	
root|word	*lit*	
ropeband	*travel*	
rope|ring	*sport*	
ropework	*travel*	
Rosalind	*Shakesp*	
Rosalind	*names*	
Rosaline	*Shakesp*	
Rosamund	*names*	
Rosebery	*leaders*	
rosebowl	*house*	
rose|bush	*flowers*	
rose|fish	*fish*	
Rosemary	*names*	
rosemary	*trees*	
rosemary	*veg*	
roseroot	*flowers*	
rosewood	*trees*	
Rossetti	*artists*	
Rossetti	*writers*	
rotarian	*jobs*	
rotation	*agric*	
rotation	*geog*	
rotavate	*agric*	
Rothesay	*herald*	
rotovate	*agric*	
rough|sea	*marine*	
roulette	*sport*	
rounders	*sport*	
round|lot	*trade*	
round|sum	*trade*	
Rousseau	*artists*	
Rousseau	*writers*	
royalist	*govt*	
royal|oak	*trees*	
rubidium	*chem*	
rubidium	*mineral*	
ruby|port	*drink*	
ruby|type	*lit*	
rucksack	*sport*	
rucksack	*travel*	
rudiment	*biol*	
rugmaker	*jobs*	
ruminant	*animals*	
rum|punch	*drink*	
runabout	*travel*	
runagate	*war*	
run|ahead	*travel*	
runner|up	*sport*	
Runstedt	*war*	
rush|hour	*trade*	
rush|hour	*travel*	
rutabaga	*veg*	
Ruy|Lopez	*sport*	
rye|bread	*food*	
ryegrass	*plants*	
Sabazius	*myth*	
sabotage	*govt*	
saboteur	*govt*	
saboteur	*jobs*	
sabulose	*geog*	
sacellum	*relig*	
sack|race	*sport*	
sacristy	*archit*	
sacristy	*relig*	
safehold	*war*	
sage|cock	*birds*	
sago|palm	*trees*	
sailboat	*travel*	
sailfish	*fish*	
sail|free	*travel*	
sail|loft	*travel*	
sainfoin	*fruit*	
Sakhalin	*islands*	
salaried	*trade*	

Salarino	Shakesp	sapgreen	colour	scansion	lit
saleroom	trade	sapindus	trees	scanties	clothes
salesman	jobs	sapijutan	animals	scaphoid	medic
salesman	trade	sapphire	colour	scapular	clothes
Saliclaw	govt	sapphire	jewels	scapular	relig
salivary	medic	sapphire	mineral	scarabee	insects
salmonid	fish	saraband	music	scarcity	trade
Salonika	cities	saraband	sport	Scarlett	names
saltbeef	food	Sarajevo	cities	scarring	medic
saltdown	trade	Sarasate	music	scenario	theatre
saltlake	geog	Sarastro	lit	sceneman	theatre
saltpork	food	sardines	sport	schedule	trade
saltwort	plants	Sardinia	islands	schedule	travel
salvager	jobs	sardonyx	jewels	Schiller	writers
Samantha	names	sardonyx	mineral	schnapps	drink
samarium	chem	sargasso	plants	scholion	lit
samarium	mineral	Sarpedon	myth	scholium	lit
samphire	plants	Satanism	myth	schooner	drink
sanatory	medic	satirist	jobs	schooner	travel
sanction	govt	satirist	lit	Schubert	music
sanction	trade	Saturday	time	Schumann	music
sanctity	relig	saucebox	people	sciatica	medic
sandbank	geog	saucepan	house	Scillies	islands
sandbank	marine	sauropod	animals	scimitar	war
sanddart	insects	Sauterne	drink	sciolist	educ
sanddune	geog	Savannah	rivers	sciolist	jobs
sandflea	insects	sawbones	jobs	scissile	physics
sandhill	geog	sawknife	tools	scissors	house
SanDiego	cities	sawsmith	jobs	scissors	tools
sandiron	sport	saxeblue	colour	scorcher	weather
sandlark	birds	sayonara	foreign	scordato	music
sandling	fish	scabbard	war	scorpion	insects
sandmole	animals	scabiosa	flowers	scotfree	law
sandpeep	birds	scabious	flowers	scoutcar	travel
sandreef	marine	scaffold	archit	Scrabble	sport
sandshoe	clothes	scaffold	law	scragend	food
sandsole	fish	scaffold	machine	scramble	food
sandspit	geog	scalawag	people	scramble	sport
sandtrap	sport	scallion	veg	screamer	birds
sandwasp	insects	scallops	herald	Scriabin	music
sandwich	food	scalping	trade	scribble	lit
sanguine	colour	scandium	chem	scrofula	medic
sanguine	herald	scandium	mineral	scrubber	house
Santiago	cities	scanning	lit	scrumcap	sport
SaoPaulo	cities	scanning	physics	scullery	archit

scullery	*house*	sea snake	*insects*	septette	*music*
sculling	*sport*	sea snipe	*birds*	septimal	*maths*
scullion	*jobs*	seasonal	*time*	septuple	*maths*
sculptor	*art*	sea swine	*animals*	sequence	*maths*
Sculptor	*astron*	sea trout	*fish*	sequence	*music*
sculptor	*jobs*	seawrack	*plants*	seraphic	*relig*
sea acorn	*fish*	secretin	*medic*	seraphim	*relig*
sea adder	*fish*	security	*govt*	serenade	*music*
sea beast	*fish*	security	*trade*	serenata	*music*
seaberry	*plants*	sedation	*medic*	sergeant	*jobs*
sea blite	*plants*	sedative	*medic*	sergeant	*law*
seaboard	*geog*	sediment	*chem*	serology	*medic*
seaboard	*marine*	scdiment	*geog*	serotine	*animals*
sea bream	*fish*	seedcase	*flowers*	servitor	*educ*
sea devil	*fish*	seedcase	*plants*	servitor	*jobs*
Sea Drift	*titles*	seed leaf	*plants*	sessions	*law*
sea eagle	*fish*	seedling	*flowers*	set forth	*travel*
seafarer	*jobs*	seedsman	*jobs*	set piece	*theatre*
seafarer	*travel*	seedtime	*geog*	set point	*sport*
sea floor	*marine*	seedtime	*time*	sex ratio	*biol*
seagoing	*travel*	segreant	*herald*	sextette	*music*
seagrape	*plants*	seigneur	*govt*	sextolet	*music*
seagreen	*colour*	selector	*jobs*	sextuple	*maths*
sea heath	*flowers*	selector	*machine*	shadbush	*trees*
sea holly	*plants*	selector	*sport*	shaddock	*fruit*
sea horse	*animals*	selenite	*mineral*	shallows	*geog*
sea hound	*fish*	selenium	*chem*	shamrock	*plants*
sea lemon	*fish*	Seleucus	*Shakesp*	Shanghai	*cities*
sea level	*geog*	self heal	*fruit*	shanghai	*govt*
sealskin	*clothes*	self made	*trade*	shanghai	*travel*
sea lungs	*fish*	semester	*educ*	Shantung	*clothes*
sea lyham	*animals*	semester	*time*	Sharrapu	*myth*
seamless	*clothes*	semi dome	*archit*	shearing	*agric*
sea nymph	*myth*	seminary	*educ*	sheepdip	*agric*
sea otter	*animals*	seminary	*flowers*	sheep dog	*animals*
sea perch	*fish*	semissis	*money*	sheer leg	*travel*
seapiece	*art*	semitone	*music*	sheer off	*travel*
seaplane	*travel*	semolina	*cereal*	shelduck	*birds*
sea robin	*fish*	semplice	*music*	shell out	*sport*
sea route	*travel*	semuncia	*money*	shepherd	*animals*
seascape	*art*	senility	*medic*	shepherd	*jobs*
seascape	*marine*	sentence	*law*	Shepherd	*relig*
seashore	*geog*	sentence	*lit*	Sheridan	*writers*
seashore	*marine*	sentinel	*jobs*	Sherlock	*names*
sea snail	*fish*	sentinel	*war*	Shetland	*animals*

shilling	*money*	Sibelius	*music*	Sisyphus	*myth*
shinbone	*medic*	sick|abed	*medic*	sitology	*biol*
shingles	*medic*	sickling	*medic*	sitz|bath	*house*
ship|ahoy	*travel*	sickness	*medic*	sixpence	*money*
shipmate	*jobs*	sickroom	*medic*	skean|dhu	*war*
shipmate	*travel*	side|arms	*war*	skeletal	*medic*
shipment	*trade*	side|blow	*sport*	skeleton	*lit*
ship|oars	*travel*	sideburn	*clothes*	skeleton	*medic*
shipping	*travel*	side|dish	*food*	sketcher	*art*
shipworm	*insects*	side|door	*archit*	sketcher	*jobs*
shipyard	*trade*	side|door	*house*	skewback	*archit*
shirring	*clothes*	side|drum	*music*	skewbald	*animals*
shirting	*clothes*	side|kick	*jobs*	skiagram	*art*
shirt|pin	*clothes*	side|line	*sport*	ski|boots	*clothes*
shoebill	*birds*	sideline	*trade*	skidding	*travel*
shoehorn	*clothes*	sidereal	*astron*	skid|mark	*travel*
shoehorn	*house*	siderite	*mineral*	skin|deep	*medic*
shoelace	*clothes*	side|road	*travel*	skin|dose	*medic*
shoe|tree	*clothes*	side|show	*theatre*	skin|game	*sport*
Sholapur	*cities*	sideslip	*travel*	skinhead	*people*
shooting	*sport*	sidesman	*jobs*	ski|pants	*clothes*
shopgirl	*jobs*	side|step	*travel*	skirmish	*war*
shopping	*trade*	side|vent	*clothes*	ski|slope	*sport*
short|bit	*money*	sidewalk	*travel*	ski|stick	*sport*
short|bob	*clothes*	siege|cap	*clothes*	skittles	*sport*
short|hop	*travel*	siege|cap	*herald*	skua|gull	*birds*
short|leg	*sport*	siege|cap	*war*	skullcap	*clothes*
short|run	*trade*	silencer	*machine*	skullcap	*relig*
short|ton	*measure*	silencer	*travel*	skylight	*archit*
shot|silk	*clothes*	silicate	*chem*	skylight	*house*
shoulder	*archit*	silicone	*chem*	skyscape	*art*
shoulder	*food*	silk|gown	*jobs*	sky|scout	*jobs*
shoulder	*medic*	silkworm	*insects*	slapdash	*art*
shoulder	*travel*	Silurian	*geog*	slattern	*people*
show|a|leg	*travel*	Silvanus	*names*	slave|ant	*insects*
showboat	*theatre*	sinapism	*medic*	sledging	*sport*
showboat	*travel*	Sinclair	*names*	Sleipnir	*myth*
showcase	*trade*	Sinclair	*writers*	Slightly	*lit*
showgirl	*jobs*	sinecure	*jobs*	slip|case	*lit*
showroom	*trade*	sinecure	*trade*	sliphorn	*music*
shrapnel	*war*	sine|wave	*physics*	slipover	*clothes*
shredder	*house*	Sing|Sing	*law*	slippers	*clothes*
shredder	*machine*	sing|song	*music*	slip|ring	*machine*
shutters	*archit*	sinister	*herald*	slip|road	*travel*
shutters	*house*	sink|unit	*house*	slipslop	*lit*

sloebush	*fruit*	soft|soap	*house*	southpaw	*sport*
sloetree	*trees*	software	*comput*	soy|beans	*veg*
slop|bowl	*house*	software	*machine*	soy|flour	*cereal*
slop|pail	*house*	softwood	*trees*	soy|sauce	*food*
slow|ball	*sport*	solar|day	*time*	Space|Age	*physics*
slow|down	*travel*	solarium	*archit*	Space|Age	*time*
slow|lane	*travel*	solarium	*astron*	space|gun	*war*
slow|pile	*physics*	solarium	*house*	spaceman	*jobs*
slow|worm	*insects*	solation	*chem*	spaceman	*travel*
slum|area	*archit*	solatium	*govt*	spadroon	*war*
small|fry	*jobs*	solatium	*trade*	spagyric	*chem*
small|pox	*medic*	soldiery	*war*	spandril	*archit*
small|sum	*trade*	solecism	*lit*	spar|deck	*travel*
smarting	*medic*	sol|faist	*music*	sparling	*fish*
smash|hit	*theatre*	solidity	*trade*	sparring	*sport*
smelting	*mineral*	solitary	*jobs*	spawning	*fish*
smithery	*machine*	solleret	*war*	spearman	*jobs*
smocking	*clothes*	solo|stop	*music*	spearman	*war*
Smollett	*writers*	solstice	*time*	specimen	*biol*
smuggler	*jobs*	solution	*chem*	specimen	*medic*
smuggler	*law*	solvency	*trade*	spectrum	*art*
snack|bar	*archit*	somatist	*medic*	spectrum	*geog*
snap|brim	*clothes*	sombrero	*clothes*	spectrum	*physics*
snap|roll	*travel*	somebody	*people*	speculum	*medic*
snapshot	*art*	Somerset	*Shakesp*	speed|cop	*jobs*
snapshot	*sport*	Somerset	*herald*	speed|cop	*law*
sneakers	*clothes*	Somerset	*names*	speeding	*travel*
snowball	*geog*	some|time	*time*	speedway	*sport*
snowball	*sport*	sonatina	*music*	spelling	*educ*
snowbird	*birds*	songbird	*birds*	spelling	*lit*
snowdrop	*flowers*	songbird	*music*	spending	*trade*
snowfall	*weather*	song|book	*music*	spergula	*plants*
snowland	*geog*	songplay	*music*	sphenoid	*biol*
snow|line	*geog*	songster	*jobs*	sphenoid	*medic*
snow|line	*sport*	songster	*music*	spheroid	*maths*
snub|nose	*clothes*	son|in|law	*family*	sphygmus	*medic*
snuff|box	*house*	Son|of|Man	*relig*	spianato	*music*
soap|dish	*house*	soothing	*medic*	spice|jar	*house*
soapsuds	*house*	sorcerer	*jobs*	spigelia	*plants*
soapwort	*plants*	sorcerer	*myth*	spikelet	*plants*
Sobranje	*govt*	sorehead	*people*	spinette	*music*
sociable	*travel*	soreness	*medic*	spinster	*family*
softball	*sport*	sore|spot	*medic*	spit|curl	*clothes*
soft|cell	*trade*	sounding	*marine*	spitfire	*people*
soft|drug	*medic*	sour|note	*music*	Spithead	*seas*

spittoon *house*	standoff *sport*	stockcar *travel*
spitzdog *animals*	standpat *sport*	stocking *clothes*
splenium *medic*	Stanford *music*	stockman *jobs*
splinter *govt*	stanhope *travel*	stockpot *food*
splitpea *veg*	stapelia *flowers*	StoneAge *geog*
spondaic *lit*	starfish *fish*	StoneAge *time*
spontoon *war*	starling *birds*	stonefly *insects*
spoonful *measure*	startoff *travel*	stopbath *art*
spoonoar *sport*	startout *travel*	stopover *travel*
Sporades *islands*	starturn *jobs*	Stoppard *writers*
sporadic *time*	starturn *theatre*	stopshot *sport*
sporting *sport*	StarWars *war*	storeman *jobs*
spotcash *trade*	starwort *plants*	storeyed *archit*
spotsale *trade*	stasimon *theatre*	Stormont *govt*
spraygun *tools*	stations *sport*	stowaway *jobs*
sprinter *jobs*	statuary *art*	stowaway *travel*
sprinter *sport*	staveoff *war*	StPierre *islands*
sprocket *machine*	staysail *travel*	Strachey *writers*
spurgear *machine*	stealage *law*	straddle *sport*
squadcar *law*	stealing *law*	strafing *war*
squadcar *travel*	steatite *mineral*	straggle *travel*
squadron *war*	steerage *travel*	straight *sport*
squareup *trade*	steering *travel*	straight *theatre*
squeezer *house*	stegodon *animals*	strainer *house*
squiffer *music*	steinbok *animals*	stranger *jobs*
squirrel *animals*	Stendhal *writers*	stranger *people*
SriLanka *islands*	Stephano *Shakesp*	strategy *war*
Srinagar *cities*	sterling *trade*	strawhat *clothes*
stabbing *war*	sternway *travel*	straycat *animals*
staccato *music*	Steropes *myth*	straydog *animals*
staffcar *travel*	StHelena *islands*	straying *travel*
Stafford *Shakesp*	stibnite *mineral*	streamer *clothes*
stagedom *theatre*	stickpin *clothes*	streamer *herald*
stageman *jobs*	stiletto *war*	Strephon *lit*
stageman *theatre*	Stilwell *war*	striatum *medic*
stageset *theatre*	stimulus *biol*	strikeup *music*
stagnant *geog*	stinging *medic*	stripper *jobs*
staining *art*	stingray *fish*	stroller *jobs*
stairway *archit*	stitches *medic*	stroller *theatre*
stairway *house*	StMartin *islands*	struggle *war*
stalking *sport*	stoccado *sport*	strummer *music*
stallion *animals*	stockade *archit*	studious *educ*
stalwart *war*	stockade *war*	studying *educ*
standard *herald*	stockcar *sport*	stuffing *food*
standard *measure*		stuntman *jobs*

stuntman	travel	surfbird	birds	tabletop	house
sturgeon	fish	surgical	medic	tachisme	art
subacute	medic	suricate	animals	tackling	travel
subatoms	physics	surplice	clothes	tagalong	travel
subimago	insects	surplice	relig	taglioni	clothes
suborder	animals	surprise	war	tailboom	travel
suborder	biol	surround	house	tailcoat	clothes
subpoena	law	surround	war	tailpipe	travel
subtitle	lit	surveyor	jobs	tailrace	geog
subtitle	theatre	survivor	jobs	tailskid	travel
subtopia	archit	Suwannee	rivers	tailspin	travel
subtract	maths	suzerain	govt	takeabow	theatre
subucula	clothes	Svengali	lit	takearms	war
suburban	geog	swaddled	clothes	takeaway	food
suburbia	archit	swagsman	jobs	takeover	trade
succubus	myth	SwanLake	titles	takeroot	plants
Suckling	writers	swansong	music	takesick	medic
sudarium	medic	swapping	trade	takesilk	law
suddenly	time	swastika	herald	taketime	time
sufferer	medic	sweetbay	trees	talesman	law
suffrage	govt	sweetpea	flowers	talisman	myth
suitcase	travel	sweetsop	trees	tallyman	jobs
Sullivan	music	swellbox	music	tallyman	trade
sulphate	chem	swelling	medic	tamarack	trees
sulphide	chem	swiftlet	birds	tamarind	food
sulphite	chem	swimsuit	clothes	tamarind	trees
summitry	govt	swindler	law	tamarisk	plants
sumtotal	maths	swindler	people	tamboura	music
sunblind	house	sybarite	people	tanaiste	govt
sunburst	weather	sycamine	trees	tantalum	chem
sundries	trade	sycamore	trees	tantalum	mineral
sundrops	flowers	syllable	lit	tantalus	drink
sungrebe	birds	syllabub	food	Tantalus	myth
sunlight	weather	syllabus	lit	tapaculo	birds
sunporch	archit	symbolic	art	tapdance	sport
sunshine	weather	symphony	music	tapedeck	film/TV
sunspots	astron	symploce	lit	tapestry	art
sunstone	jewels	synapsis	biol	tapestry	clothes
sunstone	mineral	syncline	geog	tapestry	house
superior	jobs	syndesis	biol	tapeworm	insects
superman	jobs	synopsis	lit	tarboosh	clothes
supertax	trade	synoptic	lit	tarlatan	clothes
supplier	jobs	tabbycat	animals	tarragon	food
supplies	food	tableleg	house	tarragon	plants
supplies	trade	tablemat	house	Tartarus	myth

tartrate	*chem*	tenement	*archit*	the|dance	*theatre*
Tashkent	*cities*	tenement	*law*	the|Deuce	*myth*
Tasmania	*islands*	tenendum	*law*	the|field	*sport*
tau|cross	*herald*	Tenerife	*islands*	the|front	*war*
Taverner	*music*	Tennyson	*writers*	The|Hague	*cities*
tawny|owl	*birds*	tenor|cor	*music*	The|Idiot	*titles*
taxation	*govt*	tenoroon	*music*	The|Iliad	*titles*
taxation	*trade*	tentacle	*fish*	thematic	*lit*
tax|dodge	*trade*	tent|pole	*sport*	The|Minch	*seas*
taxi|rank	*travel*	teocalli	*archit*	the|Muses	*music*
taxonomy	*biol*	Teraphim	*myth*	the|Muses	*myth*
taxpayer	*jobs*	teratoma	*medic*	Theodora	*names*
taxpayer	*trade*	terminal	*comput*	Theodore	*names*
teabread	*food*	terminal	*machine*	theology	*relig*
tea|break	*food*	terminal	*travel*	theorist	*people*
tea|caddy	*drink*	terminus	*travel*	the|Press	*lit*
tea|chest	*house*	terraced	*archit*	theropod	*animals*
teaching	*educ*	terrapin	*animals*	the|Seven	*myth*
tea|cloth	*house*	Tertiary	*geog*	Thespian	*jobs*
teal|duck	*birds*	Terylene	*clothes*	Thespian	*theatre*
team|game	*sport*	terzetto	*music*	the|stage	*theatre*
tear|drop	*medic*	tessella	*art*	the|sword	*war*
tear|duct	*medic*	testamur	*law*	The|Waves	*titles*
teaspoon	*house*	test|case	*law*	thiamine	*biol*
teaspoon	*measure*	test|tube	*chem*	thievery	*law*
tea|table	*house*	tetragon	*maths*	thin|skin	*medic*
tectonic	*archit*	textbook	*educ*	third|act	*theatre*
teddy|boy	*jobs*	textbook	*lit*	third|man	*sport*
teenager	*jobs*	Thai|silk	*clothes*	thirlage	*law*
teething	*medic*	thalamus	*archit*	this|week	*time*
teetotum	*machine*	thalamus	*medic*	tholepin	*machine*
telecast	*film/TV*	Thaliard	*Shakesp*	tholepin	*sport*
telefilm	*film/TV*	thallium	*chem*	tholepin	*travel*
telegram	*travel*	thallium	*mineral*	Thompson	*writers*
Telemann	*music*	Thanatos	*myth*	thoracic	*medic*
teletype	*machine*	thatcher	*jobs*	thousand	*measure*
teletype	*travel*	Thatcher	*leaders*	thrasher	*birds*
tell|tale	*people*	thearchy	*govt*	threnody	*music*
telluric	*geog*	The|Ashes	*sport*	thresher	*machine*
template	*machine*	The|Bells	*titles*	thriller	*lit*
temporal	*medic*	the|Bench	*law*	throstle	*birds*
temporal	*time*	the|bends	*medic*	throttle	*machine*
tenaille	*war*	the|brush	*art*	throttle	*travel*
ten|cents	*money*	The|Cenci	*titles*	thruster	*physics*
tenebrae	*relig*	the|chair	*govt*	thurible	*relig*

thurifer	*jobs*	tolbooth	*archit*	trachyte	*mineral*
thurifer	*relig*	tolbooth	*trade*	tracking	*sport*
Thursday	*time*	tollgate	*travel*	track|rod	*machine*
Thyestes	*myth*	tomahawk	*war*	tractate	*lit*
thyroxin	*medic*	Tom|Jones	*lit*	traction	*medic*
Tibullus	*writers*	Tom|Jones	*titles*	trade|gap	*trade*
tidal|rip	*marine*	tommy|bar	*tools*	trade|off	*trade*
tide|gate	*geog*	Tommy|gun	*war*	tragical	*theatre*
tide|race	*geog*	tomorrow	*time*	tragopan	*birds*
tie|break	*sport*	Tom|Pinch	*lit*	trailing	*sport*
Tien|Shan	*mounts*	Tom|Thumb	*jobs*	training	*educ*
Tientsin	*cities*	tonalist	*music*	training	*sport*
tiger|cat	*animals*	tonality	*music*	trainman	*jobs*
tiger|nut	*fruit*	tone|deaf	*music*	train|set	*sport*
tightwad	*people*	tone|down	*music*	tramline	*travel*
tile|roof	*archit*	tone|poem	*music*	transect	*biol*
Timandra	*Shakesp*	tone|poet	*jobs*	transept	*archit*
time|bill	*trade*	tone|poet	*music*	transept	*relig*
time|bomb	*machine*	tonguing	*music*	transfix	*war*
time|bomb	*war*	tonic|key	*music*	trap|door	*archit*
timeless	*time*	Tonle|Sap	*lakes*	trap|door	*house*
time|worn	*time*	too|early	*time*	trappist	*jobs*
time|zone	*geog*	tool|shop	*trade*	traprock	*mineral*
Timor|Sea	*seas*	toolwork	*trade*	traverse	*archit*
tinction	*art*	top|boots	*clothes*	traverse	*travel*
tincture	*art*	top|brass	*govt*	travesty	*theatre*
tincture	*chem*	top|brass	*jobs*	treasure	*trade*
tincture	*colour*	top|floor	*archit*	treasury	*govt*
tincture	*herald*	toponymy	*lit*	treasury	*lit*
tingling	*medic*	toponymy	*medic*	Treasury	*trade*
tin|miner	*jobs*	top|price	*trade*	treatise	*educ*
tinsmith	*jobs*	toreador	*jobs*	treatise	*lit*
tinstone	*mineral*	toreador	*sport*	tree|fern	*plants*
tipstaff	*law*	tortilla	*food*	tree|frog	*animals*
titanium	*chem*	tortoise	*animals*	tree|lily	*plants*
titanium	*mineral*	torturer	*jobs*	tree|moss	*plants*
Tithonus	*myth*	total|war	*war*	trembler	*birds*
Titinius	*Shakesp*	totitive	*maths*	tremella	*plants*
titmouse	*birds*	Totopoly	*sport*	trencher	*biol*
toad|fish	*birds*	Toulouse	*cities*	trenches	*war*
toad|flax	*plants*	town|hall	*archit*	trephine	*medic*
toboggan	*travel*	town|hall	*govt*	trespass	*law*
tocogony	*medic*	township	*geog*	tressure	*herald*
tocology	*medic*	townsman	*jobs*	triangle	*maths*
toilette	*clothes*	trachoma	*medic*	triangle	*music*

triarchy	govt	tumerous	medic	ulcerous	medic
Triassic	geog	tunalfish	fish	ultimate	time
tribasic	chem	tunester	jobs	ultraist	govt
tribrach	lit	tunester	music	umbrella	clothes
tribunal	law	tungsten	chem	unacorda	music
tricycle	travel	tungsten	mineral	unciform	biol
triglyph	archit	tuppence	money	unciform	medic
trigonal	maths	Turandot	lit	UncleSam	govt
trigraph	lit	Turandot	titles	UncleTom	lit
trillium	flowers	turbofan	machine	underarm	sport
trimaran	travel	turbojet	machine	underbid	trade
trimeter	lit	turbojet	travel	undercut	sport
trimming	clothes	Turgenev	writers	undercut	trade
trimsail	travel	turmeric	plants	underdog	people
trimship	travel	turmeric	veg	underlay	house
Trinculo	Shakesp	turnapot	art	underlay	machine
Trinidad	islands	turnaway	travel	underpar	sport
trioxide	chem	turnback	war	underpin	archit
tripeman	jobs	turncoat	people	undertow	geog
triplets	family	turncoat	war	underway	travel
trippant	herald	turnover	food	undulate	geog
triptych	archit	turnover	trade	ungulate	animals
tristich	lit	turnover	travel	unicycle	travel
Tristram	myth	turnpike	travel	unionist	jobs
Tristran	myth	turnspit	animals	unionman	jobs
trochaic	lit	turntail	animals	unitcell	physics
trochoid	maths	turntail	war	univalve	fish
Trollope	writers	tutelate	educ	universe	astron
trombone	music	tutorage	educ	unstable	chem
trotcozy	clothes	tutoress	educ	untilnow	time
trotters	food	tutorial	educ	untimely	time
troupial	birds	tutoring	educ	upheaval	geog
trousers	clothes	tweezers	clothes	upinarms	war
troutlet	animals	tweezers	tools	upperair	astron
trouvere	lit	twilight	time	uppercut	sport
trouvere	music	twopence	money	upperten	govt
trouveur	lit	twopiece	clothes	uprising	war
truckler	people	twotimer	people	upstairs	archit
truebill	law	tympanon	music	upstairs	house
trueskin	medic	tympanum	archit	uptodate	time
tubercle	medic	tympanum	medic	uricacid	chem
tuberose	plants	typecast	theatre	uroscopy	medic
tuberose	veg	typeface	lit	usheress	theatre
tubeworm	insects	typepage	lit	usufruct	trade
tugofwar	sport	typesize	lit	vacation	educ

vaccinia	*medic*	
vagabond	*jobs*	
vagabond	*people*	
valerian	*medic*	
valerian	*plants*	
Valhalla	*myth*	
Valkyrie	*myth*	
valorize	*trade*	
valuable	*trade*	
valuator	*jobs*	
vambrace	*herald*	
vambrace	*war*	
vamp|horn	*music*	
vamplate	*war*	
vanadium	*chem*	
vanadium	*mineral*	
Vanbrugh	*artists*	
Van|Buren	*USpres*	
Vanburgh	*writers*	
vanguard	*jobs*	
vanguard	*war*	
vanquish	*war*	
vargueno	*house*	
variable	*maths*	
variance	*maths*	
variolar	*medic*	
vascular	*biol*	
vascular	*medic*	
vasculum	*plants*	
vaseline	*medic*	
vaulting	*sport*	
velocity	*maths*	
velocity	*physics*	
velocity	*travel*	
vena|cava	*medic*	
venality	*trade*	
venation	*sport*	
vendetta	*govt*	
vendetta	*war*	
vendible	*trade*	
venotomy	*medic*	
verandah	*archit*	
verbatim	*govt*	
verbatim	*lit*	
verbiage	*lit*	

verjuice	*drink*	
Verlaine	*writers*	
vermouth	*drink*	
Veronese	*artists*	
veronica	*flowers*	
Veronica	*names*	
versed|in	*educ*	
verselet	*lit*	
verseman	*lit*	
versicle	*lit*	
versicle	*relig*	
vertebra	*medic*	
Verwoerd	*leaders*	
vesicant	*medic*	
vespiary	*insects*	
vestment	*clothes*	
vestment	*relig*	
Vesuvius	*mounts*	
vexillum	*herald*	
viameter	*measure*	
viaticum	*food*	
viaticum	*relig*	
vibrator	*machine*	
viburnum	*trees*	
vicarage	*relig*	
vice|king	*govt*	
vicenary	*maths*	
vice|ring	*law*	
vicinity	*geog*	
Victoria	*names*	
victoria	*travel*	
Victrola	*music*	
victuals	*food*	
vignette	*art*	
vignette	*lit*	
Villette	*titles*	
vinculum	*maths*	
vine|leaf	*fruit*	
vineyard	*agric*	
vineyard	*fruit*	
Violenta	*Shakesp*	
Violetta	*lit*	
Violette	*names*	
viperish	*insects*	
viperous	*insects*	

Virgilia	*Shakesp*	
virginal	*music*	
Virginia	*names*	
viridian	*colour*	
virology	*biol*	
virtuosa	*music*	
virtuosi	*music*	
virtuoso	*art*	
virtuoso	*jobs*	
virtuoso	*music*	
viscacha	*animals*	
viscount	*govt*	
vitality	*medic*	
vitamin|A	*biol*	
vitamin|B	*biol*	
vitamin|C	*biol*	
vitamin|D	*biol*	
vitamin|E	*biol*	
vitellus	*biol*	
vivarium	*animals*	
Vlaminck	*artists*	
vocalion	*music*	
vocalism	*music*	
vocalist	*jobs*	
vocalist	*music*	
vocation	*jobs*	
vocation	*trade*	
vocative	*lit*	
volatile	*chem*	
volatile	*travel*	
volcanic	*mineral*	
volplane	*travel*	
Voltaire	*writers*	
Volumnia	*Shakesp*	
vomiting	*medic*	
Vorspiel	*music*	
voussoir	*archit*	
wagon|lit	*travel*	
wainscot	*archit*	
wainscot	*house*	
waitress	*jobs*	
walkover	*sport*	
wall|eyed	*medic*	
wallfish	*fish*	
wall|game	*sport*	

wall newt	insects	Water Rat	lit	white fly	insects
wall safe	house	water tap	house	white fox	animals
wall tent	archit	waterway	travel	white tie	clothes
wandered	medic	watt hour	measure	Whitmore	Shakesp
wanderoo	animals	watt hour	physics	Whittier	writers
Wanganui	rivers	wave form	physics	whittler	jobs
warbling	music	waybread	plants	whizz kid	people
war cloud	war	wayfarer	jobs	whodunit	lit
warcraft	war	wayfarer	travel	wig block	clothes
war dance	war	wayfarer	war	wig block	house
ward maid	jobs	way train	travel	wigmaker	jobs
wardmote	govt	weakfish	fish	wigmaker	theatre
wardress	jobs	weakling	medic	wild boar	animals
wardrobe	clothes	weaponry	war	wild duck	birds
wardrobe	house	wear ship	travel	wildfowl	birds
wardrobe	theatre	web press	lit	wild goat	animals
wardroom	travel	web press	machine	wild life	animals
warfarer	war	weeklong	time	wild oats	cereal
warhorse	animals	well read	educ	wild rose	flowers
warhorse	war	well to do	trade	WildWest	geog
war hound	war	werefolk	myth	Williams	Shakesp
warm cell	geog	werewolf	myth	wind band	music
warm wave	geog	Wesleyan	relig	wind belt	weather
war paint	clothes	westerly	geog	wind cock	weather
war paint	war	west wind	weather	wind cone	travel
warplane	travel	wet nurse	jobs	wind cone	weather
warraga l	animals	wet nurse	medic	wind drag	travel
war whoop	war	wharfage	trade	windlass	machine
wash sale	trade	wharf rat	animals	windmill	archit
watchdog	animals	wheatear	birds	windmill	machine
watchdog	trade	wheat eel	insects	wind pump	machine
watchman	jobs	wheatfly	insects	wind sock	travel
water boa	insects	wheelies	travel	windvane	weather
water bug	insects	wheelman	jobs	windward	travel
water bus	travel	whenever	time	wing area	sport
water cow	animals	Whiggism	govt	wing over	travel
water dog	animals	whimbrel	birds	wingspan	birds
water fly	insects	whinchat	birds	Winifred	names
water gap	geog	whip hand	jobs	Winnipeg	cities
waterhen	birds	whip jack	jobs	wireless	house
water ice	food	whiskers	clothes	wireless	machine
water jug	house	whistler	animals	wireless	theatre
Waterloo	war	Whistler	artists	wireless	travel
waterman	jobs	white ant	insects	wireworm	insects
water rat	animals	white cap	birds	wiseacre	people

wise|fool	*people*	
wishbone	*food*	
wistaria	*flowers*	
witch,elm	*trees*	
withdraw	*travel*	
wolf,fish	*fish*	
wolf|pack	*animals*	
woodbind	*flowers*	
woodbine	*flowers*	
woodchat	*birds*	
wood|club	*sport*	
woodcock	*birds*	
wood|duck	*birds*	
wood|ibis	*birds*	
woodland	*trees*	
woodlark	*birds*	
woodlice	*insects*	
woodmite	*insects*	
wood|pulp	*trees*	
wood,sage	*flowers*	
woodshed	*house*	
wood|shot	*sport*	
woodsman	*jobs*	
wood,tick	*insects*	
Woodvile	*Shakesp*	
Woodward	*war*	
wood,wasp	*insects*	
woodwind	*music*	
woodworm	*archit*	
woodworm	*insects*	
wood,wren	*birds*	
woof|woof	*animals*	
woollens	*clothes*	
Wool|Sack	*govt*	

Wool|Sack	*law*
wordbook	*educ*
wordbook	*lit*
word|form	*lit*
workaday	*trade*
workfolk	*jobs*
workgirl	*jobs*
workhand	*jobs*
workings	*geog*
work|late	*trade*
workroom	*trade*
workshop	*trade*
world|war	*war*
wrangler	*educ*
wrangler	*jobs*
wrestler	*jobs*
wrestler	*sport*
wristlet	*clothes*
write|off	*trade*
xanthein	*colour*
xanthium	*plants*
Xenephon	*writers*
xenogamy	*biol*
xenolith	*mineral*
X,ray|tube	*machine*
X,ray|tube	*physics*
yachting	*sport*
yachting	*travel*
Yale|lock	*house*
Yale|lock	*machine*
yeanling	*animals*
yearbook	*lit*
yearbook	*time*
yearling	*animals*

yearlong	*time*
years|ago	*time*
yeomanry	*war*
Ygdrasil	*myth*
yodeller	*jobs*
yodeller	*music*
yoghourt	*food*
yoke,toed	*birds*
Yokohama	*cities*
yoldring	*birds*
yoretime	*time*
Yuletide	*time*
zambomba	*music*
Zanzibar	*islands*
zarzuela	*music*
zastruga	*geog*
zecchino	*money*
Zephyrus	*myth*
Zeppelin	*travel*
zero|hour	*travel*
zero|hour	*war*
ziggurat	*archit*
ziggurat	*relig*
zoetrope	*physics*
zoolater	*myth*
zoolatry	*myth*
zoom|lens	*art*
zoom|lens	*machine*
zoom|lens	*physics*
zoospore	*biol*
zoot|suit	*clothes*
zucchini	*veg*
zwieback	*food*

9 LETTERS

Aaron's|rod	*flowers*	
Aaron's|rod	*relig*	
abduction	*govt*	

Abimelech	*Bible*
ab|origine	*foreign*
aborigine	*jobs*

about,ship	*travel*
absconder	*govt*
absconder	*jobs*

absconder	trade	advalorem	trade	alarmbell	govt
abseybook	educ	advantage	sport	alarmbell	machine
absorbent	chem	advection	physics	albatross	birds
absurdist	theatre	adventure	lit	albespyne	trees
acappella	music	adverbial	lit	alchemist	chem
Acarnania	myth	adversary	people	alchemist	jobs
accession	govt	Aegisthus	myth	alcoholic	medic
accessory	govt	aepyornis	birds	alcoholic	people
accessory	people	aerialist	jobs	Aldebaran	astron
accidence	lit	aerodrome	travel	Aldebaran	myth
accompany	music	aeromotor	travel	Aleutians	islands
accordion	music	aeroplane	travel	Alexander	Shakesp
accoutred	war	Aeschylus	writers	Alexander	myth
aceydeucy	sport	aesthetic	art	Alexander	names
aciddrops	food	affidavit	law	Alexander	war
Aconcagua	mounts	affiliate	trade	Alexandra	names
acoustics	archit	affluence	geog	algarroba	trees
acoustics	music	affluence	trade	algebraic	maths
acoustics	physics	afortiori	foreign	algorithm	maths
acquittal	law	afterdeck	travel	Aliceband	clothes
acropolis	archit	afternoon	time	alignment	archit
acrospire	plants	afterthat	time	alkalizer	medic
acrostics	lit	aftertime	time	allaboard	travel
actinides	chem	Agamemnon	Shakesp	allabreve	music
actionist	govt	Agamemnon	myth	Allahabad	cities
activated	physics	Agamemnon	titles	allatonce	time
activator	physics	Agapemone	myth	allcomers	sport
adagietto	music	aggregate	maths	Allegheny	mounts
Adamswine	drink	aggregate	trade	Allelujah	relig
adansonia	trees	aggressor	war	allemande	music
addledegg	food	Aguecheek	Shakesp	alleviate	medic
addressee	travel	Ahasuerus	Bible	alligator	fruit
ademption	law	Ahmedabad	cities	alligator	insects
adhominem	foreign	Aigialeus	myth	allograph	lit
adiabatic	physics	airbridge	travel	allopathy	medic
adjective	lit	airengine	machine	allotment	agric
adlibitum	music	airhammer	tools	allotropy	chem
Admiralty	govt	airpocket	physics	allowance	trade
admission	medic	airpocket	travel	allsquare	sport
adnauseam	foreign	airsleeve	travel	almamater	educ
adoration	relig	airtoship	war	almshouse	archit
adrenalin	medic	airworthy	travel	aloeswood	trees
adulterer	people	aitchbone	food	Alphonsus	names
adulthood	time	aitchbone	medic	alpinefir	trees
adumbrate	geog	alabaster	mineral	altardesk	relig

altar|rail	*relig*	anchorite	*jobs*	antiquary	*jobs*
altimeter	*machine*	anchor|man	*sport*	antiquity	*time*
altimeter	*physics*	andantino	*music*	antiserum	*medic*
altimeter	*travel*	Andromeda	*astron*	antispast	*lit*
aluminium	*mineral*	Andromeda	*myth*	antitoxin	*medic*
Amagasaki	*cities*	andromeda	*trees*	ant|patrol	*insects*
amarantus	*flowers*	anecdotal	*lit*	ant|thrush	*birds*
amaryllis	*flowers*	anemology	*weather*	apartheid	*govt*
amaurosis	*medic*	anemostat	*weather*	apartment	*archit*
amazon|ant	*insects*	angel|cake	*food*	apartment	*house*
ambergris	*biol*	angel|fish	*fish*	Apemantus	*Shakesp*
ambulance	*medic*	angle|iron	*archit*	Apennines	*mounts*
ambulance	*travel*	anglesite	*chem*	aperiodic	*physics*
ambuscade	*war*	anglesite	*mineral*	aphid|pest	*insects*
amendment	*govt*	angleworm	*insects*	Aphrodite	*myth*
americium	*chem*	Angora|cat	*animals*	Apocrypha	*relig*
americium	*mineral*	anhydride	*chem*	apologist	*jobs*
amidships	*travel*	animation	*theatre*	apostille	*lit*
amino|acid	*chem*	anklebone	*medic*	apparatus	*chem*
amoebaean	*lit*	ankylosis	*medic*	apparatus	*machine*
amount|due	*trade*	Annabella	*names*	apparatus	*physics*
ampersand	*lit*	annealing	*physics*	appellant	*law*
Amphiarus	*myth*	annotator	*jobs*	appellate	*law*
amphibian	*animals*	annotator	*lit*	appetiser	*drink*
amphibian	*travel*	announcer	*jobs*	applecart	*travel*
amphibole	*mineral*	announcer	*theatre*	apple|tree	*fruit*
amphigory	*lit*	annuitant	*jobs*	applicant	*jobs*
amplifier	*machine*	annulment	*govt*	appraisal	*trade*
amplitude	*physics*	anonymous	*lit*	appraiser	*jobs*
Amsterdam	*cities*	Ansaphone	*house*	aqua|regia	*chem*
anabolism	*biol*	Anschluss	*foreign*	aquarelle	*art*
anabranch	*geog*	antarctic	*geog*	aqua|vitae	*drink*
anacrusis	*lit*	antenatal	*medic*	aquilegia	*flowers*
anaerobic	*biol*	anthelion	*astron*	arabesque	*music*
analeptic	*medic*	anthemion	*archit*	arabesque	*sport*
analgesia	*medic*	anthology	*lit*	arabesque	*theatre*
analgesic	*medic*	Anticleia	*myth*	arachnoid	*insects*
anamnesis	*medic*	anticline	*geog*	aragonite	*mineral*
anarchist	*govt*	Antigonus	*Shakesp*	arbitrage	*trade*
Anastasia	*names*	antihelix	*medic*	arboretum	*trees*
anastasis	*art*	anti|novel	*lit*	arc|en|ciel	*foreign*
anastatic	*art*	Antiochus	*Shakesp*	Archangel	*cities*
anatomist	*jobs*	antipasto	*food*	archangel	*myth*
anchorage	*travel*	antiphony	*music*	archangel	*relig*
anchoress	*jobs*	antipodes	*geog*	arch|druid	*relig*

archenemy	jobs	art|minded	art	athletics	sport
archenemy	relig	art|school	art	Atlantica	myth
archenemy	war	art|school	educ	atmolysis	chem
archetype	biol	Arvigarus	Shakesp	atmometer	chem
archfiend	myth	Asahikawa	cities	atom|blast	physics
archfiend	relig	Ascension	islands	Atomic|Age	time
Archibald	Shakesp	Ascension	relig	atomic|gun	war
Archibald	names	Asclepiad	myth	atomicity	physics
archilute	music	Asclepios	myth	atomic|war	war
architect	archit	Asclepius	myth	atom|liner	travel
architect	jobs	Ashtaroth	myth	atomology	physics
archivist	jobs	asparagus	veg	atonement	relig
archivolt	archit	aspirator	chem	at|present	time
Arctic|fox	animals	aspirator	machine	attacking	war
arc|welder	tools	aspirator	medic	attainder	law
Areopagus	govt	assailant	war	attendant	jobs
Areopagus	law	Assaracus	myth	attenuate	biol
argentite	mineral	assez|bien	foreign	attestant	law
Argus|eyed	myth	assigning	herald	Attic|base	archit
aria|buffa	music	assistant	educ	Attic|salt	lit
Arimathea	Bible	assistant	jobs	Attic|salt	myth
Aristaeus	myth	associate	educ	attribute	lit
Aristotle	writers	associate	jobs	attrition	war
armadillo	animals	assonance	lit	aubergine	veg
armorials	herald	assuasive	medic	au|courant	foreign
Armorican	geog	assurgent	herald	audiology	medic
army|corps	war	Astrakhan	cities	Augustine	names
army|issue	war	astrakhan	clothes	au|naturel	foreign
army|lists	war	astrodome	sport	Aunt|Sally	people
arrearage	trade	astrodome	theatre	Aunt|Sally	sport
arrowhead	plants	astrodome	travel	auriscopy	medic
arrowhead	war	astrofell	plants	au|secours	foreign
arrowroot	food	astrolabe	astron	Ausgleich	foreign
arrowroot	plants	astrolabe	measure	authoress	jobs
arrow|shot	sport	astrology	astron	authoress	lit
art|critic	art	astronaut	jobs	authority	govt
art|critic	jobs	astronaut	travel	authority	jobs
art|dealer	jobs	astronomy	astron	autoclave	chem
artemisia	plants	Astydamia	myth	autocracy	govt
arthritis	medic	Atalantis	myth	autograph	lit
arthropod	animals	Atargatis	myth	Autolycus	Shakesp
artichoke	veg	atavistic	biol	Autolycus	myth
artificer	jobs	Athabaska	rivers	automatic	machine
artillery	war	Athenaeum	educ	automatic	war
art|lesson	art	Athenaeum	lit	automaton	jobs

automaton	machine	baldmoney	plants	barmaster	law
autopilot	machine	Balearics	islands	barmbrack	food
autopilot	travel	balladist	jobs	barndance	sport
autopista	travel	balldress	clothes	barnstorm	theatre
autorifle	war	ballerina	jobs	barograph	physics
autoroute	foreign	ballerina	music	barometer	house
autotimer	house	ballerina	theatre	barometer	measure
avalanche	geog	ballistic	war	barometer	physics
avizandum	law	ballotbox	govt	barometer	weather
avocation	trade	ballpoint	lit	baroscope	physics
Axiocersa	myth	balmasque	foreign	baroscope	weather
axlesmith	jobs	balsamfir	trees	barracuda	fish
azureblue	colour	balsawood	trees	barricade	chem
babirussa	animals	Balthasar	Shakesp	barrister	jobs
babygrand	music	Balthazar	Shakesp	barrister	law
babylinen	clothes	Baltimore	cities	barrowboy	jobs
babyrussa	animals	bandaging	medic	barrowboy	trade
bacchanal	people	bandalore	sport	bartering	trade
bacchante	myth	banderole	archit	basemetal	mineral
backbench	govt	banderole	herald	basicload	travel
backcloth	theatre	banderole	war	basicsalt	chem
backcourt	sport	bandicoot	animals	basrelief	archit
backedges	sport	bandmajor	music	basrelief	art
backplate	herald	bandolier	war	Bassianus	Shakesp
backplate	war	bandstand	music	bastinado	war
backropes	travel	bandstand	theatre	Bathchair	medic
backshift	trade	bandwagon	travel	Bathchair	travel
backstage	theatre	bandyball	sport	bathsalts	clothes
backswing	sport	baneberry	fruit	bathsalts	house
backwater	geog	Bangalore	cities	Bathsheba	Bible
backwater	travel	bangsring	animals	bathtowel	house
backwoods	geog	banjolele	music	battalion	war
bacterium	medic	bankclerk	trade	battleaxe	people
badcheque	trade	bankstock	trade	battleaxe	war
badgerdog	animals	banquette	archit	battlecry	war
badminton	sport	banquette	food	battology	lit
bagatelle	music	BantryBay	seas	baulkline	sport
bagatelle	sport	barbarian	people	baywindow	archit
bailiwick	govt	barbarian	relig	baywindow	house
bakingtin	house	barbitone	medic	beachball	sport
balaclava	clothes	barcarole	music	beachhead	war
balalaika	music	Barcelona	cities	beadhouse	archit
baldachin	clothes	bargainer	jobs	beafeater	birds
baldachin	relig	bargepole	travel	beanfeast	food
baldeagle	birds	barmagnet	machine		

bean goose	*birds*	Benbecula	*islands*	bird's nest	*plants*
bearberry	*plants*	Ben Gurion	*leaders*	bird table	*birds*
Beardsley	*artists*	bent grass	*plants*	birthmark	*medic*
bear panic	*trade*	ben venuto	*foreign*	birthwort	*plants*
bear's foot	*flowers*	berg adder	*insects*	bisulcate	*biol*
Beatitude	*relig*	berkelium	*chem*	bite to eat	*food*
Beau Geste	*titles*	Bernstein	*music*	bit player	*jobs*
beaux arts	*art*	beryllium	*chem*	bit player	*theatre*
beaux yeux	*foreign*	beryllium	*mineral*	bivalence	*chem*
beaver rat	*animals*	best bower	*sport*	bivariant	*chem*
beccafico	*birds*	bete noire	*foreign*	black bass	*fish*
bedded out	*flowers*	Bethlehem	*Bible*	black bear	*animals*
bed jacket	*clothes*	Bethphage	*Bible*	black belt	*sport*
bedridden	*medic*	Bethsaida	*Bible*	Black Bess	*animals*
bed settee	*house*	bevel gear	*machine*	blackbird	*birds*
bedspread	*house*	bewitcher	*myth*	blackbook	*govt*
bee beetle	*insects*	biathlete	*sport*	blackbuck	*animals*
beech fern	*plants*	bifarious	*biol*	blackcock	*birds*
beefeater	*jobs*	Big Bertha	*war*	blackdrop	*drink*
beefeater	*war*	big dipper	*sport*	blackface	*lit*
beefsteak	*food*	bigeneric	*biol*	blackfish	*fish*
bee keeper	*jobs*	bilateral	*biol*	blackgame	*birds*
Beelzebub	*Bible*	bilge keel	*travel*	blackgang	*travel*
Beelzebub	*myth*	bilge pump	*machine*	blackhead	*birds*
Beelzebub	*relig*	bilge pump	*travel*	blackhead	*medic*
beer glass	*food*	billabong	*geog*	blackjack	*herald*
beer glass	*house*	billiards	*sport*	blackjack	*sport*
beermaker	*jobs*	Bill Sikes	*lit*	blackjack	*war*
Beer sheba	*Bible*	Billy Budd	*lit*	blacklead	*mineral*
Beethoven	*music*	Billy Budd	*titles*	blackmail	*law*
beet sugar	*veg*	billycock	*clothes*	blackmass	*myth*
beggarman	*jobs*	billy goat	*animals*	blackmass	*relig*
beleaguer	*war*	bimonthly	*lit*	Blackmore	*writers*
bel esprit	*foreign*	bimonthly	*time*	blackonyx	*jewels*
belle amie	*foreign*	binocular	*physics*	blackopal	*jewels*
bellicism	*war*	binturong	*animals*	blackpawn	*sport*
bellicose	*war*	biography	*lit*	blackswan	*birds*
bellmaker	*jobs*	biologist	*jobs*	blacktern	*birds*
bell tower	*archit*	Biondello	*Shakesp*	blackware	*art*
bellyache	*medic*	bionomics	*biol*	bladework	*sport*
below deck	*travel*	bipyramid	*maths*	blaeberry	*fruit*
below zero	*weather*	birdhouse	*birds*	blank door	*house*
belt punch	*tools*	birdlouse	*insects*	blasphemy	*relig*
belvedere	*archit*	bird's foot	*plants*	blast wave	*physics*
Ben Battle	*lit*	bird's nest	*birds*	blindfish	*fish*

blindness	*medic*	Boccaccio	*writers*	bookstall	*lit*
blind|pool	*trade*	body|check	*sport*	bookstand	*lit*
blind|spot	*medic*	body|clock	*biol*	bookstore	*lit*
blindworm	*insects*	bodyguard	*govt*	book|token	*lit*
blockship	*travel*	bodyguard	*jobs*	book|trade	*lit*
blood|bank	*medic*	bodymaker	*jobs*	boomerang	*war*
blood|feud	*govt*	body|odour	*medic*	bootblack	*jobs*
bloodroot	*plants*	body|of|law	*law*	bootmaker	*jobs*
bloodshed	*war*	body|punch	*sport*	boric|acid	*chem*
blood|test	*medic*	Boëllmann	*music*	boric|acid	*medic*
blow|a|horn	*music*	bog|myrtle	*plants*	borrowing	*trade*
blow|torch	*tools*	bog|orchid	*plants*	bossa|nova	*sport*
Bluebeard	*people*	boiled|egg	*food*	bottle|tit	*birds*
blueberry	*fruit*	boilerman	*jobs*	bottoming	*archit*
blue|black	*colour*	bold|faced	*lit*	boulevard	*travel*
blue|blood	*govt*	bolection	*archit*	bound|over	*law*
blue|blood	*medic*	bolometer	*physics*	bourasque	*weather*
bluegrass	*plants*	bolshevik	*govt*	Bourchier	*Shakesp*
blue|heron	*birds*	boltsmith	*jobs*	bourgeois	*govt*
blue|jeans	*clothes*	bombardon	*music*	bourgeois	*lit*
blue|movie	*film/TV*	bombasine	*clothes*	bower|bird	*birds*
blue|peter	*herald*	bomb|happy	*war*	bow|fiddle	*music*
blue|peter	*travel*	bombs|away	*war*	bow|a|long	*travel*
blueprint	*archit*	bombshell	*war*	bow|legged	*medic*
blueprint	*art*	bombsight	*war*	bowler|hat	*clothes*
blue|shark	*fish*	Bonaparte	*leaders*	bowstring	*sport*
blue|sheep	*animals*	Bonaparte	*war*	bow|window	*archit*
blue|skies	*weather*	bond|issue	*trade*	box|camera	*art*
blues|song	*music*	bonus|bond	*trade*	box|girder	*archit*
blue|whale	*animals*	bon|vivant	*foreign*	Boxing|Day	*time*
blusterer	*people*	bon|viveur	*foreign*	box|office	*theatre*
Boanerges	*Bible*	bon|voyage	*travel*	box|office	*trade*
board|foot	*measure*	booby|trap	*machine*	box|waggon	*travel*
board|room	*trade*	booby|trap	*war*	boy|friend	*family*
boarhound	*animals*	bookboard	*lit*	Boyle's|law	*physics*
boarhound	*sport*	book|cloth	*lit*	boy|wonder	*people*
boar|spear	*sport*	book|cover	*lit*	Brabantio	*Shakesp*
boathouse	*travel*	bookcraft	*lit*	bracteole	*plants*
Boatswain	*Shakesp*	book|louse	*insects*	brain|cell	*medic*
boatswain	*jobs*	booklover	*educ*	brain|wash	*govt*
boatswain	*travel*	booklover	*lit*	brainwave	*educ*
boat|train	*travel*	bookmaker	*jobs*	brainwork	*educ*
bobbin|net	*clothes*	bookmaker	*lit*	brake|drum	*machine*
bobsleigh	*sport*	bookshelf	*house*	brake|shoe	*machine*
bobsleigh	*travel*	bookshelf	*lit*	brambling	*birds*

brandling	*fish*	broomcorn	*cereal*	burrstone	*mineral*
brandling	*insects*	broomrape	*plants*	bus|driver	*jobs*
brand|name	*trade*	brown|bear	*animals*	bus|driver	*travel*
brass|band	*music*	brown|belt	*sport*	bush|pilot	*jobs*
brasserie	*house*	Brown|Bess	*war*	bush|shirt	*clothes*
brass|hats	*jobs*	brown|bill	*war*	bussu|palm	*trees*
brassiere	*clothes*	Brunswick	*cities*	buttercup	*flowers*
Brazil|nut	*food*	brush|deer	*animals*	butterfly	*insects*
Brazil|nut	*fruit*	brushland	*geog*	butternut	*trees*
breadline	*trade*	brush|wolf	*animals*	butter|pat	*food*
breakaway	*theatre*	brushwood	*trees*	butt|joint	*archit*
breakdown	*medic*	brushwork	*art*	Buxtehude	*music*
breakfast	*food*	bubble|car	*travel*	buy|in|bulk	*trade*
breast|pin	*clothes*	bubble|gum	*food*	by|auction	*trade*
breeze|fly	*insects*	buccaneer	*govt*	by|bidding	*trade*
breezeway	*archit*	buccaneer	*jobs*	by|product	*trade*
Breton|hat	*clothes*	Bucharest	*cities*	byrewoman	*jobs*
bric\,a\,brac	*art*	bucketing	*trade*	bystander	*jobs*
bric\,a\,brac	*house*	buck|hound	*animals*	caballine	*animals*
brick|kiln	*art*	buckthorn	*trees*	cab|driver	*jobs*
brickwork	*archit*	buckwheat	*cereal*	cab|driver	*travel*
bridewell	*law*	bucoliast	*lit*	cabin|crew	*jobs*
brief|case	*law*	bugle|call	*music*	cable|code	*trade*
brier|bush	*trees*	bugle|horn	*music*	cablegram	*travel*
brigadier	*jobs*	bulb|field	*flowers*	cable|rate	*trade*
Brigg|Fair	*titles*	bulldozer	*machine*	cabriolet	*travel*
brilliant	*jewels*	bulldozer	*travel*	cacodemon	*myth*
brilliant	*lit*	bull|finch	*birds*	cacophony	*music*
brilliant	*mineral*	bull|panic	*trade*	caddie|car	*sport*
brilliant	*weather*	bull|snake	*insects*	caddis|fly	*insects*
brimstone	*insects*	bull|trout	*fish*	cadet|line	*herald*
brimstone	*mineral*	bully|beef	*food*	Caesarean	*medic*
brimstone	*myth*	bully|tree	*trees*	cafe|owner	*jobs*
bring|suit	*law*	bumble|bee	*insects*	cafeteria	*archit*
Britannia	*myth*	Bumbledom	*law*	Caffre|cat	*animals*
broadcast	*film/TV*	Bundesrat	*govt*	cairngorm	*jewels*
broadloom	*clothes*	Bundestag	*govt*	cairngorm	*mineral*
broadside	*travel*	bunkhouse	*archit*	Caithness	*Shakesp*
broadside	*war*	bunny|girl	*jobs*	cakemaker	*jobs*
broken|arm	*medic*	buona|sera	*foreign*	cakestand	*house*
broken|leg	*medic*	burlesque	*theatre*	calamanco	*clothes*
brokerage	*trade*	burnisher	*machine*	calendula	*flowers*
Bronze|Age	*geog*	burnt|lake	*colour*	calenture	*medic*
Bronze|Age	*time*	burnt|rose	*colour*	calf's|head	*food*
brood|mare	*animals*	burro|deer	*animals*	caliphate	*govt*

callipers	*maths*	cantharis	*insects*	carpe|diem	*foreign*
callipers	*measure*	cantharus	*house*	carpenter	*jobs*
callipers	*medic*	cantharus	*relig*	carpenter	*relig*
callosity	*medic*	canticles	*relig*	carpenter	*theatre*
call|price	*trade*	cantilena	*music*	carpet|bag	*travel*
calmative	*medic*	canvasser	*jobs*	carpeting	*house*
Calpurnia	*Shakesp*	capacitor	*machine*	carpet|rod	*house*
Calvinist	*relig*	capacitor	*physics*	carrageen	*plants*
calvities	*medic*	caparison	*animals*	carronade	*war*
camass|rat	*animals*	caparison	*clothes*	carry|arms	*war*
Cambridge	*Shakesp*	caparison	*war*	Cartagena	*cities*
Cambridge	*cities*	Capernaum	*Bible*	cart|horse	*animals*
camel|coat	*clothes*	capillary	*physics*	cartilage	*medic*
camel|hair	*clothes*	cap|in|hand	*clothes*	cartouche	*archit*
camel|spin	*sport*	capitular	*govt*	cartouche	*war*
Camembert	*food*	capitulum	*flowers*	cartridge	*art*
cameo|pink	*colour*	cappucino	*drink*	cartridge	*war*
cameo|ware	*art*	cap|rhymes	*lit*	cartulary	*archit*
cameraman	*art*	capriccio	*music*	cartulary	*relig*
cameraman	*film/TV*	Capriccio	*titles*	cartwheel	*sport*
cameraman	*jobs*	Capricorn	*zodiac*	cartwheel	*travel*
camouflet	*war*	cap|sleeve	*clothes*	caruncula	*medic*
campanero	*birds*	captaincy	*govt*	case|lists	*law*
campanile	*archit*	cap|verses	*lit*	casemaker	*jobs*
campanula	*flowers*	carbonate	*chem*	casemated	*war*
canalboat	*travel*	carbonize	*chem*	case|sheet	*medic*
Canaletto	*artists*	carbuncle	*jewels*	cashew|nut	*food*
canal|rays	*physics*	carbuncle	*medic*	cashew|nut	*fruit*
candidate	*govt*	carbuncle	*mineral*	cash|grain	*trade*
candidate	*jobs*	carcinoma	*medic*	Cassandra	*Shakesp*
candle|fly	*insects*	cardsharp	*jobs*	Cassandra	*myth*
Candlemas	*time*	card|table	*house*	Cassandra	*names*
candle|nut	*fruit*	card|trick	*sport*	cassation	*law*
candytuft	*flowers*	careerist	*people*	casserole	*house*
cane|chair	*house*	career|man	*people*	cassimere	*clothes*
cane|sugar	*plants*	caretaker	*jobs*	castanets	*music*
canicular	*geog*	cargo|boat	*travel*	castellan	*war*
canicular	*time*	Carmelite	*relig*	castor|oil	*medic*
canker|fly	*insects*	carnation	*flowers*	casuarina	*trees*
cankerous	*medic*	carnelian	*jewels*	catacombs	*relig*
cannonade	*war*	carnelian	*mineral*	catalepsy	*medic*
cannoneer	*war*	carnivore	*animals*	catalogue	*lit*
canonical	*relig*	carnotite	*mineral*	catalogue	*trade*
can|opener	*tools*	carob|bean	*veg*	catalysis	*chem*
cantabile	*music*	carolling	*music*	catalytic	*chem*

catamaran	*travel*	
catamount	*animals*	
cat|and|dog	*animals*	
cataplasm	*medic*	
cataplexy	*medic*	
catatonia	*medic*	
catatonic	*medic*	
catch|cold	*medic*	
catch|line	*lit*	
catchment	*geog*	
catchpole	*govt*	
catchweed	*plants*	
catchword	*lit*	
catechism	*educ*	
catechism	*relig*	
catechize	*educ*	
caterwaul	*animals*	
catharsis	*medic*	
cathartic	*medic*	
cathedral	*archit*	
cathedral	*relig*	
Catherine	*names*	
Catskills	*mounts*	
cauchemar	*foreign*	
cauliculi	*archit*	
cauterize	*medic*	
cavalcade	*sport*	
Cavalcade	*titles*	
cave|canem	*foreign*	
cease|fire	*war*	
cedarbird	*birds*	
celandine	*flowers*	
celebrant	*relig*	
celebrity	*jobs*	
celestial	*astron*	
celestina	*music*	
cellarage	*trade*	
cellarman	*jobs*	
cell|block	*law*	
celluloid	*chem*	
cellulose	*chem*	
cement|gun	*tools*	
centaurea	*plants*	
Centaurus	*astron*	
Centaurus	*myth*	

centenary	*time*	
centigram	*measure*	
centipede	*insects*	
centumvir	*govt*	
centurion	*jobs*	
Cephissus	*myth*	
ceratodus	*animals*	
cerecloth	*relig*	
cerements	*relig*	
cerograph	*art*	
Cervantes	*writers*	
cha|cha|cha	*sport*	
chaetopod	*insects*	
chaffinch	*birds*	
chain|fern	*plants*	
chain|gang	*govt*	
chain|gang	*jobs*	
chain|mail	*war*	
chain|shot	*war*	
chair|lift	*sport*	
chalkdust	*educ*	
chalk|talk	*educ*	
challenge	*sport*	
challenge	*war*	
chalumeau	*music*	
chameleon	*insects*	
chamfrain	*war*	
champagne	*colour*	
champagne	*drink*	
champaign	*educ*	
champerty	*law*	
champleve	*art*	
chantilly	*clothes*	
chantress	*music*	
chaparral	*trees*	
charabanc	*travel*	
character	*film/TV*	
character	*lit*	
character	*people*	
character	*theatre*	
charivari	*music*	
charlatan	*people*	
charlotte	*food*	
Charlotte	*names*	
chartered	*jobs*	

charterer	*jobs*	
charwoman	*jobs*	
Charybdis	*myth*	
chassepot	*war*	
Chatillon	*Shakesp*	
chatterer	*people*	
chauffeur	*jobs*	
chauffeur	*travel*	
cheapjack	*trade*	
checkmate	*sport*	
Checkmate	*titles*	
check|rate	*trade*	
cheekbone	*medic*	
cheesefly	*insects*	
chemiatry	*chem*	
chemurgic	*chem*	
Chengchow	*cities*	
cherimoya	*fruit*	
cherry|red	*colour*	
Cherubini	*music*	
Cherubino	*lit*	
chess|game	*sport*	
chevelure	*clothes*	
chickadee	*birds*	
chickaree	*animals*	
chick|peas	*veg*	
chickwood	*plants*	
chief|mate	*travel*	
chieftain	*govt*	
Chief|Whip	*govt*	
chihuahua	*animals*	
Chihuahua	*cities*	
chilblain	*medic*	
childhood	*time*	
chiliagon	*maths*	
Chilterns	*mounts*	
china|clay	*art*	
china|clay	*mineral*	
China|root	*plants*	
China|rose	*flowers*	
China|silk	*clothes*	
chinaware	*art*	
chinaware	*house*	
chincapin	*trees*	
chinch|bug	*insects*	

chincough	*medic*	civil|case	*law*	clog|dance	*sport*
chinstrap	*clothes*	civil|list	*law*	clogmaker	*jobs*
chiropody	*medic*	civil|suit	*law*	cloisters	*relig*
chiseller	*art*	civil|time	*time*	closing|in	*sport*
chiseller	*people*	civil|year	*time*	cloud|bank	*weather*
Choephori	*titles*	clapboard	*archit*	cloudland	*myth*
chophouse	*archit*	clarendon	*lit*	cloud|over	*weather*
choppy|sea	*marine*	claret|red	*colour*	clove|pink	*flowers*
choralist	*jobs*	clarionet	*music*	club|chair	*house*
choralist	*music*	classical	*archit*	clubhouse	*archit*
chorister	*music*	classical	*lit*	club|house	*sport*
chorus|boy	*jobs*	classical	*music*	club|steak	*food*
chorus|boy	*theatre*	classmate	*educ*	coach|road	*travel*
chorus|man	*theatre*	classroom	*educ*	coachwork	*travel*
Chou|en|Lai	*leaders*	class|rule	*govt*	coadjutor	*jobs*
Christian	*names*	claustral	*relig*	coadjutor	*relig*
Christian	*relig*	claustrum	*medic*	coalfield	*geog*
Christina	*names*	clavicorn	*insects*	coal|house	*archit*
Christine	*names*	claviharp	*music*	coalition	*govt*
Christmas	*time*	clean|line	*art*	coal|miner	*jobs*
chromatic	*art*	cleansing	*medic*	coastland	*geog*
chromatic	*music*	clearance	*trade*	coastline	*geog*
chromatin	*biol*	clearance	*travel*	coastline	*marine*
chrome|red	*colour*	clear|soup	*drink*	coat|frock	*clothes*
chronicle	*lit*	cleithral	*archit*	coat|tails	*clothes*
chronicle	*time*	Cleomenes	*Shakesp*	cochineal	*food*
chrysalis	*insects*	Cleopatra	*Shakesp*	cochineal	*insects*
chthonian	*myth*	Cleopatra	*myth*	cochleate	*maths*
Churchill	*leaders*	clepsydra	*house*	Cockaigne	*myth*
Churchill	*rivers*	clepsydra	*time*	cockatiel	*birds*
Churchill	*writers*	clergyman	*jobs*	cocked|hat	*clothes*
churchman	*people*	clergyman	*relig*	cock|robin	*birds*
churchman	*relig*	Cleveland	*USpres*	cockscomb	*birds*
cicatrice	*medic*	Cleveland	*cities*	cockscomb	*plants*
cicindela	*insects*	clew|lines	*travel*	cocoa|wood	*trees*
cigarette	*house*	clientage	*trade*	coco|de|mer	*fruit*
Cimmerian	*myth*	clientele	*trade*	coelostat	*astron*
cinematic	*theatre*	cliff|face	*geog*	co|emption	*trade*
cineraria	*flowers*	clinician	*jobs*	coenobite	*jobs*
Cio|Cio|San	*lit*	clip|joint	*theatre*	coenobium	*biol*
cirrhosis	*medic*	clippings	*lit*	coffee|bug	*insects*
cisalpine	*geog*	cloakroom	*archit*	coffee|cup	*house*
citharist	*music*	cloakroom	*house*	coffer|dam	*archit*
cityscape	*art*	clock|golf	*sport*	coffering	*archit*
city|state	*geog*	clockwork	*machine*	coin|a|word	*lit*

coin|money	*trade*	
Cointreau	*drink*	
colcannon	*food*	
colchicum	*flowers*	
cold|cream	*clothes*	
cold|drink	*drink*	
cold|frame	*veg*	
cold|front	*weather*	
cold|short	*physics*	
cold|spell	*weather*	
cold|steel	*war*	
cole|garth	*veg*	
coleopter	*animals*	
Coleridge	*writers*	
Coleville	*Shakesp*	
collation	*food*	
colleague	*jobs*	
collector	*jobs*	
collector	*lit*	
collector	*sport*	
collegian	*educ*	
collegian	*govt*	
collision	*travel*	
collodion	*art*	
colloidal	*chem*	
collotype	*art*	
collotype	*lit*	
collyrium	*medic*	
colocynth	*veg*	
colonelcy	*govt*	
colonnade	*archit*	
colorific	*art*	
Colosseum	*archit*	
Colosseum	*theatre*	
colourful	*art*	
colouring	*art*	
colourist	*art*	
coltsfoot	*flowers*	
columbary	*birds*	
columbine	*birds*	
columbine	*flowers*	
Columbine	*theatre*	
columella	*archit*	
columnist	*jobs*	
columnist	*lit*	

combatant	*jobs*	
combatant	*sport*	
combatant	*war*	
combat|car	*travel*	
combative	*war*	
comforter	*clothes*	
comforter	*people*	
comic|book	*lit*	
Cominform	*govt*	
Comintern	*govt*	
commander	*govt*	
commander	*jobs*	
commenter	*lit*	
committee	*govt*	
commodity	*trade*	
commodore	*jobs*	
common|law	*law*	
Communion	*relig*	
communism	*govt*	
communist	*govt*	
companion	*jobs*	
compasses	*maths*	
complaint	*govt*	
complaint	*medic*	
component	*machine*	
composing	*lit*	
composite	*archit*	
composite	*flowers*	
concentus	*music*	
concierge	*jobs*	
concordat	*govt*	
Concordia	*myth*	
concourse	*geog*	
concourse	*travel*	
concubine	*jobs*	
concubine	*relig*	
condensed	*lit*	
condenser	*machine*	
condenser	*physics*	
condiment	*food*	
condition	*medic*	
conductor	*jobs*	
conductor	*music*	
conductor	*physics*	
conductor	*travel*	

confessor	*jobs*	
confessor	*relig*	
confidant	*jobs*	
confiture	*food*	
conger|eel	*fish*	
Coningsby	*titles*	
conjugate	*biol*	
conjugate	*lit*	
conjuring	*sport*	
conqueror	*war*	
conqueror	*jobs*	
conscious	*medic*	
conscript	*jobs*	
conscript	*war*	
consenter	*people*	
consonant	*lit*	
consonate	*music*	
Constable	*artists*	
constable	*govt*	
constable	*jobs*	
Constance	*Shakesp*	
Constance	*names*	
Constanze	*lit*	
consulate	*govt*	
contactor	*machine*	
contagion	*medic*	
container	*house*	
contender	*jobs*	
contender	*sport*	
continent	*geog*	
continual	*time*	
contralto	*jobs*	
contralto	*music*	
contusion	*medic*	
conundrum	*lit*	
converted	*archit*	
converted	*relig*	
converter	*machine*	
converter	*physics*	
convolute	*biol*	
cookhouse	*house*	
coparceny	*law*	
copolymer	*chem*	
copy|chief	*lit*	
copy|paper	*lit*	

copyright	*law*	costerman	*trade*	crayonist	*jobs*
copyright	*lit*	cost|price	*trade*	crazyweed	*plants*
coral|reef	*marine*	costumier	*jobs*	cream|cake	*food*
coral|root	*plants*	costumier	*theatre*	cream|horn	*food*
corduroys	*clothes*	cotangent	*maths*	cream|puff	*food*
coreopsis	*flowers*	cothurnus	*theatre*	cremation	*relig*
coriander	*plants*	cotillion	*sport*	crepuscle	*time*
coriander	*veg*	Cotswolds	*mounts*	crescendo	*music*
cork|borer	*chem*	cotton|gin	*machine*	cretinism	*medic*
corkscrew	*house*	cotton|rat	*animals*	cricketer	*jobs*
corkscrew	*tools*	cotyledon	*flowers*	cricketer	*sport*
corn|borer	*insects*	couchette	*travel*	crinoline	*clothes*
cornbrash	*geog*	cough|drop	*food*	criticism	*lit*
corn|bread	*cereal*	cough|drop	*medic*	criticism	*theatre*
corncrake	*insects*	cough|drop	*people*	crocodile	*animals*
Corneille	*writers*	countdown	*physics*	crocodile	*travel*
cornelian	*jewels*	countdown	*travel*	croissant	*food*
Cornelius	*Shakesp*	coup|detat	*govt*	croon|song	*music*
Cornelius	*names*	court|card	*sport*	croquette	*food*
cornerboy	*jobs*	court|fool	*jobs*	crossbeam	*archit*
cornfield	*agric*	court|list	*law*	crossbeam	*house*
cornfield	*cereal*	court|roll	*law*	crossbill	*birds*
cornflour	*cereal*	courtroom	*law*	crossette	*archit*
cornopean	*music*	courtyard	*archit*	cross|eyed	*medic*
corn|salad	*cereal*	couturier	*jobs*	cross|fire	*war*
corozo|nut	*fruit*	covalence	*chem*	crossfish	*fish*
corposant	*astron*	covalency	*chem*	crosshead	*machine*
corposant	*weather*	covergirl	*jobs*	cross|jack	*sport*
corpuscle	*medic*	Cox|and|Box	*titles*	cross|jack	*travel*
Correggio	*artists*	crab|apple	*fruit*	cross|road	*travel*
corrosion	*chem*	crab|grass	*plants*	crosstree	*travel*
cortisone	*medic*	crackling	*food*	crossword	*lit*
cosmetics	*clothes*	crackshot	*jobs*	crossword	*sport*
cosmic|ray	*physics*	crackshot	*sport*	crosswort	*plants*
cosmocrat	*govt*	crackshot	*war*	croustade	*food*
cosmogony	*astron*	cracksman	*jobs*	crowberry	*trees*
cosmogony	*educ*	cracksman	*law*	crowd|sail	*travel*
cosmogony	*physics*	craftsman	*trade*	crown|post	*archit*
cosmology	*astron*	cranberry	*fruit*	crow|snest	*travel*
cosmology	*geog*	crankcase	*machine*	crucifera	*veg*
cosmology	*physics*	crankcase	*travel*	cryogenic	*physics*
cosmonaut	*jobs*	crash|boat	*travel*	cryoscope	*physics*
cosmonaut	*travel*	crash|diet	*medic*	cryptogam	*plants*
cosmotron	*physics*	crash|land	*travel*	Cuban|heel	*clothes*
cost|clerk	*jobs*	crayonist	*art*	cubby|hole	*archit*

cubbyhole	*house*	dairymaid	*agric*	decastere	*measure*
cubicfoot	*measure*	DalaiLama	*govt*	decastyle	*archit*
cubicinch	*measure*	Dalmatian	*animals*	decathlon	*sport*
cubicmile	*measure*	danceband	*music*	deceleron	*travel*
cubiculum	*archit*	danceform	*music*	decennary	*time*
cubicyard	*measure*	dancestep	*sport*	decennial	*time*
cuckoofly	*insects*	dandelion	*flowers*	decennium	*time*
cufflinks	*clothes*	DandyDick	*titles*	deciduous	*trees*
cullender	*house*	Dardanius	*Shakesp*	decilitre	*measure*
culverkey	*flowers*	darkbread	*food*	decimetre	*measure*
cuneiform	*lit*	darkhorse	*animals*	deckchair	*house*
cuneiform	*medic*	darkhorse	*people*	decorator	*art*
cupbearer	*jobs*	dartboard	*sport*	decorator	*jobs*
cupbearer	*myth*	dashboard	*travel*	decoyduck	*sport*
cupbearer	*relig*	dasheisst	*foreign*	deduction	*trade*
Cupidines	*myth*	davenport	*house*	deerhound	*animals*
cuplichen	*plants*	DavyJones	*myth*	deermouse	*animals*
curbstone	*travel*	DavyJones	*travel*	deertiger	*animals*
currawong	*birds*	daylabour	*jobs*	defaulter	*trade*
currycomb	*animals*	dayletter	*travel*	defeatist	*people*
curtilage	*archit*	dayreturn	*travel*	defective	*medic*
curvature	*archit*	dayschool	*educ*	defendant	*jobs*
curvature	*geog*	daysofold	*time*	defendant	*law*
curvature	*maths*	dayspring	*time*	defensive	*war*
curvature	*medic*	deaconess	*jobs*	deflation	*trade*
custodian	*govt*	deaconess	*relig*	deflector	*physics*
custodian	*jobs*	deadfaint	*medic*	defrauder	*people*
cutandrun	*travel*	deadmarch	*music*	Deianeira	*myth*
cutthroat	*jobs*	deadpoint	*physics*	deigratia	*relig*
cyanotype	*art*	deadstage	*theatre*	deionizer	*physics*
cyclerace	*sport*	deadtired	*medic*	Deiphobus	*Shakesp*
cycletour	*sport*	deadwater	*geog*	dekametre	*measure*
cyclorama	*art*	deanofmen	*educ*	Delacroix	*artists*
cyclorama	*theatre*	deanofmen	*jobs*	DelaRoche	*writers*
cyclotron	*physics*	deathblow	*govt*	delftware	*art*
cymarecta	*archit*	deathduty	*law*	delirious	*medic*
cymbalist	*jobs*	deathduty	*trade*	Delphinia	*myth*
cymbalist	*music*	deathsong	*music*	Delphinus	*astron*
Cymbeline	*Shakesp*	debenture	*trade*	Delphinus	*myth*
Cymbeline	*titles*	debutante	*jobs*	demagogue	*govt*
cytoplasm	*biol*	decagonal	*maths*	demagogue	*people*
dachshund	*animals*	decalitre	*measure*	Demetrius	*Shakesp*
dailyhelp	*jobs*	decalogue	*relig*	demitasse	*house*
dairyfarm	*agric*	Decameron	*lit*	demobsuit	*clothes*
dairyherd	*animals*	decametre	*measure*	democracy	*govt*

demulcent	*medic*	deuterium	*chem*	directors	*trade*
Dendrites	*myth*	developer	*art*	directory	*house*
dentistry	*medic*	developer	*chem*	directory	*lit*
deodorant	*clothes*	devil|fish	*fish*	directrix	*maths*
departure	*travel*	devil|lore	*myth*	direct|tax	*law*
dependent	*jobs*	devotions	*relig*	direct|tax	*trade*
depiction	*lit*	diablerie	*myth*	dirigible	*travel*
depictive	*lit*	diabolism	*myth*	dirt|cheap	*trade*
depositor	*trade*	diaeresis	*lit*	dirt|track	*travel*
depot|ship	*travel*	diagnosis	*medic*	disc|brake	*machine*
deprogram	*comput*	dialogist	*jobs*	discharge	*law*
depth|dose	*medic*	diaphonia	*music*	discharge	*medic*
DeQuincey	*writers*	diaphragm	*machine*	discharge	*physics*
de|rigueur	*foreign*	diaphragm	*medic*	discharge	*trade*
derringer	*war*	diarrhoea	*medic*	discharge	*war*
descanter	*lit*	diathermy	*medic*	Discordia	*myth*
Descartes	*writers*	diatomite	*mineral*	discourse	*educ*
Desdemona	*Shakesp*	dichotomy	*biol*	discourse	*lit*
Desdemona	*lit*	dichotomy	*medic*	discovery	*theatre*
desecrate	*relig*	dicky|bird	*birds*	disc|valve	*machine*
desertion	*govt*	didactics	*educ*	disc|wheel	*machine*
desert|pea	*plants*	diesel|oil	*travel*	disembark	*travel*
desert|rat	*animals*	die|sinker	*tools*	disengage	*sport*
desert|rat	*war*	dietician	*jobs*	dishcloth	*house*
desiccant	*chem*	diet|sheet	*medic*	dishonour	*trade*
designate	*jobs*	digitalis	*flowers*	dish|towel	*house*
designing	*art*	digitalis	*medic*	dishwater	*drink*
desk|bound	*educ*	dignitary	*people*	dismissal	*trade*
desk|clerk	*jobs*	dignitary	*relig*	dispenser	*chem*
desk|light	*house*	diligence	*educ*	dispenser	*jobs*
DesMoines	*cities*	diligence	*travel*	dispenser	*medic*
desperado	*govt*	dimension	*maths*	disseisin	*law*
desperado	*people*	dime|store	*trade*	disseizin	*law*
destroyer	*travel*	dimorphic	*biol*	dissenter	*people*
detective	*jobs*	dimorphic	*chem*	distemper	*art*
detective	*law*	dineutron	*physics*	distemper	*house*
detention	*law*	dining|car	*travel*	distemper	*medic*
detergent	*chem*	dinothere	*animals*	distiller	*chem*
detergent	*house*	diphthong	*lit*	distraint	*law*
deterrent	*war*	diplomacy	*govt*	dithyramb	*lit*
detonator	*chem*	dip|switch	*travel*	dithyramb	*music*
detonator	*physics*	direction	*educ*	dittander	*plants*
detonator	*war*	direction	*film/TV*	diversion	*travel*
detrition	*geog*	direction	*theatre*	dizzy|turn	*medic*
Deucalion	*myth*	direction	*travel*	djellabah	*clothes*

dock|cress	*plants*	
doctorate	*educ*	
dodgem|car	*travel*	
dog|basket	*house*	
dog|collar	*animals*	
dog|collar	*clothes*	
dog|collar	*relig*	
dog|kennel	*animals*	
dogmatics	*relig*	
dogmatist	*govt*	
dogmatist	*people*	
dog|racing	*sport*	
dog|salmon	*fish*	
dog|violet	*flowers*	
dog|walker	*jobs*	
doing|time	*law*	
Dolabella	*Shakesp*	
dolce|vita	*foreign*	
dollar|gap	*trade*	
dollmaker	*jobs*	
doll's|pram	*sport*	
dolly|bird	*people*	
Dolomites	*mounts*	
Dominican	*relig*	
Donalbain	*Shakesp*	
Donatello	*artists*	
Don|Carlos	*lit*	
Don|Carlos	*titles*	
Donizetti	*music*	
Donna|Anna	*lit*	
doodlebug	*war*	
door|frame	*archit*	
door|frame	*drink*	
door|panel	*archit*	
doorplate	*house*	
doorstone	*archit*	
Dorabella	*lit*	
dormitory	*archit*	
dorsal|fin	*fish*	
dosimeter	*medic*	
dosimetry	*medic*	
doss|house	*archit*	
double|bar	*music*	
double|bed	*house*	
double|sap	*war*	

Dover|sole	*fish*	
down|right	*theatre*	
downstage	*theatre*	
down|under	*geog*	
drag|force	*travel*	
drainpipe	*archit*	
drainpipe	*clothes*	
drainpipe	*house*	
drain|tube	*medic*	
dramatics	*theatre*	
dramatist	*jobs*	
dramatist	*lit*	
dramatist	*theatre*	
dramatize	*theatre*	
drape|suit	*clothes*	
drawn|game	*sport*	
draw|wages	*trade*	
dray|horse	*animals*	
dreamland	*myth*	
dress|coat	*clothes*	
dress|ring	*clothes*	
dress|suit	*clothes*	
dribbling	*sport*	
dried|eggs	*food*	
dried|peas	*veg*	
drift|wire	*travel*	
drip|stone	*archit*	
drip|stone	*mineral*	
drive|away	*travel*	
Dr|Manette	*lit*	
dromedary	*animals*	
drone|bass	*music*	
drop|a|bomb	*war*	
drop|a|line	*travel*	
drop|drill	*tools*	
drop|forge	*machine*	
drop|press	*machine*	
drop|scene	*theatre*	
drop|scone	*food*	
dropsical	*medic*	
Dr|Proudie	*lit*	
drug|squad	*law*	
drug|store	*trade*	
drum|corps	*music*	
drum|major	*jobs*	

drum|major	*music*	
drumstick	*food*	
drumstick	*music*	
drum|table	*house*	
dry|fresco	*archit*	
dry|garden	*flowers*	
drysalter	*jobs*	
dry|sherry	*drink*	
Dr|Zhivago	*titles*	
Dubliners	*titles*	
duck|green	*colour*	
duck's|foot	*flowers*	
duck's|meat	*plants*	
due|season	*time*	
duffel|bag	*clothes*	
duffel|bag	*travel*	
dulcitone	*music*	
Du|Maurier	*writers*	
dunce's|cap	*educ*	
dungarees	*clothes*	
duodenary	*maths*	
duple|time	*music*	
duplicate	*biol*	
dupondius	*money*	
dura|mater	*medic*	
dust|devil	*weather*	
dust|sheet	*house*	
dust|storm	*weather*	
Dutch|oven	*house*	
Dutch|pink	*colour*	
Dutch|wife	*house*	
dwarf|tree	*trees*	
dyer's|weed	*plants*	
dysentery	*medic*	
dyspepsia	*medic*	
dyspeptic	*medic*	
dystrophy	*medic*	
dziggetai	*animals*	
eagle|eyed	*birds*	
earliness	*time*	
early|bird	*people*	
early|bird	*time*	
Early|Bird	*travel*	
ear|of|corn	*cereal*	
earphones	*travel*	

earth|star	plants	elevenses	food	engrosser	jobs
earth|wave	geog	Elimelech	Bible	enlighten	educ
earth|wolf	animals	Elisabeth	Bible	Enobarbus	Shakesp
earthwork	archit	Elisabeth	lit	en|passant	foreign
earthwork	war	Elizabeth	Shakesp	en|passant	sport
earthworm	insects	Elizabeth	names	entertain	film/TV
East|Lynne	titles	ellipsoid	maths	entertain	theatre
easy|chair	house	emaciated	medic	entourage	jobs
easy|money	trade	emanation	chem	en|tout|cas	sport
easy|terms	trade	embalming	relig	entrechat	music
eccentric	maths	embattled	herald	entrechat	theatre
eccentric	people	embattled	war	entremets	food
echolalia	medic	ember|days	time	epaulette	clothes
echo|organ	music	embezzler	jobs	epaulette	herald
ecologist	jobs	embezzler	law	ephedrine	medic
economics	trade	embracery	law	ephemeral	time
economies	trade	embrocate	medic	ephemerid	insects
economise	trade	emergency	medic	ephemeris	astron
economist	jobs	emollient	medic	ephemeris	lit
ecossaise	music	emolument	jobs	ephemeris	time
ectoplasm	biol	emolument	trade	epicedium	music
edelweiss	flowers	empennage	travel	epicentre	geog
edificial	archit	emphasize	lit	epicurean	food
Edinburgh	cities	Empire|Day	time	epic|verse	lit
editorial	lit	enactment	govt	epidermis	medic
education	educ	enactment	law	epileptic	medic
Edwardian	people	enamelist	jobs	epinicion	music
effluvium	biol	enameller	art	epiphyses	medic
egg|beater	house	encaustic	art	epirrhema	theatre
egg|powder	food	enchanter	jobs	episcopal	relig
egg|slicer	house	enchanter	myth	episcopus	relig
eglantine	flowers	enchasing	art	epithesis	lit
eiderdown	house	enclosure	sport	epizeuxis	lit
eider|duck	birds	encompass	war	epochally	time
eidograph	tools	endocrine	medic	eponymism	lit
eightfold	measure	endolymph	medic	epopoeist	lit
elastance	physics	endoplasm	biol	epulation	food
elastomer	chem	endosperm	biol	equalizer	sport
elaterite	mineral	endospore	biol	equipoise	maths
electrode	machine	end|reader	lit	equipoise	physics
electrode	physics	enemy|camp	war	equity|bar	law
Electryon	myth	enemy|fire	war	Erpingham	Shakesp
electuary	medic	energumen	medic	errand|boy	jobs
elemental	chem	en|famille	foreign	erstwhile	time
elevation	archit	engraving	art	erudition	educ

erythrite	*chem*	exchanger	*jobs*	eye doctor	*jobs*
erythrose	*chem*	exchanger	*relig*	eye doctor	*medic*
Erzebirge	*mounts*	exchequer	*govt*	eyelashes	*medic*
escalator	*machine*	exchequer	*jobs*	eye shadow	*clothes*
escalator	*travel*	exchequer	*trade*	facecloth	*house*
Escamillo	*lit*	exciseman	*govt*	face cream	*clothes*
escopette	*war*	exciseman	*jobs*	face guard	*herald*
Esdraelon	*Bible*	exciseman	*trade*	face guard	*sport*
Eskimo dog	*animals*	excise tax	*trade*	face guard	*war*
Esmeralda	*names*	ex convict	*law*	face lathe	*machine*
esotropia	*medic*	excursion	*travel*	face towel	*house*
espionage	*govt*	execution	*law*	face value	*trade*
espionage	*jobs*	execution	*music*	fair price	*trade*
espionage	*war*	executive	*govt*	fair trade	*trade*
esplanade	*archit*	executive	*jobs*	fair trial	*law*
esplanade	*geog*	executive	*trade*	fairyfolk	*myth*
esplanade	*travel*	exegetics	*lit*	fairyland	*myth*
establish	*trade*	exercises	*sport*	fairy ring	*myth*
estaminet	*archit*	exhibitor	*film/TV*	fairy ring	*plants*
estate car	*travel*	ex officio	*govt*	fairytale	*lit*
estimator	*jobs*	exonerate	*law*	faith cure	*medic*
estuaries	*geog*	exosphere	*geog*	Falklands	*islands*
estuarine	*geog*	exotropia	*medic*	fallopian	*medic*
Ethelbert	*names*	expansion	*trade*	fallotomy	*medic*
et tu Brute	*foreign*	expensive	*trade*	false face	*clothes*
etymology	*lit*	exploiter	*people*	false keel	*travel*
Eucharist	*relig*	exploiter	*trade*	false ribs	*medic*
Euclidean	*maths*	explosion	*physics*	family car	*travel*
Eumenides	*myth*	explosive	*machine*	family man	*people*
Eumenides	*titles*	explosive	*war*	family pew	*relig*
euphemism	*lit*	export tax	*trade*	fan window	*archit*
euphonium	*music*	expositor	*lit*	farandine	*clothes*
euphorbia	*plants*	expounder	*lit*	farandole	*music*
Euphorbus	*myth*	extempore	*educ*	fare stage	*travel*
Euphrates	*rivers*	extempore	*music*	far future	*time*
Euripides	*writers*	extension	*archit*	farmhouse	*archit*
Euryanthe	*titles*	extension	*travel*	fastigium	*archit*
everglade	*geog*	extortion	*law*	fat profit	*trade*
evergreen	*trees*	extortion	*trade*	favourite	*people*
ever since	*time*	extrabold	*lit*	favourite	*sport*
every hour	*time*	extra time	*sport*	featuring	*theatre*
evolution	*biol*	extravert	*people*	febrifuge	*medic*
evolution	*geog*	extremist	*govt*	febrility	*medic*
Excalibur	*myth*	extremity	*medic*	fee simple	*law*
excavator	*tools*	extrovert	*people*	felonious	*law*

fence|wall	*war*	fingering	*clothes*	five|a|side	*sport*
fenestral	*astron*	fingering	*music*	fixed|arch	*archit*
fenugreek	*plants*	fire|alarm	*govt*	fixed|star	*astron*
feralized	*animals*	fire|alarm	*house*	flagellum	*plants*
Ferdinand	*Shakesp*	fire|alarm	*machine*	flageolet	*music*
Ferdinand	*names*	fire|a|shot	*war*	flagstone	*archit*
ferrotype	*art*	firecrest	*birds*	flagstone	*mineral*
ferryboat	*travel*	fire|eater	*people*	flag|waver	*people*
fertility	*agric*	fireguard	*house*	Flaminius	*Shakesp*
festering	*medic*	fireguard	*jobs*	flashback	*film/TV*
fetishism	*medic*	fire|irons	*house*	flashbulb	*art*
feudalism	*govt*	firelight	*house*	flashbulb	*machine*
feudal|law	*law*	fireplace	*archit*	flash|lamp	*machine*
feudal|tax	*law*	fireplace	*house*	flash|note	*trade*
feudatory	*govt*	firepower	*war*	flash|tube	*art*
fever|heat	*medic*	firewater	*drink*	flat|broke	*trade*
fever|ward	*medic*	fireworks	*war*	flathouse	*archit*
fiat|money	*trade*	firmament	*astron*	flatulent	*medic*
fictional	*lit*	firmament	*relig*	flaunches	*herald*
field|army	*war*	firm|offer	*trade*	fletching	*sport*
field|coil	*physics*	firm|price	*trade*	flight|bow	*sport*
fieldfare	*birds*	firstborn	*family*	flintlock	*war*
field|game	*sport*	firstborn	*relig*	flocculus	*astron*
fieldlark	*birds*	first|form	*educ*	floodgate	*machine*
fieldsman	*sport*	first|half	*sport*	flood|tide	*marine*
fieldwork	*jobs*	first|lady	*govt*	floor|plan	*archit*
fieldwork	*war*	first|line	*war*	floor|show	*theatre*
fifth|form	*educ*	firstling	*relig*	flophouse	*archit*
figurante	*jobs*	first|lord	*govt*	floss|silk	*clothes*
figurante	*music*	first|mate	*jobs*	flotation	*physics*
figurante	*theatre*	first|mate	*travel*	flotation	*trade*
figure|out	*maths*	first|rate	*travel*	flour|mill	*machine*
fill|horse	*animals*	first|seed	*sport*	flour|moth	*insects*
film|actor	*film/TV*	first|slip	*sport*	flowerage	*flowers*
film|actor	*jobs*	first|time	*time*	flower|bed	*flowers*
film|extra	*film/TV*	first|year	*educ*	flowering	*flowers*
film|extra	*jobs*	fisherman	*jobs*	flowerpot	*flowers*
film|maker	*jobs*	fisherman	*relig*	flowerpot	*house*
film|strip	*film/TV*	fisherman	*sport*	flow|meter	*physics*
filoselle	*clothes*	fishgarth	*fish*	flow|valve	*machine*
final|year	*educ*	fish|knife	*house*	fluid|dram	*measure*
financial	*trade*	fish|louse	*fish*	fluorspar	*mineral*
financier	*jobs*	fish|slice	*house*	flute|a|bec	*music*
financier	*trade*	fisticuff	*sport*	flute|bird	*birds*
fine|toned	*music*	Fitzwater	*Shakesp*	fluxional	*maths*

flyagaric	plants	fortalice	war	frithgild	govt
flycutter	tools	forthwith	time	frockcoat	clothes
flyingfox	animals	fortified	war	frogmouth	birds
flyingjib	travel	fortitude	virtues	frogspawn	animals
flyingsap	war	fortnight	time	fromnowon	time
flyweight	sport	FortWorth	cities	frontdoor	archit
focimeter	physics	fortylove	sport	frontdoor	house
focuslamp	machine	fossicker	people	frontline	war
fogginess	weather	foundling	jobs	frontroom	archit
foliation	geog	fourpence	money	frontseat	travel
folicacid	biol	fourpenny	money	frostbite	medic
folkdance	music	fourtharm	war	frostbite	weather
Folketing	govt	FoxeBasin	seas	Fructidor	time
folkmusic	music	fragments	lit	fruitbowl	house
folkstory	lit	Fragonard	artists	fruitcake	food
foodmixer	house	framework	archit	fruitdish	house
foodmixer	machine	Francesca	names	fruiterer	jobs
foodstuff	food	franchise	govt	fruitmoth	insects
fool'sgold	mineral	Francisca	Shakesp	fruittree	fruit
footbrake	machine	Francisco	Shakesp	fryingpan	house
footfault	sport	Frankfurt	cities	fuelgauge	travel
foothills	geog	Frederica	names	fugueform	music
footropes	travel	Frederick	Shakesp	fulgurite	war
footstick	machine	Frederick	names	fullbloom	flowers
footstone	archit	freeagent	people	fullclose	music
footstone	relig	freeboard	travel	fulldress	clothes
footstool	house	freelance	jobs	fullfaced	lit
foragecap	clothes	freelance	lit	fullhouse	sport
forcemeat	food	freelance	war	fullorgan	music
forcepump	machine	freemason	jobs	fullpurse	trade
forebears	family	freereach	sport	fullscore	music
forebrace	travel	freestone	mineral	fullskirt	clothes
forebrain	medic	freestyle	sport	fulminate	chem
forecourt	archit	freetrade	trade	fumigator	machine
foregoing	time	freeverse	lit	fumigator	medic
foreigner	jobs	freewheel	sport	fundament	archit
foreroyal	sport	freewheel	travel	fungicide	chem
foreroyal	travel	freighter	travel	fungosity	medic
foresheet	travel	Frenchlug	travel	funicular	travel
foreshore	geog	frequency	physics	funnybone	medic
forestfly	insects	FriarTuck	myth	furnisher	jobs
foretaste	food	fricassee	food	furniture	house
formalist	educ	friedrice	food	fuseboard	machine
formality	govt	friedsole	food	fuselinks	machine
forsythia	trees	frithborh	law	fusillade	war

gabardine	clothes	
gaberdine	clothes	
gable roof	archit	
gain speed	travel	
Gaitskell	leaders	
galactose	chem	
galantine	food	
Galatians	Bible	
gale force	weather	
galingale	plants	
galleries	sport	
gallinazo	birds	
gallinule	birds	
gallivant	travel	
gall midge	insects	
galvanize	physics	
gama grass	plants	
game point	sport	
gamma rays	physics	
gangplank	travel	
garden hut	house	
gardening	sport	
garden pea	veg	
garderobe	archit	
Garibaldi	leaders	
garreteer	jobs	
garrotter	jobs	
gas attack	war	
gas burner	house	
gas cooker	house	
gas engine	machine	
gas fitter	jobs	
gas holder	machine	
gasometer	machine	
gaspereau	fish	
gastritis	medic	
gastropod	fish	
gathering	medic	
gather way	travel	
gaudeamus	educ	
gazehound	animals	
gazetteer	educ	
gazetteer	jobs	
gazetteer	lit	
gear lever	machine	

gear lever	travel	
gear train	machine	
gearwheel	machine	
gelignite	war	
gelsemium	flowers	
gem cutter	jobs	
gemmation	plants	
gemmology	jewels	
gemmology	mineral	
gemutlich	foreign	
genealogy	herald	
generalcy	govt	
generator	machine	
Genevieve	names	
gentleman	people	
geobiotic	biol	
geodesist	measure	
geography	geog	
geologist	jobs	
georgette	clothes	
Geraldine	names	
gerfalcon	birds	
geriatric	medic	
germander	plants	
germanium	chem	
germanium	mineral	
germicide	medic	
gerundive	lit	
gestation	biol	
ghost crab	fish	
ghost ship	travel	
ghost town	geog	
ghost word	lit	
giant star	astron	
gier eagle	birds	
gift horse	animals	
Gilgamesh	myth	
gilt edged	trade	
ginger ale	drink	
ginger pop	drink	
ginger tom	animals	
Giorgione	artists	
gipsy moth	insects	
girandole	clothes	
girandole	house	

girl guide	jobs	
give a ring	travel	
give birth	medic	
glacieret	geog	
gladiator	jobs	
gladiator	sport	
gladiator	war	
gladiolus	flowers	
gladiolus	medic	
Gladstone	leaders	
glandular	medic	
Glansdale	Shakesp	
glass door	house	
glassware	art	
glasswort	plants	
Glazounov	music	
gleanings	lit	
Glendower	Shakesp	
Glendower	war	
glissando	music	
globe fish	fish	
globe trot	travel	
glory hole	archit	
glory hole	house	
glucoside	chem	
gluemaker	jobs	
glutinous	chem	
glycerine	chem	
glycerine	medic	
gnomonics	time	
go aground	travel	
goalposts	sport	
go between	jobs	
godfather	family	
godfather	relig	
godliness	relig	
godmother	family	
godmother	relig	
godparent	relig	
goggle box	film/TV	
going rate	trade	
go karting	sport	
goldcrest	birds	
gold crown	money	
golden age	myth	

Golden Age	*time*	grand aunt	*family*	gregarine	*insects*
golden egg	*myth*	grand duke	*govt*	Gregorian	*music*
goldeneye	*birds*	grandioso	*music*	Gregorian	*time*
golden rod	*flowers*	grand jury	*law*	grenadier	*jobs*
goldfinch	*birds*	grand prix	*sport*	grenadier	*war*
goldfinny	*fish*	grand slam	*sport*	grenadine	*clothes*
gold medal	*sport*	grand tour	*travel*	Grenville	*war*
gold penny	*money*	Grand Turk	*govt*	greygoose	*birds*
gold piece	*money*	granulite	*mineral*	greyhound	*animals*
gold piece	*trade*	grapeshot	*war*	grillroom	*house*
gold plate	*house*	grape tree	*trees*	grimalkin	*animals*
goldsinny	*fish*	grapevine	*fruit*	grisaille	*art*
goldsmith	*art*	grapevine	*jobs*	gritstone	*mineral*
goldsmith	*jobs*	grapevine	*travel*	groceries	*food*
Goldsmith	*writers*	grassland	*agric*	grosgrain	*clothes*
goldspink	*birds*	graticule	*measure*	gross lift	*travel*
goldstone	*mineral*	graveside	*relig*	grotesque	*art*
gold watch	*clothes*	graveyard	*relig*	groundash	*trees*
golf links	*sport*	gravy boat	*house*	groundhog	*animals*
golf range	*sport*	gravy soup	*food*	groundhog	*travel*
golf shoes	*sport*	grease gun	*tools*	ground ivy	*plants*
golf widow	*sport*	Great Arms	*herald*	groundnut	*food*
gondolier	*jobs*	great aunt	*family*	groundnut	*fruit*
gondolier	*travel*	Great Bear	*astron*	groundsel	*plants*
gonfannon	*herald*	Great Bear	*myth*	grugrunut	*fruit*
good fairy	*myth*	great coat	*clothes*	guarantee	*trade*
good loser	*sport*	Great Dane	*animals*	guarantor	*jobs*
good mixer	*people*	great seal	*herald*	guarantor	*trade*
good price	*trade*	Great Seal	*law*	guard ring	*jewels*
good sport	*sport*	great work	*lit*	guardroom	*law*
good works	*relig*	great year	*time*	guard ship	*travel*
goosander	*birds*	Greek lace	*clothes*	guardsman	*jobs*
goosefoot	*plants*	greenback	*trade*	guardsman	*war*
goose step	*travel*	green bean	*veg*	guard's van	*travel*
Gorbachev	*leaders*	green belt	*archit*	Guayaquil	*cities*
gospeller	*relig*	green belt	*geog*	Guenevere	*myth*
Gothicism	*art*	green bone	*fish*	guerrilla	*jobs*
go to press	*lit*	greengage	*fruit*	guerrilla	*war*
governess	*educ*	greenhorn	*educ*	guesswarp	*travel*
governess	*jobs*	greenhorn	*people*	guest room	*food*
grace note	*music*	Greenland	*islands*	guest room	*house*
gradgrind	*people*	green peas	*veg*	guest rope	*travel*
grain moth	*insects*	greenroom	*theatre*	guest star	*film/TV*
gramineae	*plants*	greenweed	*plants*	guest star	*jobs*
Grampians	*mounts*	greenwood	*trees*	guest star	*theatre*

Guglielmo	*lit*	
guidebook	*lit*	
Guiderius	*Shakesp*	
Guildford	*Shakesp*	
guildhall	*archit*	
guillemot	*birds*	
guinea hen	*birds*	
guinea pig	*animals*	
Guinevere	*lit*	
Guinevere	*myth*	
guitarist	*jobs*	
guitarist	*music*	
gumshield	*sport*	
gun battle	*war*	
guncotton	*war*	
gunpowder	*war*	
gunrunner	*jobs*	
gun turret	*war*	
Gurnemanz	*lit*	
guttering	*archit*	
Gwendolyn	*names*	
gymnasium	*archit*	
Gymnasium	*educ*	
gymnasium	*sport*	
gynophore	*flowers*	
gypsymoth	*insects*	
gyrfalcon	*birds*	
gyropilot	*travel*	
gyroplane	*machine*	
gyroplane	*travel*	
gyroscope	*machine*	
gyroscope	*physics*	
habergeon	*herald*	
habergeon	*war*	
haematite	*mineral*	
hagiarchy	*relig*	
hagiology	*relig*	
hailstone	*weather*	
hailstorm	*weather*	
hairbrush	*clothes*	
hair cloth	*clothes*	
hair drier	*tools*	
hair grass	*plants*	
hairpiece	*clothes*	
hair shirt	*clothes*	

hair space	*lit*	
half a loaf	*food*	
half close	*music*	
half crown	*money*	
half eagle	*money*	
half hardy	*flowers*	
half noble	*money*	
halfpenny	*money*	
half price	*trade*	
half shaft	*machine*	
half title	*lit*	
halitosis	*medic*	
Hallowe'en	*time*	
Hallowmas	*time*	
hallstand	*house*	
halophily	*biol*	
halophyte	*plants*	
ham acting	*theatre*	
hamadryad	*myth*	
Hamamatsu	*cities*	
hamburger	*food*	
hammer toe	*medic*	
hamstring	*medic*	
hand bells	*music*	
handbrake	*machine*	
handbrake	*travel*	
hand cream	*clothes*	
handcuffs	*law*	
hand drill	*tools*	
handiwork	*trade*	
hand organ	*music*	
hand sewer	*jobs*	
handspike	*tools*	
handstand	*sport*	
hand towel	*house*	
hansom cab	*travel*	
Hans Sachs	*lit*	
happy days	*time*	
harbinger	*jobs*	
harbourer	*jobs*	
hard court	*sport*	
hard cover	*lit*	
hard frost	*weather*	
hard goods	*trade*	
hard graft	*jobs*	

hard money	*trade*	
Hard Times	*titles*	
harebrain	*people*	
harlequin	*jobs*	
harlequin	*theatre*	
harmattan	*weather*	
harmonica	*music*	
harmonics	*music*	
harmonist	*jobs*	
harmonist	*music*	
harmonium	*music*	
harmonize	*music*	
harpooner	*jobs*	
harquebus	*war*	
harvester	*agric*	
harvester	*jobs*	
harvester	*machine*	
Hary Janos	*lit*	
Hasdrubal	*war*	
hatchback	*travel*	
hatchment	*herald*	
haut monde	*foreign*	
haversack	*travel*	
hawksbill	*insects*	
Hawksmoor	*artists*	
hawse hook	*travel*	
hawsepipe	*travel*	
haymaking	*agric*	
headboard	*archit*	
head buyer	*trade*	
head clerk	*jobs*	
headdress	*clothes*	
headlight	*machine*	
headliner	*theatre*	
headlines	*lit*	
headmould	*archit*	
headphone	*travel*	
headpiece	*archit*	
headpiece	*art*	
headpiece	*clothes*	
headpiece	*herald*	
headpiece	*war*	
headstone	*relig*	
head voice	*music*	
heartbeat	*medic*	

heartburn	*medic*	Hexateuch	*relig*	HoChiMinh	*leaders*
heartwood	*trees*	hierarchy	*relig*	Hoddinott	*music*
heath cock	*birds*	hierology	*relig*	hodmandod	*insects*
heat index	*physics*	Hieronimo	*lit*	hodometer	*measure*
heavy cost	*trade*	high altar	*relig*	hoist sail	*travel*
heavy fire	*war*	high birth	*govt*	Holarctic	*geog*
heavy lead	*theatre*	high chair	*house*	holly ferm	*plants*
heavy rain	*weather*	high cloud	*weather*	hollyhock	*flowers*
heavy wine	*drink*	High Court	*law*	holocaust	*relig*
hectogram	*measure*	high horse	*animals*	holograph	*lit*
Heimdallr	*myth*	high jinks	*sport*	holograph	*physics*
heir at law	*law*	highlands	*geog*	holy cross	*relig*
Helicanus	*Shakesp*	high pitch	*music*	Holy Ghost	*relig*
helidrome	*travel*	high price	*trade*	Holy Grail	*myth*
heliostat	*astron*	high stock	*clothes*	Holy Grail	*relig*
heliostat	*physics*	high value	*trade*	holy grass	*plants*
heliotype	*art*	high water	*marine*	holy stone	*trade*
heliotypy	*art*	hillbilly	*jobs*	holy table	*relig*
hellebore	*flowers*	hill climb	*sport*	holy water	*relig*
Hellenist	*people*	Himalayas	*mounts*	homecroft	*archit*
Helvellyn	*mounts*	Hindemith	*music*	home grown	*flowers*
hemicycle	*maths*	Hindu Kush	*mounts*	home grown	*fruit*
Hemingway	*writers*	hip pocket	*clothes*	HomeGuard	*war*
hemiptera	*insects*	Hippocoon	*myth*	home maker	*jobs*
Henrietta	*names*	Hippolyta	*Shakesp*	homeopath	*jobs*
heptapody	*lit*	Hippolyte	*myth*	homeopath	*medic*
herbalist	*jobs*	hired hand	*jobs*	homestall	*archit*
herbarium	*biol*	hired help	*jobs*	homestead	*archit*
herbarium	*plants*	Hiroshima	*cities*	homiletic	*educ*
herbivore	*animals*	histamine	*medic*	homocycle	*chem*
herb Paris	*flowers*	histidine	*chem*	homophony	*music*
Hereafter	*relig*	histogram	*maths*	homotaxis	*geog*
hereafter	*time*	histology	*biol*	honest man	*people*
Herodotus	*writers*	historian	*jobs*	honey bear	*animals*
heroic act	*war*	historian	*lit*	honeymoon	*time*
heronshaw	*birds*	historify	*lit*	honour man	*educ*
herpestes	*animals*	hit and run	*law*	honour man	*people*
heterodox	*relig*	hit and run	*travel*	hoodmould	*archit*
heteronym	*lit*	hitch hike	*sport*	hoofprint	*animals*
heterosis	*biol*	hitch hike	*travel*	hook a ride	*travel*
hexachord	*music*	hit parade	*music*	hoop skirt	*clothes*
hexagonal	*maths*	hit wicket	*sport*	hopscotch	*sport*
hexameter	*lit*	hoardings	*theatre*	horehound	*medic*
hexastich	*lit*	hoar frost	*weather*	horehound	*plants*
hexastyle	*archit*	Hobgoblin	*myth*	horned bug	*insects*

horned owl	*birds*	
hornet fly	*insects*	
hornwrack	*plants*	
horny head	*fish*	
horseback	*sport*	
horseback	*travel*	
horsehair	*clothes*	
horseplay	*sport*	
horse race	*sport*	
horseshoe	*animals*	
horseshoe	*theatre*	
horsetail	*plants*	
horsewhip	*animals*	
hortatory	*educ*	
Hortensio	*Shakesp*	
hostility	*war*	
hot market	*trade*	
Hottentot	*jobs*	
hour angle	*geog*	
hourglass	*house*	
hourglass	*time*	
houseboat	*archit*	
houseboat	*travel*	
housecoat	*clothes*	
house dick	*jobs*	
household	*house*	
house leek	*plants*	
housemaid	*jobs*	
house plan	*archit*	
house room	*house*	
housewife	*house*	
housework	*house*	
Houyhnhnm	*animals*	
Houyhnhnm	*myth*	
Huascaran	*mounts*	
huckaback	*clothes*	
Hudson Bay	*seas*	
humble bee	*insects*	
humble pie	*food*	
hump speed	*travel*	
hunchback	*medic*	
hurricane	*weather*	
husbandry	*agric*	
husbandry	*jobs*	
hush money	*trade*	

Hyderabad	*cities*
hydrangea	*trees*
hydration	*physics*
hydrazine	*chem*
hydrobomb	*war*
hydrofoil	*machine*
hydrofoil	*travel*
hydrolist	*chem*
hydrolyte	*chem*
hydrostat	*physics*
hydroxide	*chem*
hygrostat	*physics*
hymnology	*music*
hypallage	*lit*
hyperbola	*maths*
hyperbole	*lit*
hypnotist	*jobs*
hypocrite	*people*
hypogaeum	*geog*
Hyppolita	*myth*
ice action	*geog*
ice hockey	*sport*
ice skates	*sport*
ice skates	*travel*
ichneumon	*animals*
ichthyoid	*fish*
I Claudius	*titles*
Identi kit	*law*
idioblast	*plants*
idiomatic	*lit*
idiopathy	*medic*
idioticon	*lit*
ignoramus	*educ*
ignoramus	*people*
iguanodon	*animals*
ill health	*medic*
Ilmarinen	*myth*
imitation	*music*
immediacy	*time*
immediate	*time*
immigrant	*jobs*
immigrant	*travel*
immigrate	*travel*
Immortals	*myth*
impartial	*govt*

impatient	*medic*
imperator	*govt*
implement	*agric*
implement	*tools*
import tax	*trade*
impromptu	*archit*
impromptu	*music*
improvise	*music*
inamorata	*people*
in arrears	*trade*
in a second	*time*
in blossom	*fruit*
in blossom	*trees*
incentive	*trade*
inch along	*travel*
Incitatus	*animals*
inclement	*weather*
incognito	*govt*
incognito	*theatre*
income tax	*law*
income tax	*trade*
increment	*jobs*
increment	*maths*
incubator	*agric*
incubator	*biol*
incubator	*machine*
incubator	*medic*
incumbent	*govt*
incumbent	*jobs*
incumbent	*relig*
incurable	*medic*
incursion	*war*
incursive	*war*
in defence	*war*
in deficit	*trade*
indemnity	*law*
indemnity	*trade*
Indian fig	*fruit*
Indian Ink	*lit*
Indian red	*colour*
indicator	*machine*
indicator	*physics*
indicator	*travel*
induction	*physics*
in due time	*time*

inebriate	*people*	inter|alia	*foreign*	isocyclic	*chem*
inelastic	*physics*	interlock	*machine*	isolation	*medic*
in|fashion	*clothes*	interlude	*music*	isomerism	*chem*
infection	*medic*	interlude	*theatre*	isosceles	*maths*
infielder	*sport*	interlude	*time*	isosteric	*physics*
infirmary	*medic*	interment	*relig*	isotropic	*biol*
infirmity	*medic*	interview	*film/TV*	Israelite	*relig*
inflation	*trade*	interview	*jobs*	itinerant	*travel*
inflexion	*music*	intestate	*law*	itinerary	*travel*
influence	*govt*	in|the|city	*trade*	ivory|palm	*trees*
influenza	*medic*	in|the|past	*time*	ivory|tree	*trees*
infusoria	*animals*	introvert	*people*	Jack|Frost	*weather*
ingestion	*educ*	intrusion	*geog*	jackfruit	*fruit*
ingestion	*medic*	invalided	*medic*	Jack|Ketch	*law*
inglenook	*archit*	invention	*music*	jackknife	*sport*
inglenook	*house*	invention	*trade*	jackknife	*tools*
ingleside	*archit*	inventory	*law*	Jack|Point	*lit*
inhalator	*medic*	inventory	*physics*	jackscrew	*machine*
inhibitor	*chem*	inventory	*trade*	jacksnipe	*birds*
initiator	*biol*	Inverness	*clothes*	jackstone	*mineral*
injection	*biol*	inversion	*maths*	Jacquetta	*names*
injection	*medic*	inversion	*music*	jade|green	*colour*
injustice	*law*	involucre	*plants*	jadestone	*jewels*
inlet|port	*machine*	Ionian|Sea	*seas*	jadestone	*mineral*
in|measure	*lit*	ipse|dixit	*foreign*	Jagannath	*myth*
inner|city	*archit*	ipso|facto	*foreign*	jailbreak	*law*
inner|city	*geog*	I|Puritani	*titles*	jail|fever	*medic*
Innisfree	*islands*	Irish|bull	*lit*	janissary	*war*
innkeeper	*jobs*	Irish|moss	*plants*	japanning	*house*
inoculate	*medic*	Irish|stew	*food*	jaunty|car	*travel*
in|plaster	*medic*	ironbound	*war*	jaywalker	*jobs*
inscriber	*art*	Iron|Guard	*govt*	jaywalker	*travel*
inscriber	*jobs*	ironminer	*jobs*	jazz|stick	*music*
in|service	*jobs*	iron|pills	*medic*	Jean|Paget	*lit*
inside|man	*jobs*	ironsmith	*jobs*	Jefferson	*USpres*
insolvent	*trade*	ironstone	*mineral*	jelly|baby	*food*
inspector	*educ*	iron|tonic	*medic*	jellyfish	*fish*
inspector	*jobs*	Irrawaddy	*rivers*	jenneting	*fruit*
inspector	*law*	irregular	*war*	Jenny|wren	*birds*
instanter	*time*	irruption	*war*	jequirity	*fruit*
instantly	*time*	Isherwood	*writers*	Jersey|cow	*animals*
institute	*educ*	isinglass	*chem*	Jerusalem	*Bible*
insulator	*machine*	Isle|of|Ely	*islands*	Jerusalem	*cities*
insurance	*trade*	Isle|of|Man	*islands*	Jerusalem	*relig*
intensive	*lit*	isoclinal	*geog*	jesserant	*war*

jet bomber	travel	kent bugle	music	labyrinth	medic
jet engine	machine	kerb drill	travel	labyrinth	myth
jet setter	people	kerbstone	travel	laccolite	mineral
jewel case	house	Kerry blue	animals	laccolith	mineral
jewellery	jewels	key worker	jobs	lacemaker	jobs
jitterbug	jobs	kick pleat	clothes	lachrymal	medic
jitterbug	music	kick start	travel	lactation	biol
Joan of Arc	war	kid gloves	clothes	ladies man	people
jobholder	jobs	Kidnapped	titles	lady's maid	jobs
job of work	trade	kidnapper	jobs	lady smock	flowers
jockey cap	clothes	kidnapper	law	Lafayette	leaders
joint bank	trade	kid sister	family	lag behind	travel
jollyboat	travel	kilocycle	measure	lake basin	geog
Josephine	lit	kilohertz	physics	Lake Garda	lakes
Josephine	names	kilolitre	measure	Lake Huron	lakes
joss house	relig	kilometre	measure	Lake Mweru	lakes
joss stick	house	king apple	fruit	Lake Nyasa	lakes
joss stick	relig	king cobra	insects	Lake Taupo	lakes
Judas goat	animals	kingcraft	govt	lake trout	fish
Judas kiss	relig	king eider	birds	lamb chops	food
Judas tree	trees	kingmaker	govt	lamb fries	food
judge made	law	King Marke	lit	Lamb of God	relig
judgement	law	king's evil	medic	lambswool	clothes
judicator	law	king snake	insects	Lammas day	time
judiciary	law	king's rook	sport	lamplight	house
judo throw	sport	kinswoman	family	lampmaker	jobs
Julian day	time	kirby grip	clothes	lampooner	jobs
Juliet cap	clothes	Kissinger	leaders	lampshade	house
Juneberry	fruit	Kitchener	war	lamp shell	animals
jungle law	animals	kittiwake	birds	lampstand	house
jungle law	law	kiwi fruit	fruit	Lancaster	Shakesp
jury woman	law	klinostat	biol	Lancaster	herald
justiciar	law	knee joint	medic	lance jack	war
Kainozoic	geog	knee socks	clothes	lancewood	trees
kalamkari	art	knock down	trade	land agent	jobs
kaolinite	mineral	knotgrass	plants	landaulet	travel
Karlsruhe	cities	knowledge	educ	land force	jobs
katabasis	war	koala bear	animals	landgrave	govt
Katharina	Shakesp	Krasnodar	cities	land of Nod	relig
Katharine	Shakesp	krummhorn	music	landowner	jobs
Katharine	names	Kubla Khan	titles	landplane	travel
keep books	trade	Kuibyshev	cities	landreeve	jobs
keep guard	war	Kumarpish	myth	land rover	machine
keep vigil	war	Kwangchow	cities	land rover	travel
kennelman	sport	Labourite	govt	landscape	archit

landscape	*art*	
landscape	*geog*	
land|shark	*jobs*	
landslide	*geog*	
landslide	*govt*	
Landsting	*govt*	
langouste	*fish*	
langridge	*war*	
langspiel	*music*	
lanthanum	*chem*	
lanthanum	*mineral*	
lapideous	*mineral*	
lapse|rate	*weather*	
larcenist	*jobs*	
larghetto	*music*	
laser|beam	*physics*	
laserwort	*plants*	
Las|Palmas	*cities*	
last|ditch	*war*	
last|rites	*relig*	
late|extra	*lit*	
later|date	*time*	
late|riser	*people*	
late|shift	*trade*	
latration	*animals*	
latter|day	*time*	
laudation	*relig*	
Launcelot	*myth*	
launching	*travel*	
launch|pad	*travel*	
launderer	*jobs*	
laundress	*jobs*	
lawmonger	*jobs*	
lawn|bowls	*sport*	
lawn|mower	*tools*	
law|reform	*law*	
law|report	*law*	
law|school	*educ*	
law|school	*law*	
layer|cake	*food*	
lay|figure	*art*	
lay|figure	*jobs*	
lay|reader	*jobs*	
lay|reader	*relig*	
lay|sister	*jobs*	

lay|sister	*relig*	
lazaretto	*medic*	
lazybones	*people*	
leaf|green	*colour*	
leaf|mould	*plants*	
leaf|table	*house*	
leasehold	*law*	
leave|home	*travel*	
Leavisite	*lit*	
left|bower	*sport*	
left|inner	*sport*	
left|overs	*food*	
left|stage	*theatre*	
legal|bond	*trade*	
legal|heir	*law*	
legal|term	*law*	
legal|year	*law*	
leg|before	*sport*	
legendary	*lit*	
leger|line	*music*	
legionary	*jobs*	
legionary	*war*	
leg|of|lamb	*food*	
leg|spread	*sport*	
Leicester	*cities*	
Leitmotiv	*music*	
lemon|peel	*fruit*	
lemon|sole	*fish*	
lemon|weed	*plants*	
lend|lease	*govt*	
Leningrad	*cities*	
lensmaker	*jobs*	
Leporello	*lit*	
Les|Biches	*titles*	
letter|box	*house*	
letter|box	*travel*	
lettering	*lit*	
leucocyte	*medic*	
leviathan	*travel*	
levin|bolt	*weather*	
levy|war|on	*war*	
Leyden|jar	*physics*	
liability	*trade*	
libertine	*people*	
librarian	*jobs*	

librarian	*lit*	
libration	*physics*	
licitness	*law*	
liege|lord	*govt*	
lie|in|wait	*war*	
life|cycle	*biol*	
life|force	*medic*	
lifeguard	*jobs*	
life|owner	*govt*	
life|story	*lit*	
life's|work	*jobs*	
life's|work	*trade*	
light|blue	*colour*	
light|blue	*sport*	
light|bulb	*house*	
light|bulb	*machine*	
lightface	*lit*	
lightning	*weather*	
lightship	*travel*	
light|wave	*physics*	
light|wine	*drink*	
light|year	*astron*	
light|year	*measure*	
light|year	*physics*	
light|year	*time*	
lilac|tree	*trees*	
Lima|beans	*veg*	
lime|green	*colour*	
limelight	*machine*	
limelight	*theatre*	
limestone	*mineral*	
limnology	*biol*	
limousine	*travel*	
limp|cover	*lit*	
linenette	*clothes*	
Linklater	*writers*	
linotyper	*jobs*	
lion|heart	*animals*	
lion|heart	*war*	
liontamer	*jobs*	
lip|reader	*jobs*	
liquefier	*machine*	
liquidate	*trade*	
liquorice	*food*	
liquorice	*plants*	

list|price	trade	long|lived	time	Lucretius	writers
lithology	mineral	long|loser	sport	lucubrate	educ
lithotint	art	long|purse	trade	Luftwaffe	war
lithotype	art	long|range	war	lumberman	jobs
lithotype	lit	long|sight	medic	lump|sugar	food
lithotype	machine	long|since	time	lunar|base	travel
litigator	law	long|spell	time	lunar|halo	astron
litigious	law	long|tacks	sport	lunar|rays	astron
little|auk	birds	long|waves	physics	lunar|year	time
Liverpool	cities	long|while	time	lunchroom	house
Liverpool	leaders	loose|ball	sport	luxuriant	plants
liverwort	plants	loose|maul	sport	luxury|tax	trade
liveryman	jobs	loose|rein	sport	Lychorida	Shakesp
live|stage	theatre	LordMayor	govt	Lycomedes	myth
livestock	agric	LordMayor	jobs	lyme|grass	plants
livestock	animals	lorgnette	clothes	lymphatic	medic
livid|pink	colour	lose|speed	travel	Lyonnesse	myth
livraison	lit	lossmaker	trade	lyric|bass	music
loadstone	geog	lost|sheep	people	lyrichord	music
loadstone	machine	LostSheep	relig	macaronic	lit
loaf|sugar	food	loudmouth	people	MacArthur	war
loan|agent	jobs	LoughDerg	lakes	Macdonald	leaders
local|room	lit	LoughErne	lakes	MacDowell	music
local|time	time	love|apple	fruit	macedoine	food
LochLeven	lakes	love|apple	veg	Mach|front	physics
LochMaree	lakes	love|charm	myth	machinist	jobs
lockmaker	jobs	love|forty	sport	Mach|meter	travel
locksmith	jobs	love|match	sport	Mackenzie	rivers
logarithm	maths	love|scene	theatre	Mackenzie	writers
log|basket	house	love|story	lit	Macmillan	leaders
logistics	war	loving|cup	house	Macmorris	Shakesp
logogriph	lit	low|comedy	theatre	Macquarie	rivers
logomachy	lit	lower|boom	travel	macrocosm	geog
logroller	govt	lower|case	lit	macrodome	physics
logroller	jobs	lower|deck	travel	mactation	relig
logroller	people	low|ground	geog	madder|red	colour
Lohengrin	lit	lowlander	jobs	Madeleine	names
Lohengrin	titles	low|priced	trade	maelstrom	geog
loincloth	clothes	low|relief	archit	maelstrom	myth
loincloth	relig	low|relief	art	Magdalena	rivers
London|fog	weather	LowrieTod	animals	Magdalene	Bible
longcloth	clothes	low|volley	sport	Magdalene	names
longcoats	clothes	lubricant	physics	Magdalene	relig
longevity	time	luciferin	biol	Magdeburg	cities
longitude	geog	lucky|bean	myth	magic|wand	myth

magic word	*myth*	man Friday	*jobs*	Marspiter	*myth*
magnesite	*mineral*	manganese	*chem*	marsupial	*animals*
magnesium	*chem*	manganese	*mineral*	marsupium	*animals*
magnesium	*mineral*	Manhattan	*islands*	Martinmas	*time*
magnetism	*physics*	manifesto	*govt*	martyrdom	*relig*
magnetite	*mineral*	manoeuvre	*travel*	masculine	*lit*
magnetron	*physics*	manoeuvre	*war*	Masefield	*writers*
magnifier	*physics*	man of mark	*people*	masochist	*people*
magnitude	*geog*	man of note	*people*	masonwork	*archit*
maharajah	*govt*	manometer	*measure*	mass media	*travel*
maharanee	*govt*	manometer	*physics*	masterate	*educ*
maid's room	*house*	manticora	*animals*	master key	*house*
mail coach	*travel*	manticore	*animals*	matchlock	*war*
mail order	*trade*	manual art	*art*	match play	*sport*
mainbrace	*travel*	manubrium	*medic*	maternity	*medic*
mainframe	*comput*	many a time	*time*	matricide	*law*
mainroyal	*travel*	many times	*time*	mattamore	*geog*
mainsheet	*travel*	manzanita	*fruit*	mature age	*time*
major domo	*govt*	maple leaf	*trees*	matutinal	*time*
major domo	*jobs*	Maracaibo	*cities*	Mauritius	*islands*
major mode	*music*	marcasite	*mineral*	mausoleum	*archit*
major poet	*jobs*	Marcellus	*Shakesp*	mausoleum	*relig*
major poet	*lit*	March hare	*animals*	maxillary	*medic*
major road	*travel*	marchpane	*food*	mayflower	*flowers*
major role	*theatre*	march past	*war*	mayoralty	*govt*
majorship	*govt*	Mardi Gras	*time*	means test	*trade*
majuscule	*lit*	mare's nest	*animals*	meanwhile	*time*
make a sale	*trade*	mare's tail	*geog*	meat paste	*food*
make haste	*travel*	mare's tail	*plants*	mechanics	*maths*
make up man	*jobs*	margarine	*food*	mechanics	*physics*
make up man	*theatre*	marigraph	*marine*	mechanism	*machine*
make war on	*war*	marihuana	*medic*	medallion	*art*
malachite	*mineral*	marijuana	*medic*	medallist	*jobs*
malaguena	*music*	marijuana	*plants*	medallist	*sport*
malar bone	*medic*	market day	*trade*	medal play	*sport*
male model	*jobs*	marketing	*trade*	meden agan	*foreign*
male nurse	*jobs*	marlstone	*mineral*	mediaeval	*time*
malic acid	*chem*	Marmaduke	*names*	mediation	*music*
malignant	*medic*	marmalade	*food*	medicated	*medic*
malleolus	*medic*	marquetry	*archit*	medicinal	*medic*
Mamillius	*Shakesp*	marquetry	*house*	megacurie	*measure*
mammalian	*animals*	Marrakesh	*cities*	megacurie	*physics*
man at arms	*jobs*	marsh fern	*plants*	megacycle	*measure*
man at arms	*war*	marshland	*geog*	megacycle	*physics*
mandoline	*music*	marshwort	*plants*	megascope	*physics*

megathere	*animals*	
Meilanion	*myth*	
Mein|Kampf	*titles*	
Melanesia	*islands*	
Melbourne	*cities*	
Melbourne	*leaders*	
Meliboean	*lit*	
Melisande	*lit*	
melocoton	*fruit*	
melodious	*music*	
melodrama	*lit*	
melodrama	*music*	
melodrama	*theatre*	
melomania	*music*	
Melpomene	*muses*	
Melpomene	*myth*	
Melpomene	*theatre*	
menagerie	*animals*	
menagerie	*theatre*	
Men|at|Arms	*titles*	
mendicant	*jobs*	
Menippean	*lit*	
menshevik	*govt*	
menstrual	*time*	
mercenary	*jobs*	
mercenary	*war*	
mercy|seat	*law*	
mercy|seat	*relig*	
merganser	*birds*	
mesentery	*medic*	
mesic|atom	*physics*	
mesmerist	*jobs*	
mesocolon	*medic*	
mesophyte	*plants*	
mesotrons	*physics*	
messenger	*jobs*	
metalloid	*chem*	
metalloid	*mineral*	
metameric	*chem*	
metaplasm	*biol*	
meteorite	*astron*	
meteoroid	*astron*	
metheglin	*drink*	
Methodist	*relig*	
metric|ton	*measure*	

metronome	*music*
metronome	*time*
Meyerbeer	*music*
mezzanine	*archit*
mezzanine	*house*
mezza|voce	*music*
mezzotint	*art*
microcopy	*art*
microfilm	*art*
microfilm	*physics*
microlite	*mineral*
microsome	*biol*
microtome	*biol*
microtron	*physics*
microwave	*physics*
midday|sun	*time*
midday|sun	*weather*
middle|age	*time*
middle|ear	*medic*
middleman	*jobs*
middleman	*trade*
Middleton	*writers*
mid|mashie	*sport*
midstream	*geog*
midsummer	*time*
midwifery	*medic*
midwinter	*time*
migration	*birds*
migratory	*birds*
mild|spell	*weather*
milestone	*measure*
milestone	*travel*
militancy	*war*
milk|churn	*machine*
milkfloat	*travel*
milk|shake	*drink*
milk|snake	*insects*
milkstone	*mineral*
milk|teeth	*medic*
milk|vetch	*plants*
millepede	*insects*
Millicent	*names*
milligram	*measure*
millinery	*clothes*
millipede	*insects*

mill|wheel	*machine*
milometer	*machine*
milometer	*travel*
Milwaukee	*cities*
mincemeat	*food*
minefield	*war*
mine|layer	*travel*
miniature	*art*
miniskirt	*clothes*
Minnehaha	*lit*
minometer	*measure*
minor|mode	*music*
minor|poet	*jobs*
minor|poet	*lit*
minor|role	*theatre*
mint|julep	*drink*
mint|sauce	*food*
minuscule	*lit*
minuteman	*war*
Mirabelle	*names*
miscreant	*law*
mispickel	*mineral*
Miss|Pross	*lit*
miss|stays	*travel*
mistiming	*time*
mistiness	*weather*
mistletoe	*plants*
Mitchison	*writers*
mizzentop	*travel*
Mnemosyne	*myth*
mobocracy	*govt*
mock|Tudor	*archit*
model|girl	*jobs*
model|gown	*clothes*
modelling	*art*
moderator	*physics*
modern|art	*art*
modernism	*art*
modillion	*archit*
modulator	*music*
molecular	*physics*
momentary	*time*
monastery	*relig*
monatomic	*physics*
moneybags	*trade*

money|belt	*trade*	
mongolism	*medic*	
monitress	*jobs*	
monkey|nut	*food*	
monkey|nut	*fruit*	
monk's|hood	*plants*	
monoceros	*animals*	
Monoceros	*astron*	
monochord	*music*	
monodrama	*theatre*	
monograph	*lit*	
monologue	*theatre*	
monomachy	*war*	
monophony	*music*	
monoplane	*travel*	
monoscope	*machine*	
monostich	*lit*	
monotreme	*animals*	
Monsignor	*relig*	
Montaigne	*writers*	
Mont|Blanc	*mounts*	
Mont|Cenis	*mounts*	
Monte|Rosa	*mounts*	
Montezuma	*war*	
monthlong	*time*	
moon|daisy	*flowers*	
moonlight	*astron*	
moonraker	*jobs*	
moonraker	*travel*	
moonshine	*astron*	
moonstone	*jewels*	
moonstone	*mineral*	
moot|court	*law*	
moot|point	*law*	
moral|code	*govt*	
morbidity	*medic*	
morganite	*jewels*	
morganite	*mineral*	
morphosis	*biol*	
morse|code	*travel*	
mortcloth	*relig*	
mortgagee	*law*	
mortgagee	*trade*	
mortgager	*law*	
mortgager	*trade*	
mortician	*jobs*	
mortified	*medic*	
Mosaic|Law	*law*	
Mosaic|law	*relig*	
moss|agate	*jewels*	
moss|green	*colour*	
motocross	*sport*	
motorbike	*travel*	
motorboat	*travel*	
motorcade	*travel*	
mouldings	*archit*	
mouldwarp	*animals*	
mound|bird	*birds*	
Mount|Cook	*mounts*	
Mount|Etna	*mounts*	
Mount|Meru	*mounts*	
mouse|deer	*animals*	
mouse|grey	*colour*	
mousehole	*animals*	
mousetrap	*house*	
moustache	*clothes*	
mouthwash	*medic*	
movie|goer	*film/TV*	
movie|show	*film/TV*	
movie|star	*film/TV*	
Mr|Justice	*law*	
Mr|Podsnap	*lit*	
Mrs|Grundy	*lit*	
muckender	*clothes*	
mule|train	*animals*	
mule|train	*travel*	
multipole	*physics*	
multi|prop	*travel*	
mummy|case	*relig*	
munitions	*war*	
Murchison	*rivers*	
muscadine	*drink*	
muscadine	*fruit*	
muscle|man	*jobs*	
music|hall	*music*	
music|hall	*sport*	
music|hall	*theatre*	
music|roll	*music*	
music|room	*house*	
music|room	*music*	
music|wire	*music*	
musketeer	*jobs*	
musketeer	*war*	
musketoon	*war*	
muskmelon	*fruit*	
musk|plant	*plants*	
musk|shrew	*animals*	
Mussolini	*leaders*	
Mussulman	*relig*	
mustachio	*clothes*	
mute|pedal	*music*	
myography	*biol*	
myriagram	*measure*	
Myrmidons	*myth*	
mysticism	*relig*	
mythmaker	*jobs*	
mythmaker	*lit*	
naked|lady	*flowers*	
Nanda|Devi	*mounts*	
Nandi|bear	*animals*	
nanny|goat	*animals*	
Nantucket	*islands*	
Naples|red	*colour*	
nappy|rash	*medic*	
narcissus	*flowers*	
Narcissus	*myth*	
narcotics	*medic*	
narration	*lit*	
narrative	*lit*	
nasal|duct	*medic*	
Nathaniel	*Shakesp*	
Nathaniel	*names*	
native|cat	*animals*	
nauseated	*medic*	
nauticals	*clothes*	
navelwort	*plants*	
navigable	*travel*	
navigator	*jobs*	
navigator	*travel*	
navy|beans	*veg*	
near|sight	*medic*	
neat|drink	*drink*	
neat|house	*animals*	
neat|price	*trade*	
neat|stall	*animals*	

nebulizer	medic	night fowl	birds	numerator	maths
neckcloth	clothes	nightgown	clothes	numerical	maths
neckpiece	clothes	nighthawk	birds	nun's habit	clothes
necrology	lit	nightlong	time	Nuremberg	cities
nectarine	fruit	night safe	trade	nursemaid	jobs
needle gun	war	nighttide	time	nutriment	food
negotiate	trade	night time	time	nutrition	biol
neighbour	jobs	nightwear	clothes	nutrition	medic
nelumbium	flowers	Nile green	colour	Nuts in May	sport
neodymium	chem	nimbosity	weather	nux vomica	fruit
neodymium	mineral	nisi prius	law	nux vomica	medic
neoGothic	archit	Nissen hut	archit	nystagmus	medic
Neolithic	geog	nitration	chem	obbligato	music
neologism	lit	nocturnal	birds	objection	law
neon light	machine	nocturnal	time	objet d'art	art
neophobia	medic	No Highway	titles	objet d'art	house
neoterism	lit	nonce word	lit	obsequent	geog
nephology	weather	noncompos	medic	obsequial	relig
nephritis	medic	nonentity	people	obsequies	relig
neptunium	chem	nonillion	measure	occipital	medic
nerve cell	medic	nonpareil	lit	occlusion	biol
net income	trade	non smoker	people	occlusion	weather
neuralgia	medic	nor'easter	weather	occultism	myth
neurology	medic	Northants	abbrev	occultist	jobs
neuropath	medic	north east	geog	ocean lane	travel
nevermore	time	northerly	geog	ocean trip	travel
New Guinea	islands	north pole	geog	octachord	music
Newmarket	sport	North Star	geog	octagonal	maths
new potato	veg	North Uist	islands	octastich	lit
newsagent	jobs	north west	geog	octastyle	archit
newsflash	travel	north wind	weather	octennial	time
newshound	jobs	nor'wester	weather	odd job man	jobs
newspaper	lit	nose guard	herald	odd man out	people
newsprint	lit	nose guard	war	off colour	art
Newtonian	maths	nosepiece	herald	off colour	medic
Newtonian	physics	nosepiece	war	Offenbach	music
next of kin	family	nosewheel	travel	offensive	war
next of kin	govt	note paper	educ	offertory	music
Nicodemus	Bible	note paper	lit	offertory	relig
Nicolette	names	not guilty	law	office boy	jobs
Nietzsche	writers	not proven	law	officiant	relig
nightbird	birds	novelette	lit	officiate	trade
night club	theatre	novitiate	educ	officinal	medic
night crow	birds	novo damus	law	off market	trade
nightfall	time	numbering	maths	offspring	family

off|the|map	geog	orange|tip	insects	overshoes	clothes
off|the|peg	clothes	orangutan	animals	overshoot	travel
oftentime	time	orchestra	music	overskirt	clothes
oiling|can	machine	orchestra	theatre	overspend	trade
oil|paints	art	order|book	trade	overthrow	war
Old|Bailey	law	ordinance	law	overtones	music
old|master	art	organ|stop	music	oviparous	animals
old|master	jobs	orientate	travel	ovulation	biol
old|stager	jobs	orienteer	sport	owl|parrot	birds
old|stager	theatre	oriflamme	herald	oxidation	chem
oleograph	art	orlop|deck	travel	ozocerite	mineral
olfactory	medic	orography	educ	pacemaker	medic
oligarchy	govt	orpharion	music	pacemaker	people
Oligocene	geog	orthodoxy	relig	pacemaker	sport
olive|drab	colour	osmometer	measure	Pachelbel	music
Ombudsman	govt	ossifrage	birds	pachyderm	animals
ombudsman	jobs	ossuarium	relig	pack|horse	travel
ombudsman	law	osteology	medic	pademelon	animals
on|account	trade	osteopath	jobs	pageantry	govt
onion|soup	drink	osteopath	medic	pageantry	herald
On|Liberty	titles	other|side	war	page|gauge	machine
onomastic	lit	otologist	jobs	page|proof	lit
onslaught	war	otologist	medic	paintress	art
on|the|hoof	animals	oubliette	law	paintwork	archit
on|the|mend	medic	ounce|troy	measure	palaestra	educ
on|the|move	travel	outer|bark	trees	palaestra	sport
on|the|nail	trade	outfitter	jobs	Palamedes	myth
on|the|wing	birds	outgoings	trade	palanquin	travel
on|the|wing	travel	out|of|date	time	Palestine	relig
open|court	law	out|of|debt	trade	palillogy	lit
open|floor	archit	out|of|tune	music	palladium	chem
open|notes	music	out|of|work	trade	palladium	mineral
open|order	war	outrigger	travel	Palladium	myth
open|score	music	outskirts	archit	palm|civet	animals
opera|pink	colour	outworker	trade	palsgrave	govt
operation	medic	overboard	travel	Panama|hat	clothes
operation	war	overcloud	weather	pancaking	travel
operative	jobs	overdraft	trade	Pandareus	myth
operative	trade	overdrawn	trade	panel|game	sport
Ophiuchus	astron	overdress	clothes	panel|game	theatre
opportune	time	overdrive	machine	panelling	archit
optic|disc	medic	overdrive	travel	panelling	house
optometry	medic	overgrown	plants	panellist	jobs
orangeade	drink	overheads	trade	panoplied	war
orange|pip	fruit	overnight	time	pantalets	clothes

pantaloon	theatre
pantomime	jobs
pantomime	sport
pantomime	theatre
papal|bull	relig
paparazzo	jobs
paper|back	lit
paper|clip	art
paper|doll	sport
paper|wasp	insects
Papillons	titles
parabasis	theatre
parabolic	lit
parachute	sport
parachute	travel
parachute	war
Paraclete	relig
paragraph	lit
parallels	geog
paralyser	biol
paralysis	medic
parameter	maths
paramount	govt
parchment	educ
parchment	lit
parchment	relig
paregoric	medic
pargeting	art
parge|work	art
parhelion	astron
pariah|dog	animals
pari|passu	foreign
Paris|doll	clothes
Parnassus	lit
Parnassus	myth
parotitis	medic
parquetry	house
parrakeet	birds
parricide	law
parsonage	relig
Parthenon	archit
Parthenon	myth
partition	archit
partition	house
partitive	lit

part|music	music
part|owner	jobs
partridge	birds
party|game	sport
party|line	govt
party|line	travel
party|whip	govt
pas|de|deux	music
pas|de|deux	theatre
paso|doble	sport
passenger	jobs
passenger	travel
passepied	music
passepied	sport
passerine	birds
Pasternak	writers
pasticcio	art
pasticcio	music
pastorale	music
past|tense	lit
pasturage	agric
patchwork	house
pathology	medic
patriarch	family
patriarch	govt
patriarch	relig
patrician	govt
patrician	people
patrimony	law
Patroclus	Shakesp
patrol|car	law
patrol|car	travel
patrolman	jobs
patrolman	law
patronage	govt
patronage	theatre
patronage	trade
patroness	jobs
patroness	theatre
patronize	trade
patty|cake	food
Paul|Jones	sport
paulownia	trees
pay|dearly	trade
pay|homage	relig

pay|in|kind	trade
paymaster	jobs
paymaster	trade
paysagist	jobs
peach|palm	trees
pea|jacket	clothes
peaked|cap	clothes
peanut|bar	food
pearl|grey	colour
Pecksniff	people
peculator	law
peculator	people
pecuniary	trade
pecunious	trade
pedagogic	educ
pedagogue	educ
pedagogue	educ
pedal|note	music
pedentive	archit
pedometer	measure
peel|house	war
peel|tower	war
pegmatite	mineral
Pekingese	animals
pellitory	plants
pelmanism	sport
penal|code	law
pen|and|ink	art
pen|and|ink	lit
pendragon	govt
peneplain	geog
pen|friend	jobs
pen|friend	sport
peninsula	geog
penniless	trade
penny|wise	trade
pennywort	plants
pen|pusher	jobs
penscript	lit
pensioner	educ
pensioner	jobs
pentapody	lit
Pentecost	relig
Pentecost	time
penthouse	archit

penthouse	*sport*	
percaline	*clothes*	
per|capita	*foreign*	
per|cheron	*animals*	
per|contra	*foreign*	
peregrine	*birds*	
Peregrine	*names*	
perennial	*flowers*	
perennial	*time*	
performer	*film/TV*	
performer	*jobs*	
performer	*music*	
performer	*theatre*	
Pergolesi	*music*	
periclase	*mineral*	
peridrome	*archit*	
perilymph	*medic*	
perimeter	*maths*	
peripatus	*insects*	
periscope	*machine*	
periscope	*travel*	
peristyle	*archit*	
permanent	*time*	
perpetual	*flowers*	
persimmon	*fruit*	
personage	*jobs*	
personage	*theatre*	
personify	*lit*	
personnel	*jobs*	
persuader	*people*	
pertussis	*medic*	
pessimist	*people*	
pesthouse	*medic*	
petersham	*clothes*	
petit|four	*food*	
petit|jury	*law*	
petri|dish	*biol*	
petroleum	*chem*	
petroleum	*mineral*	
petrology	*mineral*	
petrology	*mineral*	
Petruchio	*Shakesp*	
petticoat	*clothes*	
petty|cash	*trade*	
petty|jury	*law*	

petty|whin	*trees*	
phacolith	*geog*	
phagocyte	*medic*	
phalanger	*animals*	
phalanges	*medic*	
phalarope	*birds*	
Phantasus	*myth*	
Pharisees	*Bible*	
phenolite	*mineral*	
phenology	*biol*	
phenomena	*geog*	
phenotype	*biol*	
philately	*sport*	
phillibeg	*clothes*	
philology	*lit*	
Philomelo	*myth*	
phlebitis	*medic*	
phone|book	*house*	
phone|book	*travel*	
phone|call	*travel*	
phone|girl	*jobs*	
phonemics	*lit*	
phonemics	*physics*	
phonetics	*lit*	
phonology	*lit*	
phosphate	*agric*	
phosphate	*chem*	
phosphate	*food*	
phosphide	*chem*	
phosphite	*chem*	
photocell	*physics*	
photocopy	*art*	
photogene	*chem*	
photogram	*art*	
photoplay	*film/TV*	
photostat	*art*	
phototypy	*lit*	
phrenetic	*medic*	
phycology	*biol*	
physician	*jobs*	
physician	*medic*	
physicist	*jobs*	
physicist	*physics*	
physic|nut	*fruit*	
phytotron	*biol*	

piacevole	*music*
piangendo	*music*
piano|keys	*music*
pianolist	*music*
piano|wire	*music*
pickaback	*sport*
picksmith	*jobs*
picnic|ham	*food*
pictorial	*art*
pictorial	*lit*
piecework	*trade*
pied|piper	*myth*
pie|funnel	*house*
pierglass	*house*
Pierrette	*jobs*
Pierrette	*theatre*
pier|table	*house*
piggy|bank	*trade*
pig|trough	*agric*
pike|perch	*fish*
Pikes|Peak	*mounts*
pikestaff	*war*
pilfering	*law*
pillar|box	*travel*
pilot|ball	*sport*
pilot|boat	*travel*
pilot|fish	*fish*
pimpernel	*flowers*
pin|and|web	*medic*
pinchbeck	*measure*
pinch|draw	*sport*
pineapple	*fruit*
pine|finch	*birds*
Pinkerton	*lit*
pinnipede	*animals*
pinstripe	*clothes*
pinto|bean	*veg*
pipe|organ	*music*
piping|hot	*food*
pipistrel	*animals*
pirouette	*sport*
pirouette	*theatre*
pistachio	*food*
pistachio	*fruit*
pistareen	*money*

pistoleer	*jobs*	pocket|rat	*animals*	polygonum	*plants*
piston|rod	*machine*	poetaster	*jobs*	Polynesia	*islands*
pitch|camp	*sport*	poetaster	*lit*	polyphony	*music*
pitchfork	*tools*	poetaster	*people*	polythene	*chem*
pitch|pine	*trees*	poetastry	*lit*	pompadour	*clothes*
pitch|pipe	*music*	poetcraft	*lit*	pontlevis	*archit*
pitot|tube	*physics*	poeticule	*lit*	poodle|dog	*animals*
pituitary	*medic*	Poet's|Poet	*lit*	poorly|off	*trade*
pitwright	*jobs*	pogo|stick	*sport*	pop|artist	*jobs*
pixie|hood	*clothes*	point|duty	*travel*	poppy|head	*flowers*
pizzicato	*music*	point|lace	*clothes*	pop|record	*music*
place|card	*house*	poisoning	*medic*	pop|singer	*jobs*
plainsong	*music*	poison|ivy	*plants*	porbeagle	*fish*
plaintiff	*jobs*	poison|nut	*fruit*	porcelain	*art*
plaintiff	*law*	poison|oak	*trees*	porcelain	*house*
planetary	*astron*	poison|pen	*people*	porcupine	*animals*
planetoid	*astron*	poker|dice	*sport*	Porcupine	*rivers*
plane|tree	*trees*	polar|axis	*geog*	porringer	*house*
plant|life	*plants*	polar|axis	*physics*	portfolio	*govt*
plasterer	*jobs*	polar|bear	*animals*	portfolio	*trade*
platitude	*lit*	polar|star	*astron*	portfolio	*travel*
play|actor	*theatre*	pole|vault	*sport*	portioner	*educ*
play|by|ear	*music*	police|car	*law*	portrayal	*art*
play|group	*educ*	police|car	*travel*	portrayal	*lit*
playhouse	*theatre*	police|dog	*animals*	portrayal	*theatre*
plaything	*sport*	police|dog	*law*	portrayer	*art*
pleadings	*law*	policeman	*jobs*	portrayer	*jobs*
ploughboy	*jobs*	policeman	*law*	portreeve	*jobs*
ploughing	*agric*	police|van	*law*	portreeve	*law*
ploughman	*jobs*	police|van	*travel*	portulaca	*plants*
plug|point	*machine*	Politburo	*govt*	possessor	*jobs*
plumb|line	*physics*	political	*govt*	postcenal	*time*
plumb|line	*tools*	Polixenes	*Shakesp*	post|haste	*travel*
plume|moth	*insects*	pollen|sac	*flowers*	Posthumus	*Shakesp*
plunderer	*jobs*	pollinate	*flowers*	postilion	*travel*
plus|fours	*clothes*	pollution	*medic*	postulant	*jobs*
plutocrat	*govt*	polonaise	*music*	postwoman	*jobs*
plutocrat	*people*	polonaise	*sport*	potassium	*chem*
plutocrat	*trade*	polo|shirt	*clothes*	potato|bug	*insects*
plutonium	*chem*	polyandry	*law*	potboiler	*lit*
plutonium	*mineral*	polybasic	*chem*	potentate	*govt*
pneumatic	*machine*	polychord	*music*	potential	*lit*
pneumatic	*physics*	Polydorus	*myth*	potential	*physics*
pneumeter	*medic*	polyester	*chem*	potholing	*sport*
pneumonia	*medic*	polygonal	*maths*	pothunter	*people*

potometer	biol	
potometer	measure	
potpourri	food	
potpourri	music	
poulterer	jobs	
pound|cake	food	
pound|note	trade	
pourboire	trade	
pourpoint	clothes	
powdering	herald	
powerboat	travel	
power|dive	travel	
power|game	govt	
power|line	machine	
power|pack	machine	
power|pack	physics	
pozzolana	geog	
practical	trade	
prayer|dog	animals	
prayer|mat	relig	
prayer|rug	relig	
precedent	govt	
preceding	time	
precentor	educ	
precentor	jobs	
precentor	music	
precentor	relig	
preceptor	educ	
precipice	geog	
precisely	time	
precuneus	medic	
precursor	jobs	
predatory	animals	
predicate	lit	
prefigure	art	
preheater	machine	
prelector	educ	
prelector	jobs	
premature	medic	
premature	time	
presbyter	jobs	
presbyter	relig	
pre|school	educ	
prescribe	medic	
prescript	govt	
presently	time	
preserves	food	
president	govt	
president	jobs	
presidium	govt	
pressgang	travel	
pressroom	lit	
press|stud	clothes	
presswork	lit	
pretender	govt	
pretender	people	
preterite	lit	
priceless	trade	
price|list	trade	
price|ring	trade	
price|rise	trade	
prick|spur	herald	
prick|spur	war	
priestess	jobs	
priestess	relig	
Priestley	writers	
prime|cost	trade	
prime|song	relig	
princedom	govt	
princelet	govt	
principal	educ	
principal	jobs	
principal	music	
principal	trade	
print|shop	lit	
Priscilla	names	
prismatic	art	
privateer	govt	
privateer	jobs	
privateer	travel	
privy|seal	herald	
prize|crew	travel	
probation	law	
proboscis	animals	
procedure	govt	
processed	biol	
profanity	relig	
professor	educ	
professor	jobs	
profiteer	jobs	
profiteer	trade	
prognosis	medic	
programme	comput	
programme	film/TV	
programme	govt	
programme	music	
programme	theatre	
projector	art	
projector	film/TV	
projector	machine	
projector	war	
Prokoviev	music	
prolamine	chem	
prolation	music	
prolative	lit	
prolepsis	lit	
prolicide	law	
prolixity	lit	
promenade	music	
promenade	travel	
promotion	trade	
prompt|box	theatre	
pronghorn	animals	
pronounce	law	
proofread	lit	
proofroom	lit	
pro|patria	foreign	
propeller	machine	
propeller	travel	
prophasis	medic	
propshaft	machine	
pro|re|nata	foreign	
prosecute	law	
proselyte	educ	
proselyte	relig	
proseuche	archit	
proseuche	relig	
protamine	chem	
protector	govt	
protector	war	
prothesis	archit	
prothesis	relig	
protogyny	biol	
proton|gun	physics	
prototype	biol	

prototype	*machine*	pyrometer	*measure*	radiation	*physics*
protozoan	*animals*	pyroxylin	*war*	radiobeam	*travel*
provender	*food*	quadratus	*medic*	radiogram	*house*
provision	*food*	quadrille	*music*	radiogram	*machine*
prud'homme	*jobs*	quadrille	*sport*	radiogram	*medic*
psalmbook	*relig*	quadruped	*animals*	radiogram	*travel*
pseudonym	*lit*	quadruple	*maths*	radiology	*medic*
psoriasis	*medic*	quail dove	*birds*	radiology	*physics*
ptarmigan	*birds*	qualified	*educ*	radio rays	*physics*
pterosaur	*insects*	qualified	*trade*	radio star	*astron*
publicist	*govt*	qualifier	*lit*	raffinose	*chem*
publicist	*jobs*	quarterly	*herald*	rain cloud	*weather*
publicist	*lit*	quarterly	*lit*	rain gauge	*weather*
publicity	*theatre*	quarterly	*time*	rainmaker	*jobs*
public law	*law*	quarter to	*time*	rainspout	*weather*
publisher	*jobs*	quartette	*music*	rainstorm	*weather*
puff adder	*insects*	quartzite	*mineral*	rainwater	*geog*
pugnacity	*war*	quasi star	*astron*	ram rocket	*travel*
puissance	*sport*	quebracho	*trees*	ram rocket	*war*
pulmonary	*medic*	queenship	*govt*	ransacker	*jobs*
punchball	*sport*	queer fish	*people*	ranzelman	*jobs*
punchbowl	*house*	quicklime	*geog*	Rarotonga	*islands*
punch card	*machine*	quicksand	*marine*	Ras Dashan	*mounts*
punch line	*lit*	quickstep	*sport*	raspberry	*fruit*
punch line	*theatre*	quillwort	*plants*	ratefixer	*jobs*
punch tape	*machine*	quintette	*music*	ratepayer	*jobs*
punctuate	*lit*	quintuple	*maths*	ratepayer	*trade*
puppeteer	*jobs*	quittance	*govt*	rationale	*lit*
purchaser	*trade*	quittance	*trade*	raw comedy	*theatre*
purgative	*medic*	quodlibet	*lit*	raw sienna	*colour*
purgatory	*myth*	quodlibet	*music*	razor back	*animals*
purifying	*medic*	quotation	*lit*	razorbill	*birds*
push parry	*sport*	quotation	*trade*	razorfish	*fish*
put in suit	*govt*	quotidian	*time*	reach land	*travel*
Puy de Dome	*mounts*	rabbit pie	*food*	ready cash	*trade*
Pygmalion	*titles*	racehorse	*animals*	readymade	*clothes*
pyracanth	*trees*	race track	*sport*	real wages	*trade*
pyramidal	*maths*	rachidial	*medic*	rearguard	*war*
pyrethrum	*flowers*	racing car	*sport*	rebel call	*war*
pyrogenic	*biol*	racing car	*travel*	rebellion	*war*
pyrolater	*myth*	racketeer	*law*	recaption	*law*
pyrolatry	*myth*	racketeer	*people*	receiving	*law*
pyrolysis	*chem*	raconteur	*jobs*	reception	*archit*
pyrometer	*chem*	raconteur	*lit*	receptive	*educ*
pyrometer	*machine*	radar nose	*travel*	recession	*trade*

reckoning	maths	registrar	govt	ressaldar	war
reckoning	trade	registrar	jobs	restraint	trade
recording	film/TV	registrar	law	retelling	lit
recording	music	registrar	trade	retriever	animals
recording	physics	regularly	time	reverence	relig
recordist	jobs	regulator	machine	revetment	archit
recountal	lit	rehearsal	film/TV	Reykjavik	cities
recounter	lit	rehearsal	theatre	Rhine|wine	drink
rectangle	maths	reimburse	trade	rhodonite	mineral
rectifier	machine	relay|race	sport	rhombical	maths
recurrent	time	relay|team	sport	rhymester	jobs
redbreast	birds	relief|map	geog	rhymester	lit
red|clover	plants	reliquary	relig	rhynchota	insects
red|ensign	herald	remainder	govt	rhythmics	music
red|grouse	birds	Rembrandt	artists	rice|paddy	cereal
red|handed	law	remission	law	rice|paper	art
redingote	clothes	remontant	flowers	rice|paper	food
red|mullet	fish	remote|age	time	rice|paper	house
red|pepper	food	remote|key	music	ricercare	music
red|pepper	veg	rendering	music	richardia	flowers
red|setter	animals	rendition	music	Richelieu	leaders
red|spider	insects	repayment	trade	ridgeback	animals
red|tapism	govt	repertory	theatre	ridgepole	archit
reduction	maths	represent	art	rifle|ball	war
reduction	trade	represent	govt	rifle|bird	birds
redundant	trade	represent	law	right|back	sport
reed|grass	plants	represent	lit	right|bank	geog
reed|organ	music	represent	theatre	righteous	relig
reef|point	travel	reprimand	law	right|half	sport
re|entrant	maths	reprobate	people	right|hand	music
refectory	archit	reptilian	insects	right|hook	sport
refectory	house	rerebrace	herald	right|time	time
reference	jobs	rerebrace	war	right|wing	govt
reference	lit	rescue|dog	animals	right|wing	sport
reference	trade	resection	medic	rigid|arch	archit
refinance	trade	reservoir	archit	rigmarole	lit
reflation	trade	reservoir	chem	Rigoletto	lit
reflector	art	reservoir	geog	Rigoletto	titles
reflector	machine	reservoir	physics	rime|frost	weather
reflector	physics	resetting	law	ring|fence	archit
reflexive	lit	residence	archit	ringouzel	birds
refluence	geog	residency	jobs	ringsider	jobs
refractor	astron	resonance	music	ringsider	sport
refresher	educ	resonance	physics	ring|snake	insects
regardant	herald	resources	trade	Rio|Grande	rivers

riot|squad	law	rose|elder	flowers	rudder|bar	travel
river|boat	travel	rose|noble	money	Ruddigore	titles
riverhead	geog	Rosinante	animals	rule|of|law	law
riverside	geog	rotary|gap	machine	rump|steak	food
road|block	travel	rotavator	agric	rum|runner	jobs
road|drill	tools	rotograph	art	runesmith	lit
roadhouse	archit	rotograph	lit	Runnymede	islands
roadmaker	jobs	rotor|ship	travel	rural|dean	jobs
road|sense	travel	rotovator	agric	rural|dean	relig
roadstead	travel	Rotterdam	cities	Ruritania	myth
road|works	travel	rough|arch	archit	rus|in|urbe	archit
roast|beef	food	roughcast	archit	ruthenium	chem
robber|fly	insects	rough|copy	art	ruthenium	mineral
Robin|Hood	myth	roughneck	people	Ruwenzori	mounts
rocambole	plants	rough|note	educ	rye|whisky	drink
rock|basis	geog	round|arch	archit	saccharin	chem
rock|brake	plants	round|clam	fish	sackcloth	relig
rock|candy	food	roundelay	lit	sack|dress	clothes
rock|climb	sport	roundelay	music	sackmaker	jobs
rockcress	plants	roundelay	sport	sacrament	relig
rock|drill	tools	round|game	sport	sacrarium	relig
rocket|car	travel	round|hand	lit	sacrifice	relig
rocketeer	jobs	roundhead	war	sacrifice	trade
rocket|gun	war	round|neck	clothes	sacrilege	relig
rocket|man	jobs	round|shot	war	sacristan	jobs
rocket|man	travel	roundsman	jobs	sacristan	relig
rocket|man	war	round|trip	sport	saddlebag	travel
rock|perch	fish	round|trip	travel	Sadducees	Bible
rock|pipit	birds	roundworm	insects	safemaker	jobs
rock|plant	plants	Rousillon	Shakesp	safety|net	sport
rock|snake	insects	rover|hoop	sport	safety|pin	clothes
roisterer	people	rowan|tree	trees	safety|pin	house
romancist	lit	rowel|spur	war	sagebrush	trees
Roman|lace	clothes	royal|blue	colour	sailcloth	clothes
rondo|form	music	royal|coat	herald	sailmaker	jobs
rood|stair	relig	royal|fern	plants	sailor|hat	clothes
rood|tower	relig	royal|fish	fish	sailplane	travel
Roosevelt	USpres	royal|mast	travel	sainthood	relig
root|house	agric	Royal|Navy	war	Saint|Joan	titles
root|prune	flowers	royal|palm	trees	Saint|s|day	time
rootstock	flowers	royal|road	travel	saintship	relig
ropemaker	jobs	royal|sail	travel	salad|bowl	house
Roquefort	food	royal|seal	herald	salad|days	time
Rosabella	names	Royal|seal	law	salad|herb	fruit
rose|apple	trees			salangane	birds

sale block	trade	sapodilla	trees	schnauzer	animals
salesgirl	jobs	sapsucker	birds	schnorkel	sport
salesgirl	trade	Saragossa	cities	scholarch	educ
sales talk	trade	Sarah Gamp	lit	scholarly	educ
salesteam	jobs	Sarasvati	myth	scholiast	lit
Salisbury	Shakesp	sarcodina	animals	schoolboy	educ
Salisbury	cities	sartorius	medic	school cap	clothes
Salisbury	leaders	sassafras	medic	school hat	clothes
sally port	archit	sassafras	trees	schooling	educ
sally port	travel	sassenach	jobs	schoolish	educ
sally port	war	sassenach	people	school kid	educ
saloon car	travel	satellite	astron	school lad	educ
saltmarsh	geog	satellite	geog	schoolman	educ
saltpetre	chem	satellite	travel	schoolman	relig
saltpetre	war	satin moth	insects	scientist	biol
saltwater	marine	satinwood	trees	scientist	chem
salvation	relig	satirical	lit	scientist	jobs
Samaritan	Bible	sauceboat	house	scientist	physics
Samaritan	people	saucerman	travel	scintilla	astron
Samaritan	relig	sauna bath	medic	scintilla	physics
Samarkand	cities	sauna bath	sport	sclerosis	medic
Sam Weller	lit	saxcornet	music	sclerotic	medic
sanctions	govt	saxifrage	flowers	scoop neck	clothes
sanctions	law	saxophone	music	score card	sport
sanctuary	birds	scagliola	archit	Scotch egg	food
sanctuary	relig	scaldfish	fish	Scotch elm	trees
sand blast	weather	scale moss	plants	Scotch fir	trees
sand devil	weather	scamp duck	birds	Scots pine	trees
sand dunes	geog	scantling	archit	scoundrel	people
sandglass	time	Scapa Flow	seas	scrapbook	sport
sand grain	plants	scapegoat	people	scrapegut	jobs
sand grass	plants	scapegoat	relig	scrapegut	music
sandmason	insects	scapulary	relig	screwball	people
sandpaper	machine	scarecrow	jobs	screw dive	sport
sandpiper	birds	Scarlatti	music	screw pine	plants
sandpride	fish	scavenger	animals	scribbler	jobs
sandspout	weather	scavenger	jobs	scribbler	lit
sandstone	mineral	scenarist	jobs	scrimmage	sport
sandstorm	weather	scenarist	theatre	scrimshaw	art
sand yacht	sport	scene plot	theatre	scription	lit
sand yacht	travel	Schaunard	lit	Scripture	relig
Sangarius	myth	scheelite	mineral	scrivener	jobs
sanhedrin	govt	scherzoso	music	scrivener	lit
sans serif	lit	schilling	money	scrivenry	lit
sapodilla	fruit	schnapper	fish	scrubbird	birds

scrum半half	*sport*	seed|pearl	*jewels*	sgraffito	*art*
scrummage	*sport*	seed|plant	*flowers*	sgraffito	*lit*
sculpture	*art*	seed|snipe	*birds*	shade|tree	*trees*
scutcheon	*herald*	selachian	*fish*	shaftment	*sport*
sea|anchor	*travel*	selection	*lit*	shakedown	*house*
sea|battle	*war*	selectman	*govt*	shamateur	*sport*
sea|bottle	*plants*	sell|short	*trade*	Shangri|la	*myth*
sea|breeze	*marine*	semanteme	*lit*	shantyman	*music*
sea|canary	*animals*	semantics	*lit*	sharkskin	*clothes*
sea|dragon	*birds*	semaphore	*travel*	sharp|bend	*travel*
seafaring	*travel*	semestral	*time*	sheepskin	*clothes*
sea|gasket	*travel*	semibreve	*music*	sheep|tick	*insects*
sea|girdle	*plants*	semicolon	*lit*	sheer|drop	*geog*
sea|lawyer	*jobs*	semi|final	*sport*	sheer|hulk	*travel*
sea|margin	*marine*	semi|lunar	*medic*	sheetwork	*lit*
sea|nettle	*fish*	semimetal	*mineral*	Sheffield	*cities*
Sea|of|Azov	*lakes*	semiotics	*lit*	Shelburne	*leaders*
Sea|of|Azov	*seas*	semitonic	*music*	sheldrake	*birds*
sea|parrot	*birds*	Sempronia	*names*	shellfire	*war*
sea|salmon	*fish*	seneschal	*govt*	shellfish	*fish*
sea|sleeve	*fish*	seneschal	*jobs*	sheriffry	*govt*
seasoning	*food*	sensorium	*medic*	Shetlands	*islands*
sea|squirt	*animals*	sentry|box	*war*	shewbread	*relig*
sea|tangle	*plants*	sentryman	*jobs*	shift|work	*trade*
seat|of|war	*war*	separates	*clothes*	shinguard	*sport*
sea|turtle	*insects*	separator	*machine*	Shintoist	*relig*
sea|urchin	*fish*	September	*time*	shipboard	*travel*
seaworthy	*travel*	sepulchre	*relig*	ship|of|war	*travel*
sebaceous	*medic*	sepulture	*relig*	ship|plane	*travel*
Sebastian	*Shakesp*	Seraphina	*names*	ship|route	*travel*
Sebastian	*names*	seraphine	*music*	ship's|crew	*travel*
secateurs	*tools*	seraskier	*jobs*	shipshape	*travel*
second|act	*theatre*	serenader	*jobs*	shipwreck	*travel*
secondary	*art*	serenader	*music*	shirt|band	*clothes*
Secondary	*geog*	sermonist	*jobs*	shirt|stud	*clothes*
second|row	*sport*	sermonize	*educ*	shirt|tail	*clothes*
secretary	*govt*	serviette	*house*	shoeblack	*house*
secretary	*jobs*	Servilius	*Shakesp*	shoemaker	*jobs*
secretary	*lit*	servitude	*jobs*	shop|floor	*trade*
secretary	*trade*	set|on|foot	*travel*	shopfront	*archit*
secret|ink	*lit*	set|square	*maths*	shore|bird	*birds*
secretion	*medic*	set|square	*measure*	shoreline	*geog*
sedge|bird	*birds*	sevenfold	*measure*	shortcake	*food*
sedge|wren	*birds*	seven|seas	*marine*	short|game	*sport*
seediness	*medic*	sforzando	*music*	shorthand	*lit*

shorthorn	*agric*	silver|fir	*trees*	slide|rule	*maths*
shorthorn	*animals*	silver|fox	*animals*	slide|rule	*measure*
short|odds	*sport*	Simonides	*Shakesp*	slingshot	*war*
short|ribs	*food*	simpleton	*people*	slip|cover	*lit*
short|sale	*trade*	sine|prole	*foreign*	sloethorn	*trees*
short|side	*trade*	Singapore	*cities*	slop|basin	*house*
shortstop	*sport*	Singapore	*islands*	sloppy|Joe	*clothes*
short|term	*time*	single|jet	*travel*	sloth|bear	*animals*
short|time	*time*	single|sap	*war*	slouch|hat	*clothes*
short|wave	*physics*	single|tax	*trade*	slowcoach	*people*
shovel|hat	*clothes*	singleton	*sport*	slowcoach	*travel*
shovel|hat	*relig*	singspiel	*music*	slow|march	*music*
shower|cap	*clothes*	sink|apace	*music*	slow|train	*travel*
shower|cap	*house*	sinusitis	*medic*	slung|shot	*war*
shrew|mole	*animals*	siren|suit	*clothes*	small|arms	*war*
shrimping	*sport*	sisal|hemp	*plants*	small|beer	*drink*
shrubbery	*trees*	situation	*geog*	small|boat	*travel*
siciliana	*music*	situation	*jobs*	small|bore	*machine*
sideboard	*house*	situation	*trade*	small|bore	*sport*
sideburns	*clothes*	sixth|form	*educ*	small|bore	*war*
side|chain	*physics*	size|stick	*measure*	small|pica	*lit*
sidelight	*house*	Skagerrak	*seas*	small|shot	*war*
sidelight	*machine*	sketching	*art*	smartweed	*plants*
sidelight	*travel*	sketch|pad	*art*	smatterer	*educ*
side|scene	*theatre*	skew|table	*archit*	smerzando	*music*
side|table	*house*	skiagraph	*art*	smoke|bomb	*war*
sidetrack	*travel*	ski|jacket	*clothes*	smoke|grey	*colour*
Siegfried	*lit*	ski|jumper	*clothes*	smuggling	*law*
Siegfried	*names*	skin|diver	*jobs*	snake|bird	*birds*
Siegfried	*titles*	skin|diver	*sport*	snakelike	*insects*
Sieglinde	*lit*	skingraft	*medic*	snakeroot	*plants*
sight|bill	*trade*	skin|tight	*clothes*	snap|beans	*veg*
sight|land	*travel*	ski|troops	*war*	snowberry	*trees*
sightseer	*travel*	skunk|bear	*animals*	snow|climb	*sport*
signal|box	*travel*	sky|diving	*sport*	snowdrift	*geog*
signal|gun	*sport*	skylarker	*people*	snowfield	*geog*
signaller	*jobs*	skyriding	*travel*	snowflake	*flowers*
signalman	*jobs*	skyrocket	*machine*	snowflake	*weather*
signalman	*travel*	skyrocket	*war*	snow|fleck	*birds*
signalman	*war*	sky|troops	*war*	snow|goose	*birds*
signature	*lit*	slabstone	*mineral*	snowplant	*plants*
signature	*music*	slapstick	*theatre*	snowscape	*geog*
Silas|Wegg	*lit*	slate|roof	*archit*	snowshoes	*clothes*
silk|grass	*plants*	slaughter	*war*	snowshoes	*travel*
silver|cup	*sport*	slide|rule	*comput*	snowstorm	*weather*

snow|under	*weather*	sonneteer	*jobs*	spacesuit	*physics*
soapberry	*trees*	sonneteer	*lit*	spacesuit	*travel*
soap|opera	*film/TV*	son|of|a|gun	*war*	space|time	*time*
soap|opera	*music*	sonometer	*music*	spacewalk	*physics*
soapstone	*mineral*	soot|black	*colour*	spacewalk	*travel*
sob|sister	*people*	sooty|tern	*birds*	spaghetti	*food*
socialism	*govt*	sophister	*educ*	spare|part	*medic*
socialist	*govt*	sophister	*jobs*	spare|part	*travel*
socialist	*people*	Sophocles	*writers*	spareribs	*food*
socialite	*people*	sophomore	*educ*	spare|room	*house*
soda|bread	*food*	sophomore	*jobs*	spare|time	*time*
soda|scone	*food*	soporific	*medic*	spearhead	*war*
soda|water	*drink*	sorceress	*jobs*	spearmint	*food*
soft|cover	*lit*	sorceress	*myth*	spearmint	*plants*
soft|drink	*drink*	sostenuto	*music*	spear|side	*herald*
soft|goods	*trade*	sotto|voce	*music*	spectacle	*film/TV*
soft|pedal	*music*	soubrette	*jobs*	spectacle	*theatre*
solar|cell	*machine*	soubrette	*theatre*	spectator	*sport*
solar|time	*time*	sou|easter	*weather*	spectator	*theatre*
solar|wind	*astron*	sound|hole	*music*	speculate	*trade*
solar|year	*time*	soundness	*trade*	speedboat	*sport*
soldierly	*war*	sound|post	*music*	speedboat	*travel*
soldier|on	*war*	sound|unit	*machine*	speedster	*jobs*
sole|agent	*trade*	sound|wave	*physics*	speedster	*travel*
solenette	*fish*	soup|plate	*house*	speedwell	*flowers*
solfatara	*geog*	soup|spoon	*house*	spendings	*trade*
solfeggio	*music*	south|east	*geog*	spend|time	*time*
solferino	*colour*	southerly	*geog*	sphendone	*clothes*
solicitor	*jobs*	south|land	*geog*	spider|man	*jobs*
solicitor	*law*	south|pole	*geog*	spikenard	*plants*
soliloquy	*theatre*	South|Uist	*islands*	spillworm	*insects*
solitaire	*birds*	Southwell	*Shakesp*	spin|a|yarn	*lit*
solitaire	*clothes*	south|west	*geog*	spin|drier	*house*
solitaire	*sport*	south|wind	*weather*	spin|drier	*machine*
sollerets	*herald*	sou|wester	*clothes*	spinnaker	*travel*
solo|organ	*music*	sou|wester	*weather*	spinneret	*insects*
solo|whist	*sport*	sovereign	*govt*	spin|parry	*sport*
solstices	*geog*	sovereign	*money*	spiritoso	*music*
sometimes	*time*	soya|beans	*veg*	spiritual	*music*
song|sheet	*music*	space|crew	*jobs*	spiritual	*relig*
songsmith	*jobs*	space|crew	*travel*	splay|feet	*medic*
songsmith	*lit*	spacedock	*travel*	split|shot	*sport*
sonic|boom	*travel*	spaceport	*travel*	spodumene	*mineral*
sonic|mine	*war*	spaceship	*physics*	spokesman	*jobs*
sonic|wall	*travel*	spaceship	*travel*	sponge|bag	*house*

spoon|bait	*sport*	star|anise	*trees*
spoonbill	*birds*	starboard	*sport*
sports|car	*travel*	starboard	*travel*
sports|day	*sport*	star|drill	*machine*
sportsman	*jobs*	star|gazer	*jobs*
sportsman	*sport*	star|grass	*plants*
spot|dance	*sport*	starlight	*astron*
spot|grain	*trade*	star|pupil	*educ*
spotlight	*machine*	star|pupil	*people*
spotlight	*theatre*	statehood	*geog*
spot|price	*trade*	statement	*govt*
springbok	*animals*	statement	*law*
spring|gun	*war*	statement	*lit*
spritsail	*travel*	statement	*trade*
spun|rayon	*clothes*	stateroom	*archit*
spun|sugar	*food*	stateroom	*travel*
spur|rowel	*herald*	statesman	*govt*
square|leg	*sport*	statesman	*jobs*
squash|bug	*insects*	stationer	*jobs*
squeamish	*medic*	statuette	*art*
squinting	*medic*	statuette	*house*
stability	*physics*	St|Bernard	*animals*
stability	*trade*	steal|away	*travel*
stable|boy	*sport*	steamboat	*travel*
staffroom	*educ*	steam|iron	*house*
stage|boat	*travel*	steam|iron	*tools*
stage|door	*theatre*	steam|line	*travel*
stagehand	*jobs*	steamship	*travel*
stagehand	*theatre*	steel|blue	*colour*
stage|idol	*jobs*	steel|grey	*colour*
stage|land	*theatre*	steel|mill	*machine*
stage|name	*theatre*	steel|wool	*house*
stage|play	*theatre*	steenkirk	*clothes*
staghound	*animals*	steersman	*jobs*
staginess	*theatre*	steersman	*sport*
staircase	*archit*	steersman	*travel*
staircase	*house*	stegosaur	*animals*
stairhead	*archit*	Steinbeck	*writers*
stalemate	*sport*	stenotype	*lit*
stamp|duty	*law*	step|aside	*travel*
stamp|duty	*trade*	step|dance	*sport*
stamp|mill	*machine*	Stephanie	*names*
stanchion	*archit*	sterilize	*medic*
stanchion	*travel*	stern|fast	*travel*
stand|fire	*war*	sternpost	*travel*
stevedore	*jobs*		
stevedore	*travel*		
Stevenson	*leaders*		
Stevenson	*writers*		
Sthenelus	*myth*		
stiff|dose	*medic*		
stiff|neck	*medic*		
stillborn	*medic*		
still|life	*art*		
still|room	*archit*		
still|room	*chem*		
still|wine	*drink*		
stilt|bird	*birds*		
stimulant	*medic*		
stink|bomb	*machine*		
stink|bomb	*war*		
stinkweed	*plants*		
stippling	*art*		
stitching	*clothes*		
stock|dove	*birds*		
Stockholm	*cities*		
stockhorn	*music*		
stockinet	*clothes*		
stock|list	*trade*		
stockpile	*trade*		
stock|rate	*trade*		
stokehold	*travel*		
stomacher	*clothes*		
stonechat	*birds*		
stonecrop	*plants*		
stonefish	*fish*		
stone|hawk	*birds*		
stone|pine	*trees*		
stone|wall	*archit*		
stoneware	*art*		
stonewort	*plants*		
stop|clock	*physics*		
stop|light	*machine*		
stopwatch	*sport*		
stopwatch	*time*		
storeship	*travel*		
storiette	*lit*		
storm|boat	*travel*		
storm|door	*archit*		
storm|door	*house*		

story|book	*lit*	sub|specie	*foreign*	surfacing	*travel*
story|line	*lit*	substance	*lit*	surfboard	*sport*
stovepipe	*house*	substance	*trade*	surfboard	*travel*
strapless	*clothes*	subsultus	*medic*	surmullet	*fish*
strategic	*war*	succentor	*music*	surprisal	*war*
Strategis	*myth*	succes|fou	*foreign*	surrender	*war*
stratojet	*travel*	succulent	*fruit*	surveying	*geog*
straw|poll	*govt*	sudorific	*medic*	surveying	*measure*
straw|vote	*govt*	Suetonius	*writers*	survey|map	*geog*
streaming	*educ*	suffering	*medic*	swaggerer	*people*
streamlet	*geog*	suffragan	*jobs*	swansdown	*clothes*
streamway	*geog*	suffragan	*relig*	sweatband	*clothes*
streetcar	*travel*	sugar|beet	*agric*	sweatband	*sport*
stretcher	*medic*	sugar|beet	*veg*	sweat|bath	*medic*
stretcher	*travel*	sugar|bowl	*house*	sweatshop	*trade*
strike|off	*lit*	sugar|cane	*plants*	sweetcorn	*cereal*
strike|out	*travel*	sugar|lump	*food*	sweet|corn	*food*
strike|pay	*jobs*	sugar|plum	*fruit*	sweet|flag	*plants*
strike|pay	*trade*	suit|at|law	*law*	sweetgale	*plants*
stringers	*travel*	suit|in|law	*law*	sweetmeat	*food*
strip|mill	*machine*	sulphacid	*chem*	sweet|shop	*trade*
Stromboli	*mounts*	summarize	*lit*	sweet|wine	*drink*
strongbox	*trade*	summation	*maths*	swellhead	*people*
strongman	*people*	summer|day	*geog*	swift|moth	*insects*
strontium	*chem*	summing|up	*law*	Swinburne	*writers*
strontium	*mineral*	sump|guard	*machine*	swineherd	*agric*
structure	*archit*	sumpsimus	*lit*	swineherd	*jobs*
studhorse	*animals*	sumptuary	*trade*	swing|band	*music*
stud|poker	*sport*	sun|bonnet	*clothes*	swing|curl	*clothes*
stuff|gown	*law*	sundowner	*people*	swing|door	*archit*
Stuttgart	*cities*	sunflower	*flowers*	swing|door	*house*
St|Vincent	*islands*	sun|helmet	*clothes*	Swiss|plan	*time*
stylobate	*archit*	sunk|fence	*archit*	Swiss|roll	*food*
subaltern	*jobs*	sun|lounge	*archit*	switch|off	*travel*
subaltern	*war*	sun|lounge	*house*	swivel|gun	*war*
subatomic	*physics*	sun|spurge	*plants*	sword|bean	*veg*
sub|chaser	*travel*	sunstroke	*medic*	swordfish	*fish*
subdivide	*biol*	super|bomb	*war*	swordplay	*sport*
subeditor	*jobs*	supernova	*astron*	swordplay	*war*
subeditor	*lit*	superstar	*theatre*	swordsman	*sport*
sub|judice	*law*	suppliant	*people*	sword|tail	*fish*
submarine	*travel*	supplicat	*educ*	sycophant	*people*
submarine	*war*	supporter	*govt*	syllabary	*lit*
subregion	*geog*	suppurant	*medic*	syllepsis	*lit*
subsidize	*trade*	surcharge	*trade*	Sylvester	*names*

symbiosis	biol	tangerine	colour	telephoto	travel
symbolism	art	tangerine	fruit	telescope	astron
symbolism	lit	tank|corps	war	telescope	physics
symbology	art	tant|mieux	foreign	telescope	tools
symphonic	music	taoiseach	govt	tellurite	chem
symposium	lit	tap|dancer	jobs	tellurium	chem
synagogue	archit	tap|dancer	theatre	tellurium	mineral
synagogue	relig	tarantula	animals	telophase	biol
syndicate	educ	target|day	war	temperate	geog
syndicate	trade	tarpaulin	clothes	tempo|mark	music
synedrion	govt	task|force	war	temporary	time
Synoptics	relig	taste|buds	medic	temporize	time
syntectic	medic	tasty|dish	food	tenebrist	art
synthesis	chem	tawny|port	drink	Tennessee	rivers
synthetic	chem	tax|evader	jobs	tennis|net	sport
synthetic	trade	taximeter	travel	tenor|clef	music
tablature	art	taxiplane	travel	tenor|drum	music
tablature	music	tax|return	trade	tenor|horn	music
table|lamp	house	teachable	educ	tenor|tuba	music
tableland	geog	tea|kettle	house	tenor|viol	music
tablemaid	jobs	tea|leaves	drink	tentmaker	jobs
tableware	house	tear|gland	medic	termagant	people
tabor|pipe	music	tear|grass	plants	terracing	sport
tabulator	machine	tea|waggon	house	territory	geog
tabulator	maths	tea|waggon	travel	terrorism	govt
tactician	people	technical	trade	terrorist	people
tailboard	travel	technique	art	tessitura	music
tail|light	machine	tectonics	geog	testament	law
tail|light	travel	teddy|bear	sport	testament	relig
tailoress	jobs	tegmentum	medic	testatrix	law
tailpiece	art	Teiresias	myth	testifier	law
tailpiece	music	telamones	archit	testimony	law
tailplane	travel	Telegonus	myth	test|match	sport
tail|rhyme	lit	telegraph	travel	test|pilot	jobs
tail|rotor	travel	telemeter	measure	test|pilot	travel
tail|shaft	travel	telemetry	measure	tetragram	maths
take|apart	theatre	telemotor	travel	tetrapody	lit
take|leave	travel	teleology	chem	tetrarchy	govt
take|notes	educ	telepathy	travel	tetraseme	lit
take|sides	war	telephone	house	tetroxide	chem
take|stock	trade	telephone	machine	Thackeray	writers
talbotype	art	telephone	travel	thanatoid	medic
talegalla	birds	telephony	physics	the|actual	trade
tall|story	lit	telephony	travel	The|Aeneid	titles
tambourin	music	telephoto	art	theatrics	theatre

the|big|top	*theatre*	thyrotomy	*medic*	title|role	*theatre*
the|boards	*theatre*	tidal|bore	*geog*	titration	*chem*
TheCritic	*titles*	tidal|flow	*geog*	toadstool	*plants*
TheEgoist	*titles*	tidal|flux	*geog*	toast|rack	*biol*
theFuries	*myth*	tidal|wave	*govt*	toast|rack	*house*
TheHobbit	*titles*	tidal|wave	*marine*	TodLowrie	*animals*
the|market	*trade*	tide|gauge	*geog*	toilet|bag	*clothes*
theme|song	*music*	tidewater	*geog*	toilet|bag	*house*
TheMikado	*titles*	tie|in|sale	*trade*	tolerance	*physics*
theocracy	*govt*	tierceron	*archit*	tollbooth	*archit*
theorbist	*music*	tiffen|bat	*animals*	tollbooth	*trade*
ThePrince	*titles*	tiger|lily	*flowers*	tollhouse	*archit*
therapist	*jobs*	tiger|milk	*drink*	tombstone	*relig*
therapist	*medic*	tiger|moth	*insects*	TomSawyer	*lit*
therewith	*time*	tiger|wolf	*animals*	TomSawyer	*titles*
TheRivals	*titles*	tight|rein	*sport*	tom|turkey	*birds*
Thermidor	*time*	till|death	*time*	tool|chest	*machine*
Thersites	*Shakesp*	timberman	*jobs*	toolsmith	*jobs*
thesaurus	*educ*	time|being	*time*	toothache	*medic*
thesaurus	*lit*	time|check	*time*	toothpick	*medic*
TheSolent	*seas*	time|clock	*physics*	toothwort	*plants*
the|sticks	*sport*	time|clock	*time*	top|burton	*machine*
the|street	*trade*	time|flies	*time*	top|drawer	*house*
TheWarden	*titles*	time|limit	*time*	top|secret	*govt*
thickness	*measure*	timenoguy	*travel*	top|twenty	*music*
thighbone	*medic*	time|of|day	*time*	torch|race	*sport*
think|tank	*govt*	timepiece	*house*	torch|song	*music*
thin|space	*lit*	timepiece	*time*	tornadoes	*geog*
third|form	*educ*	times|past	*time*	torpedoed	*war*
third|mate	*travel*	timetable	*educ*	torpedoer	*war*
third|year	*educ*	timetable	*time*	totem|pole	*myth*
Thirlmere	*lakes*	timetable	*travel*	to|this|day	*time*
thornback	*fish*	time|value	*music*	touch|down	*sport*
thorn|tree	*trees*	timocracy	*trade*	touch|down	*travel*
threefold	*measure*	timpanist	*music*	touch|goal	*sport*
three|jump	*sport*	tinder|box	*house*	touchline	*sport*
threesome	*sport*	tin|opener	*house*	tout|court	*foreign*
three|turn	*sport*	tin|opener	*tools*	towelling	*clothes*
threshing	*agric*	tip|and|run	*sport*	town|clerk	*jobs*
threshold	*archit*	tipsy|cake	*food*	towncrier	*jobs*
threshold	*biol*	Tisiphone	*myth*	town|house	*archit*
threshold	*house*	tit|for|tat	*war*	townscape	*art*
threshold	*physics*	title|deed	*law*	toy|poodle	*animals*
throw|a|pot	*art*	title|page	*lit*	trachinus	*fish*
thyristor	*machine*	title|role	*film/TV*	track|suit	*clothes*

track|suit	*sport*	triatomic	*physics*	turbopump	*travel*
trade|fair	*trade*	tribesman	*jobs*	turbulent	*weather*
trademark	*trade*	tributary	*geog*	Turkey|red	*colour*
trade|name	*trade*	tricolour	*herald*	turn|aside	*travel*
trade|sale	*trade*	tricuspid	*medic*	turnip|fly	*insects*
tradesman	*jobs*	triennial	*time*	turn|round	*travel*
tradesman	*trade*	triforium	*archit*	turnstile	*sport*
trade|wind	*weather*	triforium	*relig*	turnstone	*birds*
traffic|in	*trade*	trilobite	*animals*	turntable	*machine*
tragedian	*theatre*	trinomial	*maths*	turquoise	*colour*
trainband	*war*	triologue	*theatre*	turquoise	*jewels*
traipsing	*travel*	triptyque	*travel*	turquoise	*mineral*
tramlines	*travel*	triquetra	*art*	turret|top	*travel*
transient	*time*	triticism	*lit*	tutorhood	*educ*
transport	*travel*	Trojan|War	*myth*	tutorship	*educ*
transpose	*music*	troopship	*travel*	twenty|one	*sport*
trapezium	*maths*	troopship	*war*	twinkling	*time*
trapezium	*medic*	troubador	*jobs*	twin|screw	*travel*
trapezius	*medic*	trousseau	*clothes*	twist|dive	*sport*
trapezoid	*maths*	troutling	*fish*	two|seater	*travel*
trappings	*herald*	troy|ounce	*measure*	two|shakes	*time*
traveller	*jobs*	true|story	*lit*	tympanist	*jobs*
traveller	*travel*	trump|card	*sport*	tympanist	*music*
treadmill	*machine*	trumpeter	*birds*	tymp|stick	*music*
treadmill	*trade*	trumpeter	*jobs*	Tyndareus	*myth*
treasurer	*govt*	trumpeter	*music*	type|mould	*lit*
treasurer	*trade*	trump|suit	*sport*	type|mould	*machine*
treatment	*art*	truncheon	*law*	tyre|lever	*tools*
treatment	*lit*	truncheon	*war*	ufologist	*travel*
treatment	*medic*	trunk|call	*travel*	Ullswater	*lakes*
Trebonius	*Shakesp*	trunkfish	*fish*	ululation	*animals*
tree|house	*archit*	trunk|line	*travel*	umbilical	*medic*
tree|nymph	*myth*	trunk|road	*travel*	umbilicus	*medic*
tree|onion	*veg*	truss|beam	*archit*	umpteenth	*measure*
tree|shrew	*animals*	try|square	*measure*	under|arms	*war*
tree|snake	*insects*	tsetse|fly	*insects*	undercoat	*art*
trematode	*insects*	tube|dress	*clothes*	underfelt	*house*
tremblant	*jewels*	Tudor|arch	*archit*	under|fire	*war*
tremissis	*money*	tuitional	*educ*	underfoot	*geog*
tremulant	*music*	tulip|tree	*trees*	undergrad	*educ*
Trenchard	*war*	tumblebug	*insects*	undergrad	*jobs*
trench|gun	*war*	tummy|ache	*medic*	underling	*people*
Trevelyan	*writers*	tuning|bar	*music*	underpass	*travel*
trial|jury	*law*	turboprop	*travel*	under|sail	*travel*
triangles	*music*	turbopump	*machine*	undersell	*trade*

undersong	relig	varicella	medic	virginium	chem
undertone	music	varicosis	medic	virtuosic	music
undervest	clothes	vegetable	veg	viscosity	chem
underwear	clothes	vehicular	travel	viscounty	govt
underwood	trees	Velasquez	artists	Vishinsky	leaders
unfrocked	relig	velvet|ant	insects	visionary	people
unguentum	medic	velveteen	clothes	vitascope	art
unhealthy	medic	vendition	trade	vitelline	biol
union|card	trade	venectomy	medic	vocabular	lit
Union|Jack	herald	venerable	relig	vocalizer	music
Unitarian	relig	Ventidius	Shakesp	vogue|word	lit
unit|trust	trade	ventricle	medic	voice|over	film/TV
univalent	chem	Venusberg	titles	voice|part	music
unsalable	trade	verbalism	lit	vol|au|vent	food
unsettled	geog	verbarian	lit	volcanoes	geog
unskilled	trade	verbosity	lit	Volgograd	cities
unworldly	relig	verdigris	chem	Volkslied	music
upcountry	geog	vermifuge	medic	Voltimand	Shakesp
up|for|sale	trade	vermilion	colour	voltmeter	physics
upon|which	time	vernation	plants	Volumnius	Shakesp
upper|case	lit	Veronique	names	voluntary	music
upper|deck	travel	verse|form	lit	volunteer	jobs
uraninite	mineral	versifier	lit	volunteer	war
uranology	astron	vers|libre	lit	vorticism	art
urchin|cut	clothes	vertibrae	medic	vox|humana	music
UrsaMajor	astron	vestibule	archit	vulcanism	geog
UrsaMajor	myth	vestibule	medic	vulcanite	mineral
UrsaMinor	astron	vicennial	time	vulgarism	lit
UrsaMinor	myth	vicesimal	measure	vulnerary	medic
urticaria	medic	vice|squad	law	Vulpecula	astron
usherette	jobs	ViceVersa	titles	wage|claim	trade
usherette	theatre	victorine	clothes	wage|scale	trade
utilities	trade	video|tape	physics	waistband	clothes
utterance	trade	vigesimal	measure	waistcoat	clothes
uxoricide	law	vigilante	jobs	waistline	clothes
vaccinate	medic	vigilante	law	wake|robin	flowers
vade|mecum	lit	vigilante	war	Walcheren	islands
Valentine	Shakesp	Vincentio	Shakesp	waldgrave	govt
Valkyries	myth	vingt|et|un	sport	walkabout	govt
Valkyriur	myth	viola|alto	music	wallboard	archit
vallation	archit	violation	law	wall|clock	house
valuation	trade	violin|bow	music	wall|light	house
Vancouver	cities	violinist	jobs	wallpaper	house
VanuaLevi	islands	violinist	music	waltz|time	music
variation	music	virginals	music	wanted|man	law

war|bonnet	clothes	water|polo	sport	white|bass	fish
warehouse	archit	water|rail	birds	whitebeam	trees
warehouse	trade	watershed	geog	white|beat	animals
war|galley	travel	waterside	geog	whitefish	fish
warm|front	weather	water|tank	house	white|flag	war
warmonger	people	water|vine	plants	whitehead	birds
warmonger	war	water|vole	animals	white|line	travel
War|Office	war	waterweed	plants	white|meat	food
war|rocket	war	wattmeter	machine	white|pawn	sport
washbasin	house	wattmeter	physics	whiteware	art
washboard	house	wave|guide	physics	whitewash	archit
washed|out	medic	wax|figure	art	whitewash	art
wash|sales	trade	wax|flower	flowers	whitewash	house
washstand	house	wax|glands	medic	whitewash	trade
wasp's|nest	insects	wax|myrtle	trees	white|wine	drink
wassailer	jobs	wax|polish	house	whitewing	birds
waste|away	medic	waxworker	jobs	white|wood	flowers
wasteland	agric	weak|front	weather	whole|note	music
wasteland	geog	wealth|tax	trade	whole|rest	music
waste|time	time	web|footed	birds	wholesale	trade
Wastwater	lakes	wedge|heel	clothes	whole|step	music
watchword	war	Wednesday	time	whole|tone	music
water|bird	birds	weekender	jobs	wide|world	geog
waterbuck	animals	wellbeing	medic	widow|bird	fish
water|bull	animals	well|lined	trade	widow|wail	trees
water|butt	house	well|timed	time	wild|goose	birds
water|cock	birds	Welsh|pony	animals	wild|grape	fruit
water|cock	house	whaleback	travel	wild|honey	food
water|cock	machine	whaleboat	travel	wild|olive	fruit
water|cure	medic	whalebone	animals	wild|sheep	animals
water|deer	animals	whalebone	clothes	williwaws	weather
waterfall	geog	wheatbird	birds	wind|blown	geog
water|fern	plants	wheat|germ	food	wind|chest	music
water|flag	flowers	wheatmoth	insects	wind|gauge	weather
water|flea	fish	wheatworm	insects	windhover	birds
water|flow	geog	wheel|base	travel	windiness	weather
water|fowl	birds	wheelsman	jobs	wind|music	music
waterhole	geog	wheel|spin	travel	window|bay	archit
water|leaf	plants	wherefore	time	window|box	archit
water|lily	flowers	whereunto	time	window|box	flowers
water|line	travel	whereupon	time	window|box	house
watermill	machine	whirligig	sport	windscale	weather
water|mole	animals	whirlpool	geog	wind|speed	weather
water|opal	jewels	whirlwind	weather	windstorm	weather
water|pipe	house	whitebait	fish	windswept	weather

wind|trunk	*music*	work|force	*trade*	yesterday	*time*
wine|glass	*house*	workhouse	*trade*	Yggdrasil	*myth*
winemaker	*jobs*	work|of|art	*art*	yolk|stalk	*biol*
wing|chair	*house*	work|study	*trade*	Young|Cato	*Shakesp*
winged|cap	*myth*	workwoman	*jobs*	young|fogy	*people*
winnowing	*agric*	World|Bank	*trade*	youngling	*animals*
wire|gauge	*physics*	wormeaten	*insects*	youngster	*jobs*
wire|grass	*plants*	worm|grass	*plants*	youth|club	*sport*
wirephoto	*art*	wormwheel	*machine*	ytterbium	*chem*
wirephoto	*physics*	wrap|round	*clothes*	ytterbium	*mineral*
wirephoto	*travel*	wrestpins	*music*	Zacchaeus	*Bible*
Wisconsin	*rivers*	wristband	*clothes*	Zachariah	*Bible*
wisecrack	*theatre*	wristbone	*medic*	Zechariah	*Bible*
witch|hunt	*law*	wristlock	*sport*	Zenocrate	*lit*
witticism	*lit*	write|upon	*lit*	Zephaniah	*Bible*
Wodehouse	*writers*	wrongdoer	*people*	Zernebock	*myth*
wolfhound	*animals*	wrong|note	*music*	zeuglodon	*animals*
wolf's|bane	*flowers*	wrong|time	*time*	Zeus|Pater	*myth*
wolverine	*animals*	wulfenite	*mineral*	zincotype	*lit*
womanizer	*people*	Wuppertal	*cities*	zincotype	*machine*
womenfolk	*people*	Wycherley	*writers*	zinc|plate	*art*
wood|block	*art*	wych|hazel	*trees*	zirconium	*chem*
wood|borer	*insects*	xenophobe	*people*	zirconium	*mineral*
woodchuck	*animals*	xeroderma	*medic*	zitherist	*jobs*
woodcraft	*art*	X|ray|plate	*medic*	zitherist	*music*
woodlouse	*insects*	xylograph	*art*	zoobiotic	*biol*
wood|mouse	*animals*	xylophone	*music*	zoogamete	*biol*
wood|nymph	*myth*	yacht|club	*sport*	zoologist	*jobs*
woodprint	*art*	yacht|race	*sport*	zoophobia	*medic*
woodreeve	*jobs*	yachtsman	*jobs*	zooplasty	*medic*
wood|screw	*machine*	yachtsman	*sport*	Zoroaster	*relig*
woodshock	*animals*	yachtsman	*travel*	zucchetta	*relig*
woodwinds	*music*	yard|of|ale	*drink*	zucchetto	*clothes*
woomerang	*war*	yardstick	*machine*	zucchetto	*relig*
Worcester	*Shakesp*	yardstick	*measure*	Zugspitze	*mounts*
wordiness	*lit*	yellow|boy	*money*	Zuider|Zee	*seas*
worker|ant	*insects*	yellow|dog	*animals*	zumbooruk	*war*
worker|bee	*insects*	Yellow|Sea	*seas*	zwanziger	*money*

abdication	*govt*	active|army	*war*	afterbirth	*medic*
Abercromby	*war*	active|duty	*war*	aftergrass	*plants*
aberdevine	*birds*	active|list	*war*	afterpiece	*theatre*
abirritant	*medic*	active|verb	*lit*	after|shave	*clothes*
abiturient	*educ*	act|the|goat	*theatre*	afterwards	*time*
able|seaman	*jobs*	act|the|part	*theatre*	after|which	*time*
able|seaman	*travel*	ad|absurdum	*foreign*	aggression	*govt*
aboard|ship	*travel*	adamantine	*mineral*	aggression	*war*
abreaction	*medic*	Adam's|apple	*medic*	aggressive	*war*
abridgment	*lit*	adaptation	*lit*	agility|mat	*sport*
absente|reo	*foreign*	adaptation	*music*	agonistics	*sport*
absolution	*relig*	added|sixth	*music*	agrologist	*jobs*
absolutism	*govt*	adder|stone	*jewels*	agronomist	*agric*
abstergent	*house*	adder|stone	*mineral*	agronomist	*jobs*
academical	*educ*	Addis|Ababa	*cities*	a|head|start	*travel*
acceptance	*trade*	adjectival	*lit*	aid|and|abet	*law*
access|road	*travel*	adjustment	*trade*	aide|de|camp	*jobs*
accidental	*music*	adventurer	*people*	Ailsa|Craig	*islands*
accomplice	*jobs*	adventurer	*travel*	Air|Command	*war*
accomplice	*law*	adventurer	*war*	air|control	*travel*
accountant	*jobs*	adversaria	*lit*	air|cooling	*physics*
accountant	*trade*	advertiser	*jobs*	air|cruiser	*travel*
accounting	*trade*	advertiser	*trade*	air|current	*geog*
accumulate	*trade*	aerial|bomb	*war*	air|hostess	*jobs*
accusation	*law*	aerial|mine	*war*	air|hostess	*travel*
accusative	*lit*	aerobatics	*sport*	air|service	*travel*
acetabulum	*medic*	aerobatics	*travel*	air|service	*war*
Achitophel	*lit*	aero|engine	*machine*	air|steward	*jobs*
achromatin	*biol*	aerography	*geog*	air|steward	*travel*
acid|colour	*art*	aeronautic	*travel*	air|support	*travel*
acid|yellow	*colour*	aeronomist	*jobs*	Alanbrooke	*war*
acorn|shell	*fish*	aerophobia	*medic*	alarm|clock	*house*
acrobatics	*sport*	aerosphere	*geog*	alarm|clock	*machine*
acrophobia	*medic*	aesthetics	*art*	alarm|clock	*time*
acroterion	*archit*	affettuoso	*music*	albumblatt	*music*
act|curtain	*theatre*	affliction	*medic*	albuminoid	*biol*
activation	*war*	aficionado	*people*	Alcibiades	*Shakesp*

Alcibiades	*leaders*	
alexanders	*veg*	
Alexandria	*cities*	
Alexandros	*myth*	
algebraist	*maths*	
algophobia	*medic*	
alimentary	*medic*	
alkalinity	*chem*	
alla|Franca	*foreign*	
Allan|a|Dale	*lit*	
allargando	*music*	
allegation	*law*	
allegiance	*govt*	
allegretto	*music*	
All|for|Love	*titles*	
Allhallows	*time*	
alliterate	*lit*	
allocution	*relig*	
allotheist	*relig*	
all|the|rage	*clothes*	
all|the|time	*time*	
almacantar	*astron*	
almond|tree	*trees*	
almsgiving	*relig*	
alpha|helix	*chem*	
alphameric	*comput*	
altar|cloth	*relig*	
altar|front	*relig*	
altar|mound	*relig*	
altarpiece	*relig*	
alteration	*music*	
alternator	*machine*	
amanuensis	*jobs*	
amanuensis	*lit*	
amaranthus	*flowers*	
ambassador	*govt*	
ambassador	*jobs*	
amber|light	*travel*	
ambulation	*travel*	
ambulatory	*travel*	
ambushment	*war*	
amen|corner	*relig*	
amercement	*law*	
ammunition	*war*	
Amphiaraus	*myth*	

amphibrach	*lit*
amphimacer	*lit*
Amphitrite	*myth*
Amphitryon	*myth*
amphoteric	*physics*
amputation	*medic*
Amyas|Leigh	*lit*
amylaceous	*chem*
Anabaptist	*relig*
anaglyphic	*art*
anapaestic	*lit*
anastrophe	*lit*
anchor|deck	*travel*
Andaman|Sea	*seas*
Andromache	*Shakesp*
Andromache	*myth*
Andronicus	*Shakesp*
anecdotage	*lit*
anecdotist	*lit*
anemometer	*measure*
anemometer	*weather*
anesthesia	*medic*
Angel|Clare	*lit*
angle|block	*machine*
angle|board	*machine*
angle|brace	*machine*
angle|plate	*machine*
anglophile	*people*
anglophobe	*people*
Anglo|Saxon	*jobs*
Anglo|Saxon	*lit*
Angora|goat	*animals*
anguifauna	*insects*
angwantibo	*animals*
aniline|dye	*art*
animalcule	*animals*
Animal|Farm	*titles*
animal|life	*animals*
anisotropy	*biol*
ankle|joint	*medic*
ankle|socks	*clothes*
Anne|Boleyn	*Shakesp*
annexation	*govt*
anno|Domini	*time*
annotation	*lit*

annual|ring	*trees*
antagonism	*war*
antagonist	*people*
antecedent	*biol*
antecedent	*family*
antecedent	*lit*
anthophore	*flowers*
anthracite	*house*
antibiotic	*medic*
antibodies	*biol*
antichrist	*relig*
anticlimax	*lit*
antifreeze	*chem*
antifreeze	*travel*
antimatter	*chem*
Antipholus	*Shakesp*
antiphoner	*music*
antipoison	*medic*
antiproton	*physics*
antisepsis	*medic*
antiseptic	*medic*
antithesis	*lit*
antitoxins	*biol*
antitrades	*weather*
antitragus	*medic*
Antoinette	*names*
anvilsmith	*jobs*
apocalypse	*lit*
Apocalypse	*relig*
apoplectic	*medic*
apostrophe	*lit*
Apothecary	*Shakesp*
apothecary	*jobs*
apothecary	*medic*
apotheosis	*myth*
Appalachia	*titles*
apparition	*myth*
appearance	*theatre*
apple|cover	*food*
apple|cover	*house*
apple|green	*colour*
apple|sauce	*food*
applicator	*medic*
appreciate	*trade*
apprentice	*jobs*

apprentice	*trade*	
apron|stage	*theatre*	
aqua|fortis	*chem*	
aquamarine	*colour*	
aquamarine	*mineral*	
Arabian|Sea	*seas*	
arable|land	*geog*	
Arakam|Yoma	*mounts*	
arbitrator	*govt*	
arbitrator	*jobs*	
arbitrator	*law*	
archbishop	*jobs*	
archbishop	*relig*	
archdeacon	*jobs*	
archdeacon	*relig*	
arched|door	*archit*	
arched|roof	*archit*	
archer|fish	*fish*	
arch|flamen	*relig*	
architrave	*archit*	
archpriest	*jobs*	
archpriest	*relig*	
arc|welding	*machine*	
arena|stage	*theatre*	
arid|desert	*geog*	
Arion's|lyre	*myth*	
aristarchy	*govt*	
aristocrat	*govt*	
aristocrat	*jobs*	
aristocrat	*people*	
aristology	*food*	
arithmetic	*educ*	
arithmetic	*maths*	
Armageddon	*Bible*	
Armageddon	*myth*	
Armageddon	*war*	
Armaggedon	*relig*	
armed|force	*war*	
armed|guard	*war*	
armed|truce	*war*	
armigerous	*war*	
armipotent	*war*	
arms|length	*war*	
arrow|grass	*plants*	
Arrowsmith	*lit*	

art|gallery	*archit*	
art|gallery	*art*	
arthropoda	*animals*	
art|nouveau	*art*	
arty|crafty	*art*	
Aschenbach	*lit*	
aspidistra	*plants*	
assessment	*trade*	
assign|arms	*herald*	
assignment	*herald*	
assignment	*trade*	
astragalus	*medic*	
astringent	*clothes*	
astrologer	*jobs*	
astronomer	*jobs*	
asymmetric	*maths*	
at|a|bargain	*trade*	
at|all|times	*time*	
at|a|premium	*trade*	
at|half|mast	*herald*	
atmosphere	*geog*	
atmosphere	*lit*	
atmosphere	*physics*	
atmosphere	*weather*	
atomic|bomb	*war*	
atomic|mass	*physics*	
atomic|pile	*physics*	
atomic|pile	*war*	
atomic|unit	*physics*	
atom|rocket	*physics*	
atom|rocket	*war*	
attachment	*machine*	
at|that|time	*time*	
at|the|spear	*trade*	
at|this|time	*time*	
attunement	*music*	
auctioneer	*jobs*	
auctioneer	*trade*	
auction|off	*trade*	
audiometer	*measure*	
audit|clerk	*jobs*	
auditorium	*archit*	
auditorium	*theatre*	
au|pair|girl	*jobs*	
au|pis|aller	*foreign*	

authorship	*lit*	
automation	*machine*	
automation	*trade*	
automatism	*art*	
automobile	*machine*	
automobile	*travel*	
autonomous	*govt*	
autostrada	*foreign*	
avant|garde	*art*	
aventurine	*mineral*	
average|out	*trade*	
aviculture	*birds*	
Axiocersus	*myth*	
Ayckbourne	*writers*	
babe|in|arms	*family*	
babe|in|arms	*jobs*	
babiroussa	*animals*	
baby|sitter	*jobs*	
backgammon	*sport*	
background	*art*	
background	*lit*	
background	*music*	
back|marker	*sport*	
back|number	*lit*	
back|stroke	*sport*	
bad|grammar	*lit*	
baked|beans	*food*	
baking|bowl	*house*	
baking|tray	*house*	
Balbriggan	*clothes*	
ballad|horn	*music*	
Ballantyne	*writers*	
ballet|girl	*jobs*	
ballet|shoe	*clothes*	
ballistics	*war*	
ballistite	*chem*	
ballooning	*travel*	
balloonist	*travel*	
ball|player	*jobs*	
ball|turret	*travel*	
balneation	*sport*	
balustrade	*archit*	
balustrade	*house*	
banana|skin	*fruit*	
banderilla	*sport*	

band‖leader	music	battle‖hymn	relig	Benedictus	music
bandmaster	jobs	battle‖hymn	war	benefactor	jobs
bandmaster	music	battle‖line	war	benefactor	people
Band‖of‖Hope	relig	battlement	archit	benefactor	relig
band‖waggon	music	battlement	war	ben‖trovato	foreign
bandwaggon	theatre	battleship	travel	Berlin‖blue	colour
bank‖credit	trade	battleship	war	Berlin‖ware	art
bank‖robber	jobs	Baudelaire	writers	Berlin‖wool	clothes
bank‖robber	law	Bay‖of‖Fundy	seas	Bermuda‖rig	travel
bankruptcy	trade	beard‖grass	plants	Bernadette	names
baptistery	relig	bear‖down‖on	travel	beryl‖green	colour
Barbary‖ape	animals	bearer‖bond	trade	best‖friend	people
barbed‖wire	war	bear‖garden	animals	best‖seller	lit
barcarolle	music	bear‖leader	jobs	best‖seller	trade
Bard‖of‖Avon	lit	bear‖market	trade	better‖days	time
barge‖board	archit	beaten‖work	art	betting‖man	sport
barium‖meal	medic	Beatitudes	relig	bewitchery	myth
barkentine	travel	Beaujolais	drink	bezoar‖goat	animals
barley‖corn	cereal	beautician	jobs	Bible‖class	relig
bar‖mitzvah	relig	beauty‖spot	clothes	bibliofilm	art
Barnardine	Shakesp	beche‖de‖mer	fish	bibliology	educ
barrel‖roll	travel	Beckmesser	lit	bibliology	lit
Bartimaeus	Bible	Becky‖Sharp	lit	bibliomane	educ
barysphere	geog	bedchamber	archit	bibliomane	lit
baseballer	jobs	bedclothes	house	bibliopegy	lit
base‖course	archit	Bedlington	animals	bibliopole	lit
basketball	sport	bedsprings	house	bibliosoph	educ
basset‖horn	music	bee‖keeping	sport	bibliosoph	lit
basset‖oboe	music	beforehand	time	bibliothec	lit
bassoonist	jobs	before‖long	time	bidonville	archit
bassoonist	music	beforetime	time	Big‖Brother	govt
Bass‖Strait	seas	behindhand	time	Big‖Brother	people
bathing‖cap	clothes	behind‖time	time	bill‖broker	jobs
Bath‖oliver	food	Belisarius	war	bill‖broker	trade
bathometer	geog	belladonna	flowers	billet‖doux	lit
bathometer	measure	belladonna	medic	bill‖of‖fare	food
Baton‖Rouge	cities	bellarmine	house	bill‖of‖sale	govt
batophobia	medic	bellflower	flowers	bill‖of‖sale	trade
batten‖down	travel	bell‖ringer	jobs	billposter	jobs
battery‖hen	agric	bell‖ringer	music	binary‖form	music
battery‖hen	birds	bell‖the‖cat	animals	binoculars	sport
battery‖jar	physics	bellwether	animals	biochemics	biol
battledore	lit	Belshazzar	Bible	biochemics	chem
battledore	sport	bench‖drill	machine	biochemist	biol
battle‖flag	war	benedicite	relig	biochemist	chem

biochemist	*jobs*	
biogenesis	*biol*	
biographer	*jobs*	
biographer	*lit*	
biometrics	*biol*	
biophysics	*biol*	
biophysics	*physics*	
biorhythms	*biol*	
biquadrate	*maths*	
bird cherry	*fruit*	
bird of prey	*birds*	
bird spider	*insects*	
Birmingham	*cities*	
birthright	*govt*	
birthright	*relig*	
Birtwistle	*music*	
bisulphate	*chem*	
bisulphide	*chem*	
bitterling	*fish*	
bitterroot	*plants*	
blackberry	*fruit*	
blackboard	*educ*	
blackbully	*trees*	
Black Death	*medic*	
black dress	*clothes*	
black frost	*weather*	
blackguard	*people*	
blackheart	*fruit*	
black magic	*myth*	
Black Maria	*law*	
Black Maria	*travel*	
black pearl	*jewels*	
Black Power	*law*	
black sheep	*animals*	
black sheep	*people*	
Black Shirt	*govt*	
blacksmith	*jobs*	
black snake	*insects*	
blackthorn	*trees*	
black widow	*insects*	
bladder nut	*trees*	
bladesmith	*jobs*	
blancmange	*food*	
blank verse	*lit*	
blastoderm	*biol*	

blastomere	*biol*	
Bleak House	*titles*	
bleep bleep	*physics*	
blind alley	*archit*	
blind alley	*travel*	
blind faith	*relig*	
blind poker	*sport*	
blister fly	*insects*	
blitzkrieg	*war*	
blockhouse	*war*	
blockmaker	*jobs*	
block print	*art*	
blood count	*medic*	
blood donor	*medic*	
blood group	*medic*	
blood horse	*animals*	
bloodhound	*animals*	
blood money	*trade*	
blood royal	*govt*	
blood sport	*sport*	
bloodstain	*medic*	
bloodstone	*jewels*	
bloodstone	*mineral*	
Bloody Flux	*medic*	
Bloody Mary	*drink*	
Bloomsbury	*lit*	
bludgeoner	*jobs*	
bluebottle	*flowers*	
bluebottle	*insects*	
bluebottle	*jobs*	
bluebreast	*birds*	
blue cheese	*food*	
blue ensign	*herald*	
bluejacket	*jobs*	
Blue Mantle	*herald*	
blue murder	*govt*	
blue pigeon	*birds*	
bluethroat	*birds*	
boatwright	*jobs*	
bobbed hair	*clothes*	
bobbin lace	*clothes*	
bobbysocks	*clothes*	
bobbysoxer	*people*	
Boccherini	*music*	
body of land	*geog*	

bogtrotter	*jobs*	
Bohr theory	*physics*	
boiled fish	*food*	
boiled meat	*food*	
boiler suit	*clothes*	
bold stroke	*war*	
boll weevil	*insects*	
bombardier	*jobs*	
bombardier	*war*	
Bombay duck	*fish*	
Bombay duck	*food*	
bon appetit	*food*	
bondholder	*trade*	
bonesetter	*jobs*	
bonesetter	*medic*	
boneshaker	*travel*	
bonus clerk	*jobs*	
bonus stock	*trade*	
booby prize	*sport*	
bookbinder	*jobs*	
bookbinder	*lit*	
book dealer	*jobs*	
book dealer	*lit*	
bookfolder	*jobs*	
bookholder	*jobs*	
bookholder	*lit*	
book jacket	*lit*	
bookkeeper	*jobs*	
bookkeeper	*trade*	
book loving	*lit*	
bookmaking	*lit*	
bookmonger	*lit*	
book review	*lit*	
bookseller	*jobs*	
bookseller	*lit*	
bookwright	*jobs*	
bookwright	*lit*	
bootlegger	*jobs*	
bootlicker	*people*	
boot polish	*house*	
borderland	*geog*	
borderline	*geog*	
Boreal zone	*geog*	
Botticelli	*artists*	
bottle fish	*fish*	

bottle|nose	*animals*	brickmaker	*jobs*	bulb|grower	*jobs*
bottle|tree	*trees*	bridal|hymn	*music*	bulk|buying	*trade*
bottom|land	*geog*	bridegroom	*family*	bullet|tree	*trees*
bottom|note	*music*	bridesmaid	*family*	bull|fiddle	*music*
boudoir|cap	*clothes*	bridge|deck	*travel*	bull|roarer	*animals*
bovver|boot	*clothes*	bridgehead	*war*	bumbailiff	*jobs*
bowie|knife	*tools*	bridle|path	*travel*	bunch|grass	*plants*
bowie|knife	*war*	Brie|cheese	*food*	buon|giorno	*foreign*
box|barrage	*war*	brigandine	*herald*	bureaucrat	*govt*
boxing|ring	*sport*	brigandine	*war*	bureaucrat	*jobs*
box|spanner	*tools*	brigantine	*travel*	burlesquer	*jobs*
bradyseism	*geog*	brinometer	*measure*	Burmese|cat	*animals*
brainchild	*educ*	broad|arrow	*herald*	burnet|moth	*insects*
brainchild	*lit*	broad|beans	*veg*	burnet|rose	*flowers*
brain|drain	*jobs*	broadcloth	*clothes*	burnt|umber	*colour*
brain|fever	*medic*	broadsheet	*lit*	burrow|duck	*birds*
brain|storm	*educ*	broadsword	*war*	bush|jacket	*clothes*
brakemaker	*jobs*	broken|bone	*medic*	bushmaster	*insects*
Brakenbury	*Shakesp*	broken|dose	*medic*	bush|shrike	*birds*
branch|line	*travel*	broken|nose	*medic*	bus|service	*travel*
brandy|snap	*food*	brome|grass	*cereal*	bus|station	*travel*
brass|smith	*jobs*	bronchitis	*medic*	butter|bean	*veg*
brass|winds	*music*	brook|trout	*fish*	butter|bird	*birds*
Bratislava	*cities*	broom|maker	*jobs*	butter|dish	*house*
brazilwood	*trees*	broomstick	*myth*	butterfish	*fish*
bread|board	*house*	brown|algae	*plants*	buttermilk	*drink*
breadcrumb	*food*	brown|ochre	*colour*	butter|tree	*trees*
breadfruit	*fruit*	brownstone	*mineral*	butterwort	*plants*
breadknife	*house*	brown|sugar	*food*	button|bush	*trees*
breadmaker	*jobs*	brown|trout	*fish*	buttonhole	*clothes*
bread|sauce	*food*	Brunnhilde	*lit*	buttonhole	*flowers*
bread|stick	*food*	brushmaker	*jobs*	button|hook	*clothes*
break|of|day	*time*	bubble|bath	*clothes*	buttonwood	*trees*
breakwater	*archit*	bubble|hood	*travel*	buy|and|sell	*trade*
breakwater	*geog*	buccinator	*medic*	buy|futures	*trade*
breakwater	*travel*	Bucephalus	*animals*	by|election	*govt*
breastbone	*medic*	bucket|seat	*house*	bygone|days	*time*
breastwork	*war*	bucket|seat	*lit*	by|the|clock	*time*
breathless	*medic*	bucket|seat	*travel*	cabbage|fly	*insects*
breath|test	*law*	bucket|shop	*trade*	cabin|plane	*travel*
brent|goose	*birds*	Buckingham	*Shakesp*	cacogenics	*biol*
Brer|Rabbit	*lit*	budgerigar	*birds*	cacography	*lit*
bressummer	*archit*	buffalo|bug	*insects*	caddice|fly	*insects*
brevet|rank	*govt*	buffoonery	*theatre*	caddis|worm	*insects*
bricklayer	*jobs*	bugle|corps	*war*	Cader|Idris	*mounts*

Caesarship	govt
Cairngorms	mounts
calamander	trees
calcareous	chem
calciferol	chem
calculator	machine
calculator	maths
calculator	trade
Caledonian	geog
calf's|brain	food
Callirrhoe	myth
call|to|arms	war
calorifier	physics
camel|corps	war
camelopard	animals
camel's|hair	clothes
camel|train	animals
cameo|glass	art
camera|team	jobs
camino|real	foreign
camouflage	travel
camouflage	war
campaigner	govt
campaigner	jobs
campaigner	war
campestral	geog
Canada|rice	plants
cancellate	maths
cancionero	music
cancrizans	music
candelabra	house
candlefish	fish
candy|floss	food
canephorus	archit
Canis|major	astron
Canis|major	myth
Canis|minor	astron
canker|rash	medic
canker|worm	insects
cannelloni	food
Cannery|Row	titles
cannon|ball	war
cannon|bone	animals
cannon|shot	war
canonicals	relig

cantaloupe	fruit
Canterbury	cities
cantilever	archit
cantilever	travel
canto|fermo	music
cantonment	war
canvas|back	birds
canvassing	govt
canzonetta	music
cap|and|gown	clothes
cap|and|gown	educ
cap|and|gown	herald
Cape|doctor	weather
Cape|pigeon	birds
caper|sauce	food
capitalism	trade
capitalist	govt
capitalist	trade
capitalize	trade
capitulary	govt
cappuccino	drink
carabineer	war
Caractacus	war
carat|grain	measure
Caravaggio	artists
carbonated	physics
carbon|atom	physics
carcinogen	biol
career|girl	people
cargo|plane	travel
caricature	art
carmagnole	art
carpet|moth	insects
carpophore	flowers
carry|on|war	war
Carthusian	relig
cartoonist	art
cartoonist	jobs
Casabianca	titles
Casabianca	cities
cashiering	govt
Caspian|Sea	lakes
Caspian|Sea	seas
Cassiopeia	astron
Cassiopeia	myth

cassolette	house
cast|anchor	travel
cast|a|spell	myth
castration	medic
casual|ward	govt
catabolism	biol
catafalque	relig
catalectic	lit
catalepsis	medic
cat|breeder	jobs
cat|burglar	jobs
catch|a|crab	sport
catch|a|crab	travel
catch|a|ride	travel
catechumen	educ
catechumen	jobs
catechumen	relig
catenation	physics
cathode|ray	physics
catholicon	medic
cat's|cradle	sport
cattle|cake	agric
cattlegrid	animals
cauliculus	archit
cavalryman	jobs
cavalryman	war
Celebes|Sea	seas
cellar|door	archit
cellophane	chem
cell|tissue	biol
cement|kiln	art
censorship	govt
centennial	time
centesimal	maths
Centigrade	measure
Centigrade	physics
centilitre	measure
centimetre	measure
centistere	measure
centralism	govt
centre|half	sport
centrifuge	machine
centrifuge	physics
centrosome	biol
Cephalonia	islands

cephalopod	*animals*	cheapening	*trade*	chrematist	*govt*
ceramicist	*art*	cheap|skate	*trade*	chrematist	*trade*
ceramicist	*jobs*	checkpoint	*sport*	Christabel	*names*
cerebellum	*medic*	check|valve	*machine*	Christiana	*names*
cerography	*art*	cheep|cheep	*birds*	christiana	*sport*
certiorari	*law*	Che|Guevara	*leaders*	chromatics	*art*
chafing|pan	*house*	cheque|book	*trade*	chromatism	*art*
chain|banks	*trade*	chersonese	*geog*	chrome|alum	*chem*
chain|block	*machine*	chessboard	*sport*	chromogram	*art*
chain|drive	*machine*	chessylite	*mineral*	chromosome	*biol*
chainmaker	*jobs*	Chesterton	*writers*	chromosome	*medic*
chain|store	*trade*	chest|voice	*music*	chromotype	*art*
chairmaker	*jobs*	chevesaile	*clothes*	chromotypy	*lit*
chalcedony	*jewels*	chevrotain	*animals*	chronicler	*jobs*
chalcedony	*mineral*	chickenpox	*medic*	chronicler	*lit*
chalk|downs	*geog*	chiff|chaff	*birds*	chronogram	*time*
chalkstone	*mineral*	chiffonier	*house*	chronology	*time*
challenger	*sport*	childermas	*time*	Chrysippus	*myth*
Chamaeleon	*astron*	Chimborazo	*mounts*	chrysolite	*jewels*
Chambertin	*drink*	chime|bells	*music*	chrysolite	*mineral*
chancellor	*govt*	chimney|pot	*archit*	chrysology	*trade*
chancellor	*jobs*	chimpanzee	*animals*	Church|Army	*relig*
chancellor	*law*	China|aster	*flowers*	church|bell	*relig*
chancellor	*trade*	China|grass	*plants*	churchgoer	*people*
chandelier	*house*	china|stone	*art*	churchgoer	*relig*
changeling	*jobs*	chinchilla	*animals*	churchyard	*relig*
changeling	*myth*	chinchilla	*clothes*	cibophobia	*medic*
changeover	*sport*	Chinese|box	*sport*	cider|maker	*jobs*
chaparajos	*clothes*	Chinese|red	*colour*	cigar|maker	*jobs*
chapel|cart	*travel*	chinquapin	*trees*	Cincinnati	*cities*
chapel|text	*lit*	chiselling	*art*	Cinderella	*people*
chargeable	*trade*	chitarrone	*music*	Cinderella	*titles*
chargehand	*jobs*	chittagong	*birds*	cine|camera	*art*
chargehand	*trade*	Chittagong	*cities*	cine|camera	*machine*
charity|boy	*jobs*	chloroform	*chem*	cine|camera	*physics*
charleston	*sport*	chloroform	*medic*	cinquefoil	*archit*
Chartreuse	*drink*	choir|organ	*music*	cinquefoil	*flowers*
chartulary	*relig*	choirstall	*relig*	cinquefoil	*herald*
chatelaine	*clothes*	chokeberry	*fruit*	cinquepace	*music*
chatterbox	*people*	choppiness	*marine*	circuiteer	*law*
Chatterton	*writers*	chopsticks	*house*	circumflex	*lit*
chauffeuse	*jobs*	chorus|girl	*jobs*	cismontane	*geog*
chautauqua	*educ*	chorus|girl	*music*	Cistercian	*relig*
Chauvinism	*govt*	chorus|girl	*theatre*	citric|acid	*chem*
chauvinist	*people*	chorus|show	*theatre*	city|father	*govt*

civil|death	*govt*	
claim|agent	*jobs*	
clam|shrimp	*insects*	
clapper|boy	*jobs*	
Clarenceux	*herald*	
classicism	*art*	
classicism	*educ*	
classicism	*lit*	
classicist	*educ*	
classified	*govt*	
Clausewitz	*war*	
clavichord	*music*	
claw|hammer	*clothes*	
claw|hammer	*tools*	
clay|pigeon	*sport*	
clear|house	*travel*	
clear|skies	*weather*	
clearstory	*archit*	
clearstory	*relig*	
Clemenceau	*leaders*	
Clementine	*names*	
clerestory	*archit*	
clerestory	*relig*	
clew|garnet	*travel*	
clinkstone	*mineral*	
clinometer	*measure*	
cloakmaker	*jobs*	
clockmaker	*jobs*	
clocksmith	*jobs*	
clock|tower	*archit*	
clog|dancer	*jobs*	
clog|dancer	*theatre*	
cloistered	*relig*	
cloisterer	*jobs*	
cloistress	*jobs*	
closed|shop	*trade*	
close|of|day	*time*	
closing|bid	*trade*	
clothes|peg	*house*	
clothes|pin	*house*	
clothmaker	*jobs*	
cloud|atlas	*weather*	
cloudburst	*weather*	
cloudiness	*weather*	
cloudscape	*art*	
cloven|foot	*myth*	
clown|white	*theatre*	
clubmaster	*jobs*	
Clydesdale	*animals*	
coach|horse	*animals*	
coach|horse	*travel*	
coachmaker	*jobs*	
coal|bucket	*house*	
coal|bunker	*house*	
coal|cellar	*house*	
coalescent	*chem*	
coal|shovel	*tools*	
coastal|fog	*weather*	
coastguard	*jobs*	
coastguard	*war*	
Coast|Range	*mounts*	
coat|armour	*herald*	
coat|hanger	*clothes*	
coat|hanger	*house*	
coat|of|arms	*herald*	
coat|of|mail	*clothes*	
coat|of|mail	*war*	
cobalt|blue	*colour*	
cobalt|bomb	*machine*	
cobalt|bomb	*physics*	
cockatrice	*herald*	
cockatrice	*insects*	
Cockatrice	*myth*	
cockchafer	*insects*	
cockleboat	*travel*	
coconut|shy	*sport*	
code|of|laws	*law*	
codirector	*jobs*	
codlin|moth	*insects*	
coelacanth	*fish*	
coffee|bean	*drink*	
coffee|mill	*house*	
coffee|mill	*machine*	
coffee|shop	*archit*	
Coimbatore	*cities*	
colatitude	*geog*	
cold|chisel	*tools*	
coleoptera	*insects*	
collarbone	*medic*	
collarette	*clothes*	
collar|stud	*clothes*	
collar|work	*jobs*	
collateral	*trade*	
Collatinus	*lit*	
collection	*lit*	
collection	*relig*	
college|boy	*educ*	
college|cap	*clothes*	
collegiate	*educ*	
collimator	*astron*	
collimator	*physics*	
colloquial	*lit*	
coloration	*art*	
coloratura	*jobs*	
coloratura	*music*	
Colossians	*Bible*	
Colossians	*relig*	
colour|film	*art*	
colourless	*art*	
colportage	*lit*	
colporteur	*jobs*	
colporteur	*lit*	
colporteur	*trade*	
column|gear	*travel*	
combat|area	*war*	
combat|team	*war*	
combustion	*physics*	
comedienne	*jobs*	
comedienne	*theatre*	
comic|opera	*music*	
comic|opera	*theatre*	
comic|strip	*art*	
comic|strip	*lit*	
commandant	*govt*	
commandant	*jobs*	
commandant	*war*	
command|car	*travel*	
commentary	*lit*	
commercial	*film/TV*	
commercial	*trade*	
commissary	*govt*	
commission	*govt*	
commission	*jobs*	
commission	*trade*	
commissure	*medic*	

common|cold	*medic*	consequent	*biol*	cool|breeze	*weather*
common|noun	*lit*	consequent	*geog*	co‚ordinate	*maths*
common|room	*archit*	consequent	*time*	coparcener	*law*
common|room	*educ*	consonance	*music*	Copenhagen	*cities*
common|salt	*mineral*	con|sordini	*music*	copperhead	*insects*
common|time	*music*	consortium	*trade*	copper|mine	*mineral*
common|time	*time*	conspectus	*lit*	copperworm	*insects*
common|weal	*govt*	conspiracy	*law*	copulative	*lit*
communique	*govt*	con|spirito	*foreign*	copyholder	*lit*
commutator	*machine*	constantly	*time*	copying|ink	*lit*
compass|saw	*tools*	constraint	*law*	copyreader	*jobs*
compendium	*lit*	consultant	*jobs*	copyreader	*lit*
compensate	*trade*	consultant	*medic*	copywriter	*jobs*
competitor	*jobs*	contagious	*medic*	coral|berry	*trees*
competitor	*sport*	contestant	*jobs*	coral|snake	*insects*
complement	*maths*	contestant	*sport*	cor|anglais	*music*
compluvium	*archit*	contingent	*war*	cordillera	*geog*
compositae	*flowers*	continuity	*lit*	cordon|bleu	*foreign*
compositor	*jobs*	continuity	*theatre*	Corinthian	*archit*
compositor	*lit*	continuous	*time*	Coriolanus	*Shakesp*
compressor	*machine*	contortion	*geog*	Coriolanus	*myth*
compressor	*physics*	contour|map	*geog*	Coriolanus	*titles*
compulsion	*medic*	contraband	*law*	corking|pin	*machine*
Conan|Doyle	*writers*	contraband	*trade*	corn|beetle	*insects*
concentric	*maths*	contrabass	*music*	corncockle	*flowers*
concertina	*music*	contractor	*jobs*	corn|doctor	*jobs*
concertino	*music*	contractor	*sport*	corn|doctor	*medic*
concertist	*jobs*	contraflow	*travel*	corned|beef	*food*
concertist	*music*	contravene	*law*	corned|meat	*food*
concordant	*music*	controller	*jobs*	cornettist	*jobs*
concussion	*medic*	controller	*machine*	cornettist	*music*
conducting	*music*	controller	*physics*	cornflakes	*food*
conference	*fruit*	control|rod	*travel*	cornflower	*flowers*
conference	*trade*	convalesce	*medic*	cornucopia	*myth*
confession	*law*	convection	*physics*	Cornwallis	*war*
confession	*relig*	conversion	*archit*	coronation	*govt*
confidante	*people*	conversion	*govt*	corrective	*medic*
confiscate	*law*	conversion	*relig*	corregidor	*law*
confiserie	*foreign*	conveyance	*law*	corrugated	*physics*
confluence	*geog*	conveyance	*travel*	corruption	*govt*
congestion	*travel*	conviction	*law*	corruption	*lit*
congo|snake	*insects*	convulsion	*medic*	coryphaeus	*educ*
coniferous	*trees*	cooking|fat	*food*	coryphaeus	*jobs*
connection	*travel*	cooking|oil	*food*	Coryphaeus	*music*
consecrate	*relig*	Cook|Strait	*seas*	coryphaeus	*theatre*

cos|lettuce	veg	
cosmic|dust	geog	
cosmic|time	time	
cosmodrome	travel	
cossack|hat	clothes	
cost|centre	trade	
costumiere	theatre	
cotton|mill	machine	
cottontail	animals	
cotton|tree	veg	
cotton|wood	veg	
cotton|wool	clothes	
cotton|wool	medic	
couch|grass	plants	
cough|syrup	medic	
councillor	govt	
councillor	jobs	
councilman	govt	
counsellor	govt	
counsellor	jobs	
counted|out	sport	
country|boy	jobs	
country|bus	travel	
countryman	jobs	
coupon|bond	trade	
court|dress	clothes	
courthouse	law	
court|of|law	law	
court|order	law	
court|shoes	clothes	
court|usher	law	
couturiere	jobs	
cover|agent	jobs	
covered|way	archit	
covered|way	travel	
cover|point	sport	
covert|coat	clothes	
cow|bunting	birds	
cow|catcher	travel	
cow|chervil	plants	
cow|parsley	plants	
cow|parsnip	plants	
cowrie|pine	trees	
crab|plover	birds	
crackbrain	jobs	

cradle|book	lit	
cradlesong	music	
crane's|bill	flowers	
crankshaft	machine	
crankshaft	travel	
credit|card	trade	
credit|slip	trade	
crepuscule	time	
crested|jay	birds	
Cretan|Bull	myth	
cricket|bat	sport	
cricket|net	sport	
crime|sheet	law	
crime|squad	law	
crio|sphinx	animals	
crosshatch	art	
crossroads	travel	
cross|staff	maths	
cross|staff	war	
crosswalls	archit	
crouch|ware	art	
crowd|scene	film/TV	
crowd|scene	theatre	
Crown|Derby	art	
crown|graft	trees	
crown|green	sport	
crown|wheel	machine	
cruciferae	veg	
crustacean	fish	
cryogenics	physics	
cryptogram	lit	
crystal|set	machine	
cuckoo|pint	flowers	
cuirassier	war	
cultivator	agric	
cultivator	jobs	
cultivator	tools	
culture|jar	biol	
cummerbund	clothes	
curate's|egg	lit	
curb|broker	trade	
curb|market	trade	
curiescopy	physics	
curling|pin	clothes	
curricular	educ	

curriculum	educ	
curtain|rod	house	
custard|pie	food	
customs|man	jobs	
cut|flowers	flowers	
cuttle|fish	fish	
cyanic|acid	chem	
cyclo|cross	sport	
cyclometer	measure	
cyclopedia	lit	
cyclothyme	medic	
cynophobia	medic	
cystectomy	medic	
cystoscope	medic	
cytologist	jobs	
dachshound	animals	
daily|bread	food	
daily|bread	trade	
daily|dozen	sport	
daisy|chain	flowers	
damask|rose	flowers	
dame|school	educ	
damp|course	archit	
dance|music	music	
dandy|fever	medic	
dandy|horse	travel	
danger|list	medic	
Danish|blue	food	
danke|schon	foreign	
dapple|grey	animals	
Das|Kapital	titles	
dawn|rocket	travel	
daydreamer	people	
days|gone|by	time	
days|of|yore	time	
day|tripper	jobs	
day|tripper	travel	
dead|colour	art	
dead|finish	trees	
dead|letter	lit	
dead|market	trade	
dead|matter	lit	
dead|nettle	plants	
death|chair	law	
deathwatch	insects	

deathwatch	*medic*	densimeter	*measure*	dilettante	*educ*
decahedron	*maths*	Dent du Midi	*mounts*	dilettante	*jobs*
decampment	*travel*	denticular	*archit*	dill pickle	*food*
decathlete	*sport*	dentifrice	*clothes*	diminuendo	*music*
decinormal	*chem*	dentifrice	*medic*	diminution	*music*
deck quoits	*sport*	denudation	*geog*	dim sighted	*medic*
deck tennis	*sport*	Deo gratias	*foreign*	dining hall	*archit*
declare war	*war*	Deo volente	*foreign*	dining hall	*house*
declension	*lit*	department	*govt*	dining room	*archit*
decompound	*chem*	department	*trade*	dining room	*house*
decoration	*art*	depilatory	*biol*	dinner gong	*house*
decree nisi	*law*	deposition	*geog*	dinner gown	*clothes*
decrescent	*herald*	deposition	*law*	dinner roll	*food*
dedication	*lit*	depository	*trade*	diphtheria	*medic*
dedication	*relig*	depreciate	*trade*	dipsomania	*medic*
deepfreeze	*biol*	depression	*geog*	direct blue	*colour*
deepfreeze	*house*	depression	*trade*	direct cost	*trade*
deepfreeze	*physics*	depth gauge	*machine*	direct fire	*war*
deep in debt	*trade*	depth gauge	*measure*	dirty money	*trade*
deep litter	*birds*	derivation	*lit*	dirty nurse	*jobs*
defalcator	*trade*	dermatitis	*medic*	dirty nurse	*medic*
defendable	*war*	dermoptera	*animals*	disability	*medic*
defensible	*war*	dernier cri	*foreign*	discipline	*educ*
definition	*lit*	deshabille	*clothes*	disc jockey	*jobs*
defrayment	*trade*	desiccator	*physics*	disc jockey	*music*
degaussing	*physics*	detachment	*war*	disc jockey	*theatre*
Delagoa Bay	*seas*	devil's food	*food*	discobolus	*sport*
del credere	*trade*	Dewar flask	*physics*	discomfort	*medic*
delineator	*art*	dexter half	*herald*	discounter	*jobs*
delinquent	*law*	dexter side	*herald*	discourser	*lit*
delinquent	*people*	diaconicon	*archit*	discoverer	*jobs*
delphinium	*flowers*	diaconicon	*relig*	disemplane	*travel*
delta wings	*travel*	Diana's tree	*trees*	disfigured	*medic*
demand bill	*trade*	diaskeuast	*lit*	dishabille	*clothes*
demobilize	*war*	dichromate	*chem*	disherison	*law*
Demogorgon	*myth*	dickeybird	*birds*	dishwasher	*house*
demography	*geog*	dickey seat	*travel*	dishwasher	*jobs*
demoiselle	*birds*	dictaphone	*machine*	dishwasher	*machine*
demoiselle	*fish*	dictionary	*educ*	dispatcher	*jobs*
demoiselle	*jobs*	dictionary	*lit*	dispatches	*govt*
demonology	*myth*	didunculus	*birds*	dispensary	*medic*
denaturant	*chem*	Die Walkure	*titles*	dissection	*biol*
dendrology	*trees*	difference	*herald*	dissertate	*lit*
denotation	*lit*	difference	*maths*	dissonance	*music*
denouement	*theatre*	digger wasp	*insects*	distortion	*physics*

disulphate *chem*	double|star *astron*	Dr|Pangloss *lit*
disulphide *chem*	double|talk *govt*	drug|addict *medic*
dive|bomber *travel*	double|time *music*	drug|addict *people*
dividend|on *trade*	Douglas|fir *trees*	drug|pusher *jobs*
divination *relig*	dovetailed *herald*	druid|stone *geog*
diving|bell *machine*	downstairs *archit*	drummer|boy *jobs*
diving|bell *sport*	downstairs *house*	drummer|boy *music*
diving|bell *travel*	downstream *travel*	drummer|boy *war*
dizzy|spell *medic*	dragonnade *war*	drum|sander *machine*
doctrinism *relig*	dragon|tree *trees*	dry|battery *machine*
Dodecanese *islands*	dragoonade *war*	dry|cleaner *jobs*
dog|biscuit *food*	drainpipes *clothes*	drying|wind *weather*
dog|breeder *jobs*	drakestone *mineral*	dual|school *educ*
dog|parsley *plants*	drama|group *theatre*	Duke|of|York *Shakesp*
dog's|chance *animals*	drama|logue *theatre*	dulcetness *music*
dog's|fennel *plants*	dramatizer *jobs*	dumb|animal *animals*
dollar|bill *trade*	dramatizer *theatre*	dumb|friend *animals*
doll's|house *archit*	dramaturge *jobs*	dumb|waiter *house*
doll's|house *sport*	dramaturge *theatre*	dummy|share *trade*
dolly|catch *sport*	dramaturgy *theatre*	dung|beetle *insects*
Don|Alfonso *lit*	draughting *art*	duodecimal *maths*
Don|Basilio *lit*	draw|breath *medic*	duplicator *machine*
donkey|pump *machine*	drawbridge *archit*	Durmast|oak *trees*
donkey|work *jobs*	drawbridge *war*	dusk|rocket *travel*
Don|Quixote *people*	drawing|pin *art*	Dusseldorf *cities*
Don|Quixote *titles*	drawing|pin *house*	duster|coat *clothes*
doodlesack *music*	draw|stumps *sport*	dust|jacket *lit*
doorhandle *house*	dreikanter *geog*	Dutch|clock *house*
doorkeeper *jobs*	dressing|up *clothes*	Dutch|treat *trade*
doraphobia *medic*	dressmaker *clothes*	Dutch|tulip *flowers*
Dorian|Gray *lit*	dressmaker *jobs*	Dutch|uncle *people*
Doric|order *archit*	dress|shirt *clothes*	duty|roster *jobs*
dotted|line *govt*	dried|fruit *fruit*	duumvirate *govt*
dotted|note *music*	drift|along *travel*	dyer's|broom *plants*
Douay|Bible *relig*	drift|angle *travel*	dysprosium *chem*
double|axle *sport*	Drinkwater *writers*	dysprosium *mineral*
double|bass *music*	driven|snow *weather*	eagle|crest *herald*
double|bend *travel*	drop|anchor *travel*	eaglestone *mineral*
double|chin *clothes*	drop|cannon *sport*	early|riser *jobs*
double|flat *music*	drop|hammer *tools*	earthlight *geog*
double|game *sport*	dropped|egg *food*	earthmover *machine*
double|loin *food*	drop|serene *medic*	earthquake *geog*
double|peel *sport*	drop|volley *sport*	earthshine *geog*
double|prop *travel*	drosometer *geog*	earthworks *archit*
double|reef *travel*	drosophila *insects*	ear|trumpet *medic*

Eastertide	*time*	
Easter|time	*time*	
East|Indies	*islands*	
easy|market	*trade*	
ebb|and|flow	*marine*	
economiser	*machine*	
economizer	*trade*	
ectodermal	*medic*	
Edam|cheese	*food*	
edging|tool	*tools*	
educatress	*educ*	
Edwin|Drood	*lit*	
efficiency	*trude*	
egg|albumen	*biol*	
Eisenhower	*USpres*	
Eisenhower	*war*	
Eisteddfod	*music*	
elasticity	*physics*	
elbow|joint	*medic*	
elderberry	*fruit*	
elecampane	*plants*	
electorate	*govt*	
electronic	*physics*	
Electryone	*myth*	
elementary	*chem*	
eleven|plus	*educ*	
elongation	*maths*	
elongation	*physics*	
emaciation	*medic*	
embankment	*geog*	
embankment	*war*	
ember|goose	*birds*	
emblazonry	*art*	
embonpoint	*medic*	
embossment	*art*	
embroidery	*clothes*	
embroidery	*lit*	
embryology	*biol*	
embryology	*medic*	
emery|board	*clothes*	
emery|board	*machine*	
emery|wheel	*machine*	
emigration	*travel*	
empire|line	*clothes*	
empiricist	*jobs*	
emplastrum	*medic*	
employment	*jobs*	
employment	*trade*	
emulsifier	*chem*	
enamel|kiln	*art*	
enamelling	*art*	
enamellist	*art*	
enamelware	*art*	
encampment	*war*	
enclampsia	*medic*	
encumbered	*trade*	
encyclical	*govt*	
encyclical	*relig*	
end|product	*trade*	
energetics	*physics*	
engagement	*theatre*	
engarrison	*war*	
enharmonic	*music*	
entailment	*law*	
enterprise	*trade*	
enthusiast	*people*	
entodermal	*medic*	
entombment	*relig*	
entomology	*biol*	
enzymology	*biol*	
epanaphora	*lit*	
ephemerist	*biol*	
ephemerist	*geog*	
epic|poetry	*lit*	
Epimetheus	*myth*	
episcopacy	*relig*	
episcopant	*relig*	
epispastic	*medic*	
epithelium	*medic*	
epithermal	*physics*	
eprouvette	*war*	
Epsom|salts	*medic*	
equatorial	*geog*	
equestrian	*animals*	
equestrian	*jobs*	
equitation	*sport*	
equivalent	*chem*	
Erechtheus	*myth*	
ergophobia	*medic*	
erotomania	*medic*	
eructation	*medic*	
escalation	*war*	
escapement	*machine*	
escarpment	*geog*	
escritoire	*educ*	
escritoire	*house*	
escutcheon	*herald*	
Eskimo|roll	*sport*	
estate|duty	*trade*	
estate|tail	*law*	
estimation	*chem*	
estimation	*maths*	
estimation	*physics*	
etiolation	*biol*	
Eton|collar	*clothes*	
Eton|jacket	*clothes*	
eucalyptus	*trees*	
eudiometer	*chem*	
Eugene|Aram	*lit*	
euphonious	*music*	
Euphronius	*Shakesp*	
Euphrosyne	*myth*	
Euroclydon	*myth*	
Euroclydon	*weather*	
Eurodollar	*trade*	
Eurystheus	*myth*	
euthanasia	*medic*	
evacuation	*travel*	
evaluation	*trade*	
evanescent	*time*	
Evangeline	*titles*	
evangelist	*jobs*	
Evangelist	*relig*	
evaporator	*physics*	
evening|bag	*clothes*	
eventually	*time*	
evil|genius	*myth*	
evil|spirit	*myth*	
Evil|Spirit	*relig*	
exaltation	*relig*	
excavation	*archit*	
excavation	*geog*	
excitation	*physics*	
ex|dividend	*trade*	
exhibition	*art*	

exhibition	*theatre*	fancy|stock	*trade*	figurative	*lit*
exobiology	*biol*	Fanny|Robin	*lit*	figurehead	*art*
exorbitant	*trade*	fantoccini	*sport*	figurehead	*govt*
expedition	*travel*	fantoccini	*theatre*	figurehead	*herald*
expedition	*war*	fan|tracery	*archit*	filibuster	*govt*
experience	*jobs*	farmer's|boy	*jobs*	filing|room	*lit*
experiment	*chem*	farsighted	*medic*	film|editor	*jobs*
experiment	*physics*	fascinator	*clothes*	filter|pump	*machine*
explosives	*machine*	fast|bowler	*sport*	filter|pump	*physics*
exposition	*educ*	fast|yellow	*colour*	filter|tube	*physics*
exposition	*lit*	fatherland	*geog*	filthy|rich	*trade*
exposition	*music*	Father's|day	*time*	find|guilty	*law*
exposition	*trade*	Father|Time	*time*	fine|fettle	*medic*
expository	*theatre*	fatted|calf	*animals*	finger|bowl	*house*
expression	*lit*	fatted|calf	*food*	fingernail	*medic*
expression	*music*	fearnought	*clothes*	finite|verb	*lit*
expressway	*travel*	featherbed	*house*	Fiordiligi	*lit*
extraction	*medic*	feather|boa	*clothes*	fire|basket	*house*
extramural	*educ*	feathering	*sport*	fire|beetle	*insects*
eye|glasses	*clothes*	federation	*govt*	fire|engine	*machine*
eye|witness	*jobs*	feebleness	*medic*	fire|engine	*travel*
eye|witness	*law*	feed|system	*travel*	fire|escape	*archit*
fabricator	*jobs*	fellmonger	*jobs*	fire|escape	*house*
face|powder	*clothes*	fellowship	*educ*	firemaster	*jobs*
Fahrenheit	*measure*	fellowship	*relig*	fire|raiser	*jobs*
Fahrenheit	*physics*	Fernando|Po	*islands*	firescreen	*house*
faint|heart	*war*	fertilizer	*agric*	fire|trench	*war*
fairground	*sport*	feuilleton	*lit*	firing|area	*war*
fairy|queen	*myth*	fever|pitch	*medic*	first|blood	*sport*
fairy|story	*lit*	fianchetto	*sport*	first|class	*travel*
faith|curer	*jobs*	Fianna|Fail	*govt*	first|floor	*archit*
faith|curer	*medic*	fibrinogen	*chem*	first|house	*theatre*
Falangists	*govt*	fibrositis	*medic*	first|night	*theatre*
fall|behind	*travel*	fictionist	*jobs*	first|offer	*trade*
fallow|chat	*birds*	fictionist	*lit*	first|story	*archit*
fallow|deer	*animals*	fiddlewood	*trees*	fiscal|year	*govt*
false|money	*trade*	field|event	*sport*	fiscal|year	*time*
false|piety	*relig*	field|mouse	*animals*	fiscal|year	*trade*
false|teeth	*clothes*	fieldpiece	*war*	fishing|net	*sport*
false|teeth	*medic*	field|poppy	*flowers*	fishing|rod	*sport*
family|seat	*archit*	field|sport	*sport*	fish|kettle	*house*
family|tree	*herald*	fieldstone	*geog*	fish|ladder	*fish*
fancy|dress	*clothes*	field|train	*war*	fishmonger	*jobs*
fancy|goods	*trade*	fiery|cross	*war*	fitted|coat	*clothes*
fancy|price	*trade*	figuration	*art*	Fitzgerald	*writers*

five finger	music	flying mare	sport	four in hand	travel
five senses	medic	flying shot	sport	fourmaster	travel
fixed price	trade	flying tank	war	four poster	house
fixed trust	trade	flying wing	travel	fourth form	educ
flag bearer	jobs	folding bed	house	fox hunting	sport
flagellata	animals	folk singer	jobs	fox terrier	animals
flake white	colour	folk singer	music	fractional	maths
flak jacket	clothes	fonticulus	medic	frame maker	jobs
flank steak	food	food supply	food	Franciscan	relig
flare light	machine	footballer	jobs	frangipane	food
flashlight	art	footballer	sport	frangipani	flowers
flashlight	machine	footbridge	archit	fraternity	educ
flat market	trade	footbridge	travel	fratricide	law
flat racing	sport	foot doctor	jobs	fraud squad	law
flatulence	medic	foot doctor	medic	freebooter	jobs
flea beetle	insects	FootGuards	war	freebooter	law
fleetingly	time	footlights	theatre	free for all	sport
fleur de lis	flowers	foot rifles	war	free gratis	trade
fleur de lis	herald	forced move	sport	free market	trade
fleur de lys	herald	forced sale	trade	freemartin	animals
flight crew	jobs	forcing bag	house	free pardon	law
flight deck	travel	fore and aft	travel	free period	educ
flight path	travel	forecaster	jobs	free sample	trade
flight plan	travel	forecastle	travel	free school	educ
flight time	travel	forefather	family	free trader	trade
floatplane	travel	foreground	art	freightage	trade
floatstone	geog	forerunner	jobs	French bean	veg
floodlight	machine	forerunner	travel	French blue	colour
floor cloth	house	foresheets	travel	French cake	food
floor price	trade	fore shocks	geog	French grey	colour
floral leaf	flowers	forfeiture	govt	French harp	music
Flora Poste	lit	forge ahead	travel	French horn	music
floribunda	flowers	fork supper	food	French plum	fruit
flower girl	jobs	formic acid	biol	French roof	archit
flower head	flowers	formic acid	chem	frequently	time
flower show	flowers	form master	educ	fresh cream	food
Flugelhorn	music	fortepiano	music	freshwater	geog
fluorotype	chem	Fortinbras	Shakesp	fricandeau	food
fly by night	people	fortissimo	music	fritillary	flowers
fly by night	travel	forty niner	jobs	fritillary	insects
flycatcher	insects	fossilized	geog	frog hopper	insects
fly fishing	sport	foundation	clothes	frontal low	weather
flying boat	travel	foundation	geog	front bench	govt
flying bomb	war	foundation	sport	frozen food	food
flying fish	birds	fourchette	clothes	fruit juice	drink

fruit|knife	*house*	Gatling|gun	*war*	glossarist	*lit*
fruit|salad	*fruit*	gear|change	*travel*	glossology	*lit*
fuddy|duddy	*people*	geisha|girl	*jobs*	glottology	*lit*
full|colour	*art*	gelder|rose	*flowers*	Gloucester	*Shakesp*
full|nelson	*sport*	generation	*biol*	goal|circle	*sport*
full|pardon	*govt*	generation	*time*	goal|crease	*sport*
full|stocks	*trade*	geneticist	*jobs*	goalkeeper	*jobs*
functional	*art*	Geneva|gun	*clothes*	goalkeeper	*sport*
funded|debt	*trade*	gentlefolk	*people*	goal|tender	*sport*
fund|raiser	*jobs*	gentle|wind	*weather*	goat|sallow	*tools*
funeral|ode	*lit*	geocentric	*astron*	goat's|beard	*plants*
funeral|ode	*relig*	geochemist	*jobs*	goat's|thorn	*trees*
funeral|urn	*relig*	geographer	*geog*	goatsucker	*birds*
fustanella	*clothes*	geographer	*jobs*	godfearing	*relig*
futuristic	*art*	geophysics	*geog*	go|in|the|van	*travel*
futuristic	*time*	geophysics	*physics*	goldbeater	*jobs*
gadolinium	*chem*	geriatrics	*medic*	gold|digger	*jobs*
gadolinium	*mineral*	German|iris	*flowers*	gold|digger	*people*
gain|ground	*travel*	Gesundheit	*foreign*	golden|calf	*relig*
galleyworm	*insects*	Gethsemane	*Bible*	golden|disc	*music*
gallic|acid	*chem*	get|the|bird	*birds*	golden|mole	*animals*
gallstones	*medic*	get|the|bird	*theatre*	golden|seal	*plants*
Gallup|poll	*govt*	ghost|dance	*myth*	goldilocks	*flowers*
Galsworthy	*writers*	ghost|story	*lit*	gold|nugget	*trade*
gambit|pawn	*sport*	ghost|train	*sport*	goldworker	*jobs*
gamekeeper	*jobs*	giant|panda	*animals*	golf|course	*sport*
game|warden	*jobs*	gimmal|ring	*herald*	goniometer	*measure*
gamophobia	*medic*	ginger|beer	*drink*	goniometry	*measure*
garage|hand	*jobs*	ginger|snap	*food*	Good|Friday	*time*
garden|city	*flowers*	girl|Friday	*people*	goods|train	*travel*
garden|fork	*tools*	girl|friend	*people*	goody|goody	*people*
garden|hose	*tools*	give|credit	*trade*	goody|goody	*relig*
garden|peas	*veg*	glaciation	*weather*	go|on|strike	*trade*
garden|shed	*house*	glass|cloth	*house*	gooseberry	*fruit*
garden|wall	*archit*	glass|coach	*travel*	goosegrass	*plants*
Gargantuan	*myth*	glasshouse	*archit*	Gorgonzola	*food*
garlic|salt	*food*	glasshouse	*law*	go|shopping	*trade*
gas|chamber	*govt*	glasshouse	*plants*	Gothenburg	*cities*
gasteropod	*insects*	glassmaker	*jobs*	government	*govt*
gastronome	*people*	glass|snake	*insects*	government	*trade*
gastrotomy	*medic*	glauconite	*mineral*	grace|notes	*music*
gas|turbine	*machine*	glazed|ware	*art*	graduation	*educ*
gatekeeper	*jobs*	glebe|house	*archit*	grama|grass	*plants*
gatewright	*jobs*	globulites	*mineral*	grammarian	*jobs*
gather|head	*travel*	glossarist	*jobs*	grammarian	*lit*

gramophone	*house*	green|light	*travel*	habitation	*archit*
gramophone	*music*	green|ochre	*colour*	habit,cloth	*clothes*
granadilla	*fruit*	Green|Paper	*govt*	hackmatack	*trees*
grandchild	*family*	green|pound	*trade*	hackney|cab	*travel*
grand|juror	*law*	greenshank	*birds*	hack|writer	*lit*
Grand|Mufti	*govt*	green,snake	*insects*	hagiolatry	*myth*
grand,niece	*family*	greenstone	*mineral*	hagiolatry	*relig*
grand|opera	*music*	greensward	*plants*	hagioscope	*relig*
grand|piano	*house*	Grenadines	*islands*	hailstones	*weather*
grand|piano	*music*	grey|parrot	*birds*	hair|ribbon	*clothes*
grand|prior	*jobs*	grind|organ	*music*	hairstreak	*insects*
grandstand	*sport*	grindstone	*jobs*	halberdier	*war*
grand,stone	*art*	grindstone	*machine*	half|a|jiffy	*time*
grand,uncle	*family*	grindstone	*trade*	half|an|hour	*time*
grapefruit	*fruit*	gripe|water	*medic*	half|a|shake	*time*
grape|juice	*drink*	groceryman	*jobs*	half|bisque	*sport*
graphic|art	*art*	ground|bass	*music*	half|bottle	*drink*
graptolite	*mineral*	ground|crew	*travel*	half|circle	*maths*
grass|green	*colour*	ground|fire	*war*	half|kirtle	*clothes*
grass|roots	*govt*	ground|game	*animals*	half|nelson	*sport*
grass|skirt	*clothes*	ground|loop	*travel*	half|relief	*art*
grass|snake	*insects*	ground|mass	*geog*	half,sister	*family*
grass|widow	*family*	ground|mine	*war*	half|stocks	*trade*
grasswrack	*plants*	ground|plan	*archit*	half|volley	*sport*
gravestone	*relig*	ground|rice	*cereal*	halieutics	*sport*
gravimeter	*measure*	groundsill	*archit*	Hallelujah	*relig*
gravimeter	*physics*	groundwork	*archit*	hall|porter	*jobs*
greasewood	*trees*	ground,zero	*war*	halter|neck	*clothes*
Great|Lakes	*lakes*	growth|ring	*biol*	halved|hole	*sport*
great|organ	*music*	guardhouse	*law*	ham|and|eggs	*food*
great|stave	*music*	gubernator	*jobs*	hamesucken	*law*
great,uncle	*family*	gudgeon|pin	*machine*	hammer|beam	*archit*
Grecian|urn	*art*	guillotine	*law*	hammer,fish	*fish*
Greek|Fates	*myth*	guillotine	*machine*	hammerhead	*animals*
Greek|Ionic	*archit*	guinea|cock	*birds*	handicraft	*art*
Greek|modes	*music*	guinea,fowl	*birds*	handicraft	*trade*
green|algae	*plants*	guinea|worm	*insects*	hand|lotion	*clothes*
green|beans	*veg*	Gulf|of|Aden	*seas*	handmaiden	*jobs*
green|drake	*insects*	Gulf|of|Oman	*seas*	handmarket	*trade*
greenfinch	*birds*	Gulf|of|Riga	*seas*	handshaker	*govt*
green|flash	*astron*	Gulf|of|Siam	*seas*	handshaker	*jobs*
green|goose	*birds*	gunrunning	*law*	handspring	*sport*
greenheart	*trees*	gunslinger	*jobs*	hanging|fly	*insects*
greenhouse	*archit*	gymnastics	*sport*	Happy|Isles	*myth*
greenhouse	*plants*	gypsophila	*flowers*	hard|labour	*law*

hard|lesson	*educ*	heavy|purse	*trade*	hessian|fly	*insects*
hardly|ever	*time*	heavy|swell	*marine*	heterocera	*animals*
hard|tackle	*sport*	heavy|water	*chem*	heteronomy	*govt*
hard|winter	*geog*	hebdomadal	*time*	hexahedral	*maths*
harman|beck	*govt*	Hebrew|year	*time*	hexahedron	*maths*
harmonicon	*music*	hectograph	*machine*	hexangular	*maths*
harmonizer	*music*	hedgesmith	*jobs*	hickory|nut	*food*
harpy|eagle	*birds*	heel|and|toe	*sport*	hickory|nut	*fruit*
Harrow|game	*sport*	helianthus	*flowers*	hierolatry	*relig*
hartebeest	*animals*	helicopter	*travel*	hieromancy	*relig*
harvest|bug	*insects*	Heligoland	*islands*	hierophant	*relig*
harvesting	*agric*	heliograph	*art*	high|church	*relig*
hatchet|man	*govt*	heliolater	*myth*	high|colour	*art*
hatchet|man	*jobs*	heliolatry	*myth*	high|comedy	*theatre*
haunch|bone	*medic*	heliometer	*measure*	high|diving	*sport*
have|in|hand	*trade*	heliotrope	*colour*	high|ground	*geog*
hawsepiece	*travel*	heliotrope	*flowers*	high|jacker	*jobs*
hazard|side	*sport*	heliotrope	*mineral*	highlander	*jobs*
headhunter	*jobs*	hellbender	*fish*	high|octane	*chem*
headhunter	*sport*	Hellespont	*myth*	high|places	*relig*
headlights	*travel*	hemaglobin	*medic*	high|priced	*trade*
headmaster	*educ*	hematology	*medic*	high|priest	*jobs*
headmaster	*jobs*	hemiplegia	*medic*	high|priest	*relig*
head|office	*trade*	hemisphere	*geog*	high|relief	*art*
head|porter	*jobs*	hemisphere	*maths*	high|school	*educ*
headsquare	*clothes*	hemisphere	*medic*	High|street	*travel*
headstream	*geog*	hemophilia	*medic*	highwayman	*jobs*
head|waiter	*jobs*	hemophobia	*medic*	highwayman	*law*
headwaters	*geog*	hemp|nettle	*plants*	hinterland	*geog*
healing|art	*medic*	henceforth	*time*	hipped|roof	*archit*
health|club	*sport*	henchwoman	*jobs*	Hippocrene	*myth*
health|farm	*medic*	hen|harrier	*birds*	hippodrome	*theatre*
health|farm	*sport*	Hephaestus	*myth*	hippogriff	*animals*
hearing|aid	*machine*	heptagonal	*maths*	hippogriff	*myth*
hearing|aid	*medic*	Heptameron	*lit*	hippogryph	*animals*
heart's|ease	*flowers*	heptameter	*lit*	hippogryph	*myth*
hearty|meal	*food*	heptastich	*lit*	Hippolytus	*myth*
heat|engine	*machine*	Heptateuch	*relig*	hippomanes	*myth*
heathen|god	*myth*	herald|duck	*birds*	Hippomenes	*myth*
heat|shield	*physics*	herbaceous	*flowers*	Hispaniola	*islands*
heat|shield	*travel*	herb|garden	*plants*	historical	*lit*
heatstroke	*medic*	here|and|now	*time*	historical	*time*
heave|round	*travel*	heretofore	*time*	histrionic	*theatre*
heave|short	*travel*	hermit|crab	*fish*	hitch|hiker	*jobs*
heavy|armed	*war*	Hesperides	*myth*	hitch|hiker	*sport*

hitch|hiker	*travel*	horn|footed	*animals*	hyetometer	*weather*
Hitopadesa	*myth*	horn|player	*jobs*	hygrometer	*measure*
hit|the|deck	*travel*	hornplayer	*music*	hygrometer	*weather*
hobbyhorse	*sport*	horologist	*jobs*	hyperbaton	*lit*
hockey|team	*sport*	Horologium	*astron*	hyperdulia	*relig*
hocus|pocus	*myth*	horror|film	*film/TV*	hypocentre	*geog*
hog|hunting	*sport*	horseflesh	*animals*	hypodermic	*medic*
hold|a|brief	*law*	horse|leech	*insects*	hypodermis	*medic*
hold|office	*govt*	horse|opera	*film/TV*	hypotenuse	*maths*
hold|office	*trade*	horse|opera	*music*	hypothesis	*chem*
hole|cutter	*tools*	horse|power	*physics*	hypothesis	*physics*
Holland|gin	*drink*	horse|sense	*animals*	hypsometer	*measure*
hollow|ware	*house*	horseshoes	*sport*	hypsometer	*physics*
holly|berry	*fruit*	horsewoman	*sport*	icebreaker	*travel*
Holofernes	*Shakesp*	Hortensius	*Shakesp*	ice|crystal	*geog*
holohedral	*maths*	hot|and|cold	*food*	ice|dancing	*sport*
Holy|Family	*relig*	hot|springs	*geog*	iced|coffee	*drink*
Holy|Father	*relig*	hot|springs	*medic*	Iceland|dog	*animals*
Holy|Island	*islands*	hot|weather	*weather*	ice|skating	*sport*
holy|orders	*jobs*	hour|circle	*geog*	icing|sugar	*food*
Holy|Orders	*relig*	house|agent	*jobs*	iconoclast	*relig*
Holy|Spirit	*relig*	house|finch	*birds*	Idaean|vine	*fruit*
Holy|Willie	*lit*	House|of|God	*relig*	idiopathic	*medic*
Holy|Willie	*relig*	house|organ	*lit*	idolatrous	*myth*
home|and|dry	*travel*	hovercraft	*machine*	idolatrous	*relig*
homecoming	*travel*	hovercraft	*travel*	idolomancy	*myth*
home|movies	*film/TV*	Howards|End	*titles*	illegality	*law*
Home|Office	*govt*	hugmetight	*clothes*	illiterate	*educ*
homeopathy	*medic*	humanities	*educ*	illuminate	*art*
homochromy	*biol*	human|wreck	*people*	illuminate	*educ*
homocyclic	*chem*	humidifier	*machine*	illuminati	*educ*
homophonic	*music*	humoresque	*music*	illustrate	*art*
homosphere	*geog*	hunting|bow	*sport*	Il|Seraglio	*titles*
honey|crisp	*food*	hunting|dog	*animals*	immemorial	*time*
honey|eater	*birds*	hurdygurdy	*music*	immiscible	*chem*
honeyguide	*birds*	husbandman	*agric*	immolation	*relig*
honey|mouse	*animals*	husbandman	*jobs*	immunology	*medic*
honorarium	*jobs*	Hyacinthus	*myth*	impalement	*war*
honorarium	*trade*	hybrid|word	*lit*	impediment	*law*
hooded|crow	*birds*	hydraulics	*physics*	imperative	*lit*
hoodie|crow	*birds*	hydrolysis	*chem*	import|duty	*trade*
hook|and|eye	*clothes*	hydrolytic	*chem*	imposition	*educ*
hop|sacking	*clothes*	hydroplane	*machine*	imposition	*govt*
hornblende	*mineral*	hydroplane	*travel*	imposition	*lit*
horned|toad	*animals*	hyetograph	*weather*	imposition	*trade*

impresario	*jobs*	inflatable	*travel*	in|training	*sport*
impresario	*theatre*	inflection	*lit*	intramural	*educ*
impression	*art*	in|good|time	*time*	inundation	*geog*
impression	*lit*	ingredient	*food*	invalidate	*medic*
impression	*theatre*	inhabitant	*jobs*	invalid|car	*travel*
in|articles	*law*	inhibition	*medic*	invalidism	*medic*
in|business	*trade*	inhumation	*relig*	invalidity	*medic*
incendiary	*jobs*	in|jeopardy	*govt*	invariably	*time*
incendiary	*machine*	injunction	*law*	investment	*trade*
incendiary	*war*	injury|time	*sport*	investment	*war*
in|chancery	*law*	ink|slinger	*lit*	invocation	*govt*
incidental	*music*	in|memoriam	*relig*	invocation	*myth*
incidental	*time*	In|Memoriam	*titles*	involution	*biol*
income|bond	*trade*	Inner|House	*govt*	ion|counter	*chem*
increscent	*herald*	inquisitor	*educ*	Ionic|order	*archit*
incubation	*biol*	inquisitor	*jobs*	ionization	*chem*
incumbency	*jobs*	inside|home	*sport*	ionosphere	*astron*
incumbency	*relig*	inside|lane	*sport*	ionosphere	*physics*
incumbered	*trade*	inside|left	*sport*	I|Pagliacci	*titles*
incunabula	*lit*	inside|lock	*sport*	Irish|green	*colour*
incur|a|debt	*trade*	insolation	*medic*	ironmaster	*jobs*
Indian|club	*sport*	insolation	*weather*	ironmonger	*jobs*
Indian|corn	*cereal*	insolvency	*trade*	ironworker	*jobs*
Indian|file	*sport*	inspirator	*medic*	irrational	*maths*
Indian|hemp	*medic*	instalment	*trade*	irreligion	*relig*
Indian|hemp	*plants*	instructed	*educ*	irrigation	*agric*
Indian|kite	*birds*	instructor	*educ*	irrigation	*geog*
Indian|pink	*flowers*	instructor	*jobs*	irritation	*medic*
Indian|poke	*flowers*	instrument	*medic*	Isle|of|Dogs	*islands*
Indian|pony	*animals*	instrument	*music*	isochronon	*time*
Indian|shot	*flowers*	insularity	*geog*	isometrics	*sport*
indicative	*lit*	interferon	*medic*	isonuclear	*physics*
indictment	*law*	intermezzo	*music*	isothermal	*physics*
indigenous	*plants*	intermezzo	*theatre*	ivory|tower	*archit*
indigo|bird	*birds*	Intermezzo	*titles*	ivory|tower	*myth*
indisposed	*medic*	internship	*medic*	jackanapes	*people*
indoor|golf	*sport*	inter|urban	*travel*	jack|rabbit	*animals*
inducement	*govt*	intestines	*medic*	jackstones	*sport*
inductance	*machine*	in|the|black	*trade*	jackstraws	*sport*
inductance	*physics*	in|the|money	*trade*	Jacob's|Well	*relig*
industrial	*trade*	in|the|rough	*sport*	Jacqueline	*names*
in|excelsis	*foreign*	in|the|round	*theatre*	jaguarundi	*animals*
in|extremis	*foreign*	in|the|wings	*theatre*	Jamaica|Inn	*titles*
infectious	*medic*	intonation	*music*	Jamaica|rum	*drink*
infinitive	*lit*	intoxicant	*drink*	jam|session	*music*

Jamshedpur	*cities*	
Jaquenetta	*Shakesp*	
jardiniere	*veg*	
jasper|ware	*art*	
jaywalking	*travel*	
jerry|built	*archit*	
jersey|silk	*clothes*	
jersey|wool	*clothes*	
Jesus|freak	*people*	
jet|fatigue	*travel*	
jet|fighter	*travel*	
jet|streams	*geog*	
jewel|thief	*jobs*	
jigger|flea	*insects*	
jigger|mast	*travel*	
Jim|Hawkins	*lit*	
Jimson|weed	*plants*	
jingoistic	*war*	
job|hunting	*jobs*	
job|hunting	*trade*	
job|printer	*jobs*	
job|printer	*lit*	
Jockey|Club	*sport*	
Joe|Gargery	*lit*	
Joe|Lampton	*lit*	
John|Gilpin	*lit*	
John|Gilpin	*titles*	
joint|bonds	*trade*	
joint|stock	*trade*	
Jolly|Roger	*herald*	
Jolly|Roger	*travel*	
journalese	*lit*	
journalism	*lit*	
journalist	*jobs*	
journalist	*lit*	
Joyce|stick	*travel*	
jugged|hare	*food*	
Juggernaut	*myth*	
juggernaut	*travel*	
Julian|year	*time*	
jumble|sale	*trade*	
jump|the|gun	*sport*	
June|beetle	*insects*	
jungle|fowl	*birds*	
junior|high	*educ*	

junk|dealer	*jobs*	
Juno|Lucina	*myth*	
jury|rigged	*travel*	
jury|rudder	*travel*	
jus|commune	*law*	
jus|gentium	*foreign*	
justiciary	*law*	
just|in|time	*time*	
Kabalevsky	*music*	
kabeljauer	*fish*	
kaffir|corn	*cereal*	
Kansas|City	*cities*	
karate|chop	*sport*	
katabolism	*biol*	
Kenilworth	*titles*	
kennel|maid	*jobs*	
kettledrum	*music*	
kewpie|doll	*sport*	
keyhole|saw	*tools*	
Khyber|Pass	*mounts*	
kid|brother	*family*	
kidney|bean	*veg*	
kill|or|cure	*medic*	
kinetic|art	*art*	
King|Arthur	*myth*	
kingfisher	*birds*	
King|Magnus	*lit*	
King|of|Arms	*herald*	
King's|bench	*law*	
king's|peace	*govt*	
king's|spear	*flowers*	
kiss|of|life	*medic*	
kitchenboy	*jobs*	
kitchenman	*jobs*	
kite|flying	*sport*	
kith|and|kin	*family*	
kitten|moth	*insects*	
knickknack	*house*	
knifesmith	*jobs*	
knighthood	*govt*	
knighthood	*war*	
knobkerrie	*war*	
knockabout	*travel*	
knock|knees	*medic*	
Kodiak|bear	*animals*	

kookaburra	*animals*	
kriegspiel	*sport*	
kriegspiel	*war*	
Krivoi|Roig	*cities*	
Kublai|Khan	*war*	
laboratory	*biol*	
laboratory	*chem*	
laboratory	*medic*	
laboratory	*physics*	
laboratory	*trade*	
laceration	*medic*	
lactic|acid	*chem*	
lacustrine	*geog*	
lady|beetle	*insects*	
Lady|chapel	*relig*	
lady|killer	*people*	
lady's|smock	*flowers*	
La|Fontaine	*writers*	
La|Gioconda	*titles*	
Lake|Albert	*lakes*	
Lake|Baikal	*lakes*	
Lake|Brienz	*lakes*	
Lake|Geneva	*lakes*	
Lake|Kariba	*lakes*	
Lake|Ladoga	*lakes*	
Lake|Lugano	*lakes*	
Lake|Malawi	*lakes*	
Lake|Peipus	*lakes*	
lamb|cutlet	*food*	
lambrequin	*war*	
lame|verses	*lit*	
Lammastide	*time*	
lamp|socket	*house*	
lancet|arch	*archit*	
lancet|fish	*fish*	
land|holder	*jobs*	
landing|run	*travel*	
land|jobber	*jobs*	
landlocked	*geog*	
landlubber	*jobs*	
landlubber	*travel*	
land|pirate	*govt*	
land|pirate	*jobs*	
land|tenure	*law*	
land|waiter	*jobs*	

lansquenet	*sport*	
lantern fly	*insects*	
laparotomy	*medic*	
lapidarist	*jobs*	
lappet head	*clothes*	
lappet moth	*insects*	
large scale	*geog*	
laryngitis	*medic*	
lassa fever	*medic*	
last breath	*medic*	
last chance	*time*	
last minute	*time*	
Last Supper	*relig*	
lateen sail	*travel*	
latent heat	*geog*	
latent heat	*physics*	
La Traviata	*titles*	
laundromat	*machine*	
laundryman	*jobs*	
laurustine	*trees*	
law abiding	*law*	
lawbreaker	*law*	
lawbreaker	*people*	
lawfulness	*law*	
lawn tennis	*sport*	
law officer	*jobs*	
law officer	*law*	
Law Society	*law*	
lay brother	*jobs*	
lay brother	*relig*	
lay siege to	*war*	
lazar house	*medic*	
leadership	*govt*	
lead glance	*chem*	
lead glance	*mineral*	
leading man	*jobs*	
leading man	*theatre*	
lead pencil	*educ*	
lead pencil	*lit*	
lead the way	*travel*	
leafcutter	*insects*	
leaf hopper	*insects*	
leaf insect	*insects*	
league game	*sport*	
Lebensraum	*archit*	

lectionary	*relig*	
leechcraft	*medic*	
left winger	*govt*	
left winger	*people*	
legal right	*law*	
leger lines	*music*	
legislator	*jobs*	
legislator	*law*	
legitimacy	*govt*	
legitimate	*theatre*	
lemon grass	*plants*	
lemon juice	*drink*	
Lententide	*time*	
leopardess	*animals*	
leprechaun	*myth*	
Lesser Bear	*astron*	
Les Troyens	*titles*	
lethal dose	*medic*	
letter card	*lit*	
lettergram	*travel*	
letter rack	*house*	
Lewis Eliot	*lit*	
lexicology	*lit*	
lexiconist	*lit*	
Liberalism	*govt*	
liberty man	*jobs*	
librettist	*jobs*	
librettist	*lit*	
librettist	*theatre*	
licentiate	*jobs*	
lie athwart	*travel*	
lie in state	*relig*	
lieutenant	*govt*	
lieutenant	*jobs*	
Life Guards	*war*	
life jacket	*clothes*	
life jacket	*travel*	
light armed	*war*	
light curve	*astron*	
lighterage	*trade*	
lighterman	*jobs*	
light faced	*lit*	
lighthouse	*archit*	
lighthouse	*machine*	
lighthouse	*travel*	

light lunch	*food*	
light meter	*art*	
light music	*music*	
light opera	*music*	
light valve	*physics*	
light verse	*lit*	
lime burner	*jobs*	
line of fire	*war*	
linography	*art*	
linotypist	*jobs*	
linseed oil	*art*	
lion's share	*animals*	
lip service	*relig*	
liquidator	*trade*	
liquid diet	*drink*	
literature	*lit*	
lithograph	*art*	
lithomarge	*mineral*	
litigation	*law*	
Little Bear	*myth*	
Little John	*myth*	
little slam	*sport*	
livelihood	*jobs*	
livelihood	*trade*	
live matter	*lit*	
liverwurst	*food*	
living room	*archit*	
living wage	*trade*	
loaded cane	*war*	
loaded dice	*sport*	
loan market	*trade*	
lobsterman	*jobs*	
Loch Linnhe	*lakes*	
Loch Lomond	*lakes*	
lock keeper	*jobs*	
lock washer	*machine*	
locomotion	*travel*	
locomotive	*machine*	
loganberry	*fruit*	
loggerhead	*animals*	
loggerhead	*jobs*	
logorrhoea	*lit*	
logrolling	*govt*	
long accent	*lit*	
Longaville	*Shakesp*	

Longfellow	*writers*
Long|Island	*islands*
long|knives	*war*
long|market	*trade*
long|player	*music*
long|primer	*lit*
long|seller	*trade*
lookout|man	*war*
loom|worker	*jobs*
loose|cover	*house*
loose|scrum	*sport*
Lord's|house	*relig*
Lord's|table	*relig*
Lorna|Doone	*lit*
Lorna|Doone	*titles*
Los|Angeles	*cities*
loss|leader	*trade*
loss|of|life	*medic*
lotus|eater	*people*
Louisville	*cities*
lounge|suit	*clothes*
love|letter	*lit*
love|potion	*drink*
lover's|knot	*clothes*
love|thirty	*sport*
lower|fifth	*educ*
lower|house	*govt*
lower|sixth	*educ*
lower|third	*educ*
lucky|charm	*jewels*
lucky|charm	*myth*
lucky|piece	*myth*
luff|tackle	*machine*
luggage|van	*travel*
lumber|jack	*jobs*
lumber|room	*house*
luminarist	*art*
luminosity	*astron*
lumpsucker	*fish*
lunar|month	*time*
lustreware	*art*
luxury|flat	*archit*
lycopodium	*plants*
lymph|gland	*medic*
Lyon|depute	*herald*

lyre|guitar	*music*
lyric|drama	*music*
lyric|tenor	*music*
Lysimachus	*Shakesp*
Lysistrata	*titles*
macaronics	*lit*
mace|bearer	*govt*
machinator	*govt*
Machine|Age	*machine*
machine|gun	*war*
machineman	*jobs*
Mach|number	*physics*
Mackintosh	*artists*
mackintosh	*clothes*
macroprism	*physics*
Madagascar	*islands*
madder|blue	*colour*
madder|lake	*colour*
madder|pink	*colour*
magazinist	*lit*
magic|spell	*myth*
magistracy	*law*
magistrate	*jobs*
magistrate	*law*
Magna|Carta	*govt*
Magna|Carta	*law*
magnet|core	*machine*
magnet|pole	*physics*
magnificat	*relig*
magnum|opus	*lit*
maiden|aunt	*family*
maidenhair	*plants*
maiden|name	*govt*
maiden|over	*sport*
maiden|pink	*flowers*
maidenweed	*plants*
Maid|Marion	*myth*
mail|robber	*jobs*
mail|robber	*law*
main|artery	*travel*
mainstream	*medic*
mainstream	*music*
maisonette	*archit*
major|chord	*music*
major|party	*govt*

major|scale	*music*
major|sixth	*music*
major|third	*music*
major|triad	*music*
make|a|proof	*lit*
make|tracks	*travel*
make|up|room	*lit*
malaguetta	*plants*
malefactor	*people*
malingerer	*people*
malted|milk	*drink*
Maltese|cat	*animals*
Maltese|dog	*animals*
malt|whisky	*drink*
management	*jobs*
management	*theatre*
management	*trade*
manageress	*jobs*
Manchester	*cities*
mandragora	*plants*
mangosteen	*fruit*
manicurist	*jobs*
Manila|hemp	*plants*
manipulate	*travel*
manna|grass	*plants*
manna|larch	*trees*
manoeuvres	*travel*
man|of|means	*trade*
man|of|straw	*govt*
man|of|straw	*people*
manor|house	*archit*
manservant	*jobs*
mantel|lone	*relig*
mantel|tree	*archit*
manuscript	*lit*
manuscript	*music*
manzanilla	*drink*
Mao|Tse|tung	*leaders*
maple|syrup	*food*
mappemonde	*geog*
map|reading	*geog*
maquillage	*clothes*
maraschino	*drink*
marble|cake	*food*
marcel|wave	*clothes*

Margarelon	*Shakesp*	maturation	*biol*	metathesis	*lit*
margravine	*govt*	Maupassant	*writers*	meteor|dust	*geog*
marguerite	*flowers*	Maximilian	*names*	Methuselah	*Bible*
Marguerite	*lit*	may|blossom	*flowers*	Methuselah	*people*
Marguerite	*names*	mayonnaise	*food*	Methuselah	*time*
marimbaist	*music*	meadow|lark	*birds*	metrically	*lit*
marine|blue	*colour*	meal|ticket	*food*	metrocracy	*govt*
marionette	*sport*	meal|ticket	*trade*	metropolis	*geog*
marionette	*theatre*	medical|man	*jobs*	metropolis	*govt*
Mark|Antony	*Shakesp*	medical|man	*medic*	Metternich	*leaders*
marked|down	*trade*	medicament	*medic*	Mexico|City	*cities*
marker|buoy	*machine*	medicaster	*jobs*	mezzo|forte	*music*
marker|buoy	*sport*	medicaster	*medic*	mezzo|piano	*music*
marker|buoy	*travel*	medication	*medic*	mica|schist	*mineral*
marketable	*trade*	meerschaum	*mineral*	Michaelmas	*time*
market|hall	*trade*	megalosaur	*animals*	microcurie	*physics*
market|town	*geog*	megaparsec	*physics*	microfiche	*machine*
Mark|of|Cain	*relig*	megascopic	*physics*	micrograph	*art*
Mark|Tapley	*lit*	Melba|toast	*food*	micrograph	*physics*
marquisate	*govt*	Melicertes	*myth*	micrometer	*geog*
marrow|bone	*food*	melody|part	*music*	micrometer	*machine*
Marseilles	*cities*	member|bank	*trade*	micrometer	*measure*
marsh|locks	*flowers*	Memnonides	*myth*	microphone	*film/TV*
martiality	*war*	memorandum	*educ*	microphone	*machine*
martial|law	*law*	memorandum	*govt*	microphone	*physics*
martingale	*animals*	memory|bank	*comput*	microphone	*theatre*
martingale	*travel*	Menecrates	*Shakesp*	microprint	*art*
Martinique	*islands*	Menestheus	*myth*	microscope	*biol*
mashie|iron	*sport*	meningitis	*medic*	microscope	*medic*
masonry|pin	*archit*	mercantile	*trade*	microscope	*physics*
masonry|pin	*machine*	merchantry	*trade*	microscopy	*biol*
masquerade	*clothes*	merrymaker	*people*	Midas|touch	*myth*
masquerade	*theatre*	mesogaster	*medic*	Midas|touch	*trade*
mass|defect	*physics*	message|boy	*jobs*	midchannel	*geog*
mass|energy	*physics*	mess|jacket	*clothes*	middle|aged	*time*
mass|market	*trade*	metabolism	*biol*	Middle|Ages	*time*
mass|murder	*law*	metabolism	*medic*	middlebrow	*educ*
mass|number	*physics*	metacarpus	*medic*	middlebrow	*people*
mastermind	*people*	metacentre	*physics*	middle|deck	*travel*
masterwork	*art*	metalcraft	*art*	Middle|East	*geog*
matchmaker	*people*	metalepsis	*lit*	middle|spot	*sport*
match|point	*sport*	metallurgy	*mineral*	midmorning	*time*
matchstick	*house*	metamerism	*chem*	midshipman	*jobs*
mathematic	*maths*	metaphrase	*lit*	midshipman	*travel*
matriarchy	*govt*	metatarsus	*medic*	mignonette	*flowers*

militarism	*govt*	
militarism	*war*	
militarist	*people*	
militarize	*war*	
militiaman	*jobs*	
militiaman	*war*	
milk|a|scene	*theatre*	
milk|bottle	*house*	
millennium	*time*	
millicurie	*physics*	
millilitre	*measure*	
millstream	*geog*	
millwright	*jobs*	
mimeograph	*machine*	
mimologist	*theatre*	
mind|curist	*jobs*	
mind|healer	*jobs*	
mindreader	*jobs*	
mineralogy	*mineral*	
mineral|oil	*mineral*	
miner's|lamp	*machine*	
minestrone	*food*	
ministress	*jobs*	
minor|canon	*music*	
minor|chord	*music*	
minor|deity	*myth*	
minor|party	*govt*	
minor|piece	*sport*	
minor|scale	*music*	
minor|sixth	*music*	
minor|third	*music*	
minor|triad	*music*	
minstrelsy	*music*	
mint|humbug	*food*	
miscellany	*lit*	
misogynist	*people*	
missel|bird	*birds*	
missile|man	*war*	
missionary	*jobs*	
missionary	*relig*	
Miss|Jessel	*lit*	
mitigation	*govt*	
mitre|joint	*archit*	
mixed|drink	*drink*	
mixed|times	*music*	

mixing|bowl	*house*	
mizzenmast	*travel*	
mizzen|sail	*travel*	
mizzen|stay	*travel*	
mob|tactics	*war*	
mock|heroic	*lit*	
mock|orange	*flowers*	
mock|turtle	*drink*	
modal|scale	*music*	
model|maker	*jobs*	
modern|jazz	*music*	
modulation	*music*	
Mohammedan	*relig*	
molluscoid	*animals*	
molten|lava	*mineral*	
molybdenum	*chem*	
molybdenum	*mineral*	
monetarism	*trade*	
monetarist	*trade*	
moneyed|man	*trade*	
money|order	*trade*	
monkey|deck	*travel*	
monkey|rail	*travel*	
monk's|cloth	*clothes*	
monk's|habit	*clothes*	
monochrome	*art*	
monolithic	*archit*	
monophobia	*medic*	
monopolise	*trade*	
monopolist	*jobs*	
monopolist	*trade*	
Monostatos	*lit*	
monovalent	*chem*	
Monteverdi	*music*	
Montevideo	*cities*	
Montgomery	*Shakesp*	
Montgomery	*names*	
Montgomery	*war*	
Montserrat	*islands*	
monumental	*art*	
moonshiner	*jobs*	
moratorium	*time*	
moratorium	*trade*	
mordant|dye	*art*	
morganatic	*govt*	

morphology	*biol*	
morphology	*geog*	
morphology	*lit*	
mortadella	*food*	
mossbunker	*fish*	
mother|cell	*biol*	
mother|land	*geog*	
Mother's|day	*time*	
motherwort	*plants*	
motley|fool	*jobs*	
motley|fool	*theatre*	
motorcoach	*travel*	
motorcycle	*machine*	
motorcycle	*travel*	
motor|truck	*travel*	
mountebank	*people*	
mountebank	*theatre*	
Mount|Elgon	*mounts*	
mount|guard	*war*	
Mount|Kenya	*mounts*	
Mount|Sinai	*mounts*	
Mount|Sinai	*relig*	
Mount|Tabor	*relig*	
mousseline	*clothes*	
mouth|music	*music*	
mouth|organ	*music*	
mouthpiece	*govt*	
mouthpiece	*jobs*	
mouthpiece	*music*	
movie|actor	*film/TV*	
mozzarella	*food*	
Mr|McGregor	*lit*	
Mr|Mulliner	*lit*	
Mrs|Bardell	*lit*	
Mrs|Jellyby	*lit*	
Mrs|Miniver	*lit*	
muckraking	*govt*	
mud|skipper	*fish*	
mugwumpery	*govt*	
mulled|wine	*drink*	
multicurie	*measure*	
multicurie	*physics*	
multiplier	*maths*	
mumbo|jumbo	*myth*	
Munich|beer	*drink*	

mural|crown	*war*
Murphy's|law	*law*
musical|bow	*music*
musical|box	*house*
musical|box	*music*
musical|ear	*music*
music|drama	*theatre*
music|lover	*music*
music|maker	*music*
musicology	*music*
music|paper	*music*
music|stand	*music*
music|stool	*house*
musk|beetle	*insects*
musket|shot	*war*
musk|mallow	*plants*
Mussorgsky	*music*
mustard|gas	*war*
mustard|pot	*house*
mutilation	*medic*
mutton|bird	*birds*
mutton|chop	*food*
My|Fair|Lady	*titles*
myrmidones	*myth*
nail|matrix	*medic*
nail|polish	*clothes*
nanosecond	*physics*
napalm|bomb	*war*
napkin|ring	*house*
narcissist	*medic*
narrow|seas	*geog*
nasturtium	*flowers*
native|land	*geog*
native|soil	*geog*
natural|dye	*art*
natural|gas	*geog*
naturalism	*art*
naturalist	*jobs*
nauseation	*medic*
nautch|girl	*jobs*
naval|cadet	*jobs*
naval|cadet	*travel*
navigation	*travel*
near|future	*time*
neat|cattle	*animals*

Nebelkappe	*myth*
nebulosity	*weather*
necromancy	*myth*
necropolis	*relig*
needlecord	*clothes*
Needle's|eye	*relig*
needle|time	*film/TV*
ne'er|do|well	*people*
negotiable	*trade*
negotiator	*jobs*
Nelson|Mass	*titles*
Nemean|lion	*myth*
neoclassic	*art*
nerve|fibre	*medic*
nettle|rash	*medic*
neuropathy	*medic*
neuter|verb	*lit*
neutralism	*govt*
neutralist	*jobs*
neutrality	*govt*
neutralize	*chem*
never|never	*trade*
new|mown|hay	*plants*
New|Orleans	*cities*
newscaster	*film/TV*
newscaster	*jobs*
news|editor	*jobs*
news|editor	*lit*
newsletter	*lit*
newsreader	*film/TV*
newsvendor	*jobs*
newswriter	*jobs*
news|writer	*lit*
New|Zealand	*islands*
nick|of|time	*time*
night|churr	*birds*
nightdress	*clothes*
night|float	*jobs*
night|float	*medic*
night|heron	*birds*
night|light	*house*
night|nurse	*jobs*
night|nurse	*medic*
night|raven	*birds*
nightshade	*flowers*

nightshift	*trade*
nightshirt	*clothes*
nipplewort	*plants*
nitric|acid	*chem*
nitrometer	*measure*
Nobel|prize	*educ*
noble|birth	*govt*
noble|metal	*mineral*
noblewoman	*govt*
Nogood|Boyo	*lit*
no|man's|land	*geog*
no|man's|land	*govt*
no|man's|land	*war*
nom|de|plume	*lit*
nominal|fee	*trade*
nominal|par	*trade*
nomination	*govt*
nominative	*lit*
nomography	*law*
non|fiction	*lit*
nonpayment	*trade*
non|starter	*people*
non|starter	*sport*
nose|turret	*travel*
nosophobia	*medic*
notability	*jobs*
note|of|hand	*trade*
nothofagus	*trees*
Nottingham	*cities*
noun|clause	*lit*
now|or|never	*time*
nubilation	*weather*
nuclear|war	*war*
nucleonics	*physics*
nucleonium	*chem*
numeration	*maths*
numismatic	*trade*
nurseryman	*jobs*
nutcracker	*birds*
nutcracker	*house*
obituarist	*jobs*
object|ball	*sport*
obligation	*trade*
obligative	*lit*
oboe|d'amore	*music*

obsidional	war	on|the|block	trade	orogenesis	geog
obsoletism	lit	on|the|cheap	trade	orthoclase	mineral
obstetrics	medic	on|the|eve|of	time	orthogonal	maths
occasional	time	on|the|fence	govt	orthograph	archit
occupation	jobs	on|the|march	travel	orthopraxy	medic
occupation	trade	on|the|march	war	orthoscope	medic
occupation	war	on|the|rocks	drink	orthostyle	archit
oceangoing	travel	on|the|rocks	trade	oscillator	machine
ocean|liner	travel	on|the|rocks	travel	osmium|lamp	machine
ocean|nymph	myth	on|the|shelf	trade	ossiferous	medic
ochlocracy	govt	on|the|stage	theatre	osteoblast	biol
octahedral	maths	opening|bat	sport	osteoblast	medic
octahedron	maths	opening|bid	trade	osteoclast	medic
octavalent	chem	open|letter	lit	osteopathy	medic
odontogeny	biol	open|market	trade	Ostpolitik	govt
odontogeny	medic	open|season	sport	other|ranks	war
odorimetry	measure	open|sesame	myth	ottava|rima	lit
Oedipus|Rex	myth	open|target	sport	otterhound	animals
Oedipus|Rex	titles	open|waggon	travel	otter|shrew	animals
oesophagus	medic	opera|buffa	music	Ouija|board	sport
off|licence	trade	opera|buffa	theatre	Our|Village	titles
off|the|hook	sport	opera|house	archit	Outer|House	govt
of|the|clock	time	opera|house	theatre	outer|space	astron
oil|colours	art	opera|score	music	outer|space	travel
oil|derrick	machine	operations	war	outfielder	sport
oil|of|palms	trade	ophicleide	music	outline|map	geog
oil|painter	art	opium|poppy	flowers	out|of|court	law
oil|painter	jobs	oppressive	geog	out|of|funds	trade
old|clothes	clothes	optic|nerve	medic	out|of|sorts	medic
old|country	geog	optic|tract	medic	outpatient	medic
olden|times	time	orange|lily	flowers	oven|gloves	house
old|soldier	myth	orange|peel	fruit	overblouse	clothes
old|soldier	people	orangeroot	plants	overbridge	travel
old|soldier	war	orange|wood	trees	overcharge	trade
olive|brown	colour	orchestral	music	overshadow	geog
olive|green	colour	ordinaries	herald	over|the|top	war
olive|grove	trees	Ordovician	geog	overthrust	geog
ombrometer	measure	ore|deposit	mineral	overweight	medic
ombrometer	weather	organology	biol	oxalic|acid	chem
omnivorous	animals	organ|point	music	ox|eye|daisy	flowers
on|a|bowl|ine	travel	Orion's|belt	astron	Oxford|bags	clothes
one|fine|day	time	Orion's|belt	myth	Oxford|grey	colour
on|location	film/TV	orismology	lit	Oxford|ties	clothes
on|occasion	time	ornamental	art	oxygen|mask	medic
On|the|Beach	titles	ornithopod	animals	oxygen|tank	medic

oxygen|tent	*machine*	pantry|maid	*jobs*	pastellist	*art*
oxygen|tent	*medic*	papal|brief	*law*	pasteurise	*biol*
oyster|mine	*war*	papal|brief	*relig*	past|master	*educ*
pack|animal	*animals*	Papal|Court	*law*	past|master	*people*
packet|boat	*travel*	Papal|Court	*relig*	pastry|case	*food*
packet|line	*travel*	paper|birch	*trees*	pastrycook	*jobs*
packet|ship	*travel*	paper|chase	*sport*	pathfinder	*jobs*
pack|of|dogs	*animals*	paper|knife	*house*	pathfinder	*travel*
padded|cell	*medic*	paper|knife	*tools*	pathognomy	*medic*
paddle|boat	*travel*	papermaker	*jobs*	patriarchy	*govt*
paddlefish	*fish*	paper|money	*trade*	patrol|boat	*travel*
paddy|field	*cereal*	paper|tiger	*lit*	patter|song	*music*
paediatric	*medic*	paradoxure	*animals*	Paul|Dombey	*lit*
painkiller	*medic*	paramagnet	*machine*	paving|flag	*archit*
paintbrush	*art*	paraphasia	*medic*	pawnbroker	*jobs*
paintbrush	*house*	paraphrase	*lit*	pawnbroker	*trade*
Palaeogene	*geog*	paraphrase	*relig*	peacemaker	*jobs*
palaeotype	*lit*	paraplegia	*medic*	peach|bloom	*fruit*
Palaeozoic	*geog*	paraselene	*astron*	peach|melba	*food*
palatinate	*govt*	paratroops	*war*	peacock|ore	*mineral*
Palestrina	*music*	parcel|post	*travel*	pearl|diver	*jobs*
palimpsest	*lit*	par|contest	*sport*	pearly|king	*jobs*
palindrome	*lit*	pari|mutuel	*machine*	pebble|dash	*archit*
palinodist	*lit*	pari|mutuel	*sport*	peccadillo	*law*
Palk|Strait	*seas*	Paris|green	*colour*	pedagogics	*educ*
pallbearer	*jobs*	Paris|model	*clothes*	pedagogist	*educ*
pallbearer	*relig*	park|keeper	*jobs*	pedal|board	*music*
palliation	*law*	park|ranger	*jobs*	pedal|organ	*music*
palliative	*medic*	parliament	*govt*	pedal|point	*music*
palm|branch	*trees*	Parnassian	*lit*	pedal|wheel	*art*
Palmerston	*leaders*	paronychia	*medic*	pedestrian	*jobs*
palmer|worm	*insects*	parrotbill	*birds*	pedestrian	*travel*
Palm|Sunday	*time*	parrot|fish	*fish*	pediatrics	*medic*
Panama|City	*cities*	parson|bird	*birds*	pediatrist	*jobs*
pancration	*sport*	parted|arms	*herald*	pediatrist	*medic*
pancratium	*sport*	parted|coat	*herald*	pedicurist	*jobs*
Pantagruel	*myth*	participle	*lit*	peen|hammer	*tools*
Pantagruel	*titles*	party|dress	*clothes*	peeping|Tom	*people*
pantaloons	*clothes*	party|liner	*govt*	penalty|try	*sport*
pantheress	*animals*	passageway	*archit*	Penderecki	*music*
pantograph	*maths*	passageway	*house*	penicillin	*medic*
pantograph	*tools*	passed|pawn	*sport*	Penny|Black	*travel*
pantometer	*measure*	pass|holder	*theatre*	penny|cress	*plants*
pantomimic	*jobs*	passiflora	*flowers*	pennyroyal	*plants*
pantomimic	*theatre*	paste|jewel	*jewels*	penologist	*jobs*

pen|pushing	*lit*	Peter|Quint	*lit*	phylloxera	*insects*
pensionnat	*educ*	petitioner	*jobs*	physiology	*biol*
pentachord	*music*	petitioner	*law*	physiology	*medic*
pentagonal	*maths*	petri|plate	*biol*	pianissimo	*music*
pentameter	*lit*	petrol|bomb	*war*	pianoforte	*music*
pentastich	*lit*	petrol|pump	*machine*	pianologue	*music*
pentastyle	*archit*	petrol|pump	*travel*	piano|score	*music*
Pentateuch	*relig*	petrol|tank	*travel*	piano|stool	*house*
pentathlon	*sport*	Petronella	*names*	piano|stool	*music*
pentatomic	*physics*	Petroushka	*titles*	piano|tuner	*jobs*
pentatonic	*music*	petty|juror	*law*	picaresque	*art*
peppercorn	*fruit*	petty|theft	*law*	piccalilli	*food*
peppercorn	*trade*	Pharisaism	*relig*	piccoloist	*jobs*
pepper|mill	*house*	pharmacist	*jobs*	piccoloist	*music*
peppermint	*food*	pharmacist	*medic*	picketboat	*travel*
peppermint	*plants*	Pheidippes	*myth*	picket|duty	*trade*
pepperwort	*plants*	phenacetin	*medic*	picket|duty	*war*
percentage	*maths*	phenomenon	*astron*	pickled|egg	*food*
percentage	*trade*	phenomenon	*geog*	pickpocket	*jobs*
percolator	*house*	philatelic	*sport*	pickpocket	*law*
percolator	*machine*	Philistine	*educ*	picric|acid	*chem*
percussion	*music*	Philistine	*people*	picture|hat	*clothes*
percussion	*war*	Philistine	*relig*	piermaster	*jobs*
perdendosi	*music*	phlebotomy	*medic*	piezometer	*measure*
performing	*film/TV*	Phlegethon	*myth*	pigeon|hawk	*birds*
performing	*theatre*	phlogiston	*chem*	pigeonhole	*archit*
perihelion	*astron*	phonograph	*music*	pigeon|loft	*birds*
periodical	*lit*	Phosphoros	*myth*	pigeon|loft	*sport*
periosteum	*medic*	phosphorus	*chem*	pigeon|toed	*medic*
Peripheles	*myth*	photoflash	*art*	pig|in|a|poke	*trade*
peripheral	*comput*	photoflash	*machine*	pigmentary	*art*
peritoneal	*medic*	photoflood	*art*	pile|bridge	*archit*
peritoneum	*medic*	photoflood	*machine*	piledriver	*machine*
periwinkle	*fish*	photogenic	*art*	pilgrimage	*relig*
periwinkle	*flowers*	photograph	*art*	pilgrimage	*travel*
permissive	*lit*	photograph	*house*	pillar|rose	*flowers*
perruquier	*jobs*	photolysis	*chem*	pillowcase	*house*
Persephone	*myth*	photometer	*art*	pillow|lace	*clothes*
Persian|cat	*animals*	photometry	*plants*	pillow|slip	*house*
Persian|red	*colour*	photomural	*art*	pilothouse	*travel*
Persian|rug	*house*	photoprint	*art*	pilot|light	*house*
persiennes	*clothes*	phylactery	*art*	pilot|light	*machine*
persiennes	*house*	phylactery	*myth*	pilot|plane	*travel*
Persuasion	*titles*	phylactery	*relig*	pilot|plant	*trade*
pestilence	*medic*	phyllopoda	*animals*	pin|cushion	*clothes*

pin|cushion	*house*	
pineal|body	*medic*	
pine|beauty	*insects*	
pine|beetle	*insects*	
pine|chafer	*insects*	
pine|marten	*animals*	
pine|needle	*trees*	
pipe|aboard	*travel*	
pipes|of|Pan	*myth*	
pipe|wrench	*tools*	
Pirandello	*writers*	
piston|pump	*machine*	
piston|ring	*machine*	
pitchstone	*mineral*	
pith|helmet	*clothes*	
Pittsburgh	*cities*	
plagal|mode	*music*	
plagiarist	*jobs*	
plague|spot	*medic*	
plain|cross	*herald*	
plain|field	*herald*	
planchette	*sport*	
planimeter	*measure*	
planimetry	*measure*	
plantation	*trees*	
planthouse	*plants*	
plasticine	*art*	
plastic|mac	*clothes*	
plat|du|jour	*food*	
plate|glass	*house*	
platelayer	*jobs*	
plate|piece	*house*	
plate|proof	*lit*	
play|acting	*theatre*	
playbroker	*jobs*	
playbroker	*theatre*	
playground	*educ*	
playground	*sport*	
playreader	*theatre*	
playschool	*educ*	
playwright	*jobs*	
playwright	*lit*	
playwright	*theatre*	
playwriter	*jobs*	
playwriter	*theatre*	

plebiscite	*govt*	
pleonastic	*lit*	
plot|of|land	*geog*	
plume|grass	*plants*	
plundering	*govt*	
pluperfect	*lit*	
plural|vote	*govt*	
plutocracy	*trade*	
poached|egg	*food*	
pocketbook	*trade*	
pocket|veto	*govt*	
podiatrist	*medic*	
poet|artist	*jobs*	
poet|artist	*lit*	
poetastery	*lit*	
poet|farmer	*jobs*	
poet|farmer	*lit*	
poet|priest	*jobs*	
poet|priest	*lit*	
poinsettia	*flowers*	
point|blank	*war*	
point|of|aim	*sport*	
point|of|law	*law*	
poke|bonnet	*clothes*	
poker|chips	*sport*	
politician	*govt*	
politician	*jobs*	
poll|parrot	*birds*	
polo|ground	*sport*	
polyanthus	*flowers*	
polychrest	*medic*	
polychrome	*art*	
polyclinic	*medic*	
polycyclic	*physics*	
Polydectes	*myth*	
Polydeuces	*myth*	
polyhedral	*maths*	
polyhedron	*maths*	
Polyhymnia	*muses*	
Polyhymnia	*music*	
Polyhymnia	*myth*	
Polymestor	*myth*	
Polyneices	*myth*	
Polyphemus	*myth*	
polyphonic	*music*	

Pomeranian	*animals*	
Ponchielli	*music*	
ponticello	*music*	
pontifical	*relig*	
poor|health	*medic*	
poor|sinner	*relig*	
pop|concert	*music*	
popular|air	*music*	
population	*geog*	
portamento	*music*	
port|anchor	*travel*	
port|crayon	*art*	
portcullis	*archit*	
portcullis	*herald*	
portcullis	*war*	
port|of|call	*travel*	
Portsmouth	*cities*	
possessive	*lit*	
post|chaise	*travel*	
posthumous	*time*	
postliminy	*law*	
postmaster	*educ*	
postmaster	*jobs*	
postmortem	*law*	
postmortem	*medic*	
Post|Office	*govt*	
Post|Office	*travel*	
potamology	*geog*	
potato|peel	*veg*	
potato|race	*sport*	
pot|scourer	*house*	
pot|scraper	*house*	
potted|meat	*food*	
pouched|rat	*animals*	
powder|blue	*colour*	
powder|mill	*tools*	
powder|puff	*clothes*	
powder|snow	*weather*	
power|brake	*machine*	
power|drill	*machine*	
power|happy	*govt*	
power|plant	*physics*	
power|plant	*trade*	
power|point	*house*	
power|press	*machine*	

power|wheel	*art*	primordial	*biol*	properties	*theatre*
praesidium	*law*	Prince|Igor	*titles*	proper|time	*time*
praetorium	*relig*	princeling	*govt*	Propertius	*writers*
Praetorius	*music*	print|dress	*clothes*	prophetess	*relig*
pragmatist	*people*	printworks	*trade*	proportion	*archit*
prairie|dog	*animals*	private|eye	*jobs*	proportion	*art*
prairie|fox	*animals*	private|law	*law*	proportion	*music*
pratincole	*birds*	private|war	*war*	proprietor	*jobs*
Praxiteles	*artists*	Prix|unique	*trade*	propulsion	*physics*
pray|a|tales	*govt*	prize|court	*law*	propulsion	*travel*
prayer|bead	*fruit*	prize|fight	*sport*	propylaeum	*archit*
prayer|bead	*relig*	prize|idiot	*educ*	prosaicism	*lit*
prayer|book	*relig*	prize|money	*sport*	proscenium	*archit*
prebendary	*jobs*	procession	*govt*	proscenium	*theatre*
prebendary	*relig*	Procrustes	*myth*	prosecutor	*law*
preceptive	*educ*	Proculeius	*Shakesp*	Proserpina	*myth*
precession	*astron*	procurator	*jobs*	prospector	*jobs*
pre|emption	*trade*	procurator	*law*	prospector	*trade*
prefecture	*law*	procurator	*relig*	prospectus	*lit*
preference	*trade*	production	*film/TV*	prospectus	*trade*
prehistory	*time*	production	*lit*	prosperity	*trade*
premaxilla	*medic*	production	*theatre*	protection	*govt*
prenominal	*lit*	production	*trade*	protective	*medic*
prepayment	*trade*	profession	*jobs*	Protestant	*relig*
prep|school	*educ*	profession	*trade*	protogenic	*biol*
presbyopia	*medic*	profitable	*trade*	protoplasm	*biol*
Presbytery	*relig*	prognostic	*medic*	protractor	*maths*
present|day	*time*	programmer	*jobs*	protractor	*measure*
presenting	*theatre*	pro|hac|vice	*foreign*	proveditor	*govt*
presidency	*govt*	projectile	*physics*	proveditor	*jobs*
press|proof	*lit*	projectile	*war*	provide|for	*trade*
prevention	*medic*	projection	*archit*	Providence	*relig*
preventive	*medic*	prolocutor	*educ*	provisions	*food*
previously	*time*	prolocutor	*jobs*	psychopath	*people*
price|index	*trade*	Prometheus	*myth*	public|room	*house*
price|level	*trade*	promethium	*chem*	public|walk	*travel*
prickly|ash	*trees*	promethium	*mineral*	public|ward	*medic*
priest|hole	*archit*	promontory	*geog*	publishers	*lit*
priesthood	*jobs*	promptbook	*theatre*	publishing	*lit*
priesthood	*relig*	pronucleus	*physics*	Puerto|Rico	*islands*
prima|donna	*jobs*	proof|sheet	*lit*	puff|pastry	*food*
prima|donna	*music*	propaganda	*educ*	puff|sleeve	*clothes*
prima|donna	*people*	propellant	*physics*	Pulcinella	*theatre*
prima|donna	*theatre*	propellant	*travel*	punch|drunk	*sport*
prima|facie	*foreign*	proper|noun	*lit*	Punic|apple	*fruit*

punishment	*law*	
puppet|show	*theatre*	
purchasing	*trade*	
pure|colour	*art*	
pure|profit	*trade*	
purloining	*law*	
purple|fish	*fish*	
pursuivant	*govt*	
pursuivant	*herald*	
push|button	*machine*	
push|stroke	*sport*	
put|and|call	*trade*	
put|on|a|show	*theatre*	
put|on|trial	*law*	
put|to|press	*lit*	
pyknometer	*measure*	
pyretology	*medic*	
quack|quack	*birds*	
quadrangle	*archit*	
quadrangle	*educ*	
quadrangle	*maths*	
quadratrix	*maths*	
quadrature	*astron*	
quadrature	*maths*	
quadricone	*maths*	
quadriform	*maths*	
quadrireme	*travel*	
quadrivium	*educ*	
quadruplex	*travel*	
Quaker|bird	*birds*	
quarantine	*govt*	
quarter|day	*govt*	
quartering	*herald*	
quartz|lamp	*machine*	
quaternary	*maths*	
quatrefoil	*archit*	
quatrefoil	*herald*	
queencraft	*govt*	
queen's|pawn	*sport*	
queen's|rook	*sport*	
queen's|ware	*art*	
quercitron	*trees*	
questioner	*jobs*	
quick|march	*music*	
quid|pro|quo	*foreign*	
Quintilian	*writers*	
quizmaster	*educ*	
quizmaster	*jobs*	
Quonset|hut	*archit*	
rabbit|fish	*fish*	
rabbit|foot	*myth*	
rabbitskin	*clothes*	
raccoon|dog	*animals*	
racecourse	*sport*	
racing|cars	*sport*	
radial|tyre	*travel*	
radiogenic	*physics*	
radiograph	*medic*	
radiolaria	*animals*	
radiometer	*measure*	
radiometer	*medic*	
radiometer	*physics*	
radiometry	*measure*	
radiometry	*physics*	
radioscope	*physics*	
radioscopy	*medic*	
radioscopy	*physics*	
radiosonde	*physics*	
radiosonde	*weather*	
radium|bath	*medic*	
raffia|palm	*trees*	
railwayman	*jobs*	
rain|barrel	*house*	
rain|forest	*geog*	
rain|forest	*trees*	
raking|fire	*war*	
rally|round	*war*	
ranch|house	*archit*	
ransacking	*govt*	
ranunculus	*flowers*	
Raphaelite	*art*	
rare|earths	*chem*	
rare|metals	*mineral*	
ratcatcher	*sport*	
ration|book	*govt*	
ration|book	*house*	
ration|book	*trade*	
rat|terrier	*animals*	
raven|black	*colour*	
rave|notice	*theatre*	
Rawalpindi	*cities*	
raw|recruit	*jobs*	
raw|recruit	*war*	
Rawsthorne	*music*	
ray|therapy	*medic*	
reactivity	*chem*	
reactivity	*physics*	
readership	*educ*	
ready|money	*trade*	
real|estate	*archit*	
real|estate	*govt*	
real|estate	*trade*	
real|tennis	*sport*	
rear|mirror	*travel*	
recidivist	*law*	
recidivist	*people*	
reciprocal	*maths*	
recitalist	*jobs*	
recitalist	*music*	
recitative	*music*	
recitativo	*music*	
recognitor	*law*	
recompense	*trade*	
recounting	*lit*	
recoupment	*trade*	
recreation	*sport*	
recuperate	*medic*	
red|admiral	*insects*	
red|cabbage	*veg*	
red|currant	*fruit*	
redeemable	*trade*	
red|herring	*fish*	
red|jasmine	*flowers*	
red|sanders	*trees*	
reduce|sail	*travel*	
redundancy	*trade*	
referendum	*govt*	
reform|bill	*govt*	
refutation	*govt*	
regalement	*food*	
regenerate	*relig*	
regression	*medic*	
regulation	*govt*	
regulation	*law*	
reichsmark	*money*	

related|key	*music*
relativity	*maths*
relaxation	*sport*
relegation	*sport*
reluctance	*physics*
remand|home	*law*
remittance	*trade*
remunerate	*trade*
rendezvous	*travel*
repair|ship	*travel*
repair|shop	*trade*
reparation	*govt*
reparation	*trade*
repeatedly	*time*
repertoire	*music*
repertoire	*theatre*
repetition	*music*
report|card	*educ*
repository	*archit*
repository	*trade*
repoussage	*art*
Republican	*govt*
Republican	*rivers*
repurchase	*trade*
rescue|boat	*travel*
researcher	*jobs*
resilience	*physics*
resistance	*medic*
resistance	*physics*
Resistance	*war*
resolution	*chem*
resolution	*govt*
resolution	*music*
resolution	*physics*
respirator	*machine*
respirator	*medic*
respondent	*law*
responsory	*music*
restaurant	*archit*
restharrow	*plants*
retail|shop	*trade*
retirement	*jobs*
retirement	*trade*
retrochoir	*archit*
retrospect	*time*

rev|counter	*travel*
Revelation	*relig*
revenue|man	*jobs*
revivalist	*jobs*
revolution	*govt*
revolution	*war*
rhapsodist	*jobs*
rhapsodist	*lit*
rhapsodist	*music*
rheumatics	*medic*
rhinestone	*jewels*
rhinoceros	*animals*
rhomboidal	*maths*
rhyme|royal	*lit*
ribbed|arch	*archit*
Ribbentrop	*leaders*
ribbon|fish	*fish*
ribbon|worm	*insects*
riboflavin	*biol*
Richard|Roe	*law*
Richardson	*writers*
rich|colour	*art*
ride|and|tie	*travel*
ride|a|storm	*travel*
ridge|strut	*archit*
riding|hood	*clothes*
rifle|range	*sport*
rifle|range	*war*
rift|valley	*geog*
right|angle	*maths*
right|bower	*sport*
right|inner	*sport*
right|of|way	*govt*
right|of|way	*travel*
right|stage	*theatre*
right|swing	*sport*
right|whale	*animals*
ring|brooch	*jewels*
ring|leader	*govt*
ring|leader	*people*
ring|master	*jobs*
ring|o|roses	*sport*
ring|plover	*birds*
ripe|old|age	*time*
rising|arch	*archit*

rising|damp	*archit*
ritardando	*music*
ritornelle	*music*
ritornello	*music*
river|basin	*geog*
river|horse	*animals*
River|of|woe	*myth*
riverscape	*art*
road|bridge	*archit*
roadmender	*jobs*
road|roller	*machine*
road|runner	*birds*
road|safety	*travel*
roadworthy	*travel*
robot|pilot	*machine*
robot|plane	*travel*
rock|badger	*animals*
rock|bottom	*geog*
rock|bottom	*trade*
rock|desert	*geog*
rocket|boat	*travel*
rocket|bomb	*war*
rocket|fire	*war*
rocket|ship	*travel*
rock|garden	*flowers*
rock|hopper	*birds*
Rockingham	*art*
rock|pigeon	*birds*
rock|pillar	*geog*
rock|salmon	*fish*
rock|series	*geog*
rock|turbot	*fish*
rock|violet	*flowers*
rod|and|reel	*sport*
rolled|lamb	*food*
rolled|oats	*cereal*
rolled|pork	*food*
rolling|pin	*house*
roll|of|arms	*herald*
Roman|Curia	*relig*
Roman|Doric	*archit*
Romanesque	*archit*
Roman|snail	*insects*
romper|suit	*clothes*
rood|screen	*relig*

roof garden	*flowers*	rumpus room	*archit*	sales force	*jobs*
root sheath	*medic*	rumpus room	*house*	sales force	*trade*
rope bridge	*travel*	rumpus room	*sport*	saleswoman	*jobs*
ropedancer	*jobs*	runic verse	*lit*	salicional	*music*
ropewalker	*jobs*	runner bean	*veg*	salivation	*medic*
roquelaure	*clothes*	run through	*sport*	sally forth	*travel*
Rosa Dartle	*lit*	run through	*war*	salmagundi	*food*
Rose Aylmer	*lit*	run up a bill	*trade*	salmon pink	*colour*
rose beetle	*insects*	rupestrian	*geog*	saltarello	*music*
rose chafer	*insects*	Rural Rides	*titles*	saltcellar	*house*
rose engine	*machine*	rush stroke	*sport*	saltcellar	*medic*
rose laurel	*trees*	Russian cat	*animals*	saltworker	*jobs*
rose madder	*colour*	Russian tea	*drink*	Samothrace	*islands*
rose mallow	*flowers*	Rutherford	*measure*	Samothrace	*myth*
rose quartz	*jewels*	rutherford	*physics*	San Antonio	*cities*
rose quartz	*mineral*	Sabbath day	*relig*	sanatorium	*medic*
rose window	*archit*	Sabbath day	*time*	sanctimony	*relig*
rose window	*house*	Sabbatical	*educ*	sanctioned	*govt*
rotary pump	*machine*	sabre tooth	*animals*	sandalwood	*trees*
Rouge Croix	*herald*	saccharate	*chem*	sand binder	*plants*
roundabout	*sport*	saccharine	*food*	sand castle	*sport*
roundabout	*travel*	saccharose	*chem*	sand cherry	*fruit*
round dance	*music*	sacerdotal	*relig*	sand dancer	*jobs*
round dance	*sport*	sack barrow	*machine*	sand dollar	*fish*
round house	*travel*	Sacramento	*cities*	sanderling	*birds*
round robin	*lit*	Sacramento	*rivers*	sandgrouse	*birds*
round steak	*food*	sacredness	*relig*	sand hopper	*animals*
round table	*myth*	sacred Nine	*music*	sand launce	*fish*
round trade	*trade*	sacrosanct	*relig*	sand lizard	*insects*
roustabout	*travel*	saddleback	*animals*	sand martin	*birds*
rove beetle	*insects*	safeblower	*jobs*	sand sucker	*fish*
rowan berry	*fruit*	safety belt	*travel*	sanitarian	*medic*
rowing boat	*sport*	safety fuse	*machine*	Santa Claus	*myth*
rowing boat	*travel*	safety lamp	*machine*	sarracenia	*flowers*
Rowlandson	*artists*	safety wire	*travel*	Saturnalia	*myth*
royal crown	*herald*	sage grouse	*birds*	Saturninus	*Shakesp*
royal flush	*sport*	sailorbird	*birds*	saucer eyes	*medic*
royal icing	*food*	sailor suit	*clothes*	sauerkraut	*veg*
rubber ball	*sport*	sail teaser	*travel*	sausage dog	*animals*
rubber duck	*sport*	Saint Saens	*music*	saving bank	*trade*
rubber sole	*clothes*	salability	*trade*	saving game	*trade*
Rubinstein	*music*	salad plant	*veg*	Saxon tower	*archit*
rude health	*medic*	salamander	*fish*	saxotromba	*music*
rugby union	*sport*	salamander	*myth*	scalloping	*clothes*
rules of war	*war*	sales clerk	*jobs*	scarabaeus	*insects*

Scaramouch	*theatre*	
scarlatina	*medic*	
scatter|pin	*clothes*	
scatter|rug	*house*	
scenograph	*art*	
Scepticism	*relig*	
Schamander	*myth*	
scherzando	*music*	
schipperke	*animals*	
Schismatic	*relig*	
Schoenberg	*music*	
scholastic	*educ*	
scholastic	*relig*	
schoolbook	*educ*	
schoolbook	*lit*	
school|chum	*educ*	
schooldame	*educ*	
schoolgirl	*educ*	
schoolma'am	*educ*	
schoolma'am	*jobs*	
schoolmaid	*educ*	
schoolmarm	*educ*	
schoolmate	*educ*	
school|meal	*educ*	
school|miss	*educ*	
schoolroom	*educ*	
scientific	*biol*	
scientific	*chem*	
scientific	*physics*	
scordatura	*music*	
scoreboard	*sport*	
Scotch|kale	*veg*	
Scotch|rose	*flowers*	
Scotch|snap	*music*	
scratch|pad	*lit*	
scratchwig	*clothes*	
screech|owl	*birds*	
screenings	*archit*	
screenplay	*film/TV*	
scribbling	*lit*	
scrip|issue	*trade*	
scriptural	*lit*	
Scriptures	*relig*	
scrivening	*lit*	
scrofulous	*medic*	

scrollhead	*archit*	
scrutineer	*jobs*	
scrutinize	*educ*	
sculptress	*art*	
sculptress	*jobs*	
sculptural	*art*	
sculptured	*art*	
sculpturer	*art*	
sea|biscuit	*food*	
sea|blubber	*animals*	
sea|breezes	*marine*	
sea|burdock	*plants*	
sea|cabbage	*veg*	
sea|captain	*jobs*	
sealed|book	*lit*	
sea|leopard	*animals*	
sea|lettuce	*plants*	
sealingwax	*house*	
seamanship	*travel*	
sea|monster	*animals*	
seamstress	*jobs*	
sea|poacher	*fish*	
search|form	*govt*	
seasonable	*time*	
sea|surgeon	*fish*	
sea|swallow	*birds*	
sea|unicorn	*animals*	
sea|vampire	*birds*	
sea|whistle	*plants*	
second|crop	*plants*	
second|form	*educ*	
second|half	*sport*	
secondhand	*trade*	
secondhead	*educ*	
second|line	*war*	
second|mate	*jobs*	
second|mate	*travel*	
second|slip	*sport*	
seconds|out	*sport*	
second|wind	*sport*	
second|year	*educ*	
secretaire	*house*	
secularism	*relig*	
secularist	*people*	
securities	*trade*	

sedan|chair	*travel*	
seed|vessel	*plants*	
seersucker	*clothes*	
seguidilla	*music*	
seismic|map	*geog*	
seismology	*geog*	
selenology	*astron*	
self,taught	*educ*	
semeiology	*medic*	
semeiotics	*medic*	
semichorus	*music*	
semicircle	*maths*	
seminarian	*jobs*	
semination	*plants*	
semiquaver	*music*	
Semiramide	*titles*	
semiweekly	*time*	
semper|idem	*foreign*	
Sempronius	*Shakesp*	
sempstress	*jobs*	
senior|high	*educ*	
sense|organ	*medic*	
sensitizer	*biol*	
sens|unique	*travel*	
sentry|duty	*war*	
separation	*govt*	
septennial	*time*	
septicemia	*medic*	
Septuagint	*relig*	
sepulchral	*relig*	
sergeantcy	*law*	
serial|bond	*trade*	
serologist	*jobs*	
serologist	*medic*	
serpentine	*geog*	
serpentine	*insects*	
serve|a|writ	*law*	
serve|valve	*machine*	
serviceman	*jobs*	
serviceman	*war*	
servomotor	*machine*	
servo|pilot	*travel*	
session|man	*jobs*	
sestertius	*money*	
set|in|print	*lit*	

set|the|pace	travel	shoestring	trade	silver|disc	music
setting|hen	birds	shopfitter	jobs	silverfish	fish
settlement	geog	shopkeeper	jobs	silver|grey	colour
settlement	govt	shopkeeper	trade	silver|lame	clothes
settlement	trade	shoplifter	law	silver|mine	mineral
settle|with	trade	shoplifter	people	silverside	food
set|to|music	music	shop|window	trade	silver|tree	trees
seven|a|side	sport	short|bonds	trade	silverware	house
seventh|son	family	shortbread	food	Simnel|cake	food
Sevres|ware	art	shortcrust	food	simple|time	music
sewing|room	archit	short|range	war	sine|qua|non	foreign
sextennial	time	short|score	music	single|file	sport
Seychelles	islands	short|sheep	animals	single|game	sport
shadowgram	art	short|sight	medic	single|prop	travel
shadow|show	theatre	short|spell	time	single|vote	govt
shallow|fry	food	short|story	lit	sinologist	jobs
shanghaier	jobs	short|tacks	sport	sisal|grass	plants
shaped|note	music	short|waves	physics	six|shooter	war
share|index	trade	shovelhead	fish	sixth|sense	medic
sharp|frost	weather	show|jumper	sport	sixth|sense	myth
shaving|kit	clothes	show|of|work	art	skateboard	sport
shearwater	birds	shrew|mouse	animals	sketchbook	art
sheathbill	birds	shunt|motor	machine	skew|bridge	archit
sheep|louse	insects	Siamese|cat	animals	skew|corbel	archit
sheep's|eyes	animals	sick|as|a|dog	medic	ski|jumping	sport
sheepshank	travel	sickle|bill	birds	skilled|man	trade
sheep's|head	food	sickliness	medic	skin|diving	sport
sheet|metal	mineral	sick|market	trade	ski|running	sport
sheet|music	music	sidesaddle	sport	ski|sweater	clothes
shell|shock	war	sidesaddle	travel	sky|jumping	sport
Shibboleth	Bible	side|street	travel	skyscraper	archit
shibboleth	educ	side|stroke	sport	skyscraper	travel
shibboleth	lit	sidewinder	insects	sky|writing	travel
shibboleth	relig	siegecraft	war	slave|trade	trade
shield|fern	plants	siege|train	war	sleeveless	clothes
shillelagh	war	signal|flag	herald	slide|valve	machine
shipmaster	travel	signet|ring	jewels	slime|mould	plants
shipwright	jobs	signwriter	jobs	slim|volume	lit
Shire|horse	animals	silent|film	film/TV	sling|paint	art
shirred|egg	food	silhouette	art	slingstone	mineral
shirtdress	clothes	silhouette	clothes	slipstream	travel
shirt|frill	clothes	silk|screen	machine	slit|trench	war
shirtfront	clothes	silly|mid|on	sport	slivowitza	drink
shish|kebab	food	silly|point	sport	sloop|of|war	travel
shoe|buckle	clothes	silver|bell	trees	slow|bowler	sport

slow|market	trade	sonata|form	music
sluice|gate	machine	song|leader	music
small|hours	time	songstress	jobs
small|scale	geog	songstress	music
small|sword	war	song|thrush	birds
smart|aleck	people	song|writer	music
smart|money	trade	soon|enough	time
smattering	educ	sooth|sayer	myth
smock|frock	clothes	sooth|sayer	relig
smoke|stone	mineral	sorbic|acid	chem
smoking|cap	clothes	sore|throat	medic
smoking|car	travel	soubriquet	lit
smooth|bore	war	sound|board	music
snaffle|bit	animals	sound|mixer	jobs
snake|stone	mineral	sour|pickle	food
snap|dragon	flowers	sousaphone	music
sneak|thief	law	spacecraft	physics
sneak|thief	people	spacecraft	travel
snow|flurry	weather	spacewoman	jobs
snow|plough	machine	spallation	physics
snow|squall	weather	Spanish|fly	insects
soap|flakes	house	spare|wheel	travel
soap|powder	house	spatchcock	food
social|lion	people	speaker|key	music
social|wasp	insects	spear|grass	plants
socio|drama	lit	specialist	educ
socio|drama	theatre	specialist	jobs
soda|syphon	drink	specialist	medic
sodium|lamp	chem	speciality	trade
soft|market	trade	specialize	educ
soft|palate	medic	spectacles	clothes
solan|goose	birds	spectacles	medic
solar|cycle	astron	speculator	jobs
solar|flare	astron	speculator	trade
solar|topee	clothes	speed|limit	govt
soldier|ant	insects	speed|limit	travel
soldier|fly	insects	speed|trial	sport
sole|agency	trade	sperm|whale	animals
solo|flight	travel	sphacelate	medic
solubility	chem	sphinx|moth	insects
somatology	biol	spider|crab	fish
somatology	medic	spider's|web	insects
somersault	sport	spiderwort	plants
Somerville	Shakesp	spike|shoes	sport
son|and|heir	family	spill|blood	war

spinal|cord	medic
spin|bowler	sport
spinel|ruby	jewels
spinel|ruby	mineral
spirit|lamp	house
spirograph	medic
spirometer	biol
spirometer	measure
spirometer	medic
splanchnic	medic
split|level	archit
split|shift	trade
spoilsport	people
spondulies	trade
sponge|cake	food
spoonerism	lit
sports|coat	clothes
sport|shirt	clothes
sports|suit	clothes
sportswear	clothes
sportswear	sport
spot|stroke	sport
spotted|dog	food
spotted|ray	fish
spring|buck	animals
spring|hare	animals
spring|lock	machine
spring|tail	animals
spring|tide	marine
spring|tide	time
spring|time	geog
spring|time	time
spring|wood	trees
springwort	plants
spy|catcher	jobs
squanderer	people
square|away	travel
Square|Deal	govt
square|feet	measure
square|foot	measure
square|inch	measure
square|meal	food
square|mile	measure
square|neck	clothes
square|ring	sport

square|root	maths	step|dancer	jobs	storymaker	lit
square|sail	travel	step|dancer	theatre	stovehouse	art
square|yard	measure	stepfather	family	strabismus	medic
squeeze|box	music	step|ladder	house	Stradivari	music
squeteague	fish	stepmother	family	straitened	trade
squint|eyes	medic	step|rocket	physics	Strasbourg	cities
stabilizer	physics	step|rocket	travel	strategist	govt
stadholder	govt	stepsister	family	strategist	jobs
staff|nurse	jobs	stereotype	art	strategist	war
staff|nurse	medic	stereotype	lit	strathspey	music
stag|beetle	insects	stereotype	machine	strathspey	sport
stage|boxes	theatre	sterilizer	biol	stratiform	geog
stagecoach	travel	sterilizer	medic	Stravinsky	music
stagecraft	theatre	stewardess	jobs	strawberry	fruit
stage|fever	theatre	stewardess	travel	straw|voter	govt
stalactite	geog	St|Gotthard	mounts	streamline	travel
stalagmite	geog	stick|up|man	jobs	street|arab	people
stall|plate	herald	stiff|drink	drink	street|band	music
stamp|album	sport	stillicide	law	Stresemann	leaders
stand|first	travel	still|water	geog	strict|diet	medic
stand|guard	war	stinkstone	mineral	strike|camp	sport
staple|diet	food	stirrup|cup	drink	strike|root	plants
starmonger	jobs	stitchwort	plants	Strindberg	writers
star|stream	astron	St|Lawrence	rivers	string|bean	veg
Starveling	Shakesp	St|Nicholas	myth	stringendo	music
state|barge	travel	stock|cards	sport	strip|light	house
statecraft	govt	stockhorse	animals	strip|light	machine
Statehouse	govt	stock|issue	trade	strip|tease	theatre
state|of|war	war	stockpiles	trade	stroganoff	food
state|trial	law	stockrider	jobs	stroke|play	sport
static|tube	travel	stocktaker	jobs	stronghold	archit
statistics	govt	stonecraft	art	stronghold	trade
statistics	maths	stone|horse	animals	stronghold	war
statistics	trade	stonemason	jobs	strongroom	trade
statuesque	art	stone|snipe	birds	strong|wind	weather
statute|cap	govt	stony|broke	trade	structural	archit
statute|law	law	stop|thrust	sport	strychnine	medic
stavesacre	flowers	storage|jar	house	stuffed|egg	food
stay|tackle	machine	storehouse	archit	subalgebra	maths
steelmaker	jobs	storesmith	jobs	sub|culture	educ
steel|plate	art	storiology	lit	subheading	lit
steelworks	trade	stork's|bill	flowers	sublingual	medic
steep|price	trade	stormblast	weather	submachine	war
steep|slope	geog	storm|cloud	weather	submariner	jobs
stenograph	machine	storm|track	weather	submariner	travel

submediant	*music*	supercargo	*jobs*	swordsmith	*jobs*
submission	*sport*	supercargo	*travel*	swordstick	*war*
subscriber	*jobs*	supersonic	*physics*	sworn|enemy	*war*
subsequent	*geog*	supersonic	*travel*	symphonion	*music*
subsequent	*time*	supertonic	*music*	symphonist	*jobs*
subsidence	*geog*	supervisor	*educ*	symphonist	*music*
sub|species	*animals*	supervisor	*jobs*	synchroton	*physics*
substitute	*jobs*	supplicant	*jobs*	syncopated	*music*
substitute	*sport*	supply|ship	*travel*	syncopator	*jobs*
substitute	*theatre*	supporters	*herald*	syncopator	*music*
substratum	*geog*	suppressor	*machine*	synecdoche	*lit*
subterrene	*geog*	suprarenal	*medic*	syntactics	*lit*
subtrahend	*maths*	sure|as|a|gun	*war*	synthronus	*relig*
subtropics	*geog*	surf|riding	*sport*	Syrian|bear	*animals*
succession	*govt*	surrealism	*art*	Syrphus|fly	*insects*
sucking|pig	*animals*	surrealist	*art*	tabernacle	*relig*
sucking|pig	*food*	suspenders	*clothes*	tablecloth	*house*
suede|shoes	*clothes*	suspension	*chem*	table|knife	*house*
suffragist	*govt*	suspension	*govt*	table|linen	*house*
sugar|apple	*fruit*	suspension	*machine*	tablespoon	*house*
sugar|candy	*food*	suspension	*music*	tablespoon	*measure*
sugar|daddy	*people*	suspension	*sport*	tachometer	*machine*
sugar|maple	*trees*	suspension	*travel*	tachometer	*measure*
sugar|mouse	*food*	Sutherland	*artists*	tachometer	*travel*
sui|generis	*foreign*	suzerainty	*govt*	tachymetry	*measure*
sulphation	*chem*	Sverdlovsk	*cities*	tagged|atom	*physics*
summer|duck	*birds*	Swan|of|Avon	*lit*	tailor|bird	*birds*
summer|heat	*weather*	swap|horses	*trade*	tailor|made	*clothes*
summer|teal	*birds*	sweat|gland	*medic*	tail|wagger	*animals*
summertide	*geog*	sweat|shirt	*clothes*	take|a|flier	*trade*
summertide	*time*	sweepstake	*sport*	take|a|trick	*sport*
summertime	*geog*	sweetbread	*food*	take|to|arms	*war*
summertime	*time*	sweet|briar	*flowers*	tale|teller	*lit*
sum|of|money	*trade*	sweet|brier	*flowers*	talk|turkey	*birds*
sun|bathing	*sport*	sweetheart	*family*	Talleyrand	*leaders*
sun|bittern	*birds*	sweet|stuff	*food*	tallow|tree	*trees*
sun|compass	*travel*	swell|organ	*music*	tally|clerk	*jobs*
Sunday|best	*clothes*	swell|pedal	*music*	tallywoman	*jobs*
Sunderland	*cities*	swing|chair	*house*	tambourine	*music*
sunglasses	*clothes*	switchback	*sport*	Tananarive	*cities*
sun|parlour	*archit*	switchback	*travel*	tanker|ship	*travel*
sun|parlour	*house*	switchgear	*machine*	Tannhauser	*lit*
sunray|lamp	*machine*	sword|dance	*sport*	Tannhauser	*titles*
sun|worship	*myth*	sword|fight	*war*	tantony|pig	*animals*
superaltar	*relig*	sword|grass	*plants*	tap|dancing	*theatre*

tarantella	*music*	tennis|shoe	*sport*	thermistor	*physics*
tarantella	*sport*	ten|pounder	*war*	thermopile	*physics*
tardigrade	*animals*	teratology	*medic*	thermostat	*house*
target|boat	*travel*	terminator	*astron*	thermostat	*machine*
tartuffery	*relig*	terra|cotta	*archit*	thermostat	*physics*
taskmaster	*jobs*	terra|cotta	*art*	the|Royal|we	*govt*
taskmaster	*people*	terra|cotta	*colour*	The|Seagull	*titles*
taskmaster	*trade*	terra|firma	*geog*	The|Seasons	*titles*
tawny|eagle	*birds*	terry|cloth	*clothes*	The|Tempest	*titles*
tax|evation	*trade*	tessallate	*art*	the|Tempter	*myth*
taxi|driver	*jobs*	test|flight	*travel*	The|Trojans	*titles*
tea|biscuit	*food*	test|rocket	*travel*	the|unities	*theatre*
tea|clipper	*travel*	test|rocket	*war*	thick|knees	*birds*
team|spirit	*sport*	tetrachord	*music*	thick|space	*lit*
tear|jerker	*theatre*	tetragonal	*maths*	thill|horse	*animals*
tea|service	*house*	tetrameter	*lit*	thimbleful	*measure*
technetium	*chem*	tetrastich	*lit*	thin|margin	*trade*
technetium	*mineral*	tetratomic	*physics*	third|party	*jobs*
technician	*jobs*	thale|cress	*plants*	third|party	*law*
technician	*trade*	theatre|box	*theatre*	third|reich	*govt*
technocrat	*jobs*	theatreman	*theatre*	Third|World	*trade*
technocrat	*trade*	theatrical	*theatre*	thirty|love	*sport*
technology	*chem*	The|Borough	*titles*	this|minute	*time*
technology	*physics*	the|cap|fits	*clothes*	threadbare	*clothes*
telegraphy	*physics*	The|Citadel	*titles*	threepence	*money*
tclegraphy	*travel*	the|Commons	*govt*	three|phase	*physics*
Telemachus	*myth*	the|critics	*film/TV*	thrombosis	*medic*
telepathic	*travel*	the|critics	*theatre*	throne|room	*govt*
televiewer	*jobs*	the|Dickens	*myth*	throughput	*comput*
television	*film/TV*	The|Dunciad	*titles*	thrown|goal	*sport*
television	*house*	The|Dynasts	*titles*	Thruthvang	*myth*
television	*machine*	The|Inferno	*titles*	Thucydides	*writers*
television	*physics*	The|Kingdom	*titles*	thumb|a|lift	*travel*
television	*travel*	the|needful	*trade*	ticker|tape	*machine*
telewriter	*travel*	theodolite	*geog*	ticker|tape	*trade*
tell|a|story	*lit*	theodolite	*measure*	ticker|tape	*travel*
telpherage	*travel*	The|Odyssey	*titles*	Tiergarten	*animals*
temperance	*relig*	theologian	*relig*	tiger|badge	*sport*
temperance	*virtues*	theologist	*relig*	tiger|shark	*fish*
temptation	*relig*	The|Only|Way	*titles*	tiger|snake	*insects*
tenderfoot	*educ*	The|Planets	*titles*	tight|skirt	*clothes*
tenderfoot	*jobs*	The|Prelude	*titles*	tilewright	*jobs*
tenderfoot	*war*	thereafter	*time*	timber|wolf	*animals*
tenderloin	*food*	The|Relapse	*titles*	timekeeper	*jobs*
tennis|ball	*sport*	thermistor	*machine*	timekeeper	*sport*

timekeeper	*time*	
timeliness	*time*	
time server	*people*	
time signal	*time*	
time switch	*house*	
time switch	*machine*	
time switch	*physics*	
time thrust	*sport*	
time to come	*time*	
time to kill	*time*	
timing gear	*machine*	
Tinker Bell	*lit*	
tin soldier	*sport*	
tintometer	*measure*	
Tintoretto	*artists*	
tin whistle	*music*	
tip up lorry	*travel*	
title deeds	*law*	
title fight	*sport*	
tobacco jar	*house*	
toe scratch	*sport*	
toiletries	*clothes*	
toilet roll	*house*	
toilet soap	*clothes*	
toilet soap	*house*	
toll bridge	*travel*	
tomato soup	*drink*	
tomato worm	*insects*	
Tom Collins	*drink*	
tone poetry	*music*	
tonic chord	*music*	
tonic major	*music*	
tonic minor	*music*	
tonic sol fa	*music*	
tonic spasm	*medic*	
tonic water	*drink*	
Tono Bungay	*titles*	
toothbrush	*clothes*	
toothbrush	*house*	
toothpaste	*clothes*	
toothpaste	*house*	
toothpaste	*medic*	
topgallant	*travel*	
topography	*geog*	
toponymics	*medic*	

torrid zone	*geog*	
touch paper	*war*	
Touchstone	*Shakesp*	
touchstone	*mineral*	
touring car	*travel*	
tourmaline	*jewels*	
tourmaline	*mineral*	
tournament	*sport*	
tourniquet	*medic*	
tour of duty	*trade*	
tour skiing	*sport*	
tout de meme	*foreign*	
toxicology	*medic*	
toy soldier	*sport*	
toy spaniel	*animals*	
toy terrier	*animals*	
trace horse	*animals*	
tracker dog	*animals*	
track event	*sport*	
track layer	*travel*	
trade board	*trade*	
trade cycle	*trade*	
trade guild	*trade*	
trade price	*trade*	
trade route	*geog*	
trade route	*trade*	
trade union	*govt*	
trade union	*trade*	
traffic jam	*travel*	
trafficker	*jobs*	
trafficker	*law*	
tragicomic	*theatre*	
train ferry	*travel*	
trajectile	*war*	
trajectory	*travel*	
trajectory	*war*	
tramontana	*geog*	
trampoline	*sport*	
transcribe	*music*	
transducer	*machine*	
transistor	*house*	
transistor	*physics*	
transition	*music*	
transition	*physics*	
transitive	*lit*	

transitory	*time*	
translator	*jobs*	
transplant	*medic*	
transplant	*plants*	
traumatism	*medic*	
travelling	*travel*	
travel sick	*travel*	
travel worn	*travel*	
treaty port	*trade*	
treble clef	*music*	
treble viol	*music*	
trec mallow	*plants*	
tree of life	*trees*	
tree tomato	*trees*	
tremolando	*music*	
trench coat	*clothes*	
triaconter	*travel*	
trial match	*sport*	
trial scene	*theatre*	
triangular	*maths*	
Triangulum	*myth*	
tricennial	*time*	
trilateral	*maths*	
triniscope	*physics*	
trinket box	*house*	
tripehound	*jobs*	
tripewoman	*jobs*	
triphibian	*travel*	
triple jump	*sport*	
triple peel	*sport*	
triple time	*music*	
triple time	*time*	
triplicate	*maths*	
trivalence	*chem*	
trochanter	*medic*	
trochotron	*physics*	
troglodyte	*people*	
trolley bus	*travel*	
trombonist	*jobs*	
trombonist	*music*	
tropic bird	*birds*	
tropopause	*astron*	
troubadour	*lit*	
troubadour	*music*	
troy weight	*measure*	

true|course	*travel*	typing|pool	*trade*	urbi|et|orbi	*foreign*
true|to|form	*sport*	typography	*lit*	urinalysis	*medic*
true|to|life	*lit*	ulceration	*medic*	useful|lift	*travel*
trust|house	*archit*	ultimately	*time*	usquebaugh	*drink*
truth|serum	*medic*	ultra|vires	*foreign*	usurpation	*law*
trypan|blue	*colour*	unbeliever	*relig*	utility|man	*theatre*
tryptophan	*chem*	Uncle|Remus	*lit*	utopianist	*people*
tub,thumper	*people*	Uncle|Remus	*titles*	vacillator	*people*
tumbledown	*archit*	Uncle|Vanya	*titles*	vacuum|pump	*machine*
tumble|turn	*sport*	underagent	*jobs*	vacuum|tube	*machine*
tumbleweed	*plants*	underbrush	*trees*	Valparaiso	*cities*
tumescence	*medic*	undercliff	*geog*	vampire|bat	*animals*
tuning|fork	*music*	undercroft	*archit*	vanilla|pod	*veg*
tuning|pipe	*music*	underlinen	*clothes*	vanity|case	*clothes*
tuning|wire	*music*	underpants	*clothes*	vanity|case	*travel*
turbulence	*weather*	undershirt	*clothes*	Vanity|Fair	*titles*
turkey|cock	*birds*	undershoot	*travel*	vanity|lamp	*house*
turkey|trot	*sport*	under|siege	*war*	vanquisher	*war*
Turkish|cat	*animals*	underskirt	*clothes*	vantage|set	*sport*
turn|turtle	*insects*	under|steam	*travel*	vapour|lamp	*machine*
turpentine	*art*	understudy	*jobs*	Vardhamana	*myth*
turpentine	*trees*	understudy	*theatre*	Vardon|grip	*sport*
turret|room	*archit*	undertaker	*jobs*	variations	*music*
turret|ship	*travel*	undertaker	*relig*	varicotomy	*medic*
turtle|dove	*birds*	underworld	*govt*	variety|act	*theatre*
turtle|neck	*clothes*	underworld	*myth*	vaudeville	*theatre*
turtle|soup	*drink*	underwrite	*trade*	veal|cutlet	*food*
tweedledee	*jobs*	undress|wig	*law*	vegetarian	*jobs*
tweedledee	*music*	undulation	*geog*	vegetarian	*people*
tweedledum	*jobs*	unemployed	*trade*	vegetation	*geog*
tweedledum	*music*	unilateral	*maths*	vegetation	*plants*
twelfth|man	*sport*	union|pipes	*music*	velocipede	*travel*
twelvefold	*measure*	univalence	*chem*	veneration	*relig*
twelve|note	*music*	university	*archit*	ventilator	*archit*
twin|triode	*machine*	university	*educ*	ventilator	*house*
twist|drill	*tools*	upholstery	*house*	ventilator	*machine*
two|wheeler	*travel*	upper|class	*govt*	verbal|note	*lit*
type|matter	*lit*	upper|crust	*govt*	verbal|noun	*lit*
typescript	*lit*	upper|crust	*people*	vermicelli	*food*
typesetter	*jobs*	upper|fifth	*educ*	vernacular	*lit*
typesetter	*lit*	upper|house	*govt*	versecraft	*lit*
typewriter	*lit*	upper|sixth	*educ*	versed|sine	*maths*
typewriter	*machine*	upper|stock	*clothes*	versemaker	*jobs*
typewriter	*trade*	upper|third	*educ*	versemaker	*lit*
typing|pool	*jobs*	upset|price	*trade*	versesmith	*jobs*

versesmith	*lit*	
vertebrate	*animals*	
very⎟seldom	*time*	
vesicotomy	*medic*	
vespertime	*time*	
veteran⎟car	*travel*	
veterinary	*jobs*	
veterinary	*medic*	
V⎟formation	*travel*	
vibraphone	*music*	
vice⎟consul	*jobs*	
vice⎟master	*jobs*	
Vichy⎟water	*drink*	
Vichy⎟water	*medic*	
Victoriana	*house*	
victualler	*jobs*	
Vienna⎟loaf	*food*	
Vienna⎟roll	*food*	
view⎟finder	*art*	
vigilantes	*govt*	
Vile⎟Bodies	*titles*	
Villa⎟Lobos	*music*	
villanella	*music*	
villanelle	*lit*	
vinegar⎟eel	*fish*	
vinegar⎟fly	*insects*	
vine⎟grower	*jobs*	
vintage⎟car	*travel*	
virgin⎟knot	*clothes*	
viscometer	*chem*	
viscometer	*measure*	
visibility	*geog*	
vital⎟force	*medic*	
vital⎟spark	*medic*	
vital⎟stain	*biol*	
viviparous	*biol*	
vocabulary	*educ*	
vocabulary	*lit*	
vocal⎟cords	*medic*	
vocal⎟music	*music*	
vocal⎟score	*music*	
volitation	*travel*	
volleyball	*sport*	
volplaning	*travel*	
voltameter	*measure*	

voltameter	*physics*	
volt⎟ampere	*measure*	
volt⎟ampere	*physics*	
volunteers	*war*	
voters⎟roll	*govt*	
wading⎟bird	*birds*	
wad⎟of⎟notes	*trade*	
waffle⎟iron	*house*	
wage⎟earner	*jobs*	
wage⎟freeze	*trade*	
wage⎟policy	*trade*	
wage⎟worker	*jobs*	
wainwright	*jobs*	
Wake⎟Island	*islands*	
Waldteufel	*music*	
walk⎟of⎟life	*trade*	
walk⎟on⎟part	*theatre*	
wallflower	*flowers*	
wallflower	*people*	
wall⎟lizard	*insects*	
wall⎟pepper	*plants*	
wall⎟socket	*house*	
Wall⎟Street	*trade*	
wampum⎟belt	*clothes*	
wanderings	*travel*	
wanderlust	*travel*	
waning⎟moon	*astron*	
war⎟goddess	*war*	
warm⎟colour	*art*	
warming⎟pan	*house*	
War⎟Requiem	*titles*	
washbasket	*house*	
wash⎟bottle	*chem*	
Washington	*USpres*	
Washington	*cities*	
watch⎟chain	*clothes*	
watch⎟glass	*house*	
watchmaker	*jobs*	
watch⎟night	*relig*	
watchstrap	*clothes*	
watch⎟tower	*archit*	
waterbloom	*plants*	
water⎟clock	*house*	
water⎟clock	*machine*	
water⎟clock	*time*	

watercraft	*travel*	
water⎟cress	*veg*	
water⎟elder	*flowers*	
waterflood	*geog*	
water⎟front	*geog*	
water⎟gauge	*geog*	
water⎟gauge	*machine*	
water⎟gauge	*physics*	
water⎟glass	*art*	
water⎟guard	*jobs*	
water⎟icing	*food*	
water⎟lemon	*flowers*	
water⎟level	*physics*	
watermelon	*fruit*	
water⎟mouse	*animals*	
Water⎟Music	*titles*	
water⎟nymph	*myth*	
water⎟ousel	*birds*	
water⎟plane	*travel*	
waterproof	*clothes*	
waterscape	*art*	
water⎟snake	*insects*	
waterspout	*geog*	
water⎟still	*chem*	
water⎟table	*geog*	
watertight	*travel*	
water⎟tower	*machine*	
water⎟wheel	*machine*	
water⎟wings	*sport*	
water⎟witch	*myth*	
waterworks	*trade*	
wave⎟length	*physics*	
wavy⎟border	*herald*	
wax⎟etching	*art*	
waxing⎟moon	*astron*	
wax⎟process	*art*	
way⎟station	*travel*	
way⎟traffic	*travel*	
wealthyman	*trade*	
weather⎟eye	*weather*	
weathering	*geog*	
weatherman	*weather*	
weather⎟map	*weather*	
weaver⎟bird	*birds*	
web⎟spinner	*insects*	

wedding day	*time*	widow's mite	*relig*	winter moth	*insects*
weed killer	*agric*	widow's peak	*clothes*	wintertide	*geog*
Weimaraner	*animals*	Wieniawski	*music*	wintertide	*time*
well afford	*trade*	wild animal	*animals*	wintertime	*geog*
well heeled	*trade*	wild cherry	*fruit*	wintertime	*time*
Wellington	*cities*	wildebeest	*animals*	wireworker	*jobs*
Wellington	*clothes*	wilderness	*geog*	wishing cap	*myth*
Wellington	*war*	wilderness	*plants*	witchcraft	*myth*
well versed	*educ*	wilderness	*relig*	witch hazel	*medic*
well wisher	*people*	wild flower	*flowers*	witch hazel	*trees*
Welsh onion	*veg*	wild indigo	*plants*	with the sun	*time*
Westward Ho	*titles*	wilful foul	*sport*	witness box	*law*
wet weather	*weather*	Wilhelmina	*names*	wolframite	*mineral*
whale shark	*fish*	Williamson	*music*	wolf's peach	*veg*
wharfinger	*jobs*	Willoughby	*Shakesp*	wolf spider	*insects*
wheat field	*cereal*	willow herb	*flowers*	woman hater	*people*
wheat midge	*insects*	willow wand	*sport*	wonder drug	*medic*
wheel chair	*medic*	willow weed	*plants*	Wonderland	*myth*
wheel chair	*travel*	willow wren	*birds*	woodcarver	*art*
wheelhouse	*travel*	Willy Nilly	*lit*	woodcarver	*jobs*
whensoever	*time*	win by a head	*sport*	woodcutter	*jobs*
whippers in	*sport*	Winchester	*chem*	wooden ware	*house*
whirl drill	*tools*	Winchester	*war*	woodgrouse	*birds*
whirlybird	*travel*	Windermere	*lakes*	woodpecker	*birds*
whisk broom	*house*	wind jammer	*travel*	wood pigeon	*birds*
whisky sour	*drink*	windowpane	*house*	wood shrike	*birds*
whist drive	*sport*	window sash	*house*	wood sorrel	*flowers*
white bread	*food*	window seat	*house*	wood thrush	*birds*
white cedar	*trees*	window shop	*trade*	woodworker	*jobs*
White House	*govt*	window sill	*house*	wool carder	*jobs*
white light	*physics*	windscreen	*travel*	wool comber	*jobs*
white magic	*myth*	wind sleeve	*weather*	woolly bear	*animals*
White Paper	*govt*	Windsor tie	*clothes*	wool sorter	*jobs*
white sauce	*food*	wind tunnel	*machine*	wool winder	*jobs*
white thorn	*trees*	wind tunnel	*physics*	word coiner	*lit*
white whale	*animals*	wine basket	*house*	word seller	*lit*
Whitmonday	*time*	winebibber	*jobs*	Wordsworth	*writers*
Whitsunday	*time*	winebibber	*people*	work basket	*house*
wholesaler	*jobs*	wine bottle	*house*	workfellow	*jobs*
wholesaler	*trade*	wine cellar	*house*	working day	*trade*
whole wheat	*cereal*	wine cooler	*house*	working man	*jobs*
wicker work	*house*	winewaiter	*jobs*	workmaster	*jobs*
wicket door	*archit*	wing collar	*clothes*	workpeople	*jobs*
wicket gate	*archit*	wing mirror	*travel*	work to rule	*trade*
widely read	*educ*	winning gun	*sport*	worry beads	*house*

worshipper	*jobs*	X‚radiation	*physics*	yield|point	*chem*
worshipper	*relig*	Yap|Islands	*islands*	young|blood	*people*
wrap‚around	*clothes*	Yarborough	*sport*	young|entry	*sport*
wraprascal	*clothes*	yard|tackle	*machine*	Young|Fogey	*people*
wren‚thrush	*birds*	years|on|end	*time*	your|honour	*law*
wristwatch	*clothes*	yellow|bird	*birds*	zabaglione	*food*
wristwatch	*time*	yellow|jack	*medic*	zebra|finch	*birds*
writership	*lit*	yellow|root	*flowers*	Zerbinetta	*lit*
written|law	*law*	yellow|spot	*medic*	zero|valent	*chem*
written|off	*trade*	yellow|weed	*flowers*	zincograph	*art*
Wycliffite	*relig*	yellow|wood	*trees*	zircon|lamp	*machine*
xenophobia	*medic*	yellow|wort	*flowers*	zoophysics	*biol*
xerography	*physics*	yesteryear	*time*	zwitterion	*physics*
xiphopagus	*animals*	Yggdrasill	*myth*	zylography	*art*

11 LETTERS

Aaron's|beard	*flowers*	accountancy	*trade*
abandon|ship	*travel*	account|book	*trade*
abecedarian	*educ*	accumulator	*machine*
abecedarian	*jobs*	accumulator	*physics*
abecedarian	*lit*	accumulator	*sport*
abecedarium	*educ*	achievement	*herald*
Abergavenny	*Shakesp*	achromatism	*art*
abnormality	*medic*	achromatism	*physics*
abortionist	*medic*	acidulation	*chem*
abracadabra	*myth*	acquittance	*trade*
abstract|art	*art*	acrylic|acid	*chem*
abstraction	*art*	actinic|rays	*physics*
academician	*educ*	actinometer	*measure*
academician	*jobs*	actinometer	*physics*
accelerando	*music*	active|voice	*lit*
accelerator	*biol*	actor's|agent	*jobs*
accelerator	*chem*	actor's|agent	*theatre*
accelerator	*machine*	actor's|lines	*theatre*
accelerator	*physics*	acute|accent	*lit*
accelerator	*travel*	Adam's|needle	*plants*
accipitrine	*birds*	ad|avizandum	*foreign*
accompanist	*jobs*	ad|infinitum	*foreign*
accompanist	*music*	Adirondacks	*mounts*

adjournment	*govt*	all,star,cast	*theatre*	
adjournment	*time*	almond|icing	*food*	
adolescence	*time*	almond|paste	*food*	
A|Doll's|House	*titles*	alphabetics	*lit*	
adventuress	*people*	alpine|plant	*plants*	
adversative	*lit*	altar|carpet	*relig*	
advertising	*trade*	altar|facing	*relig*	
Aeolian|harp	*music*	alto,relievo	*art*	
aeronautics	*travel*	amboyna|wood	*trees*	
Aesculapius	*myth*	American|elm	*trees*	
aetatis|suae	*foreign*	amontillado	*drink*	
Afghan|hound	*animals*	amor|patriae	*foreign*	
African|teak	*trees*	amour,propre	*foreign*	
afterburner	*machine*	amphetamine	*medic*	
afterburner	*travel*	amphisbaena	*myth*	
aftercooler	*machine*	anachronism	*lit*	
after|dinner	*time*	anachronism	*time*	
after|shroud	*travel*	anacoluthia	*lit*	
against|time	*time*	Anacreontic	*lit*	
agglomerate	*chem*	anaesthesia	*medic*	
agglutinate	*biol*	anaesthetic	*medic*	
agnosticism	*relig*	anaglyptics	*art*	
agrarianism	*govt*	an|apple|a|day	*fruit*	
agriculture	*agric*	an|apple|a|day	*medic*	
agriculture	*trade*	anchor|fluke	*travel*	
ahead|of|time	*time*	anchor|light	*machine*	
aide|memoire	*foreign*	anchovy|pear	*fruit*	
aiguillette	*clothes*	ancient|coat	*herald*	
air|controls	*travel*	Andromedids	*astron*	
airsickness	*medic*	animal|lover	*people*	
airsickness	*travel*	anniversary	*time*	
air|terminal	*travel*	antechamber	*archit*	
airtight|jar	*house*	anticathode	*physics*	
air,to|ground	*war*	anticyclone	*weather*	
air|umbrella	*travel*	antifebrile	*medic*	
alexandrine	*lit*	anti,missile	*war*	
alexandrite	*clothes*	antineutron	*physics*	
alexandrite	*mineral*	antiphrasis	*lit*	
Alfred|Polly	*lit*	antipyretic	*medic*	
aliquot|part	*maths*	antiquarian	*jobs*	
alla|tedesca	*music*	antique|shop	*trade*	
allez,vous,en	*foreign*	antirrhinum	*flowers*	
All|Fool's|day	*time*	antispastic	*lit*	
All|Souls|day	*time*	antistrophe	*lit*	
all,star|bill	*theatre*	anti,tank|gun	*war*	

antonomasia *lit*
Aonian|fount *myth*
Aonian|mount *myth*
aphrodisiac *medic*
apologetics *relig*
a|posteriori *foreign*
appeal|court *law*
apple|brandy *drink*
application *medic*
appointment *govt*
appointment *jobs*
appointment *trade*
arbitration *law*
Arcades|ambo *foreign*
archduchess *govt*
arch,heretic *relig*
archipelago *geog*
arch,prelate *relig*
arctic|front *weather*
area|bombing *war*
aristocracy *govt*
Aristomenes *myth*
armed|combat *war*
armed|forces *war*
arm|of|the|law *law*
arm|of|the|sea *marine*
armoured|car *travel*
armoured|car *war*
army|officer *jobs*
arraignment *law*
arrangement *music*
arrivederci *foreign*
arsenic|acid *chem*
Artemidorus *Shakesp*
arteriotomy *medic*
Arthur|Kipps *lit*
articulated *travel*
arts|college *educ*
asking|price *trade*
aspergillum *relig*
assassin|bug *insects*
assault|boat *travel*
assignments *herald*
association *trade*
assumed|name *law*

a|star|is|born *theatre*
astigmatism *medic*
astrologist *jobs*
astronomist *jobs*
As|You|Like|It *titles*
A|Tale|of|a|Tub *titles*
at|face|value *trade*
at|intervals *time*
atmospheric *archit*
atom|counter *physics*
atomic|clock *physics*
atomic|power *machine*
atomic|table *chem*
atomologist *chem*
atomologist *physics*
atom|smasher *physics*
attack|plane *travel*
attainments *educ*
attenuation *biol*
attestation *law*
attributive *lit*
au|contraire *foreign*
auction|ring *trade*
audio|typist *jobs*
Auger|effect *physics*
Augustinium *relig*
auscultator *medic*
Austral|zone *geog*
authorcraft *lit*
authorities *govt*
author's|copy *lit*
autostarter *machine*
auxanometer *biol*
auxiliaries *war*
avec|plaisir *foreign*
avocado|pear *fruit*
avoirdupois *measure*
backbencher *govt*
back|country *geog*
backroom|boy *jobs*
bactericide *medic*
baffle|plate *physics*
bag|of|tricks *theatre*
bag|snatcher *jobs*
bag|snatcher *law*

Baily's beads	*astron*
baker's dozen	*measure*
baking sheet	*house*
ballad maker	*lit*
ballad maker	*music*
ballad opera	*music*
ball bearing	*machine*
balletomane	*theatre*
balloon sail	*travel*
banana split	*food*
bank account	*trade*
bank balance	*trade*
bank cashier	*jobs*
bank holiday	*trade*
bank manager	*jobs*
bank manager	*trade*
bank of issue	*trade*
bank robbery	*law*
Baranquilla	*cities*
barbiturate	*medic*
Barclaycard	*trade*
bargain sale	*trade*
barge couple	*archit*
bargemaster	*jobs*
barge stones	*archit*
barley broth	*drink*
barley sugar	*food*
barley water	*drink*
barnstormer	*theatre*
barnstormer	*war*
barrel dress	*clothes*
barrel organ	*music*
barrel scale	*machine*
barrel vault	*archit*
barrier lake	*geog*
bar sinister	*herald*
Bartholomew	*Bible*
Bartholomew	*names*
barycentric	*physics*
baseball bat	*sport*
basket cells	*medic*
basket chair	*house*
basketmaker	*jobs*
basset hound	*animals*
bass passage	*music*

bastard type	*lit*
bastard wing	*birds*
bathing suit	*clothes*
bathysphere	*geog*
battery lamp	*machine*
battle array	*war*
battledress	*war*
battlefield	*war*
battle order	*war*
battleplane	*travel*
battle plane	*war*
battle royal	*war*
Bay of Bengal	*seas*
Bay of Plenty	*seas*
beachcomber	*people*
beach master	*war*
bead curtain	*house*
beaker flask	*chem*
beam antenna	*machine*
beam balance	*machine*
bear account	*trade*
bearbaiting	*sport*
bear's breech	*flowers*
bear the cost	*trade*
bear witness	*law*
beast of prey	*animals*
beat a tattoo	*music*
beaten track	*travel*
beat the drum	*music*
Beaufort Sea	*seas*
beauty queen	*jobs*
beauty sleep	*clothes*
bedevilment	*myth*
beef extract	*drink*
beef sausage	*food*
beehawk moth	*insects*
belaying pin	*travel*
Belgian hare	*animals*
bellbottoms	*clothes*
belle epoque	*foreign*
Bellerophon	*myth*
bell founder	*jobs*
bellheather	*plants*
bellows fish	*fish*
bell ringing	*music*

bell|ringing	*sport*
below|stairs	*house*
Benedictine	*drink*
Benedictine	*relig*
benediction	*relig*
beneficiary	*jobs*
Bengal|spear	*sport*
benthoscope	*biol*
benzene|ring	*chem*
benzoic|acid	*chem*
bersaglieri	*war*
besiegement	*war*
best|clothes	*clothes*
betting|ring	*sport*
betting|shop	*trade*
bevel|square	*machine*
biased|bowls	*sport*
Bible|reader	*people*
Bible|school	*educ*
bibliolater	*lit*
bibliolatry	*educ*
bibliomania	*educ*
bibliophage	*lit*
bibliophile	*educ*
bibliophile	*lit*
bibliotheca	*lit*
bicarbonate	*chem*
bicentenary	*time*
bicycle|pump	*machine*
bid|farewell	*travel*
bien|entendu	*foreign*
bifocal|lens	*physics*
big|business	*trade*
big|game|hunt	*sport*
bill|chamber	*law*
billionaire	*trade*
bill|of|costs	*trade*
billsticker	*jobs*
binary|digit	*comput*
binary|digit	*maths*
binary|scale	*comput*
binary|scale	*maths*
bingo|caller	*jobs*
bioengineer	*biol*
biographist	*lit*

bipartition	*biol*
bipartition	*maths*
biquadratic	*maths*
bird|fancier	*jobs*
bird|watcher	*jobs*
bishop's|lawn	*herald*
bishop's|ring	*jewels*
bishop's|ring	*relig*
Bismarck|Sea	*seas*
bitter|herbs	*relig*
bittersweet	*fruit*
black|and|tan	*govt*
Black|Beauty	*titles*
black|beetle	*insects*
black|butter	*food*
black|cattle	*animals*
black|coffee	*drink*
black|comedy	*lit*
black|comedy	*theatre*
black|grouse	*birds*
black|letter	*lit*
blackmailer	*law*
blackmailer	*people*
black|market	*law*
black|market	*trade*
black|martin	*birds*
black|patent	*clothes*
black|pepper	*food*
black|velvet	*clothes*
blank|cheque	*trade*
blasphemous	*relig*
blind|corner	*travel*
blind|flying	*travel*
blockbuster	*war*
blood|sister	*family*
blood|stream	*medic*
blood|stroke	*medic*
bloodsucker	*animals*
bloodsucker	*insects*
blood|vessel	*medic*
bloody|shirt	*war*
Blucher|boot	*clothes*
blue|clothes	*clothes*
blue|eyed|boy	*people*
blues|singer	*music*

blue|thistle	*plants*		brace|and|bit	*tools*
blunderbuss	*war*		Brackenbury	*Shakesp*
board|member	*jobs*		braggadocio	*people*
board|school	*educ*		Brahmaputra	*rivers*
boating|pond	*sport*		brain|teaser	*educ*
Bob|Cratchit	*lit*		brake|lining	*machine*
body|and|soul	*relig*		bramble|bush	*fruit*
body|builder	*jobs*		brandy|sauce	*food*
body|politic	*govt*		brandy|smash	*drink*
body|servant	*jobs*		breadcrumbs	*food*
boiled|shirt	*clothes*		breadwinner	*jobs*
boilermaker	*jobs*		breadwinner	*trade*
boilersmith	*jobs*		break|ground	*travel*
Bolingbroke	*Shakesp*		breaking|out	*medic*
bombardment	*war*		breastplate	*herald*
Bombay|spear	*sport*		breastplate	*war*
bomber|pilot	*war*		breathalyse	*law*
bomb|release	*war*		Brenner|Pass	*mounts*
bonne|bouche	*food*		bridgemaker	*jobs*
bonus|scheme	*trade*		bright|pupil	*educ*
book|binding	*lit*		brine|shrimp	*fish*
bookishness	*educ*		bring|to|book	*lit*
bookishness	*lit*		brisk|market	*trade*
book|keeping	*trade*		bristletail	*insects*
book|learned	*lit*		British|Army	*war*
Book|of|books	*lit*		British|Navy	*war*
Book|of|Books	*relig*		Britomartis	*myth*
book|of|verse	*lit*		brittleness	*chem*
book|printer	*lit*		broadcaster	*film/TV*
book|selling	*lit*		broadcaster	*jobs*
bookshelves	*house*		broad|comedy	*theatre*
book|support	*lit*		Brobdingnag	*myth*
booster|dose	*medic*		broken|chord	*music*
bottle|green	*colour*		bronze|medal	*sport*
bottom|glade	*geog*		bronzesmith	*jobs*
bottom|price	*trade*		Brooks|Range	*mounts*
boulder|clay	*geog*		broom|handle	*house*
Boule|de|Suif	*titles*		brown|madder	*colour*
boutonniere	*clothes*		brush|stroke	*art*
boutonniere	*flowers*		brush|turkey	*birds*
bow|and|arrow	*sport*		buck|private	*war*
bow|and|arrow	*war*		budget|price	*trade*
boxer|shorts	*clothes*		Buenos|Aires	*cities*
boxing|match	*sport*		buffalo|wolf	*animals*
boysenberry	*fruit*		buffer|state	*geog*

buffer|state	govt
built|up|area	travel
bull|account	trade
bull|baiting	sport
bulletproof	war
bullfighter	jobs
bull|mastiff	animals
bullock|cart	travel
bull|terrier	animals
bunny|rabbit	animals
buoyant|mine	war
bureaucracy	govt
burglarious	law
burgomaster	govt
Buridan's|ass	animals
bur|marigold	plants
burning|bush	relig
burning|bush	trees
burnt|almond	food
burnt|orange	colour
burnt|sienna	colour
bushfighter	jobs
bushwhacker	war
businessman	jobs
businessman	trade
butcher|bird	birds
butcher's|saw	tools
Butskellism	govt
butter|beans	veg
butter|knife	house
Butterworth	music
button|shoes	clothes
buttressing	archit
butyric|acid	chem
bygone|times	time
cabbage|moth	insects
cabbage|palm	trees
cabbage|rose	flowers
cabbage|tree	trees
cabbage|worm	insects
cable|length	measure
Cabot|Strait	seas
cabriole|leg	house
caesarotomy	medic
Caius|Lucius	Shakesp

cajuput|tree	trees
Cakes|and|Ale	titles
calceolaria	flowers
calcination	chem
calculation	maths
calibration	chem
calibration	measure
californium	chem
calling|crab	fish
calliophone	music
calorimeter	chem
calorimeter	measure
calorimetry	chem
calorimetry	measure
camel's|thorn	trees
cameraderie	war
cam|follower	machine
campaign|hat	clothes
campaniform	archit
campanology	music
Canada|goose	birds
canary|grass	plants
candelabrum	house
candidature	govt
candleberry	fruit
candlemaker	jobs
candle|power	measure
candlestick	house
candy|stripe	clothes
canine|tooth	medic
canned|music	music
canoe|slalom	sport
canvas|shoes	clothes
cap|and|bells	clothes
cap|and|bells	theatre
Cape|buffalo	animals
capillarity	physics
capital|city	geog
capital|city	govt
capital|gain	trade
capriccioso	music
Capricornus	myth
Captain|Ahab	lit
Captain|Hook	lit
Captain|Vere	lit

caravansary *archit*
carbonation *chem*
carbon|light *machine*
carbon|paper *trade*
carburetter *travel*
carburettor *machine*
card|compass *travel*
cardinal|red *colour*
cardiograph *medic*
cardophagus *animals*
carminative *medic*
carmine|lake *colour*
carnot|cycle *physics*
carriage|dog *animals*
carriageway *travel*
carrick|bend *travel*
carrion|crow *birds*
car|salesman *jobs*
car|sickness *medic*
carte|du|jour *foreign*
cartography *geog*
Carver|Doone *lit*
case|history *medic*
cash|account *trade*
cassiterite *mineral*
castellated *war*
caster|sugar *food*
Castile|soap *food*
casting|vote *govt*
castle|guard *war*
Castlereagh *leaders*
casual|shoes *clothes*
casual|water *sport*
catachresis *lit*
cataclastic *geog*
catallactic *trade*
catastrophe *theatre*
catch|a|train *travel*
catch|phrase *lit*
caterpillar *insects*
caterpillar *machine*
caterpillar *travel*
caterpillar *war*
cathode|rays *physics*
Catholicism *relig*

cats|and|dogs *weather*
cat's|concert *music*
cat's|pyjamas *animals*
cat's|squirrel *animals*
cat's|whisker *travel*
cattle|thief *law*
cattle|thief *people*
caught|short *trade*
cauliflower *veg*
Cavaradossi *lit*
cavo|relievo *art*
ceaselessly *time*
celery|stick *veg*
cellulation *biol*
centenarian *people*
centigramme *measure*
central|bank *trade*
centreboard *travel*
centrepiece *house*
cephalalgia *medic*
ceramic|ware *art*
cerographer *art*
ceroplastic *art*
certificate *educ*
certificate *trade*
chafing|dish *house*
chain|smoker *people*
chairperson *govt*
chamberlain *govt*
chamberlain *jobs*
Chamberlain *leaders*
chamberlain *trade*
chambermaid *jobs*
chancellery *trade*
change|sides *war*
channel|bass *fish*
Channel|swim *sport*
chansonette *music*
chanterelle *music*
chanterelle *plants*
Chanticleer *birds*
chapel|royal *relig*
charcoalist *art*
charcoalist *jobs*
chariot|race *sport*

charity|show	*theatre*
Charlemagne	*war*
charmed|life	*myth*
charm|school	*educ*
Charpentier	*music*
cheer|leader	*jobs*
cheer|leader	*sport*
cheese|board	*house*
cheese|cloth	*clothes*
cheese|maker	*jobs*
cheese|parer	*people*
chef|d'oeuvre	*art*
Chelyabinsk	*cities*
chemiatrist	*medic*
chemist|shop	*trade*
che|sera|sera	*foreign*
Cheshire|cat	*animals*
chiaroscuro	*art*
chicken|farm	*agric*
chicken|feed	*food*
chicken|soup	*drink*
chilli|sauce	*food*
chimney|tops	*archit*
china|figure	*house*
Chinese|clay	*art*
Chinese|silk	*clothes*
Chinoiserie	*house*
Chippendale	*house*
chiroplasty	*medic*
chiropodist	*jobs*
chiropodist	*medic*
chiropraxis	*medic*
chive|garlic	*plants*
chloric|acid	*chem*
chlorophyll	*biol*
chloroplast	*biol*
choirmaster	*jobs*
choirmaster	*music*
choir|stalls	*relig*
chokecherry	*fruit*
choking|coil	*machine*
chorography	*geog*
choroid|coat	*medic*
Christendom	*relig*
christening	*relig*
Christopher	*names*
chrome|green	*colour*
chrome|lemon	*colour*
chromic|acid	*chem*
chromoplast	*biol*
chronograph	*time*
chronometer	*time*
chronometry	*measure*
chronoscope	*time*
chrysoberyl	*jewels*
chrysoberyl	*mineral*
chrysocracy	*trade*
chrysoprase	*jewels*
chrysoprase	*mineral*
church|court	*relig*
church|mouse	*animals*
church|mouse	*relig*
cinder|track	*sport*
Cinemascope	*people*
circular|saw	*tools*
circulation	*lit*
circulation	*medic*
circulation	*trade*
circumpolar	*geog*
cirrus|cloud	*weather*
citrus|fruit	*fruit*
City|of|David	*relig*
civil|arrest	*law*
civil|rights	*govt*
civil|rights	*law*
civvy|street	*govt*
clairvoyant	*jobs*
clam|chowder	*food*
clarinetist	*music*
clarion|call	*music*
class|fellow	*educ*
class|racing	*sport*
clavicymbal	*music*
cleft|palate	*medic*
clergywoman	*jobs*
cliff|hanger	*lit*
cliff|hanger	*theatre*
climate|zone	*geog*
climatology	*geog*
clinochlore	*mineral*

clodhoppers *clothes*
cloisonnage *art*
closed chain *chem*
close friend *people*
close hauled *travel*
close season *sport*
closing down *trade*
clothes line *house*
clothes moth *insects*
clothes pole *house*
cloth of gold *clothes*
clove pepper *food*
club topsail *travel*
coach driver *travel*
coachwright *jobs*
coagulation *biol*
coal scuttle *house*
coat of paint *art*
coauthoress *jobs*
cobalt bloom *chem*
cobalt green *colour*
Cochin china *birds*
cock a doodle *birds*
cockleshell *travel*
cock sparrow *birds*
coconscious *medic*
coconut moth *insects*
coconut palm *trees*
codling moth *insects*
cod liver oil *biol*
cod liver oil *medic*
coeducation *educ*
coefficient *maths*
coefficient *physics*
coexistence *govt*
coffee break *drink*
coffee house *archit*
coffee table *house*
coffin maker *jobs*
cognoscenti *jobs*
coincidence *time*
cold therapy *medic*
cold weather *weather*
cold welding *machine*
collectanea *lit*

college bred *educ*
college girl *educ*
collegianer *educ*
Collingwood *war*
colonelship *govt*
colonialism *govt*
colorimeter *art*
colorimetry *geog*
colouration *art*
colour blind *art*
colour blind *medic*
colour cycle *art*
colour gamut *art*
colour print *art*
columbarium *birds*
combat plane *travel*
combat train *war*
combination *maths*
comedy drama *theatre*
come forward *travel*
comestibles *food*
come to terms *trade*
comic relief *theatre*
commandment *relig*
comme il faut *foreign*
commentator *jobs*
commentator *lit*
commentator *theatre*
commodities *trade*
common chord *music*
Common Pleas *law*
common scold *people*
common stair *archit*
common stock *trade*
communicant *relig*
compact disc *music*
compact disc *sport*
company rule *trade*
compartment *archit*
compartment *travel*
compendious *lit*
compensator *machine*
competition *trade*
competitive *trade*
compilation *lit*

complainant	*law*	Continental	*geog*
composition	*art*	continually	*time*
composition	*lit*	contract|law	*law*
composition	*music*	contractual	*law*
comptometer	*machine*	contraprops	*travel*
comptometer	*maths*	contrapunto	*music*
comptometer	*trade*	contredanse	*music*
compurgator	*law*	contributor	*jobs*
computation	*maths*	contributor	*lit*
concertante	*music*	convallaria	*flowers*
concert|band	*music*	conventicle	*relig*
concert|hall	*archit*	convergence	*geog*
concert|hall	*music*	convertible	*travel*
concert|hall	*theatre*	conveyancer	*jobs*
concordance	*lit*	conveyancer	*law*
concurrence	*time*	Convocation	*relig*
conditional	*lit*	convolution	*medic*
condominium	*govt*	convolvulus	*flowers*
conductance	*physics*	convulsions	*medic*
confederate	*govt*	cookery|book	*house*
confessions	*lit*	cooking|wine	*drink*
confinement	*law*	cooling|coil	*machine*
confinement	*medic*	cooling|tray	*house*
congressman	*govt*	cool|million	*trade*
congressman	*jobs*	cooperative	*trade*
conjugation	*lit*	coordinates	*maths*
conjunction	*lit*	coordinator	*jobs*
conjunctiva	*medic*	coparcenary	*law*
conjunctive	*lit*	coping|stone	*archit*
connoisseur	*art*	copper|beech	*trees*
connoisseur	*people*	copperplate	*art*
connotation	*lit*	coppersmith	*jobs*
consecutive	*music*	copperworks	*trade*
conspirator	*jobs*	coral|island	*geog*
Constantine	*names*	coram|populo	*foreign*
constituent	*chem*	corn|ear|worm	*insects*
constituent	*govt*	cornerstone	*archit*
constrictor	*insects*	corn|in|Egypt	*cereal*
consumption	*medic*	corn|in|Egypt	*trade*
consumption	*trade*	corn|plaster	*medic*
consumptive	*medic*	coronagraph	*astron*
contact|lens	*clothes*	corporation	*govt*
contact|lens	*medic*	corporation	*trade*
contaminate	*chem*	correlative	*lit*
contentious	*war*	corrigendum	*lit*

corroborate	law	crawl|stroke	sport
cosmography	astron	crazy|paving	archit
cosmosphere	astron	cream|cheese	food
cost,benefit	trade	credit|title	film/TV
cotoneaster	trees	crematorium	relig
cottage|loaf	food	crenellated	archit
cotton|grass	plants	crepuscular	time
cottonmouth	insects	crested|helm	herald
cotton|plant	plants	cricket|ball	sport
counterbase	music	cricket|pads	sport
counterfeit	trade	crimewriter	jobs
counterflux	geog	criminal|law	law
counterglow	geog	criminology	law
countermine	war	crimson|lake	colour
counterpane	house	crocodilian	insects
counterseal	herald	croquet|arch	sport
counterterm	lit	croquet|ball	sport
countervair	herald	croquet|hoop	sport
country|girl	people	croquet|lawn	sport
country|road	travel	cross|swords	sport
country|rock	mineral	crowd|of|sail	travel
country|seat	archit	crown|antler	animals
countryside	geog	crowned|head	govt
country|town	geog	crown|lawyer	jobs
country|walk	sport	crown|prince	govt
county|court	law	cruciferous	plants
county|match	sport	crucifixion	relig
coup|de|grace	sport	crystalline	physics
court|jester	jobs	cubic|system	maths
court|tennis	sport	cub|reporter	jobs
cover|charge	food	cub|reporter	lit
cover|charge	trade	cuckoo|clock	house
cover|ground	travel	cuckoo|clock	time
cowslip|wine	drink	cultivation	agric
crabbed|hand	lit	culture|tube	biol
crack|of|dawn	time	cum|dividend	trade
crack|troops	war	Curia|Romana	relig
crag|and|tail	geog	curling|pond	sport
crambo|clink	lit	curling|rink	sport
crane|driver	jobs	curry|powder	food
crash|course	educ	curtain|call	theatre
crash|helmet	clothes	curtain|hook	house
crash|helmet	sport	curtain|rail	house
crash|helmet	travel	curtain|ring	house
crash|waggon	travel	custard|tart	food

custom house	*trade*	delinquence	*trade*
customs duty	*trade*	delinquency	*law*
cutaway coat	*clothes*	delivery man	*jobs*
cyanine blue	*colour*	delivery van	*travel*
cycle racing	*sport*	demand curve	*trade*
cyma reversa	*archit*	demarcation	*trade*
cypher clerk	*jobs*	demibastion	*war*
cypress knee	*plants*	demigoddess	*myth*
cytophysics	*physics*	demi₁leopard	*herald*
Dail Eireann	*govt*	demographer	*jobs*
dairy cattle	*animals*	demonolatry	*myth*
daisy cutter	*animals*	Demosthenes	*leaders*
daisy cutter	*sport*	denominator	*maths*
dame's violet	*plants*	Denry Machin	*lit*
damper pedal	*music*	deobstruent	*medic*
danger money	*trade*	deposit slip	*trade*
Daniel Quilp	*lit*	de profundis	*foreign*
Dardanelles	*seas*	depth charge	*machine*
Dar es Salaam	*cities*	depth charge	*war*
dark glasses	*clothes*	dermaplasty	*medic*
dark lantern	*machine*	dermatology	*medic*
day after day	*time*	descant viol	*music*
day and night	*time*	description	*lit*
day in day out	*time*	descriptive	*lit*
day labourer	*jobs*	desert snail	*insects*
dead as a dodo	*birds*	dessert fork	*house*
deadly enemy	*people*	destination	*travel*
dead of night	*time*	devaluation	*trade*
dean of women	*jobs*	devilled egg	*food*
decanal side	*relig*	devilled ham	*food*
deck of cards	*sport*	diagnostics	*medic*
declaration	*govt*	Diana monkey	*animals*
declaration	*war*	diaphoretic	*medic*
decolletage	*clothes*	dichromatic	*art*
decrepitude	*medic*	diet of proof	*law*
decrescendo	*music*	differenced	*herald*
deep blue sea	*marine*	diffraction	*physics*
deep fine leg	*sport*	digest of law	*law*
deep therapy	*medic*	dimidiation	*herald*
deerstalker	*clothes*	dining table	*house*
defence bond	*trade*	dinner dress	*clothes*
degringoler	*foreign*	dinner party	*food*
de haut en bas	*foreign*	diplomatics	*govt*
dehydration	*chem*	dipsomaniac	*people*
delineation	*art*	direct party	*sport*

directrices	*maths*	dormant|lion	*herald*
disarmament	*govt*	Dostoievsky	*writers*
discography	*music*	dotted|minim	*music*
discoloured	*art*	double|agent	*jobs*
discotheque	*music*	double|chant	*music*
disjunctive	*lit*	double|check	*sport*
dislocation	*medic*	double|cream	*food*
display|arms	*herald*	double|cross	*law*
display|case	*trade*	double|eagle	*money*
dissertator	*lit*	double|entry	*trade*
dissolution	*chem*	double|fault	*sport*
dissolution	*govt*	double|fugue	*music*
dissyllable	*lit*	double|helix	*chem*
distaff|side	*herald*	double|march	*travel*
distributor	*jobs*	double|sharp	*music*
distributor	*machine*	double|touch	*music*
distributor	*trade*	Douglas|Home	*leaders*
distributor	*travel*	dovetail|saw	*tools*
dithyrambic	*lit*	downhill|run	*sport*
dithyrambus	*lit*	down|payment	*trade*
Dittersdorf	*music*	Drakensberg	*mounts*
dittography	*lit*	drama|school	*theatre*
dive|bombing	*war*	dramatic|art	*theatre*
divided|stop	*music*	dramaticism	*theatre*
dividend|off	*trade*	dramaturgic	*theatre*
divine|right	*govt*	draught|beer	*drink*
Divine|right	*relig*	draughtsman	*art*
diving|board	*sport*	draughtsman	*jobs*
diving|dress	*sport*	drawing|room	*archit*
doctrinaire	*govt*	drawing|room	*house*
documentary	*film/TV*	dreadnought	*clothes*
dodecagonal	*maths*	dreadnought	*travel*
dog's|mercury	*plants*	Dresden|blue	*colour*
dolly|camera	*machine*	dress|circle	*theatre*
Dolly|Varden	*fish*	dressed|crab	*food*
Dolly|Varden	*lit*	dress|length	*clothes*
dominant|key	*music*	dressmaking	*clothes*
Don|Giovanni	*lit*	dress|shield	*clothes*
Don|Giovanni	*titles*	drilling|rig	*tools*
Donna|Elvira	*lit*	drill|master	*jobs*
Don|Pasquale	*lit*	drinker|moth	*insects*
Don|Pasquale	*titles*	drive|a|trade	*trade*
door|knocker	*house*	driving|iron	*sport*
Dora|Spenlow	*lit*	driving|rain	*weather*
Dorian|modes	*music*	driving|test	*travel*

Dr Malatesta	*lit*
drop curtain	*theatre*
drug peddler	*jobs*
drusy cavity	*geog*
dulcet tones	*music*
dull sighted	*medic*
duplex house	*archit*
dust counter	*geog*
dusty miller	*flowers*
Dutch cheese	*food*
duty officer	*govt*
duty officer	*jobs*
dyer's rocket	*plants*
dynamometer	*machine*
dynamometer	*measure*
dynamometer	*physics*
eager beaver	*animals*
eager beaver	*people*
ear for music	*music*
earn a living	*trade*
earthenware	*art*
earthenware	*house*
earth metals	*mineral*
earth pillar	*geog*
earth's crust	*geog*
earth tremor	*geog*
eating apple	*fruit*
eating house	*archit*
eating irons	*house*
eccrinology	*biol*
eccrinology	*medic*
echo chamber	*film/TV*
echo sounder	*machine*
echo sounder	*marine*
echo sounder	*physics*
eclecticism	*art*
economic law	*trade*
economic man	*trade*
economy size	*trade*
Edgar Linton	*lit*
egg and spoon	*sport*
Egyptian cat	*animals*
Einsteinium	*physics*
ejector seat	*travel*
Elastoplast	*medic*

elbow grease	*house*
electioneer	*govt*
electric arc	*machine*
electric eel	*fish*
electric eye	*machine*
electrician	*jobs*
electrician	*theatre*
electricity	*physics*
electric saw	*tools*
electrolyte	*physics*
electron gun	*tools*
electronics	*physics*
electrotype	*art*
electrotype	*lit*
electrotype	*machine*
elephantine	*animals*
elimination	*biol*
elixir vitae	*medic*
Ellen Orford	*lit*
Elzevir book	*lit*
embarrassed	*trade*
embracement	*law*
embrocation	*medic*
embroiderer	*jobs*
empanelment	*govt*
emperor moth	*insects*
emplacement	*war*
enchantment	*myth*
enchiridion	*lit*
endless time	*time*
endocardium	*medic*
endorsement	*trade*
endothermal	*chem*
enemy action	*war*
enfeoffment	*law*
engaged line	*travel*
engine block	*machine*
engineering	*physics*
engine gauge	*travel*
engine of war	*machine*
engine of war	*war*
English horn	*music*
English pink	*colour*
engrailment	*herald*
engravement	*art*

engrossment	*law*	everlasting	*time*
engrossment	*lit*	every|moment	*time*
enlargement	*art*	Eve's|pudding	*food*
enlightened	*educ*	examination	*educ*
enlisted|man	*jobs*	examination	*law*
enlisted|man	*war*	examination	*medic*
entablature	*archit*	exclamation	*lit*
entertainer	*film/TV*	exculpation	*law*
entertainer	*jobs*	executioner	*jobs*
entertainer	*theatre*	executioner	*law*
entire|horse	*animals*	exeunt|omnes	*theatre*
entrainment	*travel*	exhaust|pipe	*machine*
enumeration	*maths*	exhaust|pipe	*travel*
envelopment	*sport*	exhaust|port	*machine*
envelopment	*war*	ex|hypothesi	*foreign*
environment	*biol*	exoneration	*law*
environment	*geog*	exoskeleton	*medic*
epidiascope	*physics*	expectorant	*medic*
Epistle|side	*relig*	expenditure	*trade*
equal|voices	*music*	exploration	*geog*
equidistant	*maths*	ex|post|facto	*foreign*
equilateral	*maths*	extemporize	*music*
equilibrium	*maths*	extenuation	*law*
equinoctial	*geog*	extortioner	*jobs*
equity|court	*law*	extradition	*law*
ergatocracy	*govt*	extremities	*medic*
escape|hatch	*travel*	fabrication	*trade*
escape|route	*travel*	face|lifting	*medic*
eschatology	*relig*	facial|nerve	*medic*
escheatment	*law*	factory|acts	*law*
established	*trade*	factory|hand	*jobs*
estate|agent	*jobs*	fair|hearing	*law*
estate|agent	*trade*	faith|healer	*jobs*
estate|in|fee	*law*	falling|star	*astron*
etching|ball	*art*	fallow|finch	*birds*
etymologist	*jobs*	false|acacia	*plants*
eurhythmics	*music*	false|arrest	*law*
eurhythmics	*sport*	false|attack	*sport*
evaporation	*chem*	family|album	*house*
evening|gown	*clothes*	family|bible	*relig*
evening|mist	*weather*	famine|fever	*medic*
evening|star	*astron*	fan|tail|dove	*birds*
ever|and|a|day	*time*	fan|vaulting	*archit*
ever|and|anon	*time*	fares|please	*travel*
everlasting	*flowers*	farm|produce	*agric*

farthingale	*clothes*
fast breeder	*physics*
fata Morgana	*geog*
Father Brown	*lit*
father in law	*family*
fatty tissue	*medic*
faux bourdon	*music*
feature film	*film/TV*
feeler gauge	*machine*
fellow pupil	*educ*
femme fatale	*people*
fence lizard	*insects*
fencing mask	*sport*
Ferris wheel	*machine*
Ferris wheel	*sport*
festal board	*food*
festschrift	*lit*
fetch a price	*trade*
fetch candle	*myth*
fibre optics	*medic*
fibre optics	*physics*
fiddlestick	*music*
field events	*sport*
field magnet	*machine*
field worker	*jobs*
fieri facias	*law*
fife and drum	*music*
fifteen love	*sport*
fifth column	*govt*
fifth column	*jobs*
fighting man	*jobs*
fighting man	*war*
figured bass	*music*
figure eight	*sport*
Fiji Islands	*islands*
filing block	*machine*
filing clerk	*jobs*
fillet steak	*food*
filter paper	*chem*
filthy lucre	*trade*
fin de siecle	*time*
find one's way	*travel*
fine feather	*clothes*
finger board	*music*
finger grass	*plants*

fingerprint	*law*
fingersmith	*jobs*
fingerstall	*medic*
fipple flute	*music*
fire a volley	*war*
fire brigade	*jobs*
fire curtain	*theatre*
firelighter	*house*
fireside rug	*house*
fire tactics	*war*
fire watcher	*jobs*
fire worship	*myth*
firing party	*war*
firing squad	*law*
firing squad	*war*
firing table	*war*
first aid box	*house*
first attack	*sport*
first cousin	*family*
first eleven	*sport*
first fiddle	*music*
first fruits	*relig*
first person	*lit*
first strike	*war*
first violin	*music*
fishing boat	*travel*
fishing dory	*travel*
fishing frog	*animals*
fishing line	*sport*
fishtailing	*travel*
fissionable	*physics*
fission bomb	*war*
fixed assets	*trade*
fixed income	*trade*
flag captain	*jobs*
flag officer	*herald*
flag officer	*jobs*
flaming June	*weather*
flank mutton	*food*
flannelette	*clothes*
flared skirt	*clothes*
flare rocket	*war*
flash camera	*art*
flat dweller	*jobs*
fleet of foot	*travel*

Fleet|Street	*lit*
flesh¦colour	*colour*
fleurs¦de¦lys	*herald*
flickertail	*animals*
flick|stroke	*sport*
flight|strip	*travel*
floating|rib	*medic*
floor|broker	*trade*
floor|polish	*house*
floor|trader	*trade*
Florida|Keys	*islands*
flour|weevil	*insects*
flower|nymph	*myth*
flower|of|age	*time*
flow|of|words	*lit*
fluctuation	*trade*
fluorescent	*physics*
fluoroscope	*medic*
fluoroscope	*physics*
fluoroscopy	*physics*
flying|corps	*war*
flying|kites	*travel*
flying|lemur	*animals*
flying|panel	*clothes*
flying|speed	*travel*
flying|squad	*jobs*
flying|squad	*law*
flying|squid	*fish*
flying|start	*sport*
flying|visit	*travel*
fold¦away¦bed	*house*
fomentation	*medic*
football|fan	*sport*
footed|arrow	*war*
footslogger	*war*
foot|soldier	*jobs*
foot|soldier	*war*
foot|the|bill	*trade*
forced|error	*sport*
forced|march	*travel*
forced|march	*war*
force|of|arms	*war*
foreclosure	*law*
foreclosure	*trade*
fore¦topsail	*travel*
for|evermore	*time*
forget¦me¦not	*flowers*
formal|dress	*clothes*
former|pupil	*educ*
former|times	*time*
fortnightly	*lit*
fortnightly	*time*
forward|deck	*travel*
forward|line	*sport*
forward|pass	*sport*
foster|child	*family*
foundations	*archit*
found|guilty	*law*
fountain|pen	*lit*
fox|and|geese	*sport*
Fra|Angelico	*artists*
francophile	*people*
francophobe	*people*
frankfurter	*food*
free|harbour	*trade*
free|radical	*physics*
free|skating	*sport*
freethinker	*people*
French|beans	*veg*
French|berry	*plants*
French|bread	*food*
French|chalk	*art*
French|chalk	*house*
French|pitch	*music*
French|sixth	*music*
French|toast	*food*
French|wines	*drink*
fresh|breeze	*weather*
fresh|butter	*food*
friend|or|foe	*war*
frigid|zones	*weather*
fritto|misto	*foreign*
frontal|wave	*geog*
frontal|zone	*weather*
frozen|north	*geog*
frozen|stiff	*weather*
frozen|water	*weather*
fruit|picker	*jobs*
fuller's|herb	*plants*
full|harness	*war*

full|of|fight	*war*
fulmination	*geog*
fume|cabinet	*chem*
funambulist	*jobs*
fun|and|games	*sport*
functionary	*govt*
functionary	*jobs*
fundamental	*music*
funeral|pile	*relig*
funeral|pyre	*relig*
funeral|song	*music*
furnishings	*house*
future|grain	*trade*
future|price	*trade*
future|tense	*lit*
galanty|show	*theatre*
gale|warning	*weather*
gall|bladder	*medic*
galley|proof	*lit*
galley|slave	*jobs*
galley|slave	*travel*
gallows|bird	*law*
gallows|bird	*people*
gambit|piece	*sport*
gambling|man	*sport*
gambrel|roof	*archit*
games|master	*jobs*
gaming|house	*sport*
gaming|table	*sport*
gammon|steak	*food*
gang|warfare	*war*
garden|chair	*house*
garden|glass	*flowers*
garden|party	*house*
garden|party	*sport*
garden|spade	*tools*
garden|stuff	*plants*
garden|swing	*house*
garnishment	*law*
gas|detector	*chem*
gastrectomy	*medic*
gate|crasher	*people*
gather|speed	*travel*
Gay|Nineties	*time*
Gegenschein	*astron*
generalship	*govt*
generalship	*war*
generic|name	*biol*
Geneva|bands	*relig*
Geneva|cloak	*relig*
Genghis|Khan	*war*
gentlewoman	*govt*
gentlewoman	*jobs*
geopolitics	*govt*
German|flute	*music*
German|sixth	*music*
germination	*agric*
germination	*plants*
germ|warfare	*war*
gerontology	*medic*
gerrymander	*govt*
get|under|way	*travel*
Ghirlandaio	*artists*
ghostwriter	*jobs*
ghostwriter	*lit*
giant|cactus	*plants*
giant|powder	*war*
Gila|monster	*insects*
gilded|spurs	*herald*
gild|the|lily	*art*
gild|the|pill	*medic*
gillyflower	*flowers*
gingerbread	*food*
gingerbread	*trade*
ginger|group	*jobs*
ginger|punch	*drink*
give|a|lesson	*educ*
glass|blower	*art*
glass|blower	*jobs*
glass|cutter	*jobs*
glass|cutter	*tools*
globigerina	*animals*
glottal|stop	*lit*
glove|puppet	*sport*
glyphograph	*art*
gnatcatcher	*birds*
gnawing|pain	*medic*
go|alongside	*travel*
Gog|and|Magog	*myth*
goldenberry	*fruit*

Golden|Bough	*myth*
golden|eagle	*birds*
golden|goose	*myth*
golden|hours	*time*
golden|toned	*music*
golden|trout	*fish*
gold|therapy	*medic*
gone|fishing	*sport*
good|innings	*sport*
good|offices	*govt*
good|old|days	*time*
goods|waggon	*travel*
good|tidings	*relig*
go|overboard	*travel*
Gorgon's|head	*myth*
Gouda|cheese	*food*
grade|school	*educ*
gradiometer	*measure*
graft|hybrid	*plants*
grain|beetle	*insects*
grain|of|sand	*geog*
grammatical	*lit*
Grand|Canary	*islands*
grandfather	*family*
grandmother	*family*
grand|nephew	*family*
grandparent	*family*
grand|salute	*sport*
grand|vizier	*govt*
granny|dress	*clothes*
grant|of|arms	*herald*
Gran|Turismo	*travel*
granule|cell	*medic*
graphic|arts	*art*
graphophone	*music*
grasshopper	*insects*
grave|accent	*lit*
grave|digger	*jobs*
gravel|stone	*mineral*
graven|image	*relig*
grave|robber	*law*
grave|robber	*people*
gravitation	*physics*
gravity|cell	*physics*
grease|paint	*clothes*

grease|paint	*theatre*
great|circle	*geog*
great|octave	*music*
great|primer	*lit*
Greek|chorus	*theatre*
Greek|Church	*relig*
green|bottle	*insects*
green|dragon	*plants*
greengrocer	*jobs*
green|linnet	*birds*
Greenmantle	*titles*
green|pepper	*food*
green|pepper	*veg*
green|turtle	*animals*
griddlecake	*food*
grizzly|bear	*animals*
gross|income	*trade*
ground|floor	*archit*
ground|frost	*weather*
ground|robin	*birds*
groundsheet	*sport*
ground|sloth	*animals*
ground|speed	*travel*
ground|spice	*food*
ground|state	*physics*
ground|swell	*marine*
ground|table	*archit*
ground|to|air	*war*
growing|pain	*medic*
Guadalajara	*cities*
Guadalcanal	*islands*
guelder|rose	*flowers*
guerrillero	*war*
guilty|party	*law*
guinea|grass	*plants*
guipure|lace	*clothes*
Gulf|of|Aqaba	*seas*
Gulf|of|Lions	*seas*
guncarriage	*war*
gunman's|moll	*jobs*
gutter|press	*lit*
guttersnipe	*people*
gynaecology	*medic*
gynecocracy	*govt*
gyrocompass	*travel*

haberdasher	*jobs*	health|salts	*medic*
haemorrhage	*medic*	heart|attack	*medic*
hagiographa	*relig*	hearth|brush	*house*
hagiologist	*relig*	hearthstone	*archit*
hairdresser	*jobs*	heart|urchin	*fish*
hairpin|bend	*sport*	heat|barrier	*physics*
hair|stylist	*jobs*	heavy|armour	*war*
hair|trigger	*machine*	heavy|bomber	*war*
hair|trigger	*war*	heavyweight	*sport*
halcyon|days	*time*	hebdomadary	*time*
half|a|second	*time*	hebephrenia	*medic*
half|brother	*family*	hectic|fever	*medic*
half|cadence	*music*	hectic|flush	*medic*
half|passage	*sport*	Hedda|Gabler	*titles*
halfway|line	*sport*	hedgepriest	*jobs*
haloid|acids	*chem*	heir|general	*govt*
hammersmith	*jobs*	Helen|of|Troy	*myth*
hand|grenade	*war*	heliochrome	*art*
handicapped	*medic*	helping|hand	*people*
hand|me|downs	*clothes*	Henry|Scobie	*lit*
handservant	*jobs*	Heppelwhite	*house*
handwriting	*lit*	heptahedron	*maths*
hanging|post	*archit*	heptavalent	*chem*
happy|ending	*lit*	hereinafter	*time*
Happy|Valley	*myth*	heroic|verse	*lit*
hard|bargain	*trade*	herringbone	*clothes*
hard|drinker	*people*	hesperidium	*fruit*
hardwareman	*jobs*	heterocycle	*chem*
hardy|annual	*flowers*	heteropathy	*medic*
harmonizing	*music*	heterotopes	*biol*
Harp|Quartet	*titles*	hibernation	*animals*
harpsichord	*music*	hide|and|seek	*sport*
Harris|tweed	*clothes*	hierography	*relig*
hart's|tongue	*plants*	high|dudgeon	*war*
harvest|moon	*weather*	higher|court	*law*
harvest|time	*geog*	high|fashion	*clothes*
hasta|manana	*foreign*	high|finance	*trade*
hatchettite	*mineral*	Highland|cow	*animals*
hawse|timber	*travel*	high|sheriff	*govt*
head|for|home	*travel*	high|sheriff	*jobs*
head|of|state	*govt*	high|society	*govt*
head|teacher	*educ*	high|society	*jobs*
head|teacher	*jobs*	high|steward	*govt*
health|foods	*food*	high|treason	*law*
healthiness	*medic*	high|voltage	*physics*

highway|code	*travel*	hound's|berry	*trees*
High|Windows	*titles*	house|arrest	*law*
hill|station	*war*	housekeeper	*jobs*
hippocampus	*fish*	housemaster	*educ*
hippocampus	*myth*	housemaster	*jobs*
Hippocratic	*medic*	housemother	*jobs*
hircocervus	*animals*	House|of|Keys	*govt*
histrionics	*theatre*	housewright	*jobs*
histrionism	*theatre*	huckleberry	*fruit*
hitch|hiking	*sport*	hug|the|shore	*travel*
hit|the|trail	*travel*	human|nature	*people*
HMS|Pinafore	*titles*	Humperdinck	*music*
hobble|skirt	*clothes*	hunger|march	*govt*
hockey|match	*sport*	hunter's|moon	*weather*
hockey|stick	*sport*	hunting|horn	*music*
Hollandaise	*food*	hunting|pink	*colour*
holohedrism	*maths*	hydrocarbon	*chem*
home|and|away	*sport*	hydrogen|ion	*chem*
home|crofter	*jobs*	hydrogenoid	*chem*
homogenizer	*biol*	hydrography	*marine*
homo|sapiens	*people*	hydrometeor	*weather*
honey|badger	*animals*	hydrophobia	*medic*
honey|locust	*trees*	hydrosphere	*marine*
honey|sucker	*birds*	hygroscopic	*biol*
honeysuckle	*flowers*	Hymn|of|Jesus	*titles*
hormonology	*medic*	hyperborean	*weather*
horned|horse	*animals*	hypermarket	*trade*
horned|snake	*insects*	Hypermestra	*myth*
hors|d'oeuvre	*food*	ice|cream|man	*jobs*
horse|doctor	*jobs*	Iceland|moss	*plants*
horse|doctor	*medic*	ice|lollipop	*food*
Horse|Guards	*war*	ice|movement	*geog*
horse|litter	*travel*	ice|yachting	*sport*
horse|market	*trade*	ichnography	*archit*
horse|pistol	*war*	ichnography	*art*
horse|racing	*sport*	ichnography	*geog*
horseradish	*plants*	icosahedron	*maths*
horseradish	*veg*	ides|of|March	*time*
horse|riding	*sport*	igneous|rock	*mineral*
horse|trader	*jobs*	ignis|fatuus	*geog*
hospital|bed	*medic*	ignition|key	*travel*
hospitalize	*medic*	I|Like|it|Here	*titles*
hostilities	*war*	illuminator	*art*
hot|cross|bun	*food*	illuminator	*jobs*
hot|luncheon	*food*	illusionist	*jobs*

illusionist	*theatre*
illustrator	*art*
illustrator	*jobs*
Il|Penseroso	*titles*
Il|Trovatore	*titles*
immediately	*time*
immigration	*travel*
impeachment	*law*
impecunious	*trade*
imperialist	*govt*
imperialist	*people*
impermeable	*chem*
impermeable	*geog*
impersonate	*theatre*
impoundment	*law*
in|an|instant	*time*
incarcerate	*law*
incarnadine	*colour*
incarnation	*relig*
incessantly	*time*
incriminate	*law*
inculcation	*educ*
inculpation	*law*
incunabulum	*lit*
indentation	*geog*
independent	*govt*
Indian|berry	*fruit*
Indian|cress	*flowers*
Indian|Ocean	*seas*
Indian|shawl	*clothes*
indigestion	*medic*
indirect|tax	*law*
indirect|tax	*trade*
in|due|course	*time*
in|duplicate	*govt*
industrials	*trade*
inexpensive	*trade*
infanticide	*law*
infantryman	*jobs*
infantryman	*war*
information	*educ*
informative	*educ*
inhabitancy	*archit*
inheritance	*law*
in|low|relief	*art*

in|medias|res	*foreign*
inner|circle	*govt*
Inner|Temple	*law*
Inns|of|Court	*law*
inoculation	*medic*
inopportune	*time*
in|principio	*foreign*
inquisition	*law*
inscription	*lit*
inscription	*music*
insculpture	*art*
insectarium	*insects*
insecticide	*agric*
insecticide	*biol*
insectivore	*animals*
inside|right	*sport*
inspiration	*lit*
institution	*educ*
institution	*govt*
institution	*trade*
instruction	*educ*
instructive	*educ*
insufflator	*law*
integration	*maths*
intelligent	*educ*
interaction	*chem*
interceptor	*travel*
intercessor	*govt*
intercourse	*trade*
internal|ear	*medic*
interpreter	*jobs*
interregnum	*time*
interrupter	*machine*
interviewer	*jobs*
interviewer	*lit*
in|the|groove	*music*
in|the|saddle	*travel*
in|the|wake|of	*travel*
intravenous	*medic*
invalid|fare	*food*
investiture	*govt*
invigilator	*educ*
ipecacuanha	*medic*
iridescence	*physics*
Irish|coffee	*drink*

Irish|Guards	*war*
Irish|setter	*animals*
Iron|Curtain	*govt*
iron|founder	*jobs*
ironmongery	*machine*
ironmongery	*trade*
iron|pyrites	*mineral*
iron|rations	*food*
iron|rations	*war*
irradiation	*medic*
irradiation	*physics*
irreligious	*relig*
Isle|of|Wight	*islands*
isochronism	*physics*
isodose|line	*medic*
isogeotherm	*geog*
Italian|blue	*colour*
Italian|pink	*colour*
Jack|and|Jill	*titles*
Jack|Dawkins	*lit*
jackpudding	*theatre*
Jaffa|orange	*fruit*
jam|turnover	*food*
Japanese|red	*colour*
Japan|laurel	*trees*
jaunting|car	*travel*
Jehoshaphat	*Bible*
jellied|eels	*food*
Jess|Oakroyd	*lit*
Jimmy|Porter	*lit*
John|of|Gaunt	*Shakesp*
joint|return	*trade*
journeyings	*travel*
Journey's|End	*titles*
journey's|end	*travel*
Judgment|day	*time*
Judith|Paris	*lit*
Judith|Paris	*titles*
jugular|vein	*medic*
jumper|cable	*machine*
jumping|bean	*sport*
junction|box	*machine*
juniper|tree	*trees*
Juno|Curitis	*myth*
jury|process	*law*
Kabibonokka	*myth*
kangaroo|rat	*animals*
katabothron	*geog*
kedge|anchor	*travel*
keep|station	*travel*
Kellogg|pact	*govt*
Kelper's|laws	*astron*
Kelvin|scale	*geog*
keyed|guitar	*music*
key|industry	*trade*
kidney|basin	*medic*
kidney|vetch	*plants*
Kilimanjaro	*mounts*
Kilkenny|cat	*animals*
killer|whale	*animals*
kilted|skirt	*clothes*
kinetic|body	*physics*
kingdom|come	*myth*
Kingdom|Come	*relig*
king|penguin	*birds*
king's|bishop	*sport*
king's|knight	*sport*
king's|ransom	*trade*
king's|speech	*govt*
king's|yellow	*colour*
king|vulture	*birds*
kirk|session	*relig*
kitchenette	*archit*
kitchenette	*house*
kitchen|maid	*jobs*
kitchen|sink	*house*
kitchen|sink	*theatre*
kitchen|unit	*house*
kite|balloon	*travel*
Korea|Strait	*seas*
Koryak|Range	*mounts*
Kuala|Lumpur	*cities*
Labour|party	*govt*
lacing|shoes	*clothes*
lactalbumin	*biol*
lactoflavin	*biol*
Lady|Billows	*lit*
Lady|Capulet	*Shakesp*
lady's|finger	*plants*
lady's|mantle	*flowers*

lake dweller	*geog*
Lake Lucerne	*lakes*
Lake Nipigon	*lakes*
Lake Ontario	*lakes*
laminar flow	*travel*
lammergeier	*birds*
Lammermuirs	*mounts*
lamplighter	*jobs*
lancet style	*archit*
land feature	*geog*
landing beam	*physics*
landing deck	*travel*
landing skis	*travel*
land measure	*geog*
landscapist	*art*
landscapist	*jobs*
land spaniel	*animals*
land steward	*jobs*
land surface	*geog*
land warfare	*war*
lantern fish	*fish*
lanthanides	*chem*
laparoscopy	*medic*
lapis lazuli	*jewels*
lapis lazuli	*mineral*
lap of honour	*sport*
lap of luxury	*trade*
lapse of time	*time*
last offices	*relig*
last request	*law*
laterigrade	*fish*
latticework	*archit*
latus rectum	*maths*
laughing gas	*medic*
laundrymaid	*jobs*
laundry room	*archit*
laundry room	*house*
laurustinus	*trees*
law and order	*law*
law breaking	*law*
lawlessness	*law*
law merchant	*law*
lawn sleeves	*clothes*
lawn sleeves	*relig*
layer of rock	*mineral*

lazy painter	*travel*
leaded glass	*archit*
leading edge	*travel*
leading lady	*jobs*
leading lady	*theatre*
leading note	*music*
league table	*astron*
league table	*sport*
leaseholder	*jobs*
leatherback	*insects*
leatherette	*clothes*
leave taking	*travel*
Le Corbusier	*artists*
lecture hall	*archit*
lecture hall	*educ*
lecture room	*educ*
lectureship	*educ*
ledger clerk	*jobs*
legal action	*law*
legal battle	*law*
legal estate	*law*
legal record	*law*
legal reform	*law*
legal remedy	*law*
legal tender	*law*
legal tender	*trade*
legislation	*law*
legislative	*law*
legislature	*law*
leg of mutton	*clothes*
leg of mutton	*food*
leisure time	*time*
lemon yellow	*colour*
Leoncavallo	*music*
leopardbane	*plants*
leopardskin	*clothes*
lepidoptera	*insects*
lese majeste	*law*
letter paper	*lit*
letterpress	*lit*
letterpress	*machine*
libel action	*law*
liberal arts	*educ*
liberty bond	*trade*
library book	*lit*

lickspittle	*people*	littleboxes	*archit*
liedetector	*law*	LittleEyolf	*titles*
liedetector	*machine*	littlewhile	*time*
lieutenancy	*govt*	LittleWomen	*titles*
lifeboatman	*jobs*	livelongday	*time*
lifedrawing	*art*	livingimage	*art*
lifemanship	*people*	livingimage	*people*
lifesavings	*trade*	LloydWebber	*music*
lightbomber	*war*	loafofbread	*food*
lightbreeze	*weather*	localbranch	*trade*
lightcomedy	*theatre*	localcolour	*art*
lightrepast	*food*	localcolour	*lit*
lightshield	*physics*	localoffice	*trade*
lightswitch	*house*	Lochaberaxe	*war*
lightweight	*sport*	LochKatrine	*lakes*
lignumvitae	*trees*	LochRannoch	*lakes*
limberboard	*travel*	lockforward	*sport*
limitedveto	*govt*	LocrianAjax	*myth*
limitswitch	*machine*	locumtenens	*jobs*
Limogesware	*art*	locumtenens	*medic*
Lincoln'sInn	*law*	locusvector	*maths*
Lindisfarne	*islands*	logarithmic	*maths*
lineengaged	*travel*	loggerheads	*war*
linenbasket	*house*	logographer	*lit*
linencloset	*archit*	lollipopman	*jobs*
lineofgoods	*trade*	Londonpride	*flowers*
lineshooter	*people*	loneprairie	*geog*
linguistics	*lit*	longaccount	*trade*
linksausage	*food*	longlasting	*time*
linographer	*art*	longoverdue	*time*
lionhearted	*animals*	longplaying	*music*
lionhearted	*war*	longservice	*trade*
lionpassant	*herald*	longsighted	*medic*
lionrampant	*herald*	longstretch	*law*
lionsalient	*herald*	lookdaggers	*war*
lipoprotein	*biol*	looptheloop	*sport*
lipoprotein	*chem*	looptheloop	*travel*
liquidation	*trade*	loosechange	*trade*
literaryman	*educ*	loosestrife	*flowers*
literaryman	*lit*	lophobranch	*fish*
lithography	*art*	LordJustice	*law*
lithosphere	*mineral*	LordofHosts	*relig*
litmuspaper	*chem*	LordProvost	*jobs*
litterateur	*educ*	Lord'sprayer	*relig*
litterateur	*lit*	Lord'ssupper	*relig*

lorry driver	*jobs*
lorry driver	*travel*
lose one's way	*travel*
lotus eaters	*myth*
loud speaker	*machine*
Lough Corrib	*lakes*
love fifteen	*sport*
Love for Love	*titles*
love in a mist	*flowers*
loving spoon	*house*
low comedian	*theatre*
lowering sky	*weather*
low pressure	*weather*
lucubration	*lit*
luggage rack	*travel*
Luisa Miller	*lit*
Luisa Miller	*titles*
lunar crater	*astron*
lunar module	*travel*
Lupin Pooter	*lit*
Lutoslawski	*music*
luxuriation	*plants*
lycanthrope	*myth*
lycanthropy	*medic*
Lydian modes	*music*
Lydian stone	*mineral*
lyophilizer	*physics*
lyric poetry	*lit*
Machiavelli	*govt*
Machiavelli	*leaders*
machine made	*machine*
machine made	*trade*
machine shop	*machine*
machine shop	*trade*
machine tool	*tools*
machine work	*machine*
mackerel sky	*weather*
macroscopic	*physics*
madder bloom	*art*
Madeira cake	*food*
made of money	*trade*
Mad Margaret	*lit*
Madonna lily	*flowers*
madrigalist	*jobs*
madrigalist	*music*

Maeterlinck	*writers*
magazine gun	*war*
magic carpet	*myth*
magic carpet	*travel*
magic circle	*myth*
Maginot line	*war*
magisterial	*law*
maidservant	*jobs*
main skysail	*travel*
maintenance	*govt*
main topsail	*travel*
major planet	*astron*
major second	*music*
make believe	*theatre*
make headway	*travel*
make sea room	*travel*
make strides	*travel*
malapropism	*lit*
Malayan bear	*animals*
malfunction	*medic*
malibu board	*sport*
malpractice	*law*
mammee apple	*fruit*
mammoth tree	*trees*
mandolinist	*jobs*
mandolinist	*music*
man from Mars	*travel*
manipulator	*jobs*
manipulator	*physics*
manna lichen	*plants*
man of genius	*people*
man on the run	*law*
man o war bird	*birds*
mansard roof	*archit*
mantelpiece	*archit*
mantelpiece	*house*
mantelshelf	*archit*
manufactory	*trade*
manufacture	*trade*
marchioness	*govt*
march of time	*time*
Mar del Plata	*cities*
Marine Corps	*war*
market place	*trade*
market price	*trade*

Marlborough	*war*
marquisette	*clothes*
marram grass	*plants*
marshalling	*herald*
marshmallow	*food*
Mary Poppins	*titles*
masonry arch	*archit*
masquerader	*jobs*
mass produce	*trade*
master baker	*jobs*
masterpiece	*art*
materialist	*people*
mathematics	*maths*
matinee coat	*clothes*
matinee idol	*jobs*
matinee idol	*theatre*
Mayor of York	*Shakesp*
meadow brown	*insects*
meadow nymph	*myth*
meadow pipit	*birds*
meadow sweet	*flowers*
meat chopper	*house*
meat cleaver	*house*
mechanician	*jobs*
Mechlin lace	*clothes*
median nerve	*medic*
medicine man	*jobs*
medicine man	*medic*
medicine man	*myth*
Megapenthes	*myth*
Meissen ware	*art*
mellifluent	*music*
mellifluous	*music*
mellisonant	*music*
memorabilia	*lit*
memorialist	*jobs*
memorialist	*lit*
memory tubes	*machine*
Menai Strait	*seas*
mendelevium	*chem*
Mendelssohn	*music*
Mendip Hills	*mounts*
mensuration	*chem*
mensuration	*maths*
mensuration	*measure*
mental giant	*people*
merchandise	*trade*
merchantman	*jobs*
merchantman	*travel*
mercury lamp	*machine*
meritocracy	*govt*
merry andrew	*people*
merry andrew	*theatre*
mess steward	*travel*
metal polish	*house*
metalworker	*jobs*
metaphysics	*maths*
meteorology	*weather*
method actor	*jobs*
method actor	*theatre*
mews cottage	*archit*
microscopic	*biol*
microsecond	*time*
microswitch	*machine*
Middlemarch	*titles*
middle years	*time*
middy blouse	*clothes*
midnight sun	*astron*
might of arms	*war*
military law	*law*
military man	*jobs*
military man	*war*
milk pudding	*food*
millionaire	*jobs*
millionaire	*trade*
millisecond	*time*
mimographer	*jobs*
mimographer	*theatre*
mineral coal	*mineral*
mineral salt	*mineral*
mineral vein	*mineral*
minesweeper	*travel*
mine thrower	*war*
miniaturist	*art*
miniaturist	*jobs*
minimum wage	*trade*
ministerial	*govt*
Minnesinger	*music*
minor planet	*astron*
minor second	*music*

mint|of|money	*trade*
Minute|Waltz	*titles*
miracle|drug	*medic*
miracle|play	*lit*
miracle|play	*theatre*
mirror|image	*maths*
misanthrope	*people*
miscarriage	*medic*
miscellanea	*lit*
mise|en|scene	*theatre*
missal|stand	*relig*
Mississippi	*rivers*
mitral|valve	*medic*
mixed|number	*maths*
mixed|voices	*music*
mizzen|royal	*travel*
modern|times	*time*
modern|waltz	*sport*
molybdenite	*mineral*
momentarily	*time*
monasterial	*relig*
money|broker	*trade*
money|dealer	*trade*
moneylender	*jobs*
moneylender	*trade*
money|s|worth	*trade*
money|to|burn	*trade*
monographer	*lit*
monomorphic	*biol*
monovalence	*chem*
monsoon|wind	*weather*
montgolfier	*travel*
monticolous	*geog*
moon|goddess	*myth*
moon|landing	*travel*
moonlighter	*jobs*
moon|station	*travel*
mooring|buoy	*travel*
mooring|mast	*travel*
moral|defeat	*war*
moral|lesson	*educ*
Morgan|le|Fay	*myth*
morning|coat	*clothes*
morning|gown	*clothes*
morning|roll	*food*
morning|room	*archit*
morning|room	*house*
morning|star	*astron*
morning|tide	*time*
morning|time	*time*
morris|dance	*music*
morris|dance	*sport*
morse|signal	*travel*
mortal|wound	*medic*
mortarboard	*clothes*
mortarboard	*educ*
mortarboard	*herald*
mortice|lock	*machine*
Moses|basket	*travel*
mosstrooper	*law*
mother|earth	*myth*
mother|in|law	*family*
mother|s|help	*jobs*
motor|launch	*travel*
motor|racing	*sport*
motor|vessel	*travel*
motu|proprio	*foreign*
mountain|ash	*trees*
mountaineer	*jobs*
mountaineer	*sport*
mountain|gun	*war*
mountaintop	*geog*
Mountbatten	*war*
Mount|Carmel	*mounts*
Mount|Elbert	*mounts*
Mount|Elbrus	*mounts*
Mount|Erebus	*mounts*
Mount|Hermon	*mounts*
Mount|Katmai	*mounts*
Mount|Kazbek	*mounts*
Mr|Pecksniff	*lit*
Mr|Rochester	*lit*
Mrs|Dalloway	*titles*
Mrs|Malaprop	*lit*
Mrs|Slipslop	*lit*
Mr|Standfast	*titles*
Mudjekeavis	*myth*
Mudjekeewis	*lit*
mudslinging	*govt*
multi|access	*comput*

mural circle	*geog*	neck and neck	*sport*
murder squad	*law*	neckerchief	*clothes*
muscovy duck	*birds*	necromancer	*myth*
musculature	*medic*	needle point	*clothes*
museum piece	*art*	needlewoman	*jobs*
musica ficta	*music*	negotiation	*govt*
musical copy	*music*	negotiation	*trade*
musical joke	*music*	Neoptolemus	*myth*
musical note	*music*	ne plus ultra	*foreign*
music critic	*jobs*	neritic zone	*marine*
music lesson	*educ*	nerve ending	*medic*
music lesson	*music*	nerve supply	*medic*
music loving	*music*	nest factory	*trade*
music school	*educ*	netherworld	*myth*
music school	*music*	net interest	*trade*
muskellunge	*fish*	net receipts	*trade*
Mustardseed	*Shakesp*	neurologist	*jobs*
mutton chops	*clothes*	neurologist	*medic*
myrtle grass	*plants*	neuroplasty	*medic*
mystery tour	*sport*	neutralizer	*chem*
mystery tour	*travel*	neutralizer	*medic*
nailed boots	*sport*	never ending	*time*
nail varnish	*clothes*	New Hebrides	*islands*
name dropper	*people*	Newman Noggs	*lit*
Nancy pretty	*flowers*	New Year's day	*time*
Nanga Parbat	*mounts*	New Year's eve	*time*
Napier's rods	*maths*	New York City	*cities*
nasopharynx	*medic*	niacinamide	*chem*
nationalism	*govt*	Nicene Creed	*relig*
nationalist	*people*	Nick Charles	*lit*
nationality	*geog*	nickelodeon	*music*
Nationalrat	*govt*	night and day	*time*
native heath	*geog*	night flower	*flowers*
native lands	*geog*	night hunter	*jobs*
native stone	*mineral*	nightingale	*birds*
naturopathy	*medic*	night letter	*travel*
naval bomber	*war*	night porter	*jobs*
naval forces	*war*	night school	*educ*
naval rating	*jobs*	night sister	*jobs*
naval rating	*travel*	night worker	*jobs*
naval school	*educ*	nihil obstat	*foreign*
naval vessel	*travel*	nitre powder	*war*
navel orange	*fruit*	nitrocotton	*war*
nearsighted	*medic*	nom de guerre	*lit*
near the wind	*travel*	nonpartisan	*govt*

non,stick,pan	*house*	Oliver Twist	*lit*
normal pitch	*music*	Oliver Twist	*titles*
Norman tower	*archit*	olla,podrida	*food*
northeaster	*weather*	Olympic team	*sport*
northwester	*weather*	Omar Khayyam	*writers*
nosey,parker	*people*	omnibus bill	*law*
nous verrons	*foreign*	omniscience	*educ*
novelettist	*jobs*	once or twice	*time*
novelettist	*lit*	on easy terms	*trade*
Novosibirsk	*cities*	on good terms	*trade*
Now We Are Six	*titles*	onion Johnny	*jobs*
Noye's Fludde	*titles*	on,off switch	*machine*
nuclear bomb	*war*	onomasticon	*lit*
nuisance tax	*trade*	onomatology	*lit*
null and void	*govt*	on the boards	*theatre*
nullifidian	*relig*	on the market	*trade*
number field	*maths*	on the morrow	*time*
numismatics	*trade*	opalescence	*chem*
numismatist	*jobs*	opeidoscope	*physics*
nursery tale	*lit*	open account	*trade*
nursing home	*medic*	open circuit	*physics*
nyctophobia	*medic*	open country	*geog*
Nymphagetes	*myth*	open end bond	*trade*
obiter dicta	*foreign*	open verdict	*law*
object of art	*art*	open warfare	*war*
observation	*medic*	opera ballet	*music*
observatory	*astron*	opera bouffe	*music*
obstruction	*medic*	opportunely	*time*
obtometrist	*medic*	opportunist	*people*
obtuse angle	*maths*	opportunity	*time*
occultation	*astron*	optometrist	*jobs*
ocean depths	*marine*	orange grass	*flowers*
Ode to Autumn	*titles*	orange juice	*drink*
oeil de boeuf	*archit*	orangestick	*clothes*
off Broadway	*theatre*	orang outang	*animals*
office party	*jobs*	orchestrate	*music*
officialdom	*govt*	orchestrion	*music*
officialism	*govt*	Organ Morgan	*lit*
offset litho	*machine*	organophone	*music*
offshore rig	*machine*	organ player	*music*
offside rule	*sport*	oriel window	*archit*
oil painting	*art*	Oriental rug	*house*
oil painting	*house*	orientation	*travel*
oil refinery	*machine*	original sin	*relig*
olive branch	*trees*	Orion's hound	*myth*

Orion's|sword	*astron*
Orion's|sword	*myth*
ornamentist	*art*
ornamentist	*jobs*
ornithopter	*travel*
ornithosaur	*animals*
orthodontia	*medic*
orthography	*lit*
orthopaedic	*medic*
orthopedics	*medic*
orthopedist	*jobs*
orthopedist	*medic*
outbuilding	*archit*
out|of|bounds	*sport*
out|of|pocket	*trade*
out|of|season	*time*
out,of,the,way	*travel*
outside|home	*sport*
outside|left	*sport*
outside|loop	*travel*
outstanding	*trade*
over|blowing	*music*
overgarment	*clothes*
overpayment	*trade*
Oxford|shoes	*clothes*
oxidization	*chem*
oxygen|meter	*chem*
oyster|plant	*plants*
package|deal	*trade*
package|tour	*travel*
pack|of|cards	*sport*
paddle|wheel	*travel*
painted|lady	*insects*
pair|skating	*sport*
Palaearctic	*geog*
palaestrian	*jobs*
palaestrian	*sport*
Pallantides	*myth*
palm|cabbage	*trees*
palpitation	*medic*
pampas|grass	*plants*
pamphleteer	*jobs*
pamphleteer	*lit*
pancake|race	*sport*
pancratiast	*sport*

Pandean|pipe	*music*
Pandemonium	*myth*
Pandora's|box	*medic*
Pandora's|box	*myth*
panel|beater	*jobs*
panel|doctor	*jobs*
pantile|roof	*archit*
pantomimist	*theatre*
panty|girdle	*clothes*
Papal|Nuncio	*govt*
papal|nuncio	*jobs*
paper|credit	*trade*
paperhanger	*jobs*
paper|sailor	*animals*
paperweight	*house*
papier|mache	*art*
parachutist	*travel*
paragrapher	*jobs*
paragrapher	*lit*
parathyroid	*medic*
paratrooper	*travel*
parenthesis	*lit*
parish|clerk	*jobs*
parish|clerk	*relig*
Paris|yellow	*colour*
parlour|game	*sport*
parlour|maid	*jobs*
Parma|violet	*flowers*
parson's|nose	*food*
partial|tone	*music*
participial	*lit*
partisanism	*govt*
partnership	*govt*
partnership	*trade*
part|playing	*music*
part|singing	*music*
parturition	*medic*
part|writing	*music*
party|member	*govt*
pas|de|quatre	*theatre*
passacaglia	*music*
passage|beds	*geog*
passing|bell	*music*
passing|note	*music*
Passion|play	*lit*

Passion play	*theatre*	penultimate	*time*
Passion week	*time*	peppergrass	*plants*
passive verb	*lit*	peptic ulcer	*medic*
pastoral god	*myth*	peptization	*chem*
past perfect	*lit*	percussives	*music*
pasture land	*agric*	peregrinate	*travel*
patent right	*law*	perennially	*time*
patent rolls	*law*	perfect year	*time*
patent space	*lit*	performance	*film/TV*
paternoster	*relig*	performance	*music*
pathologist	*jobs*	performance	*theatre*
pathologist	*law*	pericardium	*medic*
pathologist	*medic*	peripatetic	*travel*
patron saint	*myth*	perissology	*lit*
patron saint	*relig*	peristalith	*mineral*
pattern bomb	*war*	peristaltic	*medic*
paving stone	*archit*	peritonitis	*medic*
Pavlov's dogs	*animals*	permutation	*maths*
pawn and move	*sport*	perpetually	*time*
pax vobiscum	*foreign*	persecution	*relig*
pay cash down	*trade*	Persephassa	*myth*
pay on demand	*trade*	Persian blue	*colour*
pay spot cash	*trade*	Persian Gulf	*seas*
pay the piper	*trade*	Persian lamb	*clothes*
peace treaty	*govt*	personality	*people*
peace treaty	*war*	personality	*theatre*
peach brandy	*drink*	personation	*theatre*
pearlfisher	*jobs*	perspective	*art*
pearl oyster	*fish*	Peter Grimes	*lit*
pearly queen	*jobs*	Peter Grimes	*titles*
pectization	*chem*	Peter Rabbit	*lit*
pelican fish	*fish*	Peter Simple	*titles*
pelvic colon	*medic*	petits fours	*food*
penal reform	*law*	petrography	*mineral*
penalty area	*sport*	petrol gauge	*travel*
penalty goal	*sport*	petrologist	*jobs*
penalty kick	*sport*	pettifogger	*law*
penalty line	*sport*	pettifogger	*people*
pendant post	*archit*	phantom gnat	*insects*
penny a liner	*jobs*	pharyngitis	*medic*
penny a liner	*lit*	philanderer	*people*
pentahedral	*maths*	philatelist	*jobs*
pentahedron	*maths*	Philippians	*Bible*
pentavalent	*chem*	Philippides	*myth*
penteconter	*travel*	Philippines	*islands*

Philistines	*Bible*	pillion|seat	*travel*
Philoctetes	*myth*	pillow|fight	*sport*
philologist	*jobs*	pilot|jacket	*clothes*
philosopher	*jobs*	pilot|scheme	*trade*
Philostrate	*Shakesp*	pinacotheca	*art*
Phineas|Finn	*lit*	Pindaric|ode	*lit*
phone|number	*travel*	Pippa|Passes	*titles*
phonologist	*jobs*	piranha|fish	*fish*
phosphorous	*chem*	piscatology	*sport*
photo|finish	*sport*	piscatorial	*fish*
photography	*art*	pissasphalt	*mineral*
photography	*physics*	pitch|accent	*music*
photorelief	*art*	pitch|and|run	*sport*
photosphere	*astron*	pitchblende	*chem*
photosphere	*physics*	pitchblende	*mineral*
phrasemaker	*lit*	pitched|roof	*archit*
phraseology	*lit*	place|of|work	*trade*
Phrygian|cap	*clothes*	plagal|modes	*music*
phyllomania	*flowers*	planetarium	*astron*
phyllomania	*fruit*	planisphere	*astron*
physiognomy	*medic*	Plantagenet	*Shakesp*
piano|player	*music*	plant|holder	*house*
piano|violin	*music*	plantigrade	*animals*
pickelhaube	*herald*	plasmolysis	*chem*
picket|fence	*archit*	plaster|cast	*medic*
picket|guard	*war*	plasterwork	*archit*
pick|up|speed	*travel*	plate|armour	*war*
picture|book	*lit*	platen|press	*machine*
picture|card	*sport*	platoon|fire	*war*
picture|rail	*house*	play|actress	*theatre*
picture|show	*film/TV*	player|piano	*house*
picturesque	*art*	player|piano	*music*
piece|of|work	*trade*	play|for|time	*time*
piece|worker	*jobs*	playing|card	*sport*
pied|wagtail	*birds*	playing|line	*sport*
pigeon|flier	*sport*	play|on|words	*lit*
pigeon|house	*birds*	play|the|fool	*theatre*
pigeon|house	*sport*	play|the|game	*sport*
pigeon's|milk	*birds*	play|the|part	*theatre*
pigeon|timer	*sport*	plein|airist	*art*
pig|sticking	*sport*	ploughshare	*tools*
pig's|trotter	*food*	plum|blossom	*flowers*
pile|dweller	*geog*	plum|pudding	*food*
pillar|drill	*tools*	pluviometer	*weather*
pillar|saint	*relig*	poached|fish	*food*

pocket|flask	*house*	polytechnic	*trade*
pocketknife	*tools*	polyvalence	*chem*
pocketmoney	*trade*	pomegranate	*fruit*
pocketmouse	*animals*	pompelmoose	*fruit*
poetic|prose	*lit*	Pondicherry	*cities*
poetic|works	*lit*	pontificals	*relig*
poet|patriot	*lit*	pontificate	*relig*
poet|pilgrim	*lit*	pony|and|trap	*travel*
poet|thinker	*lit*	pop|rivet|gun	*machine*
poet|warrior	*lit*	popular|tune	*music*
point|a|moral	*educ*	pork|sausage	*food*
pointed|arch	*archit*	portmanteau	*travel*
pointillism	*art*	portraitist	*jobs*
pointillist	*art*	portraiture	*art*
point|of|time	*time*	positive|ray	*physics*
point|tenses	*lit*	possessions	*trade*
poison|sumac	*trees*	postal|order	*trade*
polar|aurora	*astron*	postern|gate	*war*
polar|circle	*geog*	potato|crisp	*food*
polarimeter	*measure*	potato|salad	*food*
polarimeter	*physics*	pots|of|money	*trade*
polarimetry	*measure*	potter's|clay	*art*
polarimetry	*physics*	potter's|clay	*mineral*
polar|lights	*astron*	potting|shed	*plants*
polarograph	*physics*	poultry|farm	*agric*
polar|region	*geog*	pouring|rain	*weather*
pole|vaulter	*sport*	poverty|line	*trade*
police|cadet	*jobs*	poverty|trap	*trade*
police|court	*law*	powder|grain	*war*
police|force	*law*	powermonger	*govt*
police|judge	*law*	power|of|veto	*govt*
police|squad	*law*	power|shovel	*tools*
police|state	*law*	practicable	*theatre*
policewoman	*jobs*	prairie|wolf	*animals*
policewoman	*law*	prayer|shawl	*relig*
policy|maker	*govt*	prayer|wheel	*relig*
politbureau	*govt*	Pre|Cambrian	*geog*
pollen|grain	*flowers*	preceptress	*educ*
pollination	*flowers*	precipitate	*weather*
Polly|Garter	*lit*	predecessor	*jobs*
poltergeist	*myth*	premium|bond	*trade*
Polymnestor	*myth*	preparation	*educ*
polymorphic	*chem*	preparation	*food*
polyphonism	*music*	preparation	*music*
polytechnic	*educ*	preposition	*lit*

prerogative	*govt*
preselector	*machine*
present|time	*time*
press|camera	*art*
pressed|beef	*food*
press|revise	*lit*
Prester|John	*myth*
prestissimo	*music*
pretty|penny	*trade*
Pretty|Polly	*birds*
price|fixing	*trade*
price|freeze	*trade*
price|spiral	*trade*
price|ticket	*trade*
prickly|heat	*medic*
prickly|pear	*fruit*
prickly|pear	*trees*
primary|cell	*physics*
prime|factor	*maths*
prime|number	*maths*
prime|of|life	*time*
primitivism	*art*
primus|stove	*house*
Princess|Ida	*titles*
printed|word	*lit*
printer's|ink	*lit*
private|line	*travel*
private|ward	*medic*
privy|signet	*herald*
prizegiving	*educ*
prizewinner	*educ*
prizewinner	*jobs*
prizewinner	*sport*
probationer	*educ*
probationer	*jobs*
probationer	*medic*
proceedings	*govt*
procuration	*govt*
prodigal|son	*people*
Prodigal|Son	*relig*
prognostics	*medic*
progression	*maths*
progression	*music*
progressive	*govt*
Prohibition	*govt*

proletariat	*govt*
prominences	*geog*
promptitude	*time*
proofreader	*jobs*
proofreader	*lit*
propagation	*flowers*
property|tax	*trade*
prop|forward	*sport*
prophylaxis	*medic*
proportions	*art*
proposition	*maths*
proposition	*trade*
prosecution	*law*
protagonist	*jobs*
protagonist	*theatre*
proteolysis	*chem*
protest|vote	*govt*
protomartyr	*relig*
provided|for	*trade*
Provisional	*law*
Provisional	*war*
pruning|bill	*tools*
pruning|hook	*tools*
Prussian|red	*colour*
prussic|acid	*chem*
psalm|singer	*music*
psychedelic	*art*
psychodrama	*lit*
psychodrama	*theatre*
pterodactyl	*birds*
publication	*lit*
public|enemy	*govt*
public|games	*sport*
public|house	*archit*
public|press	*lit*
public|works	*govt*
pudding|bowl	*house*
puisne|judge	*law*
pulley|block	*machine*
pullulation	*plants*
pumice|stone	*house*
punched|card	*comput*
punched|tape	*comput*
Punchinello	*theatre*
punctuality	*time*

punctuation	*lit*	Rachmaninov	*music*
purchase|tax	*trade*	racing|craft	*sport*
pure|culture	*biol*	racing|shell	*sport*
pure|in|heart	*relig*	racing|shell	*travel*
purple|finch	*birds*	racket|court	*sport*
purpleheart	*trees*	radiant|heat	*physics*
purseholder	*jobs*	radioactive	*physics*
push|bicycle	*travel*	radio|beacon	*machine*
Puss|in|Boots	*titles*	radio|beacon	*physics*
pussy|willow	*trees*	radio|beacon	*travel*
put|into|port	*travel*	radiocarbon	*chem*
put|to|flight	*war*	radio|caster	*film/TV*
put|up|market	*trade*	radiography	*medic*
pyramid|spot	*sport*	radiologist	*jobs*
quack|remedy	*medic*	radiologist	*medic*
quacksalver	*medic*	radiologist	*physics*
quacksalver	*people*	radio|mirror	*travel*
quadrennial	*time*	radiopraxis	*medic*
quantometer	*chem*	radio|source	*astron*
quantometer	*measure*	radiothermy	*medic*
quantum|jump	*physics*	ragged|robin	*flowers*
quarrystone	*mineral*	rag|merchant	*jobs*
quarterback	*sport*	ragtime|band	*music*
quarter|deck	*travel*	rainy|season	*weather*
quarter|jack	*travel*	raised|beach	*geog*
quarter|note	*music*	raison|d'etre	*foreign*
quarter|past	*time*	rallentando	*music*
quarter|rest	*music*	rallying|cry	*war*
queen|mother	*govt*	rambler|rose	*flowers*
Queen's|bench	*law*	rampant|arch	*archit*
Queen's|peace	*law*	rampant|lion	*herald*
Queer|Street	*trade*	range|finder	*art*
questioning	*law*	range|finder	*machine*
questionist	*educ*	rank|and|file	*jobs*
questionist	*jobs*	rank|and|file	*war*
quicksilver	*chem*	ransom|money	*law*
quicksilver	*mineral*	rapscallion	*people*
quill|driver	*jobs*	rate|capping	*govt*
quince|jelly	*fruit*	rationalist	*people*
quinquereme	*travel*	rattlesnake	*insects*
quoted|price	*trade*	raw|material	*geog*
rabbit|fever	*medic*	raw|material	*trade*
rabbit|hutch	*animals*	reactionary	*govt*
rabbit|punch	*sport*	reactionary	*people*
race|meeting	*sport*	reactor|pile	*physics*

read|a|lesson	*educ*
reading|desk	*educ*
reading|desk	*relig*
reading|lamp	*house*
reading|room	*lit*
ready|to|wear	*clothes*
real|meaning	*lit*
rear|admiral	*govt*
rear|admiral	*jobs*
rebel|action	*war*
reclamation	*geog*
reconnoitre	*war*
record|album	*house*
record|break	*sport*
recruitment	*war*
rectangular	*maths*
Redgauntlet	*titles*
red|hot|poker	*flowers*
red|squirrel	*animals*
reed|bunting	*birds*
reed|sparrow	*birds*
re|education	*educ*
reed|warbler	*birds*
roflex|angle	*maths*
Reformation	*relig*
reformatory	*law*
refreshment	*food*
regenerator	*physics*
regimentals	*clothes*
regular|army	*war*
relative|key	*music*
relic|monger	*jobs*
relief|valve	*machine*
religiosity	*relig*
remembrance	*relig*
reparteeist	*people*
request|stop	*travel*
Requiem|mass	*music*
requiem|mass	*relig*
rescue|plane	*travel*
researchist	*educ*
research|man	*jobs*
reservation	*animals*
reservation	*travel*
reserve|bank	*trade*

resignation	*jobs*
resignation	*trade*
respiration	*medic*
responsions	*educ*
rest|in|peace	*relig*
restoration	*archit*
restorative	*medic*
restriction	*trade*
retardation	*music*
retiring|age	*trade*
retold|story	*lit*
retort|stand	*chem*
retroaction	*travel*
retro|rocket	*physics*
retro|rocket	*travel*
retro|rocket	*war*
reverse|turn	*travel*
rhetorician	*jobs*
Rhett|Butler	*lit*
rheumaticky	*medic*
rhinoplasty	*medic*
Rhode|Island	*islands*
rhopalocera	*insects*
rhyme|scheme	*lit*
rhynchodont	*animals*
ribbon|grass	*plants*
rice|pudding	*food*
riddle|me|ree	*sport*
riding|habit	*clothes*
right|angled	*maths*
right|angles	*maths*
right|to|vote	*govt*
right|winger	*govt*
right|winger	*people*
rigor|mortis	*medic*
ringed|snake	*insects*
ring|spanner	*tools*
rising|coast	*geog*
risk|capital	*trade*
river|course	*geog*
river|Jordan	*relig*
river|keeper	*jobs*
river|system	*geog*
river|valley	*geog*
road|haulage	*travel*

road|licence	*travel*	rouge|et|noir	*sport*
road|scraper	*machine*	rough|sketch	*art*
roadsweeper	*jobs*	round|number	*maths*
road|traffic	*travel*	round|of|golf	*sport*
roast|grouse	*food*	Royal|Assent	*govt*
roasting|tin	*house*	royal|family	*govt*
roast|potato	*food*	royal|palace	*govt*
robe|of|state	*herald*	royal|pardon	*govt*
Robespierre	*leaders*	royal|person	*govt*
rock|and|roll	*music*	royal|tennis	*sport*
rock|crystal	*mineral*	rubber|plant	*plants*
rocket|motor	*machine*	rubber|stamp	*govt*
rocket|motor	*travel*	rugby|league	*sport*
rocket|pilot	*jobs*	rugby|player	*jobs*
rocket|plane	*travel*	rule|of|three	*maths*
rocket|power	*travel*	rule|of|thumb	*chem*
rock|sparrow	*birds*	rule|of|thumb	*govt*
Rodney|Stone	*lit*	rule|of|thumb	*physics*
rod|of|empire	*herald*	ruling|class	*govt*
roentgen|ray	*medic*	rummage|sale	*trade*
rolling|fire	*war*	run|into|debt	*trade*
rolling|mill	*machine*	runner|beans	*veg*
roll|top|desk	*house*	running|knot	*travel*
Roman|candle	*sport*	running|nose	*medic*
Roman|nettle	*plants*	Russian|jade	*colour*
romanticism	*art*	Sabbatarian	*people*
Rontgen|rays	*physics*	Sacred|Heart	*relig*
roofing|tile	*archit*	sacred|music	*music*
room|divider	*archit*	saddle|girth	*animals*
room|service	*food*	saddle|horse	*animals*
rooster|fish	*birds*	sad|to|relate	*lit*
root|climber	*plants*	safe|breaker	*jobs*
rose|campion	*flowers*	safe|conduct	*govt*
Rosencrantz	*Shakesp*	safe|conduct	*war*
Rosicrucian	*myth*	safecracker	*jobs*
Rosmersholm	*titles*	safecracker	*law*
Rostov|on|Don	*cities*	safe|deposit	*trade*
rotary|drill	*tools*	safety|catch	*war*
rotary|press	*lit*	safety|razor	*tools*
rotary|press	*machine*	safety|valve	*machine*
rotary|whisk	*house*	Sagittarius	*myth*
rotogravure	*art*	Sagittarius	*zodiac*
rotogravure	*lit*	sailing|boat	*travel*
rotor|blades	*travel*	sailing|ship	*travel*
Rouge|Dragon	*herald*	saintliness	*relig*

salad|burnet	*plants*
sal|ammoniac	*chem*
sal|ammoniac	*medic*
sales|ledger	*trade*
sales|person	*trade*
salinometer	*measure*
salmon|trout	*fish*
Salut|d'Amour	*titles*
sal|volatile	*chem*
sal|volatile	*medic*
Sanctus|bell	*relig*
sanding|disc	*tools*
sand|skipper	*animals*
sands|of|time	*time*
sandwichman	*jobs*
San|Salvador	*cities*
San|Salvador	*islands*
sansculotte	*govt*
sarcophagus	*relig*
Saronic|Gulf	*seas*
sarsen|stone	*mineral*
Satsuma|ware	*art*
sauce|bottle	*house*
sausage|roll	*food*
savings|bank	*trade*
savoir|faire	*foreign*
saxophonist	*jobs*
saxophonist	*music*
Scafell|Pike	*mounts*
scaffolding	*archit*
scaffolding	*machine*
scale|insect	*insects*
Scamandrius	*myth*
scaremonger	*people*
scarlet|bean	*veg*
scat|singing	*music*
scene|change	*theatre*
scenewright	*art*
scenewright	*theatre*
scenography	*art*
schistosity	*mineral*
schizoidism	*medic*
scholarship	*educ*
School|Board	*educ*
school|dress	*clothes*
school|nurse	*jobs*
Schottische	*music*
Schottische	*sport*
scissorbill	*birds*
scissor|tail	*insects*
scolopendra	*insects*
scorekeeper	*jobs*
scorpion|fly	*insects*
Scotch|broth	*drink*
Scotch|catch	*music*
Scots|Guards	*war*
scouring|pad	*house*
scoutmaster	*jobs*
scrap|dealer	*jobs*
screwdriver	*tools*
scriptorial	*lit*
sculpturing	*art*
scurvy|grass	*plants*
scuttlebutt	*travel*
scythesmith	*jobs*
sea|colewort	*veg*
sea|cucumber	*fish*
sea|dotterel	*birds*
sea|elephant	*animals*
sea|furbelow	*plants*
sea|hedgehog	*fish*
sea|lavender	*plants*
sea|longworm	*insects*
seam|bowling	*sport*
sea|milkwort	*plants*
sea|purslane	*plants*
searchlight	*machine*
search|party	*jobs*
search|plane	*travel*
sea|scorpion	*fish*
seasickness	*medic*
seasickness	*travel*
Sea|Symphony	*titles*
second|class	*travel*
second|sight	*myth*
secret|agent	*jobs*
secretariat	*govt*
seismic|zone	*geog*
seismograph	*geog*
self|defence	*sport*

selfmademan	*people*
self service	*food*
self service	*trade*
self starter	*machine*
self starter	*travel*
sellataloss	*trade*
sellforward	*trade*
sellfutures	*trade*
semanticist	*jobs*
semantology	*lit*
semaphorist	*jobs*
semasiology	*lit*
semimonthly	*time*
semiskilled	*jobs*
senatorship	*govt*
sendpacking	*travel*
seniledecay	*medic*
seniorclerk	*jobs*
Sennacherib	*Bible*
sensitivity	*biol*
seriesmotor	*machine*
servicecall	*war*
servicegrip	*sport*
servicehold	*sport*
servicelane	*archit*
servicelift	*archit*
serviceline	*sport*
serviceside	*sport*
servingdish	*house*
sesamegrass	*plants*
sesquialter	*maths*
setdesigner	*theatre*
setinmotion	*travel*
setinsleeve	*clothes*
setthescene	*theatre*
setthestage	*theatre*
shadowgraph	*art*
Shaftesbury	*leaders*
Shakespeare	*writers*
shanghaiing	*law*
Shanks'smare	*travel*
Shanks'spony	*travel*
sharebroker	*jobs*
sharebroker	*trade*
shareholder	*trade*
shareledger	*trade*
sharplesson	*educ*
shavingsoap	*clothes*
Shawandasee	*myth*
shawlcollar	*clothes*
sheepfarmer	*jobs*
sheetanchor	*travel*
sheetofrain	*weather*
shelljacket	*clothes*
shelterdeck	*travel*
shepherddog	*animals*
shepherdess	*jobs*
sheriffwick	*law*
shingleroof	*archit*
shininghour	*time*
shintystick	*sport*
shipbiscuit	*food*
shipbuilder	*jobs*
shipofstate	*govt*
ship'scooper	*jobs*
ship'stailor	*jobs*
ship'swriter	*jobs*
shiptheoars	*travel*
shiptoshore	*war*
shirtbutton	*clothes*
shittahtree	*trees*
shockheaded	*clothes*
shocktroops	*war*
shoeleather	*clothes*
shootingwar	*war*
shoottokill	*war*
shoplifting	*law*
shoppingbag	*house*
shoppingbag	*trade*
shopsteward	*jobs*
shorepatrol	*govt*
shortaccent	*lit*
shortchange	*trade*
shortnotice	*time*
shortoctave	*music*
shortseller	*trade*
shoulderbag	*clothes*
shovelboard	*sport*
showercloth	*house*
showjumping	*sport*

showmanship	*theatre*	skeleton key	*house*
show of hands	*govt*	skiing field	*sport*
show stopper	*theatre*	skin disease	*medic*
shroud lines	*travel*	skirt dancer	*theatre*
shuttlecock	*sport*	Skye terrier	*animals*
shuttle raid	*war*	skysail mast	*travel*
shuttle trip	*travel*	slaughterer	*jobs*
side of bacon	*food*	slave bangle	*jewels*
Sierra Madre	*mounts*	slave labour	*jobs*
sightseeing	*sport*	slave trader	*jobs*
sightseeing	*travel*	sleeping bag	*sport*
Signal Corps	*war*	sleeping bag	*travel*
signal light	*machine*	sleeping car	*travel*
Silas Marner	*lit*	sleepwalker	*people*
Silas Marner	*titles*	sleuth hound	*animals*
silver birch	*trees*	sliced bread	*food*
silver medal	*sport*	sliding door	*house*
silver penny	*money*	slippery elm	*trees*
silver plate	*house*	slot machine	*machine*
silversmith	*art*	slot machine	*trade*
silversmith	*jobs*	slow foxtrot	*sport*
silver spoon	*house*	small change	*trade*
silver toned	*music*	smallholder	*jobs*
Simon Legree	*lit*	small octave	*music*
Simon Legree	*theatre*	small trader	*trade*
simple curve	*maths*	smell powder	*war*
simple parry	*sport*	smoke rocket	*war*
simple Simon	*people*	smoke screen	*war*
Simplon Pass	*mounts*	smoking room	*archit*
singing bird	*birds*	smorgasbord	*food*
singing game	*sport*	snaffle rein	*animals*
singing sand	*music*	snap shooter	*art*
single cream	*food*	snapshotter	*art*
single entry	*trade*	snatch block	*machine*
sinking fund	*trade*	sneak attack	*war*
sinking ship	*travel*	snout beetle	*insects*
Sir Bedivere	*lit*	snow blanket	*weather*
Sir Lancelot	*lit*	snow bunting	*birds*
sister in law	*family*	snow crystal	*weather*
sister tutor	*jobs*	snow glasses	*sport*
sitting duck	*birds*	snow leopard	*animals*
sitting room	*archit*	snowshoeing	*sport*
sitting room	*house*	social whale	*animals*
sixpenny bit	*money*	sociologist	*jobs*
skating rink	*sport*	soft landing	*sport*

soft|landing	*travel*	spanker|boom	*travel*
solar|corona	*astron*	spanker|gaff	*travel*
solar|energy	*astron*	Sparafucile	*lit*
solar|engine	*machine*	sparrowhawk	*birds*
solar|plexus	*medic*	spatterdash	*clothes*
solar|rocket	*travel*	spawning|bed	*fish*
solar|system	*astron*	spectacular	*theatre*
soldatesque	*war*	speculation	*sport*
soldier|crab	*fish*	speculation	*trade*
soldierlike	*war*	speechmaker	*govt*
soldiership	*war*	speechmaker	*jobs*
sole|emption	*trade*	speedometer	*machine*
solid|colour	*art*	speedometer	*travel*
solid|matter	*lit*	spelaeology	*geog*
soliloquist	*people*	spellbinder	*myth*
solmization	*music*	spelling|bee	*educ*
solution|set	*maths*	spell|of|rain	*weather*
Solway|Firth	*seas*	spendthrift	*people*
somatic|cell	*biol*	spent|bullet	*war*
some|time|ago	*time*	spindle|side	*herald*
song|sparrow	*birds*	spindle|tree	*trees*
soprano|clef	*music*	spinning|top	*sport*
sorrel|horse	*animals*	spirit|level	*machine*
soteriology	*relig*	spirit|level	*measure*
sound|effect	*film/TV*	Spitzbergen	*islands*
sound|effect	*theatre*	split|second	*time*
sound|in|tune	*music*	sponsorship	*trade*
Southampton	*cities*	sporting|dog	*animals*
southeaster	*weather*	sportswoman	*sport*
South|Riding	*titles*	spotted|Dick	*food*
southwester	*weather*	spread|eagle	*herald*
sovereignty	*govt*	spreadeagle	*sport*
space|centre	*travel*	springboard	*sport*
space|doctor	*jobs*	spring|clean	*house*
space|flight	*travel*	spring|onion	*veg*
space|island	*travel*	square|dance	*sport*
space|patrol	*travel*	square|metre	*measure*
space|rocket	*physics*	square|piano	*music*
space|rocket	*travel*	square|tango	*sport*
space|travel	*travel*	squash|court	*sport*
spacewriter	*jobs*	squirearchy	*govt*
spade|mashie	*sport*	Stabat|Mater	*music*
Spanish|comb	*clothes*	staff|of|life	*food*
Spanish|fowl	*birds*	stage|design	*theatre*
Spanish|moss	*plants*	stage|effect	*theatre*

stage|fright	*theatre*
stage|player	*jobs*
stage|player	*theatre*
stage|school	*theatre*
stagestruck	*theatre*
stageworthy	*theatre*
stagewright	*jobs*
stagewright	*theatre*
stagflation	*trade*
stagger|wire	*travel*
staghunting	*sport*
Stalky|and|Co	*titles*
stallholder	*jobs*
stand|at|ease	*war*
standing|lug	*travel*
stand|of|arms	*war*
star|billing	*theatre*
Star|Chamber	*law*
star|cluster	*astron*
star|quality	*theatre*
star|studded	*theatre*
starting|gun	*sport*
star|vehicle	*theatre*
stately|home	*archit*
stateswoman	*govt*
statute|book	*govt*
statute|book	*law*
statute|mile	*measure*
steal|a|march	*travel*
steam|engine	*machine*
steam|engine	*travel*
steam|hammer	*tools*
steam|launch	*travel*
steam|roller	*machine*
steam|shovel	*tools*
steeplejack	*jobs*
stella|maris	*astron*
Stenka|Razin	*titles*
stenography	*lit*
stenotypist	*jobs*
step|brother	*family*
stephanotis	*flowers*
step|rockets	*travel*
step|rockets	*war*
step|terrace	*archit*
stereotyper	*jobs*
stern|anchor	*travel*
stern|sheets	*travel*
stethoscope	*medic*
stick|insect	*insects*
stickleback	*fish*
stiff|collar	*clothes*
still|camera	*art*
stilt|plover	*birds*
stimulation	*biol*
stipendiary	*jobs*
stirrup|bone	*medic*
stirrup|pump	*machine*
St|John's|wort	*flowers*
stockbroker	*jobs*
stockbroker	*trade*
stock|dealer	*trade*
stockfarmer	*jobs*
Stockhausen	*music*
stockholder	*trade*
stock|jobber	*jobs*
stock|jobber	*trade*
stock|ledger	*trade*
stock|market	*trade*
stockpiling	*trade*
stocktaking	*trade*
stock|ticker	*machine*
stolen|goods	*law*
stomach|ache	*medic*
stomach|pump	*medic*
stomatology	*medic*
stone|circle	*mineral*
stone|curlew	*birds*
stonecutter	*jobs*
stone|falcon	*birds*
stone|marten	*animals*
stone|plover	*birds*
stony|ground	*geog*
stool|pigeon	*law*
stool|pigeon	*people*
stopped|pipe	*music*
storage|cell	*machine*
storekeeper	*jobs*
storekeeper	*trade*
storm|centre	*weather*

stormtroops	*war*	subtropical	*geog*
stormwindow	*house*	suckingfish	*fish*
storyteller	*jobs*	suctionpump	*machine*
storyteller	*lit*	suddendeath	*medic*
storywriter	*lit*	suddendeath	*sport*
straightbat	*sport*	suedegloves	*clothes*
straightman	*jobs*	suetpudding	*food*
straightman	*theatre*	suffragette	*govt*
straightway	*time*	suffragette	*people*
straphanger	*travel*	summerhouse	*archit*
stratocracy	*govt*	summerhouse	*house*
stratopause	*astron*	summittalks	*govt*
straybullet	*war*	summumbonum	*foreign*
streetfloor	*archit*	sumptermule	*animals*
streetorgan	*music*	Sundayblack	*clothes*
streetpiano	*music*	sunkenfence	*archit*
strikerball	*sport*	supercooled	*physics*
stringalong	*travel*	supermarket	*trade*
stringbeans	*veg*	superscribe	*lit*
stringmusic	*music*	suppuration	*medic*
stringplate	*music*	surgeon'ssaw	*medic*
stripedbass	*fish*	surgeon'ssaw	*tools*
stripteaser	*jobs*	surrebutter	*jobs*
stripteaser	*theatre*	suwarrownut	*fruit*
stroboscope	*physics*	swaggercoat	*clothes*
strongdrink	*drink*	swallowdive	*sport*
studentbody	*educ*	swallowhole	*geog*
studiocouch	*house*	swallowtail	*birds*
stuffingbox	*machine*	swallowtail	*clothes*
stuntflying	*travel*	swallowwort	*plants*
Stygianoath	*myth*	swamprabbit	*animals*
subcingulum	*clothes*	sweeprowing	*sport*
subcritical	*chem*	sweetalmond	*food*
subdivision	*war*	sweetcherry	*fruit*
subdominant	*music*	sweetpepper	*food*
subjunctive	*lit*	sweetpickle	*food*
submergence	*geog*	sweetpotato	*veg*
submersible	*travel*	sweetsherry	*drink*
submultiple	*maths*	sweetvoiced	*music*
subordinary	*herald*	sweetwillow	*trees*
subordinate	*jobs*	Swisscheese	*food*
subsistence	*trade*	SwissGuards	*war*
subsonicjet	*travel*	switchboard	*machine*
substantive	*lit*	switchboard	*travel*
subtraction	*maths*	switchgrass	*plants*

swivel|chair	*house*
sword|in|hand	*war*
swordmaster	*jobs*
sylvan|deity	*myth*
sympathiser	*people*
sympathizer	*govt*
Symplegades	*myth*
synchromesh	*machine*
synchromesh	*travel*
synchronism	*music*
synchronism	*time*
synchronize	*time*
syncopation	*music*
syndicalism	*govt*
synoecology	*biol*
systematics	*biol*
Szymanowski	*music*
table|napkin	*house*
table|tennis	*sport*
tachygraphy	*lit*
tackle|block	*machine*
tagliatelle	*food*
tailless|jet	*travel*
tail|of|comet	*astron*
tailor|tacks	*clothes*
take|by|storm	*war*
take|home|pay	*trade*
take|over|bid	*trade*
take|the|lead	*travel*
take|the|veil	*relig*
take|to|court	*law*
talent|scout	*jobs*
talent|scout	*theatre*
taletelling	*lit*
talking|film	*film/TV*
Tamburlaine	*lit*
Tammany|Hall	*govt*
tam|o|shanter	*clothes*
Tam|o|Shanter	*lit*
Tam|o|Shanter	*titles*
tamping|iron	*tools*
tandem|plane	*travel*
tape|measure	*house*
tape|measure	*measure*
target|arrow	*sport*

Tattersall's	*trade*
tax|assessor	*trade*
tax|gatherer	*trade*
taxidermist	*jobs*
Tchaikovsky	*music*
teachership	*educ*
teacher's|pet	*educ*
teacher's|pet	*people*
teaching|aid	*educ*
teaspoonful	*measure*
tea|strainer	*house*
technocracy	*chem*
technocracy	*govt*
technocracy	*physics*
technocracy	*trade*
teeny|bopper	*people*
telecontrol	*travel*
telegrapher	*jobs*
telepathist	*jobs*
telephonist	*jobs*
teleprinter	*machine*
teleprinter	*travel*
Telescopium	*astron*
telpher|line	*travel*
temperament	*music*
temperature	*medic*
temperature	*physics*
temperature	*weather*
tempestuous	*weather*
tempo|giusto	*music*
tempus|fugit	*time*
tenant|right	*law*
tennis|court	*sport*
tennis|dress	*clothes*
tennis|match	*sport*
tennis|shoes	*clothes*
tent|pegging	*sport*
terminology	*lit*
ternary|form	*music*
Terpsichore	*jobs*
Terpsichore	*muses*
Terpsichore	*music*
Terpsichore	*myth*
Terpsichore	*sport*
Terpsichore	*theatre*

terra|sienna	*colour*	thermometer	*physics*
terrestrial	*geog*	thermometer	*weather*
tertium|quid	*foreign*	the|sniffles	*medic*
testamental	*law*	The|Sorcerer	*titles*
testimonial	*jobs*	Thespian|art	*theatre*
testing|area	*travel*	The|Talisman	*titles*
tetrahedron	*maths*	The|Wild|Duck	*titles*
tetravalent	*chem*	The|Wrong|Box	*titles*
The|American	*titles*	thin|red|line	*war*
The|Apostles	*titles*	third|degree	*law*
theatregoer	*sport*	third|person	*lit*
theatregoer	*theatre*	third|player	*sport*
theatreland	*theatre*	this|morning	*time*
theatricals	*theatre*	thistledown	*plants*
theatrician	*theatre*	this|very|day	*time*
The|Big|Sleep	*titles*	three|Graces	*myth*
the|black|art	*myth*	three|in|hand	*travel*
The|Blue|Bird	*titles*	three|legged	*sport*
The|Colossus	*wonders*	three|master	*travel*
The|Creation	*titles*	thrust|plane	*geog*
The|Cruel|Sea	*titles*	thunderball	*weather*
The|Dormouse	*lit*	thunderbolt	*myth*
The|Firebird	*titles*	thunderbolt	*weather*
The|Georgics	*titles*	thunderclap	*weather*
the|Good|Book	*lit*	thunderpeal	*weather*
the|have|nots	*trade*	ticket|agent	*jobs*
The|Loved|One	*titles*	ticking|over	*travel*
thenceforth	*time*	tiddlywinks	*sport*
The|Newcomes	*titles*	tiger|beetle	*insects*
theological	*relig*	tiger|flower	*flowers*
the|Olympics	*sport*	tight|budget	*trade*
the|other|day	*time*	tight|market	*trade*
The|Princess	*titles*	tile|painter	*art*
The|Pyramids	*wonders*	time|and|tide	*time*
therapeutic	*medic*	time|bargain	*trade*
thermal|unit	*measure*	time|drags|by	*time*
thermionics	*physics*	time|machine	*time*
thermoduric	*physics*	time|pattern	*music*
thermograph	*physics*	time|sharing	*sport*
thermograph	*weather*	time|to|spare	*time*
thermolysis	*biol*	Tin|Pan|Alley	*music*
thermolytic	*biol*	tired|market	*trade*
thermometer	*house*	tissue|paper	*art*
thermometer	*measure*	titanothere	*animals*
thermometer	*medic*	toastmaster	*jobs*

tobacconist	*jobs*
tobacco worm	*insects*
tobogganing	*sport*
toffee apple	*food*
toilet water	*clothes*
tomato juice	*drink*
tomato sauce	*food*
Tommy Atkins	*jobs*
Tommy Atkins	*war*
Tom Traddles	*lit*
Tom Tulliver	*lit*
tonic accent	*music*
tonsillitis	*medic*
tooth doctor	*jobs*
tooth drawer	*jobs*
tooth powder	*clothes*
tooth powder	*medic*
torchon lace	*clothes*
torch singer	*music*
torpedo boat	*travel*
torpedo boat	*war*
torridonian	*geog*
tossed salad	*food*
totalisator	*machine*
totalisator	*sport*
to the tune of	*trade*
touring club	*sport*
tout le monde	*foreign*
town dweller	*people*
town planner	*jobs*
toxophilite	*jobs*
toxophilite	*sport*
track record	*sport*
track rod end	*machine*
Tracy Tupman	*lit*
trade school	*educ*
trade school	*trade*
trading post	*trade*
trafficator	*travel*
traffic duty	*govt*
tragedienne	*theatre*
tragic drama	*theatre*
tragicomedy	*lit*
tragicomedy	*theatre*
train bearer	*jobs*
training run	*sport*
train robber	*jobs*
train robber	*law*
transaction	*trade*
transalpine	*geog*
transandine	*geog*
transceiver	*machine*
transcriber	*jobs*
transcriber	*lit*
transfer fee	*sport*
transformer	*machine*
transformer	*physics*
transfusion	*medic*
translation	*lit*
translunary	*astron*
transmarine	*geog*
transmitter	*machine*
transmitter	*physics*
transmitter	*travel*
transporter	*travel*
transposing	*music*
transuranic	*chem*
trapezoidal	*maths*
travel agent	*jobs*
travel agent	*trade*
travel agent	*travel*
treacle tart	*food*
tree creeper	*plants*
tree surgeon	*jobs*
tree swallow	*birds*
trefoil arch	*archit*
trencher cap	*clothes*
trench fever	*medic*
trench knife	*war*
trench mouth	*medic*
trial by jury	*law*
Trial by Jury	*titles*
trigger talk	*war*
triple crown	*herald*
triple crown	*relig*
triple crown	*sport*
triple plume	*herald*
tripod stand	*chem*
tripod stand	*physics*
Triptolemos	*myth*

triumvirate	*govt*
Trojan|horse	*myth*
troposphere	*geog*
troposphere	*physics*
trouser|suit	*clothes*
truck|farmer	*jobs*
truck|system	*trade*
true|colours	*herald*
true|colours	*war*
true|heading	*travel*
true|horizon	*geog*
true|meaning	*lit*
trumpet\,fish	*fish*
trusty|sword	*war*
trysail|gaff	*travel*
tube|station	*travel*
tumble|drier	*machine*
tumefaction	*medic*
tunefulness	*music*
tuning|slide	*music*
Turkish|bath	*medic*
Turkish|bath	*sport*
turret|clock	*time*
Tuscan|order	*archit*
tussock|moth	*insects*
tutelary|god	*myth*
tutti\,frutti	*fruit*
twelvemonth	*time*
type|foundry	*lit*
type|foundry	*machine*
typesetting	*lit*
typographer	*jobs*
typographer	*lit*
typographic	*lit*
ultima|Thule	*myth*
ultramarine	*colour*
ultramodern	*time*
ultrasonics	*physics*
ultra\,violet	*geog*
unconscious	*medic*
undecennary	*measure*
undecennial	*measure*
under|arrest	*law*
under|a|spell	*myth*
under|attack	*war*

under|canvas	*travel*
undercharge	*trade*
underground	*geog*
underground	*travel*
Underground	*war*
undergrowth	*trees*
undersigned	*govt*
under|the|sun	*geog*
underwriter	*trade*
und|so|weiter	*foreign*
unfold|a|tale	*lit*
unicellular	*biol*
universally	*geog*
up|and|at|them	*war*
upholsterer	*jobs*
upper|circle	*theatre*
upper|fourth	*educ*
urban|sprawl	*archit*
utility|room	*archit*
utility|room	*house*
vaccination	*medic*
vacuum|flask	*house*
vacuum|flask	*physics*
Vanga|shrike	*birds*
van|salesman	*jobs*
vapour|trail	*travel*
varnish|tree	*trees*
Vatican|City	*relig*
Vendemiaire	*time*
vendibility	*trade*
venesection	*medic*
Venetian|red	*colour*
ventilation	*archit*
ventriloquy	*theatre*
verbigerate	*lit*
vermiculite	*mineral*
versemaking	*lit*
versemonger	*jobs*
vers|librist	*lit*
vesuvianite	*mineral*
vicar|choral	*music*
vice\,admiral	*govt*
vice\,admiral	*jobs*
Vienna|green	*colour*
Vienna|steak	*food*

vinaigrette	*house*
vindication	*govt*
vine dresser	*jobs*
vine fretter	*insects*
vine of Sodom	*relig*
vintage wine	*drink*
viola d'amore	*music*
viola player	*jobs*
viol da gamba	*music*
violin piano	*music*
violoncello	*music*
viper's grass	*plants*
Virgin's Well	*relig*
viscountess	*govt*
vivacissimo	*music*
Vladivostok	*cities*
voided cross	*herald*
voix celeste	*music*
volatile oil	*chem*
volcanic ash	*mineral*
voting paper	*govt*
vulcanicity	*geog*
vulcanology	*geog*
waggon trail	*travel*
waggon wheel	*travel*
wainscoting	*archit*
waiting game	*sport*
waiting line	*theatre*
waiting room	*archit*
waiting room	*travel*
waiting time	*time*
walking part	*theatre*
walking race	*sport*
walking shoe	*clothes*
walking tour	*travel*
walk through	*theatre*
Walter Mitty	*lit*
Walter Mitty	*people*
ward of court	*law*
ware animals	*myth*
warlikeness	*war*
warm springs	*geog*
warm springs	*medic*
war of nerves	*war*
war reporter	*jobs*

war reporter	*lit*
warriorlike	*war*
war to end war	*war*
washerwoman	*jobs*
washing line	*house*
washing soap	*house*
washing soda	*house*
wash leather	*clothes*
wassail bowl	*house*
watch pocket	*clothes*
water beetle	*insects*
water canker	*medic*
water cannon	*war*
water closet	*archit*
water closet	*house*
water colour	*art*
watercourse	*geog*
water doctor	*jobs*
watered silk	*clothes*
water finder	*jobs*
water garden	*flowers*
water hazard	*sport*
water heater	*house*
watering can	*tools*
water meadow	*plants*
water pepper	*plants*
water pocket	*geog*
water skiing	*sport*
water spirit	*myth*
water sports	*sport*
water sprite	*myth*
water violet	*plants*
wattled crow	*birds*
wave erosion	*marine*
weathercock	*archit*
weathercock	*weather*
weather deck	*travel*
weather side	*travel*
weathervane	*weather*
weaver finch	*birds*
wedding cake	*food*
wedding ring	*jewels*
wedding song	*music*
weigh anchor	*travel*
weighbridge	*machine*

welfare|work	*jobs*
Welsh|rabbit	*food*
Western|roll	*sport*
Westminster	*govt*
whalefisher	*jobs*
What|Katy|Did	*titles*
wheaten|loaf	*food*
wheel,animal	*animals*
wheelbarrow	*tools*
wheelbarrow	*travel*
wheelwright	*jobs*
whereabouts	*geog*
wherewithal	*trade*
white|bottle	*flowers*
white|cliffs	*geog*
white|coffee	*drink*
white|collar	*clothes*
white|collar	*jobs*
white|ensign	*herald*
white|ermine	*animals*
white|horses	*marine*
white|hunter	*jobs*
white|pepper	*food*
white|poplar	*trees*
white|potato	*food*
whitethroat	*birds*
whiting,pout	*fish*
Whitsuntide	*time*
whole|number	*maths*
wicker|chair	*house*
wide|reading	*educ*
widow's|weeds	*clothes*
wild|flowers	*flowers*
William|Tell	*titles*
willow|cabin	*archit*
willow|pipes	*music*
windbreaker	*clothes*
windcheater	*clothes*
wind|erosion	*geog*
window|blind	*house*
window|frame	*archit*
window|frame	*house*
window|glass	*archit*
window,light	*house*
Windsor|knot	*clothes*
wine|tasting	*sport*
wing|forward	*sport*
wing|loading	*travel*
winning|post	*sport*
winning|time	*sport*
win|on|points	*sport*
winter|cress	*veg*
wintergreen	*house*
wintergreen	*plants*
wintersweet	*trees*
wirepulling	*govt*
wisdom|tooth	*medic*
Wise|Virgins	*relig*
wishing|well	*myth*
wishtonwish	*animals*
witch|doctor	*jobs*
witch|doctor	*myth*
witches|meat	*plants*
with|the|lark	*time*
wolf|whistle	*animals*
Women|in|Love	*titles*
wood|anemone	*flowers*
wood|carving	*art*
woodchopper	*jobs*
wooden|horse	*myth*
wooden|horse	*sport*
wooden|horse	*war*
wooden|shoes	*clothes*
wooden|spoon	*house*
wooden|walls	*war*
wood|fretter	*insects*
wood,swallow	*birds*
wood|warbler	*birds*
wool|stapler	*jobs*
word|history	*lit*
word|painter	*lit*
word|perfect	*theatre*
word|picture	*lit*
work|clothes	*clothes*
working|girl	*jobs*
working|life	*trade*
workmanlike	*jobs*
workmanlike	*trade*
workmanship	*trade*
works|outing	*trade*

work surface	*house*
world market	*trade*
world record	*sport*
woven fabric	*clothes*
writing desk	*educ*
writing desk	*house*
writ of error	*law*
written word	*lit*
wrong number	*travel*
wrought iron	*archit*
wrought iron	*house*
xanthophyll	*chem*
xanthoxylum	*trees*
X chromosome	*biol*
X ray machine	*machine*
X ray machine	*medic*
X ray therapy	*medic*
xylographer	*art*

xylophagous	*insects*
xylophonist	*jobs*
yarn spinner	*lit*
Y chromosome	*biol*
Year of Grace	*time*
yellow fever	*medic*
yellow ochre	*colour*
Yellow press	*lit*
Yellowstone	*rivers*
Yevtushenko	*writers*
Young Siward	*Shakesp*
your worship	*law*
youth hostel	*sport*
youth leader	*jobs*
zincography	*art*
zoochemical	*biol*
zooplankton	*biol*

12 LETTERS

abbreviation	*lit*
abbreviature	*lit*
Abel Magwitch	*lit*
absolute veto	*govt*
abstract noun	*lit*
academy award	*film/TV*
academy award	*theatre*
acceleration	*biol*
acceleration	*chem*
acceleration	*physics*
acceptor atom	*physics*
acciaccatura	*music*
accompanyist	*music*
accordionist	*music*
Achilles heel	*myth*
acid solution	*chem*
acoustic bass	*music*
acoustic mine	*war*
acting device	*theatre*

actinic glass	*physics*
active market	*trade*
actor manager	*jobs*
actor manager	*theatre*
Adam's flannel	*flowers*
adherent noun	*lit*
adhesive tape	*house*
adjudication	*law*
adjutant bird	*birds*
administrate	*govt*
ad valorem tax	*trade*
advance agent	*theatre*
advance party	*jobs*
advance proof	*lit*
aerial camera	*machine*
aerodynamics	*physics*
aero embolism	*medic*
Aesop's fables	*myth*
aestheticism	*art*

afterburning	*physics*
afternoon|tea	*food*
after|the|fact	*govt*
agogic|accent	*music*
agricultural	*agric*
air|commodore	*jobs*
aircraftsman	*jobs*
aircraftsman	*travel*
air|force|blue	*colour*
airfreighter	*travel*
air|sea|rescue	*jobs*
air|sea|rescue	*travel*
Aladdin's|lamp	*myth*
alexipharmic	*medic*
Alfred|Jingle	*lit*
alkali|metals	*mineral*
alliteration	*lit*
all|of|a|sudden	*time*
All|Saints|day	*time*
all|systems|go	*travel*
alluvial|flat	*geog*
a|long|time|ago	*time*
alpha|blocker	*medic*
alpine|flower	*flowers*
amalgamation	*trade*
ambulance|man	*jobs*
American|aloe	*fruit*
American|lion	*animals*
amicus|curiae	*law*
amortisement	*law*
amortization	*trade*
amortizement	*trade*
Amphion's|lyre	*myth*
amphitheatre	*archit*
amphitheatre	*educ*
amphitheatre	*theatre*
anaesthetist	*jobs*
anaesthetist	*medic*
anchor|cannon	*sport*
ancien|regime	*govt*
ancient|times	*time*
Angstrom|unit	*physics*
Anna|Karenina	*titles*
Annunciation	*relig*
Annunciation	*time*
antediluvian	*time*
antemeridian	*time*
ante|meridiem	*time*
anthraconite	*mineral*
anthropogeny	*biol*
anthropology	*biol*
anthropotomy	*biol*
anthropotomy	*medic*
anti|aircraft	*war*
anticipation	*music*
antigropelos	*clothes*
antimacassar	*house*
antineutrino	*physics*
antiparticle	*physics*
antithrombin	*biol*
Appalachians	*mounts*
appassionata	*music*
appeal|motion	*law*
appeal|to|arms	*war*
appendectomy	*medic*
appendicitis	*medic*
apple|blossom	*flowers*
apple|crumble	*food*
apple|fritter	*food*
apple|of|Sodom	*fruit*
apple|strudel	*food*
appoggiatura	*music*
apprehension	*law*
approach|road	*travel*
approach|shot	*sport*
apron|strings	*clothes*
apron|strings	*house*
aptitude|test	*educ*
aquapuncture	*medic*
Arcadian|hind	*myth*
Archangel|cat	*animals*
Archduke|Trio	*titles*
Archie|Traill	*lit*
architecture	*archit*
architecture	*art*
arctic|circle	*geog*
Areopagitica	*titles*
argillaceous	*mineral*
Aristophanes	*writers*
arithmograph	*maths*

arithmometer	*machine*
arithmometer	*maths*
arithmometer	*trade*
Armistice\day	*time*
armorial\seal	*herald*
armour\bearer	*jobs*
armour\plated	*war*
army\reserves	*war*
arrester\hook	*travel*
arriere\garde	*foreign*
arsenopyrite	*mineral*
arterial\road	*travel*
artesian\well	*geog*
artful\dodger	*people*
Arthur\Norris	*lit*
artilleryman	*jobs*
artilleryman	*war*
artist's\model	*art*
artist's\proof	*art*
Ascension\day	*time*
Ashley\Wilkes	*lit*
Ash\Wednesday	*time*
Ash\Wednesday	*titles*
asparagus\tip	*veg*
aspartic\acid	*chem*
assembly\hall	*archit*
assembly\line	*machine*
assembly\line	*trade*
assimilation	*educ*
astrobiology	*biol*
astronautics	*physics*
astronomical	*astron*
astrophysics	*astron*
astrophysics	*physics*
at\death's\door	*medic*
Athena\Pallas	*myth*
athlete's\foot	*medic*
atomic\cannon	*war*
atomic\energy	*physics*
atomic\number	*physics*
atomic\theory	*chem*
atomic\theory	*physics*
atomic\weight	*chem*
atomic\weight	*physics*
atom\smashing	*physics*

auction\stand	*trade*
audience\hall	*archit*
Augean\stable	*myth*
augmentation	*music*
auld\lang\syne	*time*
auscultation	*medic*
author's\proof	*lit*
autorotation	*travel*
autumn\crocus	*flowers*
ave\atque\vale	*foreign*
avenging\fury	*myth*
Avogadro's\law	*chem*
awkward\squad	*people*
awkward\squad	*war*
baby\carriage	*travel*
baby\elephant	*animals*
babysnatcher	*people*
baccalaureus	*educ*
back\straight	*sport*
backwoodsman	*people*
bacon\and\eggs	*food*
bacteriology	*biol*
bacteriology	*medic*
Baffin\Island	*islands*
Bailey\bridge	*archit*
Bailey\bridge	*travel*
bakewell\tart	*food*
balance\sheet	*trade*
balance\wheel	*machine*
balladmonger	*jobs*
balladmonger	*lit*
balladmonger	*music*
ballad\singer	*jobs*
ballad\singer	*music*
ballet\dancer	*jobs*
ballet\dancer	*theatre*
balletomania	*theatre*
ball\of\string	*house*
ballon\d'essai	*foreign*
ballpoint\pen	*lit*
balm\of\Gilead	*medic*
balsam\of\Peru	*trees*
balsam\of\Tolu	*trees*
balustrading	*archit*
Bandaranaike	*leaders*

banjo ukelele	*music*	belligerence	*war*
bank examiner	*trade*	belly landing	*travel*
bantamweight	*sport*	bench warrant	*law*
banzai charge	*war*	bend sinister	*herald*
bargain offer	*trade*	bespectacled	*clothes*
bargain price	*trade*	between decks	*travel*
Barnaby Rudge	*lit*	bib and tucker	*clothes*
Barnaby Rudge	*titles*	bible thumper	*people*
barndoor fowl	*birds*	bibliography	*lit*
barnyard fowl	*birds*	bibliologist	*jobs*
bar of justice	*law*	bibliologist	*lit*
Barquisimeto	*cities*	bibliomaniac	*educ*
barrel plater	*machine*	bibliomaniac	*lit*
barren ground	*geog*	bibliopegist	*jobs*
barrier cream	*chem*	bibliopegist	*lit*
barter system	*trade*	bibliopolist	*lit*
base shilling	*money*	bibliotheque	*lit*
basking shark	*fish*	bicarbonates	*chem*
bass baritone	*music*	bicycle clips	*clothes*
bass clarinet	*music*	bide one's time	*time*
basso relievo	*art*	Bight of Benin	*seas*
bass trombone	*music*	Bilbo Baggins	*lit*
bathing dress	*clothes*	billiard ball	*sport*
battering ram	*tools*	billiard hall	*sport*
battering ram	*war*	billiard room	*archit*
battery plate	*machine*	billiard room	*sport*
batting order	*sport*	billiard spot	*sport*
battleground	*war*	bill of health	*medic*
battle of wits	*educ*	bill of lading	*trade*
bay at the moon	*animals*	Bill of Rights	*law*
beachcombing	*sport*	binder's title	*lit*
beaching gear	*travel*	binding screw	*machine*
beacon lights	*travel*	bingo session	*sport*
beaded lizard	*insects*	biochemistry	*biol*
bead moulding	*archit*	biochemistry	*chem*
beard the lion	*animals*	biogeography	*geog*
bearing plate	*travel*	biosatellite	*biol*
beat a retreat	*music*	biosynthesis	*biol*
beat a retreat	*war*	bird's eye view	*birds*
Beaumarchais	*writers*	bird watching	*sport*
Becher's brook	*sport*	birthday cake	*food*
bedside light	*house*	birthday suit	*clothes*
bedside table	*house*	bishop's apron	*herald*
bedtime story	*lit*	bismuth salts	*medic*
be in business	*trade*	bitter almond	*food*

bitterly cold	*weather*
black and blue	*medic*
Black country	*geog*
blackcurrant	*fruit*
black diamond	*mineral*
black pudding	*food*
bladderwrack	*plants*
blast furnace	*machine*
blind landing	*travel*
blinker light	*machine*
Blithe Spirit	*titles*
block capital	*lit*
Bloemfontein	*cities*
blood brother	*family*
bloodletting	*medic*
blood pudding	*food*
blow up a storm	*weather*
bluestocking	*clothes*
bluestocking	*educ*
bluestocking	*people*
board meeting	*jobs*
board meeting	*trade*
Board of Trade	*govt*
Board of Trade	*trade*
bobby dazzler	*people*
body building	*sport*
body snatcher	*jobs*
body stocking	*clothes*
bog pimpernel	*flowers*
boiling point	*physics*
bond to bearer	*trade*
bonnet monkey	*animals*
boogie woogie	*music*
booking agent	*theatre*
booking clerk	*jobs*
book learning	*educ*
book learning	*lit*
book reviewer	*lit*
book scorpion	*insects*
bookstitcher	*jobs*
bookstitcher	*lit*
border gobony	*herald*
border lights	*theatre*
border sentry	*jobs*
bottled fruit	*fruit*
bottle opener	*house*
bottlewasher	*jobs*
bottom animal	*animals*
bottom dollar	*trade*
bottom drawer	*house*
bottomry bond	*trade*
bougainvilia	*trees*
Bougainville	*islands*
boulevardier	*jobs*
bouquet garni	*food*
Bower of Bliss	*myth*
bowling alley	*sport*
bowling green	*sport*
boxing gloves	*sport*
brachygraphy	*lit*
brain twister	*educ*
bramble finch	*birds*
branchiopoda	*fish*
branch office	*trade*
brass buttons	*clothes*
brass rubbing	*art*
brass section	*music*
Braunschweig	*cities*
break dancing	*sport*
break the bank	*sport*
breakthrough	*war*
breast of lamb	*food*
breast of veal	*food*
breast pocket	*clothes*
breast stroke	*sport*
breastsummer	*archit*
breathalyser	*drink*
breathalyser	*law*
breathalyzer	*chem*
breath of life	*medic*
breechloader	*war*
brewer's yeast	*food*
bridal wreath	*flowers*
bridgemaster	*jobs*
brigade major	*jobs*
bright colour	*art*
Brighton Rock	*titles*
brilliantine	*clothes*
bring charges	*law*
brinkmanship	*jobs*

British Isles	*islands*
broker's agent	*trade*
brokers board	*trade*
brontosaurus	*animals*
brother in law	*family*
brown pelican	*birds*
buccaneering	*war*
Buddenbrooks	*titles*
buenas noches	*foreign*
buffalo grass	*plants*
building line	*archit*
bull fighting	*sport*
Bull Poseidon	*myth*
bunsen burner	*chem*
burette stand	*chem*
burglar alarm	*law*
burglar alarm	*machine*
burial ground	*relig*
burning glass	*physics*
burning point	*physics*
burnt carmine	*colour*
burrowing owl	*birds*
bushfighting	*war*
business deal	*trade*
business life	*trade*
businesslike	*trade*
business suit	*clothes*
bustard quail	*birds*
butcher's meat	*food*
butterfly net	*sport*
butterscotch	*food*
buttress pier	*archit*
buyer's market	*trade*
buying public	*trade*
buzzard clock	*insects*
cabbage patch	*veg*
cabbage white	*insects*
cabin cruiser	*travel*
cabinet maker	*jobs*
cable railway	*travel*
cadet's shield	*herald*
Caesar Borgia	*lit*
Cairn terrier	*animals*
calabash tree	*trees*
calendar year	*time*

callable bond	*trade*
calligrapher	*jobs*
calligrapher	*lit*
callisthenic	*sport*
camera lucida	*art*
camp follower	*jobs*
Canada balsam	*trees*
canary yellow	*colour*
candid camera	*art*
candleholder	*house*
candle sconce	*house*
candlewright	*jobs*
Canis majoris	*astron*
cannon fodder	*war*
cannon's mouth	*war*
canonization	*relig*
Canvey Island	*islands*
capercaillie	*birds*
capercailzie	*birds*
capital gains	*trade*
capital goods	*trade*
capital stock	*trade*
cap of liberty	*clothes*
capstan lathe	*machine*
Captain Reece	*lit*
carat balance	*physics*
caravanserai	*archit*
caraway seeds	*food*
carbohydrate	*biol*
carbolic acid	*chem*
carbonic acid	*chem*
cardinal bird	*birds*
cardinal's hat	*clothes*
cardinal's hat	*herald*
cardinal's hat	*relig*
caricaturist	*art*
caricaturist	*jobs*
Carolina pink	*flowers*
carpenter ant	*insects*
carpenter bee	*insects*
carpetbagger	*jobs*
carpetbagger	*law*
carpet beater	*house*
carpet fetter	*jobs*
carpet knight	*people*

carpet|python	*insects*
carriage|lamp	*house*
Carrie|Pooter	*lit*
carte|blanche	*foreign*
cartographer	*geog*
cartographer	*jobs*
carving|knife	*house*
carving|knife	*tools*
cash|and|carry	*trade*
Cashmere|goat	*animals*
cash|register	*machine*
cash|register	*trade*
casual|labour	*jobs*
casual|labour	*trade*
casualty|ward	*medic*
catallactics	*trade*
catamountain	*animals*
cathetometer	*measure*
cat's|whiskers	*animals*
cattle|lifter	*jobs*
cattle|market	*animals*
caulking|iron	*travel*
cause|celebre	*law*
cause|in|court	*law*
cavalry|twill	*clothes*
caveat|emptor	*foreign*
cave|painting	*art*
cecropia|moth	*insects*
cell|division	*biol*
central|canal	*medic*
central|force	*physics*
centre|anchor	*travel*
century|break	*sport*
century|plant	*flowers*
ceramography	*art*
cerographist	*jobs*
ceroplastics	*art*
cerulean|blue	*colour*
chain|reactor	*physics*
chaise|longue	*house*
chalcopyrite	*mineral*
chaleography	*art*
chamber|music	*music*
chamber|organ	*music*
championship	*sport*
chancel|table	*relig*
change|bowler	*sport*
change|course	*travel*
change|of|ends	*sport*
changing|note	*music*
changing|room	*sport*
channel|patch	*travel*
chapel|of|ease	*relig*
chapterhouse	*archit*
chapterhouse	*relig*
characterize	*theatre*
character|man	*theatre*
charged|field	*herald*
Charles|swain	*astron*
Charley's|Aunt	*titles*
charnel|house	*archit*
charnel|house	*relig*
chart|a|course	*travel*
Charterhouse	*relig*
chastity|belt	*clothes*
chattels|real	*law*
checkerberry	*trees*
checkerboard	*sport*
check|weigher	*jobs*
cheeseburger	*food*
cheese|grater	*house*
chemical|bond	*chem*
chemical|pump	*chem*
chemotherapy	*medic*
cherry|laurel	*fruit*
chesterfield	*clothes*
chesterfield	*house*
chestnut|tree	*trees*
chest|of|viols	*music*
Cheviot|Hills	*mounts*
chiaro|oscuro	*art*
chicken|house	*birds*
chicken|thief	*jobs*
chief|cashier	*jobs*
chief|justice	*jobs*
Chief|Justice	*law*
chief|mourner	*jobs*
chief|of|staff	*jobs*
Childe|Harold	*titles*
chiliahedron	*maths*

chilli|pepper	*food*		cinnamon|bear	*animals*
chilli|pepper	*veg*		circuit|court	*law*
chiming|clock	*house*		circuit|judge	*law*
chimney|piece	*house*		circuit|rider	*jobs*
chimney|shaft	*archit*		circular|note	*trade*
chimney|stack	*archit*		cirro|cumulus	*weather*
chimney|stack	*house*		cirro|stratus	*weather*
chimney|sweep	*jobs*		citizen's|band	*travel*
chimney|swift	*birds*		City|of|Refuge	*relig*
Chinese|paper	*art*		city|planning	*archit*
Chinese|white	*colour*		civil|defence	*govt*
chin|whiskers	*clothes*		civil|defence	*war*
chirographer	*jobs*		civil|servant	*jobs*
chiropractic	*medic*		civil|service	*govt*
chiropractor	*jobs*		civil|service	*jobs*
chiropractor	*medic*		clapperboard	*film/TV*
chitterlings	*food*		clarinettist	*jobs*
chlorination	*chem*		classicalism	*lit*
chlorous|acid	*chem*		classicalist	*educ*
chocolate|box	*food*		classic|races	*sport*
choice|morsel	*food*		clavicembalo	*music*
choreography	*theatre*		clearing|bank	*trade*
chorus|singer	*music*		clear|the|land	*travel*
Chosen|People	*relig*		clerk|of|works	*jobs*
chrestomathy	*lit*		cliff|swallow	*birds*
Christianity	*relig*		climbing|fern	*plants*
Christmas|day	*time*		climbing|rope	*sport*
Christmas|eve	*time*		closing|price	*trade*
Christ's|thorn	*trees*		clothes|brush	*clothes*
chromaticity	*art*		clothes|brush	*house*
chrome|orange	*colour*		clothes|drier	*house*
chrome|yellow	*colour*		clothes|horse	*clothes*
chromosphere	*astron*		clothes|horse	*house*
chronography	*lit*		clotted|cream	*food*
Chrysomallus	*myth*		cloud|chamber	*physics*
church|living	*relig*		club|sandwich	*food*
churchmaster	*relig*		Clytemnestra	*myth*
church|nation	*relig*		coach|and|four	*travel*
church|parade	*relig*		coach|and|pair	*travel*
church|school	*educ*		coachbuilder	*jobs*
churchwarden	*jobs*		coachbuilder	*travel*
churchwarden	*relig*		coal|measures	*mineral*
cigarette|box	*house*		cobalt|glance	*chem*
cinnabar|moth	*insects*		cockfighting	*sport*
cinnamon|ball	*food*		Cocos|Islands	*islands*

codification	law	concert|music	music
cold|compress	medic	concert|party	theatre
collaborator	jobs	concert|pitch	music
collaborator	lit	Concertstuck	music
collaborator	people	condemnation	law
collar|and|tie	clothes	condemned|man	law
collectarium	lit	condensation	lit
collectarium	relig	condensation	physics
collectivism	govt	conditioning	medic
College|Board	educ	confectioner	jobs
college|scarf	clothes	confessional	relig
Colonel|Blimp	govt	confirmation	relig
Colonel|Blimp	people	confiscation	law
colour|circle	art	conglomerate	geog
colour|filter	art	congregation	relig
combinations	clothes	conic|section	maths
combinations	maths	conning|tower	travel
come|down|with	medic	conquistador	jobs
comedy|ballet	music	conscription	govt
comedy|ballet	theatre	consecration	relig
Commandments	relig	conseil|d'etat	foreign
commentation	lit	consequences	sport
commissariat	govt	consequently	time
commissioner	govt	conservatism	govt
commissioner	jobs	Conservative	govt
common|bricks	archit	conservative	people
common|factor	maths	conservatory	archit
common|lawyer	law	conservatory	educ
common|market	trade	conservatory	music
Common|Prayer	relig	conservatory	plants
commonwealth	geog	console|table	house
commonwealth	govt	constabulary	law
companion|set	house	constipation	medic
companion|way	travel	constituency	govt
compass|point	geog	constituents	chem
compensation	govt	constitution	govt
compensation	trade	construction	archit
complete|work	lit	construction	lit
complication	lit	consultation	medic
complication	medic	consumer|good	trade
compos|mentis	foreign	contemporary	jobs
compound|time	music	contemporary	time
compurgation	law	contour|chair	house
concert|grand	music	contra|mundum	foreign
concertinist	music	contrapuntal	music

control|panel	*machine*
control|stick	*travel*
control|tower	*travel*
control|valve	*machine*
convalescent	*medic*
convex|mirror	*house*
conveyancing	*law*
conveyor|belt	*machine*
cooking|apple	*fruit*
cooking|range	*house*
cook|the|books	*trade*
cooling|tower	*machine*
Coptic|church	*relig*
copying|press	*machine*
corn|chandler	*jobs*
corn|in|Israel	*cereal*
Cornish|pasty	*food*
corn|marigold	*flowers*
corn|on|the|cob	*cereal*
corn|on|the|cob	*veg*
coronary|vein	*medic*
coroner's|jury	*law*
Cosi|fan|Tutte	*titles*
cosmopolitan	*people*
costermonger	*jobs*
costermonger	*trade*
cost|of|living	*trade*
cottage|china	*art*
couchant|lion	*herald*
cough|mixture	*medic*
council|of|war	*war*
Count|Dracula	*lit*
counter|march	*travel*
counter|march	*war*
counterpoint	*music*
counter|tenor	*music*
countervenom	*medic*
counting|room	*trade*
country|dance	*music*
country|dance	*sport*
country|house	*archit*
coupe|Jacques	*food*
course|of|time	*time*
court|martial	*law*
court|martial	*war*

court|of|wards	*law*
court|plaster	*medic*
cousin|german	*family*
Covent|Garden	*veg*
covetousness	*sins*
cradle|cannon	*sport*
crap|shooting	*sport*
crash|barrier	*travel*
crash|landing	*travel*
credit|rating	*trade*
creme|caramel	*foreign*
crepe|de|Chine	*clothes*
crescent|moon	*astron*
crested|swift	*birds*
crewel|needle	*clothes*
cricket|boots	*sport*
cricket|pitch	*sport*
criminal|code	*law*
criminal|suit	*law*
critical|list	*medic*
critical|mass	*physics*
critical|path	*maths*
critical|path	*trade*
croquet|court	*sport*
cross|bedding	*geog*
cross|botonny	*herald*
cross|country	*sport*
cross|examine	*law*
cross|section	*biol*
crowned|eagle	*birds*
crust|of|bread	*food*
cryoplankton	*biol*
crystallites	*physics*
cuckoo|flower	*flowers*
cuckoo|roller	*birds*
cuckoo|shrike	*birds*
cucumber|flea	*insects*
cucumber|tree	*trees*
culture|flask	*biol*
cumulo|cirrus	*weather*
cumulo|nimbus	*weather*
cumulus|cloud	*weather*
curds|and|whey	*food*
curietherapy	*medic*
curling|stone	*sport*

curling|tongs	*clothes*
currency|note	*trade*
current|price	*trade*
cushion|dance	*music*
custard|apple	*fruit*
custard|sauce	*food*
customs|clerk	*jobs*
customs|union	*govt*
customs|union	*trade*
cut|and|thrust	*sport*
cut|and|thrust	*war*
cylinder|head	*machine*
cylinder|head	*travel*
daggers|drawn	*war*
Damascus|road	*relig*
Danish|pastry	*food*
Danse|Macabre	*titles*
Danzig|brandy	*drink*
Darby|and|Joan	*family*
Das|Rheingold	*titles*
Day|of|the|Lord	*relig*
deactivation	*chem*
dead|ball|line	*sport*
dead|language	*lit*
deadly|weapon	*war*
Dead|Sea|apple	*fruit*
Dead|Sea|fruit	*fruit*
death|penalty	*law*
death|warrant	*law*
debilitation	*medic*
debtor's|court	*law*
deceleration	*physics*
December|moth	*insects*
decimal|point	*maths*
decimal|point	*measure*
decisive|hour	*time*
Decius|Brutus	*Shakesp*
decline|of|day	*time*
declinometer	*measure*
decorticated	*cereal*
decorticated	*trees*
deep|sea|diver	*jobs*
deep|sea|diver	*sport*
deflagration	*physics*
degringolade	*foreign*
deionization	*chem*
delicatessen	*food*
deliquescent	*chem*
demi|culverin	*war*
demonstrator	*jobs*
den|of|thieves	*law*
denomination	*relig*
denomination	*trade*
deponent|verb	*lit*
depreciation	*trade*
depth|sounder	*machine*
Derwentwater	*lakes*
design|centre	*art*
desk|sergeant	*jobs*
desobligeant	*travel*
dessert|spoon	*house*
Devil's|Island	*islands*
dialling|code	*travel*
dialling|tone	*travel*
Dick|Datchery	*lit*
dictatorship	*govt*
diesel|engine	*machine*
dietotherapy	*biol*
dietotherapy	*medic*
differencing	*herald*
differential	*machine*
differential	*maths*
dinner|jacket	*clothes*
direct|cannon	*sport*
direct|labour	*trade*
direct|object	*lit*
directors|box	*sport*
direct|speech	*lit*
disbursement	*trade*
disciplinary	*educ*
discount|rate	*trade*
disinfectant	*biol*
disinfectant	*house*
disinfectant	*medic*
dispatch|boat	*travel*
dispensation	*law*
displacement	*physics*
disqualified	*sport*
disquisition	*educ*
disquisition	*lit*

dissertation	*lit*
dissociation	*chem*
distillation	*chem*
distribution	*trade*
divertimento	*music*
divided skirt	*clothes*
dividing wall	*archit*
diving beetle	*insects*
diving petrel	*birds*
divorce court	*law*
doctor's round	*jobs*
dodecahedron	*maths*
dog in a manger	*animals*
do it yourself	*sport*
dollar crisis	*trade*
Dombey and Son	*titles*
domestic fowl	*birds*
dominant note	*music*
dominion rule	*govt*
domino theory	*govt*
donkey engine	*machine*
donkey jacket	*clothes*
donkey's years	*time*
Donnerwetter	*foreign*
Doppelganger	*myth*
doppelganger	*people*
Dormer window	*archit*
dotted quaver	*music*
double boiler	*house*
double dagger	*lit*
double decker	*travel*
double glazed	*archit*
double jersey	*clothes*
double scroll	*archit*
double sculls	*sport*
doubles match	*sport*
double threes	*sport*
dragon lizard	*insects*
dragon's blood	*trees*
dramatic play	*theatre*
dramaturgist	*jobs*
dramaturgist	*theatre*
draught horse	*animals*
draught horse	*travel*
drawing board	*art*
drawing paper	*art*
Dresden china	*art*
dressing case	*clothes*
dressing down	*law*
dressing gown	*clothes*
dressing room	*clothes*
dressing room	*house*
dressing room	*sport*
dressing room	*theatre*
dress uniform	*clothes*
drift current	*marine*
drinking song	*music*
driving force	*machine*
dropped waist	*clothes*
dual controls	*travel*
duchesse lace	*clothes*
ducking stool	*law*
duffel jacket	*clothes*
Duke of Omnium	*lit*
dumb creature	*animals*
dumdum bullet	*war*
durable goods	*trade*
duraluminium	*mineral*
Dutch auction	*trade*
Dutch courage	*war*
Dutch dresser	*house*
Dyanean rocks	*myth*
early closing	*trade*
early edition	*lit*
earned income	*trade*
earth stopper	*sport*
East China Sea	*seas*
Easter bonnet	*clothes*
Easter Island	*islands*
East Indiaman	*travel*
eau de Cologne	*clothes*
eavesdropper	*people*
eccentricity	*maths*
ecclesiastic	*jobs*
ecclesiastic	*relig*
econometrics	*trade*
economy drive	*trade*
effervescent	*chem*
ejection seat	*travel*
electric blue	*colour*

electric cell	*physics*
electric cord	*machine*
electric fire	*house*
electric fire	*machine*
electric iron	*house*
electric iron	*tools*
electric lamp	*house*
electric lamp	*physics*
electric wire	*machine*
electrolysis	*medic*
electrometer	*measure*
electron bomb	*war*
electron pair	*physics*
electronvolt	*measure*
electronvolt	*physics*
electroplate	*mineral*
electroscope	*physics*
electrotyper	*jobs*
elegiac verse	*lit*
elephant bird	*birds*
elevated area	*geog*
eleventh hour	*time*
Elgin marbles	*art*
elixir of life	*medic*
elocutionist	*jobs*
embezzlement	*law*
emerald green	*colour*
emergency bed	*house*
emergency bed	*medic*
encephalitis	*medic*
encirclement	*war*
encyclopedia	*educ*
encyclopedia	*lit*
end of the line	*travel*
endoskeleton	*medic*
engines of war	*war*
enshrinement	*relig*
entomologist	*jobs*
entrance hall	*archit*
entrance lock	*travel*
entrenchment	*war*
entrepreneur	*jobs*
entrepreneur	*theatre*
entrepreneur	*trade*
epigrammatic	*lit*
Epithalamion	*titles*
eppur si muove	*foreign*
equestrienne	*jobs*
Erichthonius	*myth*
escape rocket	*travel*
escapologist	*jobs*
escaramouche	*war*
espagnolette	*archit*
esparto grass	*plants*
essential oil	*biol*
estate at will	*law*
estate in tail	*law*
Esther Waters	*lit*
etching point	*art*
eternity ring	*jewels*
etesian winds	*weather*
Eton wall game	*sport*
Eugene Onegin	*titles*
eurythermous	*biol*
evaporimeter	*geog*
evening cloak	*clothes*
evening dress	*clothes*
evening shoes	*clothes*
exchange rate	*trade*
exercise book	*educ*
exhaust price	*trade*
exhibitioner	*educ*
exhibitioner	*jobs*
experimental	*biol*
experimental	*chem*
experimental	*physics*
experimenter	*jobs*
experto crede	*foreign*
ex serviceman	*jobs*
exsufflation	*myth*
extend credit	*trade*
extended play	*music*
extensometer	*measure*
exterminator	*jobs*
extractor fan	*house*
extranuclear	*physics*
extravagance	*trade*
extravaganza	*music*
extravaganza	*theatre*
fair exchange	*trade*

fait accompli	*foreign*
faith healing	*medic*
falcon gentil	*birds*
fallen arches	*medic*
false bedding	*geog*
false cadence	*music*
false ceiling	*archit*
false colours	*herald*
false colours	*war*
false horizon	*geog*
false witness	*law*
family doctor	*jobs*
family doctor	*medic*
Farne Islands	*islands*
Faroe Islands	*islands*
fashion house	*clothes*
fashion plate	*art*
fashion plate	*clothes*
fast and loose	*sport*
fat faced type	*lit*
father figure	*jobs*
fatigue dress	*clothes*
Feast of Weeks	*time*
feather brain	*people*
feather grass	*plants*
Federal Union	*govt*
felinophobia	*medic*
fennel flower	*flowers*
ferae naturae	*foreign*
fermentation	*biol*
ferrous oxide	*chem*
feudal estate	*govt*
feudal system	*govt*
feud artifice	*foreign*
fever blister	*medic*
feverishness	*medic*
fiddlesticks	*music*
fiddlestring	*music*
field glasses	*sport*
field marshal	*jobs*
field of blood	*war*
field officer	*jobs*
field of force	*geog*
field spaniel	*animals*
fiery serpent	*relig*
fighter pilot	*travel*
fighting cock	*birds*
fighting fish	*fish*
figure dancer	*jobs*
figure skater	*sport*
filament lamp	*machine*
filibusterer	*jobs*
fill an office	*trade*
fillet of sole	*food*
film director	*jobs*
film festival	*film/TV*
film producer	*jobs*
finnan haddie	*food*
firelighters	*house*
fireside seat	*house*
First Chamber	*govt*
first defence	*sport*
first edition	*lit*
first innings	*sport*
first nighter	*theatre*
first offence	*law*
first officer	*jobs*
first refusal	*trade*
first reserve	*jobs*
first reserve	*sport*
first service	*sport*
fiscal policy	*trade*
fish and chips	*food*
fish dressing	*food*
fishing fleet	*travel*
fishing smack	*travel*
fitted carpet	*house*
fixed capital	*trade*
flame thrower	*machine*
flame thrower	*war*
flashing lamp	*machine*
flaxen haired	*clothes*
flight tester	*travel*
flittermouse	*people*
floating debt	*trade*
floating mine	*war*
floating vote	*govt*
flocculation	*chem*
florid phrase	*music*
flower border	*flowers*

flower‖delice	*flowers*	fowling‖piece	*war*
flower‖de‖luce	*flowers*	frankalmoign	*law*
flower‖garden	*flowers*	Frankenstein	*titles*
flower‖holder	*house*	frankincense	*relig*
flower‖of‖Jove	*flowers*	frankincense	*trees*
flower‖pecker	*birds*	freewheeling	*sport*
flower‖people	*people*	freewheeling	*travel*
fluorescence	*physics*	freezing‖cold	*weather*
fluorocarbon	*chem*	freight‖train	*travel*
fluorography	*chem*	French‖boxing	*sport*
fluted‖column	*archit*	French‖Gothic	*archit*
flying‖circus	*travel*	French‖lesson	*educ*
flying‖column	*jobs*	French‖pastry	*food*
flying‖column	*war*	French‖polish	*house*
flying‖doctor	*jobs*	French‖poodle	*animals*
flying‖lizard	*insects*	french‖window	*archit*
flying‖saucer	*travel*	fresh‖flowers	*flowers*
flying‖tackle	*sport*	friar's‖balsam	*medic*
flying‖tanker	*travel*	from‖that‖time	*time*
folding‖money	*trade*	frontispiece	*archit*
following‖day	*time*	frontispiece	*lit*
fool's‖parsley	*plants*	frozen‖tundra	*geog*
football‖boot	*clothes*	fruit‖machine	*machine*
footplate‖man	*jobs*	fruit‖machine	*sport*
force‖majeure	*foreign*	fuel‖injector	*travel*
forcing‖house	*plants*	fuller's‖earth	*mineral*
foreign‖trade	*trade*	full‖mourning	*clothes*
forestaysail	*travel*	fully‖fledged	*birds*
Forfar‖bridie	*food*	fume‖cupboard	*chem*
forge‖foundry	*machine*	funeral‖march	*music*
formaldehyde	*biol*	Gainsborough	*artists*
formaldehyde	*medic*	galilee‖porch	*archit*
form‖mistress	*educ*	galligaskins	*clothes*
forward‖march	*travel*	gallinaceous	*birds*
forward‖march	*war*	galvanometer	*physics*
foster‖father	*family*	game‖of‖chance	*sport*
foster‖mother	*family*	game‖of‖points	*sport*
foster‖parent	*family*	gamesmanship	*sport*
foster‖sister	*family*	Garden‖of‖Eden	*myth*
foundry‖proof	*lit*	Garden‖of‖Eden	*relig*
fountainhead	*geog*	garden‖roller	*tools*
Four‖Quartets	*titles*	garden‖shears	*tools*
foursome‖reel	*sport*	garden‖spider	*insects*
fourth‖estate	*lit*	garden‖suburb	*archit*
fourth‖of‖July	*time*	garden‖trowel	*tools*

garret master	*jobs*
gastric juice	*medic*
gastroplasty	*medic*
gate leg table	*house*
gate receipts	*trade*
gazelle hound	*animals*
geanticlinal	*geog*
general agent	*jobs*
general store	*trade*
genre painter	*art*
geochemistry	*chem*
geochemistry	*geog*
geographical	*geog*
geomagnetism	*geog*
geomagnetism	*physics*
geometrician	*maths*
geosynclinal	*geog*
geotectonics	*geog*
geriatrician	*jobs*
geriatrician	*medic*
gerontocracy	*govt*
Gesellschaft	*foreign*
get rich quick	*trade*
Giant Despair	*lit*
glacial drift	*geog*
glacial epoch	*geog*
glaciologist	*geog*
gladiatorial	*war*
Gladstone bag	*travel*
glass slipper	*clothes*
glide landing	*travel*
globetrotter	*jobs*
globetrotter	*travel*
glockenspiel	*music*
glutamic acid	*chem*
glycoprotein	*chem*
glyphography	*art*
gnomic aorist	*lit*
goat antelope	*animals*
gobbledegook	*lit*
go by the board	*travel*
going concern	*trade*
golden apples	*myth*
golden fleece	*myth*
golden guinea	*measure*

golden haired	*clothes*
Golden Legend	*myth*
golden oriole	*birds*
golden plover	*birds*
golden salmon	*fish*
golden yellow	*colour*
goldfish bowl	*fish*
gold standard	*trade*
gone to ground	*sport*
goods for sale	*trade*
Good Shepherd	*relig*
go over the top	*war*
gossip column	*lit*
gram molecule	*chem*
gram molecule	*measure*
grand duchess	*govt*
Grand Guignol	*theatre*
grand juryman	*law*
grand larceny	*law*
grand quarter	*herald*
grandstander	*jobs*
grand tactics	*war*
Gran Paradiso	*mounts*
granting arms	*herald*
grants of arms	*herald*
granular snow	*geog*
grated cheese	*food*
gravicembalo	*music*
grease nipple	*machine*
Great Britain	*islands*
great expense	*trade*
Greek calends	*time*
Greek theatre	*theatre*
green fingers	*plants*
Greenland Sea	*seas*
grey eminence	*people*
grey squirrel	*animals*
grilled steak	*food*
grinding mill	*machine*
grinding pain	*medic*
ground almond	*food*
ground beetle	*insects*
ground cherry	*fruit*
ground cuckoo	*birds*
ground feeder	*fish*

ground|forces	*war*
ground|ginger	*food*
ground|pepper	*food*
ground|school	*educ*
ground|stroke	*sport*
ground|tester	*travel*
group|captain	*jobs*
Guadal|quivir	*rivers*
guardianship	*govt*
guerrilla|war	*war*
guessing|game	*sport*
guest|speaker	*jobs*
guided|weapon	*war*
Guildenstern	*Shakesp*
Guinea|baboon	*animals*
Gulf|of|Darien	*seas*
Gulf|of|Guinea	*seas*
Gulf|of|Mannar	*seas*
Gulf|of|Mexico	*seas*
Gulf|of|Panama	*seas*
Gulf|of|Tonkin	*seas*
Gulley|Jimson	*lit*
gun|metal|grey	*colour*
Guy|Mannering	*titles*
gynecologist	*jobs*
gynecologist	*medic*
habeas|corpus	*law*
haberdashery	*clothes*
haberdashery	*trade*
hackney|coach	*travel*
hagiographer	*relig*
hair|dressing	*clothes*
hair|follicle	*medic*
hair|restorer	*clothes*
hair|restorer	*medic*
hairsbreadth	*measure*
hair|splitter	*people*
half|mourning	*clothes*
Halley's|comet	*astron*
halting|rhyme	*lit*
Hamburg|steak	*food*
handicap|race	*sport*
handkerchief	*clothes*
Handley|Cross	*titles*
hanging|judge	*law*
happy|landing	*travel*
harbour|light	*travel*
hard|currency	*trade*
hare|and|hound	*animals*
haricot|beans	*veg*
harlequinade	*theatre*
harmoni|chord	*music*
harmonic|tone	*music*
harvest|mouse	*animals*
hassock|grass	*plants*
hasta|la|vista	*foreign*
hasty|pudding	*food*
haute|couture	*clothes*
haute|cuisine	*food*
headmistress	*educ*
headmistress	*jobs*
head|moulding	*archit*
head|scissors	*sport*
headshrinker	*jobs*
headshrinker	*people*
health|resort	*medic*
heart|disease	*medic*
heart|failure	*medic*
heavenly|body	*astron*
heavenly|host	*myth*
heavy|cruiser	*travel*
heavy|dragoon	*war*
hedge|hopping	*travel*
hedge|sparrow	*birds*
hedge|trimmer	*tools*
hedge|warbler	*birds*
heir|apparent	*family*
heir|apparent	*govt*
heir|apparent	*jobs*
heliogravure	*art*
hell|grammite	*insects*
Henry|Higgins	*lit*
Henry|Willcox	*lit*
herald|angels	*relig*
heraldic|seal	*herald*
hereditament	*law*
hermeneutics	*lit*
hermit|thrush	*birds*
Hesperethusa	*myth*
Hessian|boots	*clothes*

heterocyclic	*chem*
hidden|fifths	*music*
hieroglyphic	*lit*
high|fidelity	*machine*
high|fidelity	*physics*
high|official	*jobs*
high|pressure	*trade*
high|pressure	*weather*
hill|climbing	*sport*
hippocentaur	*myth*
hippopotamus	*animals*
hire|purchase	*trade*
hitching|post	*archit*
hockey|player	*jobs*
hold|the|stage	*theatre*
holidaymaker	*jobs*
hollow|relief	*art*
Holy|Alliance	*relig*
Holy|of|Holies	*relig*
Holy|Thursday	*relig*
Holy|Thursday	*time*
home|reserves	*war*
home|straight	*sport*
homing|pigeon	*birds*
homing|pigeon	*sport*
homing|rocket	*war*
homme|du|monde	*foreign*
honey|buzzard	*birds*
honoris|causa	*foreign*
hoofed|animal	*animals*
horned|lizard	*insects*
horn|of|plenty	*myth*
hors|concours	*foreign*
hors|de|combat	*foreign*
horse|and|foot	*war*
horse|blanket	*animals*
horsemanship	*sport*
horse|marines	*war*
horticulture	*agric*
hospital|ship	*travel*
hot|chocolate	*drink*
hotel|de|ville	*archit*
hotel|manager	*jobs*
hot|gospeller	*relig*
hot|water|tank	*house*

hound's|tongue	*plants*
housebreaker	*jobs*
housebreaker	*law*
household|god	*myth*
House|of|Lords	*govt*
House|of|Lords	*law*
House|of|Peers	*govt*
housepainter	*jobs*
housey|housey	*sport*
Hudibrastics	*lit*
humanitarian	*people*
hummel|bonnet	*clothes*
Humpty|Dumpty	*lit*
hundred|yards	*sport*
hungry|market	*trade*
hunting|groom	*sport*
hunting|lodge	*archit*
hurdy|gurdist	*music*
hyacinth|blue	*colour*
hydraulic|ram	*tools*
hydrocarbons	*chem*
hydrogen|atom	*chem*
hydrogen|bomb	*war*
hydropathist	*jobs*
hydropathist	*medic*
hydrostatics	*chem*
hydrotherapy	*medic*
hymnographer	*music*
hyperalgebra	*maths*
Hyperboreans	*myth*
hyperphysics	*physics*
hypertension	*medic*
hysterectomy	*medic*
iatrochemist	*chem*
iatrochemist	*medic*
iatrophysics	*medic*
iatrophysics	*physics*
ice|cream|cone	*food*
ice|cream|soda	*drink*
Iceland|poppy	*flowers*
ichthyopsida	*fish*
if|the|cap|fits	*clothes*
illumination	*art*
illustration	*art*
immune|bodies	*biol*

immunization	*medic*
immunologist	*jobs*
immunologist	*medic*
imperial|coin	*money*
Imperial|Diet	*govt*
imperial|pint	*measure*
imperial|seal	*herald*
impersonator	*jobs*
impersonator	*theatre*
imprisonment	*law*
improvisator	*jobs*
improvisator	*music*
impulse|buyer	*trade*
inactivation	*chem*
inclinometer	*measure*
inclinometer	*travel*
in|conference	*jobs*
in|conference	*trade*
incriminator	*law*
in|days|of|yore	*time*
indebtedness	*trade*
indelible|ink	*lit*
independence	*govt*
Indianapolis	*cities*
Indian|summer	*time*
Indian|summer	*weather*
indoctrinate	*educ*
inescutcheon	*herald*
infant|school	*educ*
inflammation	*medic*
infra,red|lamp	*physics*
in|high|relief	*art*
initial|rhyme	*lit*
in|litigation	*law*
inner|sanctum	*archit*
inner|sanctum	*house*
Innocents|day	*time*
in|olden|times	*time*
insemination	*agric*
inseparables	*jobs*
instructress	*educ*
instructress	*jobs*
instrumental	*lit*
instrumental	*music*
integral|dose	*medic*
intellectual	*educ*
intelligence	*educ*
interest|rate	*trade*
interference	*physics*
interjection	*lit*
intermediary	*jobs*
intermission	*time*
internal|bond	*trade*
in|the|gazette	*trade*
in|the|running	*sport*
in|the|train|of	*travel*
intoxication	*medic*
intransitive	*lit*
in|triplicate	*govt*
introduction	*lit*
introduction	*music*
introduction	*theatre*
intromission	*law*
inverted|spin	*travel*
inverted|turn	*music*
investigator	*law*
investigator	*sport*
invisible|ink	*lit*
ion|exchanger	*chem*
Irish|terrier	*animals*
Irish|whiskey	*drink*
ironing|board	*house*
ironing|table	*house*
island|of|Reil	*medic*
Isle|of|Apples	*myth*
Isle|of|Thanet	*islands*
isolationism	*govt*
Italian|sixth	*music*
ivory|thumper	*music*
ivory|tickler	*music*
Jack|Absolute	*lit*
Jack|in|office	*govt*
jack|in|the|box	*sport*
jack|o'|lantern	*geog*
Jacksonville	*cities*
Jacob's|ladder	*plants*
Jacob's|ladder	*relig*
Jacob's|ladder	*travel*
jail|sentence	*law*
jazz|musician	*jobs*

jazz musician	*music*	king of beasts	*animals*
jet propelled	*travel*	king's counsel	*jobs*
Johannesburg	*cities*	King's counsel	*law*
John Jarndyce	*lit*	king's English	*lit*
John Jorrocks	*lit*	king's highway	*travel*
John Worthing	*lit*	King's Proctor	*law*
joint account	*trade*	kitchen staff	*jobs*
jot and tittle	*relig*	kitchen table	*house*
judge and jury	*law*	kleptomaniac	*people*
judge made law	*law*	knee breeches	*clothes*
judgment debt	*law*	kneehold desk	*house*
judgment hall	*law*	knifegrinder	*jobs*
Judgment Hall	*relig*	knifethrower	*jobs*
judgment seat	*law*	knight errant	*govt*
Judgment Seat	*relig*	knitting wool	*clothes*
judicial oath	*law*	knockout drop	*medic*
Julius Caesar	*Shakesp*	knucklebones	*sport*
Julius Caesar	*leaders*	Kreisleriana	*titles*
Julius Caesar	*titles*	Kriss Kringle	*myth*
jumping mouse	*animals*	labour of love	*trade*
jumping shrew	*animals*	labour saving	*house*
junior rating	*jobs*	lady from hell	*war*
junior school	*educ*	lady's fingers	*plants*
Junius Brutus	*Shakesp*	lady's slipper	*flowers*
Juno Quiritis	*myth*	lady's thistle	*plants*
jurisdiction	*law*	lady superior	*jobs*
jurisprudent	*law*	Laestrygones	*myth*
Justice clerk	*law*	laissez faire	*govt*
juvenile lead	*jobs*	laissez faire	*trade*
juvenile lead	*theatre*	Lake Balkhash	*lakes*
kaleidoscope	*art*	Lake District	*geog*
kaleidoscope	*sport*	lake dwelling	*archit*
Kanchenjunga	*mounts*	lake dwelling	*geog*
Karelia Suite	*titles*	Lake Maggiore	*lakes*
keep accounts	*trade*	Lake Manitoba	*lakes*
keratogenous	*biol*	Lake Michigan	*lakes*
keraunograph	*weather*	Lake Superior	*lakes*
kettle holder	*house*	Lake Tiberias	*lakes*
kettle of fish	*fish*	Lake Titicaca	*lakes*
key signature	*music*	Lake Tritonis	*myth*
Khachaturian	*music*	Lake Victoria	*lakes*
Khovanschina	*titles*	Lake Wakatipu	*lakes*
kilowatt hour	*measure*	Lake Winnipeg	*lakes*
kindergarten	*educ*	lamb's lettuce	*veg*
Kinderscenen	*titles*	lampadedromy	*sport*

lancet|window	*archit*
landed|gentry	*govt*
landed|gentry	*jobs*
landing|craft	*travel*
landing|field	*travel*
landing|light	*machine*
landing|light	*travel*
landing|speed	*travel*
landing|stage	*sport*
landing|stage	*travel*
landing|strip	*travel*
Land|o|the|Leal	*myth*
Land|Registry	*law*
land|surveyor	*jobs*
lantern|slide	*art*
lap|of|the|gods	*myth*
lapsus|calami	*foreign*
laser|surgery	*medic*
La|Sonnambula	*titles*
Last|Judgment	*relig*
late|in|the|day	*time*
launching|pad	*travel*
launching|pad	*war*
laurel|wreath	*herald*
lavender|blue	*colour*
law|of|gravity	*geog*
law|of|gravity	*physics*
law|of|the|land	*law*
law|stationer	*jobs*
layout|artist	*jobs*
leader|writer	*jobs*
leader|writer	*lit*
leading|light	*govt*
learn|by|heart	*educ*
leather|goods	*trade*
leathernecks	*jobs*
leathernecks	*war*
left|luggage	*govt*
legal|adviser	*jobs*
legal|adviser	*law*
legal|aid|fund	*law*
legal|fiction	*law*
legal|history	*law*
legally|bound	*law*
legal|redress	*law*
legal|science	*law*
Leopold|Bloom	*lit*
Le|Pere|Goriot	*titles*
Lernean|Hydra	*myth*
Les|Huguenots	*titles*
less|semitone	*music*
Les|Sylphides	*titles*
letter|writer	*jobs*
letter|writer	*lit*
level|landing	*travel*
level|pegging	*sport*
lexicography	*lit*
lexicologist	*jobs*
Leyden|cheese	*food*
Liberal|party	*govt*
library|table	*house*
life|sentence	*law*
Light|Brigade	*war*
light|cruiser	*travel*
light|dragoon	*war*
light|fitting	*house*
light|harmony	*music*
lightning|bug	*insects*
lightning|rod	*machine*
lightning|zip	*clothes*
light|therapy	*medic*
lignographer	*art*
limnophilous	*insects*
Lincoln|green	*colour*
line|engraver	*art*
line|geometry	*maths*
line|of|action	*war*
line|of|battle	*war*
line|of|credit	*trade*
line|sergeant	*jobs*
link|bracelet	*jewels*
Linz|Symphony	*titles*
liquefaction	*chem*
liquid|oxygen	*chem*
lite|pendente	*foreign*
literary|hack	*jobs*
literary|hack	*lit*
literary|lion	*jobs*
literary|lion	*lit*
lithographer	*art*

lithographer *jobs*
lithographic *art*
lithogravure *art*
Little Dorrit *titles*
little people *myth*
live in clover *trade*
lively market *trade*
lock hospital *medic*
Locksley Hall *titles*
lodging place *archit*
logodaedalus *lit*
London Bridge *sport*
long distance *sport*
long distance *travel*
long division *maths*
long interest *trade*
longshoreman *jobs*
longshoreman *travel*
long standing *time*
looking glass *house*
loose forward *sport*
Lord Advocate *law*
lord temporal *govt*
lose one's head *medic*
lose strength *medic*
losing hazard *sport*
loss adjuster *jobs*
loss of memory *medic*
lost and found *travel*
lounge lizard *people*
lower chamber *govt*
Lucie Manette *lit*
luggage label *travel*
luggage train *travel*
lumber jacket *clothes*
luminescence *physics*
lunch counter *house*
luncheon meat *food*
lying in state *govt*
lyric cantata *music*
lysergic acid *chem*
Macchiavelli *writers*
machicolated *archit*
machicolated *war*
machine ruler *machine*

macroclimate *weather*
macrophysics *physics*
Madame Bovary *titles*
mad as a hatter *people*
madder orange *colour*
madder violet *colour*
madder yellow *colour*
magazine rack *house*
magic lantern *art*
magic lantern *machine*
magistrature *law*
magnetic axis *geog*
magnetic mine *war*
magnetic pole *geog*
magnetic tape *machine*
magnetometer *measure*
Magnitogorsk *cities*
magyar sleeve *clothes*
maiden assize *law*
Maiden Castle *archit*
maiden flight *travel*
maiden speech *govt*
maiden stakes *sport*
maiden voyage *travel*
maid of honour *jobs*
main entrance *archit*
main sequence *geog*
main staysail *travel*
maitre d'hotel *jobs*
Major Barbara *titles*
major general *jobs*
majority rule *govt*
majority vote *govt*
major prophet *relig*
major seventh *music*
major surgery *medic*
make a bargain *trade*
make a fortune *trade*
make delivery *trade*
make good time *travel*
make one's pile *trade*
make progress *travel*
make the grade *educ*
make up artist *jobs*
make up artist *theatre*

malnutrition	*medic*	mass|producer	*jobs*
mammary|gland	*medic*	master|at|arms	*jobs*
man|about|town	*people*	master|of|arts	*educ*
mandarin|duck	*birds*	mastersinger	*jobs*
mangel|wurzel	*veg*	mating|season	*animals*
man|in|the|moon	*astron*	matter|of|fact	*educ*
manipulation	*trade*	mean|sea|level	*geog*
manned|rocket	*travel*	mean|semitone	*music*
man|of|letters	*educ*	measured|mile	*measure*
man|of|letters	*jobs*	Medical|Corps	*war*
man|of|letters	*lit*	medicine|ball	*sport*
man|of|science	*jobs*	medieval|mode	*music*
man|of|war|fish	*fish*	medium|bomber	*war*
Manon|Lescaut	*titles*	meeting|house	*archit*
man|overboard	*travel*	Meg|Merrilies	*lit*
mansion|house	*archit*	melding|score	*sport*
manslaughter	*law*	mellifluence	*music*
mantis|shrimp	*fish*	melodic|minor	*music*
manual|worker	*jobs*	melodramatic	*theatre*
manufacturer	*jobs*	melting|point	*chem*
manufacturer	*trade*	memorization	*educ*
many|a|long|day	*time*	Mendes|France	*leaders*
Marathon|bull	*myth*	mental|labour	*educ*
marathon|race	*sport*	mercantilism	*trade*
marbled|white	*insects*	merchant|ship	*travel*
march|against	*war*	mercy|killing	*law*
marching|song	*music*	merry|go|round	*sport*
marching|song	*war*	merrythought	*birds*
Marcus|Brutus	*Shakesp*	mesomorphous	*chem*
marginal|cost	*trade*	metachronism	*time*
marginal|land	*geog*	metal|fatigue	*mineral*
marine|engine	*machine*	metallograph	*art*
market|garden	*agric*	metallurgist	*jobs*
market|garden	*veg*	metamorphism	*geog*
marlinespike	*tools*	metaphorical	*lit*
marmalade|cat	*animals*	metasomatism	*geog*
marriage|vows	*relig*	meteor|crater	*astron*
marrow|fat	*veg*	meteorograph	*astron*
marrow|squash	*veg*	meteorograph	*weather*
marsh|harrier	*birds*	method|acting	*theatre*
martial|music	*music*	metrical|foot	*lit*
masked|comedy	*theatre*	metrical|unit	*lit*
masonry|drill	*tools*	metric|system	*maths*
massaranduba	*trees*	metric|system	*measure*
mass|produced	*trade*	metropolitan	*govt*

metropolitan	*jobs*	mixed|doubles	*sport*
mezzo‚relievo	*art*	mobile|camera	*machine*
mezzo‚soprano	*jobs*	mobilization	*war*
mezzo‚soprano	*music*	moderate|wind	*weather*
Michelangelo	*artists*	modern|ballet	*theatre*
microammeter	*physics*	modest|violet	*people*
microbalance	*chem*	modus|vivendi	*govt*
microburette	*chem*	Moll|Flanders	*lit*
micro|circuit	*machine*	Moll|Flanders	*titles*
microclimate	*weather*	monetization	*trade*
microelement	*chem*	moneychanger	*jobs*
microohmeter	*measure*	moneychanger	*relig*
microphysics	*physics*	moneychanger	*trade*
microspecies	*biol*	moneygrubber	*people*
midcontinent	*geog*	money|matters	*trade*
middle|school	*educ*	monkey‚flower	*flowers*
midnight|blue	*colour*	monkey|jacket	*clothes*
migratory|low	*weather*	monkey|puzzle	*trees*
miles|per|hour	*measure*	monkey‚rigged	*travel*
military|band	*music*	monkeywrench	*machine*
military|zone	*war*	monkish|Latin	*lit*
millerontgen	*physics*	monochordist	*music*
miller's|thumb	*fish*	monographist	*jobs*
millirontgen	*measure*	monomorphous	*biol*
mincing|steps	*sport*	monosyllable	*lit*
mine|detector	*machine*	Monte|Cassino	*mounts*
mine|detector	*war*	Mont|St|Michel	*islands*
mineralogist	*jobs*	moral|courage	*war*
mineral|pitch	*mineral*	morality|play	*lit*
mineral|water	*drink*	morality|play	*theatre*
minor|element	*chem*	moral|support	*war*
minor|prophet	*relig*	moral|victory	*war*
minor|seventh	*music*	morbid|growth	*medic*
minor|surgery	*medic*	morning|dress	*clothes*
minstrel|show	*theatre*	morning|glory	*flowers*
minstrel|song	*music*	mortgage|bond	*trade*
mirror|nuclei	*physics*	mosquito|hawk	*insects*
misdemeanour	*law*	mother|tongue	*lit*
missel‚thrush	*birds*	motorcyclist	*jobs*
Miss|Havisham	*lit*	motor|scooter	*travel*
Miss|La|Creevy	*lit*	mountain|goat	*animals*
mistle‚thrush	*birds*	mountain|hare	*animals*
mitotic|index	*biol*	mountain|lion	*animals*
mixed|cadence	*music*	mountain|pass	*geog*
mixed|decimal	*maths*	mountain|peak	*geog*

Mount Helicon	*myth*	naval academy	*educ*
Mount Illampu	*mounts*	naval militia	*war*
Mount Olympus	*mounts*	naval officer	*jobs*
Mount Olympus	*myth*	naval reserve	*war*
Mount Palomar	*mounts*	naval warfare	*war*
Mount Rainier	*mounts*	nearest offer	*trade*
Mount Roraima	*mounts*	near relation	*family*
Mount Ruapehu	*mounts*	Ned Cheeryble	*lit*
Mount Triglav	*mounts*	neighbouring	*geog*
Mount Whitney	*mounts*	neoclassical	*art*
mourning dove	*birds*	nephelometer	*weather*
mourning ring	*jewels*	nest of tables	*house*
mousquetaire	*clothes*	neurasthenia	*medic*
Mrs Millamant	*lit*	New Caledonia	*islands*
mulberry bush	*fruit*	Newfoundland	*animals*
mulligan stew	*food*	Newfoundland	*islands*
mulligatawny	*food*	newspaperman	*jobs*
multiangular	*maths*	newspaperman	*lit*
multilateral	*maths*	New Testament	*relig*
multiplicand	*maths*	nicotinamide	*chem*
multivalence	*chem*	night clothes	*clothes*
municipality	*geog*	night fighter	*travel*
municipality	*govt*	nine till five	*trade*
muriatic acid	*chem*	nitromethane	*chem*
Murrumbidgee	*rivers*	Noah Claypole	*lit*
muscle fibres	*medic*	noble science	*sport*
musical scale	*music*	nolens volens	*foreign*
musical score	*music*	nomenclature	*lit*
musicianship	*music*	nominal price	*trade*
musicologist	*jobs*	nominal value	*trade*
musicologist	*music*	non alcoholic	*drink*
mutation stop	*music*	normal school	*educ*
muzzle loader	*war*	Norway spruce	*trees*
nail clippers	*clothes*	notary public	*jobs*
nail scissors	*clothes*	nouveau riche	*trade*
Napier's bones	*maths*	nuclear force	*physics*
national bank	*trade*	nuclear power	*machine*
national grid	*machine*	nuclear power	*physics*
National Hunt	*sport*	nursery rhyme	*lit*
national park	*animals*	nursery slope	*sport*
native metals	*mineral*	nutritionist	*jobs*
natural child	*family*	nychthemeron	*time*
natural death	*medic*	obiter dictum	*foreign*
nature ramble	*sport*	oblique angle	*maths*
nautical mile	*measure*	obstacle race	*sport*

obstetrician	*jobs*
obstetrician	*medic*
occasionally	*time*
oceanography	*geog*
oceanography	*marine*
odd lot dealer	*trade*
offered price	*trade*
offer for sale	*trade*
office bearer	*govt*
office bearer	*jobs*
officeholder	*govt*
office junior	*jobs*
office junior	*trade*
office of arms	*herald*
off like a shot	*travel*
offshore wind	*weather*
oil of vitriol	*chem*
Oklahoma City	*cities*
old fashioned	*clothes*
old fashioned	*time*
old man's beard	*flowers*
Old Mortality	*titles*
old stage hand	*theatre*
Old Testament	*relig*
old time dance	*sport*
old Worcester	*art*
Olympic games	*sport*
Olympic title	*sport*
Olympic torch	*sport*
once in a while	*time*
one horse town	*geog*
one upmanship	*people*
onomatopoeia	*lit*
on the instant	*time*
on the warpath	*war*
opaque colour	*art*
open end trust	*trade*
opening notes	*music*
opening price	*trade*
open sentence	*maths*
opera comique	*music*
opera glasses	*theatre*
opposing side	*sport*
opposite tide	*marine*
optical laser	*physics*
optic chiasma	*medic*
orange flower	*flowers*
orange madder	*colour*
orchard grass	*plants*
orchestra pit	*music*
orchestra pit	*theatre*
orchestrator	*music*
ordeal by fire	*myth*
ordinary foul	*sport*
organ grinder	*music*
organization	*trade*
oriental opal	*mineral*
orienteering	*sport*
orthodiagram	*medic*
orthodontics	*medic*
orthodontist	*medic*
orthopaedics	*medic*
orthopaedist	*medic*
orthorhombic	*maths*
oscilloscope	*physics*
ossification	*medic*
otherworldly	*geog*
out of fashion	*clothes*
outside right	*sport*
overnight bag	*travel*
Owen Wingrave	*titles*
oxycellulose	*chem*
oxychromatin	*chem*
packing house	*trade*
paddling pool	*sport*
painted snipe	*birds*
painting book	*educ*
paint the lily	*art*
pair of scales	*machine*
Paisley shawl	*clothes*
palaeobotany	*biol*
palaeobotany	*geog*
palaeography	*lit*
Palaeolithic	*geog*
palette knife	*art*
palette knife	*tools*
Pallas Athene	*myth*
palpitations	*medic*
panchromatic	*art*
pangamic acid	*chem*

pantechnicon	*travel*
pantisocracy	*govt*
pantophagous	*animals*
parachronism	*time*
paradise|fish	*fish*
Paradise|Lost	*titles*
paraffin|lamp	*house*
paragraphist	*lit*
parallel|bars	*sport*
parasitology	*medic*
parcel|of|land	*geog*
parietal|bone	*medic*
Paris|fashion	*clothes*
parish|school	*educ*
parking|light	*travel*
parking|meter	*travel*
parking|orbit	*travel*
parlour|grand	*music*
parotid|gland	*medic*
parted|shield	*herald*
Parthian|shot	*myth*
Parthian|shot	*war*
part|of|speech	*lit*
party|machine	*govt*
pasque|flower	*flowers*
passe|partout	*house*
passing|place	*travel*
passion|fruit	*fruit*
passion|music	*music*
passive|voice	*lit*
pass|sentence	*law*
pastel|colour	*colour*
pastoral|poet	*jobs*
pastoral|poet	*lit*
patent|office	*jobs*
Patent|Office	*law*
paternal|arms	*herald*
pay|as|you|earn	*trade*
pay|in|advance	*trade*
peace|officer	*govt*
peach|blossom	*flowers*
Peak|District	*mounts*
peanut|butter	*food*
Pearl|Harbour	*war*
Peaseblossom	*Shakesp*
pease|pudding	*food*
pedal|pushers	*clothes*
pediatrician	*jobs*
pediatrician	*medic*
pegged|market	*trade*
peg|the|market	*trade*
pelvic|girdle	*medic*
penalty|bully	*sport*
penalty|throw	*sport*
Penang|lawyer	*clothes*
penitentiary	*jobs*
penitentiary	*law*
penny|whistle	*music*
people's|front	*govt*
Pepper's|ghost	*theatre*
perambulator	*house*
perambulator	*travel*
perfect|fifth	*music*
perfect|pitch	*music*
perfect|rhyme	*lit*
perfect|tense	*lit*
Periclymenus	*myth*
periodically	*time*
permanganate	*chem*
permeability	*chem*
perscrutator	*educ*
Persian|berry	*fruit*
Persian|melon	*fruit*
perspiration	*medic*
pestilential	*medic*
petrol|engine	*machine*
petty|juryman	*law*
petty|larceny	*law*
petty|officer	*jobs*
petty|officer	*travel*
pharmaceutic	*medic*
pharmacology	*medic*
pharmacopeia	*medic*
Philadelphia	*cities*
Philadelphus	*trees*
philharmonic	*music*
phlebotomist	*medic*
photocathode	*machine*
photochemist	*chem*
photoengrave	*art*

photoetching	*art*
photofission	*physics*
photographer	*art*
photographer	*jobs*
photographic	*art*
photogravure	*art*
photomontage	*art*
photoneutron	*physics*
phototherapy	*medic*
phrontistery	*archit*
phrontistery	*educ*
Phrygian mode	*music*
physical jerk	*sport*
physiologist	*jobs*
piassava palm	*trees*
picked troops	*war*
pickled onion	*food*
picnic basket	*house*
picnic hamper	*house*
picture frame	*art*
picture frame	*house*
picture house	*film/TV*
piece of eight	*money*
pier buttress	*archit*
piercing wind	*weather*
Piers Plowman	*titles*
pigeon flying	*sport*
Pigling Bland	*lit*
pigmentation	*medic*
pigs knuckles	*food*
pillar box red	*colour*
pilot balloon	*travel*
Pilsener beer	*drink*
ping pong ball	*sport*
piobaireachd	*music*
pioneer corps	*war*
pipe and tabor	*music*
pistachio nut	*food*
pistachio nut	*fruit*
piston engine	*machine*
pitch and putt	*sport*
pitch and toss	*sport*
place setting	*house*
plain clothes	*clothes*
plain clothes	*law*

plain English	*lit*
plain sailing	*travel*
planked steak	*food*
plantain tree	*trees*
plant manager	*jobs*
plaster board	*archit*
platanna frog	*animals*
platform deck	*travel*
Platonic body	*maths*
playing cards	*sport*
playing field	*sport*
plea for mercy	*law*
pleasure boat	*travel*
pleasure trip	*sport*
pleasure trip	*travel*
Plimsoll line	*travel*
Plimsoll mark	*travel*
ploughwright	*jobs*
plumber's mate	*jobs*
plunging fire	*war*
plural voting	*govt*
ply one's trade	*trade*
pocket gopher	*animals*
poetastering	*lit*
poetic genius	*lit*
poet laureate	*jobs*
poet laureate	*lit*
poet novelist	*lit*
poet satirist	*lit*
pointelliste	*art*
pointillisme	*art*
point of order	*govt*
point to point	*sport*
poison laurel	*trees*
polarization	*geog*
polarization	*physics*
pole position	*sport*
police cordon	*law*
police office	*law*
police patrol	*law*
politicaster	*govt*
pollice verso	*foreign*
polling booth	*govt*
Polly Peachum	*lit*
polysyllable	*lit*

polytonality	*music*
pons asinorum	*maths*
pony trekking	*sport*
poor relation	*people*
Popilius Lena	*Shakesp*
Popocatepetl	*mounts*
popular front	*govt*
popular music	*music*
Porgy and Bess	*titles*
pork and beans	*food*
Port au Prince	*cities*
porte cochere	*archit*
porte monnaie	*trade*
portrait bust	*art*
positive rays	*physics*
postage stamp	*travel*
postdiluvian	*time*
poster colour	*art*
postgraduate	*educ*
postgraduate	*jobs*
postmeridian	*time*
postmeridiem	*time*
postmistress	*jobs*
postponement	*time*
postprandial	*time*
potato crisps	*food*
potter's earth	*art*
potter's wheel	*art*
potter's wheel	*machine*
powder charge	*war*
power reactor	*physics*
power station	*machine*
power station	*physics*
powers that be	*govt*
practitioner	*jobs*
praesodymium	*mineral*
praseodymium	*chem*
prayer carpet	*relig*
Precious Bane	*titles*
prefabricate	*archit*
prescription	*govt*
prescription	*medic*
preselection	*educ*
presentation	*theatre*
present tense	*lit*

press officer	*jobs*
press release	*lit*
pressure belt	*trade*
pressure belt	*weather*
pressure mine	*machine*
pressure suit	*clothes*
pressure suit	*travel*
pressure wave	*weather*
prevaricator	*people*
preventative	*medic*
price ceiling	*trade*
price control	*trade*
price current	*trade*
price of money	*trade*
price rigging	*trade*
Prince Albert	*clothes*
Prince Regent	*govt*
Princess line	*clothes*
principal boy	*jobs*
principal boy	*theatre*
principality	*geog*
prison warder	*jobs*
prison warder	*law*
prison worker	*jobs*
Private Lives	*titles*
privy chamber	*archit*
Privy council	*govt*
prize fighter	*sport*
probate court	*law*
probate judge	*law*
productivity	*trade*
professional	*sport*
professional	*trade*
professorate	*educ*
professorial	*educ*
profiteering	*trade*
profit margin	*trade*
profit motive	*trade*
programmable	*comput*
Promised Land	*myth*
Promised Land	*relig*
prophylactic	*medic*
protactinium	*mineral*
protectorate	*govt*
protest march	*govt*

Prothalamion	*titles*	quince|yellow	*colour*
pruning|knife	*tools*	quinquennial	*time*
Prussian|blue	*colour*	quinquennium	*time*
psychometric	*educ*	racing|driver	*jobs*
psychrometer	*measure*	radar|scanner	*travel*
psychrometer	*medic*	radar|station	*travel*
publicity|man	*theatre*	radial|engine	*machine*
pudding|basin	*house*	radiant|plate	*house*
puddle|jumper	*travel*	radiobiology	*biol*
pulley|tackle	*machine*	radiochemist	*chem*
pumpernickel	*food*	radio|compass	*machine*
Punch|and|Judy	*sport*	radio|compass	*physics*
Punch|and|Judy	*theatre*	radio|compass	*travel*
punto|reverso	*sport*	radiodontist	*jobs*
pupil|teacher	*educ*	radioelement	*chem*
puppet|regime	*govt*	radiographer	*jobs*
purblindness	*medic*	radioisotope	*chem*
purple|ermine	*herald*	radio|monitor	*travel*
purse|strings	*trade*	radionuclide	*chem*
pursuit|plane	*travel*	radio|station	*travel*
putting|green	*sport*	radiosurgery	*medic*
pyridoxamine	*biol*	radiotherapy	*medic*
pyrotechnics	*war*	radish|maggot	*insects*
quadrangular	*maths*	raffle|ticket	*sport*
Quadrigesima	*time*	raglan|sleeve	*clothes*
quadrinomial	*maths*	rags|to|riches	*trade*
quadrivalent	*chem*	rainbow|trout	*fish*
quaking|aspen	*trees*	rainy|weather	*weather*
quantization	*physics*	raise|the|dead	*travel*
quarrymaster	*jobs*	rambling|rose	*flowers*
quarter|final	*sport*	ramification	*trees*
quarter|horse	*animals*	random|access	*comput*
quarter|light	*travel*	rare|occasion	*time*
quarter|noble	*money*	ratchet|drill	*tools*
quarter|staff	*war*	rate|of|growth	*trade*
queen|dowager	*govt*	reactivation	*chem*
queen's|bishop	*sport*	reactivation	*physics*
queen's|knight	*sport*	reactivation	*war*
queen's|speech	*govt*	receiving|end	*sport*
queen|termite	*insects*	receptionist	*jobs*
quelque|chose	*foreign*	reciting|note	*music*
question|mark	*lit*	record|holder	*sport*
question|time	*govt*	record|player	*house*
quill|driving	*lit*	record|player	*machine*
Quiller|Couch	*writers*	record|player	*music*

redeployment	*trade*	Rhadamanthus	*myth*
red|letter|day	*time*	rhesus|monkey	*animals*
redoublement	*sport*	rhododendron	*flowers*
red|sandstone	*mineral*	rhododendron	*trees*
reel|of|cotton	*house*	rhombohedron	*maths*
reel|of|thread	*house*	rhyming|slang	*lit*
referee's|hold	*sport*	rhythmic|mode	*music*
reflex|action	*biol*	ride|at|anchor	*travel*
reflex|action	*medic*	ride|bareback	*travel*
reflex|camera	*art*	Rider|Haggard	*writers*
reform|school	*law*	ride|to|hounds	*sport*
refrigerator	*house*	riding|school	*educ*
refrigerator	*machine*	riding|school	*sport*
refrigerator	*physics*	rienne|va|plus	*foreign*
regency|chair	*house*	rifled|cannon	*war*
regeneration	*biol*	rifle|grenade	*war*
regional|bank	*trade*	rifleman|bird	*birds*
registration	*govt*	rigged|market	*trade*
registration	*music*	right|hand|man	*people*
rehabilitate	*medic*	right|of|entry	*law*
religious|war	*war*	rig|the|market	*trade*
remuneration	*jobs*	ring|dotterel	*birds*
remuneration	*trade*	Rio|de|Janeiro	*cities*
remuneration	*trade*	riot|of|colour	*art*
rent|tribunal	*law*	Rip|Van|Winkle	*titles*
repercussion	*music*	rising|ground	*geog*
reproduction	*art*	rising|prices	*trade*
reproduction	*house*	road|junction	*travel*
resectoscope	*medic*	robust|health	*medic*
reserve|price	*trade*	rock|climbing	*sport*
residual|clay	*mineral*	rocket|assist	*travel*
resist|arrest	*law*	rocket|attack	*war*
respirometer	*measure*	rocket|engine	*machine*
respirometer	*medic*	rocket|engine	*travel*
restaurateur	*jobs*	rocket|glider	*travel*
resting|place	*relig*	rocking|chair	*house*
rest|one's|case	*law*	rocking|horse	*sport*
Resurrection	*relig*	rock|squirrel	*animals*
resuscitator	*machine*	Roentgen|rays	*physics*
resuscitator	*medic*	Rogue|Herries	*titles*
retaining|fee	*jobs*	roller|skates	*sport*
retaining|fee	*trade*	roller|skates	*travel*
retrenchment	*trade*	rolling|stock	*trade*
return|crease	*sport*	rolling|stock	*travel*
return|ticket	*travel*	rolling|stone	*people*

rolling|stone	*travel*	San|Francisco	*cities*
roll|of|honour	*educ*	Santo|Domingo	*cities*
rooming|house	*archit*	sapphire|blue	*colour*
rose|of|Sharon	*flowers*	Sardanapalus	*titles*
Rose|of|Sharon	*relig*	sarrusophone	*music*
Rosetta|stone	*lit*	sarsaparilla	*drink*
Rosie|Probert	*lit*	Saskatchewan	*rivers*
rough|diamond	*people*	sassafras|nut	*fruit*
rough|draught	*art*	satisfaction	*trade*
rough|justice	*law*	sauve|qui|peut	*foreign*
rough|outline	*art*	scarlet|fever	*medic*
rough|passage	*travel*	scarlet|ochre	*colour*
rowelled|spur	*herald*	scatterbrain	*people*
royal|charter	*govt*	scene|of|crime	*law*
royal|command	*govt*	scene|painter	*art*
rubber|cheque	*trade*	scene|painter	*jobs*
rubber|gloves	*medic*	scene|painter	*theatre*
rubber|hammer	*machine*	sceneshifter	*jobs*
run|for|office	*govt*	sceneshifter	*theatre*
running|board	*travel*	scene|stealer	*theatre*
running|light	*travel*	scenic|effect	*theatre*
running|strip	*sport*	Schiehallion	*mounts*
running|water	*geog*	school|dinner	*educ*
Russian|salad	*food*	schoolfellow	*educ*
sacred|ground	*relig*	schoolkeeper	*educ*
sacrilegious	*relig*	schoolmaster	*educ*
safe|breaking	*law*	schoolmaster	*jobs*
safe|cracking	*law*	scintillator	*physics*
sage|and|onion	*food*	scissors|jump	*sport*
sailing|barge	*travel*	scorpion|fish	*fish*
sailing|canoe	*travel*	Scotland|Yard	*law*
sailing|yacht	*travel*	scrambled|egg	*food*
Saint|Bernard	*animals*	screenwriter	*jobs*
salamandrian	*insects*	screenwriter	*theatre*
sale|by|outcry	*trade*	scriptwriter	*film/TV*
sale|or|return	*trade*	scriptwriter	*jobs*
sales|gimmick	*trade*	scullery|maid	*jobs*
sales|manager	*jobs*	sculptograph	*art*
sales|manager	*trade*	sea|buckthorn	*trees*
salesmanship	*trade*	sea|butterfly	*fish*
salle|a|manger	*archit*	Sea|of|Galilee	*lakes*
salted|peanut	*food*	Sea|of|Galilee	*relig*
Salt|Lake|City	*cities*	Sea|of|Marmora	*seas*
salvationist	*people*	sea|porcupine	*fish*
sand|yachting	*sport*	seaside|grape	*fruit*

season ticket	*theatre*
season ticket	*travel*
second attack	*sport*
Second Coming	*relig*
second cousin	*family*
second eleven	*sport*
second person	*lit*
second player	*sport*
second strike	*war*
secret police	*law*
security risk	*govt*
sedge warbler	*birds*
seignioralty	*govt*
selenium cell	*physics*
selenography	*astron*
self educated	*educ*
self governed	*govt*
self portrait	*art*
sell on credit	*trade*
semi detached	*archit*
semi diameter	*geog*
semi precious	*jewels*
sempiternity	*time*
senior school	*educ*
sentinel crab	*fish*
Sergeant Cuff	*lit*
sergeant fish	*fish*
sergeantship	*law*
Sergeant Troy	*lit*
serial number	*maths*
Serpentarius	*myth*
serpent eater	*birds*
serpentiform	*insects*
serum albumin	*biol*
serum therapy	*medic*
service berry	*fruit*
serving hatch	*house*
serving spoon	*house*
sesamoid bone	*medic*
sesquialtera	*music*
set one's cap at	*clothes*
severance pay	*trade*
sewing needle	*house*
shadow boxing	*sport*
shadow figure	*art*
shaking palsy	*medic*
shape a course	*travel*
share company	*trade*
shareholding	*trade*
sharpshooter	*sport*
sharpshooter	*war*
sheep's fescue	*plants*
sheepskin rug	*house*
sheriff court	*law*
sherry trifle	*food*
Shetland pony	*animals*
shipping line	*travel*
Shirley poppy	*flowers*
shock tactics	*war*
shock therapy	*medic*
shoot ballast	*travel*
shooting pain	*medic*
shooting star	*astron*
shopping list	*house*
short account	*trade*
short circuit	*machine*
short circuit	*physics*
short commons	*food*
short pinocle	*sport*
shortsighted	*medic*
Shostakovich	*music*
shoulder a gun	*war*
shoulder arms	*war*
shove ha'penny	*sport*
show business	*film/TV*
show business	*theatre*
show business	*trade*
show must go on	*theatre*
shrimping net	*sport*
shuffleboard	*sport*
shutting post	*archit*
side chancery	*sport*
sidereal time	*time*
sidereal year	*time*
siege warfare	*war*
Sierra Nevada	*mounts*
signal beacon	*machine*
signal rocket	*machine*
signal rocket	*war*
silk gownsman	*law*

silver dollar	money
silver polish	house
silver salmon	fish
silver screen	film/TV
s'il vous plait	foreign
simple attack	sport
simple reflex	medic
simple tissue	biol
simultaneous	time
sing in chorus	music
single combat	sport
single combat	war
single decker	travel
single person	people
single sculls	sport
singles match	sport
single tackle	machine
sinister half	herald
sinister side	herald
sinking coast	geog
sirloin steak	food
Sir Toby Belch	Shakesp
sister german	jobs
site engineer	jobs
skating boots	sport
skiffle group	music
skipping rope	sport
skunk cabbage	plants
slacken speed	travel
slanting hand	lit
sledgehammer	tools
sleep inducer	medic
sleeping pill	medic
sleepwalking	medic
slender means	trade
slice service	sport
sliding scale	trade
slimming diet	medic
slip of the pen	lit
slippery pole	sport
slow movement	music
smallholding	agric
smallholding	archit
smash and grab	law
smash the atom	physics

smoked salmon	food
snake charmer	jobs
sneak preview	art
snow blizzard	weather
snowdrop tree	trees
snow in summer	flowers
snubbing post	archit
snuff box bean	plants
soapbox derby	sport
social insect	insects
social worker	jobs
society verse	lit
soil mechanic	jobs
solar battery	machine
solar battery	physics
solar physics	physics
solar therapy	medic
soldering gun	tools
sole occupant	jobs
Solomon's seal	flowers
Solzhenitsyn	writers
somnambulism	medic
somnambulist	people
song and dance	theatre
sonic barrier	travel
sound barrier	travel
sound effects	film/TV
sound effects	theatre
sound limiter	machine
South Georgia	islands
space capsule	travel
space fiction	lit
space station	astron
space station	physics
space station	travel
Spanish broom	trees
Spanish cress	plants
Spanish grass	plants
Spanish horse	animals
Spanish onion	veg
Spanish sheep	animals
spanker sheet	travel
spare bedroom	house
spark chamber	chem
sparking plug	machine

sparking plug	*travel*		stage setting	*theatre*
speaking stop	*music*		stage whisper	*theatre*
special agent	*jobs*		staghorn moss	*plants*
specific heat	*physics*		stained glass	*archit*
specific name	*biol*		stained glass	*art*
spectrograph	*art*		stain remover	*house*
spectrograph	*astron*		stall for time	*time*
spectrometer	*measure*		stall landing	*travel*
spectroscope	*astron*		standard lamp	*house*
spectroscopy	*astron*		standard time	*time*
speechwriter	*jobs*		standing army	*govt*
speed of sound	*travel*		standing army	*war*
speed skating	*sport*		standing room	*theatre*
speed writing	*lit*		stand off half	*sport*
spelling book	*educ*		starring role	*theatre*
spelling book	*lit*		star sapphire	*mineral*
sphygmograph	*medic*		star spangled	*astron*
sphygmometer	*medic*		starting grid	*sport*
Spice Islands	*islands*		starting post	*sport*
spider monkey	*animals*		state lottery	*trade*
spinal column	*medic*		Staten Island	*islands*
spirit of wine	*drink*		statistician	*jobs*
spiritualist	*jobs*		status symbol	*govt*
split the atom	*physics*		steady market	*trade*
split the vote	*govt*		steal the show	*theatre*
sponge finger	*food*		steam turbine	*machine*
sporting life	*sport*		steam whistle	*music*
sport of kings	*sport*		steel erector	*jobs*
sportscaster	*jobs*		steeplechase	*sport*
sports master	*jobs*		steer clear of	*travel*
sportswriter	*jobs*		steering gear	*machine*
spotted fever	*medic*		steering gear	*travel*
spring beetle	*insects*		stenographer	*jobs*
spring greens	*veg*		stepdaughter	*family*
spring keeper	*fish*		stereo camera	*art*
Spring Sonata	*titles*		stereophonic	*physics*
spring washer	*machine*		stereopticon	*physics*
spurge laurel	*trees*		stereotypist	*jobs*
square rigged	*travel*		sterling area	*trade*
square rigger	*travel*		sticky wicket	*sport*
stabbing blow	*sport*		still of night	*time*
stabbing pain	*medic*		stilt walking	*sport*
staff officer	*jobs*		stitch in time	*time*
stage manager	*jobs*		St John's bread	*veg*
stage manager	*theatre*		stock company	*theatre*

stock|company	*trade*	stuffed|shirt	*people*
stock|dealing	*trade*	St|Vitus|dance	*medic*
stock|holding	*trade*	Stygian|creek	*myth*
stock|in|trade	*trade*	Stygian|gloom	*myth*
stock|jobbery	*trade*	subcommittee	*govt*
stock|of|words	*lit*	subcontinent	*geog*
Stoke|on|Trent	*cities*	subcutaneous	*medic*
stole|the|show	*theatre*	substitution	*maths*
stonechatter	*birds*	substructure	*archit*
stonedresser	*jobs*	subterranean	*geog*
stormtrooper	*jobs*	sudden|attack	*war*
stormtrooper	*war*	Suffolk|punch	*animals*
stormy|petrel	*birds*	summary|trial	*law*
story|telling	*lit*	summer|school	*educ*
stouthearted	*war*	sumpter|horse	*animals*
St|Peter's|wort	*flowers*	Sunday|driver	*sport*
straddle|jump	*sport*	Sunday|driver	*travel*
Stradivarius	*music*	Sunday|school	*educ*
straight|line	*maths*	Sunday|school	*relig*
straight|part	*theatre*	sunken|garden	*flowers*
straitjacket	*law*	sunshine|roof	*travel*
straitjacket	*medic*	superannuate	*trade*
stranglehold	*sport*	supercharger	*machine*
stratigraphy	*geog*	supernaculum	*drink*
stratosphere	*astron*	supernatural	*myth*
stratosphere	*physics*	supply|troops	*war*
streaky|bacon	*food*	supreme|court	*law*
stream|anchor	*travel*	surgical|boot	*medic*
streamlining	*travel*	survival|suit	*travel*
street|artist	*art*	sustain|a|loss	*trade*
street|market	*trade*	suture|needle	*medic*
street|singer	*music*	swashbuckler	*people*
street|trader	*jobs*	sweep|oarsman	*sport*
street|urchin	*people*	sweet|alyssum	*flowers*
streptomycin	*medic*	sweet|and|sour	*food*
stress|accent	*music*	sweet|William	*flowers*
strike|action	*trade*	swimming|crab	*fish*
strike|it|rich	*trade*	swimming|gala	*sport*
string|course	*archit*	swimming|pool	*sport*
strip|cartoon	*lit*	swinging|post	*archit*
strong|finish	*sport*	swizzle|stick	*house*
strong|market	*trade*	sword|bayonet	*war*
stubble|goose	*birds*	sword|fencing	*sport*
student|nurse	*medic*	Sydney|Carton	*lit*
stuffed|shirt	*govt*	symphonic|ode	*music*

tabard|of|arms	*herald*
tabasco|sauce	*food*
table|lighter	*house*
table|service	*house*
table|turning	*sport*
tactical|unit	*war*
take|bearings	*travel*
take|off|strip	*travel*
take|the|field	*war*
take|the|floor	*theatre*
talcum|powder	*house*
tally|counter	*maths*
tallyho|coach	*travel*
tantalum|lamp	*machine*
tape|recorder	*house*
tape|recorder	*machine*
tape|recorder	*music*
tartare|sauce	*food*
tax|collector	*jobs*
tax|collector	*trade*
tax|exemption	*trade*
teach|a|lesson	*educ*
tearing|hurry	*travel*
technicolour	*art*
technicolour	*film/TV*
technologist	*jobs*
telecomputer	*machine*
telegraph|boy	*jobs*
telephone|man	*jobs*
tenant|at|will	*law*
ten|cent|store	*trade*
tender|rocket	*travel*
tennis|player	*jobs*
tennis|player	*sport*
tennis|racket	*sport*
tennis|stroke	*sport*
tercentenary	*time*
terminus|a|quo	*foreign*
test|engineer	*jobs*
tetrahedroid	*maths*
thanksgiving	*relig*
thatched|roof	*archit*
thaumaturgus	*myth*
The|Alchemist	*titles*
The|Antiquary	*titles*
The|Apple|Cart	*titles*
theatrecraft	*theatre*
theatre|nurse	*jobs*
theatre|of|war	*war*
theatre|organ	*music*
theatromania	*theatre*
the|bitter|end	*travel*
The|Caretaker	*titles*
the|dawn|of|day	*time*
The|Decameron	*titles*
The|Dogs|of|War	*titles*
The|Excursion	*titles*
The|Golden|Ass	*titles*
The|Grand|Duke	*titles*
the|long|green	*trade*
The|Lost|Chord	*titles*
The|March|Hare	*lit*
Themistocles	*leaders*
The|Moonstone	*titles*
then|and|there	*time*
theologician	*relig*
therapeutics	*medic*
therapeutist	*medic*
thermocouple	*chem*
thermoscopic	*physics*
thermos|flask	*house*
The|Romany|Rye	*titles*
the|seven|seas	*marine*
Thesmophorus	*myth*
The|Valkyries	*titles*
the|year|round	*time*
thirdborough	*law*
thorough|bass	*music*
thoroughbred	*animals*
thoroughfare	*travel*
thousandfold	*measure*
three|quarter	*sport*
three|wheeler	*travel*
Three|Wise|Men	*relig*
through|train	*travel*
thundercloud	*weather*
thunderstorm	*weather*
thyroid|gland	*medic*
ticker|market	*trade*
ticket|holder	*jobs*

ticket office	*travel*
ticket writer	*jobs*
tidal current	*marine*
tiddleywinks	*sport*
time and again	*time*
time exposure	*art*
time honoured	*time*
timelessness	*time*
time will tell	*time*
Timothy grass	*plants*
tintinnabula	*music*
Titus Lartius	*Shakesp*
toasting fork	*house*
tobacco plant	*plants*
tone measurer	*music*
tone painting	*music*
tonsillotomy	*medic*
tooth and nail	*war*
top executive	*jobs*
top of the bill	*theatre*
top of the pops	*music*
Torres Strait	*seas*
toss the caber	*sport*
totalitarian	*govt*
touch the wind	*travel*
tourist class	*travel*
Tower of Babel	*relig*
town planning	*archit*
trace element	*biol*
trachypterus	*fish*
tracing paper	*art*
trade balance	*trade*
trade mission	*trade*
trading stamp	*trade*
traffic light	*travel*
trained nurse	*jobs*
trained nurse	*medic*
training slip	*educ*
train service	*travel*
train spotter	*sport*
Traitor's gate	*govt*
tranquillize	*medic*
transgressor	*people*
transleithan	*geog*
transmission	*machine*

transmission	*physics*
transmission	*travel*
transmundane	*geog*
transoceanic	*geog*
transuranian	*chem*
transvestite	*people*
trapshooting	*sport*
travel agency	*trade*
travel agency	*travel*
treasure hunt	*sport*
treasury bill	*trade*
treasury note	*trade*
treble chance	*sport*
tree of heaven	*trees*
tree squirrel	*animals*
trench mortar	*war*
trestle table	*house*
trial balance	*trade*
trichologist	*jobs*
trick cyclist	*jobs*
trick cyclist	*sport*
trigger happy	*sport*
trigger happy	*war*
trigonometry	*maths*
tripod camera	*art*
trolley track	*travel*
tromba marina	*music*
tropical bird	*birds*
tropical fish	*fish*
tropical heat	*geog*
tropical moth	*insects*
tropical zone	*geog*
troublemaker	*people*
trout breeder	*jobs*
trout nursery	*fish*
Trout Quintet	*titles*
truce breaker	*people*
trumpet major	*music*
trustee stock	*trade*
tubeless tyre	*travel*
tuberculosis	*medic*
tungsten lamp	*machine*
tunnel of love	*sport*
turkish towel	*house*
turn a deaf ear	*medic*

turning|point	*time*
turn|of|phrase	*lit*
Twelfth|night	*time*
Twelfth|Night	*titles*
twelve|o'clock	*time*
two|handed|saw	*tools*
type|printing	*lit*
ugly|customer	*people*
ugly|duckling	*birds*
ugly|duckling	*people*
ultramicrobe	*biol*
ultramontane	*relig*
umbelliferae	*plants*
umbrella|bird	*birds*
umbrella|tree	*trees*
umpire's|chair	*sport*
uncial|letter	*lit*
unconformity	*geog*
undercurrent	*geog*
undermanager	*jobs*
underpinning	*archit*
under|teacher	*educ*
under|the|flag	*war*
unemployment	*trade*
unified|field	*physics*
unseasonable	*time*
unwritten|law	*law*
upper|chamber	*govt*
upper|partial	*music*
upright|piano	*house*
upright|piano	*music*
upset|the|boat	*travel*
urban|renewal	*archit*
ursine|monkey	*animals*
user|friendly	*house*
utility|plane	*travel*
Van|Allen|belt	*physics*
vantage|point	*sport*
vaporization	*physics*
vapourer|moth	*insects*
variable|star	*astron*
variable|zone	*geog*
varicose|vein	*medic*
variety|store	*trade*
vaudevillian	*theatre*
vaudevillist	*jobs*
vaudevillist	*theatre*
vegetable|oil	*food*
velvet|scoter	*birds*
Venus|fly|trap	*plants*
Verdant|Green	*lit*
vernier|scale	*maths*
versemongery	*lit*
vertical|fire	*war*
vertical|rays	*astron*
vestal|virgin	*myth*
vice|director	*jobs*
vice|governor	*jobs*
Victoria|plum	*fruit*
viola|da|gamba	*music*
violent|death	*law*
violent|death	*medic*
VIP|transport	*travel*
virgin|forest	*trees*
Virginia|deer	*animals*
Virginia|reel	*sport*
virgin's|bower	*flowers*
virus|warfare	*war*
viscountship	*govt*
visiting|card	*house*
vitaminology	*biol*
vitreous|body	*medic*
vocalization	*music*
volcanic|cone	*geog*
volcanic|rock	*geog*
volcanic|wind	*weather*
Waldorf|salad	*food*
walkie|talkie	*machine*
walking|stick	*insects*
walk|the|plank	*travel*
wall|painting	*art*
Wandering|Jew	*myth*
Wandering|Jew	*travel*
warehouseman	*jobs*
warmongering	*war*
washing|board	*house*
washing|cloth	*house*
water|biscuit	*food*
water|blister	*medic*
waterboatman	*insects*

water buffalo	*animals*
water colours	*art*
water culture	*biol*
water diviner	*jobs*
watered stock	*trade*
water flowers	*flowers*
water hemlock	*plants*
water milfoil	*plants*
water parsnip	*veg*
water spaniel	*animals*
water strider	*insects*
water wagtail	*birds*
wave function	*physics*
wax engraving	*art*
wax modelling	*art*
wear the cloth	*relig*
weatherboard	*archit*
weatherboard	*travel*
weather chart	*weather*
weather gauge	*weather*
weatherglass	*weather*
weather sheet	*travel*
wedding march	*music*
Wedgwood ware	*art*
weightlifter	*sport*
Weird Sisters	*myth*
welfare state	*govt*
welfare state	*trade*
well composed	*art*
wellingtonia	*trees*
Welsh dresser	*house*
Welsh rarebit	*food*
Welsh terrier	*animals*
welterweight	*sport*
Westmoreland	*Shakesp*
wheel bearing	*machine*
whipped cream	*food*
whipping post	*law*
whip poor will	*birds*
Whisky Galore	*titles*
white admiral	*insects*
white currant	*fruit*
white feather	*war*
white heather	*plants*
white herring	*fish*

white pottery	*art*
who goes there	*war*
whortleberry	*fruit*
wicket keeper	*sport*
wild hyacinth	*flowers*
William M Turk	*lit*
will o the wisp	*geog*
Will Scarlett	*myth*
winding sheet	*relig*
wind musician	*jobs*
wind musician	*music*
wind velocity	*weather*
windward side	*travel*
wine merchant	*jobs*
winged insect	*insects*
wingless bird	*birds*
Winston Smith	*lit*
Winterhalter	*artists*
winter sports	*sport*
wishing stone	*myth*
witches coven	*myth*
witching hour	*time*
without a bean	*trade*
without delay	*time*
witness stand	*law*
Wittgenstein	*writers*
wollastonite	*mineral*
wood engraver	*jobs*
wood pheasant	*birds*
wool gatherer	*people*
word deafness	*medic*
word of honour	*law*
word painting	*lit*
worker priest	*jobs*
working class	*trade*
working order	*trade*
working party	*jobs*
work mistress	*jobs*
works manager	*jobs*
worldly goods	*govt*
worms eye view	*insects*
writer's cramp	*lit*
writing paper	*lit*
writing table	*educ*
writing table	*house*

X-ray spectrum	*physics*
yarn spinning	*lit*
yellowhammer	*birds*
yellow streak	*war*
zantedeschia	*plants*
Zigeunerlied	*music*

zincographer	*art*
zinc ointment	*medic*
zoochemistry	*biol*
zoochemistry	*chem*
zoogeography	*biol*
zoogeography	*geog*

13 LETTERS

Aberdeen Angus	*animals*
above sea level	*geog*
Abraham's bosom	*relig*
absence of mind	*people*
absolute power	*govt*
absolute ruler	*govt*
ab urbe condita	*foreign*
academic dress	*educ*
accident prone	*people*
accommodation	*archit*
accompaniment	*music*
acotyledonous	*biol*
actinotherapy	*medic*
action painter	*art*
active service	*war*
active volcano	*geog*
adding machine	*comput*
adenoidectomy	*medic*
administrator	*govt*
advanced level	*educ*
advertisement	*trade*
aerial railway	*travel*
aerodynamical	*machine*
affenpinscher	*animals*
afforestation	*trees*
again and again	*time*
against the law	*law*
aggiornamento	*relig*
agriculturist	*agric*
agrobiologist	*agric*
ailourophilia	*animals*

ailourophobia	*animals*
air compressor	*machine*
Albert Herring	*lit*
Albert Herring	*titles*
alcoholometer	*measure*
alcoholometry	*measure*
All Hallows eve	*time*
alligator pear	*fruit*
all in wrestler	*sport*
Almayer's Folly	*titles*
almond blossom	*trees*
alongshoreman	*jobs*
alpha and omega	*lit*
American organ	*music*
amplification	*physics*
amygdalaceous	*trees*
anagrammatist	*lit*
anaphrodisiac	*medic*
anastigmatism	*medic*
Ancient of days	*relig*
Andrea Chenier	*titles*
Andrew Ferrara	*war*
Angel Pavement	*titles*
Anglo American	*people*
Anglo Catholic	*relig*
angry young man	*people*
animalisation	*animals*
animal kingdom	*animals*
animal worship	*animals*
anthropomorph	*people*
anthropophagi	*people*

anthroposophy	*relig*
antichristian	*people*
anticlockwise	*measure*
anticoagulant	*medic*
antihistamine	*medic*
antilogarithm	*maths*
antimarketeer	*govt*
antiquedealer	*jobs*
antiscorbutic	*medic*
antisocialism	*govt*
anythingarian	*people*
Apostles|creed	*relig*
apple|dumpling	*food*
apple|fritters	*food*
apple|pie|order	*people*
Appleton|layer	*physics*
apple|turnover	*food*
apportionment	*maths*
appropriation	*govt*
approximately	*maths*
approximation	*maths*
apricot|brandy	*drink*
April|Fools|Day	*time*
arachnologist	*insects*
arboriculture	*trees*
archaeologist	*jobs*
archbishopric	*relig*
archidiaconal	*relig*
architectonic	*archit*
architectural	*archit*
ariston|metron	*foreign*
arithmetician	*maths*
armaments|race	*war*
armed|conflict	*war*
armoured|train	*travel*
Arms|and|the|Man	*titles*
arms|and|the|man	*war*
army|exercises	*war*
arriere|pensee	*foreign*
art|exhibition	*art*
articled|clerk	*jobs*
articled|clerk	*law*
articles|of|war	*war*
Ascensiontide	*time*
assassination	*law*

assault|course	*war*
assembly|rooms	*archit*
asset|stripper	*trade*
associateship	*govt*
associativity	*maths*
astrophysical	*physics*
at|short|notice	*time*
auction|bridge	*sport*
audio|engineer	*jobs*
Augean|stables	*myth*
Auger|electron	*physics*
authorisation	*govt*
authoritarian	*govt*
authoritative	*govt*
autobiography	*lit*
avant|gardiste	*foreign*
avis|au|lecteur	*foreign*
baccalaureate	*educ*
back|formation	*lit*
backscratcher	*house*
bacteriolysin	*medic*
bacteriolysis	*medic*
bacteriolytic	*medic*
bacteriophage	*medic*
baggage|animal	*animals*
bank|messenger	*trade*
Bank|of|England	*trade*
bank|overdraft	*trade*
bank|statement	*trade*
baptism|of|fire	*war*
barbarousness	*people*
barbecue|sauce	*food*
barber|surgeon	*jobs*
bare|faced|liar	*people*
bargain|hunter	*people*
barnacle|goose	*birds*
basso|profondo	*foreign*
battle|cruiser	*war*
battle|honours	*war*
battle|scarred	*war*
bayonet|charge	*war*
beast|of|burden	*animals*
beatification	*relig*
Beaufort|scale	*weather*
beauty|contest	*sport*

beauty|parlour	*clothes*
begging|letter	*travel*
beleaguerment	*war*
Belisha|beacon	*travel*
belles|lettres	*lit*
Berkeleianism	*educ*
Bertie|Wooster	*lit*
best|of|friends	*people*
beyond|measure	*maths*
bibliographer	*lit*
bibliophilist	*lit*
bidding|prayer	*relig*
big|game|hunter	*sport*
billiard|table	*sport*
biodegradable	*biol*
biogeographer	*biol*
bird|of|passage	*birds*
bird's|eye|maple	*trees*
black|and|white	*art*
black|and|white	*colour*
Black|Mischief	*titles*
blanket|finish	*sport*
blanket|stitch	*house*
blastogenesis	*biol*
blind|man's|buff	*sport*
blood|brothers	*family*
blood|pressure	*medic*
blood|relation	*family*
blotting|paper	*house*
Blue|Mountains	*mounts*
boarding|house	*archit*
Bob's|your|uncle	*family*
bomber|command	*war*
booking|office	*travel*
book|of|the|film	*lit*
book|of|the|play	*lit*
border|ballads	*lit*
Boris|Godounov	*titles*
Boston|terrier	*animals*
bottomless|pit	*relig*
bougainvillea	*flowers*
bouillabaisse	*food*
boustrophedon	*lit*
bowling|crease	*sport*
box|the|compass	*machine*
brainsickness	*medic*
branch|officer	*govt*
brandy|and|soda	*drink*
brass|farthing	*money*
Brave|New|World	*titles*
bread|and|water	*food*
breakdown|gang	*travel*
breakfast|food	*food*
break|the|peace	*law*
break|the|rules	*law*
Brecon|Beacons	*mounts*
breechloading	*war*
bridge|of|sighs	*travel*
British|Consul	*govt*
British|Legion	*war*
broad|daylight	*time*
brotherliness	*family*
bubonic|plague	*medic*
budget|account	*trade*
budget|surplus	*trade*
building|block	*archit*
building|board	*archit*
bulls|and|bears	*trade*
bunch|of|grapes	*fruit*
burden|of|proof	*law*
bureaucratist	*govt*
burial|society	*trade*
burnt|offering	*food*
bush|telegraph	*travel*
business|hours	*trade*
Butcher|Benyon	*lit*
butler's|pantry	*archit*
buttered|toast	*food*
calendar|month	*time*
calligraphist	*art*
callisthenics	*sport*
call|the|police	*law*
Cambridge|blue	*colour*
camel|hair|coat	*clothes*
camera|obscura	*physics*
campanologist	*jobs*
candle|snuffer	*house*
capellmeister	*music*
Captain|Grimes	*lit*
carbon|dioxide	*chem*

carboniferous	*mineral*
carbonisation	*chem*
cardiac arrest	*medic*
cardinal point	*geog*
cardinal point	*geog*
cardiographer	*medic*
careers master	*educ*
Carmina Burana	*titles*
carpet slipper	*clothes*
carpet sweeper	*house*
carriage clock	*house*
carriage drive	*travel*
carrier pigeon	*birds*
cartridge belt	*war*
cash dispenser	*trade*
cash in advance	*trade*
cash on the nail	*trade*
cast iron alibi	*law*
casual clothes	*clothes*
catchment area	*geog*
cat o nine tails	*law*
cattle breeder	*agric*
cattle farming	*agric*
cauterisation	*medic*
cavalry charge	*war*
cayenne pepper	*food*
Cayman Islands	*islands*
cello concerto	*music*
centre forward	*sport*
ceremonialism	*govt*
chain of office	*govt*
chain reaction	*chem*
chain reaction	*physics*
Champs Elysees	*foreign*
change ringing	*sport*
Channel tunnel	*travel*
Chanson de Nuit	*titles*
charity school	*educ*
Charles Darnay	*lit*
Charles Pooter	*lit*
charm bracelet	*jewels*
chateaubriand	*food*
cheddar cheese	*food*
cheese biscuit	*food*
chequered flag	*sport*

cherry blossom	*flowers*
cheval de frise	*war*
Chiang kai Shek	*war*
chicken farmer	*agric*
chief of police	*law*
Chiltern Hills	*mounts*
chimney corner	*archit*
Chinese puzzle	*film/TV*
choir practice	*music*
chopping block	*house*
chopping board	*house*
choral society	*music*
choreographer	*music*
Christmas cake	*food*
Christmas rose	*flowers*
Christmas tide	*time*
Christmas time	*time*
Christmas tree	*trees*
chrome plating	*mineral*
chronographer	*time*
chronological	*time*
chrysanthemum	*flowers*
Churchill tank	*war*
church officer	*jobs*
church officer	*relig*
church service	*relig*
cinematograph	*film/TV*
cine projector	*film/TV*
cinnamon stone	*mineral*
circumference	*maths*
civil engineer	*jobs*
clapperboards	*film/TV*
clapperclawer	*people*
Clara Peggotty	*lit*
class struggle	*govt*
clearance sale	*trade*
clearing house	*trade*
climatography	*weather*
climatologist	*weather*
climbing frame	*sport*
clishmaclaver	*people*
Clock Symphony	*titles*
closed circuit	*film/TV*
close relative	*family*
clothes basket	*house*

coach|building	travel
coarse|fishing	sport
coastguardman	jobs
cobelligerent	war
cocker|spaniel	animals
cocktail|dress	clothes
cocktail|stick	house
code|of|conduct	law
coeducational	educ
coffee|grounds	drink
cogito|ergo|sum	foreign
College|of|Arms	herald
colloquialism	lit
combat|fatigue	war
command|module	travel
commercialism	trade
commercialist	trade
committee|room	govt
committeeship	govt
common|assault	law
common|law|wife	jobs
common|measure	measure
communication	travel
communion|card	relig
communist|bloc	govt
community|home	archit
commutability	maths
companionship	people
company|lawyer	law
company|report	trade
compassionate	people
compatibility	chem
complementary	maths
complex|number	maths
comprehension	educ
comprehensive	educ
compressed|air	physics
computational	maths
comrade|in|arms	war
conceitedness	people
concentration	educ
concentricity	maths
conceptualism	educ
conceptualist	educ
concessionary	trade
concrete|mixer	machine
concrete|music	music
condemned|cell	law
condensed|milk	drink
condescending	people
condescension	people
conducted|tour	travel
conductor|rail	travel
conductorship	music
confectionery	food
confetti|money	trade
confidence|man	trade
confined|to|bed	medic
confrontation	govt
congressional	govt
congresswoman	govt
Coniston|Water	lakes
connecting|rod	machine
conquistadors	lit
consanguinity	family
conscientious	people
conservatoire	music
consideration	govt
constellation	astron
consternation	people
consul|general	govt
consumer|goods	trade
container|port	travel
container|ship	travel
contamination	food
contemplation	educ
contemplative	educ
contentiously	govt
continuity|man	film/TV
contortionist	jobs
contrabandist	jobs
contrabassoon	music
contraception	medic
contraceptive	medic
contradiction	educ
contrafagotto	music
contrapuntist	music
contravention	govt
controversial	people
convalescence	medic

cook‚housemaid	*jobs*
cooking‚sherry	*drink*
copartnership	*trade*
copper‚pyrites	*mineral*
co‚religionist	*relig*
cornet‚a‚piston	*music*
coroner's‚court	*law*
corps‚de‚ballet	*music*
corpus‚delicti	*foreign*
correspondent	*lit*
corresponding	*maths*
corridor‚train	*travel*
corroboration	*law*
corroborative	*law*
corrosiveness	*chem*
cost‚effective	*trade*
Cotswold‚Hills	*mounts*
cottage‚cheese	*food*
cotton‚spinner	*jobs*
couleur‚de‚rose	*foreign*
council‚estate	*archit*
Count‚Almaviva	*lit*
counter‚attack	*war*
countercharge	*law*
counterfeiter	*law*
counter‚jumper	*jobs*
counter‚motion	*machine*
counting‚house	*trade*
country‚cousin	*people*
county‚borough	*govt*
county‚council	*archit*
county‚cricket	*sport*
court‚circular	*govt*
courteousness	*people*
courtesy‚title	*govt*
Court‚of‚Appeal	*law*
courts‚martial	*law*
craftsmanship	*jobs*
cranberry‚tree	*trees*
credit‚account	*trade*
credit‚balance	*trade*
credit‚company	*trade*
credit‚squeeze	*trade*
creme‚de‚menthe	*drink*
cribbage‚board	*sport*
criminal‚trial	*law*
criminologist	*law*
critical‚angle	*physics*
croix‚de‚guerre	*foreign*
crossbreeding	*biol*
crossed‚cheque	*trade*
cross‚hatching	*art*
cross‚question	*law*
cross‚the‚floor	*govt*
cross‚vaulting	*archit*
crown‚imperial	*govt*
Crown‚Imperial	*titles*
crown‚princess	*govt*
cruiser‚weight	*sport*
cruising‚speed	*measure*
cryptographer	*jobs*
cubic‚capacity	*measure*
cultured‚pearl	*jewels*
cum‚grano‚salis	*foreign*
cumulostratus	*weather*
current‚assets	*trade*
curtain‚raiser	*theatre*
curtain‚speech	*theatre*
custard‚powder	*food*
cylinder‚block	*machine*
daddy‚long‚legs	*insects*
daguerreotype	*art*
dancing‚master	*jobs*
dandelion‚wine	*drink*
Dandie‚Dinmont	*animals*
darning‚needle	*house*
daughter‚in‚law	*family*
day‚of‚judgment	*relig*
days‚of‚the‚week	*time*
dead‚reckoning	*measure*
Dean‚of‚Faculty	*law*
Death‚in‚Venice	*titles*
decomposition	*chem*
decompression	*physics*
deforestation	*trees*
demonstration	*chem*
demonstration	*govt*
demonstration	*physics*
dendrological	*trees*
dental‚surgeon	*jobs*

dental|surgery	*medic*
dentist's|chair	*medic*
deoch|an|doruis	*drink*
depressed|area	*trade*
Der|Freischutz	*titles*
dermatologist	*medic*
desert|warfare	*war*
deserving|poor	*people*
determination	*people*
deus|ex|machina	*foreign*
devolutionist	*govt*
diagnostician	*medic*
diamond|brooch	*jewels*
Dido|and|Aeneas	*titles*
differentiate	*maths*
diffusion|tube	*chem*
dihedral|angle	*maths*
dinner|service	*house*
diplomatic|bag	*govt*
direct|current	*physics*
direct|descent	*family*
discharge|tube	*physics*
discount|house	*trade*
discount|store	*trade*
disengagement	*war*
dishonourable	*people*
dispassionate	*people*
dispatch|rider	*war*
disproportion	*maths*
dissolubility	*chem*
distant|cousin	*family*
distant|signal	*travel*
distinguished	*people*
district|nurse	*jobs*
divine|justice	*relig*
divine|service	*relig*
division|lobby	*govt*
Doctor|Bartolo	*lit*
Doctor|Faustus	*titles*
Doctor|Zhivago	*titles*
Doll|Tearsheet	*Shakesp*
Doppler|effect	*physics*
dormitory|town	*archit*
double|crosser	*people*
double|dealing	*people*
double|glazing	*archit*
double|meaning	*lit*
double|or|quits	*sport*
Downing|Street	*govt*
Down's|syndrome	*medic*
drainage|basin	*geog*
dramatic|irony	*theatre*
dramatisation	*theatre*
draught|animal	*animals*
draught|screen	*house*
dressing|table	*house*
drill|sergeant	*war*
driving|lesson	*travel*
driving|mirror	*travel*
driving|school	*travel*
dwelling|house	*archit*
dwelling|place	*archit*
dyed|in|the|wool	*people*
Earl|Tolloller	*lit*
east|north|east	*geog*
east|south|east	*geog*
echinodermata	*animals*
ecumenicalism	*relig*
Edinburgh|rock	*food*
educationally	*educ*
egocentricity	*people*
egotistically	*people*
election|fever	*govt*
electoral|roll	*govt*
electric|chair	*law*
electric|drill	*machine*
electric|fence	*agric*
electric|field	*physics*
electric|light	*physics*
electric|meter	*physics*
electric|mixer	*house*
electric|motor	*machine*
electric|organ	*music*
electric|razor	*house*
electric|storm	*weather*
electric|train	*travel*
electromagnet	*physics*
electrostatic	*physics*
elephant|grass	*plants*
Ellice|Islands	*islands*

Elysian|fields	*myth*
emergency|exit	*archit*
emergency|exit	*theatre*
eminence|grise	*foreign*
emulsion|paint	*house*
encephalogram	*medic*
encyclopaedia	*educ*
endocrinology	*medic*
engine|failure	*machine*
enlightenment	*educ*
entertainment	*film/TV*
entertainment	*theatre*
entomological	*insects*
epigrammatist	*lit*
equestrianism	*sport*
eschatologist	*relig*
eschscholtzia	*flowers*
establishment	*govt*
estate|bottled	*drink*
evasive|action	*war*
every|few|hours	*time*
every|few|years	*time*
every|other|day	*time*
excess|luggage	*travel*
excess|profits	*trade*
excitableness	*people*
excommunicate	*relig*
exempli|gratia	*foreign*
exhibitionism	*people*
exhibitionist	*people*
Exocet|missile	*war*
expert|witness	*law*
exponentially	*maths*
expressionism	*art*
expressionist	*art*
express|letter	*travel*
expropriation	*law*
ex|proprio|motu	*foreign*
exterior|angle	*maths*
extragalactic	*astron*
extra|judicial	*law*
eye|to|business	*trade*
faculty|of|arts	*educ*
faites|vos|jeux	*foreign*
falling|prices	*trade*
fall|overboard	*marine*
false|evidence	*law*
Fame|is|the|Spur	*titles*
family|reunion	*family*
fashion|parade	*clothes*
Faulconbridge	*Shakesp*
feather|duster	*house*
featherweight	*sport*
feature|editor	*jobs*
fellow|citizen	*govt*
fellow|servant	*jobs*
fencing|master	*jobs*
ferroconcrete	*archit*
ferromagnetic	*physics*
fertilisation	*biol*
fertility|drug	*medic*
fever|hospital	*medic*
field|dressing	*medic*
field|hospital	*medic*
field|hospital	*war*
field|of|battle	*war*
fighter|patrol	*war*
figure|of|eight	*sport*
figure|skating	*sport*
filibustering	*govt*
filing|cabinet	*trade*
financial|year	*time*
financial|year	*trade*
find|on|haddock	*fish*
finishing|post	*sport*
finnan|haddock	*fish*
finnan|haddock	*food*
Finnegans|Wake	*titles*
fire|insurance	*trade*
fire|resistant	*house*
fire|resisting	*archit*
first|begotten	*family*
first|offender	*law*
first|world|war	*war*
fishing|tackle	*sport*
flame|coloured	*colour*
Flammenwerfer	*war*
Flanders|poppy	*flowers*
Flemish|school	*art*
flesh|and|blood	*family*

floating voter	*govt*
floodlighting	*archit*
floricultural	*flowers*
flying colours	*war*
flying machine	*travel*
flying officer	*war*
flying pickets	*law*
follow through	*sport*
food poisoning	*food*
food poisoning	*medic*
food processer	*house*
foolhardiness	*people*
fools paradise	*people*
football match	*sport*
football pools	*sport*
foot passenger	*travel*
force de frappe	*war*
forced landing	*travel*
foreign legion	*war*
Foreign Office	*govt*
foreign policy	*govt*
forgetfulness	*people*
for the present	*time*
fortification	*war*
fortune hunter	*people*
fortune teller	*jobs*
foster brother	*family*
founder member	*govt*
franchisement	*govt*
Franklin Blake	*lit*
free trade area	*trade*
freezing point	*physics*
French mustard	*food*
fresh air fiend	*people*
fringe benefit	*trade*
frivolousness	*people*
from the outset	*time*
from the word go	*time*
fruit cocktail	*food*
fuel injection	*machine*
funny business	*law*
funny peculiar	*sport*
furnished flat	*archit*
gadarene swine	*animals*
Geiger counter	*physics*
Gelsenkirchen	*cities*
generalissimo	*war*
generation gap	*time*
gentian violet	*medic*
gentle hearted	*people*
gentlemanlike	*people*
gentlewomanly	*people*
geometrically	*maths*
geometric mean	*maths*
German measles	*medic*
gerund grinder	*lit*
getting on a bit	*time*
ghetto blaster	*sport*
gin and bitters	*drink*
glass printing	*art*
global village	*film/TV*
globe trotting	*travel*
go as you please	*people*
going for a song	*trade*
golden jubilee	*time*
golden section	*maths*
golden thistle	*plants*
golden wedding	*time*
good influence	*people*
good Samaritan	*people*
go the whole hog	*people*
Gothic revival	*archit*
governing body	*govt*
grammar school	*educ*
granddaughter	*family*
grandiloquent	*people*
Grand National	*sport*
graticulation	*physics*
Great Bear Lake	*lakes*
great grandson	*family*
Great Salt Lake	*lakes*
Greenwich time	*time*
Gregorian mode	*music*
Grossglockner	*mounts*
ground control	*travel*
group practice	*medic*
guardian angel	*jobs*
guard of honour	*war*
Guatemala City	*cities*
guided missile	*war*

Gulf of Bothnia	*seas*
Gulf of Corinth	*seas*
Gulf of Finland	*seas*
Gulf of Fonseca	*seas*
Gulf of Taranto	*seas*
gunnery school	*war*
gynaecologist	*jobs*
gynaecologist	*medic*
hacking jacket	*clothes*
haematologist	*medic*
hair splitting	*people*
half heartedly	*people*
half sovereign	*money*
half time score	*sport*
harbour master	*jobs*
hare and hounds	*sport*
harmonic scale	*music*
Harold in Italy	*titles*
harvest spider	*insects*
Harz Mountains	*mounts*
Hatter's Castle	*titles*
healthfulness	*medic*
health service	*medic*
health visitor	*jobs*
health visitor	*medic*
heartlessness	*people*
Heath Robinson	*machine*
heat resistant	*physics*
heat treatment	*medic*
helter skelter	*sport*
Henry Dashwood	*lit*
Hercule Poirot	*lit*
hermaphrodite	*biol*
herpetologist	*insects*
heterogenesis	*biol*
heterogenetic	*biol*
hide and go seek	*sport*
high churchman	*relig*
High Constable	*law*
high explosive	*war*
high frequency	*physics*
Highland dress	*clothes*
Highland fling	*sport*
Highland games	*sport*
high water mark	*marine*

hole and corner	*people*
holy innocents	*relig*
home economics	*educ*
Homeric simile	*lit*
Home Secretary	*govt*
homeward bound	*travel*
homoeopathist	*medic*
honeydew melon	*fruit*
honours degree	*educ*
horse and buggy	*travel*
horse chestnut	*trees*
horse mackerel	*fish*
horse mushroom	*plants*
horticultural	*agric*
house breaking	*law*
household gods	*house*
household gods	*relig*
housing estate	*archit*
hundredweight	*measure*
hunger marcher	*law*
hunger marcher	*people*
hunger striker	*law*
hunting ground	*sport*
hurricane lamp	*house*
hydraulic jack	*machine*
hydrochloride	*chem*
hydrodynamics	*maths*
hydroelectric	*physics*
hydrosulphide	*chem*
hydrosulphite	*chem*
hydroxylamine	*chem*
hypercritical	*people*
hypochondriac	*people*
ichthyologist	*fish*
identical twin	*family*
idiosyncratic	*people*
impassiveness	*people*
impersonation	*law*
impersonation	*theatre*
imperturbable	*people*
impetuousness	*people*
impressionism	*art*
impressionist	*art*
impulse buying	*trade*
impulsiveness	*people*

incarceration	*law*
incense|burner	*relig*
incomes|policy	*govt*
inconsiderate	*people*
inconsistency	*people*
incorporation	*trade*
incorruptible	*people*
indefatigable	*people*
indeterminate	*maths*
indisposition	*medic*
individualist	*people*
industrialism	*trade*
industrialist	*jobs*
infant|baptism	*relig*
infant|prodigy	*educ*
infant|prodigy	*people*
in|honour|bound	*people*
Inland|Revenue	*govt*
in|Queer|Street	*trade*
insignificant	*people*
instant|coffee	*drink*
insubordinate	*people*
intensive|care	*medic*
interior|angle	*maths*
intermarriage	*family*
internal|rhyme	*lit*
international	*govt*
international	*sport*
interrogation	*law*
intransigence	*people*
introspective	*people*
Inverness|cape	*clothes*
investigation	*law*
investigative	*law*
in|vino|veritas	*foreign*
Ionian|Islands	*islands*
irrationality	*maths*
irrepressible	*people*
irresponsible	*people*
Isle|of|Purbeck	*islands*
Isle|of|Sheppey	*islands*
jerry|building	*archit*
Jerry|Cruncher	*lit*
jet|propulsion	*machine*
jet|propulsion	*travel*

jiggery|pokery	*law*
Joan|la|Pucelle	*Shakesp*
Jolyon|Forsyte	*lit*
judge|advocate	*law*
jurisprudence	*law*
Just|So|Stories	*titles*
juvenile|court	*law*
kaleidoscopic	*colour*
kangaroo|court	*law*
kapellmeister	*music*
Karl|Marx|Stadt	*cities*
kettle|drummer	*music*
kidney|machine	*medic*
kinetic|energy	*physics*
King's|evidence	*law*
kitchen|garden	*agric*
kitchen|garden	*veg*
knuckleduster	*law*
Kurile|Islands	*islands*
La|Cenerentola	*titles*
lackadaisical	*people*
Lady|Bountiful	*lit*
Lady|Bountiful	*people*
Lady|Bracknell	*lit*
lady|in|waiting	*jobs*
lady's|bedstraw	*plants*
Lady|Sneerwell	*lit*
laissez|passer	*foreign*
Lake|Champlain	*lakes*
Lake|Constance	*lakes*
Lake|Maracaibo	*lakes*
Lake|Trasimene	*lakes*
Lambeth|degree	*relig*
lance|corporal	*war*
landing|ground	*travel*
lapsus|linguae	*foreign*
latchkey|child	*people*
Latin|American	*geog*
lattice|girder	*archit*
laughing|stock	*people*
lavender|water	*clothes*
lawn|sprinkler	*house*
learning|curve	*educ*
leather|jacket	*clothes*
leather|jacket	*insects*

left hand drive	*travel*	manufacturing	*machine*
L'Elisir d'Amore	*titles*	marriage lines	*family*
lemon coloured	*colour*	marsh marigold	*flowers*
lemon meringue	*food*	mashie niblick	*sport*
letters patent	*govt*	Massif Central	*mounts*
level crossing	*travel*	master builder	*archit*
lexicographer	*lit*	master builder	*jobs*
licensing laws	*law*	master mariner	*jobs*
life assurance	*trade*	master mariner	*marine*
life insurance	*trade*	materfamilias	*family*
lift attendant	*jobs*	mathematician	*maths*
lighthouseman	*jobs*	matinee jacket	*clothes*
light infantry	*war*	matriculation	*educ*
light of nature	*relig*	Maxwell Davies	*music*
line of defence	*war*	meadow saffron	*flowers*
Lipari Islands	*islands*	meadow saffron	*plants*
liqueur brandy	*drink*	meals on wheels	*food*
liquid measure	*drink*	measuring tape	*measure*
listening post	*war*	meat and two veg	*food*
literary agent	*lit*	mechanisation	*machine*
litigiousness	*law*	medicine chest	*medic*
livery servant	*jobs*	Mediterranean	*geog*
lollipop woman	*jobs*	Mediterranean	*seas*
Lombard Street	*trade*	meistersinger	*music*
London Gazette	*govt*	melodiousness	*music*
long suffering	*people*	melodramatist	*theatre*
Lord Greystoke	*lit*	mental cruelty	*law*
Lord President	*govt*	Messerschmitt	*war*
Lord Privy Seal	*govt*	mess of pottage	*food*
Louis quatorze	*house*	metalliferous	*mineral*
lunatic fringe	*people*	metallurgical	*mineral*
Lydia Languish	*lit*	metamorphosis	*myth*
machine gunner	*war*	Metamorphosis	*titles*
Madame Defarge	*lit*	metaphysician	*educ*
made to measure	*clothes*	meteorologist	*weather*
made to measure	*measure*	Michaelmas day	*time*
magna cum laude	*foreign*	microcomputer	*comput*
magnetic field	*physics*	micro organism	*biol*
magnetic north	*physics*	microwave oven	*house*
magnetic poles	*physics*	mild and bitter	*drink*
magnetisation	*physics*	Military Cross	*war*
maid of all work	*jobs*	Military Medal	*war*
mangold wurzel	*veg*	milk chocolate	*food*
man of business	*trade*	millionairess	*trade*
Mansfield Park	*titles*	millstone grit	*mineral*

minced|collops *food*
mine|detection *war*
mineralogocal *mineral*
mini|submarine *war*
minority|group *govt*
mirabile|dictu *foreign*
misadventurer *people*
misanthropist *people*
mischief|maker *people*
misgovernment *govt*
mismanagement *govt*
misunderstand *educ*
mixed|foursome *sport*
mixed|metaphor *lit*
modernisation *trade*
modus|operandi *foreign*
moment|of|truth *educ*
money|no|object *trade*
monochromatic *colour*
moonlight|flit *law*
moral|theology *relig*
morning|coffee *drink*
morning|prayer *relig*
mother|country *govt*
mother|of|pearl *jewels*
motion|picture *film/TV*
mountain|chain *geog*
mountain|sheep *animals*
Mount|Cameroun *mounts*
mounted|police *law*
Mount|Kinabalu *mounts*
Mount|McKinley *mounts*
Mount|Mitchell *mounts*
Mount|of|Olives *mounts*
move|mountains *mounts*
mowing|machine *house*
mowing|machine *machine*
multicoloured *colour*
multinational *trade*
multiple|store *trade*
multum|in|parvo *foreign*
musical|comedy *theatre*
music|mistress *music*
musicological *music*
muzzle|loading *war*

Mycroft|Holmes *lit*
nationalistic *govt*
nature|reserve *animals*
Neapolitan|ice *food*
New|Providence *islands*
night|watchman *jobs*
night|watchman *sport*
nitro|compound *chem*
nitrogen|cycle *chem*
noli|me|tangere *foreign*
noli|me|tangere *plants*
nolle|prosequi *foreign*
non|appearance *law*
non|attendance *law*
non|collegiate *educ*
non|compliance *law*
non|conducting *physics*
nonconformist *relig*
nonconformity *relig*
non|fulfilment *law*
non|observance *law*
non|resistance *war*
nonsense|verse *lit*
North|Atlantic *geog*
north|easterly *geog*
north|eastward *geog*
north|westerly *geog*
north|westward *geog*
Nouvelle|Vague *film/TV*
nuclear|weapon *war*
nulli|secundus *foreign*
number|engaged *travel*
nursery|school *educ*
nursery|slopes *sport*
oceanographer *machine*
office|manager *jobs*
old|as|the|hills *time*
old|clothes|man *jobs*
once|upon|a|time *time*
one|night|stand *theatre*
open|plan|house *archit*
orange|blossom *flowers*
Orb|and|Sceptre *titles*
orchestration *music*
order|of|battle *war*

order|of|the|day	*govt*	Peg|Woffington	*lit*
order|of|the|day	*war*	Peg|Woffington	*titles*
ordinary|level	*educ*	penalty|clause	*trade*
ornithologist	*birds*	Peninsular|War	*war*
over|confident	*people*	penny|dreadful	*lit*
overcredulous	*people*	penny|farthing	*travel*
overexcitable	*people*	penny|pinching	*people*
overindulgent	*people*	Pentland|Firth	*seas*
owner|occupied	*archit*	pepper|and|salt	*colour*
oyster|catcher	*birds*	peregrination	*travel*
paddle|steamer	*travel*	perfect|number	*maths*
paediatrician	*medic*	period|costume	*clothes*
pain|in|the|neck	*people*	periodic|table	*chem*
Palace|of|Cyrus	*wonders*	peripatetical	*travel*
palaeographer	*lit*	perpendicular	*maths*
palaeontology	*lit*	Persian|carpet	*house*
palais|de|danse	*archit*	perspicacious	*people*
panda|crossing	*travel*	petrification	*mineral*
panic|stricken	*people*	petrochemical	*chem*
pantheistical	*relig*	petrol|lighter	*house*
pantheologist	*relig*	petrol|station	*travel*
pantomime|dame	*theatre*	petticoat|lane	*trade*
parallelogram	*maths*	Petty|Sessions	*law*
parish|council	*govt*	pharmaceutics	*medic*
parking|ticket	*law*	pharmaceutist	*medic*
Parkinson's|Law	*trade*	pharmacopoeia	*medic*
parliamentary	*govt*	philosophical	*educ*
parliament|man	*govt*	Phoebus|Apollo	*myth*
parrot|fashion	*educ*	photo|electric	*physics*
particoloured	*colour*	physical|jerks	*sport*
partition|wall	*archit*	physicianship	*medic*
party|politics	*govt*	physiognomist	*medic*
passage|of|arms	*war*	physiotherapy	*medic*
passion|flower	*flowers*	piano|concerto	*music*
Passion|Sunday	*time*	pick|and|shovel	*tools*
patent|leather	*clothes*	pickled|walnut	*food*
Paul|Bultitude	*lit*	picture|palace	*film/TV*
payment|in|kind	*trade*	picture|window	*archit*
payment|in|lieu	*trade*	pidgin|English	*lit*
peace|and|quiet	*govt*	pieces|of|eight	*money*
peace|offering	*sport*	pinking|shears	*house*
peach|coloured	*colour*	pitched|battle	*war*
peacock|throne	*govt*	plain|speaking	*people*
pease|porridge	*food*	Platonic|solid	*maths*
pectoral|cross	*relig*	plenary|powers	*govt*

pocket|borough	*govt*
pocket|edition	*lit*
poetical|works	*lit*
poetic|justice	*law*
poetic|licence	*lit*
poetry|reading	*lit*
poisson|davril	*foreign*
police|officer	*law*
police|station	*law*
poliomyelitis	*medic*
polysyllabism	*lit*
pontoon|bridge	*travel*
popping|crease	*sport*
Port|Elizabeth	*cities*
Portland|stone	*mineral*
postal|address	*travel*
postal|service	*travel*
poste|restante	*travel*
poultry|farmer	*jobs*
power|assisted	*machine*
power|politics	*govt*
power|steering	*travel*
prairie|oyster	*drink*
prayer|meeting	*relig*
praying|mantis	*insects*
precious|stone	*jewels*
precipitation	*chem*
precision|tool	*tools*
prefabricated	*archit*
prehistorical	*lit*
pre|Raphaelite	*art*
preserving|pan	*house*
press|campaign	*travel*
press|cuttings	*travel*
pressure|cabin	*travel*
pressure|group	*govt*
price|increase	*trade*
primary|colour	*art*
primary|school	*educ*
prime|minister	*govt*
prince|consort	*govt*
Prince|of|Wales	*govt*
Princess|Royal	*govt*
printed|matter	*astron*
printer's|devil	*jobs*

printing|press	*machine*
printing|press	*travel*
prisoner|of|war	*war*
prisoner's|base	*sport*
prison|visitor	*jobs*
Private|Angelo	*titles*
private|income	*trade*
private|school	*educ*
private|sector	*trade*
prizefighting	*sport*
process|server	*jobs*
proconsulship	*govt*
procrastinate	*people*
professorship	*educ*
profitability	*trade*
profit|and|loss	*trade*
profit|sharing	*trade*
progenitorial	*family*
promenade|deck	*travel*
prophet|of|doom	*people*
protectionism	*trade*
protectionist	*trade*
protectorship	*govt*
psychoanalyst	*educ*
psychotherapy	*medic*
public|address	*travel*
public|company	*trade*
public|gallery	*archit*
public|highway	*travel*
public|library	*archit*
public|records	*govt*
Public|Trustee	*govt*
purchase|price	*trade*
purple|passage	*lit*
pusillanimous	*people*
put|pen|to|paper	*lit*
put|to|the|sword	*war*
quadratic|mean	*maths*
quadrilateral	*maths*
quadrumvirate	*govt*
quadruplicate	*measure*
quantum|number	*maths*
quantum|theory	*physics*
quarter|gunner	*war*
quartermaster	*war*

quartier|latin	*foreign*	return|service	*sport*
quartz|crystal	*mineral*	Rev|Eli|Jenkins	*lit*
Queen's|counsel	*law*	revolving|door	*archit*
Queen's|highway	*travel*	revolving|door	*house*
questionnaire	*govt*	Rhodes|scholar	*educ*
quiet|as|a|mouse	*people*	rhythm|section	*music*
quincentenary	*time*	Ribston|pippin	*fruit*
Quinquagesima	*time*	Richard|Hannay	*lit*
quizzing|glass	*clothes*	Riesengebirge	*mounts*
race|relations	*law*	rightful|owner	*law*
rack|and|pinion	*machine*	right|of|appeal	*law*
radioactivity	*chem*	right|up|to|date	*time*
radioactivity	*physics*	riotous|living	*people*
radiolocation	*physics*	road|transport	*travel*
radiotelegram	*travel*	Robin|Oakapple	*lit*
rag|and|bone|man	*jobs*	rogue|elephant	*animals*
railway|engine	*travel*	rogues|gallery	*law*
railway|system	*travel*	roll|and|butter	*food*
railway|tunnel	*travel*	roller|coaster	*travel*
raise|the|money	*trade*	roller|skating	*sport*
Ralph|Nickleby	*lit*	roll|on|roll|off	*travel*
rasher|of|bacon	*food*	romantic|novel	*lit*
raspberry|cane	*fruit*	Ronnie|Winslow	*lit*
rate|for|the|job	*trade*	room|with|a|view	*house*
rates|and|taxes	*trade*	root|vegetable	*veg*
ray|of|sunshine	*people*	rough|and|ready	*people*
read|for|the|bar	*law*	rough|customer	*people*
reading|matter	*lit*	rough|shooting	*sport*
ready|reckoner	*maths*	round|of|drinks	*drink*
reception|room	*house*	round|the|clock	*time*
recorded|music	*music*	round|the|twist	*people*
reducing|agent	*chem*	royal|air|force	*war*
reference|book	*lit*	royal|standard	*govt*
regular|income	*trade*	rugby|football	*sport*
reincarnation	*relig*	rule|of|the|road	*travel*
reinforcement	*war*	running|battle	*war*
reinstatement	*law*	Russian|ballet	*sport*
Religio|Medici	*titles*	sabre|rattling	*war*
remittance|man	*people*	Sackville|West	*writers*
remote|control	*machine*	safety|curtain	*theatre*
rent|collector	*jobs*	sailing|orders	*travel*
restaurant|car	*travel*	salad|dressing	*food*
retaining|wall	*archit*	Salvation|Army	*relig*
retrospective	*time*	sanctimonious	*people*
return|journey	*travel*	Saratoga|trunk	*house*

savanna forest	*trees*
scandalmonger	*people*
Scarlett O'Hara	*lit*
scenic railway	*travel*
Schadenfreude	*foreign*
Schindler's Ark	*titles*
scholasticism	*educ*
school leaving	*educ*
school prefect	*educ*
schoolteacher	*educ*
scorched earth	*war*
Scotch and soda	*drink*
Scotch terrier	*animals*
Scotch thistle	*plants*
scrambled eggs	*food*
scrap merchant	*jobs*
search warrant	*law*
seat of justice	*law*
second chamber	*govt*
second innings	*sport*
second opinion	*medic*
second reading	*govt*
Secret Service	*govt*
secret session	*govt*
security check	*law*
seismographer	*geog*
seismological	*geog*
self appointed	*people*
self approving	*people*
self assertive	*people*
self conceited	*people*
self conscious	*people*
self deceitful	*people*
self governing	*govt*
self important	*people*
self indulgent	*people*
self satisfied	*people*
sellers market	*trade*
semiconductor	*physics*
senior service	*war*
sense of humour	*people*
sense of values	*people*
sergeant major	*war*
service charge	*trade*
Seville orange	*fruit*
sewing machine	*house*
sewing machine	*machine*
shadow cabinet	*govt*
Shakespearean	*lit*
sharp practice	*law*
sharp practice	*people*
sheep and goats	*animals*
sheep shearing	*agric*
sheep stealing	*law*
sheriff depute	*law*
shift register	*comput*
Shihkiachwang	*cities*
ship's chandler	*jobs*
ship's register	*marine*
shock absorber	*travel*
shooting brake	*travel*
shooting lodge	*archit*
shooting range	*sport*
shooting stick	*sport*
shop assistant	*jobs*
shop detective	*jobs*
short division	*maths*
short tempered	*people*
shoulder strap	*clothes*
Shrove Tuesday	*time*
Siegfried line	*war*
Sierra Maestra	*mounts*
signature tune	*music*
sign the pledge	*people*
silver jubilee	*time*
silver wedding	*time*
singing master	*music*
sit on the fence	*people*
sitting target	*sport*
sitting tenant	*law*
skateboarding	*sport*
skeleton staff	*jobs*
Sketches by Boz	*titles*
skilled worker	*jobs*
Skimbleshanks	*lit*
skirting board	*house*
slate coloured	*colour*
sleight of hand	*sport*
small business	*trade*
small investor	*trade*

smear campaign	govt
smelling salts	medic
smoked sausage	food
smokeless fuel	mineral
smoking jacket	clothes
smoothing iron	house
smooth tongued	people
snap judgement	govt
Soames Forsyte	lit
soap box orator	people
sober as a judge	people
social climber	people
social outcast	people
social science	educ
sock suspender	clothes
soldering iron	house
some of the time	time
some other time	time
Songs of Travel	titles
Sons and Lovers	titles
sooner or later	time
sophisticated	people
soul searching	people
sound proofing	archit
soused herring	food
South China Sea	seas
south easterly	geog
south eastward	geog
Southern Cross	astron
south westerly	geog
south westward	geog
Space Invaders	sport
space platform	travel
sparkling wine	drink
speaking clock	time
Special Branch	law
speech therapy	educ
speed merchant	travel
spending spree	trade
spinning jenny	machine
spinning wheel	machine
splinter group	govt
splinter party	govt
sportsmanlike	sport
sportsmanship	sport
sports stadium	sport
spring balance	physics
spring chicken	birds
spring cleaner	lit
square dancing	sport
squash rackets	sport
staff notation	music
staff sergeant	war
stalking horse	sport
Stamboul Train	titles
standard error	maths
standing order	govt
Stanovoi Range	mounts
starboard side	marine
starch reduced	food
starting price	sport
starting stall	sport
statesmanlike	govt
statesmanship	govt
station master	travel
statistically	maths
St Crispin's day	time
steeplechaser	sport
steering wheel	travel
stepping stone	travel
sterilisation	biol
stick in the mud	people
stiff upper lip	people
still room maid	jobs
stilton cheese	food
St Luke's summer	time
stock breeding	agric
stock exchange	trade
stone coloured	colour
storage heater	house
straight fight	govt
straight flush	sport
strato cruiser	travel
strawberry ice	food
strawberry jam	food
straw coloured	colour
street sweeper	jobs
strike breaker	trade
striking force	war
string quartet	music

string|quintet	*music*	temperate|zone	*geog*
structuralism	*lit*	Temple|of|Diana	*wonders*
St|Swithin's|day	*time*	tender|hearted	*people*
styptic|pencil	*medic*	ten|dollar|bill	*money*
subcontractor	*trade*	ten|minute|rule	*govt*
subject|matter	*lit*	ten|pin|bowling	*sport*
subject|object	*lit*	The|Art|of|Fugue	*titles*
sublieutenant	*war*	theatre|school	*theatre*
sub|machine|gun	*war*	theatricalism	*theatre*
succes|d'estime	*foreign*	The|Bab|Ballads	*titles*
sugar|and|spice	*food*	The|Black|Arrow	*titles*
Sulaiman|Range	*mounts*	The|Blue|Danube	*titles*
sulphuric|acid	*chem*	The|Cancer|Ward	*titles*
sulphur|yellow	*colour*	The|Ghost|Train	*titles*
summa|cum|laude	*foreign*	The|Gondoliers	*titles*
summer|holiday	*time*	The|Jungle|Book	*titles*
summer|pudding	*food*	the|law|is|an|ass	*law*
supercritical	*people*	The|Mabinogion	*titles*
superstitious	*people*	The|Magic|Flute	*titles*
supranational	*govt*	The|Magistrate	*titles*
Supreme|Soviet	*govt*	The|Mock|Turtle	*lit*
surface|worker	*sport*	The|Nutcracker	*titles*
suspender|belt	*clothes*	The|Odessa|File	*titles*
sweet|tempered	*people*	The|Path|to|Rome	*titles*
swelled|headed	*people*	The|Pirate|King	*lit*
swollen|headed	*people*	thermonuclear	*physics*
sycophantical	*people*	Thessalonians	*Bible*
symphonic|poem	*music*	the|time|is|ripe	*time*
synchronology	*time*	The|Virginians	*titles*
Table|Mountain	*mounts*	The|White|Devil	*titles*
table|skittles	*sport*	The|Winslow|Boy	*titles*
tablespoonful	*measure*	three|day|event	*sport*
tape|recording	*film/TV*	three|line|whip	*govt*
Tarka|the|Otter	*titles*	through|ticket	*travel*
tax|deductible	*trade*	thunder|shower	*weather*
tea|plantation	*agric*	time|after|time	*time*
telegraph|pole	*travel*	time|marches|on	*time*
telegraph|wire	*travel*	time|of|arrival	*time*
telephone|book	*travel*	time|out|of|mind	*time*
telephone|call	*travel*	time|signature	*music*
telephone|line	*travel*	Timon|of|Athens	*titles*
telephoto|lens	*physics*	toad|in|the|hole	*food*
telerecording	*film/TV*	toastmistress	*jobs*
television|set	*film/TV*	tomorrow|night	*time*
temperamental	*people*	tongue|in|cheek	*people*

tongue twister	*lit*		underclothing	*clothes*
tonsillectomy	*medic*		undergraduate	*educ*
tortoise shell	*animals*		Under Milk Wood	*titles*
tortoise shell	*colour*		under pressure	*physics*
tracer element	*physics*		under sentence	*law*
trade discount	*trade*		understanding	*educ*
trade unionism	*trade*		undisciplined	*people*
trade unionist	*trade*		unenlightened	*people*
trading estate	*trade*		unfashionable	*clothes*
traffic island	*travel*		ungentlemanly	*people*
traffic lights	*travel*		unimaginative	*people*
traffic warden	*jobs*		unintelligent	*people*
train spotting	*sport*		United Kingdom	*govt*
tranquilliser	*medic*		United Nations	*govt*
transatlantic	*geog*		universal aunt	*jobs*
transportable	*travel*		unlawful entry	*law*
transport cafe	*food*		unscutcheoned	*herald*
transport cafe	*travel*		unsympathetic	*people*
transport ship	*travel*		untrustworthy	*people*
transposition	*music*		unworkmanlike	*people*
transshipping	*travel*		up to the minute	*time*
traveller's joy	*flowers*		up with the lark	*time*
Treasury bench	*govt*		urban district	*govt*
trench warfare	*war*		Utopia Limited	*titles*
tres au serieux	*foreign*		vacuum cleaner	*house*
Trinity Sunday	*time*		valuation roll	*govt*
Triple Entente	*govt*		value added tax	*trade*
triumphal arch	*archit*		Van Diemen Gulf	*seas*
tropical month	*time*		veal and ham pie	*food*
trumpeter swan	*birds*		vegetable dish	*food*
trunk dialling	*travel*		venetian blind	*house*
turkey buzzard	*birds*		ventriloquism	*sport*
turning circle	*travel*		ventriloquist	*sport*
turn of the year	*time*		vernal equinox	*time*
turn the corner	*travel*		versification	*lit*
twelve tone row	*music*		vice president	*educ*
two edged sword	*war*		vice principal	*educ*
Tyrrhenian Sea	*seas*		vicious circle	*educ*
umbrella stand	*house*		Victoria Cross	*war*
unadopted road	*travel*		video cassette	*film/TV*
unadventurous	*people*		video recorder	*film/TV*
unarmed combat	*war*		Vincent Perrin	*lit*
uncomplaining	*people*		violoncellist	*music*
uncooperative	*people*		Virgin Islands	*islands*
undercarriage	*travel*		viticulturist	*agric*

vulnerability	*sport*
walking on part	*theatre*
War Department	*govt*
war department	*war*
war to the death	*war*
wash hand basin	*house*
washing powder	*house*
watching brief	*law*
water crowfoot	*plants*
water softener	*house*
wattle and daub	*archit*
weather report	*weather*
weather symbol	*weather*
week in week out	*time*
weeping willow	*trees*
weight lifting	*sport*
well respected	*people*
well thought of	*people*
wheeler dealer	*people*
whisky and soda	*drink*
white elephant	*trade*
whooping cough	*medic*
wild cat strike	*trade*
Will Honeycomb	*lit*

willing helper	*people*
willing worker	*people*
willow pattern	*art*
willow warbler	*birds*
window cleaner	*jobs*
window dresser	*jobs*
wing commander	*war*
Winnie the Pooh	*lit*
Winnie the Pooh	*titles*
Wolverhampton	*cities*
word blindness	*educ*
word processor	*comput*
work of fiction	*lit*
world premiere	*theatre*
X ray apparatus	*medic*
year in year out	*time*
yellow bunting	*birds*
yeoman service	*war*
Young Clifford	*Shakesp*
Zarathustrism	*relig*
zebra crossing	*travel*
Zuleika Dobson	*lit*
Zuleika Dobson	*titles*

14 LETTERS

a book at bedtime	*film/TV*
absolute decree	*law*
accident policy	*trade*
accomplishment	*jobs*
according to law	*law*
accountability	*govt*
action for libel	*law*
action painting	*art*
action stations	*war*
Act of Indemnity	*law*
administration	*govt*
administrative	*govt*
admiralty chart	*machine*

advancing years	*time*
aerobic dancing	*sport*
aerobiological	*biol*
affairs of state	*govt*
aggressiveness	*law*
Agnes Wickfield	*lit*
A Handful of Dust	*titles*
airborne forces	*war*
airborne troops	*war*
aircraftswoman	*war*
airing cupboard	*house*
Air Vice Marshal	*war*
Albemarle Sound	*seas*

Alfredo Germont	*lit*	astrogeologist	*astron*
Alfred Salteena	*lit*	astrophysicist	*physics*
almighty dollar	*money*	asymmetrically	*maths*
alphanumerical	*maths*	asymptotically	*maths*
ambassadorship	*govt*	A Town Like Alice	*titles*
a minori ad majus	*foreign*	audio frequency	*physics*
ammunition dump	*war*	audiometrician	*jobs*
anacoustic zone	*physics*	auf Wiedersehen	*foreign*
analog computer	*comput*	aurora borealis	*weather*
ancient history	*lit*	autobiographer	*lit*
Andrea del Sarto	*titles*	automatic pilot	*travel*
Anglican church	*relig*	auto suggestion	*people*
annular eclipse	*astron*	axis of symmetry	*maths*
annus mirabilis	*foreign*	back scratching	*people*
antaphrodisiac	*medic*	back seat driver	*people*
anthropologist	*biol*	bacteriologist	*biol*
anticonvulsant	*medic*	balance of power	*govt*
antilymphocyte	*medic*	balance of trade	*trade*
antimonarchist	*govt*	ballet mistress	*music*
anti perspirant	*clothes*	banana fritters	*food*
antiseptically	*medic*	banana republic	*govt*
apartment house	*archit*	bangers and mash	*food*
apartment to let	*archit*	banqueting hall	*archit*
apostolic vicar	*relig*	bargain counter	*trade*
appendicectomy	*medic*	bar of chocolate	*food*
apple charlotte	*food*	barrage balloon	*war*
apple of discord	*lit*	bathing costume	*sport*
apple of discord	*myth*	bathing machine	*sport*
applied science	*physics*	battle stations	*war*
apprenticeship	*jobs*	Battle Symphony	*titles*
approach stroke	*sport*	beat generation	*people*
approved school	*educ*	beatific vision	*relig*
arboricultural	*trees*	bed sitting room	*archit*
archaeological	*lit*	before and after	*time*
archiepiscopal	*relig*	beg the question	*educ*
arithmetically	*maths*	behind schedule	*time*
army cadet force	*war*	Betsey Trotwood	*lit*
army manoeuvres	*war*	bill discounter	*trade*
arrondissement	*geog*	billiard marker	*sport*
art for art's sake	*art*	biodegradation	*biol*
artificial silk	*clothes*	bioelectricity	*physics*
as drunk as a lord	*drink*	bioengineering	*biol*
A Shropshire Lad	*titles*	bird of paradise	*birds*
asset stripping	*trade*	black marketeer	*jobs*
as the crow flies	*measure*	Black Mountains	*mounts*

bladder campion *flowers*
blank cartridge *war*
blockade runner *war*
blood poisoning *medic*
boa constrictor *insects*
boarding school *educ*
bottle of brandy *drink*
bottle of claret *drink*
bottle of Scotch *drink*
bottle of whisky *drink*
bowdlerisation *lit*
bread and butter *food*
bread and cheese *food*
bread and scrape *food*
breakdown truck *travel*
breakfast table *house*
breathing space *time*
breathlessness *medic*
breeder reactor *physics*
breeding ground *biol*
Brief Encounter *titles*
Bright's disease *medic*
bring to justice *law*
Bristol Channel *seas*
British embassy *govt*
bunch of flowers *flowers*
bureau de change *foreign*
bus conductress *jobs*
busman's holiday *jobs*
butterfly screw *machine*
cabbage lettuce *veg*
cabinet pudding *food*
cairngorm stone *jewels*
Canterbury bell *flowers*
Canterbury lamb *food*
capitalisation *trade*
captain general *war*
carbon monoxide *chem*
carcinogenesis *medic*
carcinological *medic*
cardinal number *maths*
cardinal virtue *relig*
cardiovascular *medic*
cartographical *geog*
cartridge paper *house*

casement window *house*
cash on delivery *trade*
casual labourer *jobs*
catenary system *travel*
catherine wheel *sport*
cathode ray tube *physics*
cavalry officer *war*
cedar of Lebanon *trees*
central heating *house*
certain annuity *trade*
ceteris paribus *foreign*
champagne lunch *drink*
champion jockey *sport*
chancellorship *govt*
Chancery Office *law*
changeableness *people*
Channel Islands *islands*
channel swimmer *sport*
Chanson de Matin *titles*
character actor *theatre*
characteristic *people*
charcoal burner *jobs*
Charlie Allnutt *lit*
charlotte russe *food*
cheese sandwich *food*
Cheshire cheese *food*
chest of drawers *house*
chest protector *clothes*
chevaux de frise *war*
Chief Constable *law*
Children's Panel *law*
chimney sweeper *jobs*
chincherinchee *plants*
Chinese lantern *house*
Choral Symphony *titles*
Christopher Sly *Shakesp*
chromatic scale *music*
chronometrical *time*
church militant *relig*
Cider with Rosie *titles*
cinematography *film/TV*
circuit breaker *physics*
circumlocution *lit*
circumlocutory *lit*
circumnavigate *marine*

circumnutation	*plants*
citizen's arrest	*law*
civil liberties	*law*
class conscious	*people*
classical music	*music*
classification	*plants*
Claudius the God	*titles*
claustrophobia	*people*
cleansing cream	*clothes*
clearance house	*trade*
clerical collar	*clothes*
clerical worker	*jobs*
Cleveland Hills	*mounts*
cloak and dagger	*war*
Clumber spaniel	*animals*
coaling station	*travel*
coastal battery	*war*
coastal command	*war*
coastguardsman	*jobs*
cock a doodle doo	*sport*
cocktail shaker	*drink*
cocktail shaker	*house*
coconut matting	*house*
code of practice	*law*
coffee strainer	*drink*
coin of the realm	*money*
collar attached	*clothes*
collected poems	*lit*
collective farm	*agric*
college pudding	*food*
Colonel Fairfax	*lit*
colonel in chief	*war*
Colorado beetle	*insects*
colour sergeant	*war*
commensuration	*measure*
commissionaire	*jobs*
commit for trial	*law*
committee stage	*govt*
commit to prison	*law*
common informer	*jobs*
common multiple	*maths*
common or garden	*people*
Common Sergeant	*law*
communion bread	*relig*
communion table	*relig*

communist party	*govt*
company meeting	*trade*
compass bearing	*geog*
compass reading	*geog*
compound engine	*machine*
comrades in arms	*war*
concerto grosso	*music*
concessionaire	*trade*
concrete poetry	*lit*
conference pear	*fruit*
conjugal rights	*law*
conjunctivitis	*medic*
conjuring trick	*sport*
conquering hero	*war*
constitutional	*govt*
consulting room	*archit*
consulting room	*medic*
consumer demand	*trade*
contagiousness	*medic*
continuity girl	*film/TV*
contract bridge	*sport*
contrary motion	*music*
controllership	*govt*
copper bottomed	*mineral*
cornflower blue	*colour*
corporate state	*govt*
corporation tax	*trade*
correspondence	*lit*
corrugated iron	*house*
cost accountant	*trade*
cost accounting	*trade*
cost efficiency	*trade*
council chamber	*govt*
counterbalance	*measure*
counter current	*physics*
counter measure	*measure*
counter passant	*herald*
country cottage	*archit*
country dancing	*sport*
court of inquiry	*law*
court of justice	*law*
Court of Session	*law*
court procedure	*law*
covering letter	*lit*
credibility gap	*govt*

credibility|gap	*people*
creme|de|la|creme	*foreign*
crime|of|passion	*law*
criminal|charge	*law*
criminal|lawyer	*law*
criminal|record	*law*
crocodile|tears	*people*
cross|infection	*medic*
cross|reference	*lit*
Crotchet|Castle	*titles*
crown|and|anchor	*sport*
Cuisenaire|rods	*educ*
culture|vulture	*people*
current|account	*trade*
current|affairs	*govt*
curried|chicken	*food*
customs|barrier	*law*
customs|officer	*law*
cut|throat|razor	*house*
cystic|fibrosis	*medic*
dangerously|ill	*medic*
Darkness|at|Noon	*titles*
data|processing	*comput*
Davis|apparatus	*machine*
day|in|and|day|out	*time*
daylight|saving	*time*
dead|man's|handle	*travel*
Dean|and|chapter	*relig*
Dear|John|letter	*lit*
debased|coinage	*money*
decimal|coinage	*money*
decimalisation	*maths*
Decline|and|Fall	*titles*
declining|years	*time*
decree|absolute	*law*
defence|counsel	*law*
defence|witness	*law*
demisemiquaver	*music*
demobilisation	*war*
democratically	*govt*
denominational	*relig*
deposit|account	*trade*
design|engineer	*machine*
detective|novel	*lit*
detective|story	*lit*

detention|order	*law*
Deuxieme|Bureau	*foreign*
devil's|advocate	*law*
devil's|advocate	*relig*
diamantiferous	*jewels*
diamond|jubilee	*time*
diamond|wedding	*time*
diesel|electric	*travel*
Die|Zauberflote	*titles*
direct|debiting	*trade*
dis|aliter|visum	*foreign*
disciplinarian	*people*
discount|broker	*trade*
disembarkation	*travel*
disenfranchise	*govt*
disinheritance	*law*
disintegration	*physics*
distilled|water	*chem*
distressed|area	*trade*
divide|et|impera	*foreign*
Dnepropetrovsk	*cities*
dog|in|the|manger	*people*
dolce|far|niente	*foreign*
domestic|animal	*animals*
double|breasted	*clothes*
double|entendre	*foreign*
double|stopping	*music*
doubting|Thomas	*people*
dramatic|critic	*jobs*
dramatic|critic	*theatre*
dress|rehearsal	*theatre*
driving|licence	*law*
during|the|night	*time*
early|day|motion	*govt*
early|Victorian	*lit*
Easter|holidays	*time*
easy|come|easy|go	*people*
ecclesiastical	*relig*
educationalist	*educ*
Edward|Tulliver	*lit*
eigen|frequency	*physics*
Ein|Heldenleben	*titles*
ejusdem|generis	*foreign*
elderberry|wine	*drink*
elder|statesman	*govt*

elder|statesman	*jobs*
electioneering	*govt*
electric|cooker	*house*
electric|guitar	*music*
electric|kettle	*house*
electric|shaver	*house*
electrobiology	*biol*
electrochemist	*chem*
electronically	*physics*
electroplating	*mineral*
Eliza|Doolittle	*lit*
Emperor|Quartet	*titles*
encephalograph	*medic*
encyclopaedist	*educ*
enfant|terrible	*foreign*
engagement|ring	*jewels*
English|Channel	*seas*
epigrammatical	*lit*
epistemologist	*educ*
Eroica|Symphony	*titles*
eschatological	*relig*
espresso|coffee	*drink*
ethnologically	*geog*
et|in|Arcadia|ego	*foreign*
etymologically	*lit*
evangelicalism	*relig*
evaporated|milk	*drink*
evening|clothes	*clothes*
evergreen|plant	*plants*
excursion|train	*travel*
existentialism	*educ*
existentialist	*educ*
expense|account	*trade*
extreme|unction	*relig*
eye|for|business	*trade*
facile|princeps	*foreign*
factitiousness	*people*
fairy|godmother	*family*
false|pretences	*law*
family|business	*trade*
family|planning	*medic*
fancy|dress|ball	*sport*
fastidiousness	*people*
feature|picture	*film/TV*
features|editor	*film/TV*
field|ambulance	*war*
field|artillery	*war*
fifth|columnist	*war*
fighter|command	*war*
fight|to|a|finish	*war*
figure|of|speech	*lit*
filling|station	*travel*
finance|company	*trade*
finders|keepers	*law*
finger|printing	*law*
fireman's|helmet	*clothes*
firm|government	*govt*
first|class|mail	*travel*
first|class|post	*travel*
fisherman's|ring	*relig*
fish|out|of|water	*people*
flag|lieutenant	*war*
flight|recorder	*travel*
floating|bridge	*travel*
floriculturist	*flowers*
flower|children	*people*
flowering|plant	*plants*
flowering|shrub	*trees*
follow|my|leader	*sport*
football|ground	*sport*
football|league	*sport*
forbidden|fruit	*law*
forbidden|fruit	*relig*
foreign|affairs	*govt*
foreshortening	*art*
for|ever|and|a|day	*time*
for|ever|and|ever	*time*
formidableness	*people*
for|the|duration	*time*
foster|daughter	*family*
four|letter|word	*lit*
freedom|fighter	*war*
free|enterprise	*trade*
free|of|interest	*trade*
free|spokenness	*people*
French|dressing	*food*
French|polisher	*house*
French|vermouth	*drink*
Frisian|Islands	*islands*
frolicsomeness	*people*

from time to time	*time*
full employment	*trade*
fullness of time	*time*
full of mischief	*people*
full speed ahead	*measure*
full steam ahead	*travel*
fully fashioned	*clothes*
funeral parlour	*archit*
further outlook	*weather*
Galty Mountains	*mounts*
general amnesty	*law*
general council	*govt*
general damages	*law*
gentleman usher	*jobs*
geographically	*geog*
geological time	*time*
Gilbert Islands	*islands*
glossy magazine	*lit*
glowing colours	*colour*
glutton for work	*people*
gnomes of Zurich	*trade*
golf tournament	*sport*
Goodbye Mr Chips	*titles*
good for nothing	*people*
gooseberry bush	*fruit*
gooseberry fool	*food*
Gossamer Beynon	*lit*
go to the country	*govt*
government whip	*govt*
grace and favour	*govt*
gracious living	*people*
grammaticaster	*lit*
Great Slave Lake	*lakes*
green vegetable	*veg*
greyhound Derby	*sport*
grouse shooting	*sport*
guerrilla chief	*war*
guerrilla force	*war*
guilty of murder	*law*
habit and repute	*law*
half a sovereign	*money*
half pennyworth	*money*
halloween party	*sport*
hammer and tongs	*tools*
Hanging Gardens	*wonders*

hapax legomenon	*foreign*
head for figures	*maths*
hearty appetite	*food*
heather mixture	*colour*
heavenly bodies	*astron*
heavier than air	*physics*
Heaviside layer	*physics*
heavy artillery	*war*
hell for leather	*people*
heraldic colour	*herald*
heraldic device	*herald*
heraldic shield	*herald*
herald's college	*herald*
herpetological	*insects*
herring fishery	*marine*
high cockalorum	*sport*
High Commission	*govt*
high court judge	*law*
high handedness	*people*
Highland cattle	*animals*
high mindedness	*people*
high priesthood	*relig*
high principled	*people*
high technology	*educ*
highway robbery	*law*
hobnailed boots	*clothes*
holding company	*trade*
hole in the heart	*medic*
holier than thou	*people*
Home Department	*govt*
homme d'affaires	*foreign*
honorary degree	*educ*
honorary fellow	*educ*
hop skip and jump	*sport*
horse artillery	*war*
horse of the year	*animals*
hostile witness	*law*
hot air merchant	*people*
hotel detective	*jobs*
hot water bottle	*house*
hot water system	*house*
house decorator	*jobs*
house detective	*jobs*
household goods	*house*
household linen	*house*

housemaid's|knee *medic*
House|of|Commons *govt*
house|physician *medic*
housing|problem *archit*
housing|project *archit*
hunt|the|slipper *sport*
husband|and|wife *family*
hydraulic|brake *machine*
hypersensitive *people*
ice|cream|sundae *food*
identical|twins *family*
identification *law*
identity|parade *law*
imperative|mood *lit*
imperfect|tense *lit*
imperial|purple *colour*
imperial|weight *measure*
impressionable *people*
imprest|account *trade*
in|ancient|times *time*
incendiary|bomb *war*
incident|centre *law*
in|course|of|time *time*
Indian|elephant *animals*
indicative|mood *lit*
indirect|object *lit*
indirect|speech *lit*
inertia|selling *trade*
infectiousness *medic*
infinite|number *maths*
Inigo|Jollifant *lit*
inland|waterway *travel*
in|loco|parentis *family*
Inns|of|Chancery *law*
insulating|tape *house*
intelligentsia *educ*
intercommunion *relig*
interior|design *archit*
interpretation *lit*
interval|of|time *time*
in|the|afternoon *time*
in|the|beginning *time*
in|the|meanwhile *time*
inverted|commas *lit*
inveterate|liar *people*

ipsissima|verba *foreign*
jealous|husband *people*
Joan|Hunter|Dunn *lit*
John|barleycorn *drink*
Jude|the|Obscure *titles*
Julian|calendar *time*
Jupiter|Pluvius *myth*
Kailyard|school *lit*
Karakoram|Range *mounts*
keep|early|hours *time*
king's|messenger *jobs*
kitchen|cabinet *house*
kitchen|dresser *house*
kitchen|utensil *house*
knitting|needle *house*
knives|and|forks *house*
Kreutzer|Sonata *titles*
labour|exchange *jobs*
labour|movement *govt*
lack|of|evidence *law*
Lake|Tanganyika *lakes*
larger|than|life *people*
Latter|day|saint *relig*
Launcelot|Gobbo *Shakesp*
lawful|occasion *law*
law|of|the|jungle *law*
learned|counsel *law*
Leeward|Islands *islands*
legal|liability *law*
legally|binding *law*
legal|ownership *law*
legal|procedure *law*
lemonade|shandy *drink*
Le|Morte|d'Arthur *titles*
lending|library *educ*
letter|of|credit *trade*
letter|of|the|law *law*
liaison|officer *war*
licensing|court *law*
light|artillery *war*
lighting|up|time *trade*
limited|company *trade*
limited|edition *lit*
linear|equation *maths*
listed|building *archit*

little|brown|jug	*drink*	marching|orders	*war*
livery|coloured	*colour*	Marcus|Aurelius	*writers*
living|language	*lit*	market|gardener	*agric*
Lloyd's|register	*trade*	market|gardener	*jobs*
loaded|question	*educ*	market|research	*trade*
loaded|question	*law*	mark|of|the|Beast	*relig*
local|authority	*govt*	marriage|broker	*jobs*
locus|classicus	*lit*	masculine|rhyme	*lit*
Lofoten|Islands	*islands*	mass|production	*trade*
Lombardy|poplar	*trees*	Masterman|Ready	*titles*
London|Symphony	*titles*	master|of|hounds	*sport*
Long|John|Silver	*lit*	mathematically	*maths*
Lord|Chancellor	*law*	matron|of|honour	*jobs*
Lord|of|the|Flies	*titles*	matters|of|state	*govt*
Lord|of|the|Rings	*titles*	Maundy|Thursday	*time*
lords|and|ladies	*flowers*	maxima|cum|laude	*foreign*
Lords|spiritual	*govt*	McNaghten|rules	*law*
love|in|idleness	*flowers*	medical|officer	*medic*
Lucretia|Borgia	*lit*	medical|student	*medic*
luggage|carrier	*travel*	medicine|bottle	*medic*
luncheon|basket	*house*	member|of|the|bar	*law*
Lyon|King|at|Arms	*herald*	Mephistopheles	*lit*
Lyrical|Ballads	*titles*	merchant|banker	*trade*
macaroni|cheese	*food*	metallographer	*mineral*
Macassar|Strait	*seas*	Metellus|Cimber	*Shakesp*
Macchiavellian	*people*	metempsychosis	*educ*
Madam|Butterfly	*lit*	meteorological	*weather*
Madam|Butterfly	*titles*	microbiologist	*biol*
Magellan|Strait	*seas*	microchemistry	*chem*
Maggie|Tulliver	*lit*	microcomponent	*physics*
magnetic|needle	*physics*	microprocessor	*comput*
maidenhair|tree	*trees*	middle|distance	*measure*
maintenance|man	*jobs*	midsummer|night	*time*
Maldive|Islands	*islands*	militarisation	*war*
male|chauvinist	*people*	military|police	*law*
male|voice|choir	*music*	military|police	*war*
Man|and|Superman	*titles*	military|tattoo	*war*
mandarin|collar	*clothes*	milking|machine	*agric*
mandarin|orange	*fruit*	milking|parlour	*agric*
man|in|the|street	*people*	milk|of|magnesia	*medic*
man|of|many|parts	*people*	mineral|deposit	*mineral*
man|of|substance	*people*	mineral|kingdom	*mineral*
man|of|the|moment	*people*	mining|engineer	*jobs*
man's|best|friend	*animals*	miscalculation	*maths*
marathon|runner	*sport*	misinstruction	*educ*

mismeasurement	*measure*	Never|Never|Land	*myth*
mistletoe|bough	*trees*	New|Year|honours	*govt*
mistranslation	*lit*	Nicobar|Islands	*islands*
mock|turtle|soup	*food*	night|blindness	*medic*
mods|and|rockers	*people*	night|flowering	*flowers*
monkey|business	*law*	Nightmare|Abbey	*titles*
monthly|payment	*trade*	nimble|fingered	*people*
month|of|Sundays	*time*	nine|men's|morris	*sport*
moral|certainty	*educ*	nineteenth|hole	*sport*
morning|service	*relig*	nitroglycerine	*chem*
mother|and|child	*family*	non|cooperation	*law*
mother's|darling	*family*	non|involvement	*govt*
mother|superior	*relig*	non|operational	*war*
mountaineering	*sport*	Norman|Conquest	*lit*
mountain|sorrel	*plants*	north|eastwards	*geog*
Mount|Kosciusko	*mounts*	northern|lights	*astron*
Mount|Parnassus	*mounts*	north|north|east	*geog*
moving|pictures	*film/TV*	north|north|west	*geog*
Mrs|Sarah|Battle	*lit*	Northumberland	*Shakesp*
Mrs|Tiggy|Winkle	*lit*	north|westwards	*geog*
multiple|choice	*educ*	no|thoroughfare	*travel*
multiplication	*maths*	nuclear|fission	*physics*
multiplicative	*maths*	nuclear|physics	*physics*
multiracialism	*educ*	nuclear|powered	*physics*
multiracialism	*govt*	nuclear|reactor	*physics*
munition|worker	*jobs*	nuclear|warfare	*war*
musical|prodigy	*music*	nuclear|warhead	*war*
music|publisher	*music*	nursing|officer	*jobs*
muzzle|velocity	*war*	nutritiousness	*food*
mythologically	*myth*	obiit|sine|prole	*foreign*
Napoleon|brandy	*drink*	observation|car	*travel*
nasty|bit|of|work	*people*	obstructionist	*people*
national|anthem	*govt*	Octavius|Caesar	*Shakesp*
national|health	*medic*	office|building	*archit*
national|income	*trade*	official|secret	*govt*
National|Velvet	*titles*	off|the|shoulder	*clothes*
national|wealth	*trade*	Of|Human|Bondage	*titles*
natural|history	*biol*	open|air|concert	*music*
naturalisation	*law*	open|air|theatre	*theatre*
natural|numbers	*maths*	open|cast|mining	*mineral*
natural|science	*biol*	opening|batsman	*sport*
naval|architect	*jobs*	Open|University	*educ*
Nebuchadnezzar	*Bible*	operating|table	*medic*
negro|spiritual	*music*	operations|room	*war*
ne|obliviscaris	*foreign*	opposite|number	*jobs*

orange coloured	*colour*
orchestra stall	*theatre*
order in council	*govt*
orderly officer	*war*
ordinary seaman	*war*
ordinary shares	*trade*
Ordnance Survey	*geog*
ornithological	*birds*
Orthodox Church	*relig*
ostrich feather	*clothes*
Our Man in Havana	*titles*
over production	*trade*
overscrupulous	*people*
over the counter	*trade*
Ozark Mountains	*mounts*
package holiday	*travel*
pair of scissors	*house*
pair of slippers	*clothes*
pair of trousers	*clothes*
Pancake Tuesday	*time*
pantomime horse	*theatre*
paralellopiped	*maths*
parapsychology	*educ*
parish register	*law*
Parmesan cheese	*food*
partial eclipse	*astron*
partner in crime	*law*
passenger train	*travel*
past and present	*time*
pasteurisation	*medic*
pastoral letter	*relig*
past participle	*lit*
patchwork quilt	*house*
pate de foie gras	*food*
pavement artist	*art*
pedigree cattle	*animals*
penal servitude	*law*
penny in the slot	*trade*
peppercorn rent	*trade*
peppermint drop	*food*
personal column	*travel*
person to person	*travel*
Peter principle	*trade*
petit bourgeois	*people*
petroleum jelly	*chem*

phantom circuit	*physics*
pharmaceutical	*medic*
pharmacologist	*medic*
phenobarbitone	*medic*
philanthropist	*people*
phosphorescent	*chem*
photochemistry	*chem*
photosynthesis	*biol*
photosynthesis	*chem*
piano accordion	*music*
pickled herring	*food*
Pickwick Papers	*titles*
picture gallery	*archit*
picture gallery	*art*
pig in the middle	*sport*
Pilgrim Fathers	*lit*
pillar of the law	*law*
pincer movement	*war*
pineapple juice	*drink*
pins and needles	*medic*
Pitcairn Island	*islands*
plaice and chips	*food*
plain chocolate	*food*
plantation song	*music*
plant formation	*biol*
plaster of Paris	*mineral*
plastic surgeon	*medic*
plastic surgery	*medic*
platform ticket	*travel*
platinum blonde	*colour*
plead not guilty	*law*
pleased as Punch	*people*
pleasure ground	*archit*
pleasure seeker	*people*
pluck up courage	*people*
pneumatic drill	*machine*
pneumatic drill	*tools*
pneumoconiosis	*medic*
polling station	*govt*
polyunsaturate	*food*
pontefract cake	*food*
Portland cement	*mineral*
postmastership	*educ*
powder magazine	*war*
practical joker	*people*

Prague Symphony	*titles*
precious metals	*jewels*
predestination	*educ*
prefabrication	*archit*
pre-reformation	*lit*
presence of mind	*people*
presiding judge	*law*
pressure cooker	*house*
prima ballerina	*sport*
prima ballerina	*theatre*
primary colours	*colour*
Primrose League	*govt*
Prince Charming	*lit*
principal parts	*lit*
printed circuit	*physics*
prison governor	*jobs*
private company	*trade*
production line	*machine*
production line	*trade*
prohibitionism	*law*
prohibitionist	*law*
propeller shaft	*machine*
proper fraction	*maths*
property master	*theatre*
proscenium arch	*theatre*
provost marshal	*law*
psychoanalysis	*educ*
public nuisance	*people*
public spirited	*people*
putting the shot	*sport*
pyjama trousers	*clothes*
pyramid selling	*trade*
Pyrrhic victory	*war*
quality control	*trade*
quarantine flag	*travel*
quartz porphyry	*mineral*
Queen's evidence	*law*
Quentin Durward	*titles*
question master	*film/TV*
question of fact	*law*
radio astronomy	*astron*
radio telegraph	*travel*
radio telephone	*travel*
radio telescope	*astron*
radio telescope	*physics*
Ralph Rackstraw	*lit*
rate of exchange	*trade*
rate of interest	*trade*
rational number	*maths*
read the riot act	*govt*
read the riot act	*law*
rear view mirror	*travel*
receiving order	*law*
reconnaissance	*war*
recording angel	*relig*
reed instrument	*music*
reformed church	*relig*
regimental band	*war*
registered mail	*travel*
registered post	*travel*
registry office	*govt*
registry office	*law*
relative clause	*lit*
Remembrance Day	*time*
research worker	*jobs*
Reverend Mother	*jobs*
reversing light	*travel*
Revised Version	*relig*
Rhapsody in Blue	*titles*
rheumatic fever	*medic*
Rhode Island Red	*birds*
rhyming couplet	*lit*
rich as a Croesus	*people*
ride a cock horse	*sport*
riding breeches	*clothes*
Rikki tikki tavi	*lit*
Rimsky Korsakov	*music*
road traffic act	*travel*
roaring forties	*weather*
robin redbreast	*birds*
Robinson Crusoe	*lit*
Robinson Crusoe	*titles*
Roderick Random	*titles*
rod pole or perch	*measure*
Rogation Sunday	*time*
Romeo and Juliet	*titles*
Royal Artillery	*war*
Royal Engineers	*war*
Royal Fusiliers	*war*
Royal Tank Corps	*war*

running|repairs	*travel*	Siegfried|Idyll	*titles*
sabbatarianism	*relig*	sign|of|the|cross	*relig*
sabbath|breaker	*relig*	silence|in|court	*law*
sabbatical|year	*time*	silent|majority	*govt*
saddle|of|mutton	*food*	simple|interest	*trade*
salmon|coloured	*colour*	single|breasted	*clothes*
salt|of|the|earth	*people*	Sinister|Street	*titles*
sandwich|course	*educ*	Sins|of|my|Old|Age	*titles*
sausage|and|mash	*food*	Sir|Peter|Teazle	*lit*
scatter|brained	*people*	sit|on|the|splice	*sport*
schoolmistress	*educ*	slaughterhouse	*archit*
science|fiction	*lit*	Slavonic|Dances	*titles*
Scotch|and|water	*drink*	smoking|concert	*music*
Scotch|woodcock	*food*	smoking|concert	*sport*
scrubbing|brush	*house*	smoking|concert	*theatre*
Sebastian|Flyte	*lit*	Snowy|Mountains	*mounts*
second|hand|shop	*trade*	social|contract	*govt*
security|police	*govt*	Social|Democrat	*govt*
self|advertiser	*people*	social|security	*govt*
self|controlled	*people*	Society|of|Jesus	*relig*
self|government	*govt*	solitaire|board	*sport*
self|interested	*people*	Solomon|Islands	*islands*
self|sufficient	*people*	someone|or|other	*people*
senior|wrangler	*educ*	sonnet|sequence	*lit*
sensationalist	*people*	south|eastwards	*geog*
sentimentalist	*people*	southern|lights	*astron*
Separate|Tables	*titles*	south|south|east	*geog*
septuagenarian	*time*	south|south|west	*geog*
Sergeant|Buzfuz	*lit*	south|westwards	*geog*
service|station	*travel*	space|traveller	*travel*
Sextus|Pompeius	*Shakesp*	special|damages	*law*
shadow|minister	*govt*	special|licence	*law*
shaggy|dog|story	*lit*	spectator|sport	*sport*
Shakespeareana	*lit*	speech|training	*educ*
sheet|lightning	*weather*	speech|training	*theatre*
shepherd's|glass	*flowers*	speed|the|plough	*agric*
shepherd's|purse	*flowers*	speedway|racing	*sport*
shepherd's|purse	*plants*	sports|reporter	*jobs*
sheriff|officer	*law*	spring|cleaning	*house*
Sherlock|Holmes	*lit*	spring|mattress	*house*
ship's|carpenter	*jobs*	Spring|Symphony	*titles*
shooting|jacket	*clothes*	squadron|leader	*war*
shopping|centre	*trade*	squash|racquets	*sport*
shove|halfpenny	*sport*	Squirrel|Nutkin	*lit*
shuttle|service	*travel*	stage|carpenter	*jobs*

stage carpenter	*theatre*
stage direction	*theatre*
stainless steel	*mineral*
stamp collector	*jobs*
standard bearer	*jobs*
standing orders	*govt*
St Andrews cross	*herald*
St Anthony's fire	*astron*
starboard watch	*marine*
starting blocks	*sport*
starting handle	*machine*
starting stalls	*sport*
state ownership	*govt*
station manager	*jobs*
steak and kidney	*food*
steeplechasing	*sport*
steering column	*travel*
Stephen Dedalus	*lit*
St George's cross	*herald*
stock car racing	*sport*
stocking stitch	*clothes*
Stones of Venice	*titles*
store detective	*jobs*
straight as a die	*people*
strawberry roan	*colour*
street fighting	*war*
street musician	*jobs*
string of pearls	*jewels*
subject heading	*lit*
superannuation	*trade*
superintendent	*jobs*
supersensitive	*people*
superstructure	*archit*
supporters club	*sport*
supporting cast	*film/TV*
supporting cast	*theatre*
supporting film	*film/TV*
supporting part	*film/TV*
supporting part	*theatre*
supporting role	*film/TV*
supporting role	*theatre*
supreme command	*war*
surface tension	*physics*
surgical spirit	*chem*
surgical spirit	*medic*
surrender value	*trade*
swaddling cloth	*clothes*
sworn statement	*law*
system building	*archit*
systems analyst	*comput*
tail end Charlie	*people*
tapioca pudding	*food*
tariff reformer	*trade*
tartan trousers	*clothes*
tea and biscuits	*food*
telegraph cable	*travel*
telephone kiosk	*travel*
telephotograph	*travel*
television play	*film/TV*
terminus ad quem	*foreign*
terra incognita	*foreign*
terror stricken	*people*
tertius gaudens	*foreign*
The Ambassadors	*titles*
The Bees Wedding	*titles*
The Book of Snobs	*titles*
The Coral Island	*titles*
The Country Wife	*titles*
The Deep Blue Sea	*titles*
The Entertainer	*titles*
The Forsyte Saga	*titles*
The Four Just Men	*titles*
The Gay Lord Quex	*titles*
The Golden Bough	*titles*
The Great Gatsby	*titles*
The Horse's Mouth	*titles*
The Loom of Youth	*titles*
The Lost Horizon	*titles*
The Marschallin	*lit*
The Nine Tailors	*titles*
The Plain Dealer	*titles*
The Rights of Man	*titles*
thermodynamics	*physics*
The Time Machine	*titles*
The Vicar of Bray	*titles*
The Water Babies	*titles*
The White Rabbit	*lit*
The Winter's Tale	*titles*
The Woodlanders	*titles*
thick as thieves	*law*

third dimension	*measure*
Third Programme	*film/TV*
three bottle man	*people*
three card trick	*sport*
three mile limit	*trade*
three point turn	*travel*
three speed gear	*machine*
three speed gear	*travel*
through traffic	*travel*
Tierra del Fuego	*islands*
tobacco planter	*jobs*
Tomb of Mausolus	*wonders*
top hat and tails	*clothes*
torsion balance	*physics*
total abstainer	*people*
touring company	*theatre*
town councillor	*govt*
traction engine	*travel*
traditionalist	*people*
traffic manager	*travel*
traffic signals	*travel*
Tragic Symphony	*titles*
transformation	*maths*
transitive verb	*lit*
transportation	*travel*
transverse wave	*physics*
travel sickness	*medic*
treacle pudding	*food*
Treasure Island	*titles*
trickle charger	*physics*
Tridentine Mass	*relig*
tripe and onions	*food*
Triple Alliance	*govt*
Tristan da Cunha	*islands*
Tristram Shandy	*lit*
Tristram Shandy	*titles*
troubleshooter	*jobs*
troubleshooter	*people*
trustee account	*travel*
trust territory	*govt*
Tullus Aufidius	*Shakesp*
tuner amplifier	*physics*
turf accountant	*jobs*
Turkish delight	*food*
turquoise green	*colour*

two dimensional	*maths*
Uncle Tom's Cabin	*titles*
unconventional	*people*
under secretary	*govt*
under the hammer	*trade*
unearned income	*trade*
unenterprising	*people*
universal aunts	*people*
universal joint	*machine*
unknown soldier	*war*
unknown warrior	*war*
unostentatious	*people*
unprofessional	*people*
urban guerrilla	*war*
valet de chambre	*jobs*
vanishing cream	*clothes*
vanishing point	*art*
variety theatre	*theatre*
vegetable curry	*food*
vegetable salad	*food*
vegetarian dish	*food*
vending machine	*trade*
venetian carpet	*house*
Venus and Adonis	*titles*
verbal evidence	*law*
vested interest	*trade*
vice chancellor	*educ*
vice presidency	*govt*
violin concerto	*music*
visible exports	*trade*
Voices of Spring	*titles*
vulgar fraction	*maths*
Walpurgis Night	*myth*
Walpurgis night	*time*
ward in chancery	*law*
ward of the court	*law*
warrant officer	*war*
Wars of the Roses	*war*
washing machine	*house*
watch committee	*govt*
weather prophet	*weather*
weather station	*weather*
wedding garment	*clothes*
White Mountains	*mounts*
Widowers Houses	*titles*

wild|goose|chase	*birds*		wood|nightshade	*plants*
wild|goose|chase	*travel*		Worcester|sauce	*food*
William|Collins	*lit*		working|capital	*trade*
wind|instrument	*music*		working|clothes	*clothes*
window|shopping	*trade*		works|committee	*govt*
winter|Olympics	*sport*		wrestling|match	*sport*
winter|quarters	*war*		Yellow|Dog|Dingo	*lit*
winter|woollies	*clothes*		Young|Pretender	*govt*
witches|Sabbath	*time*		Zoroastrianism	*relig*

15 LETTERS

Aberdeen|terrier	*animals*		animated|cartoon	*film/TV*
absolute|monarch	*govt*		ankylostomiasis	*medic*
abstract|painter	*art*		anorexia|nervosa	*medic*
A|Child|of|our|Time	*titles*		Antarctic|Circle	*geog*
A|Christmas|Carol	*titles*		antenatal|clinic	*medic*
Act|of|Parliament	*govt*		antepenultimate	*measure*
adjutant|general	*war*		Anthony|Absolute	*lit*
ad|misericordiam	*foreign*		anthropological	*biol*
A|Farewell|to|Arms	*titles*		anthropomorphic	*relig*
against|the|clock	*time*		anticlericalism	*relig*
agriculturalist	*agric*		antimonarchical	*govt*
ahead|of|schedule	*time*		antivivisection	*people*
air|chief|marshal	*war*		any|port|in|a|storm	*marine*
air|conditioning	*archit*		A|Passage|to|India	*titles*
aircraft|carrier	*war*		appearance|money	*sport*
Alfred|Doolittle	*lit*		arboriculturist	*trees*
A|Life|for|the|Tsar	*titles*		archiepiscopacy	*relig*
a|little|learning	*educ*		archiepiscopate	*relig*
Allan|Quatermain	*titles*		architectonical	*archit*
ambulance|chaser	*people*		argumentum|ad|rem	*foreign*
amende|honorable	*foreign*		Ariadne|auf|Naxos	*titles*
American|Express	*trade*		Aristotelianism	*educ*
amusement|arcade	*sport*		armed|to|the|teeth	*war*
analytical|logic	*educ*		armoured|cruiser	*war*
ancestor|worship	*people*		articles|of|faith	*relig*
ancient|monument	*lit*		Astronomer|Royal	*astron*
Anderson|shelter	*war*		Attorney|General	*law*
animal|magnetism	*animals*		audio|visual|aids	*educ*

Australian rules	*sport*
aversion therapy	*medic*
awkward customer	*people*
Axminster carpet	*house*
Bachelor of Music	*music*
background music	*music*
bacteriological	*biol*
Balaclava helmet	*clothes*
bankruptcy court	*law*
banqueting house	*archit*
bargain basement	*trade*
barrister's clerk	*law*
Bartholomew Fair	*titles*
bats in the belfry	*people*
beer and skittles	*drink*
behind the scenes	*theatre*
bibliographical	*lit*
biogeochemistry	*chem*
biogeographical	*geog*
biological clock	*biol*
birds of a feather	*birds*
birds of a feather	*people*
birthday honours	*govt*
blackwater fever	*medic*
blastfurnaceman	*jobs*
Bloomsbury group	*lit*
blunt instrument	*law*
bodyline bowling	*sport*
bolt from the blue	*weather*
Bow street runner	*jobs*
box of chocolates	*food*
breach of promise	*law*
breakfast cereal	*food*
Brigade of Guards	*war*
bring in a verdict	*law*
Brussels sprouts	*veg*
bubble and squeak	*food*
building society	*trade*
business as usual	*trade*
business circles	*trade*
business contact	*trade*
business manager	*trade*
business studies	*trade*
business venture	*trade*
butterfly orchis	*flowers*

cabinet minister	*govt*
cable television	*film/TV*
Camembert cheese	*food*
capital gains tax	*trade*
capital sentence	*law*
Captain Corcoran	*lit*
Captain Smollett	*lit*
careers mistress	*educ*
carriage and pair	*travel*
carriage forward	*trade*
cash transaction	*trade*
catch as catch can	*sport*
Catherine Bennet	*lit*
centre of gravity	*physics*
cerebrovascular	*medic*
chamberlainship	*govt*
chapter and verse	*relig*
character sketch	*lit*
charcoal drawing	*art*
charged'affaires	*govt*
chemical warfare	*war*
cherchez la femme	*foreign*
chicken Maryland	*food*
chocolate eclair	*food*
chocolate sundae	*food*
Christadelphian	*relig*
Christmas Island	*islands*
Christy minstrel	*music*
chronologically	*time*
Church of England	*relig*
cigarette holder	*house*
cinematographer	*film/TV*
cinematographic	*film/TV*
circumnavigable	*marine*
circumnavigator	*marine*
civilian clothes	*clothes*
Clarissa Harlowe	*lit*
Clarissa Harlowe	*titles*
clearing station	*medic*
clerk of the court	*law*
clerk of the house	*govt*
closing down sale	*trade*
cloud cuckoo land	*lit*
clustered column	*archit*
cocktail cabinet	*house*

coffee,table,book	*lit*
Coleridge,Taylor	*music*
colliery,manager	*jobs*
colour,blindness	*colour*
colouring,matter	*colour*
combination,lock	*house*
combination,room	*educ*
commission,agent	*jobs*
commission,agent	*trade*
commit,an,offence	*law*
community,centre	*archit*
companion,ladder	*machine*
company,director	*trade*
company,promoter	*trade*
complete,annuity	*trade*
complex,sentence	*lit*
computerisation	*comput*
computer,science	*comput*
concert,overture	*music*
concert,platform	*music*
confessionalist	*relig*
confidence,trick	*law*
connoisseurship	*people*
conscience,money	*law*
conservationist	*people*
contemporaneity	*time*
contemporaneous	*time*
contempt,of,court	*law*
continental,time	*time*
continuation,day	*time*
convenience,food	*food*
conventionalist	*people*
conversationist	*people*
cooked,breakfast	*food*
cool,as,a,cucumber	*people*
cordon,sanitaire	*foreign*
coroner's,inquest	*law*
coroner's,verdict	*law*
corrugated,paper	*house*
cottage,hospital	*medic*
cottage,industry	*trade*
Council,of,Europe	*govt*
counsel's,opinion	*law*
counter,evidence	*law*
counter,irritant	*medic*

counter,movement	*govt*
crease,resistant	*clothes*
creative,writing	*lit*
crime,passionnel	*law*
cross,country,run	*sport*
crossing,sweeper	*jobs*
crossword,puzzle	*sport*
cryptocommunist	*people*
crystallography	*physics*
cuckoo,in,the,nest	*people*
cultivated,pearl	*jewels*
customs,official	*jobs*
Dangerous,Corner	*titles*
Daphnis,and,Chloe	*titles*
decarbonisation	*chem*
decimal,notation	*maths*
decree,of,nullity	*law*
deferred,annuity	*trade*
deferred,payment	*trade*
definite,article	*lit*
delirium,tremens	*medic*
democratic,party	*govt*
dental,treatment	*medic*
department,store	*trade*
detention,centre	*law*
development,area	*trade*
devil,worshipper	*relig*
Devonshire,cream	*food*
diamond,merchant	*jewels*
diamond,necklace	*jewels*
differentiation	*maths*
digital,computer	*comput*
dining,room,table	*house*
diplomatic,corps	*govt*
director,general	*govt*
discharging,arch	*archit*
disorderly,house	*law*
displaced,person	*war*
dissecting,table	*biol*
distant,relative	*family*
distress,warrant	*trade*
district,council	*govt*
district,visitor	*jobs*
dividend,warrant	*trade*
divine,messenger	*relig*

do|a|roaring|trade	*trade*
documentary|film	*film/TV*
dollar|diplomacy	*govt*
domestic|economy	*educ*
domestic|science	*educ*
dominical|letter	*time*
dormitory|suburb	*archit*
double|white|line	*travel*
dramatic|society	*theatre*
draughtsmanship	*art*
dressing|station	*medic*
drilling|machine	*machine*
drop|in|the|bucket	*measure*
drop|of|good|stuff	*drink*
dual|carriageway	*travel*
dual|personality	*people*
Duke|of|Plazo|Toro	*lit*
duplicate|bridge	*sport*
Dutch|elm|disease	*trees*
Earl|Mountararat	*lit*
Ebenezer|Scrooge	*lit*
Edward|Murdstone	*lit*
egg|and|spoon|race	*sport*
electric|blanket	*house*
electricity|bill	*trade*
electric|toaster	*house*
electrification	*physics*
electroanalysis	*physics*
electrochemical	*chem*
electrodynamics	*physics*
electrokinetics	*physics*
electromagnetic	*physics*
electronic|brain	*comput*
electronic|music	*music*
Elizabeth|Bennet	*lit*
emerald|bracelet	*jewels*
emerald|necklace	*jewels*
emergency|powers	*govt*
Emperor|Concerto	*titles*
endowment|policy	*trade*
enfranchisement	*govt*
entomologically	*insects*
entrepreneurial	*trade*
episcopalianism	*relig*
epistemological	*educ*
equalitarianism	*govt*
equinoctial|year	*time*
eternal|triangle	*people*
evening|primrose	*flowers*
every|mother's|son	*family*
every|now|and|then	*time*
exchange|control	*trade*
exclamation|mark	*lit*
excommunication	*relig*
excursion|ticket	*travel*
express|delivery	*travel*
extra|curricular	*educ*
Falkland|Islands	*islands*
falling|sickness	*medic*
false|accusation	*law*
family|allowance	*trade*
fancy|dress|dance	*sport*
Fanny|by|Gaslight	*titles*
Father|Christmas	*jobs*
Father|Christmas	*myth*
fellow|traveller	*govt*
Fibonacci|series	*maths*
fifty|pence|piece	*money*
finishing|school	*educ*
firework|display	*sport*
first|lieutenant	*war*
first|principles	*educ*
flibbertigibbet	*people*
floating|capital	*trade*
flutter|tonguing	*music*
for|a|year|and|a|day	*time*
foreign|exchange	*trade*
forked|lightning	*weather*
foundation|cream	*clothes*
foundation|stone	*archit*
fourth|dimension	*measure*
fourth|dimension	*time*
franking|machine	*trade*
French|breakfast	*food*
Frenchman's|Creek	*titles*
French|subtitles	*film/TV*
fricassee|of|veal	*food*
Friendly|Islands	*islands*
friendly|society	*trade*
From|the|New|World	*titles*

full bottomed wig	*clothes*
full bottomed wig	*law*
full dress debate	*govt*
funeral director	*jobs*
furniture polish	*house*
gala performance	*theatre*
game set and match	*sport*
gastroenteritis	*medic*
gate legged table	*house*
gaudeamus igitur	*foreign*
General Assembly	*govt*
General Assembly	*relig*
general election	*govt*
general practice	*medic*
gentleman at arms	*war*
gentleman farmer	*jobs*
George Knightley	*lit*
gin and angostura	*drink*
globe artichokes	*veg*
glorious Twelfth	*sport*
golden handshake	*trade*
golden rectangle	*maths*
golden retriever	*animals*
Gone with the Wind	*titles*
Goodbye to Berlin	*titles*
good naturedness	*people*
gossip columnist	*jobs*
Gotterdammerung	*myth*
Gotterdammerung	*titles*
governor general	*govt*
Grand Union canal	*travel*
grapefruit juice	*drink*
great grandchild	*family*
green Chartreuse	*drink*
greenery yallery	*colour*
Grenadier Guards	*war*
grilled sausages	*food*
grilled tomatoes	*food*
hackney carriage	*travel*
Haffner Symphony	*titles*
half heartedness	*people*
hammer and sickle	*tools*
handful of silver	*money*
Hansel and Gretel	*titles*
harvest festival	*relig*

Heartbreak House	*titles*
heir presumptive	*govt*
higher criticism	*lit*
higher education	*educ*
highland costume	*clothes*
Hindley Earnshaw	*lit*
Hippocratic oath	*medic*
historical novel	*lit*
hit below the belt	*sport*
Holy Roman Empire	*relig*
Homeric laughter	*myth*
honeymoon couple	*family*
hope against hope	*people*
horns of a dilemma	*educ*
horseshoe magnet	*physics*
how goes the enemy	*time*
Hubble's constant	*astron*
Huckleberry Finn	*lit*
Huckleberry Finn	*titles*
humanitarianism	*people*
Hundred Years War	*lit*
identity element	*maths*
imaginary number	*maths*
imitation pearls	*jewels*
immersion heater	*house*
inadmissibility	*law*
incidental music	*music*
income tax demand	*trade*
income tax rebate	*trade*
income tax relief	*trade*
income tax return	*trade*
indecent assault	*law*
Independence Day	*govt*
Indian rope trick	*sport*
instrumentalist	*music*
instrumentation	*music*
insubordination	*govt*
insurance broker	*trade*
insurance policy	*trade*
insurrectionist	*law*
in the nick of time	*time*
invalid carriage	*travel*
investment trust	*trade*
invisible import	*trade*
Italian Symphony	*titles*

Italian vermouth	*drink*	message received	*travel*
Jack of all trades	*jobs*	Michaelmas daisy	*flowers*
J Alfred Prufrock	*lit*	microtechnology	*physics*
James Steerforth	*lit*	middle of the road	*people*
Jehovah's witness	*relig*	military mission	*war*
judgment summons	*law*	military service	*war*
judicial trustee	*law*	miniature poodle	*animals*
Jupiter Symphony	*titles*	Minister of State	*govt*
king of the castle	*sport*	Ministry of Works	*govt*
knitting machine	*house*	Mistress Quickly	*Shakesp*
knitting machine	*machine*	model of industry	*people*
labour intensive	*trade*	molecular weight	*chem*
lateral thinking	*educ*	Molotov cocktail	*war*
laughter in court	*law*	money for old rope	*trade*
laying on of hands	*relig*	month after month	*time*
legal department	*law*	months and months	*time*
legal profession	*law*	months of the year	*time*
legal settlement	*law*	Moog synthesiser	*music*
leg before wicket	*sport*	Moonlight Sonata	*titles*
legitimate drama	*theatre*	moral philosophy	*educ*
Le Nozze di Figaro	*titles*	Moral Rearmament	*relig*
Leonardo da Vinci	*artists*	morning sickness	*medic*
Letters of Junius	*titles*	Morrison shelter	*war*
light machine gun	*war*	mother and father	*family*
lightning strike	*trade*	Mothering Sunday	*time*
lily of the valley	*flowers*	motorway madness	*travel*
Little Buttercup	*lit*	mountain railway	*travel*
little Englander	*people*	Mourne Mountains	*mounts*
local government	*govt*	moving staircase	*travel*
logical analysis	*educ*	Mulberry harbour	*war*
long arm of the law	*law*	mutatis mutandis	*foreign*
Look Back in Anger	*titles*	my learned friend	*law*
Lord Henry Wotton	*lit*	national defence	*war*
Lord High Steward	*govt*	nationalisation	*govt*
Lord Peter Wimsey	*lit*	national savings	*trade*
magneto electric	*physics*	national service	*war*
majority verdict	*law*	National Theatre	*theatre*
manic depressive	*medic*	naughty nineties	*lit*
marine insurance	*trade*	Nautical Almanac	*astron*
market gardening	*agric*	naval engagement	*war*
married quarters	*archit*	naval operations	*war*
marshalling yard	*travel*	New English Bible	*relig*
Marshall Islands	*islands*	Newfoundland dog	*animals*
mass observation	*govt*	Newgate calendar	*law*
Menenius Agrippa	*Shakesp*	night after night	*time*

nitro derivative	*chem*
no claim discount	*trade*
non commissioned	*war*
non intervention	*govt*
non professional	*people*
non profit making	*trade*
Northanger Abbey	*titles*
north eastwardly	*geog*
north westwardly	*geog*
nuclear reaction	*physics*
nursery handicap	*sport*
observation post	*war*
occasional table	*house*
odds on favourite	*sport*
odour of sanctity	*relig*
officer of the day	*war*
old age pensioner	*jobs*
Old Red Sandstone	*mineral*
on active service	*war*
once in a blue moon	*time*
once in a lifetime	*time*
one over the eight	*drink*
one parent family	*jobs*
open scholarship	*educ*
ophthalmologist	*jobs*
opposition bench	*govt*
optical illusion	*physics*
oral examination	*educ*
orange marmalade	*food*
orchestra stalls	*theatre*
orderly corporal	*war*
orderly sergeant	*war*
Our Mutual Friend	*titles*
outdoor clothing	*clothes*
overflow meeting	*govt*
owner occupation	*archit*
pair of stockings	*clothes*
palaeontologist	*jobs*
parachute troops	*war*
paragon of virtue	*people*
parliamentarian	*govt*
parliament house	*govt*
party government	*govt*
pathetic fallacy	*educ*
peace conference	*govt*
peaches and cream	*food*
peak viewing time	*film/TV*
pelican crossing	*travel*
pencil sharpener	*house*
peppermint cream	*food*
peregrine falcon	*birds*
Peregrine Pickle	*titles*
perfect interval	*music*
performing right	*law*
perpetual motion	*machine*
personality cult	*govt*
personal pronoun	*lit*
persona non grata	*foreign*
Peter and the Wolf	*titles*
Petition of Right	*govt*
philanthropical	*people*
phosphorescence	*chem*
photograph album	*house*
physiotherapist	*medic*
picture postcard	*travel*
picture restorer	*art*
pillar of society	*people*
pipped at the post	*sport*
plain clothes man	*law*
Planck's constant	*physics*
planning officer	*jobs*
platitudinarian	*people*
pleasure steamer	*travel*
plenipotentiary	*govt*
ploughman's lunch	*food*
Plymouth brother	*relig*
point of no return	*travel*
police constable	*jobs*
police constable	*law*
police inspector	*jobs*
police inspector	*law*
political asylum	*govt*
political career	*govt*
political office	*govt*
political theory	*govt*
portmanteau word	*lit*
portrait gallery	*art*
portrait painter	*art*
positive vetting	*law*
potential energy	*physics*

power|of|attorney	*law*
prairie\schooner	*travel*
preference\stock	*trade*
Presbyterianism	*relig*
press\conference	*travel*
prevailing\winds	*weather*
printing\machine	*machine*
Privy\Councillor	*govt*
programme\seller	*jobs*
proof\correcting	*lit*
proportionately	*maths*
protection\money	*law*
provost\sergeant	*law*
psychometrician	*educ*
psychotherapist	*medic*
public\ownership	*govt*
public\ownership	*trade*
public\transport	*travel*
Puck\of\Pook's\Hill	*titles*
punctuation\mark	*lit*
purchasing\power	*trade*
pure\mathematics	*maths*
puss\in\the\corner	*sport*
put\back\the\clock	*time*
Put\out\More\Flags	*titles*
put\the\clock\back	*time*
quarter\sessions	*govt*
quatercentenary	*time*
Queen\of\the\Night	*lit*
Queen's\messenger	*jobs*
quite\a\character	*people*
radiotelegraphy	*travel*
railway\carriage	*travel*
railway\crossing	*travel*
rainbow\coloured	*colour*
rain\cats\and\dogs	*weather*
Raindrop\Prelude	*titles*
rain\stopped\play	*sport*
raise\the\curtain	*theatre*
ready\and\willing	*people*
rearguard\action	*war*
reception\centre	*archit*
recruiting\drive	*war*
redcurrant\jelly	*food*
refresher\course	*educ*

refreshment\room	*travel*
regimental\march	*war*
regional\council	*govt*
registration\fee	*trade*
regius\professor	*educ*
regular\customer	*trade*
regulation\dress	*clothes*
reinterrogation	*law*
relative\pronoun	*lit*
religious\belief	*relig*
rem\acu\tetigisti	*foreign*
rent\restriction	*law*
republican\party	*govt*
research\chemist	*jobs*
reserve\currency	*trade*
retrospectively	*time*
Right\Honourable	*govt*
road\fund\licence	*travel*
Robin\Goodfellow	*Shakesp*
rock\bottom\price	*trade*
Roger\de\Coverley	*sport*
roly\poly\pudding	*food*
rotation\of\crops	*agric*
Royal\and\Ancient	*sport*
royal\commission	*govt*
rude\forefathers	*family*
Rupert\of\Hentzau	*lit*
Rupert\of\Hentzau	*titles*
Russian\roulette	*sport*
Samson\Agonistes	*titles*
Samson\and\Dalila	*titles*
sausage\and\chips	*food*
sausages\and\mash	*food*
scales\of\justice	*law*
scene\of\the\crime	*law*
schoolboy\howler	*educ*
school\inspector	*educ*
Scottish\terrier	*animals*
Sealyham\terrier	*animals*
secondary\colour	*colour*
secondary\modern	*educ*
secondary\school	*educ*
second\childhood	*people*
second\class\mail	*travel*
second\class\post	*travel*

second,in,command	*war*
Security Council	*govt*
select committee	*govt*
self considering	*people*
self destructive	*people*
self opinionated	*people*
sensation monger	*people*
sentence of death	*law*
sentence to death	*law*
Serenade to Music	*titles*
service industry	*trade*
settle an account	*trade*
seven deadly sins	*relig*
Severnaya Zemlya	*islands*
shadow pantomime	*theatre*
sheepskin jacket	*clothes*
shilling shocker	*lit*
shooting gallery	*sport*
shorthand typist	*jobs*
shorthand writer	*jobs*
shotgun marriage	*law*
shrink resistant	*clothes*
Sicinius Velutus	*Shakesp*
Simon Boccanegra	*titles*
Sir Joseph Porter	*lit*
Sir Mulberry Hawk	*lit*
situation comedy	*film/TV*
situation comedy	*theatre*
slapstick comedy	*film/TV*
slapstick comedy	*theatre*
slave trafficker	*jobs*
sleeping draught	*medic*
sleeping partner	*trade*
snake in the grass	*people*
soft furnishings	*house*
south eastwardly	*geog*
south westwardly	*geog*
Spanish chestnut	*trees*
sparring partner	*sport*
special delivery	*travel*
specific gravity	*physics*
spelling mistake	*lit*
spermaceti whale	*animals*
spiral staircase	*archit*
split infinitive	*lit*

spoils of victory	*war*
sports equipment	*sport*
spot advertising	*film/TV*
springer spaniel	*animals*
spur of the moment	*time*
square the circle	*maths*
Squire Trelawney	*lit*
stable companion	*people*
stable companion	*sport*
stage door Johnny	*people*
stamp collecting	*sport*
stamp collection	*jobs*
stamp collection	*sport*
stamping machine	*travel*
standard English	*lit*
standing ovation	*govt*
stand on ceremony	*people*
St Anthony's cross	*herald*
stark staring mad	*people*
Stars and Stripes	*govt*
state apartments	*archit*
State Department	*govt*
statement on oath	*law*
stay of execution	*law*
sticking plaster	*medic*
storage capacity	*comput*
Strait of Malacca	*seas*
Strait of Messina	*seas*
stretcher bearer	*jobs*
string orchestra	*music*
strolling player	*theatre*
strong silent man	*people*
St Valentine's day	*time*
subjunctive mood	*lit*
summer lightning	*weather*
sun moon and stars	*astron*
supply and demand	*trade*
surrogate father	*family*
surrogate father	*jobs*
surrogate mother	*family*
surrogate mother	*jobs*
surrogate parent	*family*
surrogate parent	*jobs*
suspense account	*trade*
swallow tail coat	*clothes*

swimming costume	*clothes*	thumbnail sketch	*lit*
swimming costume	*sport*	ticket collector	*jobs*
sword and buckler	*war*	ticket collector	*travel*
sword of Damocles	*myth*	ticket inspector	*travel*
symphony concert	*music*	tightrope walker	*jobs*
synoptic gospels	*relig*	tightrope walker	*theatre*
systems analysis	*comput*	Tiny Tim Cratchit	*lit*
tables and chairs	*house*	Titus Andronicus	*Shakesp*
Tanglewood Tales	*titles*	Titus Andronicus	*titles*
Tarzan of the Apes	*lit*	tomorrow evening	*time*
Taurus Mountains	*mounts*	tomorrow morning	*time*
telephone number	*travel*	too clever by half	*people*
telescopic sight	*war*	topographically	*geog*
temperance hotel	*travel*	To the Lighthouse	*titles*
ten commandments	*relig*	to the manner born	*people*
territorial army	*war*	Toulouse Lautrec	*artists*
tertiary college	*educ*	tower of strength	*people*
Thanksgiving day	*time*	training college	*educ*
The African Queen	*titles*	transfiguration	*relig*
The Beggar's Opera	*titles*	tree of knowledge	*trees*
The Commendatore	*lit*	trigonometrical	*maths*
The Divine Comedy	*titles*	trinitrotoluene	*chem*
The Emperor Waltz	*titles*	tropical climate	*weather*
The Essays of Elia	*titles*	ultra violet rays	*physics*
The Faerie Queene	*titles*	unaccommodating	*people*
The Golden Legend	*titles*	uncommunicative	*people*
The Iceman Cometh	*titles*	undemonstrative	*people*
The Invisible Man	*titles*	under cover agent	*jobs*
the morning after	*time*	under lock and key	*law*
The Old Wives Tale	*titles*	under privileged	*people*
The Pearl Fishers	*titles*	under the counter	*trade*
the powers that be	*govt*	undistinguished	*people*
The Rite of Spring	*titles*	unemployment pay	*trade*
The Scholar Gipsy	*titles*	unfurnished flat	*archit*
The Soldier's Tale	*titles*	unknown quantity	*maths*
The Statue of Zeus	*wonders*	unprepossessing	*people*
The Woman in White	*titles*	unsportsmanlike	*people*
third degree burn	*medic*	unstatesmanlike	*people*
this year of grace	*time*	up guards and at em	*war*
thorn in the flesh	*people*	Valiant for Truth	*lit*
three day eventer	*sport*	Vancouver Island	*islands*
three legged race	*sport*	Vaughan Williams	*music*
Three Men in a Boat	*titles*	vegetable garden	*veg*
three ring circus	*sport*	vegetable marrow	*veg*
throw in the towel	*sport*	vertical take off	*travel*

vice|chamberlain	*govt*
victualling|ship	*travel*
Vincent|Crummles	*lit*
Virginia|creeper	*plants*
virgin|territory	*plants*
Wackford|Squeers	*lit*
Waiting|for|Godot	*titles*
Waldstein|Sonata	*titles*
weather|forecast	*weather*
weighing|machine	*house*
weighing|machine	*machine*
Weir|of|Hermiston	*titles*
wellington|boots	*clothes*
well|intentioned	*people*
whited|sepulchre	*people*
white|man's|burden	*govt*
Wiener|schnitzel	*food*
wife|and|children	*family*
Wilkins|Micawber	*lit*
windscreen|wiper	*travel*
Windward|Islands	*islands*
wines|and|spirits	*drink*
with|bated|breath	*people*
women's|institute	*sport*
woody|nightshade	*flowers*
woody|nightshade	*plants*
working|majority	*govt*
world|government	*govt*
world|of|commerce	*trade*
world|without|end	*time*
Yarrow|Revisited	*titles*
You|Never|Can|Tell	*titles*
yours|faithfully	*people*
youth|club|leader	*jobs*
Zagros|Mountains	*mounts*